One Woman, One Vote has been indispensable to me as I've worked to learn so much of the history that I'd not been taught about the nation and its centuries-long struggle toward full enfranchisement. I had been taught very little in school — shockingly little — about the lengthy, complex, fraught movement for woman suffrage in this country. When I began to learn about the movement, I turned to this compilation of academic perspectives over and over again, learning about the movement's horrifying racial politics, the many strategic approaches taken by different activists at different stages, the arguments about whether to create a proletariat coalition or appeal to elite women, and the domestic remaking of Susan B. Anthony. It's a terrific resource for those who want to know about suffrage from many different angles.

—**Rebecca Traister,** Author of
Good and Mad: The Revolutionary Power of Women's Anger

The study of the woman suffrage movement has flourished since the first edition of the anthology *One Woman, One Vote* appeared during the celebration of the Nineteenth Amendment's 75th anniversary. Marjorie Spruill's expanded second edition, published as part of the commemoration of the amendment's centennial, is a deeply satisfying and essential update, attending as it does to the campaign in the South, the international context, and the first hundred years of women voting. As with the first edition, the suffrage story told here will be compelling for both students and general readers.

—**Louise W. Knight,** Author of *Jane Addams: Spirit in Action*

Marjorie Spruill's new edition of *One Woman, One Vote* is a welcome and timely addition to the expanding body of literature on women›s gradual political empowerment. At a time when women have expanded their political influence, when the U.S. not only has its first and long overdue female vice president, Kamala Harris, when the organizing efforts of women of color, especially in Georgia, have shifted the balance of power in the U.S. Senate, and President Joseph R. Biden has appointed the first female-majority Cabinet in history, it's only appropriate that we have this updated re-examination of "how we got here," edited by Dr. Spruill, with the critical contributions of dozens of other scholars of the domestic and international woman›s movement.

—**Adele Logan Alexander,** Author of *Princess of the Hither Isles:*
A Black Suffragist's Story from the Jim Crow South

This engaging collection tackles the complexity of the mainstream movement head on. A timeless collection of classics that helped define the field, now revised and updated to help show us where we're headed. A great place to start or pick up your learning—with stories that will keep you thinking.

—**Lisa Tetrault,** Author of *The Myth of Seneca Falls:*
Memory and the Women's Suffrage Movement, 1848-1898.
Associate Professor of History, Carnegie Mellon University

The first edition of *One Woman, One Vote* was a key entry point into women's suffrage for me and many others. The now-classic essays by path-breaking scholars helped frame the complications and impact of the struggle for votes for women, spurring my own scholarly interests. The new edition maintains those key contributions and incorporates new insights from the diverse and exciting suffrage scholarship surrounding the recent centennial of the Nineteenth Amendment. The result is an invaluable collection for anyone interested in understanding this signal moment of democratization in American history.

—**Christina Wolbrecht,** Author of *A Century of Votes for Women.*
Professor of Political Science, University of Notre Dame

In recognition of the 100th anniversary of the Nineteenth Amendment in 2020 and the election of the country's first woman, first African American and South Asian American Vice President, the new edition of *One Woman One Vote* offers much needed perspectives on the history of U.S. women's suffrage. New essays foreground race, empire, global, and Southern regional perspectives that shed light not only on the passage of the Nineteenth Amendment but also the course of events after 1920.

—**Judy Tzu-Chun Wu,** Author of *Doctor "Mom" Chung of the Fair-Haired Bastards: The Life of a Wartime Celebrity.* Professor of Asian American Studies and Director of the Humanities Center, University of California, Irvine

This fascinating, meticulously researched, and clearly written anthology elevated the suffrage movement to its rightful stature as a central and continuing theme in American politics. Along with civil rights, the quest for women's inclusion in American political life becomes a crucial chapter in the ongoing re-definition of American democracy. Indispensable for women activists, historians, and anyone interested in women's contributions to our common past.

—**Edith Mayo,** Author of *The Smithsonian Book of the First Ladies: Their Lives, Times, and Issues.* Curator Emerita, Smithsonian Institution

One Woman, One Vote has been essential reading for students of the suffrage movement since it was first published in 1995. This revised and expanded edition provides an updated overview that incorporates the rich scholarship of the last twenty-five years. New chapters place the American movement in the context of international campaigns for woman suffrage and enhance our understanding of the role of race and racism in the suffrage movement. The book also offers more information about the impact of the 1918 influenza pandemic; expanded accounts of activism by women of color; and a concluding essay that brings the struggle for voting rights up through the 2020 elections. Scholars, teachers, students, and lay readers of American women's history and political history will enthusiastically welcome this new edition.

—**Catherine Rymph,** Author of *Republican Women: Feminism and Conservatism from Suffrage through the Rise of the New Right.* Professor and Chair, Department of History, University of Missouri

In this second edition of *One Woman, One Vote*, we are reminded not only of the long struggle of women to acquire the right to vote and how that struggle was shaped by issues of race and class, but also how women asserted that right on issues that spanned the political spectrum. Never a unified voting bloc, as many politicians feared would be the case, women proved that they could be as politically conservative, or liberal, as their male counterparts. Now expanded to include new chapters and a sweeping overview incorporating new scholarship, editor Marjorie J. Spruill brings the story of woman suffrage forward to include the historic election of Vice President Kamala Harris. Indispensable for classes in U.S. History and political science and for lay readers wanting to learn more about women and the vote.

—**Karen L. Cox,** Author of *Dixie's Daughters: The United Daughters of the Confederacy and the Preservation of Confederate Culture.* Professor of History, Director of Public History, University of North Carolina, Charlotte

No other single collection presents a more thorough account of woman suffrage. But more than that, *One Woman, One Vote* tells the story of women voters—not only White women voters, but Black women voters, and Native-American women voters, and Asian-American women voters—not just during the fight for the ratification of the Nineteenth Amendment but through the 2020 elections. *One Woman, One Vote* should be on the bookshelves and on the syllabi of every historian and political scientist in the country.

—**Angie Maxwell,** Author of *The Long Southern Strategy: How Chasing White Voters in the South Changed American Politics.* Diane D. Blair Professor of Southern Studies and Associate Professor of Political Science, University of Arkansas

The updated edition of *One Woman, One Vote* both builds on and expands the original content so that it clearly illustrates for students, historians and casual readers the undeniable work of women of color and also firmly places the U.S. suffrage efforts within the international women's equality movement. Not only is it an important historic narrative, but it also serves as an essential guide to understanding the link between enfranchisement, civil rights, the politicizing of women's equality efforts, and the unrelenting voter suppression that we still see today.

Page Harrington, Author of *Interpreting the Legacy of Women's Suffrage at Museums and Historic Sites*

Marjorie Spruill's *One Woman, One Vote* remains a model in how to address a single topic from a wide variety of angles that capture the complexities of American politics and activism. With new essays that complement the timeless scholarship from the collection's first printing, this updated edition moves a century beyond 1920 through the 2020 presidential election and that year's centennial celebrations of the Nineteenth Amendment. Readers can now draw connections from the roots of the suffrage movement through the ongoing struggle to allow all women to actually cast ballots and convert voting power into equal political power.

—**Stacie Taranto,** Co-Editor of *Suffrage at 100: Women in American Politics Since 1920* Associate Professor, Ramapo College of New Jersey

*H*undreds of women gave the accumulated possibilities of an entire lifetime, thousands gave years of their lives, hundreds of thousands gave constant interest, and such aid as they could. It was a continuous, seemingly endless, chain of activity. Young suffragists who helped forge the last links of that chain were not born when it began. Old suffragists who forged the first links were dead when it ended.

— CARRIE CHAPMAN CATT AND
NETTIE ROGERS SHULER
*Woman Suffrage and Politics: The Inner
Story of the Suffrage Movement*

On March 3, 1913, thousands of suffragists marched along Pennsylvania Avenue in support of woman suffrage. The procession took place the day before Woodrow Wilson's presidential inauguration to demonstrate women's exclusion from the democratic process. LIBRARY OF CONGRESS

ONE WOMAN, ONE VOTE

ONE WOMAN, ONE VOTE

REDISCOVERING THE WOMAN SUFFRAGE MOVEMENT

Edited by
MARJORIE J. SPRUILL

NEWSAGE PRESS
Oregon

One Woman, One Vote

Rediscovering the Woman Suffrage Movement

Edited by Marjorie J. Spruill

Second Edition copyright © 2021 by NewSage Press and Marjorie J. Spruill

Paperback Original ISBN 978-0939165-76-6
Library Edition ISBN 978-0-939165-78-0
E-Book ISBN 978-0939165-77-3

Address inquiries to:

NewSage Press
PO Box 610
Tillamook, OR 97141

503-695-2211

Designed and produced by Sherry Wachter,
Sherry Wachter Designs
Printed in the United States

Cover photos, clockwise from top left: Marie Louise Bottineau Baldwin; Dora Lewis; Rose Winslow, also known as Wenclawska; Nannie Helen Burroughs; Mabel Ping-Hua Lee; Fannie Barrier Williams; and *at center*, Susan B. Anthony. Additional information on page 524. Photos from the Library of Congress, except Susan B. Anthony, which is in the public domain.

Distributed by Publishers Group West

Library of Congress Cataloging-in-Publication Data Is Available

Names: Spruill, Marjorie J., 1951-

Title: One Woman, One Vote : rediscovering the
   Woman suffrage movement / edited by Marjorie J. Spruill
Description: Second Edition / Tillamook, Oregon : NewSage Press, 2021.

   Includes biographical references and index.
   ISBN 978-0-939165-76-6

Contents

Preface

The essays in this anthology focus on different aspects of the suffrage story, but presented in roughly chronological order, tell the intriguing story of women and the vote from the failure of the Constitution to enfranchise women to the participation of women in politics after 1920. A new concluding essay continues the story of woman suffrage past 1920 through the 2020 presidential election.

The authors of the essays—scholars in the fields of History, American Studies, Political Science, and Sociology—each advance our understanding of the movement's history, at times offering conflicting interpretations and challenging widely accepted theories from past and present. I begin the book with an overview of the woman suffrage movement that provides background for the essays that follow.

Together, the essays describe why a suffrage movement was necessary, how the movement began, and how it changed over time in response to changes in American history and politics. Through the essays, we are introduced to several generations of suffrage leaders and the supportive relationships as well as the tensions that developed among them. We learn more about the growing diversity of the suffrage constituency in terms of region, religion, race, class, ethnicity, and even attitude, and that the suffrage story includes both a record of harmony and cooperation between diverse groups of suffragists, and a record of discrimination and betrayal. The essays also offer insight as to why some American men and women opposed woman suffrage, and how suffragists finally prevailed.

After the Nineteenth Amendment was added to the U.S. Constitution, the diverse suffrage coalition did not turn into a united voting "bloc." However, women continued to be politically active in a wide range of organizations and movements, sometimes with conflicting agendas. Many women, including women in the U.S. territories, immigrant women, Native American women, and African American women living in the South, had to continue to fight for enfranchisement long after 1920.

Above all, these essays make it clear that the vote was not *given* to women when the Nineteenth Amendment was ratified. Generations of suffragists labored long and hard to establish woman's right to vote in the United States. Indeed, the fight for full voting rights and political equality continues to this day.

In the wake of the voting rights movement of the 1960s and the women's rights movement of the 1960s and 1970s, women turned out to vote in larger numbers, exceeding the turnout of men for the past forty years. Though not unified, the woman's vote is recognized as massive and highly influential in the outcome of elections. Women are a force in politics, not only as voters but as organizers, and increasingly, as elected officials.

After a century of woman suffrage, women have much to celebrate, even as they continue the fight to protect voting rights, to gain more equitable representation in American government, and to fully establish women's equality under the law.

—*Marjorie J. Spruill*
April 2021

xi

ELIZABETH
CADY STANTON

LUCY STONE

LUCRETIA MOTT

SUSAN B. ANTHONY

SOJOURNER
TRUTH

IDA B. WELLS-
BARNETT

CARRIE
CHAPMAN CATT

ANNA
HOWARD SHAW

MARY
CHURCH TERRELL

ALICE PAUL

Generations of leaders of the long struggle for woman suffrage

One

HOW WOMEN WON:

The Long Road to the
Nineteenth Amendment

Marjorie J. Spruill

O N AUGUST 26, 1920, Secretary of State Bainbridge Colby signed a
proclamation officially certifying the ratification of the Nineteenth
Amendment to the U.S. Constitution. It declared that "the right of citizens
of the United States to vote shall not be denied or abridged by the United States or
by any state on account of sex."[1]

This victory was dearly won and long in coming. Between 1848, when reformers
gathered in Seneca Falls, New York and endorsed a woman suffrage resolution,
and 1920, when state legislators gathered in Nashville, Tennessee and ratified the
Nineteenth Amendment, generations of suffragists labored tirelessly for the vote.
As suffragists rejoiced, they recalled the sacrifices of their foremothers and the
many thousands of women who had been a part of this "...continuous, seemingly
endless, chain of activity." In the words of National American Woman Suffrage
Association (NAWSA) leader Carrie Chapman Catt, "Old suffragists who forged
the first links were dead when it ended," while "young suffragists who helped
forge the last links of that chain were not born when it began."[2]

Why this long arduous struggle? In framing the Constitution, women were not
explicitly excluded: the framers generally used the word "persons" when referring
to American citizens and assigned the power to decide who would be allowed to
vote to the individual states. But everywhere in the young republic the vote was
restricted to White property owners on the theory that only they could exercise
independent judgment. That automatically excluded married women, as state
laws generally followed a concept borrowed from British common law in which a
married woman's legal identify was "covered" by that of her husband, but states
also excluded widows and unmarried women with property. The only exception
was New Jersey, which, between 1776 and 1807, permitted all inhabitants who met
property requirements to vote.[3]

Most people assumed women had no independent interests beyond the interests
of their families, which were represented in politics by male heads of household. In
addition, most considered women to be unsuitable as voters—too irrational and
emotional. In the early nineteenth century, people increasingly spoke of women as

better than men in terms of morality and religiosity, but insisted they could inspire and influence male voters for good without being exposed to—and endangered by—the corrupt world of politics.[4]

Even as many states began to loosen restrictions on voting to allow all White men to qualify, including those without property, early advocates of woman suffrage found that ideas about gender and politics—along with laws stipulating qualifications for voting—were extremely resistant to change. Over time and through tremendous effort, and despite many defeats, suffragists managed to persuade many states to enfranchise women, however, some states, especially in the South, remained unwavering in their opposition. Full enfranchisement of women in the United States would ultimately depend on securing an amendment to the U.S. Constitution.

Amending the Constitution was difficult by design. Though the founding fathers intended for it to be a flexible document, they also wanted to forestall faddish changes that lacked broad, national support. To succeed, an amendment had to have the approval of two-thirds of each house of Congress and then three-fourths of the states. It followed that no reform regarded as radical by most citizens at a particular time could be added to the nation's founding document. And any proposed amendment that failed to gain at least some support in every part of the nation was destined to fail.

Thus, the story of how women won the vote in the United States of America is long and complicated. It is a tale of hard work and ingenuity; strategic adaptation to cope with changing circumstances; racial, regional, and generational tensions; struggles between ideals and political realities; and sheer perseverance. But at its core is a story about how a movement begun in one section of the nation by a small group of women considered to be radicals, managed to gain the strong, widespread support required to overcome the obstacles deliberately placed in its path.

The Beginning

The woman suffrage movement originated in the Northeastern United States in the context of antebellum reform. Women began speaking out for women's rights when their efforts to participate fully in the great reform movements of the day— most notably the movement to end slavery—were severely criticized as inappropriate for their sex. Agitation for women's rights preceded the start of a woman suffrage movement by almost two decades.

Maria W. Miller Stewart, an African American woman who grew up in Connecticut as an orphaned indentured servant, is considered the first American woman to speak in public about women's rights. While living in Boston in the early 1830s, she began lecturing and writing about racial and gender injustice. In her passionate speeches with frequent biblical references, Stewart denounced White Americans for enslaving African Americans and mistreating free Blacks in the North. Siding with abolitionist William Lloyd Garrison and other advocates of immediate and uncompensated emancipation, she denounced the more moderate critics of slavery who supported colonization and were raising money to send freeborn and emancipated African Americans to Africa. This money, she insisted, should be spent on aiding and educating them. She also had sharp words for her fellow African Americans, especially women, demanding that they stand up for their rights.[5]

Stewart's audiences were often hostile, jeering her and even throwing rotten vegetables: she not only spoke in public, she addressed what were then called "promiscuous" audiences that included both men and women and were racially mixed. But Stewart bravely defied her critics, once stating, "Shall I, for fear of feeble man who shall die, hold my peace? Shall I for fear of scoffs and frowns, refrain my tongue? Ah, no!" Garrison, who supported women's rights and published her writings, encouraged her, but wrote that Stewart "encountered an opposition even from her Boston circle of friends that would have damped the ardor of most women." She soon moved to New York but continued to support the rights of women and African Americans.[6]

Sarah and Angelina Grimké also spoke out in the 1830s on behalf of women's rights and against slavery and racial prejudice. Though members of a prominent family in Charleston, South Carolina that enslaved African Americans, their opposition to slavery led them to leave behind lives of privilege to live among Quakers in the North. Their unique qualifications led the American Anti-Slavery Society to send them on speaking tours in New York and Massachusetts beginning in 1836. When their lectures began to attract huge audiences that included men, the Grimké sisters encountered tremendous criticism, including from the Congregational ministers of Massachusetts who denounced them for assuming "the place and tone of man as public reformer" and barred them from speaking in their churches.[7]

The controversy led many abolitionists to oppose hiring women as agents, fearing it would undermine the antislavery cause. But the criticism motivated the Grimkés to speak and write to promote women's freedom as well that of the enslaved. Each sister published a series of letters affirming women's right to participate in the great moral reforms of the day. Sarah Grimké also demanded equal pay and equal educational opportunities for women, insisting "Men and women are created equal." She wrote, "All I ask our brethren is that they take their feet off our necks and permit us to stand upright on the ground which God destined for us to occupy."[8]

In 1838, Angelina Grimké became the first woman in U.S. history to address a legislative body when she spoke to the Massachusetts legislature. However, exhaustion from dealing with all the controversy contributed to the sisters' decision to retire from public life. During Angelina's last public address in the brand-new Pennsylvania Hall erected by the Philadelphia Female Anti-Slavery Society, a howling mob of thousands threw stones through the windows and later that night burned the hall to the ground. Still, the Grimké sisters continued to support the struggle to end slavery, working with Angelina's husband, abolitionist Theodore Weld, in compiling a massive collection documenting the realities of slavery later used by Harriet Beecher Stowe in writing *Uncle Tom's Cabin*.[9]

Sarah Grimké
LIBRARY OF CONGRESS

Angelina Grimké
LIBRARY OF CONGRESS

The Grimké sisters' experience inspired yet another early advocate of women's rights, Abigail (Abby) Kelley Foster. Like them, she was a Quaker, fortified in her work by the Quakers' belief that women and men were equally led by an "inner light." Convinced that improving mankind was "the only object worth living for," she, too, became an agent for the American Anti-Slavery Society. In 1839, Foster began what proved to be a long and effective career as a traveling lecturer, converting many to the antislavery and women's rights causes. Facing hostile audiences and angry mobs, she became all the more committed to her work, stating, "We have good cause to be grateful to the slave. In striving to strike his irons off, we found most surely, that we were manacled ourselves."[10]

Foster's nomination to a leadership position in the American Anti-Slavery Society, however, prompted a heated debate that culminated in a permanent schism in the organization. In 1838, Garrison, who continued to support women's full participation, proclaimed in his newspaper, *The Liberator*, "As our object is universal emancipation, to redeem women as well as men from a servile to an equal condition—we shall go for the rights of women to their utmost extent." To the Grimkés, Foster, and other champions of women's rights and of the enslaved, it was impossible to work for the rights of one and deny the rights of the other. The goal was human rights.[11]

The Seneca Falls Convention

A year later, the controversy over women's role in the antislavery movement led indirectly to a fateful meeting of two women who later issued the call for the Seneca Falls Convention. Lucretia Mott, a revered Quaker minister and a co-founder of the Philadelphia Female Anti-Slavery Society in 1833, was an inspiration to the Grimkés and many other younger women reformers. In 1840, Mott arrived in London as a

Abby Kelley Foster
LIBRARY OF CONGRESS

Frederick Douglass
LIBRARY OF CONGRESS

delegate to the World Anti-Slavery Convention, only to find that women delegates were barred from participation. There she met Elizabeth Cady Stanton, a young woman who had come to London with her new husband, a delegate to the convention. The two women were disgusted by the exclusion of women delegates and spent their time in London discussing the status of women in the United States, vowing to do something to improve it. Forming a lasting friendship, they resolved to call a women's rights convention when back in the United States.[12]

In 1848, finding that Mott was visiting nearby, Stanton called on her, suggesting that they go forward with a plan for a convention. They were amazed that with little advance publicity, approximately three hundred people, mostly women, responded to the call. Frederick Douglass, editor of the antislavery newspaper, *The North Star*, published in nearby Rochester, New York, was among them. Having escaped from slavery in 1838, Douglass had become an agent for the American Anti-Slavery Society and in 1845, published his best-selling autobiography which made him famous in the United States and abroad. He was also devoted to the cause of women's rights.[13]

Meeting beforehand, Stanton and Mott drafted a "Declaration of Sentiments" to propose to the participants, using the Declaration of Independence as their model. In it they demanded a wide range of changes in women's social, legal, educational, and economic status, including reform of unjust marriage laws. Of the eleven Resolutions, the ninth would make this gathering iconic in the history of the woman suffrage movement: "Resolved, that it is the duty of the women of this country to secure to themselves their sacred right to the elective franchise."[14]

Ironically, at this conference, which would become famous as the start of the woman suffrage movement, the right to vote was not the initial focus. Indeed, those present at the Seneca Falls Convention regarded the resolution demanding the vote as the most extreme of all the demands they put forward in the Declaration. Stanton, who had been inspired by the Chartist movement for universal manhood suffrage while she was in London, proposed the call for women's enfranchisement. The participants approved the woman suffrage resolution by a narrow margin due to the insistence of Stanton and Douglass.[15]

The Movement Grows

The first decade after the Seneca Falls Convention saw a tremendous amount of women's rights activism as reformers organized local, state, and "national" conventions in the Northeast and Midwest where they continued to debate the issues and work for change. The conventions stirred Americans to think anew about women's rights and women's place in the world.[16]

Though no formal state or national organizations were created, women's rights associations sprung up all over New England and the Midwest, as far west as Wisconsin. The frequent conventions attracted both women and men, some of whom were detractors. Having been forged in the crucible of abolitionism, the women's rights movement was firmly associated in the minds of most Americans with this cause, which was regarded by most as extremely radical. However, women's rights advocates continued to enjoy unconditional support from their allies in the antislavery movement, including Garrison, Douglass, and Wendell Phillips, a prominent abolitionist known for his oratorical skills and courage. At the World Anti-Slavery Convention in London in 1840, he had led the unsuccessful effort to have the women delegates seated.[17]

Lucretia Mott, Elizabeth Cady Stanton, Abby Kelley Foster, and others who had spoken out for women's rights before or during the Seneca Falls Convention, were soon joined by many promising newcomers, among them two women who would become some of the movement's most prominent leaders, Lucy Stone and Susan B. Anthony.[18]

Stone, who grew up on a farm in Massachusetts, was the daughter of abolitionists. She was one of the first American women to earn a B.A. degree, graduating from Oberlin College in Ohio in 1848. Oberlin, founded in 1833, was radically different from other American institutions of higher education; it began admitting women and African Americans in 1837. As a girl, Stone was inspired by Sarah and Angelina Grimké and Foster to devote her life to fighting against slavery and for women's rights. Stone began traveling as a speaker for the American Anti-Slavery Society in 1848. In 1850, she organized a convention in Worcester, Massachusetts billed as the first National Woman's Rights Convention. When she married Henry Blackwell in 1855, they wrote and published egalitarian marriage vows, and Stone made history by retaining her original name.[19]

Susan B. Anthony also became involved in the burgeoning women's rights movement, bringing her enormous talent as an organizer and campaigner to the cause. She grew up in a reform-minded family with parents committed to abolition and temperance. They moved from Massachusetts to New York when she was young, living near Rochester, New York where she met many leading abolitionists, including Frederick Douglass, William Lloyd Garrison, and Wendell Phillips. Starting her career as a teacher and outraged by the vast discrepancy in the salaries of male and female teachers, Anthony was an early advocate of equal pay for equal work. She was also involved in the temperance movement, where she encountered the same hostility to women's public speaking and leadership that characterized much of the antislavery movement. In 1851, while in Seneca Falls to hear an antislavery lecture, Anthony met Elizabeth Cady Stanton and they began working together for women's rights; it was the beginning of a fruitful collaboration that would last the rest of their lives.[20]

African American women and men also attended these conventions throughout the 1850s and 1860s, committed to expanding women's rights while working to end slavery. African American and White women reformers often worked side by side, including organizing these conventions. Most African American women pioneers in these two movements were born free and were well educated and middle class, such as Harriet Forten Purvis and Margaretta Forten of a prominent family of reformers in Philadelphia. In 1833, along with their mother, Charlotte Forten, and Lucretia Mott, they co-founded the interracial Philadelphia Female Anti-Slavery Society, joined shortly thereafter by the Grimké Sisters. Purvis and her husband, Robert Purvis, played central roles in the Underground Railroad and worked with Harriet Tubman. He joined his wife in supporting women's rights. Harriet Forten Purvis and Margaretta Forten helped organize the fifth National Women's Rights Convention in 1854. Sarah Remond, an antislavery speaker from a prominent African American family in Salem, Massachusetts, also took part in these conventions, winning acclaim as a speaker, notably at the 1858 National Women's Conference in New York.[21]

In addition, there was Sojourner Truth, who had escaped slavery in New York and went on to become an abolitionist and advocate for women's rights. Although Truth never learned to read or write, she dictated her memoirs, *The Narrative of Sojourner Truth: A Northern Slave*, to a friend, and they were published by William Lloyd Garrison in 1850. That same year, Truth began attending women's rights conventions, actively

Sojourner Truth

supporting woman suffrage and becoming one of the most renowned advocates for gender and racial equality of the nineteenth century. Her speech, often referred to as "Ain't I a Woman?" delivered at the 1851 Women's Rights Convention held in Akron, Ohio, is recognized as one of the most famous speeches in the history of the movement. Truth continued speaking for the rights of women and African Americans throughout the 1850s and beyond.[22]

As was the case at Seneca Falls, participants at these conventions addressed a wide array of issues and made recommendations for reform—then pressing legislatures to implement the reforms they recommended. The primary gain was the expansion of marital rights laws in some two dozen states. Women's rights activism in the United States cheered women's rights advocates in Britain and throughout Europe: women reformers in the United States, meanwhile, were inspired by the efforts of reformers abroad.[23]

During the Civil War, however, women's rights supporters in the United States put their nascent movement on hold to support the war effort. Along with their male allies, they worked to make it a war to end slavery as well as to save the Union. In 1863, Stanton and Anthony founded the Women's Loyal National League, which launched a massive petition drive to Congress calling for a constitutional amendment to permanently abolish slavery throughout the United States. This was necessary as the Emancipation Proclamation was a wartime measure freeing enslaved African Americans only in the states "still in rebellion." The League had five thousand members within the first year. By the end of the war, they had gathered signatures from almost four hundred thousand women and men—approximately four percent of the Union's population. Their ally, Senator Charles Sumner of Massachusetts, credited this "mighty army" as crucial to building public support for what became the Thirteenth Amendment.[24]

Dashed Hopes for Universal Suffrage

After the Civil War, women's rights leaders came to see enfranchisement as one of the most important—perhaps *the* most important—of their aims. It was essential, they believed, both as a symbol of equality and individuality, and as a means of improving one's legal and social condition. Their goal was universal suffrage, not just woman suffrage. Banding together with former antislavery movement allies, women's rights leaders formed a new group, the American Equal Rights Association (AERA) with the stated goal of securing "equal rights to all American citizens, especially the right of suffrage, irrespective of race, color or sex." Lucretia Mott served as president, and Elizabeth Cady Stanton and Frederick Douglass served as vice presidents. Other officers of this new organization included Susan B. Anthony, Lucy Stone, her husband Henry Blackwell, Harriet Forten Purvis, and Purvis's daughter Hattie Purvis. Frances Ellen Watkins Harper, a former abolitionist who was a poet, writer, and teacher, also joined the group.[25]

As Congress debated the legislation that eventually became the Fourteenth and Fifteenth Amendments, however, woman suffrage advocates found even former allies insisting that the demand for women's enfranchisement be postponed in the interest of securing suffrage for Black men. The Fourteenth Amendment, ratified in 1868, granted citizenship to all persons born or naturalized in the United States, including formerly enslaved people. But in the second section of the Fourteenth Amendment, which dealt with enforcement, Congress decreed that any state that denied the vote to "male" citizens would be punished by reduced representation. Woman suffrage advocates protested strenuously, aghast that the amendment did not call for universal suffrage for all and that the word "male" was added to the Constitution for the first time. When it appeared that further action, a Fifteenth Amendment, ratified in 1870, was required to secure the voting rights of the freedmen, women were again left out.[26]

Meanwhile, some former allies, particularly Wendell Phillips, aware there was considerable opposition to the proposed amendments, urged suffragists to desist campaigning for woman suffrage and work only to assure voting rights for the freedmen, stating, "One question at a time. This hour belongs to the Negro."[27]

Stanton and Anthony were incensed at Phillips's suggestion that the quest for woman suffrage be deferred for a generation, believing that, in Stanton's words, Reconstruction was "the opportunity, perhaps for the century," to press forward on full citizenship rights irrespective of race or sex. Anthony reportedly replied she "would rather cut off her right hand than ask for the ballot for the Black man and not for woman."[28]

Sojourner Truth was also distressed by Phillips's "Negro's hour" priority, and reminded her fellow reformers that "the Negro" included women also. Addressing the AERA, Truth said, "There is a great stir about colored men getting their rights, but not a word about the colored women, and if colored men get their rights and not colored women theirs, you see the colored men will be masters over the women, and it will be just as bad as it was before. So, I am for keeping the thing going while things are stirring."[29]

Douglass continued to affirm the desirability and justice of woman suffrage, but to him, enfranchisement of African American men—a claim made more viable by Black men's service to the Union during the Civil War—took priority. Moreover, he insisted that given the perils faced by newly freed African Americans in the South, enfranchising Black men was a matter of life and death.[30] Douglass and other advocates of Black male suffrage saw it as crucial that newly-freed African Americans be able to vote to protect themselves against Southern Whites' efforts to virtually re-enslave them.

Many Republican politicians also saw the enfranchisement of Black men as crucial for their party. Black men would almost certainly vote for Republicans, guaranteeing support for the party in the Southern states where the vast number of Whites were Democrats. Black male voters' support would enable the Republicans to maintain their dominance of national politics and carry out their plans for Reconstruction of the South. Republicans reasoned that if women were enfranchised, not only Black women would vote, and in the South the far more numerous White women, who were likely to vote for Democrats, would gain the vote.[31]

Suffragists' former allies insisted that if the controversial issue of woman suffrage was included, the Fifteenth Amendment would not be ratified, and they begged suffragists to understand. The issue of how to respond split the woman suffrage movement in two. In 1869, women suffragists divided acrimoniously, largely over the issue of whether to support ratification of the Fifteenth Amendment or not.

Suffrage Strategies During "the Schism"

Harriet Forten Purvis, 1870s
LIBRARY OF CONGRESS

Frances Harper, 1872
LIBRARY OF CONGRESS

In 1869, suffragists founded two organizations with different positions on the Fifteenth Amendment and different ideas about how best to promote woman suffrage. The National Woman Suffrage Association (NWSA), headed by Elizabeth Cady Stanton and Susan B. Anthony, actively opposed the amendment. Given their background as antislavery activists and their staunch advocacy of universal suffrage, their opposition and public statements about the Fifteenth Amendment shocked and horrified long-time allies, including Frederick Douglass and Frances Harper. Stanton and Anthony bitterly denounced the enfranchisement of what they called "ignorant" and "degraded" former slaves and recent immigrants ahead of "educated White women" as a terrible injustice that would make the task of woman suffrage advocates harder than ever. Stanton was from an upper-class background and held elitist sentiments. She expressed outrage at the idea of suffragists having to go around the country begging "paupers, knaves, and drunkards" and every "Tom, Dick, Harry, Patrick, Hans, Yung-Tung, and Sambo" to accept them as political equals. Stanton declared that she, for one, refused to do so.[32]

When the Fifteenth Amendment was ratified in 1870, Stanton, Anthony, and their associates in the NWSA called for another federal amendment—hopefully the Sixteenth Amendment—that would enfranchise women. The New York based NWSA, led exclusively by women, focused on the enfranchisement of women through federal action and promoted a wide variety of women's rights measures in its short-lived journal, *The Revolution*.[33]

The other organization founded in 1869 was the American Woman Suffrage Association (AWSA), with headquarters in Boston. Lucy Stone led the AWSA. Her husband, Henry Blackwell, played an active role in the organization, as did Antoinette Brown Blackwell, Stone's sister-in-law and a pioneering minister. Other AWSA members included Julia Ward Howe, author of the "Battle Hymn of the Republic"; Henry Ward Beecher, brother of Harriet Beecher Stowe and one of the nation's most prominent ministers; and Thomas Wentworth Higginson, White commander of African American troops during the Civil War and ardent supporter of women's rights. The AWSA supported ratification of the Fifteenth Amendment while working for woman suffrage as well. Stone explained, "I will be thankful in my soul if *any* body can get out of the terrible pit."[34]

Some African American suffrage supporters, including Harriet Forten Purvis—a close friend of Anthony—and journalist Mary Ann Shadd Cary, sided with the NWSA, however, the AWSA attracted more African American affiliates. For example, prominent businesswoman Caroline Remond Putnam helped found the Massachusetts Woman Suffrage Association under the auspices of the AWSA. Publisher and civil rights leader Josephine St. Pierre Ruffin, who was friends with Julia Ward Howe and Lucy Stone, was an early AWSA member. Frances Harper also chose the AWSA; speaking at the AWSA conference in 1873, she stated, "Much as White women need the ballot, colored women need it more." Sojourner Truth attended conferences sponsored by both groups.[35]

The AWSA endorsed adding a federal woman suffrage amendment to the U.S. Constitution, but recognizing how little backing the idea had at the time, concentrated on developing grassroots support for women's enfranchisement. The organization engaged in a massive educational campaign designed to make woman suffrage seem less radical and consistent with widely shared American values. It employed agents who traveled across the nation speaking and circulating literature, and reached a large audience through the AWSA's newspaper, *The Woman's Journal*. Members promoted state suffrage amendments and various forms of "partial suffrage" legislation, including bills giving women the right to vote on school or municipal issues, or in presidential elections. They believed that these measures were desirable in themselves and a means to the eventual end—full suffrage for women of the United States.[36]

The "New Departure"

Meanwhile, suffragists associated with the National Woman Suffrage Association (NWSA) were disheartened by the response to the proposed federal amendment and disdainful of the state-by-state approach as slow and cumbersome. Instead, they tried to win their rights by other approaches known collectively as the "New Departure." Invoking the equal protection clause of the Fourteenth Amendment, these suffragists challenged women's exclusion from voting on the grounds that, as citizens, women were entitled to vote. Victoria Woodhull, a radical, iconoclastic, and charismatic figure who briefly gained the support of Elizabeth Cady Stanton and Susan B. Anthony, had made this argument before Congress in 1871.[37]

In the early 1870s, hundreds of women claimed the right to vote based on the equal protection clause of the Fourteenth Amendment and tried to register and vote, though most were turned away. In Hyde Park, Massachusetts, a group of forty-two women, led by Sarah Grimké and Angelina Grimké Weld, made their way through a heavy snowstorm to cast their votes. Sojourner Truth attempted to vote in Battle Creek, Michigan, and Mary Ann Shadd Cary was one of sixty-four women who tried to vote in Washington, D.C. In 1872, Anthony managed to cast a vote in Rochester, New York, hoping to be arrested and then test this new strategy in the courts. She was arrested and indicted for "knowingly, wrongfully and unlawfully vot[ing] for a representative to the Congress of the United States." Found guilty and fined, Anthony insisted she would never pay a dollar of it.[38]

Virginia Minor, a suffrage leader in St. Louis, succeeded in getting the issue before the U.S. Supreme Court, but in a key decision in 1875, *Minor v. Happersett*, the court ruled unanimously that citizenship did not automatically confer the right to vote. The decision forced suffragists to face a grim reality: woman suffrage would not come swiftly from an interpretation of the U.S. Constitution that accepted women's claim to the rights and privileges of all citizens. Instead, it would have to come about by state legislation or a constitutional amendment specially worded to enfranchise women.[39]

When a federal woman suffrage amendment was introduced in the Senate in 1878, it contained the same language as the bill that would become the Nineteenth Amendment, emphasizing the distinct claims of women and prohibiting denial of voting rights to citizens "on account of sex." It would take forty-two more years and a tremendous amount of work on the part of suffragists working at the state and national levels for it to become law.[40]

Pioneering Woman Suffrage States

Even as the National Woman Suffrage Association (NWSA) and the American Woman Suffrage Association (AWSA) competed for support and tried several strategies for winning female enfranchisement to no avail, woman suffrage was making headway in the West. While most politicians in Eastern states were dead set against woman suffrage, politicians and voters in several Western states enfranchised women and, at times, battled Congress for the right to do so.

In 1869, the very year that frustrated Eastern suffragists parted ways and formed the NWSA and the AWSA, the territory of Wyoming unexpectedly led the nation in the adoption of woman suffrage. In 1890, when it appeared that Congress would not approve its application for statehood as long as Wyoming allowed woman suffrage, the territorial legislature sent a telegram to Congress declaring that they would remain out of the Union a hundred years rather than join without the women. Even the Mormon stronghold of Utah enacted woman suffrage in 1870 while still a territory; it came into the Union as a state with woman suffrage in 1896. Other pioneering suffrage states included Colorado, which enfranchised women in 1893, the first suffrage victory as a result of a state referendum, and Idaho, which enfranchised women by state constitutional amendment in 1896.[41]

Academic historians as well as proud Westerners have speculated at length about *why* the West was so precocious in its adoption of woman suffrage, putting forth a great variety of explanations. Western suffragists such as Esther Morris of Wyoming, who became a suffrage advocate after attending women's rights conferences back East, and Emmeline Wells, a Mormon suffrage leader and a "plural wife," certainly deserve part of the credit for these early victories. Credit must also be given to Eastern suffrage associations that aided suffragists in the West through speaking tours, funding, and organizational experience. Elizabeth Cady Stanton, Susan B. Anthony, Lucy Stone, and future national suffrage leaders Dr. Anna Howard Shaw and Carrie Chapman Catt all stumped for suffrage out West.[42]

However, the question remains: Why were woman suffrage advocates successful in the West when unable to make headway elsewhere in the United States? One theory is that frontier conditions undermined traditional gender roles and that women, having proven their ability to conquer difficult conditions and do "men's work," were rewarded with the vote. A related theory is that traditions and institutions in the West were less entrenched than in the East and people in the West were more open to new ideas. On the other hand, some have insisted that politicians in the West supported woman suffrage hoping that women voters would bring Eastern gender conventions along in their covered wagons and help to "civilize" as well as populate the West.[43]

Most historians stress practical politics rather than advanced thinking as the explanation, emphasizing that politicians in the West—whatever their views on woman suffrage—found it expedient to enfranchise women. For example, Wyoming was a brand-new territory, established only one year before adopting woman suffrage: Wyoming politicians hoped to gain publicity and to attract women migrants to the territory. The victory has also been attributed to Reconstruction-era politics with Republican and Democratic leaders both supporting woman suffrage, but for different reasons. Territorial Governor John Allen Campbell, a Union Army veteran appointed by President Ulysses Grant, was a Republican who believed in universal equal rights. The legislator who introduced the woman suffrage bill, William H. Bright, was a native of Virginia and a Democrat, who opposed the newly ratified Fourteenth Amendment. His wife, Julia Bright, was for woman suffrage and in his view, if African American men were going to vote, there was no reason to deny the vote to women. Bright and his Democratic colleagues also hoped that doubling the size of the White electorate might ensure White control of the territory and that grateful women would vote for the Democrats.[44]

In Utah, Mormons of both sexes believed that women's votes would aid in preserving Mormon traditions—including polygamy—and that enfranchising women would help dispel the idea widely accepted in the East that Mormon women were oppressed. More importantly, perhaps, Mormon leaders were confident that enfranchising women would tip the balance of power in their favor in their ongoing power struggle with the non-Mormon population, consisting largely of miners, railroad construction workers, cowboys, and prospectors, who tended not to have women with them.[45]

In Colorado and Idaho, two states with larger and more diverse populations, the issues were different and even more complex. Racial issues were brought into the debate over woman suffrage by people on both sides. African American women were involved in the campaign, particularly in Denver, but most suffrage supporters were White and middle class, and many of them argued that White, native-born American women should have at least equal political rights with African American men. Some White suffragists also objected to the fact that Native American men who, under an 1887 law, were allowed citizenship and voting rights if they moved off of reservations, and Chinese men, who were allowed to vote if born in the United States, were voting ahead of White American-born women. Many anti-suffragists railed against adding to the electorate what they called "Negro wenches" as well as Chinese and Native American women.[46]

Success came as local suffragists and their allies from Eastern suffrage associations became increasingly adept at building coalitions and finding ways to appeal to politicians. Suffragists in Colorado benefitted from alliances with a labor union, the Knights of Labor, and a new political movement, Populism, that aided them after they pledged to support silver as a currency basis, in addition to gold. In Idaho, all three parties—Populists, Democrats, and Republicans—endorsed woman suffrage, and in 1896 support from Populists, the labor movement, and Mormons, contributed to a victory for the woman suffrage referendum by a two-to-one margin.[47]

For whatever reasons, these four Western states were the only states to adopt woman suffrage in the nineteenth century. Many other campaigns were attempted in Western states, and in a few cases, suffragists came close to success. Most notably, back in 1854, the territory of Washington defeated a suffrage bill by a single vote. In 1868, Nevada passed an amendment eliminating the words "male" and "White" from the voting requirements in the state constitution, but Nevada law required that any constitutional change be approved by two successive legislative sessions and in 1871 the measure failed.[48]

Suffragists also made unsuccessful bids for enfranchisement in California, Oregon, and Washington. Oregon suffrage leader Abigail Scott Duniway and Susan B. Anthony made a two-thousand-mile journey through Washington and Oregon in 1871, and built considerable support for the suffrage cause. But in the 1870s and 1880s, Oregon legislatures defeated suffrage bills four times, and

Washington passed suffrage laws twice only to have the state Supreme Court invalidate them. A hard-fought referendum campaign in California in 1896 failed, despite the state's suffragists' tireless work, aided by Carrie Chapman Catt and Susan B. Anthony. Attempts in 1889 and 1898 to re-enfranchise women of Washington also failed. Suffragists in Arizona, Montana, and Nevada lobbied their legislatures repeatedly but without success. There were no other territorial or state victories in the United States for the rest of the century.[49]

Oregon Poster
LIBRARY OF CONGRESS

Oregonians began another major push in the new century, and woman suffrage was on the ballot in 1900, 1904, 1906, 1908, and 1910, but lost each time. However, when the next round of state victories took place, beginning in 1910, the victories were all in the West: Washington in 1910 and California in 1911, soon followed by Oregon, Kansas, and Arizona in 1912, and Nevada and Montana in 1914.[50]

The West's precociousness on woman suffrage was reflected in Western women's early entry into elected office. In the 1890s, Idaho, Colorado, and Utah all elected women to their state legislatures. In a bizarre historical twist, Utah suffragist, physician, and plural wife, Dr. Martha Hughes Cannon, was elected to the state senate in 1896. Her victory gained considerable national attention as she was not only the first woman elected to a state senate but she ran against and defeated her husband. Montana elected Jeannette Rankin, a leading suffragist in the state, to the U.S. House of Representatives in 1916, making her the first woman to hold federal office in the United States.[51]

Martha M. Hughes Cannon
LIBRARY OF CONGRESS

Meanwhile, Stanton and Anthony traveled to France and England in 1882 and 1883, where they found kindred spirits and instituted a committee of correspondence with the goal of establishing an international association for women's advancement. The goal was realized at the NWSA's 1888 conference in Washington, D.C. when representatives of many nations founded the International Council of Women (ICW).[52]

Suffrage sentiment was flourishing internationally, and in achieving full enfranchisement at the national level, suffragists outside the United States would be the first to taste success. In 1893, women in New Zealand won the vote, followed by Australia in 1902. These countries became the first in the world to enfranchise women, followed shortly by Finland in 1906 and Norway in 1913.[53]

Woman Suffrage and Temperance

The suffrage movement won a valuable ally when Frances Willard, as president of the Woman's Christian Temperance Union (WCTU), led thousands of otherwise quite traditional women to "convert" to the cause of woman suffrage as a means of protecting the home, women, and children. Following its official endorsement in 1881, the WCTU created a Department of Franchise under Zerelda Wallace and Dr. Anna Howard Shaw, which encouraged state WCTU chapters to endorse suffrage and distribute suffrage literature. African American suffragists also advanced the suffrage cause through the WCTU. Both Hattie Purvis and Frances Harper promoted woman suffrage in the role of WCTU Superintendent of Work Among Colored People.[54]

By 1890, the WCTU had grown into the largest woman's organization of the nineteenth century. It greatly aided the woman suffrage movement not only in the United States, but abroad. For example, the WCTU played a vital role in the victories for woman suffrage in New Zealand and Australia. In the United States, the WCTU was crucial to suffrage success both in attracting support among women who might have considered the existing suffrage organizations and their leaders eccentric or radical, and in expanding the suffrage movement's constituency to all parts of the United States. This included the South where the WCTU organized both White and Black women, though in segregated chapters.[55]

The WCTU endorsement, however, had serious repercussions for the suffrage movement; the politically powerful liquor industry concluded that woman suffrage was a threat to be stopped at all costs. At least one historian has argued that suffragists on the West Coast began to win their suffrage campaigns only after disassociating themselves from temperance. Looking back after 1920, Carrie Chapman Catt would denounce the liquor industry as "the Invisible Enemy" that "for forty years kept suffragists waiting for the woman's hour" through its corrupt manipulation of American politics.[56]

Unity Restored Through the NAWSA

One of the most important turning points in the history of the woman suffrage movement in the United States came in 1890 as the two national suffrage organizations reunited. At the instigation of younger suffragists, the movement's aging pioneers put aside their differences sufficiently to merge their rival organizations into the National American Woman Suffrage Association (NAWSA). Elizabeth Cady Stanton was chosen as president, Lucy Stone as head of the

Executive Committee, and Susan B. Anthony as Vice President, but it was Anthony who actually took command of the new organization, officially becoming president in 1892 and remaining in office until 1900.

While continuing to demand a federal amendment, NAWSA leaders concluded they must first build support within the states, eventually winning enough state suffrage amendments—and thus creating enough women voters—that Congress would be compelled to approve a federal amendment and three-fourths of the states would be sure to ratify. "I don't know the exact number of States we shall have to have," Anthony explained, "but I do know that there will come a day when that number will automatically and resistlessly [sic] act on the Congress of the United States to compel the submission of a federal suffrage amendment."[57]

Stanton continued to address a wide range of feminist issues and assert positions too radical for most suffragists; she became somewhat estranged from the movement after 1895 when she published *The Woman's Bible*, indicting Christianity for contributing to the subordination of women.[58] However, most NAWSA leaders, including Anthony, thought it imperative that the movement focus almost exclusively on winning the vote. While individual suffragists supported a wide variety of causes, they believed the national suffrage organization must work solely for enfranchisement, and as a single-issue group be able to attract the largest possible number of followers. In keeping with this strategy and influenced by the conservatism of new recruits, the suffragists went to great lengths to avoid association with radical causes.

Race, Region, and Suffrage Strategy

This new approach included attempts by White suffragists to shed the long-term association of women's rights with the rights of African Americans. Although the National American Woman Suffrage Association (NAWSA) never stopped using natural rights arguments for woman suffrage, many White suffragists were still indignant that Black men were enfranchised ahead of them and angry at the ease with which White immigrant men gained the vote. Increasingly, White suffragists departed from the movement's earlier emphasis on universal suffrage and employed racist and nativist rhetoric and tactics. Though individual friendships between White and African American suffragists continued and new ones developed, the interracial quality of woman suffrage movement in its earliest years when Blacks and Whites worked together for human equality was lost. As White suffragists no longer welcomed Black women's participation in their organizations and conferences, African American suffragists worked through their own organizations seeking to gain their own voting rights and to restore those of Black men.[59]

These changes resulted in part from the fact that the NAWSA now included thousands of younger White women from all parts of the nation who had not been a part of the earlier movements to end slavery and attain suffrage for all. Most of them shared the idea gaining currency at the time that voting should be a privilege and a duty of the best qualified. Many White suffrage advocates favored literacy tests for voting, insisting that as long as the nation provided free public education, such a requirement was acceptable, even an incentive to self-improvement.[60]

The last three decades of the woman suffrage struggle coincided with an era in which support for universal suffrage waned across the country. Numerous factors contributed to this trend, including dramatic increases in the numbers of immigrants from Southern and eastern Europe and Asia, and imperialist ventures that left the U.S. government debating what rights could be claimed by people of color who inhabited territories under its control. In addition, the stubborn resistance of Southern White conservatives to the political equality of African Americans, along with distorted negative portrayals of Reconstruction-era governments that influenced public opinion outside the South, led many White, native-born voters to demand restriction rather than expansion of the electorate. In the 1890s, African American suffragists felt betrayed as NAWSA leaders crafted new strategies designed to succeed in this inhospitable climate, especially in the South.[61]

The historic connection between the woman's movement and the antislavery movement made advocacy of woman suffrage anathema to most White Southerners, and daunting to the Southern women that NAWSA leaders hoped to recruit. Southern White women who took up the suffrage cause were denounced as traitors to their region, accused of threatening the South's key institution—White supremacy. As one Alabama legislator put it, White Southern suffragists allowed themselves "to be misled by bold women who are the product of the peculiar social conditions of our Northern cities into advocating a political innovation the realization of which would be the undoing of the South."[62]

NAWSA leaders were aware, however, that a national victory would require support from at least some Southern states. Thus, in the 1890s they went to great lengths to, in Kentucky suffragist Laura Clay's words, "bring in the South." Using a strategy first suggested by Lucy Stone's husband, Henry Blackwell, Northern and Southern leaders began to argue that woman suffrage—far from endangering White supremacy in the South—could be a means of restoring it. Perhaps leading politicians in the South, like those in the West, might be persuaded that woman suffrage was expedient, a way to realize their political goals.[63]

At that point, Southern White politicians had yet to adopt the restrictions on voter eligibility they would soon put in place that disqualified most African American men, and were casting about for means other than the usual fraud and violence to solidify White control. NAWSA leaders and their Southern allies insisted that, as White women outnumbered Black women in the South, the adoption of woman suffrage would allow the South to restore White supremacy in politics *without* disfranchising Black men and risking congressional repercussions. When reminded that there were more African Americans than Whites in some parts of the South, White suffragists suggested that educational requirements, or even property requirements, could be used to ensure that most of the new voters would be White.[64] The NAWSA spent considerable time and resources pursuing this "Southern strategy," locating suffrage sympathizers and organizing them, sending out recruiters, circulating literature, dispatching Carrie Chapman Catt and Susan B. Anthony on speaking tours through the region, and holding national conferences in Atlanta and New Orleans. However, by 1903 most suffragists recognized that the strategy had failed; the region's politicians had refused, in the words of one Mississippi politician, to "cower behind petticoats" and "use lovely women" to maintain White supremacy. Instead, these conservative men found other means to do so that did not involve the "destruction" of woman's traditional role. NAWSA leaders turned their attention elsewhere, and for a time, suffrage activity in the region declined.[65]

African Americans in the Struggle

African American suffragists were appalled by the racism White suffragists exhibited in the late nineteenth and early twentieth centuries. Still, they persisted, determined to gain the right to vote. For instance, the Rollin sisters, a family of activists in Columbia, South Carolina in the late 1860s and 1870s, were strong supporters of woman suffrage and well situated to promote it. Charlotte, Kathryn, and Louisa Rollin turned their home into a "salon" where movers and shakers in Reconstruction-era politics gathered. In addition, Frances was married to a state legislator, William J. Whipper, who promoted woman suffrage as a delegate to the 1868 South Carolina Constitutional Convention. In 1869, Charlotte "Lottie" Rollin addressed the state legislature on behalf of woman suffrage, insisting that "public opinion has had a tendency to limit woman's sphere to too small a circle" and asking for suffrage, "not as a favor, not as a privilege, but as a right."[66]

In 1870, the Rollins held a Woman's Rights Convention in Columbia attended by some of the state's most influential male Republicans, Black and White. With Lucy Stone's encouragement, in 1871 the sisters established a state suffrage organization affiliated with the American Woman Suffrage Association (AWSA) with Lottie Rollin representing South Carolina as an ex-officio member of the AWSA Executive Committee.[67]

Throughout the 1870s and 1880s, Mary Ann Shadd Cary continued to be involved in the National Woman Suffrage Association (NWSA). Cary, who became one of America's first female African American lawyers when she graduated from Howard University's school of law in 1870, joined other suffragists in testifying before the House Judiciary Committee in January 1874. Cary was disappointed when NWSA leaders rebuffed her request to include the names of ninety-four Black woman suffragists from Washington, D.C. on the Declaration of the Rights of the Women of the United States in 1876. Nevertheless, she remained a committed suffragist and attended all NWSA national conventions held in Washington, D.C.— giving an address at the 1878 convention. In 1880, Cary founded a Colored Woman's Franchise Association in Washington, D.C.

As noted, Frances Harper and Hattie Purvis promoted woman suffrage through their work with the Woman's Christian Temperance Union (WCTU) in the 1880s. Purvis, the daughter of Harriet Forten Purvis, had grown up in the suffrage movement. She was an officer in the Pennsylvania Woman Suffrage Association in 1884, and served as a delegate to NWSA meetings in that decade. When the International Council of Women (ICW) was created in 1888, African American women were involved from the beginning, including Frances Harper, who addressed the founding convention in Washington, D.C. A year later, Hattie Purvis accompanied Susan B. Anthony, a family friend, to London to attend the ICW meeting there.[68]

Even as White suffragists and suffrage groups distanced themselves from advocacy of the rights of African Americans in the late nineteenth and early twentieth centuries—a period that has been described as "the nadir" of race relations in the United States—the ranks of Black women working for the vote grew steadily. This rise in the number of African American suffragists reflected an increase in the number of educated, middle-class Black women in society and their eagerness to promote women's rights in tandem with racial uplift. The deterioration of race relations, including the rise of Jim Crow, a surge in the number of lynchings, and the Southern states' disfranchisement of Black men, made many Black women all the more determined to organize for collective self-help and resistance. Many worked through African American women's clubs affiliated with the National Association of Colored Women (NACW) founded in 1896.[69]

The NACW's first president, Mary Church Terrell, was an ardent suffragist. Born in Memphis to formerly enslaved parents who, after the Civil War, became affluent business owners, Terrell earned Bachelor's and Master's degrees at Oberlin College. She then spent several years in Europe where she became fluent in German, French, and Italian, and experienced what it was like to live free of the pervasive racism of life in the United States. Later, she settled in Washington, D.C. and became a teacher, principal, and a member of the District of Columbia Board of Education. As president of the NACW between 1896 and 1901, Terrell was a powerful advocate for woman suffrage and racial justice, and became one of the best-known African American women in the nation.[70]

When a horrific race riot in Ohio led a group of White liberals and African American leaders to issue a call for a meeting to discuss racial justice, Terrell was one of the signers. The 1909 meeting resulted in the founding of the National Association for the Advancement of Colored People (NAACP), which aimed to secure racial equality, including enforcement of the Fourteenth and Fifteenth Amendments. In the pages of the NAACP magazine, *The Crisis*, whose editor, W.E.B. DuBois, was a suffrage supporter, Terrell called on African Americans to support women's enfranchisment. Pointing out that the arguments against the Fifteenth Amendment mirrored those against women's right to vote, she wrote: "What could be more absurd and ridiculous than that one group of individuals who are trying to throw off the yoke of oppression themselves...should favor laws and customs which impeded the progress of another unfortunate group and hinder them in every conceivable way."[71]

Likewise, as a member of the National American Suffrage Association (NAWSA), Terrell challenged White suffragists to support the struggles of African Americans, including the fights for equal suffrage and against lynching. At a time when few African American women were invited to speak at White suffragists' conferences, Terrell not only addressed NAWSA conferences but also represented American suffragists at an International Council of Women (ICW) conference in Berlin, where she spoke in fluent German and French about racial prejudice in the United States.[72]

Ida B. Wells-Barnett was also a nationally and internationally prominent advocate for gender and racial justice in the late nineteenth and early twentieth centuries. She became famous as a suffragist and as a passionate crusader against lynching. Born into slavery in Mississippi in 1862, she was freed six months later by the Emancipation Proclamation. As an adult, Wells-Barnett moved to Memphis where she was co-owner of a newspaper. Her crusade against lynching began in 1892 after three Memphis men, all friends of hers, were lynched after competing successfully with White businessmen. Afterward, she began investigating other lynchings and publishing the facts behind them, challenging the pervasive fiction that lynchings were committed by White men solely to avenge White women assaulted by Black men. In response, a White mob destroyed Wells-Barnett's newspaper office while she was away, and threatened to kill her if she ever returned to Memphis. She traveled extensively, founding anti-lynching societies and lecturing, including two trips to Great Britain in 1893 and 1894. Wells-Barnett settled in Chicago and founded many organizations and programs to serve the African American community, while continuing to travel and speak nationwide. Along with Terrell, Wells-Barnett was a co-founder of the NAACP and a member of the NAWSA.[73]

In 1913, after suffragists won the right to vote in presidential and municipal elections in Illinois, Wells-Barnett organized the Alpha Suffrage Club through which Black women played an influential role in Chicago politics. Outspoken and uncompromising, Wells-Barnett famously defied White suffragists' instructions that Black women march in a separate section at the back of the 1913 NAWSA suffrage parade in Washington, D.C. Instead, Wells-Barnett claimed her place in the middle of the parade with the Illinois delegation.[74]

Frances "Fannie" Barrier Williams was also a Chicago-based reformer, lecturer, and clubwoman who worked for women's rights and racial justice. Like Terrell, Barrier Williams was a co-founder of the NACW and a NAWSA member. A native of Brockport, New York, she spent most of her life in Chicago where, as a member of the city's Black elite, she used her considerable organizing ability and influence to expand services and create new institutions to aid African Americans and other residents of the city. Her efforts included an interracial hospital with a training school for nurses, a settlement house named the Frederick Douglass Center, and the Phillis Wheatley Home for Girls. In 1895, Barrier Williams became the first African American

Fannie Barrier Williams
LIBRARY OF CONGRESS

Adella Hunt Logan
LOGAN FAMILY COLLECTION

member of the prestigious Chicago Woman's Club. She gained national fame for her successful battle for representation of African Americans in the Columbia Exposition of 1893 in Chicago, where she delivered a famous address, "The Intellectual Progress of the Colored Women of the United States Since the Emancipation Proclamation." Barrier Williams was a supporter of W.E.B DuBois, and an early member of the NAACP. An avid supporter of woman suffrage and a friend of Susan B. Anthony, she was invited to eulogize Anthony at the 1907 NAWSA convention.[75]

Nannie Helen Burroughs, a Virginia-born woman whose parents had both been enslaved, became a prominent educator and church leader as well as a suffragist. When only thirty, she founded the National Training School for Women and Girls in Washington, D.C., one of the first vocational schools in the nation for African American girls and women. Burroughs first gained national recognition through a speech, "How the Sisters are Hindered from Helping," which she gave at the 1900 conference of the large and influential National Baptist Convention (NBC). For many decades thereafter, Burroughs promoted woman suffrage as an officer of the NBC's Women's Convention. She wrote and spoke extensively on the importance of enfranchisement for women of color in order to protect themselves against discrimination and injustice, and the need for African American and White women to work together to gain the vote.[76]

Adella Hunt Logan, a faculty member at the Tuskegee Institute in Alabama, was one of the beleaguered African American women supporting woman suffrage while remaining in the South. An active member of the NACW between 1900 and 1914, Logan spoke frequently at NACW conferences and headed the organization's department of suffrage. A life member of the NAWSA, she sometimes attended its conventions held in the South that excluded African American women. Logan looked like a White woman and on rare occasions such as these passed as White in order to attend. After meeting privately with Carrie Chapman Catt at a conference in Atlanta, Logan explained (somewhat sarcastically) to a friend that she "could not resist the temptation to stay...a while, observing how the 'superior sister' does things."[77]

Logan was a great admirer of Anthony, though she deplored her concessions to racism in order to gain White support for the cause. In 1903, at Logan's invitation, Anthony and Catt visited Tuskegee, where, after an extended program, each female student "passed by in review before Miss Anthony and received each a hearty hand shake." Logan wrote articles about NACW activities for the NAWSA newspaper, the *Woman's Journal*, and promoted the suffrage cause through articles in the *Colored American* magazine and the NAACP magazine, *The Crisis*. One of her frequent themes was, if White women needed the vote to protect their rights, then Black women—victims of racism as well as sexism—needed the ballot even more.[78]

African American Suffragists' Crown of Thorns

White suffragists in this era varied in their attitudes toward African Americans and Black suffrage. Some shared the racism endemic in turn-of-the-century America; others were convinced they must cater to it in order to succeed. Some were sympathetic to Black suffrage, including Carrie Chapman Catt, who from the start of her career spoke in African American churches and clubs, published articles in the NAACP magazine, *The Crisis*, and spoke out against the discriminatory application of literacy tests. Mary Church Terrell praised Catt as being without race prejudice. However, in seeking the support of White Southerners, Catt catered to *their* racial prejudice and stated that White supremacy would be strengthened rather than weakened by woman suffrage.[79] Black suffragists accused White suffrage leaders—accurately—of being two-faced, of making concessions to White prejudice while making gestures of support to African Americans. But women's enfranchisement was also the Black suffragists' cause and they supported it regardless of the actions of White suffragists.

In 1903, Anthony and several NAWSA officials attending a Whites-only NAWSA conference in New Orleans, met separately with Black members of the Phillis Wheatley Club. The members welcomed Anthony's visit, but their leader, Sylvanie Williams, a *creole de couleur*, gently reminded her White guests of the poor treatment of Black women and the pain that it caused. According to the *History of Woman Suffrage*, Williams presented Anthony with a large bouquet tied with yellow satin ribbon and said:

> Flowers in their beauty and sweetness may represent the womanhood of the world. Some flowers are fragile and delicate, some strong and hardy, some are carefully guarded and cherished, others are roughly treated and trodden under foot. These last are the colored women. They have a crown of thorns continually pressed upon their brow, yet they are advancing and sometimes you find them further on than you would have expected. When women like you, Miss

Nannie Burroughs holding banner at Baptist convention
with church members, c. 1905

Anthony, come to see us and speak to us it helps us to believe in the Fatherhood of God and the Brotherhood of Man, and at least for the time being in the sympathy of woman.[80]

Yet, White suffrage leaders' words and gestures of appeasement were but small comfort as NAWSA leaders sought to distance the suffrage movement from advocacy of the rights of Black Americans while African American suffragists watched in dismay. It was clear to them that White suffragists' main goals were to enlarge their White constituency and to cultivate White politicians whose support they deemed essential to a national victory—and they were willing to do what was necessary to achieve their goals.

At times, White suffragists reached out to African American suffragists for help, such as in cultivating Black support for state woman suffrage referenda in Northern states where Black men could vote. But White suffragists' discriminatory behavior would continue throughout the rest of the woman suffrage movement. In 1918, when a regional body of Black clubwomen, the Northeastern Federation of Women's Clubs, applied for affiliation with the NAWSA, White leaders rebuffed them. At that time, NAWSA leaders were desperate to convert at least a few of the Southern senators and congressmen who were blocking approval of the federal suffrage amendment. Believing it to be a "critical moment when our Federal Amendment hangs in the balance," NAWSA leaders felt they were 'justified" in making the request, and begged the Black clubwomen to temporarily withdraw their application. The NAWSA leaders expected the Black suffragists to understand and not take offense. However, the applicants, who had been testing the White suffragists' commitment to the enfranchisement of African American women, understood all too well and were deeply offended.[81]

The situation was reminiscent of the Reconstruction era when it appeared that Black male suffrage could be attained if divorced from woman suffrage. At that time, former allies in a movement for universal suffrage had insisted that this was "the Negro's Hour" and that suffrage for women—White and Black—would have to wait. Now, half a century later, it appeared that "the Woman's Hour" had arrived, but White suffrage leaders were convinced that the federal woman suffrage amendment could not succeed it they defended Black suffrage. African American women were asked to *continue* to wait.

Rebuilding at the Turn of the Century

From the late 1890s to around 1910, the National American Woman Suffrage Association (NAWSA) went through a major period of change. Aging pioneers died or retired, and leadership shifted to younger women intent on modernizing NAWSA operations and bringing the movement to a successful conclusion. Historians have sometimes characterized this era as "the doldrums" of the woman suffrage movement owing to the lack of state victories. During these years, however, suffragists did much to expand the movement's constituency, retool its image, and adapt its strategy to fit current political conditions.[82]

The rebuilding effort commenced under the leadership of Susan B. Anthony's hand-picked successor, Carrie Chapman Catt, president of the NAWSA from 1900 to 1904. Catt was an early graduate of Iowa State University, the only woman in her graduating class. After a brief career in education in which she rose rapidly from teacher to principal to school superintendent, she married and moved to California, but after her husband's death in 1886, she returned to Iowa and began her crusade for woman suffrage. Catt married again, her new husband a wealthy engineer fully supportive of her suffrage work. In 1890, Catt attended the NAWSA's first convention, becoming a field organizer shortly thereafter, and soon proved to be exceptionally talented at organizing, speaking, and writing. Catt played a big role in the Colorado campaign, the first victory in which voters enfranchised women in a referendum. During the campaign, Catt traveled over a thousand miles, lecturing and establishing suffrage clubs. Her efforts extended even beyond national borders: between 1902 and 1904 she played a leading role in the creation of the International Woman Suffrage Alliance (IWSA), serving as its president from 1904 to 1923.[83]

Upon Anthony's retirement, Catt was elected to succeed the revered suffrage pioneer, but served only four years before her husband's illness led her to resign. One of Catt's earliest campaigns was the successful launch of what many called the "society plan"—an effort to recruit socially prominent and wealthy women. These included larger-than-life figures such as multi-millionaire and socialite Alva Smith (Vanderbilt) Belmont, philanthropist Katherine Dexter McCormick, and the daring and colorful newspaper publisher, Mrs. Frank Leslie (Miriam Folline Leslie legally adopted her late husband's name), who later willed her fortune to the woman suffrage movement. An unspoken assumption among the NAWSA leadership was that the "society plan" was for Whites only.[84]

As suffragists attracted the support of women philanthropists of high social standing, it became more difficult for the press to dismiss the suffrage movement as radical. In fact, suffrage work was becoming quite fashionable at home and abroad. The International Council of Women (ICW), founded in 1888 by Elizabeth Cady Stanton and Susan B. Anthony, attracted what an American suffragist described as "the most eminent women" of their respective countries, including aristocrats. During ICW conferences in London in 1899 and Berlin in 1904, delegates were entertained by Queen Victoria and German Empress Augusta Victoria. The ICW did not formally endorse women's enfranchisement, but under Catt's leadership during the Berlin meeting, members who wanted to commit themselves to the suffrage cause created the spin-off organization, the International Woman Suffrage Alliance (IWSA).[85]

In the United States, the fact that Anthony's eightieth birthday celebration in 1900 took place at the White House at the invitation of President William McKinley, was proof that suffrage leaders' efforts to shed the movement's radical image had been a success—even though McKinley did not endorse it. Suffragists' success in converting so many women of wealth ensured that at least the last phase of the suffrage campaign would be well funded. In September 1909, the NAWSA moved its headquarters from the county courthouse in Warren, Ohio—the home of the organization's treasurer, Harriet Taylor Upton—to New York City where their wealthy benefactor, Alva Belmont, had leased an entire floor of a building on the corner of Fifth Avenue and 42nd Street.[86]

Leaders of the NAWSA also cultivated as allies well-respected and well-heeled men whose support meant a lot to the movement in its last years. In 1908, a group of prominent men from New York City established an organization called the Men's League for Woman Suffrage, which consisted of more than a hundred prominent and influential men in publishing, industry, finance, law, medicine, academia, the clergy, and the military. Their ranks included men such as Oswald Garrison Villard, a progressive editor and publisher; John Dewey, a philosopher and educational reformer; George Foster Peabody, a banker and philanthropist; and Stephen S. Wise, Reform rabbi and nationally prominent Jewish leader. These self-assured men marched proudly in woman suffrage parades, often ridiculed by observers who verbally assaulted their masculinity, calling them "Suffragents." The Men's League soon had thousands of members in thirty-five states, working closely with the NAWSA to persuade waffling politicians, the press, and the public to support the suffrage cause.[87]

A primary part of the NAWSA rebuilding effort involved convincing the growing numbers of White, middle- and upper-class members of women's clubs that woman suffrage would be a boon to their civic improvement efforts.

Local and state affiliates of the General Federation of Women's Clubs (GFWC) began to support woman suffrage, which would later culminate in its endorsement at the GFWC's national convention in 1914. NAWSA leaders also reached out to the new generation of college-educated women, many of them professionals, challenging them to take up the torch for woman suffrage, reminding them that their opportunities were owed to the pioneers of the women's rights movement.[88]

The movement profited greatly from the new ideas and energy of these younger leaders, such as Radcliffe College graduates Maud Wood Park and Inez Haynes Irwin who founded the College Equal Suffrage League (CESL) in 1900. Park, who would later emerge as one of the NAWSA's most prominent leaders, played a crucial role in bringing women of her generation into the suffrage fold. As Park explained:

> After hearing Miss Anthony speak, I came to realize what her life had been, the heroism of her service not for herself but for the sex, and so for the whole human race.... I promised myself then that I would try to make more women see these things as I have seen them. College women should realize their debt to the pioneers who have made our education and competence possible. They should be made to feel the obligation of their opportunities and to understand that one of the ways to pay that debt is to fight the battle for suffrage now in the quarter of the field in which it is still unwon.

"College Evenings" in which aging pioneers were lauded by an array of college deans and grateful graduates, came to be a regular feature at annual NAWSA conventions. College evenings were also effective for recruitment between conventions, and another useful tactic for making the suffrage movement less radical and more popular.[89]

Harriot Stanton Blatch, Elizabeth Cady Stanton's daughter, also had a major impact after returning from living in England for two decades. While the "society plan" and College Evenings brought more elite women into the woman suffrage movement, Blatch emphasized working women's need for the vote and the suffrage movement's need for them. Blatch admired self-supporting women, seeing them as exemplars to women like herself and partners in the fight. Having been impressed by the success of some British suffragists in organizing across class lines, she sought to do so in New York. In 1907, Blatch brought together working women—from professionals to trade unionists—into the Equality League of Self-Supporting Women, later called the Women's Political Union (WPU). The tactics she and her associates in New York borrowed from working-class political activists and British suffragists, including open-air meetings and parades, invigorated the suffrage movement and helped to diversify the movement's constituency.[90]

The NAWSA's increased membership, diversification, and heightened visibility were not accompanied by political victories in this era. When Catt resigned as NAWSA leader in 1904, Dr. Anna Howard Shaw inherited the presidency. Though rebuilding efforts continued, under Shaw the organization became less centralized and provided little in the way of a national political strategy. She was undeniably a woman of incredible drive and ability. From a poor immigrant family on a struggling frontier farm in Michigan, Shaw overcame great obstacles to become both a Methodist minister and a physician before walking away from both professions to devote her life to woman suffrage. Shaw was also a gifted and witty orator who gave more than ten thousand speeches during her career. Catt praised Shaw as "the greatest orator among women the world has ever known." But from the late 1890s to 1910, few state campaigns were launched and all of them failed.[91]

The Suffrage Movement and Progressivism

By 1910, however, there were considerable grounds for optimism. The Progressive Movement, which had begun around 1900 at the grassroots level and swept both national political parties, was proving to be a tremendous boon to the cause of woman suffrage. Progressivism appealed especially to well-educated, middle- and upper-class women and men eager to reform government at all levels to better serve the needs of the people. Their aim was powerful, positive, and efficient government able to counter the malignant influence of giant corporations and "robber barons" that in the late nineteenth century corrupted the government and enriched themselves at the expense of consumers and workers.[92]

Progressives supported a wide variety of reforms such as pure food and drug legislation, expansion of public health programs, improvement of public schools, restrictions on child labor, and legislation to curb political corruption. They also advocated for a national income tax, believing that citizens who made the most money should pay at a higher rate than those who made less. This idea, which became known as "progressive taxation," was intended to curb the growing problem of inequality of wealth that many saw as a threat to the republic as well as to help fund the federal government.

Many Progressives were moral reformers with diverse goals ranging from stamping out prostitution to prohibiting the manufacture and sale of alcohol. Ultimately, the Progressive era would yield four amendments to the U.S. Constitution: The Sixteenth Amendment, establishing a tax on income; the Seventeenth Amendment, calling for senators to be directly elected by the people rather than by state legislators; the Eighteenth Amendment, prohibiting the manufacture and sale of alcohol; and the Nineteenth Amendment, enfranchising women.[93]

Progressives varied greatly in their attitudes on race. Some, such as the White and African American founders of the NAACP, were in the forefront of campaigns for racial justice. Other Progressives, including leading scholars and politicians—most notably President Woodrow Wilson—were profoundly racist. Particularly in the South, but in other regions of the United States as well, many White Progressives saw excluding racial minorities and illiterate Whites as Progressive reform, a means of cleaning up politics. The Progressive impulse led Americans to try to improve conditions for immigrants, but also inspired efforts to "Americanize" them and to restrict further immigration.[94]

One of the most widely-shared goals of Progressives reformers was to improve conditions for workers. While labor unions sought improvements in wages, hours, and working conditions through collective bargaining, reformers from upper-class and middle-class backgrounds called on local and state governments to address these issues through "protective legislation." Reformers and unions often worked together for laws establishing a minimum wage or setting a limit on work hours. They sought protection for workers of both sexes, though after conservatives vigorously opposed these laws through the courts, reformers emerged with dearly-won protective legislation for women, but not for men.[95]

Regarding woman suffrage, Progressive politicians believed that women voters would provide vital support for reform and many women wanted the vote in order to do just that. Across the United States, countless Progressive women, many of them members of women's clubs, enlisted in the suffrage movement as they became frustrated with their inability to secure such reforms through "indirect influence" or lobbying.[96]

Reform-minded politicians were impressed by the argument that enfranchised women, as "municipal housekeepers" seeking to make government more honest, moral, and helpful to them in carrying out their traditional duties, would support them. Some suffragists disdained appealing for enfranchisement on the basis of "woman's nature" and its compatibility to progressive reform, instead insisting that women had a right to the vote regardless of what they chose to do with it.[97] Yet, Progressivism gave suffragists a new expediency argument that suffragists put to good use in the movement's final decade. Indeed, one could argue that the woman suffrage movement finally succeeded, not because of changes in Americans' ideas about "woman's nature," but because new ideas about the nature of government and what government should do were compatible with old ideas about the nature of woman.

In 1912, for the first time in its history woman suffrage was endorsed by a major national political party, Theodore Roosevelt's Progressive Party. Roosevelt invited leading suffragist and Progressive heroine Jane Addams, the founder of the famous Chicago settlement house, Hull House, to place his name in nomination at the Progressive's national convention.[98]

Diversity Strengthens the Movement for Woman Suffrage

During the Progressive Era, the woman suffrage movement grew dramatically in size and diversity. Even as many White suffrage leaders discriminated against African American suffragists, they reached out to women from diverse class and ethnic backgrounds who saw suffrage as crucial for enhancing the status of women and improving society.

Many prominent suffragists were women from elite backgrounds who founded or joined organizations dedicated to improving conditions for workers, especially women workers. For example, Maud Nathan and Florence Kelley were daughters of privilege who were determined to aid women who were not. Both were leaders of the National Consumers League, founded in 1899 by Jane Addams and other Progressives to harness the power of consumers to obtain fair wages and safe conditions for workers as well as reliable goods and services.[99]

Nathan was from a socially prominent, Sephardic Jewish family in New York, the descendent of a long line of prominent activists and leaders dating back to the American Revolution. A founding member of the New York Consumers League, Nathan served as its president from 1897 to 1927. During years of lobbying New York legislators, she became convinced that lawmakers cared little about the views of non-voters, leading Nathan to become an ardent suffragist—despite the fact that her sister, Annie Nathan Meyer, was a leading anti-suffragist. Maud Nathan's husband, Frederick, was a staunch suffrage supporter and headed the New York Men's League for Equal Suffrage. In 1913, Theodore Roosevelt appointed Maud Nathan to chair the Suffrage Committee of the National Progressive Party.[100]

Florence Kelley, a prominent suffragist born in Philadelphia, was a leading Progressive reformer as well as a scholar, lawyer, and socialist. She was also an activist for the rights of African Americans, strongly influenced by her father, an abolitionist, a founder of the Republican Party, a judge, and a congressman from Pennsylvania, and by Quaker relatives on her mother's side. In the 1890s, she lived at Jane Addams's Hull House in Chicago, writing and lecturing about child labor and "sweatshops," and successfully lobbying the Illinois legislature for reform. In 1899, she moved to New York where she became general secretary of the newly organized National Consumers League and henceforth one of the nation's leading advocates on behalf of industrial workers.[101]

Kelley was crucial to the successful defense of maximum hour laws for women, argued and won by Louis Brandeis in the landmark Supreme Court decision *Muller v. Oregon* in 1908. Kelley also played an important role in the founding of the National Association for the Advancement of Colored People (NAACP) in 1909 and afterward in its opposition to lynching and to racism in education. In 1912, she helped establish the Children's Bureau in the U.S. Department of Labor. As a vice president of the NAWSA, Kelley contributed greatly as an organizer, speaker, and writer, calling for woman suffrage as a means of protecting the most vulnerable members of society. In a well-known pamphlet "Woman Suffrage: Its Relation to Working Women and Children," she wrote:

> It is the daughters of the poor who chiefly fall victims to the basest crimes. Poor, young, ignorant, unorganized, they depend for protection upon laws framed and enforced by persons older than themselves. Is it safe or sane to exclude from a full share of power and responsibility the mothers and teachers, the older women whose first care is for the welfare of the young?[102]

Another prominent suffragist, Inez Milholland, a New Yorker from a wealthy background, was also a lawyer, a socialist, and reformer. From her days at Vassar, when she famously defied the college president's ban on woman suffrage activities on campus and organized a rally in the cemetery, Milholland was whole-heartedly engaged in the movement, lecturing, lobbying, and participating in public demonstrations and marches. Athletic and attractive, she became popular with the public for her role in leading suffrage parades on horseback. She was an early and enthusiastic member of the NAACP along with her father, John Milholland, a wealthy businessman and newspaper editor who served as the NAACP's first treasurer. Introduced to socialism as well as militant feminism while a student in London, Milholland became a fervent advocate for the rights of workers, especially women and children, and for unionization. It was natural for her to be drawn to the Women's Trade Union League (WTUL), founded in 1903 to unionize women to gain better wages and working conditions, and full citizenship.[103]

The WTUL was unusual for bringing women of different classes together. Florence Kelley and Harriot Stanton Blatch were members, as was wealthy NAWSA benefactor Alva Vanderbilt Belmont. WTUL members of all classes believed that politicians knew little and cared less about the needs of working women who needed the power of the ballot for their demands to be addressed. As a WTUL member, Milholland supported many strikes, such as the shirtwaist and laundry workers' strikes of 1910. She walked the picket lines, raised money from wealthy friends to support the strikers, and as a lawyer gave legal counsel to workers.[104]

While women like Nathan, Kelley, and Milholland sympathized with exploited workers and the injustices heaped upon them, there were many other women who were leaders in the fight for woman suffrage who had firsthand knowledge of these conditions. Leonora O'Reilly, Mary Kenney O'Sullivan, and Rose Schneiderman, for example, began working in factories at an early age. All were women of great courage and charisma who quickly rose to positions of leadership in labor organizations and in the WTUL.[105]

Many of the women workers in the WTUL were immigrants or the daughters of immigrants. O'Reilly and O'Sullivan, whose parents were poor Irish immigrants, were forced to leave school and begin work as young girls. O'Reilly started working in a clothing factory at age eleven in 1881 and became a union member at age sixteen. After she founded the Working Women's Society to promote fair wages and better working conditions, wealthy women philanthropists enabled her to take time off from her job to study factory conditions while living in the Henry Street Settlement house in New York. After helping establish the WTUL in 1903, O'Reilly spent twelve years as a member of its executive committee as well as an organizer and recruiter, often speaking in public for labor reform and woman suffrage. In 1909, O'Reilly signed the call leading up to the founding of the NAACP, then served on the organization's executive committee. That same year, she helped organize the famous New York City strike nicknamed the "Uprising of the 20,000." After the tragic 1911

Triangle Shirtwaist Factory Fire in which 146 workers, mostly young immigrant girls, died jumping from windows or being burned to death in locked rooms with no fire escapes, she worked to build support for occupational safety laws.[106]

O'Sullivan grew up in poverty in Hannibal, Missouri, left school after the fourth-grade, and started work as an apprentice dressmaker, later becoming a bookbinder. After working in Chicago bookbinderies, she organized a women bookbinders' union. Jane Addams invited O'Sullivan to hold union meetings at Hull House and paid for printing circulars that Addams personally helped distribute to workers during their lunch hours. Soon thereafter, Samuel Gompers, head of the American Federation of Labor (AFL), hired O'Sullivan as the federation's first woman organizer, and she began organizing in New York and Massachusetts. In 1903, O'Sullivan helped found the WTUL, becoming its first secretary and then vice president. An active suffragist, she addressed the U.S. House of Representatives on behalf of a federal suffrage amendment in 1906, insisting that women were producers in American society and that every producer deserves the right to vote.[107]

Rose Schneiderman was born in Poland to a Jewish family that moved to New York City's Lower East Side in 1890 when she was eight. At thirteen, she started working in a department store, which was considered more respectable than factory work, but as it paid less, Schneiderman became a capmaker. Still, wages were low and working conditions poor, leading her to organize a branch of a capmakers' union. While leading a strike, she became involved in the New York WTUL. By 1906, Schneiderman had become the WTUL's vice president, and by 1908, its chief organizer, focusing on New York's garment district. Schneiderman was legendary as a speaker; at only four feet nine inches tall and with flaming red hair, Schneiderman delivered powerful, militant speeches that many described as the most moving they had ever heard. Her "bread and roses" speech delivered in 1912 inspired many working women and touched the hearts of their wealthy "allies":

> What the woman who labors wants is the right to live, not simply exist—the right to life as the rich woman has the right to life, and the sun and music and art. You have nothing that the humblest worker has not a right to have also. The worker must have bread, but she must have roses, too. Help, you women of privilege, give her the ballot to fight with.

Schneiderman helped found the Wage Earner's League for Woman Suffrage in 1911. Although from different class backgrounds, Schneiderman and Maud Nathan helped carry heavily Jewish districts in New York for suffrage in the crucial 1917 referendum.[108]

All of this work had a major impact on the woman suffrage movement. Large numbers of working-class women joined the movement, urged on by suffragists from similar backgrounds and by middle-class and elite allies who sought to unite women of all classes into a revitalized suffrage movement that was also increasingly diverse.

LUISA
CAPETILLO

ROSE
SCHNEIDERMAN

FLORENCE
KELLEY

MARY KENNEY
O'SULLIVAN

MAUD
NATHAN

ADELINA
OTERO-WARREN

LEONORA
O'REILLY

INEZ
MILHOLLAND

MARIA GUADALUPE
EVANGELINA LOPÉZ

All photos are courtesy of the Library of Congress
or they are in the public domain.

Beyond the Northeast and Midwest, women from different economic, ethnic, and racial backgrounds were also working to gain the vote. Bilingual suffrage advocates reached out to potential supporters from various backgrounds and cultures. Some suffrage advocates who were important in expanding and diversifying the movement were immigrants unable to become citizens and voters themselves.

In New Mexico, Adelina "Nina" Otero-Warren, a descendent of elite "Hispanos" who had long ago settled in the area, cultivated support for women's enfranchisement among Spanish-speaking residents of her state. Aurora Lucero White, a bi-lingual educator, the daughter of New Mexico's first Secretary of State, gave suffrage speeches in Spanish. Recognizing that Spanish-speaking women made up at least half of the female population of New Mexico, they made sure that suffrage literature was published in Spanish as well as English.[109]

In California, suffragists narrowly won a state referendum in part by cultivating support from diverse immigrant communities in the state. They published suffrage articles in Spanish, Chinese, German, Portuguese, and Italian. Los Angeles suffragist, Maria Guadalupe Evangelina de Lopez, an instructor at the University of California, Los Angeles, reached out to Spanish-speaking residents of her city, translating at rallies, and working with other suffragists to distribute tens of thousands of pamphlets in Spanish. Though there was hostility to Chinese Americans among some White activists, others courted their support. When Californians voted on the suffrage referendum in 1911, a majority of Chinese voters supported it.[110]

In Oregon, as in California, suffragists finally won a referendum by putting together diverse coalitions; Jewish women were among the key leaders in Portland. The Colored Women's Equal Suffrage Association organized African American clubwomen, and Portland's Chinese neighborhoods were mobilized by the Chinese American Suffrage Club.[111]

In New York, sixteen-year-old, Chinese-born Mabel Ping-Hua Lee supported the woman suffrage movement as a member of the New York Women's Political

Suffrage pamphlet of
L.A. Political Equality League
written by Maria de Lopéz
SCRIPPS COLLEGE, CLAREMONT

Equality League. At the invitation of NAWSA leaders, Lee led a 1912 suffrage parade in New York City on horseback while behind her NAWSA president Dr. Anna Howard Shaw carried a banner that read "NAWSA Catching Up with China." Shaw sought to advertise the fact that the new Chinese Republic allowed women to vote when the United States did not. Lee, along with her mother and other Chinese immigrant women from New York, supported U.S. woman's suffrage, even though as Asian immigrants, they were ineligible to become citizens and one day vote.[112]

Marie Louise Bottineau Baldwin, a Native American suffragist, was a Chippewa born in North Dakota. She later lived in Washington, D.C. where her father was a lawyer working to defend the Chippewa's treaty rights. She worked in the Office of Indian Affairs (OIA), one of only two NativeAmerican employees in the OIA. In 1912 at age forty-nine, Baldwin entered the Washington College of Law, founded by women lawyers since few traditional law schools admitted women. She became the first woman of color and the first Native American to earn a law degree from the college. When she became involved in the suffrage movement, Baldwin reminded suffragists that Native American women had had "virtual suffrage, and the power of recall, since time immemorial" in their Native American communities. Baldwin marched with her classmates and teachers in the 1913 suffrage parade in Washington, D.C., joining a contingent of women lawyers. At a time when many Native Americans lacked citizenship, and therefore the right to vote, Baldwin was also a tireless advocate of voting rights for Native peoples. She testified before Congress and even met with President Wilson on behalf of Native Americans and voting rights.[113]

Puerto Rican-born Luisa Capetillo brought the suffrage message to Cuban American, African, African American, and Italian American workers, while she worked as a *lectora* (reader) in a Florida cigar factory. As a labor union leader who traveled back and forth between the United States and Puerto Rico, Capetillo was eager to address the problems facing the working conditions of women and children. Considered the first suffragist in Puerto Rico, she was also a writer, intellectual, freethinker, and feminist—remembered by some Puerto Ricans as the first woman to wear pants in public. She is also remembered as one of the most important advocates of woman suffrage in Puerto Rico.[114]

Mexican-born Teresa Villarreal in Texas, a revolutionary labor organizer, socialist, newspaper publisher, and activist for feminist causes, was an ardent suffragist. Forced to flee Mexico with her family, which opposed the dictatorship of President Porfirio Díaz, they found allies among unionists and socialists in the United States. In 1909, they settled in San Antonio. Together with her sister, Andrea Villarreal, Teresa Villarreal published *La Mujer Moderna* (*The Modern Woman*), the state's first feminist newspaper, as well as *El Obrero* (*The Worker*).[115]

Many converts to the suffrage movement in the United States were inspired by socialism and by socialist feminists abroad. Their efforts were crucial to the first

European victory for woman suffrage in Finland in 1906. In the United States, opponents of socialism and woman suffrage were quick to point out this connection, and in some cases, "mainstream" suffragists were less than welcoming of their socialist sisters. But socialist women made invaluable contributions during suffrage battles in several states, notably the victorious suffrage campaign in California in 1911.[116]

Often, socialist suffragists in the United States—who came from all classes—served as intermediaries between working-class women and middle-class and elite suffragists. They also helped win support from labor unions and working-class men. Though some socialists such as Emma Goldman disdained the suffrage movement, thinking it foolish to expect that real progress would come from female enfranchisement, many socialist feminists were convinced that gaining the vote was crucial in order for women to realize their goals.[117]

Anti-suffragists in the Progressive Era

As in the case of temperance and suffrage, however, the idea that women would support Progressive reforms inspired opposition. As the suffrage movement became more of a threat, its opponents became more organized. In 1911, the National Association Opposed to Woman Suffrage (NAOWS) was founded. The organization was based in New York City, later adding state branches, and in 1913 a second headquarters in Washington, D.C. Josephine Jewell Dodge, the NAOWS' founder and first president, was an educated and accomplished reformer well known as a pioneer in the American day nursery movement. When the suffrage fight shifted to Washington, D.C., Alice Hay Wadsworth, wife of a prominent anti-suffrage senator from New York, James W. Wadsworth, Jr., took over as NAOWS president.[118]

The NAOWS consisted of wealthy and influential women such as Dodge and Wadsworth, but also men eager to block the enfranchisement of women out of fear that their business interests or political power would suffer at the hands of women voters. In the South, the cotton textile industry that employed large numbers of child laborers joined the liquor industry as a formidable opponent of woman suffrage, and worked with a growing number of Southern anti-suffrage organizations to oppose state suffrage referenda.[119]

In the last ten years of the suffrage struggle, anti-suffragists continued to make extensive use of the race issue, particularly in the South, even as White Southern suffragists tried to dismiss it as irrelevant. While the suffragists insisted that the recently adopted laws that disfranchised African American men would apply to Black women as well, White Southern anti-suffragists insisted Black women would register and vote in even larger numbers than White women, who would be forced to associate with African Americans at the polls. Their racist tactics included publicizing the early association between the antislavery and the women's rights movements, and the continued friendship of White suffragists such as Susan B.

Anthony with Black suffrage leaders, including Frederick Douglass, whose late-life marriage to a White woman outraged many Americans. White Southern anti-suffragists also publicized Carrie Chapman Catt's supportive statements about Black suffrage, including comments that appeared in the NAACP magazine, *The Crisis*, as "proof" that Catt supported equal rights for African Americans and was an enemy of the South. The main anti-suffrage organization in the region, the Southern Women's League for the Rejection of the Susan B. Anthony Amendment, declared its opposition to "any measure that threatens the continuation of Anglo-Saxon domination of Social and Political affairs in each and every State of the Union."[120]

Anti-suffragists also opposed woman suffrage on the grounds that African American women supported it. For instance, suffrage opponents distributed reprints of "Negro Women's Resolutions for Enforcement of Federal Suffrage Amendments" adopted by the National Association of Colored Women (NACW). The document also noted that the retiring NACW president, Mary B. Talbert, would join Carrie Chapman Catt in the U.S. delegation to the International Council of Women in Norway, and called for a federal anti-lynching law. At times, anti-suffragists insisted that enfranchised African American women would be more demanding and difficult to deter than Black men. Moreover, as the suffragists became more focused on the federal woman suffrage amendment, White Southern politicians denounced it as an unacceptable extension of the Fifteenth Amendment, a measure that would inspire new demands for Black suffrage, which they insisted was "not dead but sleeping."[121]

Anti-suffrage rhetoric continued to present woman suffrage as a threat to home and family, warning that enfranchised womanhood would neglect children and saddle husbands with cooking and childcare. It is significant, however, that in the Progressive Era, female anti-suffragists like Josephine Dodge widely proclaimed that they *favored* women's involvement in public affairs, including nonpartisan political activity. Pointing to their own records of community service, anti-suffragists insisted that they opposed woman suffrage primarily out of the belief that involvement in partisan politics would dispel women's energies and dilute, rather than enhance, women's influence.[122]

As the suffrage movement entered what proved to be its last decade, a tradition of women's civic activism had developed—and had been accepted—to the point that the argument over suffrage was more often framed in terms of how women could be most effective, rather than if women should concern themselves with life outside a narrowly defined "woman's sphere."

Alice Paul and the National Woman's Party

Around 1912, the increased support for woman suffrage resulting from the Progressive Movement, together with the series of victories in the Western states, seemed to breathe new life into suffragists nationwide. The return of Alice Paul from England, where she was inspired by the energy and boldness of the "militant" faction of British suffragists led by Emmeline Pankhurst, was also a major factor in the new suffrage activism. The Pankhursts, officially the Women's Social and Political Union (WSPU), embraced the derisive term coined by the press, "suffragettes," in part to distinguish themselves from the older, larger, and more moderate organization of British suffragists, the National Union of Women's Suffrage Societies led by Millicent Fawcett. While many American suffragists had been inspired by Pankhurst and her daughters during their speaking tours in the United States, Paul had become involved with them while a doctoral student in Britain. She participated in WSPU parades and demonstrations, and was arrested and jailed for the cause. Paul shared, as well as admired, the Pankhursts' militant spirit.[123]

Paul, along with her able associate Lucy Burns and the circle of women who gathered around them, many of them young, had no patience with the slow, state-by-state plodding that had consumed much of the National American Woman Suffrage Association's (NAWSA) energies. Paul and her cohort's militance and impatience to achieve what they considered a long-overdue victory also appealed to some older NAWSA leaders, including Harriot Stanton Blatch and the imperious NAWSA benefactor Alva Vanderbilt Belmont, who became a key financial backer and strategist.[124]

At first, these women worked through the Congressional Union, the group within the NAWSA charged with lobbying for a federal amendment. They urged the NAWSA to focus its attention almost exclusively on the federal route to enfranchisement. This infuriated some suffragists, particularly a small but vocal group of states' rights devotees led by Kate Gordon of New Orleans, who favored woman suffrage by state action only. The NAWSA did indeed step up its campaign for a federal amendment—but not before parting company with Paul and her associates who formed a separate organization, the National Woman's Party

First Picket line at the White House, 1917
LIBRARY OF CONGRESS

(NWP).[125]

The central issue in this new rift in the suffrage forces was Paul's advocacy of a strategy derived from the British suffragettes to oppose the "party-in-power"—in this case, the Democratic Party—until it compelled Congress to enfranchise women. This strategy, ill-suited to the divided party system in the United States, violated the NAWSA's longstanding policy of non-partisanship. Eventually, President Woodrow Wilson and the Democratic Party declared their support for woman suffrage by state action, but in keeping with their states' rights views, still refused to endorse a federal amendment. Paul and her associates employed a number of bold new tactics designed to force President Wilson and the Democrats to support the federal amendment, which the NWP members dubbed the "Susan B. Anthony Amendment." Their tactics ranged from mobilizing women voters in Western states to vote against all Democrats in the 1916 election—especially Wilson who was running for re-election—to publicly burning the president's war-time speeches in praise of democracy in front of the White House.[126]

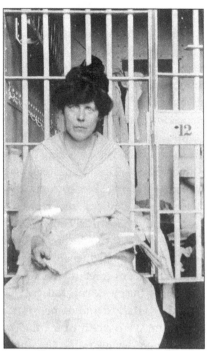

Suffragist Lucy Burns jailed at Occoquan Workhouse. Burns was arrested six times, sometimes spending months in jail.
LIBRARY OF CONGRESS

Paul proved to be brilliant at attracting and keeping the attention of the press and thereby forcing the issue of woman suffrage to the forefront of public debate. The massive, dramatic suffrage parade that she organized during Wilson's inaugural celebration in 1913 captured the attention of the nation. This spectacular event featured nine bands, four mounted brigades, and twenty-four floats. The striking Inez Milholland, already known for her role in New York suffrage campaigns and marches, led the parade dressed in flowing White robes and riding a White horse. Behind her came women from countries that had already enfranchised women, followed by the "Pioneers" who had worked for decades to gain the vote for women in the United States. Estimates varied, but around eight thousand suffragists—many dressed in White and representing every state plus a vast number of pro-suffrage organizations—participated in the march.[127]

Throngs of spectators, most of them men, many of them intoxicated, crowded

Pennsylvania Avenue sidewalks to watch the parade. Some men spit on the marchers, pelted them with lighted cigars and liquor bottles, and then began to attack them. About one hundred suffragists were injured and hospitalized as a result. The police failed to protect the marchers, either through indifference or in support of the mob's actions, which led to a congressional investigation. The whole affair attracted sympathy for the cause, not unlike the public outcry after the attacks on peaceful demonstrators during the civil rights movement of the 1960s.[128]

Paul and the NWP were among the first Americans to employ many of the tactics of civil disobedience, including being the first ever to picket the White House for a political cause. They held signs and banners designed to embarrass President Wilson and compel him to support a federal woman suffrage amendment. Nonviolent and dignified, the pickets were "silent sentinels," keeping up their demonstrations for nearly three years in every kind of weather, eventually winning the respect of many in the press who dubbed them the "Iron Jawed Angels." Many people were outraged when NWP members continued their demonstrations after the United States entered World War I in April 1917, at one point even carrying a sign calling the president "Kaiser Wilson."[129]

Crowds attacked the demonstrators as they protested in front of the White House, but the police arrested the suffragists—not their attackers. Charged with obstructing sidewalk traffic, the suffragists were sentenced to jail terms of up to six months. Most were imprisoned under deplorable conditions at the Occoquan Work House near Washington, D.C. Some of the prisoners, including elderly women,

Suffragists demonstrating against Woodrow Wilson in Chicago, 1916
NATIONAL WOMAN'S PARTY RECORDS, LIBRARY OF CONGRESS

protested this violation of their rights by going on hunger strikes, which led to forced feedings—a brutal and dangerous procedure—recorded in shocking detail in Doris Stevens's classic memoir of 1920, *Jailed for Freedom*.[130]

These horrific experiences only increased the suffragists' determination to expose the hypocrisy of a nation which, during World War I, proclaimed itself the leader of a crusade for democracy while at the same time jailing and abusing women in the United States for protesting their nation's denial of the vote to half of its adult citizens.

Carrie Chapman Catt and the "Winning Plan"

Carrie Chapman Catt was also eager for the National American Woman Suffrage Association (NAWSA) to bring the long struggle to a conclusion with the adoption of the federal suffrage amendment, but she pursued this end with a strategy that contrasted sharply with that of Alice Paul and the National Woman's Party (NWP). After stepping down as NAWSA president in 1904, Catt served as leader of the International Woman Suffrage Alliance (IWSA). But in 1915, responding to the NAWSA's call for a forceful general, Catt returned to the presidency and soon launched an initially top-secret "Winning Plan" to harness the power of the massive but sluggish NAWSA and initiate the final, victorious suffrage drive.[131]

Catt made it clear that the federal amendment was still the ultimate goal, while further state work was essential toward that end. The suffragists still had to have the support of key states on the East Coast, including "Mighty New York," which had one of the largest congressional delegations and did not adopt woman suffrage until 1917. Catt's plan called for suffragists in states that had not adopted woman suffrage—and where victories seemed possible—to launch campaigns immediately and simultaneously with strong NAWSA support. In states where defeat was likely, Catt insisted that suffragists refrain from state suffrage campaigns to avoid potential embarrassment to the cause but seek partial suffrage where possible, whether municipal, presidential, or primary suffrage. She urged suffragists in states where women already voted to pressure their national representatives to support the federal amendment.[132]

Meanwhile, Catt and key lieutenants, Maud Wood Park and Helen Gardener, worked hard to convince President Wilson to support woman suffrage by federal as well as state means, and conducted a massive lobbying effort to enlist congressional support. The press dubbed this effort the "Front Door Lobby" because of the contrast between suffragists' open and honest methods and those more common among Washington lobbyists.[133]

Women from all parts of the nation came in well-coordinated "relays" to reinforce those stationed at the NAWSA's Washington headquarters. They studied the congressmen with microscopic intensity, seeking the right words or arguments with which to persuade the politicians to support the federal amendment. It had long since become clear to the suffragists that "justice" arguments alone would not be

The first contingent of the Women's Overseas Hospitals, supported by the
National American Woman Suffrage Association

NATIONAL ARCHIVES

sufficient; politicians had to be convinced it was expedient for them personally as
well as for their party to support woman suffrage. Though some loved it and some
loathed it, suffragists found it necessary to learn the art of "practical politics."[134]

As Catt and Nettie Rogers Shuler later recalled in their book, *Woman Suffrage
and Politics,* this was an all-absorbing effort. "It is doubtful," they wrote, "if any
man, even among suffrage men, ever realized what the suffrage struggle came to
mean to women before the end was allowed in America. How much of time and
patience, how much work, energy and aspiration, how much faith, how much
hope, how much despair went into it. It leaves its mark on one, such a struggle."[135]

In these years, Catt, like Susan B. Anthony in the final decades of her life, set aside
other causes to focus exclusively on winning the suffrage battle. Catt had been a
founder of the Woman's Peace Party in 1915, but when the United States entered
World War I two years later, Catt urged suffragists to support the war effort—for
which she was expelled from the Woman's Peace Party and shunned by fellow
pacifists. The NAWSA even maintained a hospital in France for wounded soldiers.
Former NAWSA president Dr. Anna Howard Shaw chaired the Woman's Committee
of the Council of National Defense established by the Wilson administration to
coordinate the war efforts of American women. For her efforts, Shaw was awarded

the nation's Distinguished Service Medal, the first woman to receive it.[136]

Suffragists' war work enhanced the patriotic image of the movement with the public and powerful decision makers, including the president. When Wilson finally announced his support for the federal woman suffrage amendment in a September 30, 1918 speech to Congress, he stated: "We have made partners of the women in this war...Shall we admit them only to a partnership of suffering and sacrifice and toil and not to a partnership of privilege and right?"[137]

The 1918 Pandemic

At the time of Wilson's address, the House of Representatives had already approved the woman suffrage bill. The Senate would vote the next day. But even the president's plea failed to produce the last two votes from senators needed to clear the constitutional requirement of two-thirds of each chamber of Congress. Suffragists pressed on, looking toward the November mid-term elections and making plans for suffrage referenda in four states—striving for more state victories that would amplify the pressure on Congress. Suffragists were also determined to defeat four anti-suffrage senators whose challengers promised to vote for the federal amendment.[138]

Then calamity struck in the form of a massive outbreak of influenza, the deadliest in modern times. The 1918 flu pandemic lasted about fifteen months, ultimately killing up to 50 million people, including 675,000 in the United States. The death toll far exceeded that of World War I, horrific as it was. The first wave of the pandemic had come in the spring of 1918, but it roared back in the fall, worse than before. The flu killed almost 200,000 people in October alone. Washington, D.C. was hit especially hard. In a letter to supporters, Carrie Chapman Catt wrote, "These are sad times for the whole world, grown unexpectedly sadder by the sudden and sweeping epidemic of influenza. This new affliction is bringing sorrow into many suffrage homes and is presenting a serious new obstacle in our referendum campaigns and in the congressional and senatorial campaigns." Catt fell victim to the flu, described by frantic associates as "chained to her bed...and extremely ill." Nevertheless, she was determined that the suffrage movement would not lose momentum.[139]

It was a struggle. Suffragists' best-laid plans were wrecked. The U.S. Public Health Service issued a nationwide advisory prohibiting all large meetings and public gatherings. By late October of 1918, one suffragist wrote, the pandemic was "so bad that it was considered immoral for six women to meet in a parlor." Many National American Woman Suffrage Association (NAWSA) members who would have been campaigning for suffrage, instead volunteered as Red Cross workers or as nurses in hospitals. Alice Paul also faced setbacks. The National Woman's Party (NWP) had to postpone a cross-country train tour in which suffragists who had been imprisoned in their fight for suffrage, planned to don replicas of their prison uniforms and tell their story to large crowds along the way. To continue their work during the pandemic, suffragists had to be creative. They relied more heavily on telephone calls, the press, and the mail: NAWSA headquarters provided over a million pamphlets for distribution door to door and hundreds of bulletins to be sent to local newspapers.[140]

The pandemic greatly suppressed voter turnout in the fall of 1918, but when the votes were counted, suffragists were thrilled that two senators they had targeted for defeat lost and several new pro-suffrage lawmakers were voted in. And though the referendum in Louisiana—the only one in the South—failed, the other referenda in Michigan, South Dakota, and Oklahoma, passed. The month brought more great news: on November 11, 1918, World War I came to an end.[141]

Gratitude for women's service during the war, and more recently, the epidemic, contributed to the growing support for women's enfranchisement in general, and to the success of these referenda in particular. The growing number of state victories and Woodrow Wilson's conversion, finally led Congress to approve the Nineteenth Amendment and submit it to the states.

Historians sometimes debate the relative contributions of Catt and the NAWSA versus Paul and the NWP to congressional endorsement of the Nineteenth Amendment, but most agree that their strategies were inadvertently complementary. Catt's careful coordination of suffragists nationwide and her skillful political maneuvering, together with Paul and the NWP's skill in focusing attention on the federal amendment and putting pressure on Wilson and members of Congress, all were major factors.

The Fight for Ratification

On June 4, 1919, when Congress approved the federal suffrage amendment, the final chapter in the long suffrage story was still ahead—the fight for ratification. The amendment had to be approved by three-fourths of the states, which at that time was thirty-six states, in order to be added to the Constitution. As the struggle began, Illinois and Wisconsin competed for the honor of being the first to ratify. Meanwhile, Georgia and Alabama scrambled to be the first to pass a "rejection resolution" in keeping with a scheme hatched by the governor of Louisiana for thirteen Southern states to formally reject the proposed amendment and ask for a "Proclamation of Defeat."[142]

Most states took longer to act and many battles were hard fought with suffragists and anti-suffragists using all the powers of persuasion at their command. By the end of 1919, twenty-two states had ratified and suffragists were confident that victory was on its way.[143] In February 1920, the National American Woman Suffrage Association (NAWSA) held a "Victory Convention" in Chicago to celebrate the impending victory and plot its course for the future. At that convention, the NAWSA officially changed its name to the League of Women Voters (LWV), confident that the federal suffrage amendment would be ratified before the November 1920 presidential election. Plans called for the LWV, which would continue the NAWSA's non-partisan policy, to promote good government and a more just society, and to educate U.S. citizens, especially women, in becoming well-informed voters.[144]

During the spring of 1918, state ratifications continued though with more "rejection resolutions." When Mississippi voted against ratification of the amendment, the Jackson newspaper, the *Clarion-Ledger*, celebrated the defeat, proclaiming, "…the vile old thing is as dead as its author [Susan B. Anthony], the old advocate of social equality and intermarriage of the races, and Mississippi will never be annoyed with it again."[145]

By the summer of 1920, suffragists were dismayed to find that, while only one more state was needed, no further state legislative sessions were scheduled before the November 1920 election. Desperate, suffragists began working for special sessions. NAWSA leaders called on the chairs of the Republican and Democratic National Committees, insisting that women would soon be voting and the electorate would double in size: surely these leaders wanted a state controlled by their party to be "the Perfect 36." According to Catt and Shuler, "The Republican leaders were determined that their record should not be blackened at the eleventh hour, and Democratic leaders were equally sincere in the decision that defeat of final ratification not be laid at their door. So both national chairmen again issued statements and vied with each other in efforts to influence lagging states." Polls in Connecticut and Vermont, states with Republican majorities, indicated that their legislatures would ratify if called into special session, but the anti-suffrage governors refused.[146]

National Woman's Party (NWP) members picketed the Republican national convention, demanding that its nominee for president, Warren Harding, compel these GOP governors to call special sessions needed for ratification. When Harding declined, the NWP threatened to oppose all Republican candidates in 1920 as they had opposed all Democrats in 1916. Finally, President Wilson was able to pressure governors in North Carolina and Tennessee, states controlled by Democrats, into calling special sessions. North Carolina legislators refused to ratify, however, insisting they would not sacrifice their honor on the altar of political expediency, and urged Tennessee to do likewise.[147]

Armageddon

Thus, the final battle over woman suffrage took place in Nashville, Tennessee in the long, hot summer of 1920. In that final, dramatic contest, anti-suffragists as well as suffragists from across the nation descended upon the state in a bitter struggle over ideology and influence. As suffragists and their champions in the legislature began wearing yellow rose boutonnieres, and suffrage opponents donned red ones, the press began calling this unsavory struggle "The War of the Roses."[148]

Alice Paul wisely stayed away, aware that Southern Democrats were none too keen on the NWP's tactics, including opposing all Democrats back in 1916 and "harassing" their hero, President Woodrow Wilson; but she sent able lieutenants, including Sue Shelton White and Anita Pollitzer. White was a native Tennessean, well acquainted with state politics and with Tennessee suffragists affiliated with the National Woman's Party (NWP) and the National American Woman Suffrage Association (NAWSA). Pollitzer, another Southerner who grew up in Charleston, South Carolina, was a talented NWP organizer. Also an experienced lobbyist with considerable charm, she traversed the state, seeking to find and persuade legislators to vote for ratification.[149]

Carrie Chapman Catt also sent deputies, notably Marjorie Shuler, who helped smooth out problematic rifts among Tennessee NAWSA members, which had complicated the ratification campaign. But when the battle heated up, Catt rushed to Nashville and remained for over a month, determined the fight would end successfully in Tennessee. However, that the suffrage movement's "Armageddon" would take place in the South, the region where the suffrage movement had encountered the most opposition, meant that the result was far from certain.[150]

Opponents of ratification urged Tennessee legislators to "Save the South from the Susan B. Anthony Amendment and Federal Force Bills." Anti-suffrage broadsides warned, "Remember that woman suffrage means a reopening of the entire negro suffrage question, loss of State rights, and another period of reconstruction horrors, which will introduce a set of female carpetbaggers as bad as their male prototypes of the sixties."[151]

Meanwhile, the liquor industry and its corporate allies, most notably the railroads, were clearly using all of their considerable power and resources to secure the proposed amendment's defeat. A year earlier in January 1919, the Eighteenth Amendment, banning the manufacture, sale, and transportation of liquor, had been ratified, making Prohibition the law of the land. Hardly willing to accept defeat, the liquor industry immediately began campaigning for repeal—more determined than ever to stop woman suffrage.[152]

Despite the glare of national publicity, the suffragists watched with dismay as a comfortable margin in favor of ratification gradually disappeared and they were quite uncertain of the result when the vote took place. On August 18, it appeared that Tennessee had ratified the amendment after an unexpected "aye" from Harry Burn, a twenty-four-year-old Republican legislator from the mountains who was wearing an anti-suffrage red rose. Burn had been sympathetic to the suffrage cause, but he was up for re-election and under intense pressure to vote against ratification. After the vote, he explained that he changed his position at the urging of his pro-suffrage, elderly mother, Febb King Ensminger Burn, whose letter urging him to support ratification he received just prior to the vote. He added, "A mother's advice is always safest for her boy to follow." Aware of the profound impact of his vote for ratification (though vastly underestimating the number of new women voters), Burn also stated that he "appreciated the fact that an opportunity such as seldom comes to a mortal man to free seventeen million women from political slavery was mine."[153]

After Burn's aye vote, both sides were stunned. The suffragists were jubilant, but the antis refused to accept defeat, moved to reconsider, and managed to delay official ratification through parliamentary tricks. While anti-suffrage legislators fled the state to avoid a quorum, their associates held a "Mass Meeting...to Save the South" in Nashville's Ryman Auditorium and through more covert, under-the-table methods, attempted to pressure pro-suffrage legislators to change their votes.[154]

Finally, Tennessee reaffirmed its vote for ratification. Tennessee's governor, Albert H. Roberts, signed the bill and it was rushed to Washington, D.C. where Secretary of State Bainbridge Colby hastened to certify the Nineteenth Amendment in the wee hours of the morning and without ceremony, before the antis were able to gain an injunction or by any other means interfere with the ratification process.[155]

On August 26, 1920, a week after the Tennessee legislature became the thirty-sixth state to ratify, the United States officially added the Nineteenth Amendment to the Constitution.

At last, the long suffrage movement had come to an end. It had taken over seventy-two years, but the U.S. Constitution finally prohibited denying citizens the vote "on account of sex." Defying all obstacles, including the high bar for amending the Constitution deliberately set by its authors, the movement begun by a small group of women's rights advocates in one corner of the nation had grown into the massive, diverse, powerful, national coalition required for victory.

Twenty-six million American women were now eligible to vote, the largest expansion of the electorate in the history of the nation. For many women of the United States, however, the fight was still not over. In 1920, many Native Americans, residents of U.S. overseas territories, immigrants from Asia who were barred from becoming citizens, and citizens disfranchised merely by residing in Washington, D.C., the struggle for voting rights would continue. African American women living in the Southern states now had the right to vote, but for almost half a century more, they would be kept from voting by the same discriminatory laws and policies that kept most African American men away from the polls. Only after the Voting Rights Act of 1965—the result of another prolonged struggle for equal suffrage in which African American women played leading roles—were they able to claim their right to vote established by the Nineteenth Amendment.[156]

Not a Gift but a Triumph

As news of the ratification of the Nineteenth Amendment spread across the nation, whistles blew and church bells rang. In towns and cities from coast to coast, there were processions, flag raisings, wreath-layings, toasts (some appropriate for the era of Prohibition and some not), and ceremonies transforming suffrage associations into the League of Women Voters (LWV). In Seneca Falls, suffragists draped a flag over a tablet marking the site of the women's rights convention where women had first demanded the vote in 1848.[157]

After hearing that Tennessee had ratified, Alice Paul sewed the thirty-sixth star on the National Woman's Party's (NWP) ratification banner and, with great fanfare, unfurled it from the balcony of the NWP headquarters, hailing the triumph of the

Alice Paul unfurling the suffrage flag upon ratification of the
Nineteenth Amendment in 1920
LIBRARY OF CONGRESS

cause—a federal suffrage amendment—for which the NWP was founded. Earlier, Paul spoke of the emotional impact: "Women who have taken part in the long struggle for freedom feel today the full relief of the victory. Freedom has come not as a gift but as a triumph, and it is therefore a spiritual as well as political freedom which women receive."[158]

Back from Nashville, Carrie Chapman Catt was invited to the White House where she was congratulated by President Wilson, her former foe who had been, in the end, a formidable ally. Proceeding to New York City, she received a hero's welcome from Governor Al Smith who represented the Democratic Party, New York Senator William M. Calder, who represented the Republicans, and prominent New York suffragists, who presented her with an enormous victory bouquet. Catt then joined other suffragists for a final parade in which they marched together for the last time, accompanied by a regimental band and waving their worn suffrage banners.[159]

Catt and Paul often disagreed, but at this time of triumph, both rejected the rhetorical fancy that the vote had been "given" to American women. As a leader of the International Woman Suffrage Alliance (IWSA) as well as the National American Woman Suffrage Association (NAWSA), Catt found it "humiliating"

Victorious Carrie Chapman Catt receiving a hero's welcome from
Governor Al Smith as she returns to New York after ratification
LIBRARY OF CONGRESS

that so many other countries "had outdistanced America" in enfranchising women.
While thrilled that victory had come at last, as she later recalled, Catt's joy was
tempered by thoughts of its cost. The suffrage movement in the United States, Catt
wrote, "Engaged the lifelong energies of a longer list of women, called into action a
larger organization in proportion to population, and involved a greater cost in
money, personal sacrifice and ingenuity, than the suffrage campaign of any other
land." And when, in 1920, "the final victory came to the woman suffrage movement
in the land of its birth American suffragists knew that their victory had, even then,
been virtually wrung from hesitant and often resentful political leaders."[160]

In the prepared message Catt delivered on August 26, 1920, rather than thanking
the president, members of Congress, or state legislators, the NAWSA president
directed her remarks to the "women of America," reminding them of the seventy-
two years of struggle by generations of suffragists and the many sacrifices made so
that "you and your daughters might inherit political freedom. That vote has been
costly. Prize it!"[161]

Notes

1. This overview of the woman suffrage movement in the United States is meant to give readers a broad view of the movement from beginning to end as well as a solid background for the following essays in Marjorie J. Spruill, editor, *One Woman, One Vote: Rediscovering the Woman Suffrage Movement*, Second edition, (NewSage Press, 2021).

2. Carrie Chapman Catt and Nettie Rogers Shuler, *Woman Suffrage and Politics: The Inner Story of the Suffrage Movement* (Seattle & London: University of Washington Press, 1923), 107-108.

3. Linda K. Kerber, "Ourselves and Our Daughters Forever: Women and the Constitution, 1787-1876," Chapter Two, in Spruill, *One Woman, One Vote*, Second edition.

4. Nancy F. Cott, 1997. *The Bonds of Womanhood: "Woman's Sphere" in New England, 1780-1835* (New Haven: Yale University Press, 1977, 1997).

5. Eleanor Flexner, "Maria W. Miller Stewart," in Edward T. James *et al*, *Notable American Women: A Biographical Dictionary* Vol. III, (Cambridge: Harvard University Press, 1975), 377-78.

6. Ibid.; Erin Blakemore, "This Little-Known Abolitionist Dared to Speak in Public Against Slavery," *Time* January 24, 2017; Martha S. Jones, *All Bound Up Together: The Woman Question in African American Public Culture, 1830-1900* (Chapel Hill: University of North Carolina Press, 2007).

7. Gerda Lerner, *The Grimké Sisters from South Carolina: Pioneers for Women's Rights and Abolition* (University of North Carolina Press, 2004); Carol Berkin, *Civil War Wives: The Lives and Times of Angelina Grimké Weld, Varina Howell Davis, and Julia Dent Grant* (New York: Vintage Books, 2010); Nancy Woloch, *Women and the American Experience*, Fifth Edition (New York: McGraw-Hill, 2011), 180-95.

8. Ibid.; Sarah Moore Grimké. *Letters on the Equality of the Sexes and the Condition of Women* (Isaac Knapp, 1838).

9. Lerner, *The Grimké Sisters*; Berkin, *Civil War Wives*; Woloch, *Women and the American Experience*, 180-95.

10. Ibid., 183.

11. Ibid., Keith Melder, "Abigail Kelley Foster," *Notable American Women*, Vol. I, 647-50.

12. Alice S. Rossi, "A Feminist Friendship: Elizabeth Cady Stanton and Susan B. Anthony," Chapter Four, in Spruill, *One Woman, One Vote*, Second Edition.

13. Sally G. McMillen, *Seneca Falls and the Origins of the Women's Rights Movement* (New York: Oxford University Press, 2009), 81-94; Leigh Fought, *Women in the World of Frederick Douglass*, (New York: Oxford University Press, 2019).

14. McMillen, *Seneca Falls*, 88-93

15. Elizabeth Cady Stanton, Susan B. Anthony, and Matilda Gage, eds. "The Seneca Falls Convention, from *History of Woman Suffrage, 1881*," Chapter Three; Rossi, Chapter Four; Katherine M. Marino, "The International History of the U.S. Suffrage Movement," Chapter Eleven, in Spruill, *One Woman, One Vote*, Second Edition; McMillen, *Seneca Falls*; Note: In *The Myth of Seneca Falls: Memory and the Women's Suffrage Movement, 1848-1898* (University of North Carolina Press, 2014), historian Lisa Tetrault emphasizes the multiplicity of events in the early stages of the women's rights movement. She argues that the myth that celebrates the Seneca Falls Convention rather than any other pre-war event as the origin was constructed to strengthen the movement as it "imposed a sense of order and inevitability onto the whole of nineteenth-century women's rights."

16. McMillen, *Seneca Falls*, 104-48; Woloch, *Women and the American Experience*, 192.

17. Ibid., 192-95; McMillen, *Seneca Falls*, 104-48.

18. Ibid.

19. Sally G. McMillen, *Lucy Stone: An Unapologetic Life* (New York: Oxford University Press, 2015).

20. Alma Lutz, "Susan Brownell Anthony," *Notable American Women*, Vol. I, 51-59.

21. Rosalyn Terborg-Penn, "African American Women and the Woman Suffrage Movement," Chapter Ten, in Spruill, *One Woman, One Vote*, Second Edition; RosalynTerborg-Penn, *African American Women in the Struggle for the Vote, 1850-1920* (Bloomington: Indiana Univ. Press, 1999); Sharon Harley, "African American Women and the Nineteenth Amendment,"

National Park Service nps.gov/articles/african-american-women-and-the-nineteenth-amendment.htm#_ednref1

22. Terborg-Penn, Chapter Ten; Harley, "African American Women and the Nineteenth Amendment"; Nell Irvin Painter, *Sojourner Truth: A Life, A Symbol* (New York, NY: Norton, 2007).

23. Rossi, Chapter Four; Terborg-Penn, *African American Women in the Struggle for the Vote*, 16, 18; Harley, "African American Women and the Nineteenth Amendment'"; Marino, Chapter Eleven.

24. Andrea Moore Kerr, "White Women's Rights, Black Men's Wrongs, Free Love, Blackmail, and the Formation of the American Woman Suffrage Association," Chapter Five, in Spruill, *One Woman, One Vote*, Second Edition; Faye E. Dudden, *Fighting Chance: The Struggle Over Woman Suffrage and Black Suffrage in Reconstruction America* (Oxford University Press, 2014).

25. Kerr, Chapter Five; Terborg-Penn, Chapter Ten; Harley, "African American Women and the Nineteenth Amendment."

26. Dudden, *Fighting Chance.*

27. Ibid., 62.

28. Kerr, Chapter Five; Terborg-Penn, Chapter Ten; Dudden, *Fighting Chance*, 61-87, quotations Stanton 83, Anthony 86. Anthony reportedly said this to Wendell Phillips and Theodore Tilton in a private meeting in Tilton's office as the two men sought to convince her to wait for another generation to push for woman suffrage. Incident described in Ida Husted Harper, *Life and Work of Susan B. Anthony*, Vol. 1:261.

29. Truth quoted in Dudden, *Fighting Chance*, 96.

30. Ibid., 82.

31. Kerr, Chapter Five; Ellen Carol DuBois, "Taking the Law Into Our Own Hands: Bradwell, Minor, and Suffrage Militance in the 1870s, Chapter Six, in Spruill, *One Woman, One Vote*, Second Edition; Nell Irvin Painter, "Voices of Suffrage: Sojourner Truth, Frances Watkins Harper, and the Struggle for Woman Suffrage," in Jean H. Baker, *Votes for Women: The Struggle for Suffrage Revisited* (New York: Oxford University Press, 2002), 42-55; Dudden, *Fighting Chance*, 94-101, 161-66.

32. Kerr, Chapter Five; Dudden, *Fighting Chance;* On Harper, see Bettye Collier-Thomas, "Frances Ellen Watkins Harper: Abolitionist and Feminist Reformer, 1825-1911," in Ann D. Gordon and Betty Collier-Thomas, et al., *African American Women and the Vote* (Amherst: University of Massachusetts Press, 1998), 41-65; Lori D. Ginzberg, *Elizabeth Cady Stanton: An American Life* (New York: Hill and Wang, 2010).

33. Kerr, Chapter Five; DuBois, Chapter Six.

34. McMillen, *Lucy Stone;* Stone put aside previous opposition to the Fifteenth Amendment because it was crucial to the freedmen and a step toward universal suffrage. On Stone's decision, Stanton commented: "Mrs. Stone felt the slaves' wrongs more deeply than her own—my philosophy was more egotistical." Quotations, 178.

35. Kerr, Chapter Five; Terborg-Penn, Chapter Ten; Terborg-Penn, *African American Women in the Struggle for the Vote*, 47.

36. Kerr, Chapter Five; McMillen, *Lucy Stone.*

37. Kerr, Chapter Five; DuBois, Chapter Six.

38. DuBois, Chapter Six; Terborg-Penn, Chapter Ten; Kerber, Chapter Two; Berkin, *Civil War Wives*, 99; Lynn Sherr, *The Trial of Susan B. Anthony* (New York: Humanity Books, 2003); Lynn Sherr and Susan B. Anthony. *Failure Is Impossible: Susan B. Anthony in Her Own Words* (New York: Times Books, 1996); Susan Ware, *Why They Marched: Untold Stories of the Women Who Fought for the Right to Vote* (Harvard University Press, 2019).

39. Ibid.

40. Kerber, Chapter Two; DuBois, Chapter Six.

41. Beverly Beeton, "How the West Was Won for Woman Suffrage," Chapter Seven, in Spruill, *One Woman, One Vote*, Second Edition.

42. Beeton, Chapter Seven; Beverly Beeton, *Women Vote in the West: The Woman Suffrage Movement, 1869-1896* (New York: Garland Publishing, 1986); Jad Adams, *Women and the Vote: A World History* (Oxford: Oxford University Press, 2016), 149-58; Susan Ware, *Why They Marched*; Rebecca J. Mead, *How the Vote Was Won: Woman Suffrage in the Western United States, 1868-1914* (New York University Press, 2006, 2004); Jennifer Helton, "Woman Suffrage in the West," nps.gov/articles/woman-suffrage-in-the-west.htm

43. For different views on woman suffrage in the West, see Beeton, Chapter Seven; Beeton, *Women Vote in the West: The Woman Suffrage Movement, 1869-1896* (New York: Garland Publishing, 1986); Alan Pendleton Grimes, *The Puritan Ethic and Woman Suffrage* (Westport, Conn: Greenwood Press, 1967, 1980); Adams, *Women and the Vote*, 149-58; Mead, *How the Vote Was Won*; Helton, "Woman Suffrage in the West."

44. Beeton, Chapter Seven, Adams, *Women and the Vote*, 149-56; Helton, "Woman Suffrage in the West"; Jennifer Helton, "To Pass Suffrage, Wyoming Embraced Radical Innovation," *WyoFile*, December 10, 2019, wyofile.com/to-pass-suffrage-wyoming-embraced-radical-innovation/; Tom Rea, "Right Choice, Wrong Reasons: Wyoming Women Win the right to Vote," WyoHistory.org, November 8, 2014 wyohistory.org/encyclopedia/right-choice-wrong-reasons-wyoming-women-win-right-vote

45. Beeton, Chapter Seven; Adams, *Women and the Vote*, 156-58; Susan Ware, *Why They Marched*; In 1887 Utah women lost the vote when the U.S. Congress passed the Edmunds-Tucker Anti-Polygamy Act. Though it mainly targeted plural marriage, it also took away women's voting rights in the Utah territory. As a result, Utah women, both Mormon and non-Mormon, founded suffrage organizations and began working to regain their voting rights. Woman suffrage was restored when Utah was admitted as a state in 1896.

46. Beeton, Chapter Seven.

47. Ibid.

48. Helton, "Woman Suffrage in the West."

49. Ibid.

50. Ibid.

51. Ibid.; For more information, see this extensive database: "Her Hat Was In the Ring! U.S. Women Who Ran for Political Office Before 1920," herhatwasinthering.org/about.php; Martha Cannon's 1884 marriage had to be held in secret. She was her husband's fourth wife and the U.S. government was actively prosecuting polygamists, especially men. When she had a child, the prosecutors took that as proof of the plural marriage and she had to flee to England to avoid testifying against her husband as well as the husbands of other plural wives whose babies she personally delivered. She had to flee again when her second child was born. After she served in the Utah senate for four years, her public career ended when she had a third child, again showing evidence Mormons were continuing to practice polygamy, and again making national news. In 2018 the Utah legislature voted to place her statue in Statuary Hall of the U.S. Capitol beginning in 2020, the centennial of the Nineteenth Amendment. Jennifer Baker, "Martha Hughes Cannon." National Women's History Museum. 2019.www.womenshistory.org/education resources/biographies/martha-hughes-cannon.

52. Marino, Chapter Eleven; Leila J. Rupp, *Worlds of Women: The Making of an International Women's Movement* (Princeton University Press, 1998).

53. Marino, Chapter Eleven; Adams, *Women and the Vote*, 106-34, 175-87.

54. Carolyn De Swarte Gifford, "Frances Willard and the Woman's Christian Temperance Union's Conversion to Woman Suffrage," Chapter Eight, in Spruill, *One Woman, One Vote*, Second Edition; Terborg-Penn, Chapter Ten; Harley, "African American Women and the Nineteenth Amendment."

55. Gifford, Chapter Eight; Marino, Chapter Eleven; Adams, *Women and the Vote*, 109-32; Glenda Elizabeth Gilmore, *Gender and Jim Crow: Women and the Politics of White Supremacy in North Carolina, 1896-1920*. (Chapel Hill: Univ. of North Carolina Press, 2006); Anastatia Sims, *The Power of Femininity in the New South: Women's Organizations and Politics in North Carolina, 1880-1930* (Columbia: University of South Carolina Press, 1997).

56. Helton, "Woman Suffrage in the West"; Catt and Shuler, *Woman Suffrage and Politics*, 132-59, 270-79.

57. bid., 266-69; Kerr, Chapter Five; quotation from Maud Wood Park, "Campaigning State by State," in NAWSA, *Victory: How Women Won It* (New York, 1940), 69-80. Anthony made this comment in the early 1880s after the New Departure and hopes for enfranchisement through an appeal to the Supreme Court had failed.

58. Elizabeth Cady Stanton, editor, *The Woman's Bible* (New York: European Publishing Company, 1895).

59. Marjorie J. Spruill, "Bringing in the South: Southern Ladies, White Supremacy, and States' Rights in the Fight for Woman Suffrage," Chapter Nine, and Judith N. McArthur, "Minnie Fisher Cunningham's Back Door Lobby in Texas: Political Maneuvering in a One-Party State," Chapter Twenty, in Spruill, *One Woman, One Vote*, Second Edition; Harley, "African American Women and the Nineteenth Amendment."

60. Spruill, "Bringing in the South," Chapter Nine; McArthur, Chapter Twenty.

61. Aileen S. Kraditor, *The Ideas of Women Suffrage Movement 1890-1920* (New York: Columbia Univ. Press, 1965); Roger Daniels, *Guarding the Golden Door: American Immigration Policy and Immigrants Since 1882* (New York: Hill and Wang, 2005); David W. Blight, *Race and Reunion: The Civil War in American Memory* (Cambridge, Mass: Harvard University Press, 2002); Louise Michele Newman, *White Women's Rights: The Racial Origins of Feminism in the United States*. (New York, N.Y.: Oxford Univ. Press, 2010); Spruill (Wheeler), *New Women of the New South: The Leaders of the Woman Suffrage Movement in the Southern States* (Oxford University Press, 1993).

62. Ibid., quotation, 25.

63. Ibid.

64. Ibid.; Spruill, "Bringing in the South," Chapter Nine.

65. Ibid.

66. Willard Gatewood, "The Rollin Sisters: Black Women in Reconstruction South Carolina," in Marjorie J. Spruill, Valinda Littlefield, and Joan Marie Johnson, eds., *South Carolina Women: Their Lives and Times*, Vol. 2 (University of Georgia Press, 2010): 50-67; Terborg-Penn, Chapter Ten.

67. Gatewood, "The Rollin Sisters."

68. Ibid.; Megan Specia, "Overlooked No More: How Mary Ann Shadd Cary Shook Up the Abolitionist Movement," *New York Times*, June 6, 2018; Harley, "African American Women and the Nineteenth Amendment"; Terborg-Penn, *African American Women*, 50; Marino, Chapter Eleven; Nancy Santucci Cohen, "Biography of Harriet Hattie Purvis, 1839-1904," Women and Social Movements of the United States," (Alexandria, VA: Alexander Street, 2018).

69. Rayford W. Logan, *The Negro in American Life and Thought: The Nadir, 1877-1901* (New York: Dial Press, 1954); Terborg-Penn, Chapter Ten; Paula Giddings, *When and Where I Enter: The Impact of Black Women on Race and Sex in America* (New York: Harper Collins, 2007); Jones, *All Bound Up Together*, 175-77.

70. Terborg-Penn, Chapter Ten; Mary Church Terrell, *A Colored Woman in a White World* (Washington, D.C.: Ransdell, 1940), 85-87; Marino, Chapter Eleven.

71. Terborg-Penn, Chapter Ten; Mary Church Terrell, "Woman Suffrage and the 15th Amendment," *The Crisis*, August 1915.

72. Alison M. Parker, Introduction to "What Was the Relationship between Mary Church Terrell's International Experience and Her Work against Racism in the United States?" (Alexandria, VA: Alexander Street Press, 2012); Marino, Chapter Eleven; Terrell, *A Colored Woman in a White World*, 85-87; Terborg-Penn, Chapter Ten.

73. Ibid.

74. Ibid.; Wanda A. Hendricks, "Ida B. Wells-Barnett and the Alpha Suffrage Club of Chicago," Chapter Seventeen, in Spruill, *One Woman, One Vote*, Second Edition.

75. Wanda A. Hendricks, *Fannie Barrier Williams: Crossing the Borders of Region and Race* (Urbana: University of Illinois Press, 2014); Western New York Suffragists: Winning the Vote https://rrlc.org/winningthevote/biographies/fannie-barrier-williams/

76. Evelyn Brooks Higginbotham, *Righteous Discontent: The Women's Movement in the Black Baptist Church*, 1880-1920 (Harvard University Press, 1994).

77. Adele Logan Alexander, "Adella Hunt Logan, The Tuskegee Woman's Club, and African Americans in the Suffrage Movement," in Marjorie Spruill (Wheeler), ed., *Votes for Women: The Woman Suffrage Movement in Tennessee, the South, and the Nation* (University of Tennessee Press, 1995): 71-104, quotation 88.

78. Ibid.; Adele Logan Alexander, *Princess of the Hither Isles: A Black Suffragist's Story from the Jim Crow South* (New Haven: Yale University Press, 2019).

79. For example, in an essay in a 1917 special woman suffrage issue of the NAACP magazine, Catt wrote: "Everybody counts

in applying democracy. And there will never be a true democracy until every responsible and law-abiding adult in it, without regard to race, sex, color or creed has his or her own inalienable and unpurchaseable voice in government." Carrie Chapman Catt, 1917, Votes for All: A Symposium, *The Crisis* (1917) 15 (1); Jane Cox, "Racism and Carrie Chapman Catt," *Iowa State Daily*, November 8, 1995, iowastatedaily.com/racism-and-carrie-chapman-catt-today/article_d052fd29-c606-5c29-883a-068f5bce3b30.html; Robbie Sequeira, "Catt Center Continues Efforts to Clear Namesake of Racism Allegation," July 27, 2019, *Ames Tribune*, amestrib.com/news/20190727/catt-center-continues-efforts-to-clear-namesake-of-racism-allegation ; Elaine F. Weiss, *The Woman's Hour: The Great Fight to Win the Vote* (Penguin, 2019),137-41.

80. Alexander, *Princess of the Hither Isles*; Terborg-Penn, Chapter Ten; Sylvanie Williams quoted in *History of Woman Suffrage*, Vol. 5, 115.

81. Terborg-Penn, Chapter Ten; Ida Husted Harper to Mary Church Terrell, March 18, 1919, Mary Church Terrell Papers: Correspondence, 1886-1954; 1919, Jan.-Mar., Manuscripts Division, Library of Congress.

82. Sara Hunter Graham, "The Suffrage Renaissance: A New Image for a New Century, 1896-1910," Chapter Twelve, in Spruill, *One Woman, One Vote*, Second Edition; Sara Hunter Graham, *Woman Suffrage and the New Democracy* (New Haven: Yale Univ. Press, 1996); Use of the term "doldrums" for this era began with historian Eleanor Flexner in her 1959 study, *Century of Struggle: The Woman's Rights Movement in the United States* (Cambridge, Mass., Belknap Press, 1959; Catt and Shuler, *Woman Suffrage and Politics*, 266-70).

83. Biographical sketch, Iowa State University Archives of Women's Political Communication, https://awpc.cattcenter.iastate.edu/directory/carrie-chapman-catt/; Helton, "Woman Suffrage in the West."

84. Graham, Chapter Twelve; Joan Marie Johnson, *Funding Feminism: Monied Women, Philanthropy, and the Women's Movement, 1870-1967* (Chapel Hill: University of North Carolina Press, 2017; Catt and Shuler, *Woman Suffrage and Politics*, 269-270.

85. Catt resigned as NAWSA president due to the illness of her husband who soon died. Afterwards she became heavily involved in promoting woman suffrage internationally through the IWSA. She served as its president from 1904 until 1923; Rupp, *Worlds of Women*, 22, 52. The quotation describing ICW participants is from suffragist Matilda Gage, 52. The Alliance began with six countries from Europe, Australia, and the United States, to twenty-six in 1913 to fifty-one in 1929, including South Africa, China, Argentina, Uruguay, Brazil, Egypt, India, Palestine, Jamaica, Bermuda, Cuba, Peru, Puerto Rico, Japan, Turkey, Ceylon, Dutch East Indies, Syria, and Rhodesia; *History of Woman Suffrage*, Stanton, Anthony, Gage, Harper, eds. (1881-1922), Vol. 6, pp. 805—11;

86. Graham, Chapter Twelve; Kathleen Barry, *Susan B. Anthony: A Biography of a Singular Feminist* (New York University Press, 1988), 331 - 32; Johnson, *Funding Feminism*, 56-58; Catt and Shuler, *Woman Suffrage and Politics*, 266, 269-70.

87. Brooke Kroeger, *The Suffragents: How Women Used Men to Get the Vote* (Albany: State University of New York Press, 2017), 1-5.

88. Graham, Chapter Twelve; Susan Ware, *Why They Marched*; Ellen Carol DuBois, *Harriot Stanton Blatch and the Winning of Woman Suffrage* (New Haven: Yale University Press, 1999).

89. Graham, Chapter Twelve; Park quotation in clipping, Elizabeth Miller NAWSA Suffrage Scrapbooks, 1897-1911, Rare Book and Special Collections Division, Library of Congress; Ellen Carol DuBois, "Working Women, Class Relations, and Suffrage Militance: Harriot Stanton Blatch and the New York Woman Suffrage Movement, 1894-1909," Chapter Fifteen, in Spruill, *One Woman, One Vote*, Second Edition.

90. Ibid.

91. Anna Howard Shaw, *The Story of a Pioneer*, 2011; Trisha Franzen, *Anna Howard Shaw: The Work of Woman Suffrage*. (University of Illinois Press, 2014); Graham, *Woman Suffrage and the New Democracy*; Quotation, Catt and Shuler, *Woman Suffrage and Politics*, 168.

92. Victoria Bissell Brown, "Jane Addams, Progressivism, and Woman Suffrage: An Introduction to 'Why Women Should Vote'," and Jane Addams, "Why Women Should Vote," Chapter

Thirteen, in Spruill, *One Woman, One Vote*, Second Edition.

93. Ibid.; Michael McGerr, *A Fierce Discontent: The Rise and Fall of the Progressive Movement in America, 1870-1920* (New York, Oxford University Press, 2005).

94. Ibid.; Patricia O'Toole, *The Moralist: Woodrow Wilson and the World He Made* (New York: Simon & Schuster, 2019); Eric Steven Yellin, *Racism in the Nation's Service: Government Workers and the Color Line in Woodrow Wilson's America* (Chapel Hill: University of North Carolina Press, 2016); William A. Link, *The Paradox of Southern Progressivism, 1880—1930* (Chapel Hill: University of North Carolina Press, 1992); Daniels, *Guarding the Golden Door*.

95. Brown, Chapter Thirteen; McGerr, *A Fierce Discontent*; Alice Kessler-Harris, *Out to Work: A History of Wage-Earning Women in the United States* (New York: Oxford University Press, 2003).

96. Brown, Chapter Thirteen.

97. Ibid.

98. Ibid.; Graham, *Woman Suffrage and the New Democracy*; Catt and Shuler, *Woman Suffrage and Politics*, 239.

99. DuBois, Chapter Fifteen; Brown, Chapter Thirteen; Kessler-Harris, *Out to Work*.

100. Elinor Lerner, "Jewish Involvement in the New York City Woman Suffrage Movement," Turning Point Suffragist Memorial, suffragistmemorial.org/jewish-suffragists/; Maud Nathan (1862-1946), Turning Point Suffragist Memorial, suffragistmemorial.org/maud-nathan-1862-1946/; Susan Ware, "Two Sisters," in Ware, *Why They Marched*.

101. Kathryn Kish Sklar, *Florence Kelley and the Nation's Work: The Rise of Women's Political Culture, 1830-1900* (New Haven: Yale University Press, 1995); Louise C. Wade, "Florence Kelley," *Notable American Women*, Vol. II, 316-19.

102. DuBois, Chapter Fifteen; Sklar, *Florence Kelley*; Wade, "Florence Kelley"; Quotation from, Kelley, "Woman Suffrage: Its Relation to Working Women and Children," [Circa 1913-1915]," Ann Lewis Women's Suffrage Collection, https://lewissuffragecollection.omeka.net/items/show/1597

103. DuBois, Chapter Fifteen; Paul S. Boyer, "Inez Milholland Boissevain," *Notable American Women*, Vol. I, 188-90; Linda Lumsden, *Inez: The Life and Times of Inez Milholland* (Bloomington: Indiana University Press, 2004).

104. DuBois, Chapter Fifteen; Nancy Schrom Dye, *As Sisters and As Equals: Feminism, the Labor Movement and the Women's Trade Union League of New York* (Columbia: University of Missouri Press, 1980).

105. Ibid.

106. Leonora O'Reilly, Iowa State University Archives of Women's Political Communication https://awpc.cattcenter.iastate.edu/directory/leonora-oreilly/

107. Eleanor Flexner, Janet Wilson James, "Mary Kenney O'Sullivan," *Notable American Women*, Vol. II, 655-56; Barbara Mayer Wertheimer, *"We Were There": The Story of Working Women in America* (Pantheon, 1977).

108. DuBois, Chapter Fifteen; Elinor Lerner, "Jewish Involvement in the New York City Woman Suffrage Movement"; Dye, *As Sisters and As Equals*; quotation from "Annie Schneiderman Valliere, "Rose Schneiderman," Turning Point Suffragists Memorial https://suffragistmemorial.org/rose-schneiderman-april-6-1882-august-11-1972/ ; Annelise Orleck, Rose Schneiderman," Jewish Women's Archive, jwa.org/encyclopedia/article/schneiderman-rose

109. Marino, Chapter Eleven; Nina Otero-Warren, National Park Service, nps.gov/people/nina-otero-warren.htm; Suffragists in New Mexico, Turning Point Suffragist Memorial suffragistmemorial.org/suffragists-in-new-mexico/; Helton, "Woman Suffrage in the West."

110. DuBois, Chapter Fifteen; Sherry J. Katz, "A Politics of Coalition: Socialist Women and the California Suffrage Movement, 1900-1911," Chapter Sixteen, in Spruill, *One Woman, One Vote*, Second Edition; Gayle Gullett, *Becoming Citizens: The Emergence and Development of the California Women's Movement, 1880-1911* (Urbana and Chicago: University of Illinois Press, 2000); Helton, "Woman Suffrage in the West."

111. Ibid.

112. Lee later acquired her Ph.D. in economics at Columbia University and became a lifetime supporter of girls and women, mobilizing the Chinese community. Cathleen D. Cahill, "Mabel Ping-Hua Lee: How Chinese-American Women Helped Shape the Suffrage Movement," Women's Vote Centennial,

womensvote100.org/the-suff-buffs-blog/2020/4/30/mabel-ping-hua-lee-how-chinese-american-women-helped-shape-the-suffrage-movement; Mabel Pink-Hua Lee, "More to the Movement," Library of Congress loc.gov/exhibitions/women-fight-for-the-vote/about-this-exhibition/more-to-the-movement/mabel-ping-hua-lee/

113. "Marie Louise Bottineau Baldwin," National Park Service, nps.gov/people/marie-louise-bottineau-baldwin.htm; Cathleen D. Cahill and Sarah Deer, "In 1920, Native Women Sought the Vote. Here's What's Next," New York Times, July 31, 2020.

114. Vicki L. Ruiz, Virginia E. Sánchez Korrol, Latina Legacies: Identity, Biography, and Community, (New York: Oxford University Press, 2005)

115. Ibid.; Marino, Chapter Eleven.

116. Ibid.; Katz, Chapter Sixteen.

117. Ibid.

118. Manuela Thurner, "'Better Citizens Without the Ballot': American Anti-suffrage Women and Their Rationale During the Progressive Era," Chapter Fourteen, in Spruill, One Woman, One Vote, The Woman's Hour; Jo Freeman, A Room at a Time: How Women Entered Party Politics (New York: Rowman & Littlefield Publishers, Inc. 2000, 2002), 52; Catt and Shuler, Woman Suffrage and Politics, 271-79.

119. Ibid.; Spruill (Wheeler), New Women of the New South, 4, 11-13, 25, 27, 30, 35-36; Anastatia Sims, "Armageddon in Tennessee: The Final Battle Over the Nineteenth Amendment, Chapter Twenty-one, in Spruill, One Woman, One Vote, Second Edition.

120. See flyers and posters distributed by Southern anti-suffragists in Spruill (Wheeler), Votes for Women, 302-11; Sims, Chapter Twenty-one.

121. Ibid.; Spruill (Wheeler), Votes for Women, 303, 304; Terborg-Penn, Chapter Ten.

122. Sims, Chapter Twenty-one; Thurner, Chapter Fourteen; Spruill (Wheeler), Votes for Women, 300, 301.

123. Linda K. Ford, "Alice Paul and the Triumph of Militancy," Chapter Eighteen, and Robert Booth Fowler, "Carrie Chapman Catt, Strategist," Chapter Nineteen, in Spruill, One Woman, One Vote, Second Edition; Christine Bolt, "America and the Pankhursts," in Baker, Votes for Women, 143-58.

124. Fowler, Chapter Nineteen; Johnson, Funding Feminism, 67-69.

125. Ford, Chapter Eighteen; Spruill (Wheeler), New Women of the New South, 133-71; Spruill, "Bringing in the South," Chapter Nine.

126. Ford, Chapter Eighteen; Doris Stevens, Jailed for Freedom: American Women Win the Vote, 1920. New edition, Carol O'Hare, ed. (NewSage Press, 1995).

127. Sheridan Harvey, "Marching for the Vote: Remembering the Woman Suffrage Parade of 1913," Library of Congress https://guides.loc.gov/american-women-essays/marching-for-the-vote#note_3

128. Rebecca Boggs Roberts, Suffragists in Washington, D.C.: The 1913 Parade and the Fight for the Vote. (Charleston, SC: History Press, 2017); Ware, Why They Marched.

129. Ford, Chapter Eighteen; Linda Ford, "Alice Paul and the Politics of Nonviolent Protest," in Baker, Votes for Women, 174-88; Stevens, Jailed for Freedom; See also a film about Alice Paul and the National Woman's Party, Katja von Garnier, Director. Iron Jawed Angels: Lead, Follow or Get Out of the Way. Home Box Office, 2004.

130. Doris Stevens, Jailed for Freedom: The Story of the Militant American Suffragist Movement, ed. Marjorie J. Spruill (Chicago: Lakeside Press/R.R. Donnelley & Sons, 2008).

131. Fowler, Chapter Nineteen; McArthur, Chapter Twenty.

132. That "Mighty New York" had "finally caved in" was a line in a celebratory suffrage song. See "One Woman, One Vote," Educational Film Company, PBS documentary (1995, 2020); Fowler, Chapter Nineteen.

133. Catt and Shuler, Woman Suffrage and Politics, quotation, 316; McArthur, Chapter Twenty.

134. Ibid.

135. Catt and Shuler, Woman Suffrage and Politics, 462.

136. Ibid., 338-39; HWS, VI; Weiss, The Woman's Hour, 84; Fowler, Chapter Nineteen.

137. Catt and Shuler, Woman Suffrage and Politics, 325; Alisha Haridasani Gupta, "Everything Conspires Against Women (sic)

Suffrage. Now It Is the Influenza." New York Times, May 29, 2020; Catt and Shuler, Woman Suffrage and Politics, 294-96, 299, 337-39..

138. Ibid., 304-15, 324-28; Ellen Carol DuBois, A Pandemic Nearly Derailed the Women's Suffrage Movement, National Geographic, April 20, 2020.

139. Ibid.; Gupta, "Everything Conspires Against Women (sic) Suffrage"; Catt and Shuler, Woman Suffrage and Politics, 304, 314

140. Ibid.; Weiss, The Woman's Hour; DuBois, "A Pandemic Nearly Derailed the Women's Suffrage Movement."

141. Catt and Shuler, Woman Suffrage and Politics, 304-314, 328-29.

142. Spruill (Wheeler), New Women of the New South, 33,173-76;

143. Sims, Chapter Twenty-one; McArthur, Chapter Twenty; Spruill, "Bringing in the South," Chapter Nine.

144. Catt and Shuler, Woman Suffrage and Politics, Chapter Twenty-six, "Last of All Suffrage Conventions," 381-86; At the time of the Jubilee Convention, 31 states had ratified. Stanley Lemons, The Woman Citizen: Social Feminism in the 1920s (Urbana: University of Illinois Press, 1973, 1975), 50-51.

145. Spruill (Wheeler), New Women of the New South, quotation, 34.

146. Catt and Shuler, Woman Suffrage and Politics, 396-413, quotation, 398.

147. Ibid., 465, 476-80; Sims, Chapter Twenty-one; Freeman, A Room at a Time, 125; Spruill (Wheeler), New Women of the New South, 34-35.

148. Sims, Chapter Twenty-one; see also the vivid, detailed account of this final stage of the suffrage struggle in Weiss, The Woman's Hour.

149. On Tennessee Democrats' dislike of the NWP, on Sue White's role in the ratification battle, see Spruill (Wheeler), Votes for Women, 169-196; On Pollitzer, see Amy Thompson McCandless, "Anita Pollitzer: A South Carolina Advocate for Equal Rights," in Marjorie J. Spruill, Valinda W. Littlefield, and Joan Marie Johnson, South Carolina Women: Their Lives and Times Vol. 2, (Athens: University of Georgia Press, 2010), 172-74.

150. Sims, Chapter Twenty-one; Carrie Chapman Catt and Nettie Rogers Shuler, "Tennessee," their account of the suffrage battle taken from Woman Suffrage and Politics, in Spruill (Wheeler), Votes for Women, 243-74; See also the documentary produced by Nashville Public Television, "By One Vote: Woman Suffrage in the South," 2019, wnpt.org/suffrage

151. Spruill (Wheeler), Votes for Women, see anti-suffrage broadsides, 300-311, quotations, 305, 311.

152. Sims, Chapter Twenty-one.

153. Ibid.; Quotation from Harry Burn, Catt and Shuler, Woman Suffrage and Politics, 451. The number of women enfranchised was approximately 27 million.

154. Ibid., 449-55; Sims, Chapter Twenty-one; Tyler L. Boyd, Harry T. Burn: Tennessee Statesman, The History Press, 2019, 72-100.

155. Sims, Chapter Twenty-one; Catt and Shuler, Woman Suffrage and Politics, 455.

156. See Marjorie J. Spruill, "A Century of Woman Suffrage," Chapter Twenty-three in Spruill, One Woman, One Vote: Rediscovering the Woman Suffrage Movement, Second Edition.

157. Catt and Shuler, Woman Suffrage and Politics, 455-56.

158. Shall Not Be Denied: Women Fight for the Vote, Official Companion to the Library of Congress Exhibit, Rutgers University Press, 1919, 101; nps.gov/articles/celebrations-of-success.htm

159. Mary Gray Peck, Carrie Chapman Catt: A Biography (Westport, Conn: Hyperion Press, 1976), 339; Catt and Shuler, Woman Suffrage and Politics, 455-56.

160. Catt and Shuler, Woman Suffrage and Politics, 5.

161. Quotation from The Woman Citizen, September 4, 1920; Barbara Stuhler, For the Public Record: A Documentary History of the League of Women Voters (Westport, Connecticut: Greenwood Publishing Group, 2000), 26.

Two

"OURSELVES AND OUR DAUGHTERS FOREVER":

Women and the Constitution
1787—1876

Linda K. Kerber

Editor's Introduction: In this essay, Linda K. Kerber, one of the leading scholars of women in the American Revolution and the early national period, discusses why women were excluded from the vote as the new nation was launched and remained disfranchised during the nation's first one hundred years. Kerber makes it clear why a woman suffrage movement was necessary, and why suffragists came to focus on an amendment to the Constitution.

After describing the dramatic protest against women's political and legal inferiority led by Susan B. Anthony and Elizabeth Cady Stanton at the 1876 celebration of the nation's centennial, Kerber examines the assumptions held by John Adams and the other Founding Fathers who implicitly excluded women from participation in the government of the new republic. These men, says Kerber, "Shared assumptions about women and politics so fully that they did not need to debate them," including the idea that women, like propertyless men, were dependent and "lacked a will of their own," and thus were appropriately excluded from suffrage. Significantly, the American Constitution did not *explicitly* exclude women from voting or other political rights. The states—assigned the task of establishing the requirements for voting—*could* have interpreted the Constitution to justify full enfranchisement of women, or the courts could have so ruled. "Women might have been absorbed fully into the American political community," writes Kerber, "without the necessity of constitutional amendment."

In the antebellum period, as the states dropped many of the restrictions on voting and extended the franchise to virtually all White men, however, no state moved to extend suffrage to women and the one state that had allowed women to vote rescinded this privilege. Thus, in the 1820s, 1830s, and 1840s, women began to protest publicly against their legal and political inferiority. In the Declaration of Sentiments adopted at the Seneca Falls Convention in 1848, participants demanded a wide range of constitutional, legal, and social reforms—including the right to vote.

After the Civil War, as the nation experienced a revolution in politics, and Congress amended the Constitution to address—for the first time—the issue of voter qualifications, women's rights advocates hoped that universal suffrage for *all* would be the result. As Kerber describes, however, the Fourteenth and Fifteenth Amendments, adopted to enfranchise the freedmen, actually added new obstacles to woman suffrage; not only did the amendment fail to include sex as a protected category along with race, but in the Fourteenth Amendment the word "male" was added to the Constitution for the first time. Ironically, the fact that women were now demanding the vote led the authors of the amendment to believe it was necessary to specify that the amendment would *not* enfranchise women.

Initially dismayed by these events, suffragists then tried the "New Departure," claiming suffrage and other rights based on a broad interpretation of the Fourteenth Amendment. As citizens, they claimed all the "privileges and immunities" of citizens, but were rebuffed by the courts. Thus, by the centennial celebration in 1876, it had become clear that woman suffrage was not going to emerge from reinterpretations of existing laws, either state or federal. If women were to be enfranchised, said Kerber, they would have to have "either an explicit constitutional amendment or a series of revisions in the laws of the states." Suffragists now knew what they would have to do to establish their right to the vote. The long and difficult fight for enfranchisement had only begun.

★   ★   ★   ★   ★

IN 1876, THE UNITED STATES celebrated one hundred years as an independent nation dedicated to the proposition that all men are created equal. The capstone of the celebration was a public reading of the Declaration of Independence in Independence Square Philadelphia, by a descendant of a signer, Richard Henry Lee.

Elizabeth Cady Stanton, who was then president of the National Woman Suffrage Association (NWSA), asked permission to present silently a women's protest and a written women's Declaration of Rights. Her request was denied. "Tomorrow we propose to celebrate what we have done the last hundred years," replied the president of the official ceremonies, "not what we have failed to do."

Led by Susan B. Anthony, five women appeared nevertheless at the official reading, distributing copies of their own Declaration. After this mildly disruptive gesture, they withdrew to the other side of the symmetrical Independence Hall, where they staged a counter-Centennial. "With sorrow we come to strike the one discordant note, on this one-hundredth anniversary of our country's birth," Susan B. Anthony declared.

Although the rhythms of her speech echoed the Declaration of Independence, as was fitting for the day—"The history of our country the past hundred years has been a series of assumptions and usurpations of power over woman..."—the substance of her speech was built on references to the Constitution. Anthony and the women for whom she spoke were troubled by the discrepancy between the universally applicable provisions of the Constitution and the specificity of the way in which these provisions were interpreted to exclude women. For example, since all juries excluded women, women were denied the right of trial by a jury of their peers. Although taxation without representation had been a rallying cry of the Revolution, single women and widows who owned property paid taxes although they could not vote for the legislators who set the taxes. A double standard of morals was maintained in law by which women were arrested for prostitution while men went free. The introduction of the word "male" into federal and state constitutions, Anthony asserted, functioned in effect as a bill of attainder, in that it treated women as a class, denying them the right of suffrage, and "thereby making sex a crime."

Anthony ended by calling for the impeachment of all officers of the federal government on the grounds that they had not fulfilled their obligations under the Constitution. Their "vacillating interpretations of constitutional law unsettle our faith in judicial authority, and undermine the liberties of the whole people," she declared.

> Special legislation for woman has placed us in a most anomalous position. Women invested with the rights of citizens in one section—voters, jurors, office holders—crossing an imaginary line, are subjects in the next. In some states a married woman may hold property and transact business in her own name; in others her earnings belong to her husband. In some states, a woman may testify against her husband, sue and be sued in the courts; in others she has no redress in case of damage to person, property, or character. In case of divorce on account of adultery in the husband, the innocent wife is held to possess no right to children or property, unless by special decrees of the court.... In some states women may enter the law school and practice in the courts; in others they are forbidden....

> These articles of impeachment against our rulers we now submit to the impartial judgment of the people.... From the beginning of the century, when Abigail Adams, the wife of one president and mother of another, said, "We will not hold ourselves bound to obey laws in which we have no voice or representation," until now, woman's discontent has been steadily increasing, culminating nearly thirty years ago in a simultaneous movement among the women of the nation, demanding the right of suffrage.... It was the boast of the founders of the republic, that the rights for which they contended were the rights of human nature. If these rights are ignored in the case of one half the people, the nation is surely preparing for its downfall. Governments try themselves. The recognition of a governing and a governed class is incompatible with the first principles of freedom....[1]

Abigail Adams
ENGRAVING BASED ON
ORIGINAL PORTRAIT BY GILBERT STUART

John Adams
ENGRAVING BY H.B. HALLS SONS,
LIBRARY OF CONGRESS

The Founding Generation

Let us stand with Susan B. Anthony at her vantage point of 1876 and review the constitutional issues that touched women's lives in the first hundred years of the republic. During those hundred years, basic questions were defined and strategies for affecting legislation were developed. Not until after the Centennial would women direct their energies primarily to constitutional amendment. In the first century, the challenge was to understand whether and to what extent women's political status was different from that of men, and to develop a rationale for criticizing that difference.

It is intriguing to speculate how the Founders might have responded to Anthony's challenge. Throughout the long summer of 1787 in Philadelphia, the role of women in the new polity went formally unconsidered. Whether they came from small or large states, whether they favored the New Jersey or Virginia Plan, whether they hoped for a gradual end to slavery or a strengthening of the system, the men who came to Carpenters' Hall in 1787 shared assumptions about women and politics so fully that they did not need to debate them. Indeed, John Adams had missed the point in his now-famous exchange with Abigail Adams to which Anthony referred in her Centennial Address: Abigail Adams clearly had domestic violence as well as political representation in mind as she wrote; that is, she was thinking in both practical and theoretical terms.[2] Her husband refused to deal with the issue:

Abigail Adams to John Adams
March 31, 1776

...in the new Code of Laws which I suppose it will be necessary for you to make, I desire you would Remember the Ladies, and be more generous and favourable to them than your ancestors. Do not put such unlimited power into the hands of the Husbands. Remember all Men would be tyrants if they could. If perticular care and attention is not paid to the Laidies we are determined to foment a Rebelion, and will not hold ourselves bound by any Laws in which we have no voice, or Representation.

That your Sex are Naturally Tyrannical is a Truth so thoroughly established as to admit of no dispute.... Why then, not put it out of the power of the vicious and the Lawless to use us with cruelty and indignity with impunity....

John Adams to Abigail Adams
April 14, 1776
As to your extraordinary Code of Laws, I cannot but laugh. We have been told that our struggle has loosened the bonds of Government every where. That Children and Apprentices were disobedient—that schools and colleges were grown turbulent—that Indians slighted their guardians and Negroes grew insolent to their Masters. But your Letter was the first Intimation that another Tribe more numerous and powerfull than all the rest were grown discontented.... Depend upon it, We know better than to repeal our Masculine systems.... We have only the Name of Masters, and rather than give up this, which would compleatly subject Us to the Despotism of the Peticoat, I hope General Washington, and all our brave Heroes would fight....

Abigail Adams to John Adams
May 7, 1776
...Arbitrary power is like most other things which are very hard, very liable to be broken....[3]

The exclusion of married women from the vote was based on the same principle that excluded men without property from the vote. If the will of the people was in fact to be expressed by voting, it was important that each vote be independent and uncoerced. Men who had no property and were dependent on their landlords or employers for survival were understood to be vulnerable to pressure; they were, in John Adams's words, "too dependent upon other men to have a will of their own." Adams acknowledged, in fact, that excluding all women was somewhat arbitrary; but lines, as he explained in a thoughtful letter to the Massachusetts politician James Sullivan, had to be drawn somewhere.

John Adams to James Sullivan
May 26, 1776
It is certain, in theory, that the only moral foundation of government is, the consent of the people. But to what an extent shall we carry this principle?

Shall we say that every individual of the community, old and young, male and female, as well as rich and poor, must consent, expressly, to every act of legislation? No, you will say, this is impossible. How then, does the right arise in the majority to govern the minority, against their will? Whence arises the right of the men to govern the women, without their consent? Whence the right of the old to bind the young, without theirs?…

But why exclude women?

You will say, because their delicacy renders them unfit for practice and experience in the great businesses of life, and the hardy enterprises of war…. Besides, their attention is so much engaged with the necessary nurture of their children, that nature has made them fittest for domestic cares. And children have not judgment or will of their own. True, but will not these reasons apply to others? Is it not equally true, that men in general, in every society, who are wholly destitute of property, are also too little acquainted with public affairs to form a right judgment, and too dependent upon other men to have a will of their own?… They talk and vote as they are directed by some man of property….

Your idea that those laws which affect the lives and personal liberty of all, or which inflict corporal punishment, affect those who are not qualified to vote, as well as those who are, is just. But so they do women, as well as men; children, as well as adults. What reason should there be for excluding a man of twenty years eleven months and twenty-seven days old, from a vote, when you admit one who is twenty-one? The reason is, you must fix upon some period in life, when the understanding and will of men in general, is fit to be trusted by the public. Will not the same reason justify the state in fixing upon some certain quantity of property, as a qualification?

The same reasoning which will induce you to admit all men who have not property, to vote, with those who have, for those laws which affect the person, will prove that you ought to admit women and children; for, generally speaking, women and children have as good judgments, and as independent minds, as those men who are wholly destitute of property; these last being to all intents and purposes as much dependent upon others, who will please to feed, clothe and employ them, as women are upon their husbands, or children on their parents.

Depend upon it, Sire, it is dangerous to open so fruitful a source of controversy and altercations as would be opened by attempting to alter the qualifications of voters; there will be no end of it. New claims will arise; women will demand a vote; kids from twelve to twenty-one will think their rights not enough attended to; and every man who has not a farthing, will demand an equal voice with any other; in all acts of state. It tends to confound and destroy all distinctions, and prostrate all ranks to one common level....[4]

John Adams spelled out with unusual frankness what most of his colleagues believed. If dependent men were to vote, the result would not be that the will of all individuals was counted; rather the result would be that landlords and employers would in effect exercise multiple votes. Married women were thought to be in much the same state as unpropertied men. Their property, according to the traditional British law of domestic relations, came under their husbands' power when they married, a practice known as coverture. The married woman, "covered" by her husband's civic identity, lost the power to manipulate her property independently. (She remained however, an independent moral being under the law, capable of committing crimes, even treason.) To give a vote to a person so dependent on another's will seemed to give a double vote to husbands, rather than to enfranchise wives. In a society in which it was assumed that the wife did the husband's bidding, it seemed absurd to give married men a political advantage over their unmarried brothers. Instead of revising the old law of domestic relations, and taking married women out from under the "cover" of their husbands' authority, virtually all the states denied the franchise to married women.

Roads Not Taken

The logic that excluded married women should not have, on the face of it, excluded unmarried women with property—including widows—who were not under the immediate influence of an adult man, who could buy and sell their property, and who paid taxes. Single adult women might have formed a substantial electorate, even in a system of coverture. But in practice custom rather than logic prevailed; single women were treated for the most part as were their married counterparts.

Only in New Jersey, where the state constitution of 1776 enfranchised "all free inhabitants" who could meet property and residence requirements did women vote; in 1790, possibly because of Quaker influence, an election law used the phrase "he or she" in referring to voters.

The New Jersey Constitution of 1776 provided that "All Inhabitants of this colony, of full age, who are worth fifty pounds proclamation money, clear estate in the same, and have resided within the county in which they claim a vote for twelve months immediately preceding the election, shall be entitled to vote for Representatives in Council and Assembly; and also for all other public officers, that shall be elected by the people of the county at large...."

In 1797, New Jersey law explicitly recognized that women voted: "No person shall be entitled to vote in any other township or precinct, than that in which he or she doth actually reside at the time of the election.... Every voter shall openly, and in full view deliver his or her ballot...."

The general tendency in suffrage law throughout the nineteenth century was to broaden the electorate by gradually eliminating property and racial qualifications; yet the New Jersey election statute did not become a model for other states. In 1797 the women's vote was thought to have been exercised as a bloc vote in favor of the Federalist candidate for Elizabethtown in the state legislature, and it was alleged to have made a real difference in the outcome of the election.

Faced with this gender gap, the defeated Democratic-Republicans launched a bitter campaign with two themes that were to appear and reappear as long as woman suffrage was debated in this country. First, they argued that women who appeared at the polls were unfeminine, forgetful of their proper place. Second, they asserted that women were easily manipulated, if not by husbands, then by fathers and brothers. It took ten years, but in 1807 New Jersey passed a new election law excluding all women from the polls, and no other state attempted New Jersey's 1776 experiment. In the absence of a collective political movement, no delegate came to Philadelphia in 1787 prepared to make an issue of woman suffrage or of any other distinctively female political concern; no one came prepared to engage in debate over the extent to which women were an active part of the political community.

With the benefit of hindsight, it is possible for historians to identify some substantive issues that politically empowered women might well have raised had

Women voting in New Jersey, c. 1800
LIBRARY OF CONGRESS

the Constitution guaranteed their right to participate in a republican government. (Some of these issues would be addressed only a few years later, by Montagnards and Jacobins in France.) One obvious issue is divorce reform. In some states divorce was nearly impossible in 1787; in all it was extremely difficult. Since the majority of petitioners for divorce were women, the issue was one in which women had a distinctive interest. The language of republicanism, with its acknowledgment that the new order validated a search for happiness, was taken by a number of people to imply that divorce reform was a logical implication of republicanism. But the Constitution said nothing about it, and the states loosened restrictions only slowly. Two generations later women's rights activists would place divorce reform high on their political agenda; it is probable that it would also have been given priority on an agenda drafted in the 1780s.

A second concern might have been pensions for widows of soldiers. The Continental Congress authorized modest pensions for the widows of officers, but widows of soldiers would not be provided with pensions until 1832, by which time, of course, many of them were dead. It is easy to think of other issues: the right of mothers to child custody in the event of divorce, restrictions on wife abuse, the security of dower rights. But expressions of opinion on these issues remained the work of individuals; no collective feminist movement gave them articulate expression as was the case in France. No organized female political pressure was brought to bear at the Constitutional Convention; there do not seem to have been American predecessors of the female Jacobin clubs of Paris.

The Constitution reflected the experience of the White middle- and upper-class men who wrote it and the experience of their constituents, the men of the upper- and lower-middle classes, the farmers and artisans, who had, as historian Edward Countryman has observed, "established their political identity in the Revolution." Although their political choices were characterized by what the historian Michael Grossberg has called their "deep aversion to unaccountable authority," they retained the authority of husbands over wives intact.[5] All free men, rich or poor, continued to gain control of their wives' bodies and property when they married. Women had not yet, as a group, firmly established their political identity.

Gender and the Language of the Constitution

The Constitution did not explicitly welcome women as voters or take particular account of them as a class. However, what the Constitution left unsaid was as important as what it did say. The text of the Constitution usually speaks of "persons"; only rarely does it use the generic "he." Women as well as men were defined as citizens. The Constitution establishes no voting requirements, leaving it up to the states to set the terms by which people shall qualify to vote.

> **Article 1, Section 2:** The House of Representatives shall be composed of
> Members chosen every Year by the People of the several States, and the

Electors in each State shall have the qualifications requisite for Electors of the most numerous Branch of the State Legislature.

Thus women were not explicitly excluded from Congress, nor even from the presidency. The Constitution, in fact, left an astonishing number of substantive matters open to the choices of individual states; every part of it was open to change by amendment. This flexibility is an important reason for the survival of the American Constitution, as contrasted to the other republican constitutions of the era, like the French, which were far more detailed and explicit, but also less resilient. Women might have been absorbed fully into the American political community without the necessity of constitutional amendment.

Yet this absorption did not occur automatically. No state imitated New Jersey's experiment with suffrage before the Civil War; only a few—Utah, Wyoming, Colorado, Idaho—did so after the war. No state moved to place non-voters on juries, although there was obvious common sense in the argument that in order for a woman to be tried by her peers a jury should include women, whether or not women voted in that state. Although the old argument that the proper voter was a person of property eroded as liberals steadily decreased property requirements for voting by men, women were not enfranchised.

Attempts at Reform

Still, even without the vote, effective political coalitions of feminists and legal reformers developed at the end of the 1830s. They were interested in the codification and simplification of state laws. They pressed for the passage of Married Women's Property Acts that would enable married women to control property without necessitating cumbersome trusteeship arrangements. Beginning with a severely limited statute passed in Mississippi in 1839 and continuing throughout the century, state Married Women's Property Acts gradually extended the financial independence of married women, making it possible for a few feminists to entertain a vision of a full range of women's political activity, even under the older requirements of property holding. However, the new control that women achieved over their own property was not accompanied by the extension of the franchise.

The New York State Married Women's Property Act provides an example of this type of legislation:

> The real and personal property of any female [now married and] who may here-after marry, and which she shall own at the time of marriage, and the rents, issues and profits thereof shall not be subject to the disposal of her husband, nor be liable for his debts, and shall continue her sole and separate property, as if she were a single female.... It shall be lawful for any married female to receive by gift, grant, devise or bequest, from any person other than her husband and hold to her sole and separate use, as if

she were a single female, real and personal property, and the rents, issues and profits thereof and the same shall not be subject to the disposal of her husband, nor be liable for his debts....

A married woman may bargain, sell, assign, and transfer her separate personal property, and carry on any trade or business, and perform any labor or services on her sole and separate account, and the earnings of any married woman from her trade...shall be her sole and separate property, and may be used or invested by her in her own name....

Any married woman may, while married, sue and be sued in all matters having relation to her ... sole and separate property...in the same manner as if she were sole....

Every married woman is hereby constituted and declared to be the joint guardian of her children, with her husband, with equal powers, rights, and duties in regard to them, with the husband....[6]

Elizabeth Cady Stanton, who had been a strong supporter of the New York Married Women's Property Acts, was also an energizing force behind the gathering of women in Seneca Falls in 1848. She and others who prepared and signed the Declaration of Sentiments at that meeting addressed forcefully the ways in which women had not been fully absorbed into the republican political order, although they were citizens. After a preface casting "Man" in a rhetorical role comparable to that played by King George III in the Declaration of Independence, the Declaration of Sentiments addressed constitutional and legal as well as social questions: trial by jury, the relationship between taxation and representation, the persistence of coverture.

He has compelled her to submit to laws, in the formation of which she had no voice....

He has made her, if married, in the eye of the law, civilly dead....

He has taken from her all right in property, even to the wages she earns....

After depriving her of all rights as a married woman, if single, and the owner of property, he has taxed her to support a government which recognizes her only when her property can be made profitable to it....[7]

The legislative gains of the early part of the century and the emergence of a women's movement at mid-century were not, however, followed by a wave of enfranchisement. In fact, women found themselves excluded from the debate about the extension of the franchise that was engendered by the Civil War.

The Civil War Amendments, the New Departure and Its Defeat

The Civil War was not only a military crisis but also a revolution in politics, which would be validated by the Thirteenth, Fourteenth, and Fifteenth Amendments. By now there was most emphatically, a collective women's public presence—in the

Sanitary Commission, the women's abolitionist societies, the Women's National Loyal League. But the "Woman Question" had not been central to the ideology of the Civil War, and once again, women found they could not claim the benefits. Abolitionist and Republican feminists had permitted themselves to anticipate that suffrage would be the appropriate reward for their sacrifices and support of the war effort. They also believed strongly that the authentic meaning of the expanded citizenship embedded in the Fourteenth Amendment was contradicted by its enforcement clauses. That is, if indeed "all persons, born or naturalized in the United States are citizens of the United States and the state in which they reside" then, they thought, women as well as men, Black and White, should have the vote as one of the "privileges and immunities of citizenship." Their resentment was therefore all the greater when woman suffrage was not made part of the post-war amendments. The inclusion of the word "male" in the second section of the Fourteenth Amendment—a section never enforced—rubbed salt in a raw wound. The Fifteenth Amendment, guaranteeing the vote to all men despite race or previous condition of servitude, made explicit what the Fourteenth Amendment had left implicit.

Fourteenth Amendment, 1868

Section One

All persons born or naturalized in the United States, and subject to the jurisdiction thereof, are citizens of the United States and of the State wherein they reside. No State shall make or enforce any law which shall abridge the privileges or immunities of citizens of the United States; nor shall any State deprive any person of life, liberty or property, without due process of law; nor deny to any person within its jurisdiction the equal protection of the laws.

Section Two

Representatives shall be apportioned among the several States according to their respective numbers, counting the whole number of persons in each State, excluding Indians not taxed. But when the right to vote at any election for the choice of electors for President and Vice-President of the United States, Representatives in Congress, the executive and judicial officers of a State, or the members of the legislature thereof, is denied to any of the male inhabitants of such State, being twenty-one years of age and citizens of the United States, or in any way abridged, except for participation in rebellion, or other crime, the basis of representation therein shall be reduced in the proportion which the number of such male citizens shall bear to the whole number of male citizens twenty-one years of age in such State....

Holding their tempers, suffragists embarked on a national effort to test the universal possibilities of the first section of the Fourteenth Amendment, a strategy they called "the New Departure," only to discover that the Supreme Court rejected their arguments.[8] It was tested first in 1873 by Myra Bradwell, a Chicago woman who had studied law with her husband. She had been granted a special charter from the State of Illinois permitting her to edit and publish the *Chicago Legal News* as her own business, a business she carried on with distinction. (After the Chicago fire destroyed many law offices, it was the files of Bradwell's *Legal News* on which the city's attorneys relied for their records.) Bradwell claimed that one of the "privileges and immunities" of a citizen guaranteed by Section One was her right to practice law in the State of Illinois and to argue cases. The Illinois Supreme Court turned her down, on the ground that as a married woman, she was not a fully free agent.

In her appeal to the Supreme Court, Bradwell's attorney argued that among the "privileges and immunities" guaranteed to each citizen by the Fourteenth Amendment was the right to pursue any honorable profession. "Intelligence, integrity and honor are the only qualifications that can be prescribed…. The broad shield of the Constitution is over all, and protects each in that measure of success which his or her individual merits may secure." But the Supreme Court held that the right to practice law in any particular state was a right that might be granted by the individual state; it was not one of the privileges and immunities of citizenship. A concurring opinion added an ideological dimension:

> The natural and proper timidity and delicacy which belongs to the female sex evidently unfits it for many of the occupations of civil life. The constitution of the family organization, which is founded on the divine ordinance, as well as in the nature of things, indicates the domestic sphere as that which properly belongs to the domain and functions of womanhood. The harmony, not to say identity, of interests and views which belong or should belong to the family institution, is repugnant to the idea of a woman adopting a distinct and independent career from that of her husband. So firmly fixed was this sentiment in the founders of the common law that it became a maxim of that system of jurisprudence that a woman had no legal existence separate from her husband, who was regarded as her head and representative in the social state…many of the special rules of law flowing from and dependent upon this cardinal principal still exist in full force in most states. One of these is that a married woman is incapable, without her husband's consent, of making contracts which shall be binding on her or him. This very incapacity was one circumstance which the supreme court of Illinois deemed important in rendering a married woman incompetent fully to perform the duties and trusts that belong to the office of an attorney and counselor.[9]

Meanwhile, suffragists in a number of places attempted to test the other possibilities of the first section of the Fourteenth Amendment. In the presidential election of 1872, suffragist women in a number of districts appeared at the polls, arguing that if all citizens had the right to the privileges of citizenship, they could certainly exercise the right to vote. Susan B. Anthony presented herself at a barber shop in the eighth ward in Rochester, New York, which was serving as a polling place, and convinced two out of the three polling inspectors to register her, on the grounds that the New York State Constitution made no sex distinctions in the qualifications for voters. By the end of the day, fifteen more women had registered. On November 5, having first assured the inspectors that if they were prosecuted for admitting unauthorized persons to the polls, she would pay their legal fees, Anthony and the other women voted. It would be Anthony and the other women who were arrested for an illegal attempt to vote, not the inspectors. When she was judged guilty, she refused to pay her bail, hoping to force the case to the Supreme Court. A supporter, however, thinking he was doing Anthony a favor, paid it. The case was set for trial; in the interlude she voted in the Rochester city elections, and no one made a fuss. When the trial was moved to another county, Anthony and her colleagues made a whirlwind tour, speaking in approximately twenty towns each, ensuring that public opinion would not be uniformly against them even in a strange locale.

Anthony reasoned that sex was a characteristic markedly different from youth or being an alien. Although aliens could not vote, an individual alien man could choose to become a naturalized citizen. Minors could not vote, but minors, in the nature of things, grew to adulthood. "Qualifications," she argued, "can not be in their nature permanent or insurmountable. Sex can not be a qualification any more than size, race, color, or previous condition of servitude."

The judge, wanting to deny Anthony the legal system as a forum, directed the jury to bring in a verdict of guilty, and immediately discharged the jury. He fined Anthony $100. When she announced that she would "never pay a dollar of your unjust penalty," he declined to enforce the punishment. "Madam, the Court will not order you to stand committed until the fine is paid." Thus he had it both ways; a verdict of guilty, which would dissuade others from following Anthony's path, but a refusal to punish, thus avoiding making Anthony a martyr and making it impossible for her to bring the case to the U.S. Supreme Court.[10]

The president of the Woman Suffrage Association of Missouri was able to do what Anthony could not. Observing that the "power to regulate is one thing, the power to prevent is an entirely different thing," Virginia Minor attempted to vote in St. Louis. When the registrar refused to permit her to register, she and her husband Francis, an attorney who had developed the distinction between regulation and prohibition of suffrage, sued him for denying her one of the privileges and immunities of citizenship. When they lost the case they appealed to the Supreme Court.

In *Minor v. Happersett,* decided in 1875, the Court ruled that change must happen as a result of explicit legislation or constitutional amendment, rather than by interpretation of the implications of the Constitution. In a unanimous opinion the Court observed that it was "too late" to claim the right of suffrage by implication;

the Founders had been men who weighed their words carefully. Nearly a hundred years of failure to claim inclusion by implication made a difference. What might have been gradual evolution in the founders' generation was avoidance of legal due process a hundred years later—"If suffrage was intended to be included… language better adapted to express that intent would most certainly have been employed." The Court was not prepared to interpret the Constitution freshly: "If the law is wrong it ought to be changed; but the power for that is not with us...." The decision meant that woman suffrage could not emerge from reinterpretation of the Constitution; it would require either an explicit constitutional amendment or a series of revisions in the laws of the states.

> …For nearly ninety years the people have acted upon the idea that the Constitution, when it conferred citizenship, did not necessarily confer the right of suffrage. If uniform practice long continued can settle the construction of so important an instrument as the Constitution of the United States confessedly is, most certainly it has been done here. Our province is to decide what the law is, not to declare what it should be.[11]

Reluctant Realignment of Suffrage Strategy

In the years between 1848 and 1876, American women had created a collective movement. It is true that it did not include the entire female population; many women were unaware and more were hostile. But the activists had brought into being an articulate and politically sophisticated pressure group which was prepared to offer an explicit and detailed criticism of the American political system and to make direct demands for inclusion in it.

When Susan B. Anthony rose to speak on July 4, 1876, the strategies of feminist politics were being realigned. She had the court decisions in *Bradwell* and *Minor* in mind as she spoke. She addressed not only the issue of suffrage but also the exclusion of women from multiple aspects of the political community that the Constitution had created. The right to serve on a jury had been so precious to American men that some states had refused to ratify the Constitution until they were convinced it would be added; yet "the women of this nation have never been allowed a jury of their peers," even in crimes like infanticide or adultery, where women's perspective might well be different from that of men. Anthony decried the division of the community into a class of men, which governed, and a class of women, which was governed.

Anthony's generation of feminists would begin their campaign for suffrage to restore what the second section of the Fourteenth Amendment—with its introduction of the word male—had killed by implication. But as historian Ellen DuBois has shrewdly discerned, this strategy abandoned the healthier, more inclusive strategy of the pre-1876 period, when claims for the vote as part of the privileges of *all* citizens meant that women understood themselves to be part of a

Elizabeth Cady Stanton before the Senate Committee on
Privileges and Elections, *New York Daily Graphic*, January 16, 1878
LIBRARY OF CONGRESS

community that included men and women, Black and White. A suffrage
amendment would be introduced in the Senate in 1878, and a new chapter in the
political history of feminism would begin, one which emphasized the distinctive
claims of women.

It is important to recognize that Stanton and Anthony began with a definition of
equality under the Constitution that was considerably more inclusive than the vote
alone. It included a vision of egalitarianism in the process of lawmaking as well as
in the outcome. Ever since the 1848 Declaration of Sentiments, it had included a
vision of equality within the family, between husbands and wives, as well as social
equality, between male and female citizens, in the public realm. In her Centennial
Address, Anthony expressed the full range of this vision, attacking double
standards in moral codes, unequal pay scales, unequal treatment of adulterers. She
would not be surprised today to see wife abuse, female health, or the feminization
of poverty emerge as topics high on the contemporary feminist agenda. "It was the
boast of the founders of the republic, that the rights for which they contended were
the rights of human nature. If these rights are ignored in the case of one-half the
people, the nation is surely preparing for its downfall," she declared.

Anthony ended her Declaration of Rights with a ringing conclusion. If there are
any schoolchildren today who still—as children did in the nineteenth century—
memorize great moments in the oratorical tradition of this country like Webster's

reply to Hayne or Lincoln's Gettysburg Address, they should add this to their repertory:

And now, at the close of a hundred years, as the hour-hand of the great clock that marks the centuries points to 1876, we declare our faith in the principles of self government; our full equality with man in natural rights; that woman was made first for her own happiness, with the absolute right to herself—to all the opportunities and advantages life affords for her complete development; and we deny that dogma of the centuries, incorporated in the codes of all nations—that woman was made for man—her best interests ... to be sacrificed to his will. We ask of our rulers, at this hour, no special privileges, no special legislation. We ask justice, we ask equality, we ask that all the civil and political rights that belong to citizens of the United States be guaranteed to us and our daughters forever.

Notes

This essay is a slightly expanded version of "'Ourselves and Our Daughters Forever': Women and the Constitution, 1787-1876," reprinted from *This Constitution: A Bicentennial Chronicle*, Spring 1985, 25-34, published by Project '87, of the American Historical Association and the American Political Science Association.

1. This account of the July 4, 1876 protest and the text of Anthony's speech is drawn from *History of Woman Suffrage*, eds., Elizabeth Cady Stanton, Susan B. Anthony, and Matilda Joslyn Gage, (Rochester, N.Y., 1886), 3: 31-34.

2. On this point, see the shrewd comments of Nancy F. Cott, "Passionlessness: An Interpretation of Victorian Sexual Ideology, 1790-1850," *Signs: A Journal of Women in Culture and Society* 4 (1978): 228-29.

3. L.H. Butterfield, ed., *Adams Family Correspondence* (Cambridge, Mass., 1963: New York, 1965) 1: 369-70, 382, 402.

4. John Adams to James Sullivan, 26 May 1776, in Robert J. Taylor, et al, *Papers of John Adams* (Cambridge, Mass., 1979) 4: 208-213.

5. Michael Grossberg, *Governing the Hearth: Law and the Family in Nineteenth-Century America* (Chapel Hill, 1985), 5-6.

6. *Laws of the State of New-York, Passed at the Seventy-First Session of the Legislature...* (Albany, 1848), 307-8; *Laws of the State of New York, Passed at the Eighty-Third Session of the Legislature...* (Albany, 1860), 157-59.

7. The complete text of the Declaration of Sentiments can be found in "The Seneca Falls Convention," *One Woman, One Vote*, below.

8. See two brilliant essays by Ellen DuBois, "Outgrowing the Compact of the Fathers: Equal Rights, Woman Suffrage, and the United States Constitution, 1820-1878," *Journal of American History* 74 (1987): 836-62, and "Taking the Law Into Our Own Hands: *Bradwell, Minor* and Suffrage Militance in the 1870s," in *One Woman, One Vote*, below.

9. *Myra Bradwell v. State of Illinois*, 83 U.S. 130 (1873).

10. See Ida Husted Harper, ed. *The Life and Work of Susan B. Anthony* (Indianapolis, 1899), 1: 423-53.

11. *Minor v. Happersett*, 88 U.S. 162 (1875).

Three

THE SENECA FALLS
CONVENTION

Editor's Introduction: In this passage from the six-volume suffrage classic, *History of Woman Suffrage,* (Volume 1, 1881), editors Elizabeth Cady Stanton, Susan B. Anthony, and Matilda J. Gage tell the story of the 1848 convention in Seneca Falls, New York. Though there were individuals including Abigail Adams, Frances Wright, Maria W. Stewart, Sarah and Angelina Grimké, Maria Weston Chapman, Abby Kelley Foster, Ernestine Rose, Lydia Maria Child, Margaret Fuller, and Lucy Stone, speaking out in favor of women's rights before 1848, the Seneca Falls Convention is usually cited as the origin of the woman suffrage movement. The site of the Wesleyan Chapel where the convention took place and Stanton's Seneca Falls home are now National Historic Sites.

The passage contains the famous "Declaration of Sentiments" adopted at the convention, one of the most important documents in American history. The suffragists modeled their Declaration after the United States Declaration of Independence, enlisting for their cause the powerful, revolutionary rhetoric still much in the public consciousness, and indirectly making the point that women had been left out of the freedoms gained by White men as a result of the Revolution.

The women who organized the convention and drafted the Declaration—all White, middle-class, married women—were, in the words of Stanton, Anthony, and Gage, "fortunately organized and conditioned," and "had not in their own experience endured the coarser forms of tyranny resulting from unjust laws or association with unscrupulous men." As they compiled their list of grievances to present to the world, these pioneering suffragists laughed at themselves for having to go to the books to find a list sufficient to make a good case! They nevertheless felt "the wrongs of others" as well as the "insults incident to sex" contained in law, religion, literature, and custom that were an affront to "every proud, thinking woman." Foreshadowing the elitism, nativism, and racism that was later manifested in the suffrage movement, however, they expressed indignation that man "has withheld from her [woman] rights which are given to the most ignorant and degraded men—both natives and foreigners."

The Declaration of Sentiments was a fitting document for the birth of the women's movement as it addressed a wide range of issues: moral, political, religious, legal, educational, occupational, and even psychological, issues that the women's movement continues to address. It comes as a surprise to most modern readers that the ninth resolution calling for women to demand their "sacred right to the elective franchise" was the most controversial. It was adopted by a slender margin owing to the strenuous efforts of Elizabeth Cady Stanton and Frederick Douglass who insisted the vote was the means by which their other demands could be realized.

That so many people (three hundred, including forty men) responded to their "call" surprised the convention's organizers but made it clear that the time was right for their venture. That women like Stanton and Mott were daunted at the prospect of chairing such a large gathering and drafted James Mott for the job, indicates the degree to which women—even these extraordinary women—were affected by the nearly universal disdain for women speaking in public. Several of the resolutions reflect their frustration at being denied the right to participate fully in the great antebellum reform movements of their times including temperance and antislavery. Given the prevailing view that women were morally superior to men, these women found it absurd that so many men engaged in moral reforms were attempting to deny them and other women the right to preach and teach versus the social evils of their day. In fact, Stanton and Mott first met in London at the 1840 World Anti-Slavery Convention, where Mott and the other female delegates from America were rejected; rather than watch silently from the galleries, the two women took the opportunity to tour London "arm in arm" and talk of starting a women's rights movement in America.

As indicated by the concluding paragraph of the Declaration of Sentiments, the signers of the Declaration knew that they would be misrepresented and ridiculed, but they proclaimed that they would "use every instrumentality within our power to effect our object." All of this occurred as predicted. Outraged newspaper editors denounced the convention as shocking, unwomanly, monstrous, and unnatural, or ridiculed them as Amazons or love-starved spinsters. The ensuing storm of protest led some of the one hundred signers to retract their signatures. Frederick Douglass, one of their few champions in the press (and a supporter of women's rights until his death in 1895), defended the convention in *The North Star*. He was appalled that the women's rights advocates were abused and ridiculed even by those "who have at last made the discovery that negroes have some rights as well as other members of the human family." Indeed, said Douglass, "a discussion of the rights of animals would be regarded with far more complacency by many of what are called the wise and the good of our land."

However, the outraged editors inadvertently aided the movement; as word spread of the convention, women were inspired to call other conventions. In October 1850, the first National Woman's Rights Convention was held in Worcester, Massachusetts, and thereafter conventions took place every year (except 1857) until the Civil War led to a postponement of women's rights activities. Many of them were organized by a prominent antislavery orator and women's rights advocate Lucy Stone, who along with Susan B. Anthony, became fully engaged in this great movement soon after Seneca Falls.

★　★　★　★　★

Woman's rights convention—A Convention to discuss the social, civil, and religious condition and rights of woman, will be held in the Wesleyan Chapel, at Seneca Falls, N. Y., on Wednesday and Thursday, the 19th and 20th of July, current; commencing at 10 o'clock A.M. During the first day the meeting will be exclusively for women, who are earnestly invited to attend. The public generally are invited to be present on the second day, when Lucretia Mott, of Philadelphia, and other ladies and gentlemen, will address the convention.

This call, without signature, was issued by Lucretia Mott, Martha C. Wright, Elizabeth Cady Stanton, and Mary Ann McClintock ....

The eventful day dawned at last, and crowds in carriages and on foot, wended their way to the Wesleyan church. When those having charge of the Declaration, the resolutions, and several volumes of the Statutes of New York arrived on the scene, lo! the door was locked. However, an embryo Professor of Yale College was lifted through an open window to unbar the door; that done, the church was quickly filled. It had been decided to have no men present, but as they were already on the spot, and as the women who must take the responsibility of organizing the meeting, and leading the discussions, shrank from doing either, it was decided, in a hasty council round the altar, that this was an occasion when men might make themselves pre-eminent]y useful. It was agreed they should remain, and take the laboring oar through the Convention.

James Mott, tall and dignified, in Quaker costume, was called to the chair; Mary McClintock appointed Secretary, Frederick Douglass, Samuel Tillman, Ansel Bascom, E.W. Capron, and Thomas McClintock took part throughout in the discussions. Lucretia Mott, accustomed to public speaking in the Society of Friends, stated the objects of the Convention, and in taking a survey of the degraded condition of woman the world over, showed the importance of inaugurating some movement for her education and elevation. Elizabeth and Mary McClintock, and Mrs. Stanton, each read a well-written speech; Martha Wright read some satirical articles she had published in the daily papers answering the diatribes on woman's sphere. Ansel Bascom, who had been a member of the Constitutional Convention recently held in Albany, spoke at length on the property bill for married women, just passed the Legislature, and the discussion on woman's rights in that Convention. Samuel Tillman, a young student of law, read a series of the most exasperating statutes for women, from English and American jurists, all reflecting the tender mercies of men toward their wives, in taking care of their property and protecting them in their civil rights.

The Declaration having been freely discussed by many present, was re-read by Mrs. Stanton, and with some slight amendments adopted.

DECLARATION OF SENTIMENTS

When, in the course of human events, it becomes necessary for one portion of the family of man to assume among the people of the earth a position different from that which they have hitherto occupied, but one to which the laws of nature and of nature's God entitle them, a decent respect to the opinions of mankind requires that they should declare the causes that impel them to such a course.

We hold these truths to be self-evident: that all men and women are created equal; that they are endowed by their Creator with certain inalienable rights; that among these are life, liberty, and the pursuit of happiness; that to secure these rights governments are instituted, deriving their just powers from the consent of the governed. Whenever any form of government becomes destructive of these ends, it is the right of those who suffer from it to refuse allegiance to it, and to insist upon the institution of a new government, laying its foundation on such principles, and organizing its powers in such form, as to them shall seem most likely to effect their safety and happiness. Prudence indeed, will dictate that governments long established should not be changed for light and transient causes; and accordingly all experience hath shown that mankind are more disposed to suffer, while evils are sufferable, than to right themselves by abolishing the forms to which they were accustomed. But when a long train of abuses and usurpations, pursuing invariably the same object evinces a design to reduce them under absolute despotism, it is their duty to throw off such government, and to provide new guards for their future security. Such has been the patient sufferance of the women under this government, and such is now the necessity which constrains them to demand the equal station to which they are entitled.

The history of mankind is a history of repeated injuries and usurpations on the part of man toward woman, having in direct object the establishment of an absolute tyranny over her. To prove this, let facts be submitted to a candid world.

He has never permitted her to exercise her inalienable right to the elective franchise.

He has compelled her to submit to laws, in the formation of which she had no voice.

He has withheld from her rights which are given to the most ignorant and degraded men—both natives and foreigners.

Having deprived her of this first right of a citizen, the elective franchise, thereby leaving her without representation in the halls of legislation, he has oppressed her on all sides.

He has made her, if married, in the eye of the law, civilly dead.

He has taken from her all right in property, even to the wages she earns.

He has made her, morally, an irresponsible being, as she can commit many crimes with impunity, provided they be done in the presence of her husband. In the covenant of marriage, she is compelled to promise obedience to her husband, he becoming, to all intents and purposes, her master—the law giving him power to deprive her of her liberty, and to administer chastisement.

He has so framed the laws of divorce, as to what shall be the proper causes, and in case of separation, to whom the guardianship of the children shall be given, as to be wholly regardless of the happiness of women—the law, in all cases, going upon a false supposition of the supremacy of man, and giving all power into his hands.

After depriving her of all rights as a married woman, if single, and the owner of property, he has taxed her to support a government which recognizes her only when her property can be made profitable to it.

He has monopolized nearly all the profitable employments, and from those she is permitted to follow, she receives but a scanty remuneration. He closes against her all the avenues to wealth and distinction which he considers most honorable to himself. As a teacher of theology, medicine, or law, she is not known.

He has denied her the facilities for obtaining a thorough education, all colleges being closed against her.

He allows her in Church, as well as State, but a subordinate position, claiming Apostolic authority for her exclusion from the ministry, and, with some exceptions, from any public participation in the affairs of the Church.

He has created a false public sentiment by giving to the world a different code of morals for men and women, by which moral delinquencies which exclude women from society, are not only tolerated, but deemed of little account in man.

He has usurped the prerogative of Jehovah himself, claiming it as his right to assign for her a sphere of action, when that belongs to her con science and to her God.

He has endeavored, in every way that he could, to destroy her confidence in her own powers, to lessen her self-respect, and to make her willing to lead a dependent and abject life.

Now, in view of this entire disfranchisement of one-half the people of this country, their social and religious degradation—in view of the unjust laws above mentioned, and because women do feel themselves aggrieved, oppressed, and fraudulently deprived of their most sacred rights, we insist that they have immediate admission to all the rights and privileges which belong to them as citizens of the United States.

In entering upon the great work before us, we anticipate no small amount of misconception , misrepresentation, and ridicule; but we shall use every instrumentality within our power to effect our object. We shall employ agents, circulate tracts, petition the State and Nation al legislatures, and endeavor to enlist the pulpit and the press in our behalf. We hope this Convention will be followed by a series of Conventions embracing every part of the country.

The following resolutions were discussed by Lucretia Mott, Thomas and Mary Ann McClintock, Amy Post, Catharine A. F. Stebbins, and others, and were adopted:

WHEREAS, The great precept of nature is conceded to be, that "man shall pursue his own true and substantial happiness." Blackstone in his Commentaries remarks, that this law of Nature being coeval with mankind, and dictated by God himself, is of course superior in obligation to any other. It is binding over all the globe, in all countries and at all times; no human laws are of any validity if contrary to this, and such of them as are valid, derive all their force, and all their validity, and all their authority, mediately and immediately, from this original; therefore,

Resolved, That such laws as conflict, in any way, with the true and substantial happiness of woman, are contrary to the great precept of nature and of no validity, for this is "superior in obligation to any other."

Resolved, That all laws which prevent woman from occupying such a station in society as her conscience shall dictate, or which place her in a position inferior to that of man, are contrary to the great precept of nature, and therefore of no force or authority.

Resolved, That woman is man's equal—was intended to be so by the Creator, and the highest good of the race demands that she should be recognized as such.

Resolved, That the women of this country ought to be enlightened in regard to the laws under which they live, that they may no longer publish their degradation by declaring themselves satisfied with their present position, nor their ignorance, by asserting that they have all the rights they want.

Resolved, That inasmuch as man, while claiming for himself intellectual superiority, does accord to woman moral superiority, it is pre eminently his duty to encourage her to speak and teach, as she has an opportunity, in all religious assemblies.

Resolved, That the same amount of virtue, delicacy, and refinement of behavior that is required of woman in the social state, should also be required of man, and the same transgressions should be visited with equal severity on both man and woman.

Resolved, That the objection of indelicacy and impropriety, which is so often brought against woman when she addresses a public audience, comes with a very ill-grace from those who encourage, by their attendance, her appearance on the stage, in the concert, or in feats of the circus.

Resolved, That woman has too long rested satisfied in the circumscribed limits which corrupt customs and a perverted application of the Scriptures have marked out for her, and that it is time she should move in the enlarged sphere which her great Creator has assigned her.

Resolved, That it is the duty of the women of this country to secure to themselves their sacred right to the elective franchise.

Resolved, That the equality of human rights results necessarily from the fact of the identity of the race in capabilities and responsibilities.

Resolved, therefore, That, being invested by the Creator with the same capabilities, and the same consciousness of responsibility for their exercise, it is demonstrably the right and duty of woman, equally with man, to promote every righteous cause by every righteous means; and especially in regard to the great subjects of morals and religion, it is self-evidently her right to participate with her brother in teaching them, both in private and in public, by writing and by speaking, by any instrumentalities proper to be used, and in any assemblies proper to be held; and this being a self-evident truth growing out of the divinely implanted principles of human nature, any custom or authority adverse to it, whether modern or wearing the hoary sanction of antiquity, is to be regarded as a self-evident falsehood, and at war with mankind.

At the last session Lucretia Mott offered and spoke to the following resolution:

Resolved, That the speedy success of our cause depends upon the zealous and untiring efforts of both men and women, for the overthrow of the monopoly of the pulpit, and for the securing to woman an equal participation with men in the various trades, professions and commerce.

The only resolution that was not unanimously adopted was the ninth, urging the women of the country to secure to themselves the elective franchise. Those who took part in the debate feared a demand for the right to vote would defeat others they deemed more rational, and make the whole movement ridiculous.

But Mrs. Stanton and Frederick Douglass seeing that the power to choose rulers and make laws, was the right by which all others could be secured, persistently

WOMAN'S RIGHTS

CONVENTION!

COOPER UNION

New York City, Wednesday, March 20th '56,

at 8 P. M.

A Convention to discuss the social, civil, and religious
rights of women.

SUSAN B. ANTHONY

LUCRETIA MOTT

and other ladies and gentlemen will address the convention.

JAMES MOTT, Sec'y.   ELIZABETH CADY STANTON, Chairman.

the audience is requested to listen respectfully to the speeches but is invited to take part in the
discussion.

Poster announcing an
1856 Woman's Rights Convention
in New York

FRANK CORBEIL COLLECTION

advocated the resolution, and at last carried it by a small majority.

Thus it will be seen that the Declaration and resolutions in the very first Convention, demanded all the most radical friends of the movement have since claimed—such as equal rights in the universities, in the trades and professions; the right to vote; to share in all political offices, honors, and emoluments; to complete equality in marriage, to personal freedom, property, wages, children; to make contracts; to sue, and be sued; and to testify in courts of justice. At this time the condition of married women under the common law, was nearly as degraded as that of the slave on the Southern plantation. The Convention continued through two entire days, and late into the evenings. The deepest interest was manifested to its close.

The proceedings were extensively published, unsparingly ridiculed by the press, and denounced by the pulpit, much to the surprise and chagrin of the leaders. Being deeply in earnest, and believing their demands pre-eminently wise and just, they were wholly unprepared to find themselves the target for the jibes and jeers of the nation. The Declaration was signed by one hundred men, and women, many of whom withdrew their names as soon as the storm of ridicule began to break. The comments of the press were carefully preserved [and are in the Appendix to Volume I. of *History of Woman Suffrage*], and it is curious to see that the same old arguments, and objections rife at the start, are reproduced by the press of today. But the brave protests sent out from this Convention touched a responsive chord in the hearts of women all over the Country....

Four

A FEMINIST FRIENDSHIP:
Elizabeth Cady Stanton
and Susan B. Anthony

Alice S. Rossi

Editor's Introduction: In this classic essay, a favorite of suffrage scholars and students for many years, Alice Rossi brings these two suffrage leaders to life. The essay originally appeared in *The Feminist Papers: From Adams to de Beauvoir*, a collection of documents by major feminist writers edited by Rossi that was first published in 1973.

"A Feminist Friendship" describes Elizabeth Cady Stanton and Susan B. Anthony's extraordinary relationship, which lasted fifty-one years. Rossi explains how their contrasting but complementary skills and personalities empowered them both—making them such effective advocates for the cause of woman suffrage. In this essay, Rossi also offers an introduction to two of Stanton's writings: "Motherhood," and the Introduction to *The Woman's Bible*.

The two friends had quite different experiences and attitudes in regard to marriage and family. Married and the mother of seven children, Stanton took pleasure from her domestic life, but struggled to cope with the heavy burdens of housekeeping and children that left her little time to engage in the women's movement. Anthony, on the other hand, single and single-mindedly devoted to the cause of women's rights, resented the claims that marriage and childbearing exacted on other women's rights advocates. Yet she frequently came to Stanton's home and "stirred the pudding" and held the babies to free her hard pressed friend for writing.

This feminist friendship afforded Stanton moral support as well. Her women's rights activities were opposed vigorously by her conservative father and resented by her politically ambitious husband who feared her controversial activities would cost him votes. Henry Stanton actually left town on the eve of the Seneca Falls Convention when he learned the proposed Declaration of Sentiments would include a demand for the vote!

Rossi's essay also demonstrates the wide range of Stanton's and Anthony's interests regarding women's rights beyond suffrage, and discusses how their contrasting family backgrounds led to contrasting political perspectives. Rossi's analysis of the way Stanton's views changed over time—along with her personal circumstances—is intensely interesting, as is the fact that Stanton recognized that Anthony was growing more conservative while she grew more radical.

★ ★ ★ ★ ★

THE TWO WOMEN most closely associated with the emergence of the woman's rights movement in the nineteenth century are Elizabeth Cady Stanton and Susan B. Anthony. From the spring of 1851, when they first met, until Elizabeth's death in 1902 they were the most intimate of friends and the closest collaborators in the battle for women's rights in the United States. Together they were Lyceum lecturers in the 1850s, founders of equal rights and suffrage associations, organizers of annual conventions, hardy suffrage campaigners in the Western states, and coeditors of the massive first three volumes of the *History of Woman Suffrage;* the contributions of these two pioneers are so intertwined that it is nearly impossible to speak of one without the other. They were in and out of each other's personal lives and households for more than fifty years. Their friendship and shared commitment to the cause of women's rights were the solid, central anchor in both their lives. As Elizabeth wrote to Susan in 1869, "no power in heaven, hell or earth can separate us, for our hearts are eternally wedded together." [1]

It is fitting, therefore, to introduce these two remarkable women in one essay and to focus on their friendship and the nature of their collaboration. The key to their effectiveness lies in the complementary nature of their skills. It can truly be said in this instance that the sum was greater than its parts, for either woman by herself would have had far less impact on the history of women's rights than they had in combination. Elizabeth had the intellect and ability to organize thought and evidence in a pungent, punchy prose. Susan was a master strategist, the "Napoleon" of the movement, as [Unitarian minister and friend] William Channing described her, superb at managing large-scale campaigns, quick and nimble in handling the give-and-take of convention meetings, and an effective public speaker. Elizabeth had only average stage presence and delivery as a speaker, and Susan's ability to conceptualize and develop her ideas was poor. Between them, Elizabeth's effective prose found its perfect outlet in Susan's public speaking. Elizabeth summed up their complementarity very well:

> In writing we did better work together than either could alone. While she is slow and analytical in composition, I am rapid and synthetic. I am the better writer, she the better critic. She supplied the facts and statistics, I the philosophy and rhetoric, and together we have made arguments that have stood unshaken by the storms of thirty long years.[2]

Down through the years Susan turned to Elizabeth for help in drafting speeches, testimony, and letters for presentation to conventions on education, temperance, and women's rights. A good example of this pressure on Elizabeth is in a letter appealing for her help in preparing a speech for a convention of school teachers which Susan was invited to give in 1856:

> There is so much to say and I am so without constructive power to put in symmetrical order. So, for the love of me and for the saving of the

Elizabeth Cady Stanton and
Harriot, 1856. Library of Congress

Susan B. Anthony, 1848
Library of Congress

reputation of womanhood, I beg you, with one baby on your knee and another at your feet, and four boys whistling, buzzing, hallooing "Ma, Ma," set yourself about the work...Now will you load my gun, leaving me to pull the trigger and let fly the powder and ball? Don't delay one mail to tell me what you will do, for I must not and will not allow these school masters to say: "See, these women can't or won't do anything when we give them a chance." No, they sha'n't say that, even if I have to get a man to write it. But no man can write from my standpoint, nor no woman but you; for all, all would base their strongest argument on the unlikeness of the sexes.... And yet, in the schoolroom more than any other place, does the difference of sex, if there is any, need to be for gotten.... Do get all on fire and be as cross as you please.³

The letter captures several of Susan's qualities: blunt speech, a badgering of her associates to give her the help she needs (always in a hurry), a fighting spirit, and an ability to point to a central theme she wishes stressed. Elizabeth's response to this particular call for help came just five days later. She says in part:

Your servant is not dead but liveth. Imagine me, day in and day out, watching, bathing, dressing, nursing, and promenading the precious contents of a little crib in the corner of the room. I pace up and down these two chambers of mine, like a caged lioness longing to bring to a close nursing and housekeeping cares.... Is your speech to be exclusively on the point of educating the sexes together, or as to the best manner of educating women? I will do what I can to help you with your lecture.⁴

The "baby" referred to is five-month-old Harriot, Elizabeth's sixth child, and the speech, entitled "Co-education," was written by Elizabeth and delivered by Susan less than two months later.

This particular collaborative effort differed from most of their team work only in that it involved no face-to-face working out of the ideas to be developed in the speech. In most of their joint efforts they worked together more closely; Susan often visited the Stanton home in Seneca Falls for this purpose. Elizabeth described these occasions:

> Whenever I saw that stately Quaker girl coming across my lawn, I knew that some happy convocation of the sons of Adam were to be set by the ears, by one of our appeals or resolutions. The little portmanteau stuffed with facts was opened... Then we would get out our pens and write articles for papers, or a petition to the Legislature, letters to the faithful... call on *The Una, The Liberator,* and *The Standard,* to remember our wrongs as well as those of the slave. We never met without issuing a pronunciamento on some question.⁵

Thirty years later, when Elizabeth was no longer burdened with housekeeping and child-rearing responsibilities, she commented that in the 1850s, had it not been for Susan, who provided her with enough evidence of injustice to "turn any woman's thoughts from stockings and puddings," she might in time, "like too many women, have become wholly absorbed in a narrow family selfishness."

But a supportive friend who applied continual pressure to produce speeches and resolutions and articles for the press would hardly suffice to carry Elizabeth through the arduous years of child-rearing, from 1842 to the Civil War. During these years she not only bore seven children, but did a good deal of entertaining, produced reams of written material, served in temperance and abolition societies, lectured widely with the Lyceum circuit, and ran the household in Seneca Falls for long stretches of time without a man in the house. Elizabeth was clearly a woman of enormous physical energy coupled with a very strong will; these were needed to cope with such a regimen and to thrive on it. She was not a woman easily threatened by new experiences. Indeed, one of the best examples of her independence of mind and strength of body is the selection that follows, which describes her first experience of maternity. The reader will see how readily Elizabeth exercised her own judgment, even if it meant overriding medical advice. She seems to have given birth to all seven children with no aid beyond that of a friend and a nurse, commenting in a letter to Lucretia Mott after the fifth child's birth:

> Dear me, how much cruel bondage of mind and suffering of body poor woman will escape when she takes the liberty of being her own physician of both body and soul!⁶

Among Elizabeth's prescriptions for a healthy womanhood was one she clearly followed herself, but which it would take many decades for medicine and psychiatry to learn: she insightfully put her finger on an important cause of hysteria and illness among the women of her day, in a 1859 letter to a Boston friend:

> I think if women would indulge more freely in vituperation, they would enjoy ten times the health they do. It seems to me they are suffering from repression.[7]

Elizabeth was not a woman to suffer from such repression herself. She showed none of the modern ambivalence about complaining when her responsibilities became onerous. One feels sure that in the intimacy of a friendly visit she let off steam in much the way she did in her letters during the 1850s, either by frankly admitting that she longed to be "free from housekeeping and children, so as to have some time to read and think and write" or by chafing at some affront to women and writing to Susan: "I am at a boiling point! If I do not find some day the use of my tongue on this question I shall die of an intellectual repression, a woman's rights convulsion.[8]

There was probably not another woman in the nineteenth century who put her tongue and pen to better use than Elizabeth Stanton. She and Susan clearly viewed themselves as rebels in a good fight for justice and equality for women. They wrote each other in martial terms full of "triggers," "powder and balls," "Thunderbolts." Locust Hill, Elizabeth's home in Seneca Falls, was dubbed "the center of the rebellion" and from here Elizabeth "forged the thunderbolts" and Susan "fired them."

But even a close friend was no solution to the heavy family responsibilities Elizabeth carried throughout the 1850s. In the early years of her residence in Seneca Falls she was full of complaints about the unreliability of household servants falling back on a dream of some "cooperative housekeeping in a future time that might promise a more harmonious domestic life" for women. But from 1851 on she had the help of a competent housekeeper, Amelia Willard, a capable woman who could readily substitute for Elizabeth herself. It was unquestionably this household arrangement which released Elizabeth for at least periodic participation in lecture tours and convention speeches during the years of heavy family responsibilities.

> It was while living in Seneca Falls and at one of the most despairing periods of my young life, that one of the best gifts of the gods came to me in the form of a good, faithful housekeeper. She was indeed a treasure, a friend and comforter, a second mother to my children, and understood all life's duties and gladly bore its burdens. She could fill any department in domestic life, and for thirty years was the joy of our household. But for this noble, self sacrificing woman, much of my public work would have been quite impossible. If by word or deed I have made the journey of life easier for any struggling soul I must in justice share the meed of praise accorded me with my little Quaker friend Amelia Willard.[9]

It is curious that it maybe the help of a housekeeper and a friend that facilitates a woman's life's work, while the closest analogy to Elizabeth 's tribute one would find from the pen of a man is typically a tribute to his wife .

It is an interesting aspect of the friendship between Elizabeth and Susan that, while Susan was extremely critical of the energy her woman's rights friends gave to homemaking and "baby-making," as she put it, there is no written evidence that Elizabeth exerted any pressure on Susan to marry and have a family of her own, though Susan was only in her thirties during the first decade of their friendship. Elizabeth seems, in fact, to have been remarkably accepting of Susan exactly as she was; only a teasing quality in a few letters expressed any criticism of her. Susan, by contrast, showed little understanding of, and no hesitation in expressing herself strongly about, the diversion of her friends' energies away from reform causes. In the same 1856 letter in which she calls for Elizabeth's aid in writing a speech on coeducation Susan comments:

> Those of you who have the talent to do honor to poor womanhood, have all given yourself over to baby-making; and left poor brainless me to do battle alone. It is a shame . Such a body as I might be spared to rock cradles. But it is a crime for you and Lucy Stone and Antoinette Brown to be doing it.[10]

In response, Elizabeth urged her friend to let "Lucy and Antoinette rest awhile in peace and quietness," since "we cannot bring about a moral revolution in a day or year."[11] This advice from Elizabeth had no effect on Susan, however. Two years later, in learning of the birth of Antoinette Brown Blackwell's second child, she wrote the following revealing letter to Nettie (emphasis is by Susan):

> Dear Nettie:
> April 22, 1858
> A note from Lucy last night tells me that you have another *daughter.* Well, so be it. I rejoice that you are past the trial hour.

> Now Nettie, *not another baby* is my *peremptory command, two* will solve the problem whether a *woman can* be anything more than a *wife* and *mother* better than a half dozen or *ten even.*

> I am provoked at Lucy, just to think that she will attempt to speak in a course with such intellects as Brady, Curtis, and Chapin, and then as her special preparation, take upon herself in addition to baby cares, quite too absorbing for careful close and continued intellectual effort—the entire work of her house. A woman who is and must of necessity continue for the present at least, the representative woman, has no right to disqualify herself for such a representative occasion. I do feel it is so foolish for her to put herself in the position of *maid of all work and baby tender....*

> Nettie, I don't really want to be a downright scolder, but I can't help looking after the married sheep of the flock a wee bit.[12]

Three weeks later Susan sent another note to Nettie, this time adding a post script to report:

> Mrs. Stanton sends love, and says "if you are going to have a large family go right on and finish up at once," as she has done. She has only devoted 18 years out of the very heart of existence here to the great work. But I say stop now, once and for all. Your life work will be arduous enough with two.[13]

Elizabeth Stanton softened this message with her own warm congratulations in an undated letter to Nettie that must have been written during this same spring:

> How many times I have thought of you since reading your pleasant letter to Susan. I was so happy to hear that you had another daughter. In spite of all Susan's admonitions, I do hope you and Lucy will have all the children you desire. I would not have one less than seven, in spite of all the abuse that has been heaped upon me for such extravagance.[14]

Quite another aspect of the place their friendship held in their personal lives is suggested by their terms of address and reference to each other. They were not terms of "sisterhood" but of "marriage." Their hearts "are eternally wedded together," as Elizabeth put it. In 1870, when the press circulated rumors that their partnership was "dissolving," Elizabeth wrote her friend, half in jest:

> Have you been getting a divorce out in Chicago without notifying me? I should like to know my present status. I shall not allow any such proceedings. I consider that our relations are to last for life; so make the best of it.[15]

Two such passionate and committed women were bound to have differences of opinion, but once again, Elizabeth drew the analogy to marriage in explaining their conviction that differences should be confined to their private exchanges while they presented a united front in public:

> So entirely one are we, that in all our associations, ever side by side on the same platform, not one feeling of jealousy or envy has ever shad owed our lives. We have indulged freely in criticism of each other when alone, and hotly contended whenever we have differed, but in our friendship of thirty years there has never been a break of one hour. To the world we always seem to agree and uniformly reflect each other. Like husband and wife, each has the feeling that we must have no differences in public.[16]

During these years the two women were firm in their belief that the differences between men and women were rooted purely in social custom; it may be that the cultural model of differences between husband and wife made the complementarity of marital roles a closer analogy to the nature of their own relationship than the presumed similarity of sisterhood. There is nevertheless some psychological validity in the symbolic use of the marriage bond to describe their friendship.

Left: Susan B. Anthony (left) and Elizabeth Cady Stanton, c. 1870, c. 1888

Susan Anthony never married, and Elizabeth Stanton, though married for forty-six years, clearly received only shallow emotional support and no political support for her convictions from Henry Stanton. A warmth and effusiveness pervades Elizabeth's autobiography and her correspondence when she speaks of her children and of her close friends, but in hundreds of pages devoted to her personal life no comparable sentiment of warmth and mutuality appears in her rare references to her husband. It is not even clear whether Susan's frequent visits to the Stanton home coincided with Henry's stays at home. A politician, reformer, and journalist, he was clearly a traveling man. Seven children were born between 1842 and 1859, but there was a thinly disguised conflict between husband and wife on nonfamily matters. In 1855 Elizabeth wrote a few letters that permit a crack to show in the surface harmony. She had been developing plans that year to give a series of lectures on the Lyceum circuit and reports an exchange with her father concerning this plan in a letter to her cousin Elizabeth:

> We had a visit a little while ago from my venerable sire… As we sat alone one night, he asked me: "Elizabeth, are you getting ready to lecture before lyceums?" "Yes sir," I answered. "I hope," he continued, "you will never do it during my lifetime, for if you do, be assured of one thing, your first lecture will be a very expensive one." "I intend," I replied, "that it shall be a very profitable one."[17]

Her father did in fact disinherit her at this time, though he relented before his death and altered his will once again. Elizabeth does not give vent to her acute distress over this altercation with her father in writing to her cousin, but during the same month she wrote in quite a different vein to Susan. Referring to a "terrible scourging" on her last meeting with her father, she wrote:

> I cannot tell you how deep the iron entered my soul. I never felt more keenly the degradation of my sex. To think that all in me of which my father would have felt a proper pride had I been a man, is deeply mortifying to him because I am a woman. That thought has stung me to a fierce decision—to speak as soon as I can do myself credit. But the pres sure on me just now is

too great. Henry sides with my friends, who oppose me in all that is dearest to my heart. They are not willing that I should write even on the woman question. But I will both write and speak. I wish you to consider this letter strictly confidential. Some times, Susan, I struggle in deep waters.[18]

This letter is a revealing one concerning both men in her life. Elizabeth had deeply ambivalent feelings toward her father. On the one hand she admired him for his mental abilities, was grateful for the understanding he gave her of the law, and was indebted to him for his continual financial support of her and her family over the years after her marriage. On the other hand she deeply resented the fact that none of her abilities or successes either as a schoolgirl or an adult could gain any praise at all from him. The same profile seems to hold for her marriage to Henry Stanton. Though they were both active in temperance and abolition agitation, they were completely at odds on her ideas and political activity on the woman's rights issue. In the letter quoted above, the association of "father" and "husband" is immediate (Henry was ten years her senior), and Elizabeth feels herself a lone rebel in an unsympathetic social circle of family and neighbors, reaching out to the one sure friend who shares her commitments.

In this connection Henry Stanton's memoirs are interesting for what they leave unsaid. Though he wrote in the 1880s, when he was himself in his eighties, he seems unable even to mention the words "woman's rights." His wife is as absent from these pages as he is from her memoirs. The only reference in the entire book to Elizabeth's role in the woman's rights movement is the following passage, with its oblique reference to her leadership role "in another department."

The celebrity in this country and Europe of two women in another department has thrown some-what into the shade the distin-nguished service they rendered to the slave in the four stormy years preceding the war and in the four years while the sanguinary con-flict was waged in the field. I refer to Elizabeth Cady Stanton and Susan B. Anthony.[19]

The submerged conflict in the Stan-ton household was not confined to the husband and wife, for the seven children were drawn in as well. It is interesting to compare their separate memoirs on this point. Of the seven, the first four and the last-born were boys; yet it was the fourth child, a fourth son, who was to be the closest of the sons to Elizabeth. In the kind of leap across time that is perhaps characteristic of women's memories of their children she wrote:

I had a list of beautiful names for sons and daughters, from which to designate each newcomer; but, as yet, not one on my list had been used for my children. However, I put my foot down at number four, and named him Theodore, and, thus far, he has proved himself a veritable "gift of God," doing his uttermost, in every way possible, to fight the battle of freedom for woman.[20]

It was Theodore who studied the women's movement in Europe, where he lived for many years; he wrote a book entitled *The Woman Question in Europe*. In her autobiography Elizabeth noted:

> To have a son interested in the question to which I have devoted my life, is a source of intense satisfaction. To say that I have realized in him all I could desire, is the highest praise a fond mother can give.[21]

Theodore's daughter was named Elizabeth Cady Stanton Jr. That Elizabeth took pride in her two daughters and lived in close contact with them, particularly Harriot, is clear throughout her memoirs. Both Harriot and her own daughter Nora were active in the suffrage movement, carrying Elizabeth's lead into the third generation.

In contrast, Henry Stanton makes no reference at all to the three children Elizabeth talked about so warmly, though he mentions the remaining four sons with pride. Speaking of his life as a lawyer, he added:

> I have shown my regard for the profession by inducting four of my sons into its intricacies. Daniel Cady Stanton was for one year a supervisor of registration, and for two years a member of the legislature of Louisiana, in the turbulent era of reconstruction. Henry Stanton, a graduate of the law school of Columbia College, is now the official attorney of the Northern Pacific Railway Company. Gerrit Smith Stanton and Robert Livingston Stanton are also graduates of the Columbia School. The for mer cultivates the soil and dispenses the law in Iowa. The latter practices his profession in the city of New York.[22]

These are the only references Henry makes to any of his children. One senses a divisive line-up within the Stanton household that widened as the children grew up: Henry Sr. with sons Daniel, Henry, Gerrit, and Robert on the one side; Elizabeth with Theodore, Margaret, and Harriot on the other. The division, at least on the surface indications left to us, was rooted in Elizabeth's involvement in the "woman question."

It is little wonder that Elizabeth's friendship with Susan took on such intensity. While Elizabeth was torn between the love of her children and a sense of duty to home and spouse on the one hand, and the rebellious desire to be up and out fighting the battles dearest to her convictions on the other, Susan was a vital link that held these two worlds together in Elizabeth's heart and mind. Always the one to speak for both of them, and able to acknowledge tender sentiments to a far greater extent than the more purposive Susan, Elizabeth sums up the importance of their friendship:

> So closely interwoven have been our lives, our purposes, and experiences that, separated, we have a feeling of incompleteness—united, such strength of self-assertion that no ordinary obstacles, difficulties, or dangers ever appear to us insurmountable.[23]

The emotional quality of this assessment is one normally associated with the ideal, if not the reality, of a marital relationship; it is also a forerunner of the sisterly solidarity experienced in numerous feminist friendships in the 1970s.

It is much more difficult to gain a sense of Susan Anthony as a private person than it is of Elizabeth Stanton. Though she clearly reciprocated the deep friend ship Elizabeth described, her personal style was quite different. The pressures on Susan were far more of a public than a private nature throughout her life, nor did she experience the deeply ambivalent relationship to a parent as Elizabeth did. Since she did not marry, Susan had no adult conflict of loyalties between family and a public career. Indeed, she showed great impatience with her women friends in the reform movements as they married and took on family responsibilities. That reticence in an autobiographic sense may be rooted in a past of greater serenity and lack of conflict is an insight for which we are indebted to Gordon Allport:

> Autobiographical writing seems to be preoccupied with conflict... happy, peaceful periods of time are usually passed over in silence. A few lines may tell of many serene years whereas pages are devoted to a single humiliating episode or to an experience of suffering. Writers seem driven to elaborate on the conditions that have wrecked their hopes and deprived them of satisfactions.[24]

This point may apply to correspondence as much as to autobiographies; and it is consistent that, from all one knows of Susan Anthony's family background, it was far more serene and conflict-free than Elizabeth's.

Susan Anthony's parents were happily married, and her father was a strong and beloved figure throughout her life . He was a strong supporter of temperance and antislavery, even at the risk of financial penalty to himself. He took an active role in the rearing and education of his children, with consistent encouragement of their independence and initiative, and drew no distinction in such matters between sons and daughters. He supported the girls in any desire to acquire skills, believing that every girl should be trained to be self-supporting—a view the Anthony neighbors clearly did not share. Susan's first biographer and friend, Ida Harper, suggests that Daniel Anthony saw in Susan

> an ability of a high order and that same courage, persistence and aggres- siveness which entered into his own character. He encouraged her desire to go into the reforms which were demanding attention, gave her financial backing when necessary, moral support upon all occasions and was ever her most interested friend and faithful ally. [25]

While many parents of the early woman's movement leaders shared commit- ments to temperance and abolition, few were full supporters of the woman's rights movement. Susan's family was exceptional in this regard; her parents and sister attended the earliest convention on woman's rights in Rochester and were among those signing petitions in support of the convention resolutions.

Drive, executive ability, and a single-mindedness of purpose became enduring characteristics of Susan Anthony. She was impatient with whatever did not contribute directly to the battles she waged in her various campaigns for reform. She began as a teacher at the age of seventeen, and for many years she was a critical observer and then vigorous participant at teachers' association conventions. An early example of her courage and ability to press to the main point of an argument can be seen in her role at the 1853 state convention of schoolteachers. At this time women teachers could attend but could not speak at the convention meetings. Susan listened to a long discussion on why the profession of teaching was not as respected as those of law, medicine, and the ministry. When she could stand it no longer, she rose from her seat and called out, "Mr. President!" After much consternation about recognizing her, she was asked what she wished. When informed that she wished to speak to the question under discussion, a half-hour's debate and a close vote resulted in permission. Then she said:

> It seems to me, gentlemen, that none of you quite comprehend the cause of the disrespect of which you complain. Do you not see that so long as society says a woman is incompetent to be a lawyer, minister or doctor, but has ample ability to be a teacher, that every man of you who chooses this profession tacitly acknowledges that he has no more brains than a woman? And this, too, is the reason that teaching is a less lucrative profession, as here men must compete with the cheap labor of woman. Would you exalt your profession, exalt those who labor with you. Would you make it more lucrative, increase the salaries of the women engaged in the noble work of educating our future Presidents, Senators and Congressmen.[26]

Susan's point on the wage scale of occupations in which many women are employed is as pertinent today as it was in the 1850s. Equal pay for equal work continues to be seen as applying to equal pay for men and women in the same occupation, while the larger point of continuing relevance in our day is that some occupations have depressed wages because women are the chief employees. The former is a pattern of sex discrimination, the latter of institutionalized sexism.

Stanton and Anthony were of one mind on the issue of political rights for women, and this unanimity was at the core of their concerted organizational efforts during the long decades of the suffrage campaigns. Beyond this collaboration, however, they had complementary secondary interests. As a single woman and a Quaker, Susan was deeply concerned with opening the doors to women in the professions and with improving the pay scale of women workers. As a married woman and the more radical thinker of the two, Elizabeth was concerned with legislative reform of marriage, divorce, and property laws. There was much debate in the inner circle of woman's rights leaders in the 1850s on the expediency of pressing an issue such as divorce at woman's rights conventions, for it triggered far more violent responses from the public and was more divisive within their associations than even the political rights issue. It was also the case that the early leaders were not in agreement among themselves on the importance of marriage and divorce law reform or the solutions to sex inequity in the family sphere.

To trace these women leaders' views on marriage and divorce issues over the years would constitute a fascinating analysis that must remain for future scholars. I suspect, though only as a hypothesis, that the long-range trend of the woman's rights movement toward a narrower focus on the single issue of the vote was partially rooted in the aging of the leaders. Not only did these early pioneers live to a very old age, but they retained leadership positions in the movement well into their seventies. With increasing age, they may have felt far less personal involvement in such issues as marriage, child care, divorce, employment, and household management than they did in questions of political rights. Lucy Stone and Elizabeth Stanton were most concerned to press the issue of a woman's right to her own body in the 1850s, when they were young enough to be personally concerned. Thirty years later, the issue was no longer of high priority to them either personally or politically.

Some suggestion of the link between personal age and family status on the one hand and views on sex and maternity on the other can be seen in the fol lowing excerpts from writings of Elizabeth Stanton at various moments during her life. Elizabeth's age is recorded in parentheses along with the year in which she made each statement.

1853 (38) [Letter to Susan Anthony].

Man in his lust has regulated long enough this whole question of sexual intercourse. Now let the mother of mankind, whose prerogative it is to set bounds to his indulgence rouse up and give this whole matter a thorough, fearless examination.... I feel, as never before, that this whole question of woman's rights turns on the pivot of the marriage relation, and, mark my word, sooner or later, it will be the topic for discussion. I would not hurry it on, nor would I avoid it.[27]

1860 (45) [Letter to Susan Anthony].

Woman's degradation is in man's idea of his sexual rights. Our religion, laws, customs are all founded on the belief that woman was made for man. Come what will my whole soul rejoices in the truth that I have uttered. One word of thanks from a suffering woman outweighs with me the howls of all Christendom. How this marriage question grows on me. It lies at the very foundation of all progress. I never read a thing on this subject until I had arrived at my present opinion. My own life, observation, thought , feeling, reason, brought me to the conclusion. So fear not that I shall falter. I shall not grow conservative with age.[28]

1870 (55) [Letter to Susan Anthony].

Not only have I finished my lecture on marriage and divorce, but I have delivered it Women respond to this divorce speech as they never did to suffrage. In a word, I have had grand meetings. Oh, how the women flock to me with their sorrows. Such experiences as I listen to, plantation never equaled.[29]

1883 (68) [Excerpt from Diary].

I have been reading *Leaves of Grass*. Walt Whitman seems to understand everything in nature but woman. In "There is a Woman Waiting for Me," he speaks as if the female must be forced to the creative act, apparently ignorant of the great natural fact that a healthy woman has as much passion as a man, that she needs nothing stronger than the law of attraction to draw her to the male."[30]

1890 (75) [Excerpt from Diary].

Our trouble is not our womanhood, but the artificial trammels of custom under false conditions. We are, as a sex, infinitely superior to men, and if we were free and developed, healthy in body and mind, as we should be under natural conditions, our motherhood would be our glory. That function gives women such wisdom and power as no male ever can possess. When women can support themselves have their entry to all the trades and professions, with a house of their own over their heads and a bank account, they will own their bodies and be dicta tors in the social realm.[31]

There is an interesting progression in Elizabeth's ideas over the forty years covered by these excerpts, reflecting, one feels sure, not only the continuing evolution of her thought but also the subtle impact of her changing age and family status. Let us go back over these excerpts and try to see a connection between her ideas and the developmental stage she had reached in her own personal life.

The first two excerpts focus on sex and the power of men to impose their sexual demands on women: these are years during which Elizabeth was herself sexually active, with two pregnancies still ahead of her at the time of the 1853 writing, and a last birth just a year before she wrote the second excerpt in 1860.

The growing concern she felt for divorce reform was particularly apparent in the 1860s, culminating in the speech she delivered on marriage and divorce laws at numerous Lyceum lectures in 1870: with her own children now ranging in age from eleven to twenty-eight, she herself may have emerged from her peak dependent years. Indeed, since she was fifty-five years old in 1870, she was probably postmenopausal. Marital stability and termination now absorb her.

By 1883 there is a sharp shift in emphasis, with an image of woman as possessing a healthy sexual passion to match that of men: despite her age—sixty eight—she had read and traveled widely and given much thought to the question

IN MEMORIAM
ELIZABETH CADY STANTON.

On Sunday, October 26th, at three o'clock in the afternoon, Elizabeth Cady Stanton "fell asleep."

The news of her death transpired just as this department went to press. Scarcely more than a fortnight before her death Mrs. Stanton was talking with the Editor, who was impressed by the wonderful clearness of her mind and the sprightliness of her manner. At this time was taken the photograph of Mrs. Stanton reproduced herewith. The article printed with the photograph had just been dictated by Mrs. Stanton to her secretary for this department. Her signature is reproduced from a copy of "The Woman's Bible," which she had just signed and presented to the Editor.

Had Mrs. Stanton lived till November 12th she would have celebrated her eighty-seventh birthday, with Susan B. Anthony as her guest. Miss Anthony had sent her birthday greeting to Mrs. Stanton for publication in this department. The beautiful sentiment expressed by Miss Anthony in the last paragraph of this greeting makes it a fitting *in memoriam* of the noble life of her lifelong friend.

MISS ANTHONY'S BIRTHDAY GREETING TO MRS. STANTON.

My Dear Mrs. Stanton :—

I shall indeed be happy to spend with you the day on which you round out your four score and seven, over four years ahead of me, but, in age as in all else, I follow you closely. It is fifty-one years since first we met, and we have been busy through every one of them, stirring up the world to recognize the rights of women. The older we grow, the more keenly we feel the humiliation of dis-franchisement, and the more vividly we realize its disadvantages in every depart-ment of life, and most of all in the labor market.

We little dreamed when we began this contest, optimistic with the hope and buoyancy of youth, that half a century laterwewould be com-pelled to leave the finish of the battle to another generation of women. But our hearts are filled with joy to know that they enter upon this task equipped with a col-lege education, with business experience, with the fully ad-mitted right to speak in public — all of which were denied to women fifty years ago. They have practically but one point to gain —the suffrage; we had all. These strong, courageous, capable young women will take our place and complete our work. There is an army of them, where we were but a handful; ancient prejudice has become

Elizabeth Cady Stanton. Her last photograph taken about two weeks before her death.

so softened, public sentiment so liberalized, and women have so thoroughly demonstrated their ability, as to leave not a shadow of doubt that they will carry our cause to victory.

And we, dear old friend, shall move on the next sphere of existence—higher and larger, we cannot fail to believe, and one where women will not be placed in an inferior position, but will be welcomed on a plane of perfect intellectual and spiritual equality.

Ever lovingly yours,

Susan B. Anthony

Following Elizabeth Cady Stanton's death in October 1902, *Pearson's Magazine* published a birthday greeting Susan B. Anthony had prepared for Stanton's "four score and seventh" birthday, recalling their long, productive friendship.

of sexuality; but she no longer had any personal need to act upon them. She was now fully independent of her husband, seldom traveling with him, and perhaps learning a more modern view of sexuality from her own married children, Theodore and Harriot.

By 1890 the view of maternity had again shifted, and a strong positive view of women emerges: now she is no longer focusing on what women are deprived of by men or subjected to by men—a topic which had absorbed her as a younger woman; rather, she is taking pride in what women have that men do not have. Perhaps her own independence and the circumstance of married children who acknowledge her prominence and share her interests now permit her to see the power and privilege that flow from maternity at a more mature age. It may also be significant that by this date she is living in New York City, in an apartment overlooking the Hudson River, which she shared with her daughter Margaret and her youngest son, Robert. But it is also a tribute to the openness of her intellect at seventy-five that she could envisage the significance to women of an independent household and independent income, some thirty-five years before Virginia Woolf argued that "500 guineas" and a "room of one's own" were the symbols of what women needed to achieve real emancipation.[32]

Elizabeth and Susan began their lives in the same social and political climate of central New York State, absorbing the perspectives on benevolent reform that marked the region during the 1820s and 1830s. A critical difference between them was rooted in their families: Susan's family applied the lofty reformist values to their own personal lives, whereas Elizabeth's did not. Hence, when the two women turned to the cause of their own sex, it was a rebellious step for Elizabeth but an acting-out of parental values for Susan. This difference between the two women had consequences that showed throughout their lives. The more rebellious Elizabeth was in part motivated by the discord rankling within her as a result of the ambivalence in her relations with her parents and husband. She was driven to a search for a better vision of a better life, one grounded in cooperation and marked by domestic harmony. Her intellect was opened outward to the future, while her political action was held in check by the necessities of organization and the pressure of her far more conservative supporters. Since her past did not nourish her as Susan's did, the impulse to open inquiry and acceptance of change continued strong. For Susan the world looked rather different. She had no inner rebellious feelings rooted in her early family experiences, since she enjoyed the support and praise of the people important in her private life . She was therefore the executor of the reform ideas developed by her friend . But her mission was to make the system work, while Elizabeth was drawn to social innovation and more fundamental change in the system. From all the evidence available, Elizabeth seems to have been correct when she wrote, at the age of seventy-nine, that "I get more radical as I grow older, while she [Susan] seems to get more conservative."[33]

Notes

Reprinted from Alice S. Rossi, editor. *The Feminist Papers, From Adams to de Beauvoir,* Copyright 1973 by Alice S. Rossi. Reprinted with the permission of Northeastern University Press, Boston.

1. Theodore Stanton and Harriot Stanton Blatch, eds. *Elizabeth Cady Stanton as Revealed in Her Letters, Diary and Reminiscences,* 2 vols. (New York, 1922, 2: 125). This account of the friendship between Elizabeth Stanton and Susan Anthony is a partial one at best, and the interested reader can find more detail and a better chronology of their individual lives in several biographies (Ida H. Harper, *The Life and Work of Susan B. Anthony.* 3 vols. (Indi-anapolis, 1898); Katherine Anthony, *Susan B. Anthony: Her Personal History and Her Era.* (Garden City , N. Y., 1954); Alma Lutz, *Susan B. Anthony.* (Boston, 1959); see also, Alma Lutz, *Created Equal. A Biography of Elizabeth Cady Stanton.* (New York, 1940); and Stanton and Blatch, 1922) and memoirs by Elizabeth Stanton herself (E.C. Stanton, *Eighty Years and More: Reminiscences of Elizabeth Cady Stanton.* 2 vols. (New York, 1898). The best introduction to the political and organizational efforts of these two friends is in the volumes of the *History of Woman Suffrage* themselves.

2. Elizabeth Cady Stanton, Susan B. Anthony, and Matilda Joslyn Gage, eds., *History of Woman Suffrage,* (New York, 1881), 1:459. Hereafter HWS.

3. Stanton and Blatch, *Elizabeth Cady Stanton as Revealed in Her Letters ...,* 2: 64-66.

4. Ibid, 66 -67.

5. *HWS* 1:458-459. *The Una,* edited by Paulina Wright Davis, was one of the first women's rights newspapers. *The Liberator* was William Lloyd Garrison's antislavery newspaper in which he also supported women's rights.

6. Stanton and Blatch, *Elizabeth Cady Stanton as Revealed...,* 2: 45.

7. Ibid., 73-74.

8. Ibid., 41.

9. Ibid., 174 .

10. Ibid., 65. Editor's note: Lucy Stone had one child and another that lived only briefly; her sister-in-law Antoinette Brown Blackwell, a Congregational and (later) Unitarian minister, author and lecturer, had seven children, though two died in infancy. Blackwell nevertheless managed to publish nine books over her long life including an attack on the antifeminist uses of Darwinism. She was the only one of the antebellum women's rights leaders who lived long enough to vote, at age ninety-five.

11. Stanton and Blatch, *Elizabeth Cady Stanton as Revealed...,* 2:67.

12. Sarah Gilson, *Antoinette Brown Blackwell: Biographical Sketch,* 1909, 223-224. Unpublished manuscript in the Blackwell Family Papers, Schlesinger Library, Radcliffe College, Cambridge, Mass.

13. Ibid., 225.

14. Ibid., 233.

15. Stanton and Blat ch, *Elizabeth Cady Stanton as Revealed...,* 2:127.

16. *HWS* 1:459.

17. Stanton and Blatch, *Elizabeth Cady Stanton as Revealed...,* 2:61.

18. Ibid ., 59, 60.

19. Henry B. Stanton, *Random Recollections.* (New York, 1887), 68.

20. Stanton and Blatch, *Elizabeth Cady Stanton as Revealed...,* 136.

21. E.C. Stanton, *Eighty Years and More,* 399- 400 .

22. Henry Stanton, *Random Recollections,* 1887, 147.

23. Stanton and Blatch, *Elizabeth Cady Stanton as Revealed...,* 1:157.

24. Gordon W. Allport, *The Use of Personal Documents in Psychological Science,* Bulletin 49, (New York: Social Science Research Council), 78.

25. Harper, *The Life and Work of Susan B. Anthony,* 1:57, 58.

26. *HWS* 1:514.

27. Stanton and Blatch, *Elizabeth Cady Stanton as Revealed...,* 2:49 .

28. Ibid., 2:82, 83.

29. Ibid., 2:127. Editor's note: "plantation never equaled" presumably means that the problems of women needing divorces and unable to secure them exceeded even those of the slaves.

30. Ibid., 2:210.

31. Ibid. , 2:270.

31. Virginia Woolf, *A Room of One's Own,* (London, 1931).

32. Stanton and Blatch, *Elizabeth Cady Stanton as Revealed...,* 2:254.

Five

WHITE WOMEN'S RIGHTS, BLACK MEN'S WRONGS:
Free Love, Blackmail,
and the Formation of the
American Woman Suffrage Association

Andrea Moore Kerr

Editor's Introduction: In this article, Andrea Moore Kerr, author of *Lucy Stone: Speaking Out for Equality,* describes the dilemmas and difficulties the youthful suffrage movement encountered two decades after the Seneca Falls Convention. After a "golden age" of woman suffrage activity in the 1850s under the leadership of Elizabeth Cady Stanton, Susan B. Anthony, and Lucy Stone, the movement was temporarily suspended due to the Civil War. During Reconstruction, the suffragists hoped that the expansion of the electorate that had begun before the war (the extension of the vote to all White men) would continue, and that a reform-minded Congress dominated by the Republican Party would enact universal suffrage for all. But when opponents of Black suffrage appeared to be using woman suffrage for their own ends, and some who proposed an alliance with the woman suffrage movement were clearly hostile to Black suffrage, the suffragists faced difficult decisions. And when even former allies including Frederick Douglass asked the suffragists to accept exclusion from the postwar suffrage amendments rather than endanger the prospects of the newly freed Black men, the suffragists did not all resolve their dilemma in the same way.

In these troubled times, the movement was torn apart, and two rival suffrage organizations were formed, creating a schism in the movement that lasted from 1869 to 1890. Anthony and Stanton, who believed that the enfranchisement of Black and immigrant men would actually make it even *more difficult* for women to win the vote, formed the National Woman Suffrage Association (NWSA) opposing the Fifteenth Amendment and calling for a federal amendment for woman suffrage. Lucy Stone, also distressed by the failure to seek universal suffrage but unwilling to oppose the enfranchisement of the freedmen, led those who founded the American Woman Suffrage Association (AWSA)—supporting the Fifteenth Amendment but working assiduously for woman suffrage. Unlike some historians, Kerr insists that the issue of whether or not to support the Fifteenth Amendment was *the* issue leading to the great schism of 1869 and the creation of the rival suffrage associations and was recognized as such at the time. Andrea Kerr describes these years—

from the Civil War to the reunification of the AWSA and NWSA in 1890s—as very difficult ones for the movement, where support was limited and allies few. Yet accepting help from would-be allies sometimes proved to be very costly for the movement. Kerr argues that the NWSA's brief embrace of the notorious Victoria Woodhull tarnished the reputation of the entire movement despite the AWSA's attempts at "damage control." Kerr also argues for the importance of Lucy Stone and the AWSA during these years, insisting that the AWSA was larger and better organized than the NWSA during the 1870s, and that their strategy was later vindicated. Though the NWSA deprecated the AWSA's state-by-state approach and willingness to work for partial suffrage, by the 1880s they recognized that these steps were necessary in order to build enough support for woman suffrage that a federal amendment could finally be won.

In part because her rivals, Anthony and Stone, co-edited the *History of Woman Suffrage*, Stone is the lesser-known of the three pioneering suffragists. Many remember her primarily for her insistence on being known after her marriage to Henry Blackwell as "Lucy Stone only": shortly after her death in 1893 a Lucy Stone League, consisting of women who "kept their own names," was formed that continued into the 1970s. A charismatic and compelling orator, Stone had a talent for organization that greatly benefited the nineteenth-century suffrage movement.

★   ★   ★   ★   ★

AS THE WOMAN SUFFRAGE MOVEMENT entered its second decade of activity in the early 1860s, its leaders could look back on a period of extraordinary accomplishment. From its modest beginnings—an 1846 public debate on woman suffrage at Oberlin College, the first public address on the subject of woman's rights in 1847, the Seneca Falls woman's rights convention of 1848—the movement for women's rights entered a period of growth unprecedented in the annals of reform. By the time of the first national convention held in 1850 in Worcester, Massachusetts, woman's rights, including the right of suffrage, had swept the land. The reform attracted so much attention that in 1854, P.T. Barnum sought to duplicate his success with the tour of Swedish singer Jenny Lind by hiring Lucy Stone to take her series of woman's rights lectures on a national tour.[1]

Antebellum Suffrage Activity: The "Golden Age"

The decade following the Worcester convention comprises a "golden age" of woman suffrage activity. Though the movement's proximate roots were intertwined with the antislavery organization, by the 1850s, woman suffrage had assumed a distinct reform identity. Loosely organized under the leadership of Lucy Stone, Elizabeth Cady Stanton, and Susan B. Anthony, women raised funds and managed finances, organized conventions, developed strategies, delineated goals, and determined the direction of the movement. They planned and carried out petition drives and scheduled legislative hearings. With funds collected at meetings supplemented by earnings from lectures, women paid for the printing and distribution of books, tracts, and proceedings of the many local and national conventions. Groups of women formed education cadres and small political action committees in cities, towns, and rural hamlets.

The momentum gained by the fledgling movement in the 1850s came to a halt when Fort Sumter was fired upon in April of 1861. Woman suffrage activity ended while the American Civil War raged. In the war's aftermath, the fortunes of woman suffrage and the tangled politics of Reconstruction combined in a web of events and circumstances that threatened to reverse suffrage advances of the 1850s, making the enfranchisement of women an ever-more-distant goal. Out of this postwar chaos, two woman suffrage societies arose—the American and the National. For more than two decades, the two organizations labored separately toward the same goal. The story of one wing of suffragists—the National Woman Suffrage Association—has been told in the *History of Woman Suffrage*. A comprehensive history of the other wing—the American Woman Suffrage Association—has yet to be written.

Attempts to make clear distinctions between the two organizations falter before the changing tactics and strategies that marked both organizations for two decades after the war. Both labored more or less consistently for suffrage by Constitutional amendment; both eventually agreed on the need for state, municipal, and presidential suffrage. Lacking political experience, unschooled in consensus building, without the education formed in board room and back room, woman suffragists had to learn how to gain political ground the hard way—through trial and error. The ideologically driven but politically unwise actions of one wing of suffragists caused the woman suffrage movement to all but founder in the 1870s; the other association's attempt at damage control could not stem the flight of members nor turn the tide of public opinion that threatened to reverse the gains of two decades.

A look at events leading up to the division into two separate societies raises provocative questions about the politics of race and class. When the rights of two groups—in this instance, Black males and White women—came into conflict, as they did in the post-Civil War period, present-day historians face a problem of interpretation that possesses many of the same features as the original dilemma. In the years immediately after the war, the rights of women Black and White, former slaves and free, came to be counterpoised against the rights of newly emancipated Black males and free Southern Black males. The reaction to this conflict posed serious problems for woman suffragists then, and for women's historians now. In casting the Reconstruction dispute as hinging on universal suffrage versus Black male suffrage, as some historians have done, we are at risk of replicating the mistakes of those whose political misalliances and poor judgment led to a brief-but-regrettable period of egregiously racist and elitist conduct. When a small splinter group of woman suffragists chose to lobby for educated suffrage and to campaign actively to prevent Black freedmen from voting, the issues raised by their conduct transcend the theoretical. By casting this benighted campaign as a quest for universal rights, we risk perpetuating a means-and-ends argument that fails to take into account the political exigencies of a particular historical moment.[2]

The Competing Claims of Race and Sex

The first intimation of trouble arising from competing claims based upon race and sex came while the Civil War was still in progress. The war had occasioned a dramatic increase in both the size and scope of women's organized benevolent work. Seeking a wider political role for women, Elizabeth Cady Stanton and Susan B. Anthony issued a "call" in the spring of 1863 for a meeting of the "Loyal Women of the Nation." Its language both echoes Revolutionary-era notions of Republican Womanhood and rhetorically transforms them into ideas of women's full political equality. Drafted by Stanton, the call provoked women to think of themselves as equal political participants in the struggle: "Woman is equally interested and responsible with man in the final settlement of this problem of self-government; therefore let none stand idle spectators now.... [I]t is high time for the daughters of the revolution, in solemn council, to...lay hold of their birthright of freedom, and keep it a sacred trust for all coming generations."[3]

Lucy Stone presided over the gathering of leaders at the inaugural meeting of the Loyal Women. A series of resolutions committing women to an all-out effort to secure to all African Americans a full share of constitutional rights and privileges passed handily. The fifth resolution, calling for "no peace until the civil and political rights of all citizens of African descent and all women are practically established," provoked opposition from those who feared that adding woman's rights to antislavery would encumber the push for freedom and civil rights for slaves. Here was the first indication of future antagonism. Despite serious objections, the resolution passed.[4]

The women of the Loyal League, led principally by the efforts of Stanton and Anthony, eventually gathered four hundred thousand signatures on a petition urging Congress to pass a Thirteenth Amendment ending slavery. Their labors earned them praise and respect from reformers and politicians alike, but the small skirmish at the organizing convention was a bellwether of the larger conflict that would erupt over the inclusion of women in the push for civil rights at war's end. The history of events leading up to the 1869 split in the woman's rights movement furnishes a cautionary chapter on the perils of trying to compel the cart of ideology to pull the horse of politics.[5]

With the end of the war in sight in January, 1865, Stone and Anthony presented a resolution calling for combining woman's rights and antislavery organizations at a meeting of the New England Anti-Slavery Society. To their dismay, Wendell Phillips deferred action on their proposal until the May national meeting. In the months leading up to the May meeting, Stone and Anthony corresponded furiously with suffrage and antislavery leaders about the necessity for including woman suffrage in the press for Black suffrage.[6]

At the May meeting, Wendell Phillips, a longtime friend of woman suffrage, insisted that this was the "Negro's Hour," and women must wait. Where the suffragists saw the hour as propitious, Phillips believed that adding woman suffrage would doom prospects for passage of a Black suffrage amendment. The political situation of emancipated Blacks was steadily deteriorating due to the passage of harsh and punitive Black Codes in the South. Northern Republicans were also aware that counting non-voting emancipated slaves as full persons, (rather than the three-fifths status apportioned by the Constitution), would gain fifteen potentially Democratic seats in Congress for the South. By enfranchising freedmen, Republicans hoped to gain substantial voters, a prospect appealing to non-reform as well as reform Republicans. Given the urgency of the moment, Wendell Phillips and other Republican leaders believed that passage of a Black suffrage amendment was possible. They realized, however, that even if Congress were to pass the amendment, its ratification would be difficult, and they refused to endanger its passage by including women.[7]

Concerned that woman suffrage was to be abandoned in the push for Black male suffrage, Stone, Stanton, and Anthony circulated woman suffrage petitions, lobbied for universal suffrage in the District of Columbia and organized a Woman's Rights convention at which they planned to go forward with plans for an Equal Rights Association with or without the cooperation of the existing antislavery organization. At the May 1866 convention, the two groups voted to merge, and the American Equal Rights Association (AERA) was born.[8]

In June of 1866, Congress passed the Fourteenth Amendment, introducing the word "male" into the Constitution as a qualification for voting. This dashed any lingering hopes suffragists might still have nurtured regarding universal suffrage. At an AERA convention in Albany, New York, that autumn, Stanton made a speech denouncing Republicans and praising Democrats, whose support she had hoped to gain—a hope that would later prove vain. Frederick Douglass objected, pointing out that the Democratic Party was on record as opposing any move to give suffrage or civil rights to Blacks; their support for woman suffrage, warned Douglass, was but "a trick of the enemy" intended to split reformers on racial lines. Douglass begged suffragists to resist the ploy, but Stanton and Anthony ignored his warning.[9]

Following the Albany convention, Stone, Stanton, and Anthony embarked on a tour of New England and the Mid-Atlantic states. They set up AERA adjuncts, spearheaded petition drives and lobbied Republican legislators. Toward the end of January, the three suffragists were on board a train to New York when a blizzard stranded them for more than twenty-four hours. The snowbound train offered a captive audience of "doctors, lawyers, and legislators." Stanton, Stone, and Anthony "separated themselves far apart and each one gathered a crowd and talked and answered questions. They had a most merry time," an observer wrote, "and did a vast deal of good, I have no doubt."[10]

If suffragists gave the appearance of unity, differences were emerging. Though Stone protested "the poor half loaf of justice for the Negro, poisoned by its lack of justice for every woman in the land," she was growing more concerned about the deteriorating political condition of Southern Blacks. Matters came to a head in the Kansas campaign of 1867. The Kansas debacle began with a simple request to AERA headquarters from Sam Wood, a Kansas Republican. He asked if Lucy Stone and other woman suffrage workers would come to Kansas to campaign on behalf of a woman suffrage referendum. They agreed to his request.[11]

Kansas: Issues of Race and Sex Collide

Still bearing the scars of its recent bloody past, Kansas in 1867 was a hotbed of mistrust and malfeasance. The Republican-dominated legislature had ratified the Fourteenth Amendment; those who had labored since 1862 for Black suffrage then called for a November referendum on a proposal to strike the word "White" from the state's list of voter qualifications. Sam Wood, a legislator who had voted against Black suffrage every year since 1862, immediately proposed adding a referendum that would strike the word "male," thereby enfranchising women. Blacks accused Wood of deliberately trying to sabotage Black suffrage by linking it to woman suffrage.[12]

Into this political quagmire came Lucy Stone and her husband Henry Blackwell, brimming with optimism and armed with two hundred and fifty pounds of suffrage leaflets they would distribute throughout the state. Blackwell, brother to the pioneer physicians Elizabeth and Emily Blackwell, was an ebullient optimist. "This is a glorious country, Mrs. S., and a glorious people," he wrote Stanton soon after their arrival. Stone and Blackwell stayed first at the home of former governor Charles Robinson, a relative of Stone's by marriage and a Republican Party leader who warned them that Sam Wood's proposal was an attempt to defeat Black suffrage by splitting Republicans. Within weeks, it became clear that party unity was not going to withstand the test of woman suffrage. "I can not send you a telegraphic dispatch as you wish for just now there is a plot to get the Republican Party to ... agree to canvass *only* for [striking] the word 'White,'" Stone wrote Anthony in early May. Soon afterward, Republicans voted by a very narrow majority to campaign for Black suffrage only.[13]

Returning to New York, Stone took over the AERA office, while Stanton and Anthony went to Kansas to continue the campaign that was growing more and more bitterly divided along racial lines. Newspapers reported suffragist Olympia Brown as inveighing "against placing the dirty, immoral, degraded negro before a White woman." Sam Wood engaged in a nasty editorial exchange with Black leaders. Long-time Republican friends of woman suffrage questioned the political wisdom of continuing their support.[14] The situation worsened in late October when Stanton and Anthony joined forces with George Francis Train, a Copperhead (i.e. Northerner who sympathized with the South in the Civil War) and a self-

Lucy Stone, c. 1880

SOPHIA SMITH COLLECTION

Poster, 1867 Kansas campaign

SCHLESINGER LIBRARY, RADCLIFFE INSTITUTE,
HARVARD UNIVERSITY

proclaimed candidate for president. He described his purpose: "By talking woman suffrage the Democrats 'beat the Republicans.' By stumping for woman suffrage Train 'beats the Republicans.' Copperheads know that the Republicans can carry Kansas unless they are divided."[15]

Back East, suffragists were dismayed to see an AERA-funded announcement of Train's entry into their campaign. Stone begged Anthony not to use AERA funds to campaign against Black suffrage. Train was making woman suffrage "a laughingstock everywhere," she wrote, lamenting that Train's presence was "enough to condemn [woman suffrage] in the minds of all persons not already convinced." Anthony ignored her, and she and Train toured Kansas together, she speaking in favor of woman suffrage and denouncing the "rotten" Republican Party; he making derogatory and insulting remarks about Blacks and uttering demagogic pronouncements about the dangers of Black suffrage. "Carry negro suffrage," he warned, "and we shall see some White woman in a case of negro rape being tried by 12 negro jurymen." Train sent newspapers copies of his and Anthony's speeches and paid to publish and distribute booklets as well. Divisions within the Repub-lican Party in Kansas and Train's association with the suffrage leaders drew national press attention. Train's anti-

Black campaign put Republicans who had remained staunchly pro-woman suffrage into an untenable position.[16]

Both woman suffrage and Black suffrage proposals went down to defeat. Stanton and Anthony afterward publicly credited Train with delivering the 9,070 votes cast for woman suffrage, ignoring the evidence that showed that votes for woman suffrage came from heavily Republican counties. In the aftermath of the defeat, Republican Party leaders blamed the "side issue" of woman suffrage for the failure of Black suffrage, sounding the alarm for any future attempts to combine both measures at the polls.[17]

Following the Kansas campaign, Stanton and Anthony announced that Train was financing a tour in which he would share the speakers' platform with them in cities and towns throughout the Midwest and East. Abolitionist and longtime friend of woman suffrage, William Lloyd Garrison, wrote that he was "mortified and astonished beyond measure in seeing Elizabeth Cady Stanton and Susan B. Anthony traveling about the country with that harlequin and semi-lunatic George Francis Train ... denouncing Republicanism and lauding Copperheadism .... The colored people and their advocates have not a more abusive assailant than this same Train; especially when he ... delights to ring the charges upon the "nigger," "nigger," "nigger," *ad nauseum.*"[18]

Stanton and Anthony turned a deaf ear to Train's anti-Black invective, however. The connection did not end with the close of the speaking tour. Returning East, the two women accepted Train's offer to establish a newspaper that would jointly serve his political aims and the cause of woman suffrage. He named the paper *The Revolution.* "So long as Mr. Train speaks nobly for the woman," Anthony wrote, "why should we repudiate his services, even if he does ring the charges 'nigger, nigger, nigger'?" As Stanton explained, "All there is about [Train] is that he has made it possible for us to establish a paper. If the Devil himself had come up and said ladies I will help you establish a paper I should have said Amen!"[19]

Dissension Deepens, Conflict Erupts

At the May, 1868, meeting of the AERA, Olympia Brown, who had remained close to Stanton and Anthony, made a speech critical of the Republican Party. Frederick Douglass rose to object, characterizing Republicans as "largely in favor of enfranchising woman." He asked Brown: "Where is the Democrat who favors woman suffrage?" When a voice in the audience shouted "Train!" Douglass erupted: "Yes, he hates the negro, and that is what stimulates him to substitute the cry of emancipation for women." Following Douglass's speech, Anthony introduced a surprise resolution urging women to oppose the Fourteenth Amendment and to resolve to work for woman suffrage only. Her resolutions were defeated by the near-unanimous vote of all present. Immediately after the 1868 convention, Anthony set up a Woman Suffrage Society, with Stanton as president. [20]

In January 1869, Stone, Stanton, and Anthony were in Washington, where Congress was drafting the Fifteenth Amendment. The women unsuccessfully attempted to convince legislators, in particular Charles Sumner, to make it a universal suffrage amendment. Sumner apologized to the women, but he could see no political way to assure Black enfranchisement if women were to be included. On February 27, Congress passed the proposed amendment, forbidding voter discrimination on the basis of "race, color, or previous condition of servitude." Immediately afterward, on March 15, 1869, George Julian proposed a Sixteenth Amendment forbidding voter discrimination based upon sex.[21]

Throughout the spring, Stanton continued to publish anti-Fifteenth Amendment editorials in *The Revolution*. In mid-April, Anthony called an emergency meeting of the executive committee of the AERA at which she tried and failed to get the committee to pass resolutions opposing ratification of the Fifteenth Amendment. If the AERA was willing to do all in its power to obtain suffrage for women, it refused to work to prevent Black freedmen from voting. The stage was set for a major battle.[22]

"It is a pity that the cause of 'Equal Rights' should have been so disgraced by such a lawless scrabble for entrance tickets as occurred in the vestibule of the Hall last evening," said the Brooklyn *Daily Union*. "Men and women remorselessly crushing and tearing one another, and suffocating the solitary policeman who had the matter in charge." Indeed, throngs had besieged Steinway Hall, the site of the May 1869 AERA convention, hoping to witness the anticipated showdown.[23]

The opening salvo was fired by abolitionist Stephen Foster when he voiced objection to the nomination of Stanton to the vice presidency, because she had "publicly repudiated the principles of the society." Pressed by Stanton for particulars, Foster replied:

> These ladies stand at the head of a paper which has adopted as its motto "Educated Suffrage".... *The Revolution* lately had an article headed "That Infamous Fifteenth Amendment" .... I am not willing to take George Francis Train on this platform with his ridicule of the negro and opposition to his enfranchisement.

Anthony responded with an impassioned defense of Train in which she protested that he had been *"almost* sent by God to furnish funds for *The Revolution."* This was too much for Foster, who replied angrily: "If you choose to put officers here that ridicule the negro and pronounce the Fifteenth Amendment infamous, why I must retire." [24]

Frederick Douglass then came forward and denounced Stanton's insistence on characterizing Blacks as "Sambo" and "bootblacks" in *The Revolution*. He begged her to cease her anti-Fifteenth Amendment campaign. Anthony responded to his plea by laying a match to whatever oil remained on the troubled waters. If the "entire people" could not have suffrage, she said, then it must go "to the most intelligent first," for if "intelligence, justice, and morality, are to have precedence in the Government, let the question of woman be brought up first and that of the negro last." Anthony proceeded to introduce resolutions opposing ratification of the Fifteenth Amendment and in favor of educated suffrage. Lucy Stone rose and urged Anthony to withdraw the offending resolutions, arguing:

> We are lost if we turn away from the middle principle and argue for one class…. I thank God for the Fifteenth Amendment, and hope that it will be adopted in every State. I will be thankful in my soul if *any* body can get out of the terrible pit."[25]

Stanton's response to Stone's plea for withdrawal of the anti-Black resolutions was to announce that she "did not believe in allowing ignorant negroes and foreigners to make laws for her to obey."[26]

Dissidents Form New Suffrage Organization

Put to the vote, both Anthony's anti-Fifteenth Amendment and the Educated Suffrage resolutions were defeated. Instead, the AERA body voted overwhelmingly to ratify resolutions favoring ratification of the Fifteenth Amendment and calling for adoption of a Sixteenth Amendment. They also passed a resolution calling for the establishment of a national woman suffrage organization comprising a network of state and local associations. Stanton and Anthony decided to pre-empt the AERA by forming a new "national" organization immediately, rather than after preliminary correspondence and meetings, as they had earlier agreed to do.[27]

The following week's *Revolution* noted that a national woman suffrage association had been formed in the parlor of the Woman's Bureau following the close of the AERA convention. The splinter group, calling itself the National Woman Suffrage Association, immediately passed a resolution opposing the proposed amendment. "All Wise Women Will Oppose the Fifteenth Amendment," editorialized Stanton. In the summer and fall of 1869, *The Revolution* stepped up its anti-Black rhetoric, making references to the "barbarism," "brute force," and "tyranny" of Black men.[28]

The majority of woman suffragists worried about the effect of Stanton and Anthony's campaign on the prospects for ratification of the Fifteenth Amendment. "Just arouse Mrs. Stanton's ire," wrote Stone, "and with her paper circulating largely in the doubtful Western States, she can defeat the 15th Amendment." An editorial in the *Woman's Advocate* of July 1869, called for "a National Organization," that would "be careful it deny no right, even to the most hapless or degraded of God's children." The organization must concentrate its efforts "on the proposed Sixteenth Amendment and such immediate legislation by Congress as may be obtained without any Amendment." At the next meeting of the New England Woman Suffrage Association, (NEWSA) members voted to work to form "an organization at once more comprehensive and more widely representative."[29]

Formation of the American Woman Suffrage Association

Writing to Elizabeth Buffum Chace, president of the Rhode Island Woman Suffrage Association, Stone explained the need for a new organization:

> I think it is a great pity to try and create or give currency to the idea that the Woman's Movement is opposed to the 15th Amendment.
>
> At every convention ... we have adopted resolutions heartily endorsing the 15th amendment.... It is not true that our movement is opposed to the negro. But it will be very easy to make it so, to the mutual harm of both causes....[30]

Modern-day historians who describe the differences between the two suffrage associations as lying in federal versus state suffrage work, or radical versus conservative ideologies, or who ascribe the division to "personal" factors ignore the clear and compelling reasons put forward at the time of the split.

Similarly, historians who conflate woman suffrage history in the decade after the Civil War with the National wing rather than with the larger American Woman Suffrage Association formed later that year at Cleveland, Ohio, ignore such critical factors as representation, size, membership, budget, tactics, and political impact. For more than a decade, the "National" organization consisted of small meetings held in New York City, its principal effort an annual January convention in Washington D.C. Mainstream suffragists—the great majority of those in attendance at the 1869 convention—had refused to be drawn into an either/or campaign to defeat Black male suffrage, nor would they campaign for educated suffrage as a way of putting White women's interests ahead of those of freedmen.[31]

The American Woman Suffrage Association (AWSA) declared its purpose as securing the ballot to women, based upon the belief that "suffrage for woman is the great key that will unlock to her the doors of social and political equality." In pursuit of its goals, the AWSA proposed to organize for suffrage state by state, and to "prepare and circulate petitions to State Legislatures, to Congress, or to constitutional conventions in behalf of the legal and political equality of women," as well as to publish and distribute tracts and documents at below cost, and "employ lecturers and agents" to expand the organization.[32]

The volume of publications alone was staggering: in a single year AWSA sent out almost 216,000 leaflets from its Boston headquarters. At times, the organization had as many as four paid field agents who lectured and set up state and local societies in cities, towns, and villages throughout the country. AWSA's delegate basis ensured that state and local organizations would be represented at conventions held in different regions of the country so as to obtain the widest possible representation.[33]

In its early years, AWSA gained membership and auxiliaries at a rapid rate . In 1870, Lucy Stone began publication of a new woman's rights newspaper, *The Woman's Journal*. "Woman Suffrage has made astonishing progress," its editors reported. It had been "established in Wyoming, adopted in Utah, and submitted to the vote...in Vermont," while "Minnesota has passed a bill to submit it to the concurrent votes of men and women." The article enumerated those states where woman suffrage was under consideration.[34]

In May of 1870, there were two woman suffrage conventions in New York City. At the AWSA meeting, a large crowd approved resolutions promising to continue state organizational work while supporting adoption of a federal woman suffrage amendment. Across town, at the NWSA convention, Stanton delineated what she called the "essential issue" dividing the two associations. The American society wished to "carry the measure step by step, year by year through the states" thereby forcing "educated refined women ... to kneel at the feet of paupers, knaves, and drunkards." Stanton made clear her scorn for this approach, saying that "those who have the stomach for such work" could "canvass every state from Maine to California, and humbly ask Tom, Dick, and Harry, Patrick, Hans, Yung-Tung and Sambo, to recognize such women as Lucretia Mott, Ernestine Rose, Susan B. Anthony and Anna Dickinson as *their* political equals."[35]

The NWSA rejection of any state-by-state work held for almost a dozen years. The American wing, on the other hand, believed that intensive, state-by-state organization would lay the groundwork for eventual adoption and ratification of a federal amendment, should such an amendment prove constitutionally possible. The constitutionality of enfranchising women by federal amendment was brought into question by a number of court cases in the 1870s.[36]

Although partial forms of suffrage were problematic at best, they were nonetheless a factor in the final push for suffrage. When at last the Nineteenth Amendment was passed by Congress and sent to the state legislatures for ratification in June of 1919, its success was far from assured. Despite strong opposition, state legislators were aware that partial suffrage had made women's vote a force in national politics; women were able to vote for 339 of 531 presidential electors. The ratification margin was narrow, and in states where women could vote, the Nineteenth Amendment was ratified most easily.[37]

By the early 1880s, the National wing had come around to the American strategy. Anthony was quoted as saying, "I don't know the exact number of States we shall have to have... but I do know that there will come a day when that number will automatically and resistlessly act on the Congress of the United States to compel the submission of a federal suffrage amendment."[38]

The emphasis on state-by-state political organization, and the lobbying of legislators for various forms of partial suffrage was an arduous task. The slow but steady trickle of states and towns granting school suffrage, municipal suffrage, presidential suffrage, and occasionally, full voting rights to women kept suffragists' hopes alive, though the gains were painfully slow in coming, and losses often outnumbered gains.[39]

Suffrage campaigns and the weekly publication of a newspaper were costly. To raise funds, AWSA and *The Woman's Journal* editors staged a series of "bazaars" in

Boston. These were enormous undertakings, usually occupying all three major public auditoriums, where merchants, entertainers, craftsmen, and restaurateurs donated time, goods, and services. There were daily theatrical and musical offerings, booths displaying crafts and various kinds of merchandise. Cakes, containing gold rings and little china dolls, were sold by the slice. At large concessions, women could buy "cooking-stoves, clothes-reels, bed-blankets, washing machines, wringers, pianos, sewing-machines of every variety, flowers, boxes of dried fish, soap, starch.... An art gallery displayed donated works, and one entire building had been "floored over and transformed into a large dining-room and restaurant." Hundreds of workers volunteered their time, and profits, usually eight to ten thousand dollars, went back into the suffrage effort.[40]

Woman Suffrage Linked to Free Love, Blackmail

Unfortunately, many of these organizational gains were undone by another misalliance. The NWSA leaders' actions in 1871 landed suffragists in an ever widening net of scandal and intrigue that caused membership rolls to plummet and had hecklers shouting "Free Love!" at suffrage gatherings for decades to come. In January of 1871, Anthony welcomed Victoria Woodhull onto the NWSA platform in Washington following the latter's memorial before Congress claiming the right of suffrage for women based upon a Fourteenth Amendment argument. The possibility of a constitutional remedy for women's disfranchisement, accompanied by Woodhull's promise to donate ten thousand dollars to the NWSA won her acceptance among its leaders, a move they would bitterly regret.

Though only thirty-three at the time of her entrance into the woman suffrage movement, Victoria Woodhull had already led a full and remarkable life. She had worked variously as a prostitute, a mesmerist and spiritualist who claimed Demosthenes as her medium, a quack healer, blackmailer, extortionist, performance artist, stockbroker, journalist, and at the time of her entrance into the woman suffrage campaign, self-proclaimed candidate for president of the United States. Woodhull was simultaneously dubbed "Mrs. Satan" in a Nast cartoon, called "Queen of the Prostitutes" by the daily papers.[41]

Before she was eighteen, Woodhull had married, borne two children, and been charged along with other members of her family with numerous crimes. Following a "magnetic healing session" with millionaire financier Cornelius Vanderbilt, she and her sister, Tennie C. Claflin, suddenly came into enough money to purchase a stock brokerage on Wall Street and to begin publication of a newspaper, *Woodhull & Claflin's Weekly*. Both in her newspaper and in her public speeches, Woodhull championed "free love." News that Anthony had welcomed Woodhull onto the NWSA platform caused Stanton to write begging her not to "have another Train affair with Mrs. Woodhull." Stanton would come to embrace Woodhull too. The initial flurry of interest in Woodhull subsided, and for a brief period, calm reigned.[42]

The following May, Stone opened the AWSA meeting in New York City with an account of the year's progress: Woman suffrage proposals were under legislative consideration in nearly every Eastern, Northern, and Western state, and despite repeated defeats, they drew larger average votes each year. Women were enfranchised in both Utah and Wyoming. Over fifty new county societies and five new state societies had been organized in Massachusetts alone. Stone and Livermore had been accredited party delegates to the Republican convention; the December bazaar netted close to $8,000; the Sixteenth Amendment was reintroduced in Congress, and the bill to grant woman suffrage in the District of Columbia had made a good legislative showing. With the circulation of *The Woman's Journal* nearing five thousand, she told the assembled gathering, there was much to celebrate.

Had Stone seen that day's New York *Tribune* with its bold headline, "Woman Suffrage and Free Love," she might have been less sanguine. The reference was to the rival NWSA convention and "[t]he people who 'work with and for' Mrs. Woodhull, new leader of the Woman Suffrage party, Woman Suffrage candidate for the Presidency and editor of *Woodhull & Claflin's Weekly.*"[43]

Following the NWSA "Woodhull Convention," as it came to be known, membership in Anthony's society fell off so drastically that for the duration of 1871 and 1872, its leaders were able to hold "only parlor meetings." Former members set up separate suffrage organizations. Most of the New York women reorganized as the New York Central Woman Suffrage Association. The Connecticut Woman Suffrage Association led by Olympia Brown severed its tie to the NWSA and declared itself an independent society resolving to work "*only* for the elective franchise." In Iowa, Pennsylvania, Maryland, and Washington, resolutions were passed disavowing any tie to the Woodhull organization. By the end of 1871, fourteen of fifteen state suffrage societies had voted to become auxiliary to AWSA.[44]

In Boston in 1871, an Anti-Suffrage Committee was formed, and it was quick to offer Victoria Woodhull as "proof" of the serious threat to the sanctity of the family posed by those who claimed for women the right of suffrage. Propriety, no matter how numerous or decorous its adherents, was not news; Woodhull was. Waging a desperate counter-campaign, the Massachusetts AWSA paid three lecture agents/ organizers to set up twenty to thirty meetings per week in cities and towns throughout New England, a prodigious political undertaking.[45]

Following a free-love speech by Victoria Woodhull, newspaper headlines proclaimed: "Died of Free Love, November 25th In Steinway Hall the Woman Suffrage Movement." Woodhull's association with the NWSA lasted little more than a year; by May of 1872, its leaders had severed all ties to her. The New York suffragists' final disenchantment grew out of Woodhull's extortion campaign that spring, followed by her attempt to use the NWSA platform to campaign for the presidency of the United States. Woodhull's extortion methods consisted of presenting her victims with dummy copies of the front page of *Woodhull &*

Claflin's Weekly that featured detailed, wholly spurious allegations of supposed sexual indiscretions. She then demanded $500 to keep the story out of print. Woodhull tried this with many suffragists, among them Elizabeth Phelps, Laura Curtis Bullard, Lillie Devereaux Blake, and even Susan B. Anthony herself.[46]

In May, Anthony learned that Woodhull intended to take over the 1872 NWSA convention and use it as a nominating meeting for her presidential candidacy. Cutting short a lecture trip, Anthony returned to New York and ordered the janitor to douse the gas lights as Woodhull mounted the stage, afterwards writing, "A sad day for me; all came near to being lost. Our ship was so nearly stranded by leaving the helm to others, that we rescued it only by a hair's breadth." The "ship" of suffrage was not yet stranded, but it was a vessel with a serious leak.[47]

Scandal Erupts

Woodhull's withdrawal in the summer of 1872 and a split in the ranks of Republicans resulted in a momentary political triumph for the suffragists. With Horace Greeley running as an independent candidate against them, Republicans were persuaded in the 1872 election to include in their platform a carefully worded and less-than-wholehearted woman suffrage plank—a promise of "respectful consideration" of the woman suffrage question.[48]

Buoyed by this political action and free of the Woodhull alliance, Anthony proposed having the two rival associations "cooperate and make a systematic campaign covering the whole ground." Stone, in the midst of an AWSA campaign to orchestrate demonstrations involving half a million Republican women throughout New England as a means of pressuring politicians to press their claim for suffrage after the election, ignored Anthony's peace overture.[49]

Days before the November election, *Woodhull & Claflin's Weekly* appeared on the newsstands. Its lead article accused Henry Ward Beecher, president of the AWSA and one of the most famous and respected clergymen in the nation, of having seduced a number of his female parishioners, among these women, suffragist Elizabeth Tilton. The entire first printing of the *Weekly* sold out within minutes. Copies commanded up to forty dollars apiece, and newsboys and carriages created gridlock on lower Broad Street as they awaited a second edition. Along with the allegations against Beecher, the paper accused Luther Challis, a wealthy Brooklyn stockbroker, of sexual misconduct in a story replete with lurid and sensational sexual details. Woodhull was arrested under the recently- enacted Comstock Law and thrown into the Ludlow Street jail; Challis promptly sued for libel.[50]

Any hopes the suffragists had of escaping the scandal were quickly dashed. The newspapers focused on the woman's rights connection. The accused adulterer, Beecher, was president of the AWSA; the presumably wronged husband, Theodore Tilton, had headed the NWSA, and the imprisoned Victoria Woodhull was calling herself the woman suffrage candidate for president of the United States. If the connection to woman suffrage was inevitable, the tarring of all suffragists with the brush of immorality seemed an unduly harsh consequence. A Midwestern editorialist described the irrationality of the public response to the scandal, writing that he regretted the injustice to "hundreds of thousands of honest men and pure women earnestly in favor of the [suffrage] reform to say that they were following at the leadstring of the notorious female, Mrs. Wood hull...." Despite the "unreason" of linking the majority of suffragists to free love, "five out of six people think so, and cannot be led to think anything else."[51]

The Beecher-Tilton trial was the longest and most-publicized trial to have occurred up to its time. For more than six months, the testimony of its various witnesses occupied the front pages of newspapers across the country. Woman suffragists struggled unsuccessfully to keep the political question of suffrage separate from the public sensation. From Ohio, suffrage workers reported that "'free love' (whatever it may mean) is the most efficient agent employed to frighten people from our ranks." The *Des Moines Register* headlined its woman suffrage report "Halt in Progress of Woman Suffrage." Indeed, throughout the country, support at the state and local level evaporated rapidly. Formerly friendly legislators advised woman suffragists that in the "current free-love storm" it would be best to table woman suffrage legislation.[52]

Although a jury failed to convict Beecher, voting nine to three for his innocence, the damage had been done. The defection of formerly staunch supporters cut deeply into existing suffrage ranks and crippled the drive to recruit and organize new members. Meetings were canceled; proprietors refused to rent their halls to suffragists. Twenty years later, as suffragists tried to post notices of their meetings, it was not unusual to hear some man shout across the street to another, "Are you going to hear Woodhull tonight?" A Vermont suffragist insisted that the Woodhull matter "set the cause back twenty years," and that country people persisted in thinking as late as 1889 that women wanted suffrage "for free love."[53]

In the Wake of Disaster: Rebuilding Begins

Lucy Stone's anniversary address at the following spring's AWSA convention was the most negative she had ever given. Though she tried to sound upbeat, she had never felt less optimistic. Membership was falling off at such a rate that the Massachusetts Woman Suffrage Association was forced to lower the number required for a quorum at business meetings. Attendance at the May NEWSA anniversary had been down by more than a third.

As new women's organizations sprang up, leaders were careful to distance themselves from woman suffrage organizations. When the Association for the Advancement of Women was formed, newspapers characterized it as an attempt to "make a 'New Departure' from Woman Suffrage." When members tried to include woman suffrage as one of the aims of the new organization, their efforts went down to defeat.[54]

The Woodhull misalliance did incalculable harm. While present-day historians may sympathize with Woodhull's radical politics, it is nonetheless clear that

Stanton and Anthony's embrace of an exotic, blackmailing, free-love advocate in the 1870s was a political disaster for woman suffrage. While the Woodhull connection directly tarnished the image of suffragists, it indirectly controlled the direction and tactics of the AWSA from the early 1870s on, as the "other" wing struggled to counter the image of impropriety with a purity crusade. "We *need* every clean soul to help us, now when such a flood of what is fatal to the peace, and purity of the family, is rolled in on our question," Lucy Stone wrote to a suffrage supporter in the midst of the Woodhull imbroglio."[55]

Eventually, memory of the scandals faded. The AWSA, which had been the larger and stronger organization, began to lose ground to the NWSA in the early 1880s as Anthony led the latter organization in a strong campaign to "capture" New England suffrage societies. Declining membership rolls and a shift by the NWSA to both state and federal work made Stone more amenable to merging the two societies. In 1887, Lucy Stone and her daughter, Alice Stone Blackwell, met with Susan B. Anthony and her protégé, Rachel Foster. Together, they agreed upon a committee to effect a reconciliation between the two societies. It was February 1890, before the two societies would formally merge as the National American Woman Suffrage Association, (NAWSA) but the groundwork for rapprochement had been laid.

Because Stanton and Anthony wrote the history of the movement, modern historians appear to accept the authors' *ex post facto* characterization of the 1869 split as devolving from tactical differences. All parties at the time of the split understood the issue to be the acceptance or rejection of Stanton and Anthony's campaign to defeat the Fifteenth Amendment. Mainstream suffragists in the American wing—the overwhelming majority—found the anti-Fifteenth Amendment campaign not only politically unwise, but morally repugnant.[56] Marginalized by their unpopular actions, the National wing—effectively a splinter group for more than a decade—found itself involved in a series of costly misalliances. In the decades that followed, Stanton and Anthony did extraordinary work for the cause of woman's rights; nevertheless, the political consequences of their earlier actions furnish a cautionary tale to those who continue to work for full equality for women today. Consensus building, the choice of rhetoric, decisions about which issues to include or exclude, and other strategic questions are as problematic to feminists today as those that confronted our foremothers. Ignoring what is painful in woman suffrage history diminishes the capacity to build on its strengths by learning from past mistakes. Even as today's historians acknowledge early suffragists' failings, we honor their legacy of courage, brilliance, fury, and power.

Notes

1. Carrie Chapman Catt and Nettie Rogers Shuler, *Woman Suffrage and Politics: The Inner Story of the Suffrage Movement* (New York, 1923), 31; P.T. Barnum to Dr. Trall, February 11, 1854; April 27, 1854; NAWSA Collection, Library of Congress (hereafter NAWSA LC).

2. Ellen Carol DuBois in "Outgrowing the Compact of the Fathers: Equal Rights, Woman Suffrage, and the United States Constitution, 1820-1878," in *Journal of American History* 74 (December, 1987), 841, casts the dispute in these terms. In her recent introduction to the revised edition of *The Elizabeth Cady Stanton-Susan B. Anthony Reader* (Boston, 1992), DuBois admits to a "profound sense of what was lost" in the break of Stanton and Anthony with abolitionists and Republicans. In identifying the 1869 break as the "moment the case for woman suffrage became simultaneously more gender-based and more elitist and racist," (xvi), DuBois conflates the woman suffrage movement with the actions of Stanton and Anthony, whose position on the issue was very much a minority position among suffragists.

3. See Lori Ginzberg, *Women and the Work of Benevolence: Morality, Politics, and Class in the Nineteenth-Century United States* (New Haven, 1990), chpt. 5; Elizabeth Cady Stanton, with Susan B. Anthony, Ida Husted Harper, *History of Woman Suffrage*, (Rochester, N.Y., 1889), 2: 53, (hereafter *HWS*).

4. "The Loyal Women's National League" in *HWS*, Stanton, et. al., 2: 50-67.

5. Eleanor Flexner, *Century of Struggle: The Woman's Rights Movement in the United States* (Cambridge, Mass., 1959), 110-111.

6. 1865 letters in Blackwell Family Collection, Library of Congress, (hereafter B-LC).

7. *New York Times*, May 10, 1865; Ratification of the Fourteenth Amendment would take more than two years. Although Northern sympathy for former slaves ran high, support for black suffrage did not. See William Gillette, *The Right to Vote: Politics and Passage of the Fifteenth Amendment* (Baltimore, 1965), 25-27.

8. *Proceedings* of the 1866 Woman's Rights Convention, (New York, 1866).

9. Ida Husted Harper, *Life and Work of Susan B. Anthony*, 3 vols. (New York, 1969), 1: 261-64.

10. Train incident in Ralph V. Harlow, *Gerrit Smith: Philanthropist and Reformer* (New York, 1972), 471. General suffrage activity in *HWS* 2: 172-82.

11. Lucy Stone to Abby Kelley Foster, January 24, 1867, B-LC.

12. See Eugene Berwanger, *The West and Reconstruction* (Urbana, Ill., 1981), 164-175.

13. Henry Blackwell to Elizabeth Cady Stanton, April 21, 1867, in B-LC; Andrea Moore Kerr, *Lucy Stone: Speaking Out for Equality* (New Brunswick, N.J., 1992), 124; Lucy Stone to Susan B. Anthony, May 9, 1867, B-LC; Daniel Wilder, *Annals of Kansas* (Topeka, 1875), 456.

14. Berwanger, *West*, 171.

15. George Francis Train, *The Great Epigram Campaign of Kansas* (Leavenworth, 1867), 47.

16. Elinor Rice Hays, *Morning Star: A Biography of Lucy Stone, 1818-1897* (New York, 1961), 197; Train, *Epigram*, 48, 58; Gillette, *Right*, 32-33.

17. Charles Robinson to Olympia Brown, December 22, 1867, Olympia Brown Collection, Schlesinger Library, Radcliffe; *Emporia News*, November 15, 1857; Gillette, *Right*, 31-40.

18. William Lloyd Garrison to Alfred Love, December 18, 1867, in Boston Public Library.

19. *The Revolution*, January 29, 1868; Elizabeth Cady Stanton to Olympia Brown, January, 1868, in Olympia Brown Collection.

20. Harper, *Anthony*, 1: 304; *HWS*, 2: 341.

21. George W. Julian, *Political Recollections, 1840 to 1879* (Westport, Conn., 1884), 324.

22. Lucy Stone to Samuel May, April 9, 1869, in B-LC.

23. Brooklyn *Daily Union*, May 15, 1869.

24. *The Revolution*, May 20, 1869.

25. Brooklyn *Daily Union*, May 15, 1869; *The New York Times*, May 15, 1869; *HWS* 2: 383-84.

26. *The Revolution*, May 27, 1869.

27. *HWS* 2: 391-92, 320.

28. *The Revolution*, June 3, June 10, October 21, 1869.

29. Lucy Stone to Elizabeth Buffum Chace, July 11, 1869, in NAWSA-LC; *Woman's Advocate*, 2 (July, 1869).

30. Lucy Stone to Elizabeth Buffum Chace, July 11, 1869, in NAWSA-LC.

31. To date, no in-depth organizational history of either association has been done. Records indicate, however, that the AWSA dominated the 1870s, while the NWSA gained ascendance in the 1880s.

32. AWSA Convention in *HWS* 2: 763-64.

33. Lois Bannister Merk, "Massachusetts and the Woman Suffrage Movement," Ph.D. diss., Harvard University, 1961, 198.

34. *The Woman's Journal*, April 9, 1870.

35. Merk, "Massachusetts," 63; *The Revolution*, May 19, 1870.

36. See Catt and Shuler, Woman Suffrage, 96; and DuBois, "Outgrowing the Compact of the Fathers," 857-60.

37. See Catt and Shuler, *Woman Suffrage*; also see Appendix 5, "Partial Suffrage Gains," and chpt. 6, "Campaigning State by State" by Maud Wood Park in NAWSA, *Victory: How Women Won It* (New York, 1940), 69-80.

38. Anthony quote in Catt and Shuler, *Woman Suffrage*, 227.

39. See Catt and Shuler, *Woman Suffrage*; see also appendix and chart in NAWSA, *Victory*.

40. *The Woman's Journal*, December 31, 1870.

41. Emanie Sachs Arling, *The Terrible Siren* (New York, 1928), 1-15.

42. Elizabeth Cady Stanton to Susan B. Anthony, January 31, 1871, ECS Collection, LC.

43. New York *Tribune*, May 10, 1871.

44. *The Woman's Journal*, August 19, 1871; Katherine Deveraux Blake, *Champion of Woman: The Life of Lillie Deveraux Blake*, (New York, 1943), 91. Olympia Brown, *Acquaintances Old and New Among Reformers* (Milwaukee, 1911), 91; Louise Noun in *Strong-Minded Women: The Emergence of the Woman-Suffrage Movement in Iowa* (Ames, Iowa, 1986), 177-197.

45. *The Woman's Journal*, March 11, 18, 25, 1871; Merk, "Massachusetts," chpt. 10.

46. Lancaster *Gazette*, November 25, 1871; Woodhull defended her use of blackmail in *Woodhull & Claflin's Weekly*, April 6, 1872; Accounts of the blackmail scheme (which in one case included a threat on the recipient's life if she did not pay up) in Arling, *Siren*, 164-65; NAWSA-LC; Blake, *Champion*, 90; Susan B. Anthony to Isabella Beecher Hooker, June 19, 24, 1872, in Stowe-Day Collection.

47. Harper, *Anthony*, 1: 413-15.

48. *The Woman's Journal*, June 15, 1872; *HWS* 2: 517-20.

49. *The Woman's Journal*, June 29, 1872; Susan B. Anthony to Lucy Stone, September 4, 1872, in NAWSA-LC.

50. Arling, *Siren*, 176; *Woodhull & Claflin's Weekly*, November 2, 1872; Challis case in New York *Herald*, November 3, 5, 6, 8, 10, 11, 19, 1872.

51. *The Woman's Journal*, November 30, 1872; Quote in Noun, *Strong-Minded*, 200.

52. *The Woman's Journal*, November 25, 1872; Register quote in Noun, 199. Blake, *Champion*, 91.

53. See Margaret Campbell to Lucy Stone, December 28, 1872; Alice Stone Blackwell to Mary Hunter, August 12, 1838; Alice Stone Blackwell to Lucy Stone, June 12, 1889. All in NAWSA-LC.

54. *The Woman's Journal*, October 25, 1873 and November 22, 1873.

55. Lucy Stone to John K. Wildman, November 7, 1871, in B-LC.

56. Although later accounts by Stanton and Anthony ascribed the split to different causes, (*HWS* 2: 400), there was no such confusion at the time of the formation of the new organization. Both *The Revolution* (May 20, 1869) and the *Woman's Advocate* (May 29, 1869) make it clear that it was the issue of support for or opposition to the Fifteenth Amendment that precipitated the formation of the splinter group.

Satire of Anthony, Stanton, and Anna Dickinson claiming the right to vote
under the Fourteenth Amendment, 1875

Six

TAKING THE LAW INTO OUR OWN HANDS:
Bradwell, Minor, and Suffrage Militance in the 1870s
Ellen Carol DuBois

Editor's Introduction: Ellen Carol DuBois, one of the most well-known and prolific scholars of the suffrage movement in the United States, describes the militant strategy pursued by the National Woman Suffrage Association (NWSA) between the schism of 1869 and the reunification of the two suffrage camps in 1890. In contrast with Andrea Kerr, DuBois presents the actions of the NWSA and its leaders as bold and principled. This includes their association with Victoria Woodhull, whom DuBois views as a courageous defender of women's right to control their own bodies as well as an articulate and intelligent advocate of woman suffrage.

DuBois sees Susan B. Anthony, Elizabeth Cady Stanton, and the NWSA as champions of political equality for all, demanding for women the protections afforded "citizens" in the Fourteenth and Fifteenth Amendments. Furious at their abandonment by former allies in the Republican Party, who insisted that the inclusion of woman suffrage would endanger the success of these two Reconstruction amendments, Stanton and Anthony initially protested the amendments even while they simultaneously called for a separate federal woman suffrage amendment. Yet, as DuBois explains in this essay, calling for a new amendment to the Constitution was not the only constitutional approach through which these suffragists tried to secure the vote in the 1870s.

After ratification of the Fourteenth and Fifteenth Amendments, NWSA leaders came up with a bold new strategy for winning the vote by claiming that the Fourteenth and Fifteenth Amendments actually *enfranchised* women. This approach, (also described in the previous essay by Linda Kerber), was known among the suffragists as the "New Departure." Initiated by Virginia and Francis Minor of St. Louis, who pursued it through the courts, it was the principal argument developed by Victoria Woodhull in her famous speech before Congress in 1871. It also inspired Myra Bradwell to claim the right to practice law as a *citizen's right.*

The New Departure emboldened many women including Susan B. Anthony to turn to "direct action," to go to the polls and claim their right to vote as citizens of the United States. Anthony's subsequent trial for "knowingly, wrongfully, and unlawfully vot[ing]" was one of the most dramatic incidents in the history of the suffrage movement. The judge, in a statement prepared in advance of the trial, directed the jury to find Anthony guilty, and ordered her to pay a one hundred dollar fine that she, of course, refused to pay.

Rather than *plead* for the vote to be extended to them, the NWSA suffragists *demanded* a right that they insisted was already theirs. In the 1870s, however, the nation was in retreat from Reconstruction, and Congress and the courts were increasingly unwilling to protect even the newly established Black male suffrage. The suffragists' militant strategy did not succeed, and direct action to demand woman suffrage as a right rather than a privilege gave way to more conservative tactics—at least until militancy was revived during the last years of the suffrage movement.

However, drawing parallels to the equality-versus-difference debate among feminists in the 1980s and 1990s, DuBois argues that—before they began arguing for enfranchisement on the basis of woman's ability to contribute to politics owing to their differences from men—they first exhausted every possibility of gaining the right to vote as citizens of the United States entitled to equal rights under the United States Constitution. As DuBois so aptly phrases it: "They first attempted to march into power directly through the main political entrance, rather than indirectly, through the back door of the nursery or kitchen."

★　★　★　★　★

A MONG THE MOST CONTESTED ELEMENTS of the Constitution have been the Reconstruction amendments, and a crucial aspect of that contest has been the relation of the Fourteenth Amendment to women's rights. This essay addresses the early history of women's rights claims to the Fourteenth and Fifteenth Amendments. It explores the legal arguments with which woman suffragists approached the Reconstruction amendments, the popular support and militant activism they inspired, and the role that the defeat of women's rights claims played in the larger history of Reconstruction constitutionalism. This mid-nineteenth-century episode in women's rights history was extremely brief, but it reverberates richly with many important and perplexing issues facing feminist thinkers and activists today. At various moments during which I worked on this essay, I felt that this material provided the historical key to current debates within feminism over "equality," over "rights," and over "politics."

Here, in the post-Civil War years, we can see proponents of women's rights as they move from universal to particularistic arguments, providing us with the Gilded Age equivalent of the shift from "equality" to "difference" in the feminism of our own time. While many of my contemporaries emphasize the abstract and "male" character of such universalistic categories as "person" or "citizen," I have chosen to stress the many costs to the women's rights tradition of moving away from such frameworks—however "hegemonic" they may seem to our postmodern consciousness—which have helped situate women's emancipation in the larger context of humanity's freedom.[1]

Here, too, we can trace the course of the demands of a disempowered group based on the venerable but problematic constitutional concept of "rights." Of late, "rights arguments" have been criticized, not only by conservatives but also by those on the left, for the assumption that entitlement inheres "naturally" in individuals, flourishing in a "private" realm that must be protected from interference, by others and by the state. Such a concept of "rights," it is argued, masks the workings of power and favors those already privileged by existing social and political structures—men, White people, and the propertied.[2] But this episode in women's rights, perhaps the entire tradition, treats rights quite differently: as something to be won and exercised collectively rather than individually; as the object of political struggle as much as of judicial resolution; as that which government affirmatively establishes rather than negatively shields; and above all as that which has greatest meaning not to the powerful, who already enjoy their entitlements, but to the powerless, who have yet to have their full place in society recognized.

Finally, this episode has implications for the character and place of the "political" in women's history. While women's historians have deepened our knowledge of the public activism of women, even—or especially—before their enfranchisement, much of this scholarship has followed what is called (in shorthand) "the separate spheres" model. Women, it is argued, have had—and may still have—their own political culture distinct from men's, and they have chosen to work for their own and society's betterment by embracing different institutions, following different rules, and adhering to different political values.[3] This essay suggests that to the degree that nineteenth-century women abandoned a political terrain also occupied by men—of partisan power and judicial contest— they were driven from it by defeat and forced to pursue politics by other, more indirect means. This essay considers women as they attempted to march into power directly, through the main political entrance, rather than indirectly, through the back door of the nursery or kitchen.

Introduction to the New Departure

Most histories of women's rights—my own included—have emphasized the initial rage of women's rights leaders at the Radical Republican authors of the Fourteenth and Fifteenth Amendments. In 1865 Elizabeth Cady Stanton was horrified to discover what she called "the word male" in proposals for a Fourteenth Amendment. The second section of the amendment defines the basis of congressional representation as "male persons over the age of twenty-one" and in doing so makes the first reference to sex anywhere in the Constitution. The passage of the Fifteenth Amendment in 1869, a much more powerful constitutional defense of political equality, only deepened the anger of women's rights advocates because it did not include sex among its prohibited disfranchisements.[4]

In 1869 the crisis split suffragists into two camps—the National Woman Suffrage Association, which protested the omission of women from the Reconstruction amendments, and the American Woman Suffrage Association, which accepted the deferral of their claims. This part of the story is well known to students of woman suffrage, as is the National Association's concentration, through most of its twenty-one-year life (in 1890 it amalgamated with the American Association), on securing a separate amendment enfranchising women. Inasmuch as the form that federal woman suffrage ultimately took was precisely a separate constitutional amendment—the Nineteenth, ratified in 1920—this strategy is taken as the entirety of woman suffragists' constitutional claims. Yet, in the first few years after the passage of the Fourteenth and Fifteenth Amendments, suffragists in the National Association camp energetically pursued another constitutional approach. They proposed a broad and inclusive construction of the Fourteenth and Fifteenth Amendments, under which, they claimed, women were already enfranchised. This constitutional strategy, known at the time as the New Departure, laid the basis for the subsequent focus on a separate woman suffrage amendment, even as it embodied a radical democratic vision that the latter approach did not have.

The Fourteenth and Fifteenth Amendments

While the Fourteenth Amendment was in the process of being ratified, woman suffragists concentrated on its second clause, because of the offensive reference to "male persons." This phrase was included by the amendment's framers because in 1867 there was an active movement demanding the franchise for women, and it would no longer do to use such gender neutral terms as "person" to mean only men.[5] Yet such explicit exclusions of particular groups from the universal blessings of American democracy were not at all in the egalitarian spirit of the age. Perhaps it was for this reason that in writing the first section of the Fourteenth Amendment, which defines federal citizenship, the framers could not bring themselves to speak of races or sexes but instead relied on the abstractions of "persons" and "citizens." In other words, the universalities of the first section of the Fourteenth Amendment, where federal citizenship is established, run headlong into the sex-based restrictions of the second section, where voting rights are limited. Those Reconstruction Era feminists angered at the restrictive clause quickly recognized these contradictions and became determined to get women's rights demands included in the broadest possible construction of the terms "persons" and "citizens" in the first section, to use, in other words, the first section to defeat the second.

After the Fifteenth Amendment was finally ratified, the suffragists of the National Association therefore shifted from the claim that the Reconstruction amendments excluded women and began to argue instead that they were broad enough to include women's rights along with those of the freedmen. This strategic turn, the New Departure,[6] was first outlined in October 1869 by a husband and wife team of Missouri suffragists, Francis and Virginia Minor. They offered an elaborate and elegant interpretation of the Constitution to demonstrate that women already had the right to vote. Their construction rested on a consistent perspective on the whole Constitution, but especially on a broad interpretation of the Fourteenth Amendment.[7]

The Minors' first premise was that popular sovereignty preceded and underlay constitutional authority. In exchange for creating government, the people expected protection of their preeminent and natural rights. This is a familiar element of revolutionary ideology. Their second premise was to equate the power of the *federal* government with the defense of individual rights, to regard federal power as positive.[8] Historically, the federal government had been regarded as the enemy of rights; the Bill of Rights protects individual rights by enjoining the federal government from infringing on them. In the wake of the devastating experience of secession, the Fourteenth Amendment reversed the order, relying on federal power to protect its citizens against the tyrannical action of the states. The Minors thus argued in good Radical Reconstruction fashion that national citizenship had finally been established as supreme by the first section of the Fourteenth Amendment: "the immunities and privileges of American citizenship, however defined, are national in character and paramount to all state authority."

A third element in the Minors' case was that the benefits of national citizenship were equally the rights of all. This too bore the mark of the Reconstruction Era. In the words of the amendment, "all persons born or naturalized in the United States" were equally entitled to the privileges and protections of national citizenship; there were no additional qualifications. In the battle for the rights of the Black man, the rights of all had been secured. The war had expanded the rights of "proud White man" to all those who had historically been deprived of them, or so these radical recon- structionists believed.[9] In other words, the historic claim of asserting *individual* rights was becoming the modern one of realizing *equal* rights, especially for the lowly.

Finally, the Minors argued that the right to vote was one of the basic privileges and immunities of national citizenship. This was both the most controversial and the most important part of the New Departure constitutional construction. Popular sovereignty had always included an implicit theory of political power. The Minors' New Departure argument took this article of popular faith, reinterpreted it in light of Reconstruction Era egalitarianism, and gave it constitutional expression to produce a theory of universal rights to the suffrage. The New Departure case for universal suffrage brought together the Fourteenth Amendment, which nationalized citizenship and linked it to federal power, and the Fifteenth Amendment, which shifted the responsibility for the suffrage from the state to the national government.[10] This theory of the suffrage underlay much of the case for

Black suffrage as well, but because the drive for Black suffrage was so intertwined with Republican partisan interest, it was woman suffrage, which had no such political thrust behind it, that generated the most formal constitutional expression of this Reconstruction Era faith in political equality.

Women Take the Vote

The New Departure was not simply a lawyer's exercise in constitutional exegesis. Reconstruction was an age of popular constitutionalism. Although presented in formal, constitutional terms, what the Minors had to say had much support among the rank and file of the women's rights movement. The underlying spirit of the Minors' constitutional arguments was militant and activist. The basic message was that the vote was already women's right; they merely had to take it. The New Departure took on meaning precisely because of this direct action element. Many women took the argument to heart and went to the polls, determined to vote. By 1871 hundreds of women were trying to register and vote in dozens of towns all over the country.[11] In 1871 in Philadelphia, to take one of many examples, Carrie Burnham, an unmarried tax-paying woman, got as far as having her name registered on the voting rolls. When her vote was refused, she formed the Citizens Suffrage Association of Philadelphia, dedicated not only to the defense of women's political rights but also to the greater truth that the right to vote was inherent, not bestowed. If the contrary were true, if the right to vote were a gift, this "implied a right lodged somewhere in society, which society had never acquired by any direct concession from the people." Such a theory of political power was patently tyrannical.[12]

That the first examples of women's direct action voting occurred in 1868 and 1869, before the Minors made their formal constitutional argument, suggests that the New Departure grew out of a genuinely popular political faith. In 1868 in the radical, spiritualist town of Vineland, New Jersey, almost two hundred women cast their votes into a separate ballot box and then tried to get them counted along with the men's. "The platform was crowded with earnest refined intellectual women, who feel it was good for them to be there," *The Revolution* reported. "One beautiful girl said 'I feel so much stronger for having voted.'"[13] The Vineland women repeated the effort for several years, and the ballot box eventually became an icon, which the local historical society still owns. From Vineland, the idea of women's voting spread to nearby towns, including Roseville, where, despite the American Association's official disinterest in the New Departure, Lucy Stone and her mother tried—but failed—to register their votes.

On the other side of the continent, Mary Olney Brown also decided she had the right to vote because the legislature of Washington Territory had passed an act giving "all White American citizens above the age of twenty-one years the right to vote." She wrote to other "prominent women urging them to go out and vote at the coming election…[but] I was looked upon as a fanatic and the idea of woman voting was regarded as an absurdity." "Many [women] wished to vote...," she decided, "[but] had not the courage to go to the polls in defiance of custom." Finally, in 1869, she went to the polls with her husband, daughter, and son-in-law. Election officials threatened that she would not be "treated as a lady."

> Summoning all my strength, I walked up to the desk behind which sat the august officers of election, and presented my vote.... I was pompously met with the assertion, "You are not an American citizen; hence not entitled to vote." ...I said... "I claim to be an American citizen, and a native-born citizen at that; and I wish to show you from the fourteenth amendment to the constitution of the United States, that women are not only citizens having the constitutional right to vote, but also that our territorial election law gives women the privilege of exercising that right."...I went on to show them that the...emancipation of the Southern slaves threw upon the country a class of people, who, like the women of the nation, owed allegiance to the government, but whose citizenship was not recognized. To settle this question, the fourteenth amendment was adopted.

Whereupon, the local election official, "with great dignity of manner and an immense display of ignorance," insisted "that the laws of congress don't extend over Washington territory" and refused her vote. When Brown was refused again, two years later, she concluded, "It amounts to this: the law gives women the right to vote in this territory, and you three men who have been appointed to receive our votes, sit here and arbitrarily refuse to take them, giving no reason why, only that you have decided not to take the women's votes. There is no law to sustain you in this usurpation of power."[14]

News of the efforts of women to register and vote spread through formal and informal means. Women's rights and mainstream journals reported on them, but information also might have been passed by word of mouth through networks of activists. Many sisters and friends, often in different states, turn up in the stories of New Departure voting women. In her account, Mary Olney Brown tells of her sister, who was inspired by her efforts to try to vote in a nearby town. Brown's sister took a different approach and was more successful. Eager to vote in a school election, she and her friends prepared a special dinner for election officials. "When the voting was resumed, the women, my sister being the first, handed in their ballots as if they had always been accustomed to voting. One lady, Mrs. Sargent, seventy-two years old, said she thanked the Lord that he had let her live until she could vote."[15]

The voting women of the 1870s often went to the polls in groups. They believed in the suffrage as an individual right but an individual right that would be achieved and experienced collectively. The most famous of these voting groups was the nearly fifty local activists, friends, and relatives who joined Susan B.

Anthony in attempting to vote in Rochester, New York, in 1872. Virginia Minor herself was swept up in this collective activism. When she and some of her friends, all suffrage activists and Republican partisans, tried to register in St. Louis and were refused, she sued.

The congressional passage of the Enforcement Act in May 1870 to strengthen the Fifteenth Amendment greatly accelerated women's direct action voting. The Enforcement Act was meant to enforce the freedmen's political rights by providing recourse to the federal courts and penalties against local election officials who refused the lawful votes of citizens. Women who wanted to vote saw the act as a way to use the power of the federal government for their own benefit. Benjamin Quarles reports that freedwomen in South Carolina were encouraged by Freedmen's Bureau officials to attempt to vote by appealing to the Enforcement Act.[16] Some election officials responded to the Enforcement Act by accepting women's votes. When Nanette Gardner went to vote in Detroit in 1871, the ward official in her district was sympathetic to her protest and accepted her vote. The same man accepted Gardner's vote again in 1872, and she presented him with "a beautiful banner of white satin, trimmed with gold fringe on which was inscribed...'To Peter Hill, Alderman of the Ninth Ward, Detroit.... By recognizing civil liberty and equality for woman, he has placed the last and brightest jewel on the brow of Michigan.'"[17]

Most local officials, however, refused to accept women's votes. While Nanette Gardner voted successfully in Detroit, her friend Catherine Stebbins (the daughter of one of the Rochester voters) was turned away in the next ward. When Mary Brown's vote was refused in Olympia, she concluded that politicians more powerful than the local committeemen had decided to resist women's direct action efforts to vote and that "money was pledged in case of prosecution." In Santa Cruz, California, when Ellen Van Valkenberg was similarly turned back at the polls, she became the first woman to sue an election official under the Enforcement Act for refusing her vote.[18] By 1871 numerous New Departure woman suffrage cases were making their way through the federal courts.

Victoria Woodhull and the New Departure

Meanwhile, the New Departure gained an advocate who moved it from the local level into national politics: Victoria Woodhull. In January of 1871 Woodhull appeared before the House Judiciary Committee to make the constitutional case for women's right to vote. No woman had ever before been invited to address a committee of the United States Congress. Her appearance was sponsored by Massachusetts Republican Benjamin Butler, who may have helped her outline her constitutional case. The deeply felt conviction about women's rights underlying her argument was undoubtedly her own, however. Her memorial asked Congress to pass legislation clarifying the right of all women to vote under the new Reconstruction amendments.[19] The major difference between Woodhull and the Minors was tactical; she urged women to turn to Congress to resolve the question, while they relied on the courts.

Like all New Departure advocates, Woodhull embraced the premise that popular sovereignty was absolute: "the sovereign power of this country is perpetual in the politically-organized people of the United States, and can neither be relinquished nor abandoned by any portion of them." Her case for woman suffrage was simple and, from a radical Reconstruction perspective, virtually unassailable: inasmuch as the first section of the Fourteenth Amendment made no reference to sex, women along with men were citizens of the United States, and foremost among the "privileges and immunities" of national citizenship was the right to vote.[20] Like the Minors, Woodhull argued that the Fourteenth Amendment established the supremacy of national over state citizenship and the obligation of the federal government to protect the rights of all citizens equally.

Victoria Claflin Woodhull, c. 1870
MATHEW BRADY

Woodhull also argued from the Fifteenth Amendment, which she interpreted broadly, that voting is "a Right, not a privilege of citizens of the United States."[21] She directly confronted the most obvious objection to this interpretation, that the Fifteenth Amendment specifically prohibits only disfranchisements by race, color, and previous condition. First, she argued, the amendment's wording does not bestow the right to vote but assumes it to be preexisting. Although it explicitly prohibited certain disfranchisements, Woodhull argued that it could not be read to implicitly permit others. Second, the Fifteenth Amendment forbids disfranchisement "under three distinct conditions, in all of which," Woodhull argued, "woman is distinctly embraced." In other words, "a race comprises all the people, male and female." Woodhull here seems to grasp what many modern White feminists are still struggling to understand, that counterpoising the discriminations of race and sex obscures the experience of those who suffer both, that is, Black women. Finally, Woodhull argued for her broad construction of the right of suffrage on the grounds of what she called "the blending of [the Constitution's] various parts," that is, the relation between the Fourteenth Amendment, which nationalizes citizenship and links it to the power of the federal government, and the Fifteenth Amendment, which shifts the responsibility for the suffrage from the state to the national government.[22]

The first official reaction to the New Departure came in response to Woodhull's memorial. The House Judiciary Committee issued two conflicting reports on the constitutional issues she raised.[23] Here we begin to see that debate over the feminists' particular constitutional arguments was inseparable from questions of the larger meaning of the Reconstruction amendments. The Majority Report rejected Woodhull's claims. Its author was John Bingham, one of the framers of the Fourteenth Amendment. Although Bingham conceded that women enjoyed the privileges of United States citizenship along with men, he disagreed that the Fourteenth Amendment added anything new to the content of national citizenship or altered the relationship between national and state citizenship. The Minority Report, signed by William Loughridge of Iowa and Benjamin Butler of Massachusetts, supported Woodhull's memorial and the generous and radical interpretation of the amendments on which it relied. The Minority Report interpreted the Fourteenth Amendment broadly, arguing that it was intended "to secure the natural rights of citizens as well as their equal capacities before the law." The Majority Report rejected Woodhull's argument that the Fifteenth Amendment shifted responsibility for the suffrage from the state to the national level, while the Minority Report agreed that the Fifteenth Amendment "clearly recognizes the right to vote, as one of the rights of a citizen of the United States."[24] "Thus it can be seen," Woodhull observed archly, "that equally able men differ upon a simple point of Constitutional Law."[25]

The mere fact of a congressional hearing was a victory for woman suffrage leaders, and the language of constitutional principle was an improvement over the semi-sexual innuendo with which their claims were often met.[26] The favorable Minority Report meant that some of the leaders of the Republican Party supported women's rights claims on the Constitution. In 1871 two committee rooms in the Capitol were put at the disposal of the suffragists to facilitate their lobbying efforts.[27] "Could you feel the atmosphere of...Congress, to-day, you would not doubt what the end must be, nor that it will be very soon," Isabella Beecher Hooker wrote.[28] The National Woman Suffrage Association urged women to put pressure on their congressmen to support the Butler Report, as well as to continue trying to vote and to work through the courts.[29]

Free Love and the Moral Divide

It was in this context, as Republicans struggled over the claims of the New Departure and suffragists grew hopeful, that the issue of "free love" was raised. The sexual discourse that soon surrounded the New Departure played a role in shaping the political context and therefore the constitutional outcome. Woodhull is generally remembered in the history books not for her powerful constitutional arguments but for her shady sexual reputation. These sexual issues, however, were introduced not by Woodhull but by her opponents, who saw in them a way to divert attention from the constitutional arguments she made. Republican newspapers, notably the *New York Tribune*, accused Woodhull of multiple marriages, bigamy, and the advocacy of free love.[30] Suffrage leaders allied with Woodhull were either accused of sharing her "free love" sentiments or warned against the consequences of associating with disreputable women. As in other times, when politicians cannot face the genuine issues before them, the importance of "character" was asserted. "Men judge men's conventions not more by the formal platform they present than by...the character of those who are prominent in the proceedings," a New York periodical solemnly warned.[31]

Rather than react defensively to the attacks on her, Woodhull embraced the "free love" opprobrium with which she was charged. To her, the principles at the heart of sexual life were the same as those at the heart of political life, and the true basis of marriage was the same as the true basis of republican government: individual rights. Groping for a way to express her conviction that women, whether married or unmarried, must have unqualified control over their own reproductive and sexual lives, she used the language of Reconstruction constitutionalism to proclaim the doctrine of rights to and over one's own person. "Yes I am a Free lover," Woodhull responded to a heckler at one of her speeches. "I have an *inalienable, constitutional* and *natural* right to love whom I may,...to *change* that love *every day* if I please,...and it is your *duty* not only to *accord* [me my right], but, as a community, to see that I am protected in it."[32]

Such sex radicalism was not the predominant strain in nineteenth-century feminist circles. Most of the New Departure leaders (with the significant exception of Elizabeth Cady Stanton) were closer to the Victorian stereotype than Woodhull was, and they believed that the sex impulse must be tamed, not constitutionally secured. Nonetheless, even these "pious" women defended their alliance with Woodhull and rejected the conventional moral divide that separated "good" women from "bad." "God has raised up Woodhull to embody all questions of fellowship in political work [among] women irrespective of character," declared Isabella Beecher Hooker.[33] Instead of joining in a crusade against the immorality of women, New Departure suffragists began to attack the "hypocrisy" of men. Woodhull had been "raised up of God," suffragist and moral reformer Paulina Wright Davis claimed, to expose the perfidy of "a class that no one dares touch," men who said one thing and did another, men in power.[34] They shifted accusations of immorality not only from women to men but also from sexuality to politics. The true prostitutes, Woodhull asserted, were Republican leaders, who sold out principles for party power and wealth.[35]

The *Bradwell* Case

In late 1871, in the midst of this increasingly sexualized political context, the first New Departure cases began to reach the dockets of the federal courts. One was the case of Sara Spencer and seventy other women from the District of Columbia, who sued election officials under the Enforcement Act for refusing to permit them to vote. The District of Columbia was a deliberate choice for testing the New Departure argument. There, as advocates of Black suffrage had first realized in 1867, the power of the federal government over the suffrage was not complicated by questions of dual sovereignty and states' rights.[36]

In October Judge Cartter of the Supreme Court of the District of Columbia ruled against Spencer. Cartter conceded that the Fourteenth Amendment included women along with men in the privileges and immunities of national citizenship; however, he rejected the democratic theory of suffrage on which the case rested. To concede that voting was a right was, in his opinion, to open the door to anarchy and would "involve the destruction of civil government." "The right of all men to vote is as fully recognized in the population of our large centres and cities as can well be done," wrote Cartter. "The result...is political profligacy and violence verging upon anarchy."[37] The larger context of the opinion, therefore, was anxiety about democratic politics, and Cartter's concern for the proper position of women in society was secondary. This was true of the entire New Departure debate (and perhaps of judicial disposition of women's rights claims more generally); it was conducted primarily in terms of "rights," not woman's sphere. What was claimed or denied for women was claimed or denied for all citizens, especially those previously excluded from rights due them. Whether this was because the question of women's place was subsumed in a more general struggle for political democracy or because sex-prejudice was still unspeakable in constitutional terms, the consequence was the same: denying women the rights they claimed under general provisions weakened those provisions in general.

The observation that general questions of constitutional rights had overtaken the specific discourse on woman's place is even clearer in the next major New Departure decision, *Bradwell v. Illinois* (1873). *Bradwell* was the first case touching on the New Departure to reach the Supreme Court. In 1869 Myra Bradwell, a Chicago feminist and pioneering woman lawyer, was refused admission to the Illinois bar. The grounds on which the state supreme court refused her application, along with the initial brief that Bradwell submitted in response, were concerned entirely with coverture, that is, with the question of the disabilities of married women before the law. By the time Bradwell brought her case before the United States Supreme Court in October 1871, she had changed the terms radically. Her case was no longer about coverture but had been reformulated in entirely New Departure terms. Her brief argued that her right to practice law was a citizen's right and that Illinois's action in refusing her was prohibited by the Fourteenth Amendment. As for coverture, she asserted that "the great innovation of the XIV Amendment...sweeps away the principles of the common law," so that even reforms of married women's property rights were no longer necessary. The *Bradwell* case is one of the few concerning women's rights commonly included in the history of constitutional law, but in my opinion it is not correctly situated, since it is usually cited to illustrate judicial assumptions about woman's place rather than the constitutional issues of citizenship on which it was actually argued and decided.[38]

Bradwell's case was closely watched by suffragists as an indication of how much support to expect from the Republican Party. Bradwell was represented before the Supreme Court by Senator Matthew Carpenter, one of the major second-generation leaders of the Republican Party. While Carpenter took up Bradwell's case and argued it in strong Fourteenth Amendment terms, he prefaced his case with an equally strong argument about why the right to vote was not covered by the Reconstruction amendments. He

Myra Bradwell, 1870
LIBRARY OF CONGRESS

insisted, in other words, on a distinction between civil and political rights. While the federal government protected civil rights, women's as well as men's, Carpenter argued, the suffrage remained under the control of the states, beyond the lawful interference of federal power.[39]

Suffragists were understandably confused by the way Carpenter argued Bradwell's case. Was it an indication that Republican leaders were in favor of the New Departure or against it? Stanton allowed herself to be encouraged; if women were covered along with men under the Fourteenth Amendment, wasn't the fundamental point of equal rights won?[40] Victoria Woodhull, however, saw it differently; she argued that women might be admitted to the benefits of the postwar amendments only to find those amendments so narrowed that they bestowed virtually nothing at all, certainly not political rights. She charged that Republicans, "frightened by the grandeur and the extent" of the amendments they had enacted, had retreated to the enemies' doctrine of states' rights, where their own greatest achievements would ultimately be undone.[41]

The Supreme Court held back its decision on *Bradwell* until after the election. To trace the final judicial disposition of the suffragists' constitutional arguments, we have to understand what was at stake in this election and what a Republican victory would mean. The election of 1872 was a crisis for the Republicans.[42] In June 1872 an important group of reformers split off from regular Republicans to run an independent presidential campaign. These political rebels, the Liberal Republicans, based their revolt on the old opposition between central government and individual rights. From the perspective of feminists, who were also looking for a political alternative to the regular Republicans, the terms of the bolt were particularly disappointing. Feminists had learned from freedmen to see the federal government not as a threat to their rights but as the agency for winning them.

To add insult to injury, the Liberal Republicans picked as their candidate Horace Greeley, a man who had made his opposition to woman suffrage clear many years before. Infuriated by the nomination of Greeley, many New Departure suffragists campaigned actively for Ulysses Grant in 1872.[43] The regular Republicans cultivated their support, sending them about the country on official speaking tours and inserting a timid little reference to "additional rights" for women in their platform, a plank so insignificant that suffragists called it a "splinter." Holding off a decision on *Bradwell* was consistent with this temporary friendliness. Anthony expected that if Republicans won, they would reward women with the suffrage by recognizing the New Departure claims. She was so sure that when she came home from her last speaking tour on election day, she gathered together friends and relatives and went down to her local polling place to submit her vote for Grant. Although the local Republican official accepted the votes of fifteen of the demonstrators, including Anthony,[44] a few weeks later a United States marshall came to her house and arrested her for violation of federal law—the Enforcement Act.

Anthony's arrest was a signal that the Republicans were ready to dispose of the New Departure. Because she was the most famous woman suffragist in the nation, there is good reason to suspect her arrest had been authorized at the highest level of government. The conduct of her trial several months later reinforces this suspicion. The trial was moved from her home county, where she had lectured extensively to educate potential jurors, to another venue. The judge, Ward Hunt, was no small-town jurist but a recent appointee to the United States Supreme Court. He refused to submit the case to the jury, instead directing a guilty verdict from the bench, a practice that was later found unconstitutional. Years later, Anthony's lawyer observed, "There never was a trial in the country with one half the importance of Miss Anthony's.... If Anthony had won her case on the merit it would have revolutionized the suffrage of the country.... There was a prearranged determination to convict her. A jury trial was dangerous and so the Constitution was deliberately and openly violated." Anthony was not even permitted to appeal.[45]

In general, the outcome of the election cleared the way for the Republican Party to retreat from the radical implications of the postwar amendments. There is a link between the judicial dismissal of the feminists' New Departure and the larger repudiation of the postwar amendments. It is embodied in the fact that the Supreme Court's opinions on *Bradwell* and on the *Slaughterhouse* cases were delivered on the same day in 1873. *Slaughterhouse* is generally considered the fundamental Fourteenth Amendment Supreme Court decision. The case involved a group of Louisiana butchers who challenged a state law regulating their occupation on the grounds that it violated their rights as federal citizens (to practice their vocation—the same issue as *Bradwell*) and that the Fourteenth Amendment established the supremacy of national over state citizenship.[46]

Six months after the election, the Court delivered negative opinions in both cases, interpreting the Fourteenth Amendment very narrowly and finding it inapplicable in both cases. The case that the Court lingered over was *Slaughterhouse*.[47] By a bare majority, it ruled that the amendment's intent was only to ensure "the freedom of the slave race" and that it did not transfer the jurisdiction over fundamental civil rights from state to federal government. The opinion in *Bradwell* covered much less territory but did so by a larger majority. The Court merely rejected the claim that the right to practice law was one of the privileges and immunities of federal citizenship protected by the amendment. Beyond that, the Court simply commented that "the opinion just delivered in the *Slaughterhouse* Cases … renders elaborate argument in the present case unnecessary."[48] We should not be misled by this preemptory dismissal, however. The very interpretation under which the *Slaughterhouse* cases had been decided, that the Fourteenth Amendment was limited to matters of race and did not elevate national over state citizenship, had first been articulated in 1871 in the Majority Report of the House Judiciary Committee, rejecting Victoria Woodhull's claim that the Fourteenth Amendment guaranteed her right to vote.

The *Minor* Case

The Supreme Court ruled conclusively against the New Departure two years later, in 1875. The case in which it did so was *Minor v. Happersett*, brought, appropriately enough, by Virginia Minor, the woman who had first argued that as a citizen of the United States, she was constitutionally protected in her right to vote. Like Anthony, Minor had tried to vote in the 1872 election, but when her vote was refused, she brought suit under the Enforcement Act. The Missouri courts ruled against her, and she appealed to the United States Supreme Court on the grounds that constitutional protections of the citizen's right to vote invalidated any state regulations to the contrary. The Court ruled unanimously against her. Since the *Slaughterhouse* and *Bradwell* cases had disposed of the first element of the New Departure, that the Fourteenth Amendment established the supremacy of national citizenship, the decision in *Minor* concentrated on the second assertion, that suffrage was a right of citizenship. On this, the Court ruled starkly that "the Constitution of the United States does not confer the right of suffrage upon any one."[49]

Here, too, there was an intimate link between the fate of woman suffragists' constitutional claims and that of the Reconstruction amendments in general. The day after the Court delivered its opinion in *Minor*, it heard arguments in *United States v. Cruikshank*. In this case and in the *United States v. Reese*, Black men for the first time brought suit under the Enforcement Act for protection of their political rights under the Fourteenth and Fifteenth Amend-ments, and the Court ruled

Virginia Louise Minor

J.A. Scholten & J.C. Buttre

against them. In the process of ruling against the plaintiffs, the Court found the Enforcement Act, under which both feminists and freedmen had sought protection, unconstitutional. Citing the recent decision in *Minor*, the Court ruled that inasmuch as the Constitution did not bestow the suffrage on anyone, the federal courts were outside their jurisdiction in protecting the freedmen's political rights.

The rejection of woman suffrage arguments on the grounds that the Fifteenth Amendment was only intended to forbid disfran-chisement by race paved the way for a reading of the Fifteenth Amendment that was so narrow it did not even protect the freedmen themselves. In its decision in *United States v. Reese*, the Court argued that the plaintiff, although a Black man, had not proved that his vote was denied on the grounds of race and so was not covered by constitutional protections. Eventually, of course, the freedmen were effectively disfranchised on grounds of income, residence, and education, all surrogates for race. Anthony had anticipated this connection. At her own trial, she predicted that the general narrowing of the Reconstruction amendments would follow on the heels of the repudiation of women's claims of equal rights under them. "If we once establish the false principle, that United States citizenship does not carry with it the right to vote in every state in this Union," she said, "there is no end to the petty freaks and cunning devices that will be resorted to exclude one and another class of citizens from the right of suffrage."[50]

Three years after the *Minor* defeat, suffragists began their pursuit of a separate constitutional amendment to prohibit disfranchisement on account of sex. At many levels, this was a less radical strategy. With the defeat of the New Departure, winning the vote for women was no longer tied to an overall democratic interpretation of the Constitution. To the degree that the struggle for women's votes was not strategically linked to the general defense of political democracy, that its goal was "woman suffrage" not "universal suffrage," elitist and racist tendencies faced fewer barriers, had freer reign, and imparted a more conservative character to suffragism over the next half-century.

Yet, despite this very important strategic shift, the New Departure period left a deep mark on the history of feminism. From time to time, some suffragist would see possibilities in the existing propositions of the Constitution and propose some clever legal mechanism for exploiting them.[51] Even direct action voting never completely died away. Twenty years after the *Minor* decision, Elizabeth Grannis of New York City made her eighth attempt to register to vote.[52] Certainly the larger spirit of militant direct action resurfaced in a spectacular way in the last decade of the American suffrage movement. The deepest mark of the New Departure, however, was to make women's rights and political equality indelibly constitutional issues. As Susan B. Anthony wrote, she "had learned... through the passage of the Fourteenth and Fifteenth amendments that it had been possible to amend [the Constitution] in such a way as to enfranchise an entire new class of voters."[53] The *Minor* case, the historian Norma Basch has observed, "drew the inferiority of women's status out of the grooves of common law assumptions and state provisions and thrust it into the maelstrom of constitutional conflict. The demand for woman suffrage...acquired a contentious national life."[54]

Elizabeth B. Grannis, 1894

Notes

1. This essay is a reprint (with abbreviated notes) of an essay that first appeared in *Visible Women: New Essays on American Activism*, Nancy A. Hewitt and Suzanne Lebsock, eds., published in 1993 by the University of Illinois Press. It is reprinted here with permission of the press.

The literature generated by the feminist debate on equality versus difference is enormous. Two excellent analyses by historians are Linda Gordon, "On Difference," *Genders* 10 (Spring 1991): 91-111; and Joan Scott, "Constructing Equality-versus-Difference; or the Uses of Poststructuralist Theory for Feminism," *Feminist Studies* 14 (Spring 1988): 33-50.

2. For a sampling of critical legal studies scholarship on the limitations of rights thinking, see Mark Tushnet, "An Essay on Rights," *Texas Law Review* 62 (May 1984): 1386; and Peter Gabel, "The Phenomenology of Rights Consciousness and the Pact of Withdrawn Selves," ibid., 1563-99.

3. Paula Baker made this argument most forcefully for the pre-1920 period; see "The Domestication of Politics: Women and American Political Society, 1780-1920," *American Historical Review* 89 (June 1984): 620-47.

4. Ellen Carol DuBois, *Feminism and Suffrage: The Emergence of an Independent Women's Movement in America, 1848-1869*, (Ithaca, N.Y., 1978); Elizabeth Cady Stanton, *Eighty Years and More: Reminiscences, 1815-1897*, ed. Ellen Carol DuBois (1898; Boston, 1993), 242.

5. Stanton, *Eighty Years and More*, 242.

6. Elizabeth Cady Stanton, Susan B. Anthony, and Matilda J. Gage, eds., *History of Woman Suffrage*, Vol. 2 (Rochester, N.Y., 1881), 407-520; Ida Husted Harper, ed., *Life and Work of Susan B. Anthony*, (Indianapolis, 1899), 1: 409-48.

7. *HWS* 2: 407-10; on the Minors, see Louise R. Noun, *Strong Minded Women: The Emergence of the Woman Suffrage Movement in Iowa* (Ames, 1986), 168-69.

8. David Montgomery notes the importance of this Reconstruction Era shift in attitude to the positive state in *Beyond Equality: Labor and the Radical Republicans* (New York, 1967), 80-81.

9. On this aspect of Reconstruction Era constitutional thought, see Judith A. Baer, *Equality Under the Constitution: Reclaiming the Fourteenth Amendment* (Ithaca, N.Y., 1983).

10. While the Fifteenth Amendment was still pending, the Minors found an alternative constitutional basis for their claim that suffrage was a natural right in the frequently cited 1820 case *Corfield v. Coryell*, which included the franchise as one of the privileges and immunities protected in Article 4.

11. In New Hampshire in 1870, Matilda Ricker tried to vote (*HWS* 2: 586-87). In New York in 1871, Matilda Joslyn Gage tried to vote in Fayetteville, and a group of women, led by Louise Mansfield, tried to vote in Nyack (Elizabeth Cady Stanton, Susan B. Anthony, and Matilda Joslyn Gage, eds., *History of Woman Suffrage*, [Rochester, N.Y., 1887], 3: 406; Isabelle K. Savelle, *Ladies' Lib: How Rockland Women Got the Vote* (New York, 1979), 13-16; in New York City, Victoria Woodhull and Tennessee Claflin tried to vote (Johanna Johnston, *Mrs. Satan* [New York, 1967], 110).

12. *HWS* 3: 461-62, and *HWS* 2: 600-601.

13. Eleanor Flexner, *Century of Struggle: The Women's Rights Movement in the United States* (Cambridge, Mass., 1959), 168, citing *The Revolution*, November 19, 1868, 307.

14. *HWS* 3: 780-86.

15. Ibid., 784.

16. Benjamin Quarles, "Frederick Douglass and the Woman's Rights Movement," *Journal of Negro History* 25 (June 1940): 35.

17. *HWS* 3: 523-24.

18. Ibid., 766.

19. Ibid., 2: 443-48.

20. Ibid., 445.

21. Victoria C. Woodhull, *Constitutional Equality: A Lecture Delivered at Lincoln Hall, Washington, D.C., February 16, 1871* (New York, 1871).

22. *HWS* 2: 445-46. The comment on "blending" was made in Woodhull's arguments in support of her congressional memorial. These are available in Victoria Woodhull, *The Argument for Woman's Electoral Rights under Amendment XIV and XV of the Constitution of the United States* (London, 1887), 44.

23. Both reports can be found in *HWS* 2: 461-82.

24. Ibid., 469, 478. In support of their interpretation, they cited the federal district court's decision in what was called the *Crescent City* case, later renamed the *Slaughterhouse* cases.

25. Woodhull, *Constitutional Equality*, 4.

26. Martha Wright complained to Elizabeth Stanton about a congressman who "said rudely to Mrs. Davis & Mrs. Griffing, 'You just call on us because you like to,'" to which Mrs. Griffing answered "'We call on you, because it is the only way known to us, to present our appeal to you,' & Mrs. Davis said 'You must remember that we are your constituents.'" Wright to Stanton, December 29, 1870, Garrison Family Collection, Smith College, Northampton, Mass.

27. *HWS* 2: 489.

28. Isabella Beecher Hooker to the Editor, *Independent*, February 11, 1871, reprinted in *Woodhull and Claflin's Weekly*, March 4, 1871, 1.

29. Ibid.; *An Appeal to the Women of the United States by the National Woman Suffrage and Educational Committee* (Hartford, Conn., April 19, 1871).

30. Woodhull's response to the charges can be found in the *New York World*, May 22, 1871, 3.

31. "The Voice of Apollo Hall," *Every Saturday*, June 17, 1871, 554.

32. Victoria C. Woodhull, *The Principles of Social Freedom, Delivered in New York City, November 20, 1871* (New York, 1871), 23-24.

33. Isabella Beecher Hooker to Anna E. Dickenson, April 22, (1871), box 9 Dickenson Papers, Library of Congress, Washington, D.C.

34. Paulina Wright Davis to Woodhull, May 29, 1871, Victoria Woodhull Martin Collection, Southern Illinois University, Carbondale.

35. Victoria C. Woodhull, "The Speech of Victoria C. Woodhull before the National Woman's Suffrage Convention at Apollo Hall, May 11, 1871," reprinted in Woodhull, *The Argument for Women's Electoral Rights*, 137.

36. *HWS* 2: 587-99.

37. Ibid., 598.

38. Ibid., 622. The opinion in Bradwell that is usually cited is not the terse dismissal of the Fourteenth Amendment argument that settled the case, but an individual concurring opinion by Justice Bradley that addressed the coverture issues that Bradwell had removed from her argument.

39. *HWS* 2: 618.

40. Elizabeth Cady Stanton, "Argument before the Senate Judiciary Committee," January 11, 1872, reprinted in *Woodhull and Claflin's Weekly*, January 27, 1872, 7; see also Stanton to Woodhull, December 29, [1872], Stanton Miscellaneous Papers, New York Public Library, New York.

41. Victoria Woodhull, *Carpenter and Cartter Reviewed: A Speech before the National Suffrage Association at Lincoln Hall, Washington, D.C, January 10, 1872* (New York, 1872), 20.

42. Montgomery, *Beyond Equality*, 379-86.

43. Anthony to Stanton, July 10, 1872, box 38, NAWSA Papers, Library of Congress.

44. Nancy A. Hewitt, *Women's Activism and Social Change: Rochester, New York, 1822-1872* (Ithaca, N.Y., 1984), 211. Anthony to Stanton, November 5, 1872, Harper Papers, Huntington Library, San Marino, California.

45. Harper, ed., *The Life and Work of Susan B. Anthony*, 1: 423-53; Charles Fairman, *History of the Supreme Court*, (New York, 1987), 7: 224.

46. Fairman, *History of the Supreme Court*, 285. Carpenter's argument in *Slaughterhouse* can be found in 21 Court Reporters Lawyers Edition, 399-401 (1872).

47. 16 Wall. 36 (1873).

48. 16 Wall. 130 (1873).

49. *HWS* 2: 734-42.

50. Ibid., 641.

51. The most important of these was Catherine McCullough's successful argument that the Constitution permitted states legislatively to enfranchise voters for presidential electors. In 1914 Illinois passed a "presidential suffrage" law, giving women votes in the 1916 presidential election. See Steven W. Buechler, *The Transformation of the Woman Suffrage Movement: The Case of Illinois, 1850-1920* (New Brunswick, N.J., 1986), 174-76.

52. Unidentified clipping, v. 12, 75, Susan B. Anthony Memorial Library Collection, Huntington Library, San Marino, Calif.

53. Susan B. Anthony and Ida Husted Harper, eds., *History of Woman Suffrage*, (Rochester, N.Y., 1902), 4: 10.

54. Norma Basch, "Reconstructing Female Citizenship" (Paper delivered at Women and the Constitution Conference, American University and the Smithsonian, October 1987).

Seven

HOW THE WEST WAS WON FOR WOMAN SUFFRAGE

Beverly Beeton

Editor's Introduction: In 1869 and 1870, as Eastern suffrage forces were in disarray following the failure of the Reconstruction amendments to establish universal suffrage for all, the territories of Wyoming and Utah stunned the nation by announcing the enfranchisement of women. Later, as they entered the Union as states, Wyoming (1890) and Utah (1896) insisted on retaining woman suffrage despite considerable opposition from Congress. They were joined as suffrage states by Colorado (1893) and Idaho (1896), which enfranchised women through state constitutional amendments. These were the only four states to enfranchise women in the nineteenth century.

In this essay, historian Beverly Beeton answers the question students of the suffrage movement have always pondered: what was behind this pioneering embrace of woman suffrage? Why was it that the West was far ahead of the rest of the nation in enfranchising women? Beeton, the author of the book *Women Vote in the West: The Woman Suffrage Movement, 1869-1896* and numerous articles on woman suffrage in the West, explains that there were many factors contributing to the early victories in the West, and that each of the four territories/states has its unique story. She emphasizes, however, that practical politics rather than advanced ideology explain the West's precociousness in adopting woman suffrage. While most Eastern and Southern politicians saw woman suffrage as worthy of scorn or ridicule and unpopular with their constituents, Western politicians embraced it as politically expedient for a fascinating variety of purposes. As Beeton explains, there *were* Western men who wanted women enfranchised out of a sense of justice. But the votes necessary for passage of suffrage bills were there because woman suffrage served practical needs ranging from attracting women settlers (using woman suffrage as an advertising gimmick) to protecting polygamy.

Beeton also discusses the relationship between the Eastern and Western suffrage movements, a relationship of mutual influence. Some Eastern proponents— including Congressmen—saw the territories as a good place to test this controversial new idea of woman suffrage. National suffrage leaders, including Lucy Stone, Elizabeth Cady Stanton, Susan B. Anthony, Anna Howard Shaw, and Carrie Chapman Catt, assisted with Western suffrage campaigns, beginning with the unsuccessful Kansas campaign of 1867. But they benefited from the opportunity to test and develop strategies and tactics in the West that were later used elsewhere.

One fascinating aspect of the Western story told by Beeton is the relationship between Mormon suffragists and Eastern suffrage leaders who tried to welcome and support the Mormon women while avoiding the appearance of condoning polygamy. In the wake of the Victoria Woodhull affair, the public was prepared to believe the worst regarding suffragists and unconventional ideas about sex and marriage, and the National Woman Suffrage Association (NWSA) particularly was hurt by its defense of Mormon suffragists. Beeton also explains that in the West, as in the rest of the nation, racism and ethnic tensions played a role in the suffrage movement, and that in this region the controversy over voting rights involved Chinese and Native Americans as well as African Americans.

The early victories in the West were of tremendous importance in the history of the American woman suffrage movement. As Beeton notes, suffragists and anti-suffragists alike gathered data and published studies on the effects of woman suffrage on Western society and politics, with each side insisting that the Western experience proved *them* right. Of greater significance, however, was the inspiration these Rocky Mountain states provided to suffragists in other regions of the United States.

★　★　★　★　★

A HALF-CENTURY prior to the 1920 ratification of the Nineteenth Amendment women voted in the Rocky Mountain West. In December 1869, Wyoming women were granted the right to vote, and two months later in February of 1870, their sisters across the mountains in Utah gained access to polling places. In both cases, women were enfranchised through woman suffrage bills adopted by their territorial legislatures and signed by the territorial governors. As a result of an 1893 referendum women in Colorado were also enfranchised, and a state constitutional amendment in Idaho in 1896 provided woman suffrage there. Thus, Wyoming, Utah, Colorado, and Idaho were the *only* states where women were enfranchised in the nineteenth century.[1]

Why were women in the Rocky Mountain West the first to vote? There is no one simple answer. An examination of events in the four nineteenth-century suffrage states reveals a variety of motives that together caused a sufficient number of male legislators and voters to support woman suffrage. There *were* liberal-minded men who believed voting rights were an inherent right of citizenship; but pragmatic objectives, usually political ones, were necessary for enough men to vote for woman suffrage for it to become a reality. In short, women were enfranchised in the American West primarily as a matter of expediency, not ideology.

Move West and Vote

In the West, woman suffrage was often seen as a means to advertise a region in hopes of attracting settlers or investors. Sometimes it was proposed as a device to embarrass political opponents if they voted against it or vetoed it. Often, territorial residents saw it as a way to recruit Eastern support for their bids for statehood. When Black men, American-born Chinese men, and some Indian men voted, arguments for educated, property-owning, White women to have the same privilege appealed to many peoples' racial prejudices. Since the Rocky Mountain West was in the process of forming governments during the last quarter of the nineteenth century, the electorate had to be defined in the new laws and constitutions. Consequently, Westerners were forced to think about and debate the issue of who would be allowed to vote.

The fact that there was no significant, organized opposition in the four states (as there was from liquor interests in the states of Washington and California) made passage of legislation and referenda easier. Another contributing factor was the completion of the transcontinental railroad in 1869 that facilitated the quick transportation of people and ideas. Eastern lecture-bureau circuit riders, many of whom addressed women's issues, immediately toured the West, and Westerners traveled to the East more frequently and received news in a more timely fashion— including reports on Eastern debates regarding political rights for former slaves and women.

The existence of a post-Civil War woman suffrage movement also contributed to the early enfranchisement of Western women because Eastern suffragists kept the discussion of women's rights alive. It was in response to lobbyists' pressure for passage of a woman suffrage constitutional amendment that some Eastern newspapers and politicians proposed testing woman suffrage in the territories. Also, when campaigns were waged in the West, Eastern suffrage associations provided money and organizational expertise. Conversely, the suffrage movement as a whole benefited when strategies and campaign techniques were developed and tested in the Western states.

In 1867, when the Fourteenth Amendment defining national citizenship to include Black men was being ratified, a number of campaigns to amend state and territorial constitutions to provide for woman suffrage took place in the American West. The most vigorous effort was staged in Kansas where two amendments were proposed: one enfranchising Black men and one enfranchising women. Initially, the prospects appeared to be good because the 1861 Kansas constitution included school suffrage for women.[2]

Representing the American Equal Rights Association, the postwar organization advocating universal suffrage, Lucy Stone and her husband, Henry Blackwell, campaigned for a month in Kansas, and returned to Boston with optimistic reports that the Republicans had launched an irreversible movement for equal rights. However, this optimism proved premature. As the debate intensified, editors of national and local Republican and reform newspapers supported political privileges for Black men but failed to endorse equal rights for women. In the words of Horace Greeley, chair of the American Equal Rights Association, the extension of the franchise to women would be too revolutionary for public acceptance.

As the sunflowers blossomed in the late summer of 1867, Susan B. Anthony and Elizabeth Cady Stanton toured Kansas and found sentiment against woman suffrage growing. A month before the vote on the amendments, they were joined by George Francis Train, an avid Democrat and railroad financier, who brought money to the campaign. But association with Train caused abolitionists and Republicans to criticize severely Anthony and Stanton because Train used White supremacy arguments overtly to advance the women's cause. Responding to Republican critics, Anthony exclaimed: "Your test of faithfulness is the Negro, ours is the woman."[3]

Belatedly, many national newspaper editors tried to convince Kansas voters that the question was one of universal suffrage. Even Horace Greeley grudgingly acknowledged in his *New York Tribune* that while he regarded woman suffrage with distrust, he was willing to see it pioneered in Kansas.[4] Nevertheless, when the votes were tallied, both propositions failed. Neither women nor Black men were enfranchised as a result of the Kansas campaign in 1867.

Following the Kansas campaign, however, the woman suffrage movement adopted sunflower yellow as its campaign color, and the movement began to assume the form that it would take for the next quarter century. Feeling betrayed by the male equal rights reformers they had worked with for years before and after the Civil War, Stanton and Anthony launched a new organization in 1869 dedicated to woman suffrage, the National Woman Suffrage Association (NWSA), with headquarters in New York. They also founded a woman suffrage newspaper, *The Revolution*, which they used to oppose the Fourteenth and Fifteenth Amendments, advocating instead for suffrage for the educated, irrespective of sex or color. Immediate enfranchisement of all women through a federal constitutional amendment was their major focus. That same year, led by Lucy Stone, Henry Blackwell, and Julia Ward Howe, more moderate suffragists rallied to the banner of the American Woman Suffrage Association (AWSA) based in Boston. This group, which supported the Fourteenth and Fifteenth Amendments, endorsed the constitutional amendment for woman suffrage, but emphasized building support for woman suffrage in the states. This schism on goals and methods persisted until 1890 when the two factions merged into the National American Woman Suffrage Association (NAWSA).

Meanwhile, Congressmen continued to consider the idea of enfranchising women in the territories as an experiment. During the Kansas campaign, Hamilton Willcox, a representative of the New York Universal Franchise Association, proposed that women in *all* the territories be enfranchised, and *The New York Times* publicized this scheme for testing woman suffrage. Given legislative form by George Washington Julian, Republican Congressman from Indiana, the idea of women voting in the territories was appealing because it appeared to be safe from a political point of view.[5] Neither the political stability of the established states nor the national political scene would be seriously altered (since territorial residents were not allowed to vote for their own governors or the president), and the definition of the electorate could be reexamined by Congress when the territories applied for admission to the Union as states. Moreover, since Congress controlled the territories, the experiment could be halted if it went awry. And the possible defeminizing impact that politics might have on women and the impact women would have on politics could be tested safely.

In addition, Willcox and others predicted that woman suffrage would be advantageous in relieving the problem of "surplus women" in the East (more women than men available for marriage as a result of the Civil War casualties, a problem exacerbated by male migration to the West). The adoption of woman suffrage in the West, they believed, would encourage Eastern women to move to the frontier.[6] These men also predicted that woman suffrage would lead to the elimination of polygamy—the Utah Mormon practice of men marrying multiple wives.

Of course, population redistribution and Mormon plural marriage were not the primary concerns of women's rights advocates who insisted that women had inherent natural rights and demanded a constitutional amendment protecting women's political rights as the proposed Fifteenth Amendment protected the rights of freedmen. Yet, as the Fifteenth Amendment was approved, the proposed woman suffrage amendment and the proposal to test woman suffrage in the territories languished. Representative Julian's bill on woman suffrage in the territories was now limited to Utah Territory where the bill's sponsors hoped woman suffrage could eradicate polygamy—a "relic of barbarism."

While Eastern suffragists divided over the best means of attaining the vote and Eastern politicians contemplated the theoretical consequences of woman suffrage, however, women in the Rocky Mountain West were voting.

Women's Rights in Wyoming

In December of 1869, the Wyoming territorial legislature surprised the nation by passing a bill enfranchising women. While there was no organized suffrage campaign in this new territory with fewer than nine thousand residents of which only slightly more than one thousand were women of voting age, the arguments for woman suffrage were well known. Traveling on the newly completed transcontinental railroad, the lyceum bureau's stellar speaker, Anna Dickinson, visited Wyoming on her Western tour. And Redelia Bates, a woman suffrage lecturer from St. Louis, spoke to the Wyoming territorial legislature. In addition, Eastern debates over women's rights were covered by local newspapers. Yet, though there were individuals in Wyoming such as the suffrage bill's introducer, William H. Bright, who believed in women's right to vote as a matter of citizenship, the bill passed because lawmakers believed woman suffrage was a way to advertize

Women voting in Wyoming,
November 1888

LIBRARY OF CONGRESS

the territory to potential investors and settlers. Some Democrats thought it would embarrass the Republican governor, John A. Campbell, who would (they presumed) veto it, but he surprised them by quickly signing the law that even went beyond suffrage to allow women to serve on juries and hold public office.

A jubilant Susan B. Anthony reported the news of the enfranchisement of women in Wyoming to the suffragists assembled for the first NWSA convention. She urged women "to emigrate to Wyoming and make a model State of it by sending a woman Senator to the National Capital,"[7] though she planned to stay home and work for a federal constitutional amendment enfranchising all women. While Eastern women did not heed the call to go West, they did use the Wyoming example to urge their own state legislatures to extend equal rights to them and to encourage Congress to amend the Constitution.

In the summer of 1871, Stanton and Anthony went West to "the land of freedom," as they called Wyoming, where they were warmly greeted by government officials and leading citizens. Returning east in December, Anthony learned that some Wyoming Democrats, unhappy about the election of several Republicans, were trying to repeal the woman suffrage law. However, Governor Campbell vetoed the repeal act, saying, "No legislature has the right to disfranchise its own constituents."[8] When an attempt was made to overturn his veto, the members of the Council and the House divided along party lines defeating the measure by one vote.

As the first and only place where women voted and sat on juries, Wyoming was an object of curiosity. Easterners were eager to question travelers and Wyoming residents to determine what impact woman suffrage had on women and on society. Two years after passage of the law, Edward M. Lee (who reportedly had been removed as Secretary of Wyoming Territory for public drunkenness and enjoying the company of a prostitute known as "the Circassian Girl") told *The Galaxy* magazine that the powers of the ballot had not caused women to abandon any of their womanly or wifely qualities. As he saw it, the time-honored ordinance of marriage seemed to be as everlasting as the mountains; moreover, there were no signs of that "pestiferous freelove doctrine" that seemed to be gaining converts in the East.[9] At the 1874 NWSA convention, Aaron Sargent, a Congressman from California, praised woman suffrage in Wyoming "where women hold office, where they vote, where they have the most orderly society of any of the Territories."[10]

While Sargent was applauding the results of Wyoming women's new-found freedoms, however, a number of newspaper editors were questioning the experiment. When the *New York Independent* charged that only twenty-five women had voted in the last election, the AWSA investigated and its newspaper *The Woman's Journal* countered with assurances from citizens of Wyoming that women's participation in elections had "become a matter of course." Having observed women voting for four years, Governor Campbell testified he was convinced of the justice and wisdom of the measure. In 1888, the NWSA expressed its confidence in its convention banner proclaiming: "The vote of women transformed Wyoming from barbarism to civilization."

A year later, over one hundred Wyoming women demanded that woman suffrage be affirmed in the statehood constitution. Few convention delegates openly opposed woman suffrage, but nearly a third subscribed to the idea of separate submission (of woman suffrage and statehood) arguing that the citizens of Wyoming had not had an opportunity to vote on the proposition because voting rights had been granted to women by the territorial legislature. However, when the debates ended, woman suffrage was included, and two-thirds of the voters registered their support for the constitution. When Congress was about to reject Wyoming's admission into the Union because of the clause enfranchising women, Wyoming legislators telegraphed Congress saying they would remain out of the Union a hundred years rather than join without woman suffrage. Finally, the constitution was approved by a narrow margin with the controversial clause intact, and Wyoming became the first state to allow its female citizens to vote.

Utah Suffrage a Vote for Mormons

Two months after the 1869 passage of the initial woman suffrage bill in Wyoming, the Utah territorial legislature enfranchised Utah women. This move received considerable national attention because it admitted nearly forty times as many women to the polling places as had the Wyoming action; moreover, most of these women were members of the Mormon church that practiced plural marriage. Arguing that polygamy only existed where women were degraded, reformers predicted the ballot would be used to eradicate the practice. Even the NWSA proclaimed its confidence that the enfranchisement of women in Utah was the one safe, sure, and swift means to abolish polygamy. Reformers refrained, however, from claiming the vote would cause women to migrate to the territory because the Mormons promoted their marital system as a means to deal with "surplus women."

Generally, the national concern about Utah women amused the Mormons. Assuring readers that Utah women could vote "without running wild or becoming unsexed," George Q. Cannon, editor of the Mormon-controlled newspaper, the *Deseret News*, expressed pleasure in the opportunity to be an example to the world.[11]

The Mormons, of course, expected that woman suffrage would reinforce rather than undermine Mormon traditions. In fact, enfranchisement of women in Utah was primarily an effort by the Mormons to counter the image painted by lecture-bureau circuit riders of Mormon women as downtrodden slaves and to stop national efforts to eliminate polygamy. Furthermore, in 1870, just before the territorial legislature acted, reports arrived in Salt Lake City that Congress was considering a variety of threatening legislation ranging from schemes to partition Utah and give segments to the surrounding territories and states, to proposals to disfranchise the Mormons, disqualify them from holding public office and sitting on juries, and deprive them of the right to homestead or preempt public lands, or disinherit their children. Mormons were also concerned about new threats to polygamy; when enforcement of the anti-polygamy law of 1862 seemed imminent, five thousand women gathered in the Mormon Tabernacle on Temple Square for a "great indignation meeting" to decry the "mean, foul" legislation.

It was against this background that the Utah legislature passed the bill extending the ballot to women, and on February 12, 1870, the non-Mormon, Territorial Secretary S.A. Mann, serving as acting governor, signed the bill into law. Responding to a resolution of appreciation from a delegation of Utah women, Mann penned a letter philosophizing about the intelligent use of the ballot. Mormon faithful, William Clayton, was less philosophical when he noted, "The poor, enslaved downtrodden!!! women of Utah can now act for themselves and take revenge on the men of Israel." Then he gleefully exclaimed that those who expected Mormon women to use the vote against polygamy would "gnash their teeth with rage" and "foam worse than ever," for "there are not many women here but will sustain all the measures of the authorities [of the church] better than some of the men do."[12]

There were individuals in Utah in 1870 who advocated woman suffrage for liberal, human rights reasons, and there was some concern about non-Mormons coming into the territory now that the transcontinental railroad was completed. But the compelling reasons for passage of the legislation were related to polygamy and statehood. "Bah!" was the *Salt Lake Herald's* response to the accusation that the Mormon-dominated legislature gave the vote to women to strengthen Mormon political power against non-Mormons. With a total population of 87,000 of which only about 4,500 were non-Mormons, doubling the Mormon voting power was not necessary.[13]

Ironically, now that Mormon women had proven to be supporters of polygamy, Congress began to try to strip them of the franchise. During the 1870s and 1880s, Utah repeatedly petitioned for statehood as Congress continually proposed legislation designed to take voting privileges from Utah women as part of the anti-polygamy effort. And Mormons repeatedly reminded Congress that the idea of enfranchising women in Utah was being considered in the East when the Utah territorial legislature acted.

Using the church's women's auxiliary, the Relief Society, as the communications network, Mormon women became skilled at holding "mass meetings" and producing "mammoth petitions" in opposition to hostile legislation or in support of statehood. Utah women and the territory's delegate to Congress were in regular communication with national suffrage leaders and were able to solicit suffragists to lobby Congress on Utah's behalf.

In 1883, when Congress was considering a number of measures to "elevate" the women of Utah and "relieve" them from their "bondage" by repealing the territorial act conferring the vote, the Washington, D.C., attorney, suffragist, and soon-to-be presidential candidate, Belva Lockwood, launched an aggressive campaign against the legislation saying: "It is not only a fight for `Mormon' female votes—it is a contest for woman's equal rights in principle." Persuading the NWSA to adopt a resolution against the legislation, Lockwood declared: "Only a fool or a knave would deny" the bill is a direct blow at woman suffrage.[14]

When suffragists were accused by anti-polygamists of being in "an attitude not unfriendly to polygamy" and anti-polygamy societies reported that Mormon women voted as instructed by the church hierarchy, national suffrage leaders realized their image was being tarnished by identification with Utah women. Thus, Anthony went to great lengths to clarify that the NWSA's only interest in Utah was woman suffrage. As the concern with polygamy intensified in Congress, suffrage leaders continued their support of Utah women's voting rights while trying to distance themselves from polygamy.

Reverend Anna Howard Shaw, Henry Blackwell, and Mary A. Hunt presented the arguments of the AWSA to the House Committee on Territories, objecting to the proposed disfranchisement of Utah women. Instead, they petitioned for a law to give women equal suffrage in all the territories. In 1887, the NWSA urged President Grover Cleveland to veto the Edmunds-Tucker Bill that proposed to take the vote from Utah women. He responded by allowing the bill to become law without his signature.[15] And the national suffrage cause was set back further when Congress once again refused to pass the Anthony Amendment.

The suffrage movement and the NWSA in particular were greatly weakened by identification with the Mormons and their marital system. Belva Lockwood's defense of the Mormons brought the wrath of society down on the NWSA and the cause. In the 1870s, society had a similar negative reaction to feminist Victoria Woodhull who was opposed to legal and clerical marriage and instead advocated "free love" with the assumption that each woman had the right to decide whether, when, and with whom to become sexually active.[16] Women's rights advocates could no longer be critical of the institution of marriage without being accused of favoring polygamy. It was now necessary for feminists to shun all criticisms of marital and family relations and pledge their belief in the sanctity of monogamous marriage.

Elizabeth Cady Stanton and Susan B. Anthony's methods and philosophy lost credibility after 1887, and American feminism took a conservative turn. The state-by-state approach to gaining enfranchisement dominated the movement until 1914, and feminist critiques of marriage and women's roles in society were set aside as priority was given to securing the ballot. Susan B. Anthony continued to be revered, but a new and more conservative generation of suffragists emerged, and temperance was accepted as part of the movement in spite of warnings that it would rally liquor interests to work against woman suffrage. When the NWSA and the AWSA merged in 1890, only the women of Wyoming were enfranchised, because Utah women had lost the vote by Congressional action, and Washington women had, for the second time, seen their suffrage law declared invalid by that territory's supreme court.

While the relationship between women's rights leaders and the Mormons was strained, suffragists continued to visit Utah. In the spring of 1895, Anthony and Anna Howard Shaw led a three-day Rocky Mountain Suffrage Conference in Salt Lake City attended by women from Wyoming, Utah, and Colorado. National suffragists also assisted Utah women with the development of a territorial suffrage association—a step that seemed necessary because many Utah men were willing to abandon woman suffrage now that it could no longer be used to protect polygamy or advance the statehood cause. This became evident when Utah made a new bid for admission into the Union (still unsuccessful) with a constitution

Rocky Mountain Suffrage Conference, May 1895.
In the front row are Margaret N. Caine *(far right)* and Susan B. Anthony *(third from right).* In the second row are Zina D. H. Young *(second from right),* Emmeline B. Wells *(third from right),* Sarah M. Kimball *(fourth from right),* and Anna Howard Shaw *(fifth from right).* In the third row are Mary C.C. Bradford *(far right)* and Estelle Kesl *(third from right).* Theresa A. Jenkins is in the fourth row, *(third from right).* In the back row are Mattie Hughes Cannon *(far left),* Emily S. Richards *(fourth from left),* and Ellis Meredith Stansbury *(fifth from left).*

prohibiting polygamy and limiting suffrage to adult men.

The Utah feminist, Charlotte Ives Cobb Godbe Kirby, who was known for her radical rhetoric calling for women of the world to unite, wrote numerous articles and letters on behalf of the Utah Territory Woman Suffrage Association and sometimes vied with Emmeline B. Wells for the leadership role in the Utah woman suffrage movement.[17] Active on the local and nation-

Emmeline B. Wells

al scenes, Kirby and Wells were both involved in the discussion about woman suffrage in 1895 when the territory prepared to make a new bid for statehood and debated the provisions of the proposed state constitution.[18] However, two Mormon men, both of whom were historians and members of the Democratic party, led the convention debate over inclusion of women in the electorate. Brigham H. Roberts argued that women could not act independently because of relationships in the family; besides, he said, women are sufficiently represented in politics by husbands, fathers, sons, or brothers.[19] Orson F. Whitney, who compared Roberts to a bull standing in front of a train attempting to prevent it from passing ("I admire your courage but d__n your judgement"), insisted, "it is woman's destiny to have a voice in the affairs of government. She was designed for it. She has a right to it."[20]

Finally, Utah approved a constitution containing woman suffrage in 1895. Since the Mormon Church had officially abandoned polygamy in 1890, Congress approved the constitution with little protest about the enfranchisement of women, and President Cleveland did not raise the issue when he issued the proclamation admitting the territory of Utah as a state on January 4, 1896.

Colorado Suffrage, a Matter of Race

While polygamy was the major issue tied to woman suffrage in Utah, across the Rockies in Colorado racial concerns were predominant. The territorial legislature and newspapers had been discussing woman suffrage since the late 1860s, and Governor Edward M. McCook had called for Colorado to join its sister territory, Wyoming, as a leader in the cause of universal suffrage. Advocates argued it was taxation without representation when women were prohibited from voting. Opponents warned: women do not want to vote; involvement in politics might destroy "the symmetry of women's character"; only the class that goes to war should be allowed to vote; and the enfranchisement of women at this time is premature. But race was the major issue.[21]

Representative M.S. Taylor warned Colorado territorial legislators in 1870 that Black women, as well Chinese women, will vote if the woman suffrage bill passes.[22] After studying the legislation, a house committee chaired by Representative A.H. DeFrance urged passage and argued it was unfair for uneducated, non-property-holding Black men to vote on matters concerning the property of White women who were not allowed to vote. He went on to suggest that women's presence in politics would have a "purifying influence" on society and politics. It was in response to DeFrance that Taylor warned of the folly of allowing "Negro wenches" and Chinese women to vote.

Unmoved by petitions from women requesting suffrage, lawmakers refused to approve the legislation. Thus, DeFrance sought a compromise by proposing that the suffrage bill be submitted to the qualified electorate of the territory, including women, for ratification or rejection.[23] After considerable parliamentary maneuvering by the friends and foes of woman suffrage, Taylor moved for postponement, and the house effectively killed the bill by voting fifteen to ten to delay action.

Even though the legislative measure was dead, the debate was kept alive in the newspapers and was periodically enlivened by the visit of a suffrage speaker. In July of 1870, the Eastern actress and lecturer Olive Logan spoke in Denver, and one year later, Stanton and Anthony lectured to a responsive crowd in the Denver Theater. As Colorado drafted a constitution in preparation for admission as the Centennial State, woman suffrage was a major issue. Fearing rejection by the Colorado electorate or the national Congress, constitutional convention delegates limited women's involvement in the political process to school district elections, but provided for a vote on woman suffrage in the first general election after statehood.

Consequently, in 1877 a major campaign began to persuade the Colorado male electorate to fully enfranchise women. The Colorado Suffrage Association coordinated speaking tours throughout the state that included local advocates such as William H. Bright, who had initiated the suffrage bill in Wyoming and was now living in Denver, and many Eastern headliners. Susan B. Anthony stumped mining towns and outlying communities speaking in saloons, in hotel dining rooms, at railroad stations, and on a soapbox in front of a courthouse.

While newspapers in Denver generally supported the referendum, Pueblo's *Colorado Chieftain* editorialized against suffragists. Denver's Catholic Bishop Machebeuf continued his pulpit campaign against woman suffrage and was soon joined by the Presbyterian Reverend Bliss, who referred to suffragists as "bawling, ranting women, bristling for their rights." If women vote, he told parishioners, married women will live in endless bickering with their husbands and single women will never marry. On election day when Reverend Bliss encountered women handing out fliers urging men to vote in the affirmative, he identified himself and reiterated his objections to women voting. The AWSA's Lucy Stone countered, and a loud exchange ensued. Yet, when the day ended, Reverend Bliss's point of view was victorious; woman suffrage was defeated by a vote of two to one.[24]

Sixteen years passed before Colorado suffragists were once again able to get a referendum on the ballot in 1893—thanks to the support of Populist legislators and the Populist governor, David H. Waite. Colorado suffragists concentrated on converting male voters through newspapers and political parties. While they organized local suffrage leagues throughout the state, they limited the number of Eastern speakers invited to the state. When suffragists pledged their support of silver as a currency basis along with gold, miners and unionized workers seemed willing to support the referendum, and victory came within grasp when the Republican, Prohibitionist, and Populist parties endorsed equal suffrage. With strong support and little opposition the referendum passed.

National suffragists quickly seized Colorado as an attractive example because it had a large population and an urban center where the impact of women voting could be closely observed. Unlike Wyoming, Colorado did not have a reputation as a wild frontier with a high crime rate, and it was not tainted by polygamy as was Utah. Moreover, Colorado was unique as the first state to grant woman suffrage by referendum. The aggressive campaign methods used by Colorado suffragists with organizational and financial support from Eastern suffrage associations became the model for other states. The strategies of converting the male electorate through speeches, political parties, and public demonstrations, which were developed in Colorado under the guidance of NAWSA leader Carrie Chapman Catt, would be employed in other states, notably California and Idaho.

Idaho, Suffrage in Snake River Country

One year after women were enfranchised in Wyoming and Utah, Dr. Joseph William Morgan, a Democratic representative from Oneida County, announced that women in Idaho should enjoy the same rights and introduced a woman suffrage bill in the territorial legislature. However, Republican W.H. Van Slyke appealed to Blackstone's theory of the legal and political merger of the woman with the man upon marriage and warned, "that to give her the ballot would work an entire social revolution, disrupting the family tie, and bringing a conflict of sexes in the land."[25] When lawmakers put the issue to a vote, it resulted in a tie. Thus, Idaho's first woman suffrage bill died.

Occasionally, an Idaho suffragist would lecture or Abigail Scott Duniway,[26] the Oregon suffrage leader and editor of *The New Northwest* suffrage newsletter, would tour the territory speaking and soliciting subscribers, but for a decade and a half there was only limited discussion of woman suffrage in Idaho. Immigration, Mormons, prohibition, and woman suffrage were intertwined in a complex way in Idaho. One-fourth of the residents were Mormons, most of whom lived in Dr. Morgan's Southeastern part of the state along the Utah-Idaho border, and there

Abigail Scott Duniway
LIBRARY OF CONGRESS

were fears woman suffrage would give Mormons disproportionate political power because there were large numbers of women in Mormon settlements. Fearing voting rights for women might encourage more Mormons to move to Idaho some people reported: "The impression was getting abroad that Idaho was controlled by the leading Mormons in Salt Lake, and that this impression would tend to discourage [non-Mormon] immigration."[27] The underlying cause of most of this anxiety was political; at the time, most Mormons voted Democratic.

Concerns about prohibition posed a bigger problem for woman suffrage advocates in Idaho; Duniway and some other suffragists blamed the Woman's Christian Temperence Union (WCTU's) efforts to stop liquor traffic for a woman suffrage law being declared unconstitutional in Washington territory. Consequently, in 1889—when the constitutional convention was being lobbied to include woman suffrage and a clause prohibiting the sale of liquor—Duniway rushed to Boise. Arguing temperance and woman suffrage were not inexorably tied, she assured statehood constitution writers that women would not vote away beer and whiskey. However, delegates were more concerned that the document would not be accepted if Idaho was associated with the Mormons and woman suffrage than they were that women would use the ballot to bring about prohibition. Thus, both women and Mormon men were denied political rights and the opportunity to vote on the constitution that was submitted to the Idaho electorate and the United States Congress in 1890.

Abigail Scott Duniway, who now spent part of her time in Custer County, Idaho, where her sons had a homestead claim, thought woman suffrage would be submitted to the Idaho electorate in the first election after statehood as had been the case in Colorado. This did not happen, however. While Duniway, temperance advocates, and Mormon women worked in their own ways to advance the cause, six years passed before a woman suffrage amendment received the required two-thirds vote in the Idaho legislature. Anticipating that a major campaign was needed to persuade the electorate to support the amendment, Anthony told Duniway to leave suffrage in Idaho to the Eastern managers and to confine her activities to Oregon.[28] Thus, Emma Smith DeVoe of Illinois went to Idaho to manage the campaign, and Mell Woods, an active suffrage worker from Wallace, Idaho, (the daughter of the Utah's Mormon suffragist Emmeline B. Wells), was assigned to assist DeVoe.

Organizing local suffrage clubs as she traveled, DeVoe toured Idaho giving suffrage lectures. In November of 1895, delegates from these suffrage clubs converged in Boise to found the Idaho Equal Suffrage Association. Having just returned to her home in Buffalo, New York from California where she had worked

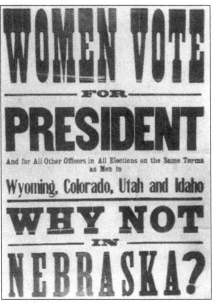

Flag with four stars representing states
where women could vote, c. 1900

SMITHSONIAN INSTITUTION

Poster from the
1911 Nebraska campaign

NEBRASKA STATE HISTORICAL SOCIETY

on that state's unsuccessful suffrage campaign, Anthony sent a telegram to Idaho suffrage conventioneers saying, "Women speakers can not reach them [male voters]."[29] Instead she advised Idaho suffragists to educate voters through political party newspapers and public meetings. Heeding Anthony's advice, Idaho suffragists organized for the upcoming campaign. In the spring of 1896, Laura M. Johns, a campaign organizer from Kansas, was coordinating activities in the Southwest part of the state. Helen Young, a lawyer from Wallace, Idaho, was in charge of the Northern part of the state, and Blanche Whitman of Montpelier was responsible for rallying the predominantly Mormon communities in the Southeast region, where Mormon men were now allowed to vote.

This approach minimized regional tensions and allowed suffragists to focus on gaining support for political rights for women. In their resolutions urging support for the amendment, Idaho suffragists pointed to the examples of women voting in the neighboring states, and called forth the principle of no taxation without representation. Appealing to racial biases, suffragists argued that White, native-born American women should be at least equal in political rights with Chinese men, who if born in the United States were allowed to vote, and Indian men, who under the the 1887 Dawes Act [dividing Western Indian reservations into individually owned land] were allowed citizenship and voting rights. In her Fourth of July speech, suffragist Laura M. Johns referred to the enfranchisement of Nez Pierce Indian men and said she believed, "Women were as much entitled to privileges of citizenship as those savages."[30] NAWSA organizer Carrie Chapman Catt, who had refined campaign strategies in Colorado, came to Idaho during the summer to assist the Idaho association's advisory board with the preparation of instructions to the local suffrage clubs. As the election approached, most of the state's newspapers declared their support, and all four political parties—Populists, Democrats, Republicans, and Silver Republicans—endorsed the amendment.

On election day men cast 12,126 votes in support and 6,282 against. However, before celebrations proclaiming Idaho the fourth woman suffrage state could be staged, the board of canvassers ruled the measure was defeated because it had not received a majority of all votes cast in the election, just a majority cast on the amendment. Determined, the Idaho suffrage association commissioned lawyers, William E. Borah and James H. Hawley, who would eventually become Idaho's senator and governor, to carry the issue to the Idaho Supreme Court where the ruling was favorable. Idaho now joined the ranks of suffrage states.

Woman suffrage was realized in Idaho in 1896 because the political parties (especially the Populists) as well as the Mormons and the WCTU supported it, and there was no significant organized opposition from liquor interests as there was in the Pacific Coast states. Idaho suffragists perfected campaign techniques developed in Colorado that proved to be the major strategies of the women's movement for the next quarter century. In 1897, Catt instructed the NAWSA conventioneers to study the Idaho methods and improve them, for: "Until we do this kind of house-to-house work we can never expect to carry any of the states in which there are large cities."[31]

Four Experiments Examined

Idaho was the last and the least famous of the nineteenth-century woman suffrage states. The Wyoming experience was the best known and the longest tested. While the Utah example was considered anomalous by some as a result of the association of polygamy, Colorado—with its large population and urban center—was considered the most reliable test of suffrage strategies and suffrage itself.

Suffragists gathered data on the four states in an attempt to demonstrate the positive impact of woman suffrage. They concluded from their findings that women's involvement in politics had resulted in calmer and more orderly polling places, in the selection of candidates of higher moral character, in better schools, in more moral and sanitary legislation, and in making "intemperance and other bad habits unpopular."[32] More colorful, but less positive conclusions appeared in popular publications. The well-known Western novelist William Macleod Raine reported access to polling booths had not "unsexed" women, and they had not "regenerated the world" with their ballots.[33] Examining the experiences in the Rocky Mountain states, the editor of the Utah *Deseret News* found the promised purification of politics had "not panned out to any very extraordinary extent";

"The Awakening" is a well-known illustration by artist Henry Mayer. Lady Liberty strides across the Western states where women already had the vote, toward the East, where women are reaching out to her. Mayer's illustration was the centerfold of a special suffrage issue of *Puck* magazine, guest-edited in 1915 by New York suffrage groups. Library of Congress

moreover, partisanship had "taken hold of the lady voter with equal if not greater force than" it had the men.[34] As one Colorado woman phrased it: "They vote with men, and for men, and just about like men."[35] A writer for *Pearson's Magazine* concluded women had used the ballot to do "nothing revolutionary, startling, uplifting, or sensational."[36]

Woman suffrage is usually viewed by historians as a middle-class reform movement; this view holds in the early experiences in the West. Most leaders and supporters of the movement in the four Rocky Mountain states were White, Protestant, protectors of the community. There was some identification of woman suffrage with temperance and Populism, but generally woman suffrage in the American West was not led by people who sought to overthrow or even radically reform the established social, economic systems. Even in the cases where the Populist Party was a prime force in bringing about their enfranchisement, after a year or two, women tended to vote for the more conventional political parties. Most Western suffragists held conservative political views and defended tradition, especially the role of wife and mother.

Arguments for and against political rights for women were often based on racist assumptions in the last quarter of the nineteenth century, in the West as elsewhere in the nation. Since White women were generally better educated and often owned property, it was argued, they should not be the political inferiors of Black, Chinese, or Indian men. The emotional appeals of equal rights workers and politicians that "my wife" or "my mother" is surely as good as a Black man were provocative, and the cry of White women's superiority to Indians and Chinese had a special appeal in the American West. On the other hand, an often-heard condemnation of woman suffrage was that Black women, Chinese women, and Indian women could not be kept out of the voting booths if women were enfranchised. These arguments were frequently used by Westerners and by Eastern politicians and suffragists who kept woman suffrage alive on the national scene.

The fact that a national suffrage movement existed in the East and that governments were in a formative stage in the West also contributed to the establishment of women's rights during the last three decades of the nineteenth century. The West was a dynamic, evolving region. Railroads ended the isolation, the frontier was closing, and territorial status was being traded for statehood. In those days of boosterism, Westerners were promoters; so it was natural for them to seize on a non-threatening scheme such as woman suffrage as a means to publicize their regions and hopefully attract settlers, investors, and support for their admission to the Union as states.

The fact that Wyoming and Utah were territories in 1869 and 1870 allowed for quick enactment of woman suffrage. Once a territorial legislature approved a bill, only the governor's signature was needed for it to become law. Moreover, when Westerners were writing statehood constitutions and preparing themselves for self-government, they had to think through and vote consciously on a form of government including a definition of the electorate.

Certainly, there were liberal, egalitarian-minded individuals in the West who supported woman suffrage for human rights reasons, but enfranchisement became a reality as a result of expediency. The motives of the legislators and governors responsible for enfranchising women were usually conservative and political rather than progressive, ideological, and egalitarian. These men were not afraid that Western women would use the ballot to reform society or seize political power; after all, with the exception of Utah, there were not many women.[37] Moreover, in these four regions, women had not formed significant social reform movements. Even the WCTU was not considered a serious threat.

Fourteen Years to Light the Other Forty-Four States

After the 1896 amendment of the Idaho constitution, however, it was fourteen years before Wyoming, Utah, Colorado, and Idaho, were joined by another suffrage state and a new star was added to the woman suffrage flag displayed annually at the national suffrage meeting. Yet, when at last the woman suffrage movement emerged from its string of defeats and began to win battles in the states, the first victories *again* were in the American West. In 1910, Washington added its star to the suffrage flag, followed by California in 1911, Oregon, Arizona, and Kansas in 1912, the Territory of Alaska in 1913, and Montana and Nevada in 1914. Thus, at the beginning of World War I, woman suffrage existed in eleven Western states and the territory of Alaska. It would be seven more years before the Nineteenth Amendment would be ratified in 1920.

Notes

1. This essay is based on Beverly Beeton's book *Women Vote in the West: The Woman Suffrage Movement, 1869-1896*, published in the American Legal and Constitutional History series, edited by Harold Hyman and Stuart Bruchey, Garland Publishing, New York, 1986.
2. Ellen Carol DuBois, *Feminism and Suffrage: The Emergence of an Independent Woman's Movement in America, 1848-1869* (Ithaca, 1978).
3. Elizabeth Cady Stanton, Susan B. Anthony, Matilda J. Gage and Ida H. Harper, eds. *History of Woman Suffrage*, 6 vols. 1881-1922. (Reprint edition, New York: Arno, 1969), 2: 264, (hereafter, *HWS*).
4. *New York Tribune*, October 1, 1867.
5. *HWS* 2: 324-325.
6. In the post-Civil War years there was a great deal of concern about what the newspapers called the "surplus women" problem. Yet census data for 1890 reveals that there were 32,067,880 men in the nation and only 30,554,370 women. It seems to have been a problem more of perception than reality; to the extent that a marriage gap existed, it was a matter of age and geographical distribution, not of actual numbers.
7. As quoted in Katharine Anthony, *Susan B. Anthony: Her Personal History and Her Era* (New York, 1954), 248.
8. Hamilton Willcox, pamphlet, "Wyoming: The True Cause and Splendid Fruits of Woman Suffrage There from Official Records and Personal Knowledge correcting the errors of Horace Plunkett and Professor Bryce and supplying omissions in the *History of Woman Suffrage* by Mrs. Stanton, Mrs. Gage, and Miss Anthony, and in the *History of Wyoming* by Hubert Howe Bancroft with other information about the state." (New York: November 1890), 17, Bancroft Library, Berkeley, Calif.
9. Extract from *The Galaxy* article, 13 (June 1872): n.p., located in the Susa Young Gates papers, Widtsoe Collection at the Utah State Historical Society, Salt Lake City, Utah.
10. *HWS* 2: 545.
11. *Deseret News*, February 15, 1870.
12. William Clayton to Brother Jesse, and Clayton to Brother East, February 13, 1870. Clayton Letterbooks, Bancroft Library.
13. In *The Puritan Ethic and Woman Suffrage* (New York, 1967), Alan P. Grimes, employing status anxiety techniques similar to those developed by Richard Hofstadter, argues that "the constituency granting woman suffrage was composed of those who also supported prohibition and immigration restriction and felt woman suffrage would further their enactment." Grimes errs in his analysis when he reads backwards into history. The issues of prohibition and immigration restriction were not significant factors in Wyoming, Utah, Colorado, and Idaho when woman suffrage was enacted there.
14. Belva A. Lockwood's speech before the NWSA, January 24, 1883, as printed in the *Ogden Daily Herald*, June 9, 1883.
15. *Salt Lake Herald*, January 29, 1887; and *Deseret News*, March 4, 1887.
16. In *Everyone Was Brave: The Rise and Fall of Feminism* (Chicago, 1969), William L. O'Neil argues that suffragists' identification with Victoria Woodhull and her views on monogamy made it impossible for women's rights advocates to be critical of the institution of marriage without being accused of favoring free love. The same thesis is valid when applied to Lockwood and the identification with polygamy.
17. Beverly Beeton, "'I Am an American Woman': Charlotte Ives Cobb Godbe Kirby," *Journal of the American West*, 27 (April 1988): 13-19.
18. See Jean Bickmore White article, *Utah Historical Quarterly*, 42 (Fall 1974): 344-69.
19. Brigham Henry Roberts autobiography, copy of manuscript at Utah State Historical Society, Salt Lake City, Utah, 117-78.
20. O.F. Whitney speech, March 30, 1895, *Men and Woman* (May 14, 1895): 10-12.
21. William B. Faherty, "Regional Minorities and the Woman Suffrage Struggle," *Colorado Magazine* (July 1956), 1.
22. "Speech of M.S. Taylor on Suffrage," *Colorado Transcript*, January 26, 1870.
23. Billie Barnes Jensen, "Woman Suffrage in Colorado," M.A.

thesis, University of Colorado, 1959, 20-21.
24. *HWS* 3: 723.
25. *Idaho Statesman*, January 10, 1871; also see the January 5, 1871 issue.
26. Abigail Scott Duniway's *Path Breaking: An Autobiographical History of the Equal Suffrage Movement in Pacific Coast States* (Portland, Oregon, 1914) is a detailed record of events in Idaho; however, Duniway had her prejudices and made herself and her point of view most important in her narration of events. *HWS* 4: 589-97 has a chapter on the suffrage campaign in Idaho written by two participants—Eunice Pond Athey and William Balderston, editor of the *Idaho Statesman*.
27. An article from the *Avalanche* as cited in the *Idaho Democrat*, a Mormon newspaper published in Southern Idaho, March 24, 1883.
28. T.A. Larson, "Woman's Rights in Idaho," *Idaho Yesterdays* 16 (Spring 1972): 2-15, 9. Larson published numerous articles on woman suffrage in the West. The most detailed version is "Emancipating the West's Dolls, Vassals and Hopeless Drudges: The Origins of Woman Suffrage in the West," in Roger Daniels, editor, *Essays in Western History in Honor of T.A. Larson*, v. 37 (Laramie: University of Wyoming Publications, 1971).
29. As quoted in *Idaho Statesman*, November 21, 1895; also see, Anthony Diary, November 18, 1895, in the Library of Congress, Manuscript Division, Washington, D.C.
30. *Caldwell Tribune*, July 4, 1896; also see, "Equal Suffragists' Desires," in the Equal Suffrage Association of Idaho file, Idaho State Historical Society, Boise, Idaho.
31. *HWS* 4: 293.
32. For detailed information on the impact of woman suffrage in the four states see Beeton, *Women Vote in the West*, 136-156.
33. As quoted in *Deseret News*, February 13, 1902.
34. *Deseret News* editorial, October 12, 1906.
35. Priscilla Leonard, "Woman Suffrage in Colorado," *Outlook*, 55 (March 2, 1897): 791.
36. Ike Russell, "What Women Have Done with Votes," *Pearson's Magazine*, n.d., 538, clipping in The Church Archives, Historical Department of the Church of Jesus Christ of Latter-day Saints, Salt Lake City, Utah.
37. The census data for 1870 indicates that when woman suffrage was being considered in the four territories the population was approximately 9,000 in Wyoming, 87,000 in Utah, 40,000 in Colorado, and 15,000 in Idaho. Utah was the only place where women represented nearly half of the total; in the other territories women composed one-fourth, or less, of the population.

Eight

FRANCES WILLARD
and the Woman's Christian
Temperance Union's Conversion
to Woman Suffrage
Carolyn De Swarte Gifford

Editor's Introduction: In the early 1880s, the woman suffrage movement received one of the most important endorsements in its history when the new president of the Woman's Christian Temperance Union (WCTU), Frances Willard, "converted" the WCTU to the suffrage cause. Willard thus brought into the movement large numbers of moderate women who were activists and would labor mightily for the "Home Protection Ballot"—women who otherwise might have avoided association with woman suffrage in an era when its national leaders were considered by many to be radical if not disreputable.

Carolyn De Swarte Gifford, editor of *"Writing Out My Heart": Selections from the Journal of Frances E. Willard, 1855-1896* and author of several articles on Willard and the WCTU, explains here that converting the WCTU to woman suffrage meant redefining the influential image of the "True Christian Woman." It meant convincing women that their God-given duty was to use their moral influence for good in the larger society—not just in the home as tradition required.

This was no easy task in late nineteenth-century America. Several generations of women had been influenced by a flood of prescriptive literature defining the "True Woman" as (in the words of historian Barbara Welter), "pure," "pious," "submissive," and "domestic." Most American women and men assumed that women were innately more religious than men and morally obligated to exercise influence for good in the world—but only through woman's "indirect influence" over husbands and children in the home. It was widely believed that participation in public affairs, particularly in the disreputable world of politics, would rob women of that very innocence and ignorance of evil that so inspired men to rule wisely for their sakes.

As early as the 1870s and 1880s, however, the women of the WCTU experienced the disillusionment with "indirect influence" that later converted many women reformers to the suffrage cause during the Progressive Era, which began around 1900. The WCTU women were convinced that their crusade would not succeed until women were enfranchised; and they insisted that if women were (as most people believed) morally superior to men, it was their *solemn duty* to enter the political arena and clean it up—if only to protect the home.

Thus many evangelical Christian women were "converted" to woman suffrage, and convinced—like Frances Willard—that God had called them to serve the cause of woman suffrage as well as temperance. Through the WCTU, the influential concept of the True Woman was revised and expanded to include, as Gifford writes, the "public space" beyond the home. The WCTU, which in the late nineteenth century was the largest woman's organization yet in existence, had branches in twenty-one countries, and opened new doors for countless women. This was true even in the South, a stronghold of evangelical Christianity and conservatism, where resistance to expansion of woman's role was strong. Not every woman in the WCTU became a suffragist; but hundreds of thousands responded to Willard's message that it was not only *acceptable* to work for woman suffrage—it was their Christian duty.

The endorsement of woman suffrage by the WCTU was a mixed blessing for the cause, however, as it attracted a formidable opponent, the liquor industry. The so-called "whisky interest," composed of brewers, distillers, distributors, and saloon keepers, often combined forces with other industries that felt threatened by woman suffrage and spent heavily to defeat it. Carrie Chapman Catt and Nettie Rogers Shuler, in their 1923 retrospective *Woman Suffrage and Politics: The Inner Story of the Suffrage Movement*, devoted an entire chapter to the "corrupt manipulations" of American politics by the liquor industry. The industry, claimed Catt and Shuler, "dictat[ed] terms to parties and politicians," "kept Legislatures from submitting suffrage amendments," "organized droves of ignorant men to vote against suffrage amendments at the polls," and "restrained both dominant parties from endorsing woman suffrage,"—an "invisible and invincible power that for forty years kept suffragists waiting for the woman's hour." The "forty years" to which Catt and Shuler referred were the years between 1880, when the WCTU endorsed woman suffrage, to 1920 when suffragists were at last victorious.

★　★　★　★　★

THE SIXTH ANNUAL CONVENTION of the Woman's Christian Temperance Union in November 1879 promised fresh direction for the organization. Its newly elected leader, Frances E. Willard, a young, vigorous educator from the West, advocated woman suffrage as the means necessary to insure prohibition. The choice of Willard as president indicated that many WCTU leaders supported her suffrage position, a stance well known to them (and to her opposition within the organization) since she had been speaking about it publicly for several years. The WCTU could expect to enter the new decade of the 1880s faced with a difficult task: convincing its rapidly growing membership of mainly evangelical Christian women that woman suffrage was not a radical idea espoused by women whose behavior was at least questionable, if not outrageous. The vote for women must be made acceptable, respectable, and in fact a part of woman's duty as a Christian. For this to occur the image of the True Christian Woman had to be redefined and broadened to include enfranchisement. This redefinition began for many WCTU members through a religious experience that they described as a conversion to woman suffrage. They claimed that God called them to work for the vote for women. Increasingly during the 1880s, evangelical women entered the struggle for woman suffrage, convinced that it was God's will that they do so.

Redefining True Womanhood

In 1880 the WCTU suffrage goal must have appeared as a vision far off in the future. Nevertheless, WCTU leaders began a campaign for woman suffrage throughout the country. Willard and other WCTU organizers traveled thousands of miles by rail and horse-drawn wagons stumping for the twin aims of prohibition and the vote for women. As they tirelessly crisscrossed the United States with their message, *Our Union* (after 1882 *The Union Signal*), the official organ of the WCTU, began to print a barrage of articles, editorials, columns, and letters, pushing woman suffrage from every angle that might appeal to its readership. Through the decade of the 1880s the organization labored to persuade its members that woman's sphere should be widened to include numerous activities believed by most Americans to be the prerogative of men.

Frances Willard announced the widening of woman's sphere in what became a favorite motto of the WCTU: "Woman will bless and brighten every place she enters, and she will enter every place."[1] The first half of the motto was not particularly alarming since "brightening every place she enters" had been woman's traditional duty and, moreover, her greatest pleasure, if one could believe the volumes of prescriptive literature written for and by women throughout the nineteenth century. The second half of the motto might prove disconcerting, however, if one grasped its full import. It boldly stated that women intended to move from the private, domestic sphere into the public world. Although the motto was constructed in the declarative rather than the imperative mode, as befitted a ladylike statement, Willard meant what she said. She was to spend her many years as WCTU president working out with determination her conviction that women belonged in every place, whether it be in the pulpit and in delegations to national church conferences or in the voting booth and in the conventions of national political parties. She envisioned a limitless space for women's abilities and talents.

Willard faced a dilemma in the 1880s: how was she to encourage and enable others to share in her vision for women? How would she inspire WCTU women to examine and reinterpret prescriptive images of woman that had shaped their lives? What motivation would compel evangelical women to work slowly and at times painfully toward a redefinition of the Christian woman?

There is power for change as well as for proscription inherent in symbols and images since they are, by their very nature, capable of revealing new depths of meaning and lending themselves to nuances of interpretation. Particular persons and specific historical contexts may shape and alter traditional symbols and images, reinvesting them with further content and renewed vigor. Such a process of change occurred in the image of the True Christian Woman during the decades of the 1870s and 1880s. Certainly it had begun earlier in the century, but the women and men who initiated the task were often isolated from one another or involved in reform goals other than that of re-visioning woman's image. Other more radical women's rights reformers such as Elizabeth Cady Stanton and Susan B. Anthony, failed to evoke images of woman that appealed to the majority of mainstream evangelical Protestant women who were more timid and loath to challenge the status quo, than Stanton and Anthony.

Frances Willard
LIBRARY OF CONGRESS

In order to understand how vast numbers of WCTU women accepted a redefinition of the True Woman image that included enfranchisement, it is necessary to follow several lines of investigation. First, one must examine the image of woman current in the evangelical milieu from which most of the WCTU women came. Second, one must determine how closely the image or ideal of Christian womanhood conformed to the realities of women's lives. Third, one must assess the ways in which influential leaders such as Frances Willard were able to infuse ideals and images with new possibilities of content and meaning. Finally, one must seek to discover what other forces were at work in the last third of the nineteenth century, in both the church and the larger world, which might call forth or allow for enlarged roles for women. In short, one must try to recreate the historical moment in which the image of woman was opened up to dimensions previously unthinkable and thus unattainable for the majority of American evangelical Protestant women during the nineteenth century.

The Traditional Meaning of True Womanhood

These evangelical Protestant women who filled the ranks of the "white ribbon army" of the WCTU proudly displayed the tiny emblem of their membership on respectable, drab-colored, high-collared dresses. The simple grosgrain ribbons, in white to symbolize the purity of the True Woman, identified those who wore them as sisters battling for prohibition, but also for the elevation of women in all areas of their lives. Quite often the white ribbon was entwined with a yellow ribbon signifying woman suffrage.[2] Both colors were worn proudly and in many cases with more than a hint of defiance. And no wonder, since these women were daring to stand up to the mighty weight of centuries of Christian tradition which taught that women were subordinate to men and to be governed by them, and therefore women had no justification for demanding the enfranchisement of their sex.

The authority of scripture was unquestionable for evangelical woman. They had grown up hearing, reading, and believing that the Bible, the word of God, decreed the dominant/subordinate male/female relationship. God had created it so, and Eve's rebellious refusal to obey God's word served to emphasize woman's fundamental irresponsibility with the corresponding necessity for male governance. The Pauline Epistles elaborated on woman's subordinate status, enjoining wives to submit to their husbands and ordering all women to keep silent in church. Along with the biblical injunctions came enormous numbers of sermons, homilies, home Bible study groups, and advice books based on biblical texts, which commented further on the attitudes and activities proper to the True Christian Woman. Often these commentaries included warnings to women who overstepped the bounds of woman's sphere, putting themselves in danger of becoming "unwomanly."

The editorial page of the February 1880 issue of *Our Union* featured an article containing such a warning, which was reprinted from an Indianapolis newspaper. The first paragraph of the article quoted from a Sunday evening sermon given November 2, 1879, by the Reverend J. Saunders Reed, priest of St. Paul's Episcopal Cathedral in Indianapolis. Reed had delivered his message just as the National WCTU, meeting in the same city, decided to embrace the goal of woman suffrage. He was obviously disturbed by the public behavior of women.

> It worries, it angers, it disheartens me to see women thrusting themselves into men's places and clamoring to be heard in our halls and churches. A woman-man I have always nauseated and loathed; but, oh, from a man-woman I would make haste to get me away as from a monstrosity of nature, a subverter of society, the cave of despair, the head of Medusa, a bird of ill-omen, a hideous specter, a travesty of all that is sacred and divine.[3]

Here was an example of a vicious verbal assault on women who ventured beyond their proper place. Why would the editors of *Our Union* choose to print such a diatribe, one invoking symbols and images that had served for centuries to proscribe women's activities and confine them to a restricted sphere?

Reed attacked women who entered the public arena, that "male territory" of church pulpit and lecture hall, and probably the city council and state legislature as well, since WCTU members had already appeared before these bodies seeking the passage of prohibition legislation. He accused women who acted in this manner of breaking down sanctified gender expectations, assuming male prerogatives, and thereby becoming masculinized. Such an accusation could not be shrugged off lightly by a generation of women who had been socialized to understand that women and men were created by God for different though complementary tasks and spheres. Usurping a role of the opposite sex was deviant behavior as Reed so clearly charged. The woman who stepped out of her space was unnatural, even monstrous. She risked destroying the social order; worse, in committing "a travesty of all that is sacred and divine" she sinned willfully against God's plan for creation.

Reed's rhetoric played upon the powerful prescriptive symbol of the woman as Other—shameful, sinful, and, finally, less than fully human. In an age that was familiar with classical Greek mythology, he called up the horrible image of Medusa with her grotesque face surrounded by ringlets of writhing serpents, a monster turning those who looked upon her to stone. He might as effectively have chosen a biblical symbol of woman as Other—Eve, Mary Magdalene, Jezebel—whose mere mention would have served the same purpose as the name of Medusa, suggesting to his listeners woman's potential for unnaturalness and wickedness. Moreover, the priest was not alone in his opinion of woman's proper sphere and the qualities of those who overstepped its bounds. Undoubtedly the majority of Americans agreed with him. Even as late as 1879 few women had the courage to challenge the men (and women as well) who employed such evocative symbols of deviance and evil to keep women in their place.[4] Wouldn't the editors of *Our Union* have been wiser to leave this attack on "the public woman" out of the WCTU paper? Why not downplay such virulent criticism by ignoring it? But the editors of *Our Union* were neither stupid nor naive; rather, they were quite shrewd. They had an excellent reason for printing Reed's thoughts on the "man-woman."

The sermon excerpt had originally appeared as the lead paragraph in an article by a reporter covering the WCTU national convention for the *Indianapolis Journal*. The entire piece was printed in *Our Union*. In it, the *Journal* reporter took Reed to task for his statements and ridiculed him for being "angered, disheartened and worried" by such women as J. Ellen Foster, Mary Livermore, Mary T. Lathrop, Annie Wittenmyer, and Frances E. Willard, the convention's leaders. These women and others, according to the reporter, were the equals of any minister in an Indianapolis pulpit: "They were logical, forcible and concise, and held the attention of an audience from their first utterance to the close. They were conservative and sensible—much more so than a like number of men have usually been when convened on a similar occasion."[5] The writer thus captured in a paragraph the tone and demeanor that the WCTU as an organization would assume throughout the 1880s. He went on to accuse Reed and those who held similar opinions about woman's sphere, of being "many generations behind the age." The article closed with a veiled challenge: "The men have not all the brains, nor all the morals, nor all the religion, and should not be afraid to compete with the women in any place they can fill with equal ability and propriety."[6]

The interplay of Reed's attack and its vigorous rebuttal by a newspaper completely independent of the WCTU served an important strategic function. The points made in the article, though thoroughly endorsed by the union, did not appear to be special pleading by a self-interested group. The newspaper labeled as old-fashioned those who conformed to the prevalent attitude toward women and pronounced a rallying cry for WCTU women in the 1880s. Although this particular challenge came from the *Indianapolis Journal*, it was in fact similar to many such challenges and exhortations from the WCTU leaders to the membership that were regularly printed in *Our Union* and *The Union Signal*. Through its national newspaper as well as through its leaders' speeches, the WCTU directly confronted the issue with which nineteenth-century American women struggled: the binding force of the American religious-cultural tradition whose institutions interlocked to uphold the image of the ideal woman as pious, pure, domestic, and submissive, shut up in the private sphere of the home and its extension, the church.[7]

Many of the women who joined the WCTU spent all their time in their homes and their churches. These two areas were literally their lives. Even as late as the 1870s only a few exceptional women had rebelled against this pleasant prison, woman's sphere. Indeed, many enjoyed and took pride in their womanly tasks. Nothing could be more satisfying they felt, than providing a haven of peace and rest from the cares of the world for the True Man, counterpart of the True Woman. If the True Woman was to be dependent, passive, yielding, the True Man, her complement, was to be independent, aggressive, and a good provider for his family.

The earliest issues of *Our Union* abounded with descriptions of the gentle wife as the "soul force" of the home, welcoming her weary husband back to his domestic retreat and comforting him after his day of battle with the bustling economic enterprises of the nation. In this shelter she was also to nurture her children in a pure, protected environment. The frequency of these cloying portrayals moved Mary A. Livermore, Massachusetts WCTU leader and woman suffrage worker, to dismiss the contents of the paper as "pious blarney."[8] Yet alongside these glorifications of the home as haven, *Our Union* printed gruesome cautionary tales depicting the disintegration of families and homes through the drunkenness of husbands and fathers. It ran true stories, contributed by readers, about young boys eight or nine years old "led down the road to ruin" by saloon keepers who tempted them with liquor-filled candies and free lunches. Always the tales included descriptions of helpless wives and mothers wringing their hands and weeping but unable to do anything to stop their men and boys from the onslaught of "Demon Rum." The apparently naive and unintended juxtaposition of the ideal of True Man and True Woman with the stark reality of women's actual experience pointed out the failure of many families to live up to the expectations generated by powerful ideal images.

Clearly a terrible tension had developed between the ideal and the real. Such tension had always existed, but events during the 1870s brought many women to the point of admitting the strain they felt themselves or observed in other women's lives. Male alcoholism was a key factor in creating this tension. Men who were drunkards often did not support their families and thus did not live up to the responsibilities of the True Man. Indeed, they were apt to abandon their families for long periods of time while they went on "binges," a pattern that one contemporary historian has described as a uniquely American phenomenon.[9] Women were unprepared to support their families economically and were thus in dire circumstances if the family wage earner disappeared or became disabled through chronic alcoholism. Excessive alcohol consumption had long been an American characteristic. Alcohol consumption had fallen in the decades just before the Civil War, partly through the efforts of the temperance movement. But it rose again rapidly during and after the war, and the number of saloons per capita grew as well. Faced with an intolerable situation, women acted in protest. In the winter of 1873-74 occurred the Ohio Women's Crusade, a spontaneous series of praying demonstrations by women aimed at forcing saloon keepers to shut down their establishments. In a welcoming address to the Fifth Annual Convention of the California WCTU in 1884, a member reminded the delegates of the crucial significance of the crusade as the start of a consciousness-raising process for women. As the news of the praying bands of women spread rapidly by telegraph throughout the nation:

> Men read and laughed and sneered; women, busy women stopped their work, read the strange lines, thought and lifted up their hearts to God in prayer. Had the time come for women to take the forefront in the battle against intemperance? Was it right? Had she not learned, and learned at her mother's knee that home is woman's sphere? Home her only safe abiding place?
>
> But on the other hand, had she not through long years been the sufferer? It was her frame that blighted and withered under the curse of this vile traffic. No wonder she was ready for acting. No wonder she sprang to the front.[10]

What had been implicit earlier in the pages of *Our Union*—the discontinuity between the ideal of the True Woman in her home and the awful reality of many women's lives—became explicit. Woman was not "safe" in her home. The lessons about womanhood that generations of mothers had taught their daughters were being seriously questioned. Woman was not necessarily the "queen" of the domestic realm; she was, in far too many cases, its victim. The corrupt world that she had attempted to shut out of the home invaded her supposedly pure, inviolate space, often through the saloon and its influence. Saloons were not a part of most women's experience. For many they epitomized male and thus public territory. The decision to move from the private to the public sphere, to assail the enemy on his own ground, was a tremendous and frightening one for women. Yet clearly, as the quote suggests, they were fed up with their situation. And just as clearly, they believed they were being called by God out of their homes into active temperance agitation.[11]

The Traditional Meaning Loses Its Power

The women of Ohio were temporarily successful in achieving their goals. Some saloon keepers actually closed their businesses and took up other lines of work or moved West, at times assisted by crusade women who provided them with small sums of money to make a new start. During the crusade, however, women discovered to their dismay how powerless they really were. They had been taught that the moral and spiritual influence they exerted over men was enormous though indirect, and thus consistent with their subordinate status. While women provided pure home life and noble Christian example, men would somehow carry that atmosphere with them into the halls of government and law and guide public life accordingly. Believing this, the Ohio Crusade women, going to court on behalf of wives who were beaten and abandoned by drunken husbands, expected to find a sympathetic hearing. When they attempted to prosecute liquor dealers under statutes that made dealers responsible for selling liquor to known drunkards, they found that the male-run judicial system figuratively (and often literally) laughed in their faces. Occasionally, at the local level where a woman did wield some influence through her husband's position, a guilty verdict was brought against a liquor dealer. But it was swiftly appealed and thrown out in appellate court.[12] When women appeared before city councils and state legislatures all over the country lobbying for various prohibition measures, they encountered male reactions ranging from polite boredom to sarcastic ridicule to open hostility. In fact Reed's sermon, quoted earlier, was typical of the hostile reactions women provoked.

At first the women were merely puzzled. They had been told that they were the guardians of morality. Sometimes it was even suggested that women were spiritually and ethically superior to men, and yet they were ignored, ridiculed, or verbally attacked by men when they attempted to raise ethical issues in saloons, courtrooms, and legislatures. Some WCTU women discovered that men found it convenient to let women attend to morality while they attended to business, law, and politics. There was, in effect, a double standard of morality in regard to the public and private spheres.

Women became painfully aware that they and their spiritual, moral influence were not welcome in men's public life. Many husbands instructed their wives, politely and no doubt gently, to stay where they belonged—at home. There women could be as pious and pure as they pleased. And men could get on with the work of the public world, where the values of home and woman seemed not to operate. Many women sensed that a deep ethical split had occurred between the public and private spheres. Different moral systems prevailed in the two separated sectors.

Drusilla Wilson, president of the Kansas WCTU, addressed herself to the conflict that had developed between women's private and men's public values, as she spoke about her leadership of Lawrence, Kansas women who knelt on the floors of saloons, fervently praying that saloon keepers would stop selling liquor.

Indelibly stamped upon some of our minds during the Crusade was the need of Prohibition, for then some of us learned that the [liquor] traffic was a child of the law. Woman saw it was inconsistent for our fathers and brothers and husbands to make laws protecting [liquor traffic] and the women follow in the wake pleading with men thus licensed [to sell liquor] to quit the business. A change must be brought about.[13]

Obviously, what many women viewed as moral—temperance, in this instance— did not accord with what the men in their own households believed to be in the interests of good business.

Wilson also emphasized what would become increasingly evident to the WCTU organization during its first decade (1874-84): "following in the wake pleading" was not an effective long-term strategy for reform. Women questioned both the dignity and the efficacy of such tactics. Drusilla Wilson, in her reserved Quaker manner, had described the methods as "inconsistent." Other women were humiliated and extremely angered by the failure of praying and pleading, typical women's tactics, to move men to support temperance reform measures. Their humiliation reflected their recognition of women's total powerlessness in the public sphere. It also reflected women's consternation in the face of the breakdown of the ideal complementary relationship of True Man and True Woman in the ethical realm.

Additionally, women began to perceive that although they were placed on a pedestal in much male rhetoric and there honored, adored, and cared for, men showed little actual sympathy for women who were victims of their dependent status, left without ways to support themselves and their children when men abandoned them. Nor did men really seem to take seriously women's ethical concerns, women's thoughts, women's activities, or women in general. It was a cruel hoax to be placed on a pedestal and dismissed with laughter, and women did not like it. Again and again in their accounts of temperance work, references appear to the indignation women felt when men found their public appearances, both praying and pleading, occasions of humorous diversion. Apparently the True Woman image functioned for many men only as a way to keep women from meddling in the male world. It was no longer an ideal they believed in but a convenient mechanism to put women in their place and out of men's way.

If this were the case, women would not be able to accomplish their temperance goals. They had to depend on male cooperation with their reform efforts, since these efforts increasingly involved legislative measures for prohibition. With few exceptions, in the 1870s and 1880s women could not vote and were not members of legislative bodies. If they were not able to persuade men to vote for prohibition they could pray and plead, but to no effect. Definitely, as Drusilla Wilson maintained, a change must be brought about.

Woman suffrage was the change for which Wilson and other WCTU leaders called.... Furthermore, as evangelical Christians they had to be able to justify their political and suffrage activity religiously. It was absolutely essential for them to believe that their behavior sprang from an experience that convinced them that God wanted them, indeed called them, to vote.

God Calls WCTU Women to Vote

During the nineteenth century, the individual conversion—a personal experience of God's saving power and will for one's life—was a weighty source of authority for religious behavior. Revivals centering on such conversions were a fundamental characteristic of American evangelical Protestant life. Within such a religious climate, if one claimed to receive a changed, reinterpreted image of woman as the content of the conversion experience, the claim would be difficult for another to challenge, particularly if the challenger shared a belief in the possibility of individual conversion. Many WCTU women came from a background of revivalism. The Ohio Women's Crusade, which came to be looked upon as the formative event for the WCTU, had strong revivalistic features, including the participants' testimony that they received a pouring out of the Holy Spirit upon them, a fresh baptism of power renewing and deepening the baptism they had previously received upon entry into the Christian faith.

Frances Willard herself claimed to have experienced God's call to advocate woman suffrage. As she traveled through Ohio in the winter of 1876 organizing for the WCTU, she took time out from her hectic schedule for Bible study and prayer on Sunday morning:

> Upon my knees alone, in the room of my hostess who was a veteran Crusader, there was borne in upon my mind, as I believe from loftier regions, the declaration, "You are to speak for woman's ballot as a weapon of protection to her home and tempted loved ones from the tyranny of drink."[14]

Not only did Willard hear God's will that she work for what she labeled "The Ballot for Home Protection," she also received "a complete line of argument and illustration"[15] for her first speech on Home Protection which she delivered later in the year at the Woman's Congress in Philadelphia and at the National WCTU Annual Meeting in Newark.

An intense wave of revivalism led by Dwight L. Moody was sweeping through America's large Eastern and Mid-western cities during the 1870s. Willard worked with Moody in Boston for a short time during the winter of 1877 but left his revival circuit to devote her energy to her own methods of temperance reform. In a letter to

Moody's wife explaining why she was leaving, Willard set forth her differences with Moody's approach to the temperance aspect of his revivals. He expected and sought individual regeneration with an accompanying pledge by the saved person to drink no more. Willard noted sharply in her letter that Moody emphasized the regeneration of men and that she as a woman found his approach inadequate. She advocated the WCTU goals of prevention through education and legislation especially, she wrote, "putting the ballot in woman's hand for the protection of her little ones and her home."[16] Willard saw no distinction as Moody did between the religious activity of revival and the political activity of securing temperance legislation. A Christian, she felt, should work through any and every means available and consonant with her faith to reform the world and its institutions as well as individual believers. She understood no separation between the public and private spheres; both were arenas for reform and they overlapped. Women must strive for the reform of society in all its aspects and one of the most powerful means toward this aim was woman suffrage. In order to be effective reformers, women must have the ballot. After all, had not God himself validated this means of reform in Willard's personal religious experience "on her knees in prayer"?

For the next two years Willard "evangelized" for her belief in woman suffrage, managing to persuade a significant number of WCTU leaders and a portion of the membership of the rightness of her position. She became president in November 1879, an event that signaled the beginning of the National WCTU campaign for endorsement of a suffrage position among its member state organizations.

On January 1, 1880, *Our Union* featured the story of "One Woman's Experience." It was nothing less than a paradigmatic example of a conversion, that form of religious experience so prevalent in American Protestant life. However, its content was quite unusual. The anonymous writer claimed a conversion to woman suffrage:

> It would sound very strange and far-fetched to many ears, even absurd, that a woman should be morally and religiously converted to Home Protection. I feel I was actually converted by the Lord's Spirit, and led to a deeper feeling, if not a deeper knowledge of the truth.[17]

She described her attendance at a WCTU Annual Meeting, where, for the first time, she had the opportunity to see and hear the "consecrated women" who led the organization. She was convinced of the sincerity of their efforts in temperance reform and of their selfless dedication to the cause.

She contrasted their demeanor with her impressions of others who advocated woman suffrage. She had come to the convention believing that suffragists were "party aspirants and women who were always howling over the wrongs of woman, and the Lord had been so good to me I did not think women had such a hard time after all; nor in fact, do I now."[18] Her attitude toward suffragists was typical of that of many WCTU women. They saw them as self-serving power seekers whose activities went beyond the bounds of propriety and who thus did not conform to the image of True Womanhood.

WCTU women were not iconoclastic. They had not abandoned or destroyed the ideal of True Woman but were in the process of dealing with some of its negative, prescriptive aspects and seeking to broaden and re-vision its possibilities. Thus they were frightened of radical suffragists who seemed to go too far, to act too boldly, and to take anticlerical, antireligious positions. Historians Nancy F. Cott and Ellen Carol DuBois have created a phrase to describe the change in religious attitude more radical suffragists underwent: "de-conversion," meaning "ideological disengagement from the convincing power of evangelical Protestantism (or inability to accept the whole of it)."[19] In contrast, one might call the experience of many WCTU women "re-conversion," an intense conviction that God demanded yet more from women, further consecration that would lead them toward places and forms of activity formerly thought off limits. "One Woman's Experience" continues with a vivid description of just such a "re-conversion."

> I had thought I had consecrated myself to the Lord, to work for Him both in the Church and in Temperance work; I thought I was willing to use any weapon for truth, justice and virtue He should place in my hand. But when I came into convention, the conviction kept forcing itself upon me that I was not wholly consecrated to His service: I was not willing to do anything and everything for Him. There was that fearful ballot woman "unsexing herself," etc., etc., according to Dr. Bushnell, whose arguments you know, and of which every letter I have hitherto endorsed.[20]

"De-conversion" implies a sharp breaking away, a definite denial of one's former tradition; "re-conversion" indicates not a rupture, but rather a deepening or re-dedication of one's life to God's service in new ways.

The Dr. Bushnell to whom the anonymous writer referred was the Reverend Horace Bushnell, a leading nineteenth-century evangelical theologian, dead for three years by the time this article was written, but whose thought obviously still wielded tremendous influence over American churchgoers. He had written a book, *Woman Suffrage: The Reform against Nature*,[21] which developed the argument that man was to govern, woman to be governed, and thus that woman could not vote since voting was governing. His views on woman's unsexing herself by the act of voting (woman as unnatural, as other) were so well known that the writer assumed she did not have to elaborate on them for her readers. And yet she was able to defy such a powerful theological figure on the strength of her personal experience of God's call to vote.

Her conversion did not come easily. She mentioned nights of "waking and weeping," during which God allowed her to "gather up her prejudices [against woman suffrage] as a bundle and lay them aside." She felt her conversion as an easing of heart and conscience, accompanying her decision to work for woman's vote as an expression of God's will for her. Historian Donald M. Scott, in his article, "Abolition as a Sacred Vocation," describes the conversion to a reform, using as his example the position of Immediatism held by radical abolitionists. "Immediatism," Scott writes, "was less a program of what to do about slavery than, in evangelical terms, a 'disposition,' a state of being in which the heart and will were irrevocably set against slavery.... Immediatism became a sign of whether or not one was a saved Christian in abolition circles." [22] Although the reform is different, the "disposition" of the convert is very similar to that described in "One Woman's Experience." Belief in woman suffrage for Home Protection signified for a large number of WCTU members the deepest commitment to temperance and to woman. The belief in temperance was assumed, but support for woman suffrage became the mark of a truly consecrated worker.

Testimonies of conversion to woman suffrage multiplied on the pages of *Our Union* as WCTU women throughout the country felt a clear call from God to support the ballot for women as a means of Home Protection. A "Home Protection" column, running throughout the 1880s in *Our Union* and *The Union Signal*, carried reports of state and local efforts for woman's vote in school, municipal, state, and territorial elections and referenda. Each new gain was celebrated on the pages of the WCTU paper and announced in meetings where it was greeted with a restrained but enthusiastic waving of handkerchiefs and the singing of the "Temperance Doxology." A Boston prayer meeting in January 1880 with several hundred women and men present was described as exceeding the great revivals of Moody in the felt presence of the Holy Spirit. [23] At the end of a long day of prayer women left the church with petitions in their hands, determined to canvass Boston for woman's limited right to vote on the single issue of prohibition.

Mary A. Livermore wrote one of the more dramatic accounts of a conversion to woman suffrage in a memorial eulogy for a Massachusetts WCTU leader. Livermore quoted a letter written in the woman's last illness and addressed to the membership of the Massachusetts Union.

Standing on the threshold of the better land, I see more clearly. I would like to urge the dear workers in our great cause to acquaint themselves more fully with the evil that destroys the beauty and glory of our nation. The desire comes strongly to me to entreat them to put aside all narrowness and prejudice in their methods of work. Dear sisters, hold yourselves open to conviction! If the ballot were in the hands of women as a temperance measure, it would be powerful for the overthrow of the liquor traffic. *Then do not fight against the movement to give the ballot to woman "lest haply you be found fighting against God."* [24]

The women of the Massachusetts WCTU were not noted at that time for their enthusiastic support of woman suffrage. But surely the deathbed pleading of one of their own would make them reexamine their "prejudices," particularly when their dying sister strongly hinted that they might be defying God by not supporting the ballot for Home Protection.

The True Woman as Voter

WCTU women were beginning to reverse the arguments used against them by those who warned that woman's voting would be an act of rebellion against God. With the strength and validation they gained from personal experience of God's will for them, the women were able to stand up to persons who cited the authority of scripture against woman's moving outside her sphere. Writings and speeches began to include many references to women of the Old and New Testaments who served God through entering the public sphere and engaging in the religious and political processes of their times. Deborah, judge of the people of Israel and leader of its armies, was a great favorite. Zerelda Wallace from Indiana, head of the WCTU franchise [suffrage] department during the 1880s and an outspoken supporter of woman suffrage, was fondly referred to as "the Deborah of the franchise movement."[25] Biblical women served as models of courage and power for WCTU women who were attempting to initiate new modes of behavior. They did not intend to question the authority of scripture but to enlist the weight of scripture in support of what they had experienced as the will of God for them. In doing so, they launched upon an extensive hermeneutical task as they pored over scriptural passages for fresh insight into their meaning.

WCTU speakers and writers began to place Galatians 3:28 ("There is neither Jew nor Greek, there is neither bond nor free, there is neither male nor female: for ye are all one in Christ Jesus" [KJV]) alongside Paul's more restrictive passages in recognition that the Bible lent itself to differing interpretations and emphases. Jesus was hailed as the friend of woman and, more boldly, as her Emancipator.[26] The WCTU had a number of excellent preachers in its membership, and these women filled pulpits across the nation speaking on temperance and other issues of concern to women. Wherever the National WCTU Annual Meeting was held, arrangements were made so that WCTU women spoke in as many churches as would receive them. Often over fifty women preached both Sunday morning and evening to packed sanctuaries. In their sermons they delivered powerful alternative understandings of scripture that inspired their listeners to re-vision woman's possibilities.

Thus the image of the True Woman went through a process of extensive reinterpretation in the 1880s. As more and more WCTU women experienced a "re-conversion" to woman suffrage, they could imagine the True Woman as a voter and her sphere as extending out from her home to include the public space beyond. The WCTU encouraged its members to try out their newly claimed power

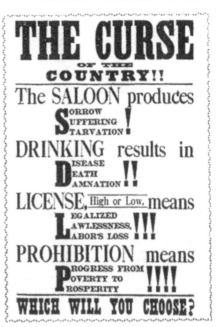

Frances Willard

FRANCES WILLARD MEMORIAL LIBRARY

Prohibition poster

WOMAN SUFFRAGE MEDIA COLLECTION

and define new roles for themselves. The WCTU functioned, historian Estelle Freedman notes, as "a strong public female sphere...mobiliz[ing] women [to gain] political leverage in the larger society."[27] As such it became far more than a temperance organization....

Frances Willard and other leaders repeatedly emphasized that the WCTU was a sisterhood that brought together women from all areas of the nation, as well as an educational endeavor that prepared them for intelligent and responsible participation in public life. As Willard declared in 1885:

> Our WCTU is a school, not founded in that thought or for that purpose, but sure to fit us for the sacred duties of patriots in the realm that lies just beyond the horizon of the coming century. Here [at the close of the nineteenth century] we try our wings that yonder [in the twentieth century] our flight may be strong and steady. Here we prove our capacity for great deeds. There we shall perform them.[28]

In this "school" WCTU members would be "educated up to the level of the equal suffrage movement" where there would be "no sex in citizenship."[29]

...The WCTU had struggled for nearly two decades reinterpreting the traditional image of woman.... The WCTU women were not discouraged from their suffrage goals by suggestions of unnaturalness or accusations of unwomanly behavior, as they had been earlier. Their deep conviction that God called them to work for the vote for women enabled thousands of WCTU members to accept wholeheartedly Frances Willard's challenging statement to them: "Woman will bless and brighten every place she enters, and she will enter every place." For the WCTU in 1890, this was a vision in the process of becoming a reality.

Notes

This is a shortened version of Gifford's original article entitled "Home Protection: The WTCU's Conversion to Woman Suffrage," that appeared in *Gender, Ideology, and Action: Historical Perspectives on Women's Public Lives,* Janet Sharistanian, ed., (Greenwood Press, 1986), 95-120, and is reprinted with permission of Greenwood Publishing Group, Inc., Westport, CT.

1. Frances E. Willard, "Work of the W.C.T.U.," in Annie Nathan Meyer, *Woman's Work in America* (New York, 1891), 410. Also see Frances E. Willard, annual address at St. Louis NWCTU Convention, in *The Union Signal,* October 30, 1884, 2.

2. In "Politics and Culture in Women's History: A Symposium," *Feminist Studies* 6, no. 1 (Spring 1980): 26-64, Ellen DuBois and Mari Jo Buhle referred to the WCTU as a key organization for understanding the nineteenth-century woman's movement. Buhle identified the twenty-year period from 1870 to 1890 as an important gap which historians needed to fill in from a feminist historical approach. Subsequent scholarship on the WCTU included: See Ruth Bordin, *Woman and Temperance: The Quest for Power and Liberty, 1873-1900* (Philadelphia, 1982); Barbara Leslie Epstein, *The Politics of Domesticity: Women, Evangelism and Temperance in Nineteenth Century America* (Middletown, Conn., 1981); and, Jack S. Blocker Jr., *"Give to the Winds Thy Fears": The Women's Temperance Crusade, 1873-1874* (Westport, Conn., 1985).

3. "They Say: From Four Standpoints," *Our Union,* February 1, 1880, 1.

4. Ellen Carol Dubois, in *Feminism and Suffrage: The Emergence of an Independent Women's Movement in America, 1848-1869* (Ithaca, 1978), mentions Elizabeth Cady Stanton's 1869 meeting with Bloomington, Ill., women who had been reminded by a clergyman of their inferiority to men. Stanton reports (in *History of Woman Suffrage,* 2: 372) that she had to moderate her usually radical stance in the face of the women's resulting demoralization. Over a decade later, the situation had not much changed.

5. "They Say: From Four Standpoints," *Our Union,* February 1, 1880, 1.

6. Ibid.

7. Barbara Welter, *Dimity Convictions: The American Woman in the Nineteenth Century* (Athens, Ohio, 1976); Nancy F. Cott, *The Bonds of Womanhood: "Woman's Sphere" in New England, 1750-1835* (New Haven, 1977); and Kathryn Kish Sklar, *Catharine Beecher: A Study in American Domesticity* (New York, 1976) on the antebellum cult of True Womanhood and women like Catharine Beecher who sought to make of woman's sphere a shaping force for American society. See Carolyn De Swarte Gifford, "For God and Home and Native Land: The WCTU's Image of Woman in the Late Nineteenth Century," in Hilah F. Thomas and Rosemary Skinner Keller, eds., *Women in New Worlds: Historical Perspectives on the Wesleyan Tradition* (Nashville, 1981): 310-27.

8. Mary A. Livermore to Frances E. Willard, November 21, 1876. WCTU National Headquarters Historical Files (joint Ohio Historical Society-Michigan Historical Collections), WCTU microfilm edition, roll 11.

9. William J. Rorabaugh, *The Alcoholic Republic: An American Tradition* (New York, 1979), 163-68. See also Jacquie Jessup, "The Liquor Issue in American History: A Bibliography," in Jack S. Blocker, Jr., ed., *Alcohol, Reform and Society: The Liquor Question in Social Context* (Westport, Conn., 1979): 259-79; and Bordin, *Women and Temperance,* intro., chpts. 1 and 2.

10. "News from the Field," *The Union Signal,* October 2, 1884, 11.

11. Gifford, "For God and Home and Native Land," 8, 9, 15.

12. See Eliza Daniel Stewart, *Memories of the Crusade: A Thrilling Account of the Great Uprising of the Women of Ohio in 1873, against the Liquor Crime,* (Columbus, Ohio, 1889).

13. *Minutes of the Fourth Annual Meeting held at Burlingame, Kansas, September 27, 28, 29, 1882,* State Woman's Christian Temperance Union of Kansas, (Burlingame, Kans., 1882), 11.

14. Frances E. Willard, *Glimpses of Fifty Years: The Autobiography of an American Woman* (Chicago, 1892), 351.

15. Ibid.

16. Ibid., 360.

17. "One Woman's Experience," *Our Union,* January 1, 1880, 3.

18. Ibid.

19. Cott, *Bonds of Womanhood,* 204, n. 10.

20. "One Woman's Experience," 3.

21. Horace Bushnell, *Woman Suffrage: The Reform against Nature,* (New York, 1869).

22. Donald M. Scott, "Abolition as a Sacred Vocation," in Lewis Perry and Michael Feldman, eds., *Antislavery Reconsidered: New Perspectives on the Abolitionists* (Baton Rouge, 1979), 53, 54, 72.

23. "Home Protection," *Our Union,* February 1, 1880, 3.

24. "In Memoriam" by Mary A. Livermore. For Mrs. Lucinda B. Barrett of the Massachusetts WCTU in *The Union Signal,* July 3, 1884, 2. Emphasis added. The phrase "Lest haply you be found fighting against God" paraphrases Acts 5: 39 (KJV).

25. "Annual Convention," *Our Messenger,* December 1887, 4.

26. In *Our Messenger,* September 1887, the Wichita, Kans. WCTU announced that it was sending Rev. Hana's leaflet "Jesus Christ, the Emancipator of Women" to every minister in town.

27. Estelle Freedman, "Separatism as Strategy: Female Institution Building and American Feminism, 1870-1930," in *Feminist Studies* 5, 3 (Fall 1979): 513.

28. Frances E. Willard, Address to the Woman's Congress at Des Moines, Iowa, 1885, as quoted in Annie Nathan Meyer, *Woman's Work in America,* 408.

29. Ibid., 404. "No sectarian in religion, no sectionalism in politics, no sex in citizenship" was a popular slogan of the WCTU.

Nine

BRINGING IN THE SOUTH:

Southern Ladies, White Supremacy, and States' Rights
in the Fight for Woman Suffrage

Marjorie J. Spruill

Editor's Introduction: There were distinct regional patterns in the history of the woman suffrage movement. It developed in the Northeast, an offshoot of the antislavery movement. The West provided the movement's crucial first victories. However, the South was notorious in the history of the woman suffrage movement as the region where the movement encountered the most resistance and experienced the least success.

In this essay, Marjorie J. Spruill, one of the first historians to focus on the Southern suffrage movement and place it in a national context, describes how and why an organized woman suffrage movement developed in such an inhospitable cultural and political climate, and why it failed to thrive, almost costing suffragists a national victory.

In the 1890s, a newly unified National American Woman Suffrage Association (NAWSA), committed to winning enough states that victory for a federal woman suffrage amendment was not only possible but inevitable, turned its attention to the South. NAWSA leaders understood that they faced a major challenge. To the elite White Southern men then seeking to restore White political supremacy in the region, Southern White womanhood—the symbol of racial purity whom Southern White men were bound to honor and defend—belonged on a pedestal and not in politics. Moreover, the suffrage movement was anathema owing to its antislavery roots.

There had been suffrage societies in the South during Reconstruction—the work of both White and African American women—that sent delegates to national suffrage conventions. The fact that these earliest suffrage groups in the region were the work of White "carpetbaggers" and "scalawags" in Virginia, and Black women active in Reconstruction-era politics in South Carolina, however, had only strengthened White conservative Southerners' disdain for the suffrage movement and reinforced their idea that advocacy of women's rights and the rights of African Americans were connected.

White Southern conservatives who perceived the Fifteenth Amendment as having been forced upon them during Reconstruction were infuriated in 1878 when suffragists from the Northeast demanded a similarly-worded Sixteenth

Amendment calling for federal protection of the voting rights of women. A few "respectable" White women of the South had dared speak out in favor of female enfranchisement in the 1870s and 1880s, but as the 1890s began, there was no organized suffrage movement in the region.

Beginning in 1892, however, a regional suffrage movement developed as a small number of White Southern women stepped up and assumed leadership of this unpopular cause. Working together, these Southern suffragists and national leaders developed a strategy they believed would succeed even in the inhospitable South.

In the first phase of the Southern suffrage movement from 1892 to 1903, most of its leaders were elite White women who sought enfranchisement primarily through amendments to state constitutions or through the new state constitutions adopted during that era. Later, between 1909 and 1916, a much larger and more diverse contingent of Southern suffragists took up the fight for enfranchisement through state action. When all of these efforts failed, most, but not all of these women, joined national leaders in supporting a federal suffrage amendment.

However, regional hostility to the suffrage movement frustrated Southern suffragists in their efforts to become enfranchised through either state or federal action. Before ratification of the Nineteenth Amendment in 1920, Southern women did not gain full enfranchisement in even one Southern state and gained partial suffrage in only four. In Congress, Southern politicians managed to block passage of the federal suffrage amendment for many years and after it was submitted to the states, made a concerted effort to prevent ratification—despite the pleas of regional favorite son President Woodrow Wilson to support the amendment for the sake of the National Democratic Party.

When victory ultimately came in 1920 through the Nineteenth Amendment, it was won with the support of four Southern states that broke ranks with the otherwise "Solid South": Kentucky, Texas, Arkansas, and the crucial thirty-sixth state, Tennessee, that ratified the amendment by just one vote. Nine of the ten states that refused to ratify were South of the Mason-Dixon line. Several Southern states passed "rejection resolutions" denouncing the federal amendment variously as "unwarranted," "unnecessary," "undemocratic," and "dangerous."

The struggle for woman suffrage in the South has received far less attention than the history of the movement in other regions. Yet, as Spruill makes clear, a full understanding of the suffrage movement in the United States requires examining its history in the region where it was least successful. In this essay, she explains why the South was so hostile to the suffrage movement, why certain Southern women signed on to lead this unpopular fight, and why and how they thought they could win it. She also explores the profound impact of race and states' rights issues, which rendered state victories in the region difficult if not impossible, and nearly prevented ratification of the Nineteenth Amendment in 1920.

★   ★   ★   ★   ★

IN 1892, KENTUCKY SUFFRAGIST Laura Clay issued a stern warning to the leaders of the National American Woman Suffrage Association (NAWSA): "Since we claim to be national let us never forget that the South cannot be left out of our calculations. You have worked for forty years and you will work for forty years more and do nothing unless you bring in the South."[1]

The woman suffrage movement, Clay realized, had begun in the Northeast and had spread to other sections of the nation. But in 1892, most White Southerners remained hostile to the movement as a product of an inferior Northern culture that, anti-suffragists insisted, had no place in the sunny South, the land of chivalry and devoted respect for women. Yet, as Clay said, the NAWSA would need support from all regions of the United States if it wanted to achieve a "national" victory. A woman suffrage amendment to the Constitution would have to be approved by two-thirds of each house of Congress and three-fourths of the states.

With this in mind, NAWSA leaders took Clay's advice to "launch their bark in the Southern sea." The NAWSA's "Southern Committee" headed by Clay, brought together a handful of Southern women already known to be suffrage sympathizers and recruited many more, especially seeking Southern White women with prestige and influence. The committee solicited and distributed funds, circulated suffrage literature, and dispatched NAWSA organizers into the region. By 1895, they had organized every Southern state. Together, Southern suffragists and their NAWSA allies launched a suffrage campaign designed to succeed in the South's exceedingly inhospitable political climate where the "Southern Lady," White supremacy, and state sovereignty were sacrosanct and perceived to be under attack.[2]

Laura Clay
LIBRARY OF CONGRESS

Why the South Was Last and Least

The unyielding opposition of the majority of White Southerners to the woman suffrage movement resulted from several interrelated cultural, political, and economic factors. The Southern suffrage movement took place from 1890 to 1920, a time when most White Southerners were devoted to preserving what they saw as a distinct and superior "Southern Civilization." They often spoke of defending the values of "the Lost Cause," those for which they claimed Confederate soldiers had fought in "the War Between the States"—most notably White supremacy and states' rights. As one regionally prominent minister put it, they were eager that the "victory over Southern arms" not be followed by "a victory over Southern opinions."[3]

A key element of this Southern Civilization most White Southerners wished to preserve was a dualistic conception of the natures and responsibilities of the sexes that precluded the participation of women in politics and cast "the Southern Lady" as the guardian and symbol of Southern virtue. Charged with transmitting Southern culture to future generations as well as inspiring current statesmen to serve as their noble defenders, Southern womanhood had a vital role to play in preserving the values of the Lost Cause. A leading Lost Cause minister, Albert Bledsoe, urged Southern women to shun the fruit offered by the women's rights movement and take as their "mission" not to "imitate a Washington, or a Lee, or a Jackson," but to "rear, and train, and educate, and mould the future Washingtons, and Lees, and Jacksons of the South, to protect and preserve the sacred rights of woman as well as of man." In addition, leaders of burgeoning industries of the New South, particularly the textile industry, wanted Southern women to confine their beneficent influence to the home rather than vote for child labor legislation and other encumbrances that would adversely affect business growth and profits.[4]

In the eyes of White Southerners, the cornerstone of Southern Civilization was White supremacy, and their determination to restore White domination of politics—and then defend the state sovereignty thought necessary to preserve it— also presented a tremendous obstacle to the Southern suffrage movement. Most viewed the women's rights movement as yet another unfortunate product of an inferior Northern culture that they were trying to resist—one led by Northern women with the abolitionists' "naive" and dangerous belief in equality. Southern suffragists were scolded for playing into the hands of social "levelers" who had no understanding of the crucial social distinctions of gender and race that accounted for the superiority of Southern Civilization, and for unwittingly complicating ongoing efforts to restore and protect White supremacy. Southern anti-suffragists charged that suffragists failed to recognize that the proposed federal woman suffrage amendment was nothing more than a "reaffirmation of the Fifteenth Amendment" and that its ratification would not only signal acceptance of Black suffrage, but also concede the right of the federal government to determine suffrage qualifications in the states.[5] In 1919, during the ratification battle, a leading anti-suffragist, James Callaway, editor of the *Macon (Georgia) Telegraph*, clearly articulated these sentiments:

> May our Southern women remain on the pedestal, forever preserve that distinctive deference which is theirs so long as they remain as they are—our highest ideals of the true, the beautiful and the good.... Deference to its womankind has always been a distinguished characteristic of the Southern people. Southern men would perpetuate it. But foreign forces have invaded us, established branches over the South of a huge National Woman's Association whose ideals are not our ideals; whose women are not like our Southern women. They are women of a different clay, and are of different mould. Should these

foreign crusaders succeed, pervert the tastes of our women, persuade them to abandon their old ideals and descend into the arena of politics... woe is the day for Southern civilization.[6]

Even after President Woodrow Wilson became convinced that woman suffrage was inevitable and that the Democrats must not allow the Republicans to claim credit for the victory, he could not convince most Southern congressmen or state legislators to support woman suffrage. Surrender of principle in anticipation of defeat was not an acceptable alternative to these children of the Confederacy who had grown up amidst tales of the heroic sacrifices of their ancestors. The majority of Southern politicians believed that their constituents required them to fight to the last ditch and then some.[7]

The Making of Southern Suffragists

The Southern women willing to embrace woman suffrage, indeed to become leaders of such an unpopular cause, were formidable individuals. In their 1923 reflective, *Woman Suffrage and Politics*, Carrie Chapman Catt and Nettie Shuler observed, "No stronger characters did the long struggle produce than these great-souled Southern suffragists. They had need to be great of soul."[8] Catt and Shuler meant, of course, that advocacy of woman suffrage in such an inhospitable climate was character-building; but the leaders of the woman suffrage movement in the Southern states had to have unusual self-confidence and determination in order to take up this cause in the first place.

It was no coincidence that the most prominent leaders of the Southern suffrage movement were the descendants of the region's social and political elite. This pattern contrasted with suffrage leaders in other parts of the nation who were more often from middle-class backgrounds. In addition to Laura Clay, the so-called "Susan B. Anthony of the South," a crucial intermediary between Northern and Southern suffragists, there were other prominent Southern women who enlisted. Among them were the Gordon sisters, Kate and Jean, "silk-stockinged reformers" from New Orleans; Nellie Nugent Somerville, daughter of one of Mississippi's most prominent attorneys who was revered by Whites for his role in restoring "home rule" and ending Reconstruction; Lila Meade Valentine of Richmond, one of the "First Families of Virginia" (FFV); Mary Johnston, also of Virginia, descendent of Confederate heroes and nationally famous as a novelist; Rebecca Latimer Felton, whose husband served several terms in the Georgia legislature and in the United States Congress; Madeline McDowell Breckinridge of Kentucky, granddaughter of Henry Clay and wife of Desha Breckinridge, son of a congressman and editor of the *Lexington Herald*; and Pattie Ruffner Jacobs of Alabama, wife of a wealthy Birmingham industrialist.[9]

These women enjoyed more opportunities for education than most Southern women of their era as well as opportunities for travel outside the region that helped undermine provincial attitudes about woman's role. Wealth gave them the leisure and the means to assume leadership roles in the suffrage movement. A few Southern leaders were members of families that were experiencing financial distress, including Mississippi's Belle Kearney, who wrote of taking in sewing for former slaves one day and the next day dancing as a debutante in the governor's mansion. There was also Tennessee's suffrage leader, Sue Shelton White, who supported herself as a court reporter. Most, however, were daughters of wealth and privilege who could hire maids, cooks, and baby tenders as well as personally finance most of the suffrage work in the South. Southern suffrage leaders generally assumed that that they should fund their own activities and sometimes expressed disdain for Mississippi's Kearney for requesting payment for her suffrage lectures in order to pay her bills.[10]

Exalted social position facilitated the work of Southern suffrage leaders, giving them familiarity and access to the political process and a degree of immunity from criticism—or at least social ostracism—not enjoyed by Southern women of lesser social standing. Well aware of the particular importance of social position in the South, national suffrage leaders sought to recruit Southern women from prominent families, women who had, as New Orleans suffragist Kate Gordon phrased it, "names to conjure with." These women could demand and receive a respectful hearing, even as Southern anti-suffragists denounced Northern suffragists in no uncertain terms. When Louisville *Courier-Journal* editor Henry Watterson dared criticize the suffragists of Kentucky, led by the women of the Breckinridge and Clay families, *Lexington Herald* editor Desha Breckinridge chastised him for assailing the reputations of these women, "the hems of whose garments he was not fit to touch."[11]

As leaders of an unpopular movement, these Southern women displayed remarkable self-confidence, in part the product of exalted social position. They were members of families that were accustomed to guiding public opinion, rather than simply being guided by it. Kate Gordon wrote, "Review every advance, moral or otherwise. Have the majority ever desired the advance? The great earnest minority always shapes thought and leads the van."[12]

Nellie Nugent Somerville and her associates in Greenville, Mississippi, signaled their attitude toward public opinion when they named their literary society after Hypatia, a learned woman stoned to death by a mob in ancient Egypt. Somerville also derived confidence from her religious convictions, and both Laura Clay and Belle Kearney felt that God had called them to serve the cause of women's rights. Still others revealed, through diaries and private correspondence, a mischievous desire to be different, deriving pleasure from going against the grain.[13]

The decisions of these suffrage leaders to take up this cause resulted from a combination of personal characteristics and experiences that made them receptive to feminism. The attitudes and actions of family members were crucial in shaping these women's views. For example, Laura Clay's family background—which would have converted almost anyone to feminism—certainly had that effect on Clay, her mother,

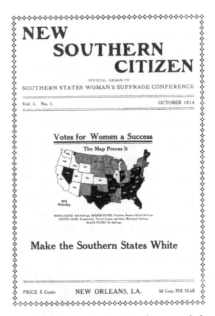

NEW
SOUTHERN
CITIZEN

OFFICIAL ORGAN OF
SOUTHERN STATES WOMAN'S SUFFRAGE CONFERENCE

Vol. 1. No. 1.   OCTOBER 1914

Votes for Women a Success
The Map Proves It

Alaska

Make the Southern States White

PRICE 5 Cents   NEW ORLEANS, LA.   50 Cents PER YEAR

Kate Gordon, President of the Southern States Woman Suffrage Conference, left. In the organization's newspaper, the *New Southern Citizen*, Gordon used racist and states' rights appeals to attempt to persuade Southern White politicians to support woman suffrage. LIBRARY OF CONGRESS

and all her sisters. After President Abraham Lincoln appointed Laura's father, Cassius Marcellus Clay as ambassador to Russia, he took his family with him to St. Petersburg. However, when living with six children and in the style expected of an ambassador proved too costly, he sent them back home. His wife, Mary Jane Clay, was somehow able to get her family back to Kentucky despite the hazards of travel in the midst of the Civil War, and managed the family plantation and a multitude of children by herself for eight years. She even remodeled and expanded their plantation and provided her daughters with a formal education despite her husband's objections. Meanwhile, Cassius Clay became involved in a well-publicized scandal involving a notorious St. Petersburg courtesan and then returned to Kentucky with a son whom he legally adopted. Advanced in his thinking when it suited his purposes, Clay divorced his wife who lost the plantation she had tended so carefully. As a result, Mary Jane Clay and her four daughters *all* became suffragists and advocates of expanded political and legal rights for women in Kentucky and the South.[14]

Positive attitudes toward women and feminism on the part of family members also played a role in the making of Southern suffrage leaders. Sue White and the Gordon sisters all had mothers who inspired them to adopt an expanded view of woman's role. Nellie Somerville's father saw to it that she received the best education available to a Southern woman and even invited his daughter to read for the law in his office, an offer she declined.[15]

Several suffrage leaders had sisters who supported them in their work. Anna Howard Shaw, president of the National American Woman Suffrage Association (NAWSA) once quipped, in reference to the Clays, the Gordons, the Johnstons, the Howards of Georgia, and the Finnegans of Texas, "If there was a failure to organize any state in the South…it must be due to the fact that no family there had three sisters to start the movement." Madeline Breckinridge, Pattie Jacobs, and Lila Meade Valentine all enjoyed the enthusiastic support of their husbands in their suffrage work. Contacts with suffragists from the North, the West, from other countries, as well as with suffragists from other Southern states, were also crucial in these key Southern women's decisions to become advocates of women's rights. And once recruited, they interested scores of other Southern women in the cause. Like all reformers, Southern suffragists came to see themselves as part of a supportive subculture and to judge themselves according to the precepts of that group, rather than those of the larger society they were trying to reform.[16]

Southern Ladies and Maternalism

The White women leading the Southern suffrage movement were reform-minded on some subjects, but nonetheless they identified strongly with the South and shared many of the attitudes of the men of their race and class. While seeking expanded rights and privileges for themselves and their gender, they nonetheless took pride in their heritage as Southern Ladies, embracing the traditional duties if not the restrictions that role entailed. Opponents called them "unconscious agents" of Northern saboteurs, but they fully understood what they were doing and why. For the most part, they considered their movement to be supportive rather than destructive of "Southern Civilization." Yet, they were clearly weary of women's indirect, limited role in politics, which they had concluded not only denied their individuality but also had proven to be inadequate for the protection of their interests or that of their "constituency," the "unprivileged" of the South— particularly women and children.[17]

In the 1890s, women who led the Southern suffrage movement fully supported the campaign led by elite Southern White men to return government to the so-called "best people." They took it for granted that it was the duty of the "most qualified" to guide and protect the rest, but they believed themselves to be among the best qualified. Indeed, their goal in fighting for suffrage was to add *maternalism* to paternalism, to carry the traditional role of the Southern Lady into politics and offer their services and unique feminine insights to the governing of their region. They sought, in fact, to restore and preserve elements they believed had once been integral in Southern politics, but were missing in the politics of the New South: morality, integrity, and the tradition of *noblesse oblige*.[18]

One important characteristic shared by these elite White Southern women that inspired them to take up this unpopular cause and continue working for it despite so many defeats, was their low opinion of the current management of the New

South. While all of the Southern suffrage leaders had friends or relatives in public office, they believed that Southern politics since the Civil War had degenerated to the point that too few honest and intelligent men were willing to serve. For example, Nellie Nugent Somerville contrasted the "boys" of the Confederacy, who "gave up prospects of material advancement to fight for principle," with the politicians of the present, who spoke of the rampant chaos and corruption in government as "practical politics," which if deplorable was nonetheless inevitable. She insisted that if "good men" continued to say "no man can go into politics and maintain his integrity and therefore hold themselves aloof and do not even vote," women would have to step in where men feared to tread. At the time of her conversion to the suffrage cause (1897), Somerville was furious about the overt bribery and coercion of voters employed by the "wets" in her county—those who opposed prohibition—with the knowledge and cooperation of local officials.[19]

A series of political murders in 1899 and 1900, including the shooting of a gubernatorial candidate by a member of a rival "gang" in the yard of the Kentucky state capitol, first prompted Madeline McDowell Breckinridge to become involved in politics. Shocked by what she considered a general atmosphere of lawlessness in her state, she organized a women's committee that pledged itself to "make every effort in our power for the overthrow of lawlessness and crime, and for the establishment of that social and political purity of righteousness which makes for good citizens and exalteth a nation."[20]

Rebecca Latimer Felton's long struggle for prohibition and against the convict lease system convinced her that women must be enfranchised; she was well aware of the "Liquor Interest's" eagerness to contain women's influence. When criticized for meddling in politics, she insisted that men's failure to give "sober homes to women and children" made it necessary for women to get involved. Although she was a member of the United Daughters of the Confederacy, she blasted Georgia politicians for invoking their war records and "waving the Bloody Shirt" to perpetuate their power and thereby extend their opportunities to fleece the public.[21]

Involvement in charitable work and reform societies led these women to a greater knowledge of social ills and a conviction that many of the social and economic problems that were formerly addressed by the private sector now required governmental attention. Yet, it seemed clear to the suffragists that Southern male politicians either failed to understand the crucial need for reforms, such as improved public education and health care, temperance, and legislation to protect women and children, or they simply preferred to use public office to line their own pockets. Indeed, the suffragists believed that in their eagerness to promote economic development, the leaders of the New South were willing to offer up the South's working class for Northern exploitation. Breckinridge accused Southern boosters of trading "ideals of the past" for material prosperity, and she expressed disgust at attempts to attract Northern manufacturers by advertising "that we have not only the cotton and the fuel ... but the cheap child labor as well."[22]

To the suffragists, this failure to live up to their responsibilities in keeping with the concept of *noblesse oblige* meant that the legislators needed women to assist them in fulfilling their moral obligations.

Inadequacy of "Indirect Influence"

Obviously, many Southern women of the same race and class, including other women attempting to influence public policy through voluntary associations, chose to rely strictly upon the traditional "weapon" of the Southern Lady—the highly touted "indirect influence." Some lacked the courage to defy public opinion; others had no desire for the vote and thought it foolish for women to insult men by demanding it. Still others insisted they had no need for the vote. For example, the president of the Georgia Federation of Women's Clubs testified that the state's women's clubs had "no difficulty getting their measures passed by the legislature" using powers of persuasion, that they were "the power behind the throne now, and would lose, not gain, by a change."[23]

It was true that Southern women lobbying their legislators through voluntary associations did achieve some successes. Suffrage clubs often worked together with traditional women's clubs and succeeded in bringing about a number of significant changes in women's status and opportunities, including the admission of women to colleges and professional schools, establishing women's right to serve on governmental commissions and boards and to work as factory inspectors in some states, and securing legal reforms regarding inheritance and custody, to name a few. But the women who became suffragists grew increasingly convinced that moral suasion was ineffective. Kentucky suffragist Madeline Breckinridge applauded the accomplishments of the women's clubs in her state, but she observed ruefully, "When one remembers that it is the result of twenty-five years of work of a group of able and determined women, it is seen to be small."[24]

To Southern suffragists, their own indirect influence seemed negligible compared to that exercised by the brewers, the "cotton men," the railroad barons, and other industrialists who regularly managed to influence politicians' decisions. As they grew increasingly frustrated by legislative resistance to the reforms they supported, the suffragists grew increasingly cynical about the celebrated chivalry of Southern men and denounced the Southern woman's enforced reliance upon indirect influence as degrading, as well as inefficient.[25]

Many Southern women were converted to what Jean Gordon called "a belief in the potency of the ballot beyond that of 'woman's influence'" after the defeat of child labor legislation. Gordon recalled that the failure of a child labor bill strongly supported by New Orleans clubwomen—including the wives of many legislators— caused many of the women to question the efficacy of indirect influence. We learned, Gordon observed, "what we had suspected," that "the much-boasted influence of the wife over the husband in matters political was one of the many theories which melt before the sun of experience."[26]

The suffragists in the South were disgusted by the way Southern politicians insisted on "chivalrously" shouldering the burden of politics for women by invoking chivalry as a reason for denying women direct influence, while refusing to offer women and children genuine legal protection. They were frustrated by the slow pace of reform as they sought to open up educational institutions to women and revise outdated guardianship and inheritance laws. Suffragists were indignant that legislators who so celebrated the influence of the mother, refused to change existing laws that gave the father full legal rights to their children, even the power to appoint a guardian for his unborn child. Breckinridge found it ironic that a society allegedly intent on protecting women clung to antiquated property and inheritance laws that left a married woman totally dependent on her husband's decency and his survival. "It was one of the anomalies of the old common law," she pointed out, "that it seemed to feel that a man left with children to support and without a wife, needed three times as much as a wife left with children and no husband."[27]

After observing the effects of the passage of woman suffrage in Colorado, Breckinridge noted that in the states where women were already enfranchised, the "age of consent" laws [laws specifying the age at which a person is able to voluntarily consent to sexual intercourse] ranged from eighteen to twenty-one, while in the South the "age of consent" ranged from ten to sixteen. Breckinridge asked, "Do Southern men protect Southern women at all comparably to the way Western women, granted the right to do it, protect their own sex?"[28]

Southern suffragists clearly saw that indirect influence was still their only weapon with which to pry suffrage from a reluctant South, so they tried to make their demand for power as unthreatening as possible. They did invoke "natural rights" arguments, insisting that, as Georgia suffragist Rebecca Latimer Felton put it, "I pay taxes and obey the laws, and I know the right belongs to me to assist in selecting those who rule over me."[29]

Somerville denied a statement by a Mississippi newspaper editor who asserted that the suffragists' chief argument was that enfranchised womanhood would "bring about great reforms." She wrote, "The orthodox suffragists do not base their claims on any such argument. We stand upon the Declaration of Independence, 'governments derive their just powers from the consent of the governed.' Any argument based on results is merely incidental and not fundamental."[30]

Yet, like many suffragists outside the South, the White women who led the Southern suffrage movement often argued for equal partnership in governing with the men of their race and class by emphasizing the differences in the interests and responsibilities of the sexes. This was a nice and less challenging way of saying that the interests of women and children would never be adequately represented as long as women were relying upon men to protect them. "Men have done remarkably well to battle so many foes of the human race and its progress," said

Pattie Jacobs, but as some "for-sighted [sic] men" now realize, woman's "highly developed moral nature and intimate knowledge of conditions governing the welfare of women and children... would ultimately result in great good to the state, the nation, and the race." Virginia suffragist Mary Johnston wrote in a similar vein: "Men have their minds too much fixed on the large political issues, and there are a multitude of details that slip through their fingers, so to speak, and which women can better attend to [including]... legislation concerning schools and children."[31]

Southern suffragists took care to look and act like ladies, avoided *additional* unpopular causes, issued press releases celebrating the beauty, femininity, and domesticity of their leaders, and sometimes addressed their legislators in such a fashion that Northern coworkers were shocked and dismayed at their "honey-tongued charm." In the last decade of the suffrage movement, most Southern suffragists strenuously avoided association with the National Woman's Party (NWP), publicly denouncing their "un-seemly," "fanatical," and "misguided" tactics, including suffragists picketing the White House and burning Woodrow Wilson's speeches in Lafayette Square. Virginia suffrage leader Lila Meade Valentine begged the public not to "condemn the suffrage cause as a whole because of the folly of a handful of women" and urged her state's suffragists to avoid all "spectacular tactics."[32]

Southern suffragists greatly resented having to stoop to wheedling and coddling male egos, however. Mary Johnston deplored the fact that society still encouraged—indeed required—women to rely upon this "sinuous, indirect way of approaching and of obtaining the object or the end which they desire...just as when they were the cowering mates of savages half as strong again as they." Johnston, a friend and admirer of author Charlotte Perkins Gilman, echoed Gilman's message that female dignity could only be won through economic independence and that marriage was somewhat akin to prostitution. She predicted that the phrase "indirect influence" would, in the near future, become "most distasteful to a naturally self-respecting and straightforward woman ... *It means, make me comfortable, and I will see what I can do about it.*"[33]

Clearly, these women recognized the contrast between rhetoric and reality when it came to discussions of woman's role in Southern society. Nellie Nugent Somerville wrote in a 1914 article:

It is quite common for men to say...that women should not vote because they are too good and must not be degraded to the level of men.... Now the facts in the case are that there is not a word of truth in this proposition. It is exasperating because it is short-sighted, unreasonably and historically false.... Exclusion from the right to vote is a degradation—always has been, always will be, never was intended as anything else, cannot be sugarcoated into anything else. The age-long cause of all of these things [discrimination against women in education, in industry, in property rights and political rights] has been the theory that women were too bad and too incompetent.[34]

Somerville and her associates in the suffrage movement demanded that men—Southern White men who surpassed all others in extolling the goodness and virtue of woman—accept woman's help in governing Southern society. These Southern ladies gladly accepted their role as soul and conscience of the South, but wanted to be in a position to actually carry out that role. They did not object to the vote being restricted so much as they wanted to be among the elect.

To them, the vote was a badge of honor as well as a tool. As Alabama suffragist Pattie Jacobs wrote, "We of all people understand the symbolism of the ballot... [as we live] in states where its use is restricted and professedly based upon virtue and intelligence."[35]

Indeed, it was largely the perception that *they*—moral, God-fearing, intelligent, educated, women whose families had been largely responsible for settling and guiding the South—were being denied the right to vote, even as inferior men were not only voting, but governing the region that fueled their activism. They wanted and believed that *they, if not all women*, deserved, in Mary Johnston's words, "the dignity of citizenship."[36]

Southern Suffragists and "The Negro Problem"

On race relations, the elite White women who took on leadership of the Southern suffrage movement were little different from the men of their race and class. White Southern suffragists, who spoke eloquently of the inalienable right of women as citizens to self-government, nevertheless advocated—or at least acquiesced in—the restoration of White political supremacy that took place contemporaneously with the Southern woman suffrage movement.

Like most elite White Southerners and a growing number of White, native-born Americans nationwide in the late nineteenth century, most Southern suffragists believed that voting was *not* a right of all citizens but the privilege and duty of those best qualified to exercise it. Indeed, to White Southern suffragists the contemporary meaning of the frequently used phrase "the negro problem" was not the use of the race issue against their cause—though this concerned them greatly—but the enfranchisement after the Civil War of several million African Americans whom Southern White conservatives considered to be ignorant, purchasable, and unfit for political participation.[37]

White Southern suffragists believed they were better qualified to participate in politics than most White men; they did not doubt that they and other White women were more desirable as voters than the African American men who had been enfranchised by the Fifteenth Amendment. Like many other elite Southerners, these privileged Southern women saw themselves as advocates for, and protectors of, Blacks. They paternalistically (or maternalistically) defended African

Woman Suffrage and White Supremacy in the South

The Federal Suffrage Amendment will not affect the negro situation in the South. It sets aside no qualification for voting except the sex qualification. It simply eliminates the word "male". The same qualifications will apply to negro women as now apply to negro men. (See Constitution of North Carolina, Article 6, Section 4.)

The Census Report of the U. S. Government Tells the Story

1910—Population of North Carolina was upwards of 2,200,000
1920—At normal rate of increase population will now be up-
wards of.. 2,800,000
The rule is one adult male to every five persons, which gives us
as adult males.. 560,000
There are fully as many adult females........................:............... 560,000

Total adult males and females.............................. 1,120,000

As the ratio in North Carolina by the census is 70% white and 30% negro, it follows that the negro adults, male and female, are 336,000 and the white adults, male and female, are 784,000. One half (392,000) of these last are, of course, white females, making 56,000 more adult white women than the 336,000 negro men and negro women combined.

IF white domination is threatened in the South, it is, therefore, DOUBLY EXPEDIENT TO ENFRANCHISE THE WOMEN QUICKLY IN ORDER THAT IT BE PRESERVED.

U. S. Senator Simmons, who waged the successful fight for White Supremacy in North Carolina in 1898, advocates ratification of the Federal Suffrage Amendment by the Legislature of North Carolina.

The Democratic State Convention asked that the Legislature ratify this Amendment.
Woodrow Wilson urges every Democratic State to ratify.
Secretary of the Navy, Josephus Daniels is eager for North Carolina to ratify.
Chief Justice John M. Anderson, of Alabama, says: "This is the most important Amendment ever proposed to the Federal Constitution; indeed, more important than any original section of that instrument, as it seeks an interpretation of that part of the Bill of Rights which proclaims that all men are born equal by interpolating therein the word WOMAN".
Chief Justice Clark, of North Carolina, says: "No matter how bad a character a man has, if he can only keep out of the penitentiary and the insane asylum we permit him to vote and to take a share in the Government, but we are afraid to trust our mothers, wives, and daughters to give us the aid of their intelligence and clear insight".

Would these representative men of the South ask that a measure be passed which would endanger the civilization of the South?

EQUAL SUFFRAGE ASSOCIATION OF NORTH CAROLINA—RALEIGH

Circular distributed by North Carolina suffragists to quiet fears that a federal amendment for woman suffrage would imperil White Democrats' dominance of state politics and to argue that it could even help to preserve White supremacy in the state. STATE ARCHIVES OF NORTH CAROLINA

Americans' rights to public education and social services, and they expressed disgust at the mistreatment of Blacks by lower-class Whites. However, political rights were another matter. Indeed, these suffragists were highly indignant that Black men had become the political superiors of "the best White women of the South."[38]

Still, there was a range of opinion within this group of Southern suffrage leaders that in part reflected the area of the South in which they lived, as well as their age. On one end were negrophobes, including older suffragists like Rebecca Latimer Felton of Georgia, Kate Gordon of Louisiana, and Belle Kearney of Mississippi who spoke of African Americans as though speaking of another, inferior species. Felton was openly and unapologetically racist in her demand for woman suffrage, declaring in a 1915 speech:

> Freedom belongs to the white woman as her inherent right. Whatever belongs to the freeman of these United States belongs to the white woman. Her Anglo--Saxon forefathers, fleeing from English tyranny won this country from savage tribes and again from English bayonets, by the expenditure of blood and treasure. Whatever was won by these noble men of the Revolution was inherited alike by sons and daughters. Fifty years from now this country will hold up hands in holy horror that... any man or set of men in America should assume to themselves the authority to deny to free white women of America the ballot which is the badge and synonym of freedom.[40]

On the other end of the scale, there was Madeline McDowell Breckinridge, a "second generation" suffragist from Kentucky and a progressive reformer. She spoke of White supremacy in politics as a temporary necessity until "undesirable" voters became "desirable" through education and gradual social progress that Whites were morally obligated to support *noblesse oblige* and believed that meanwhile, "qualified" Blacks should be allowed to vote.[41] And there was Mary Johnston of Virginia, who disdained the use of racist tactics by suffragists like Gordon and warned against it. In a 1913 letter to Lila Meade Valentine, she wrote: "I think that as women we should be most prayerfully careful lest, in the future, that women—whether colored women or White women who are merely poor, should be able to say that we had betrayed their interests and excluded them from freedom."[42]

Still, most Southern suffragists employed racist arguments to promote woman suffrage—some aggressively and enthusiastically, and others defensively and reluctantly. While there were African American women supporting women's enfranchisement from inside the South, they were systematically excluded from all White-led suffrage organizations and meetings as the suffragists sought to distance their movement from its historic association with advocacy of the rights of Black Americans.[43]

The Rise and Fall of the Suffragists' "Southern Strategy"

White Southern conservatives' devotion to White supremacy was not only a prime obstacle to the suffragists' success in the region, it was also a major *causative* factor in the development of the Southern suffrage movement in the 1890s—not in causing Southern women to *want* suffrage, but in giving them a *reason to expect that they could win it.* An organized regional movement with strong national support came into existence in the 1890s because many leading suffragists—both Southern and Northern—believed the determination of White Southern politicians to restore White supremacy might be the key to female enfranchisement.[44]

It is one of history's many ironies that this strategy was originally conceived by leading suffragist and abolitionist Lucy Stone's husband, Henry Blackwell, an antislavery activist who once risked his life to rescue an enslaved girl from her master. He began presenting his idea to Southern politicians in 1867 and managed to persuade delegates to the Mississippi Constitutional Convention of 1890 (the first of several such conventions) to give it serious consideration. This impressed Laura Clay, whose pleas for woman suffrage as "justice" were falling upon deaf ears, and she promoted the idea to other leaders of the NAWSA.[45]

They launched a major campaign based on Blackwell's Southern strategy, investing considerable time and resources. Carrie Chapman Catt and Susan B. Anthony went on separate speaking tours, sweeping through the region. In addition, the NAWSA took the unusual step of holding national conventions in Atlanta and New Orleans. Eager to avoid offending their Southern hosts at the 1895 convention in Atlanta, NAWSA leaders even asked their aging hero Frederick Douglass—an honored participant in women's rights conventions elsewhere in the nation—to stay away.[46] At the New Orleans convention, delegates formally endorsed a "states' rights" measure accepting each state suffrage organization's right to determine its own goals, tactics, and membership requirements, Some, notably Anthony, showed signs that they felt bad about these concessions to Southern racism. While in New Orleans, Anthony met separately with African American members of the Phillis Wheatley Club, and on the way home, stopped in Alabama at the Tuskegee Institute, established by Booker T. Washington for African American students, where she shook the hand of every female student. But many national suffrage leaders, including Catt and Anna Howard Shaw, shared the indignation of these elite, White Southern women that their social "inferiors"— whether African Americans in the South or immigrants in the North—had become their political "superiors."[47]

Late-nineteenth-century suffragists found it quite difficult to believe that the federal government would—as it did— abandon the defense of Black suffrage and allow the South to solve its "negro problem" by disfranchising African American men. Even after Mississippi in 1890 and South Carolina in 1895 led the South in adopting measures such as "understanding clauses" and poll taxes to "legally" keep Blacks from voting—instead of the usual fraud and violence employed for decades—suffragists who supported this Southern strategy for gaining woman suffrage insisted that the federal government would not allow these measures to stand.[48]

Southern suffragists such as Clay and Kearney warned that Congress would invoke the Fifteenth Amendment's enforcement clause, or the Supreme Court would rule the states' disfranchisement provisions unconstitutional. Yet, solving "the negro problem" by *extending* the franchise to *women* with education or property," they argued, would ensure that the vast majority of new voters would be White and still be seen as a *liberalization*, rather than a restriction of suffrage. Thus, White political supremacy could be permanently restored without risking congressional retribution or an unfavorable Supreme Court ruling.[49]

Throughout the 1890s, many Southern suffragists believed that as the men of their class cast about for a means of countering the effects of Black suffrage, they might accept woman suffrage as a solution—just as politicians in Western states had used woman suffrage to consolidate their political position. By 1903, however, it was clear to most suffragists that Southern politicians had managed to restore White supremacy by disfranchising Black men and that they were going to be allowed to get away with it. NAWSA initiatives in the South ended and, except in states such as Kentucky and Louisiana where there were exceptionally committed suffragist leaders, the Southern suffrage movement foundered.[50]

Out of desperation, in 1906 and 1907 a few Southern suffragists initiated still more blatantly racist campaigns. Belle Kearney called for a new Southern campaign explicitly asking for woman suffrage "as a solution of the race problem," and Kate Gordon initiated a scheme to get a "White women only" amendment added to the Mississippi constitution. However, the NAWSA refused to give its endorsement to either scheme. NAWSA president, Anna Howard Shaw, wrote in a letter to suffragist Laura Clay of Kentucky, "It must appeal to you as to every fair-minded woman that such a call could not be sanctioned by the National Suffrage Association." It is "contrary to the spirit of our organization" and would "re-act against ourselves" by suggesting "that we really don't believe in the justice of suffrage, but simply that certain classes or races should dominate the government."[51]

Other national suffrage leaders, notably Henry Blackwell and his daughter Alice Stone Blackwell, pleaded with advocates of the "Whites only" amendment to abandon it. Alice explained that any measure that allowed Whites to vote, "no matter how ignorant or bad in character," and shut out every Black, "no matter how intelligent or how good," was "regarded everywhere outside the Southern States as an unmitigated iniquity."[52]

Though the NAWSA had for years sought to exploit the South's "negro problem" to bring in the inhospitable South, rejection of these explicitly racist schemes indicated that there was, after all, a limit to the racism the organization would support. NAWSA leaders feared an explicitly Whites-only campaign would weigh against the woman suffrage movement in the North and in the West—the region where suffragists would finally achieve the crucial breakthroughs that gave momentum to the suffrage campaign and lead to the passage of the federal amendment.[53]

Most Southern suffrage clubs dissolved or lay dormant until approximately 1910. In the second stage of the suffrage movement in the South, 1910 to 1920, White suffragists rarely raised the race issue and were almost exclusively on the defensive in regard to race. As anti-suffragists used rabidly racist rhetoric to fight women's enfranchisement, especially by federal amendment, White suffragists now insisted that the race issue was irrelevant to the woman suffrage issue, a "non-issue" trumped up by their opponents. Even Mary Johnston denied that state suffrage amendments would enfranchise large numbers of African American women, insisting that only "a few educated, property-owning coloured women will vote, but not the mass of coloured women." Nellie Nugent Somerville brushed aside the question, "How would woman suffrage apply to the American negress?" saying, "I answer, just as it applies to the American negro."[54]

Divisions Over States' Rights

On the race issue, White Southern suffragists presented a united front. Those who questioned the use of racist tactics or disapproved of the wholesale exclusion of Blacks from the electorate, generally kept such sentiments to themselves or at least out of the public arena. They had no desire to confirm the widespread suspicion that White suffragists favored Black suffrage.[55] However, there was no such consensus or show of solidarity regarding the states' rights issue.

In the last decade of the suffrage movement, as the federal suffrage amendment gained momentum elsewhere in the nation, differences of opinion over the state sovereignty issue divided Southern suffragists into warring camps. The National American Woman Suffrage Association (NAWSA), the newly formed National Woman's Party (NWP), and a new Southern organization, the Southern States Woman Suffrage Conference (SSWSC) each followed separate strategies and competed for the loyalty of Southern suffragists. The controversy over different strategies strained, and in some cases, severed long-standing friendships and added to the difficulties the woman suffrage movement faced in the South.[56]

Southern White women who became suffragists generally identified strongly with their region and with their states. This was true even of those quite critical of the region and its institutions, such as Mary Johnston, who wrote in 1905: "In spite of all reason and [owing to] merely an ingrained and hereditary matter…Virginia (and incidentally the entire South) is my country, and not the stars and stripes but the stars and bars is my flag."[57]

In fact, reverence for their states and the South made Southern White suffragists determined to reform them. Thus, winning the suffrage battle at home was paramount. Even the suffragists with no theoretical objection to a federal amendment—those who were not states' rights devotees—longed for suffrage victories on the state level that would proclaim an acceptance of women's equality and the triumph of a new progressive spirit. This filial attachment to their states and region, together with expediency (they were well aware of the regional reverence for state sovereignty, particularly in regard to the franchise), led them to seek enfranchisement only through state action until all hope of such action was lost.

A minority of Southern suffragists could not bring themselves to support a federal suffrage amendment, however. When in 1913, the NAWSA—prodded into action by Alice Paul and her associates—renewed its campaign for a federal suffrage amendment, Kate Gordon decided it was time that Southern suffragists go their own way. Gordon, a disgruntled former NAWSA officer and a committed states' rights advocate, led in the establishment of the Southern States Woman Suffrage Conference (SSWSC).[58]

Gordon and her followers insisted that Southern states would never allow a federal amendment to be passed by Congress. By promoting a federal solution, Gordon charged, the NAWSA was just wasting its time and money, and making things even more difficult for Southern suffragists to win state victories. In her view, Southern suffragists—who must gain their rights from Southern Democrats—must never even appear to favor a federal amendment. Gordon demanded that all Southern suffragists support the SSWSC and insisted that the NAWSA turn over the South to her leadership.[59]

Most Southern suffragists, however, did not follow Kate Gordon's lead. Few were willing to renounce federal suffrage when it might be their only means of gaining enfranchisement. In fact, after one of Gordon's tirades against NAWSA leaders, state suffrage organizations in Tennessee and Alabama formally rebuked Gordon and her attempts to lead a Southern revolt against the NAWSA and the federal amendment. Tennessee's resolution declared that "the Convention of the Tennessee Equal Suffrage Association go on record as disapproving the action of Miss Kate M. Gordon in undertaking to dictate to the NAWSA or its Congressional Committee in regard to its policy, methods, or plans... and in her presuming to speak for the women of the South."[60]

As Gordon and her tactics alienated nearly all of the prominent Southern suffrage leaders, the SSWSC ceased to exist except in name only. Of the leading suffragists, only Clay and Kate and Jean Gordon were so committed to the concept of state sovereignty that they ultimately refused to support, and indeed, opposed the federal suffrage amendment.[61]

After 1916 when many pleas for state suffrage amendments had been made and rejected throughout the South, and the NAWSA was fully committed to securing enfranchisement through federal action, most Southern suffragists campaigned actively for the proposed amendment. Some, including Nellie Nugent Somerville, set aside her own reservations about federal overreach and labored to convince fellow Southerners that the amendment held "no menace for the institutions of any State or any group of States." Others had no such reservations to overcome. Anne

Dallas Dudley of Tennessee insisted that "the spirit of the New South has been misunderstood by our representatives in Congress" who so long blocked the amendment, and that Southerners were "glad and proud to acclaim ourselves loyally an integral part of our nation today."[62]

Sue Shelton White, also of Tennessee, warned that rather than expect suffragists to uphold state sovereignty, the Democrats would be well advised to modify their doctrines in order to keep the loyalty of Southern women: "Moss-backed traditions of political parties will no longer be accepted as an excuse for withholding democracy from women," she wrote. "There are suffragists born Democrats who have hoped to live and die in the political faith of their fathers who can no longer accept such an excuse."[63]

Most Southern suffragists rallied behind NAWSA President Catt when she announced her "Winning Plan" to coordinate state suffrage work through a nationwide strategy to finally secure a federal amendment. Catt's plan, however, was not satisfactory to all the NAWSA supporters in the South, partly because it largely wrote off the region until time for ratification. The NAWSA fully supported and contributed generously to state suffrage campaigns in critical states such as New York where there was a good chance of victory. But fearing that failed state suffrage campaigns would blunt momentum, Catt demanded that NAWSA affiliates in states she considered poor prospects suspend efforts at winning full suffrage through state amendment and seek only partial suffrage. Yet, to the chagrin of some Southern suffragists, especially Madeline McDowell Breckinridge who believed victory in Kentucky was quite likely, Catt's list of poor prospects included *all* Southern states.[64]

When in June 1919 Congress finally submitted the proposed Nineteenth Amendment to the states for ratification, the leaders of the woman suffrage movement in the Southern states found themselves fighting one another as well as the antis—a situation that did nothing to help the cause. In Virginia, there was open hostility between NAWSA loyalists led by Lila Meade Valentine and the state's chapter of the NWP. In Mississippi, Somerville and her associates endured the bitter experience of sitting in the gallery of the capitol while Kate Gordon denounced the federal amendment as a threat to state sovereignty and the Constitution. In Louisiana, the Gordons and other advocates of woman suffrage through state action combated both federal amendment supporters *and* the anti-suffragists, creating a three-way struggle in which no form of woman suffrage was adopted. During the final, bitter battle which took place in Nashville, Tennessee, both Gordon sisters and Laura Clay actually campaigned against ratification of "this hideous amendment" though Clay expressed "a great distaste" at being publicly associated with the despised antis.[65]

As the end of the long struggle for woman suffrage approached, those Southern suffragists who opposed the Nineteenth Amendment were bitter, disappointed in their fellow suffragists, and dismayed that the success of woman suffrage for which they had worked for so many years helped undermine another cherished political ideal—state sovereignty. Most Southern suffragists, however, were jubilant when ratification came at last and grateful to Tennessee for, in the words of Virginia suffragists, "redeeming the honor of the country."[66]

Still, their celebration was dampened by the fact that so many women had to be enfranchised "courtesy of Uncle Sam." Madeline McDowell Breckinridge, whose state was one of the four Southern states that ratified the Nineteenth Amendment, was joking when she told the NAWSA's "Jubilee Convention" in Chicago in 1920:

> We'll get all our rights with the help of Uncle Sam,
> For the way that they come, we don't give a _ _ _ _.[67]

Breckinridge fully understood the disappointment of those suffragists in the states that failed to ratify—or worse, adopted "rejection resolutions."

Pattie Ruffner Jacobs of Alabama, speaking for the "defeated" suffragists at the Jubilee Convention, observed: "It only remains for the outward and visible sign of our freedom to be put in the hands of Southern women by the generous men of other states, a situation which hurts our pride and to which we submit with deep regret but not apology."[68] Having hoped to win from their home states and region a public endorsement of woman's political equality, these Southern women—like African American men—had instead gained the right to vote over the strenuous objections of political leaders in their states.

The analogy was not lost on the suffragists. Jacobs acknowledged, "It is acutely distasteful to Southern suffragists not to be enfranchised by Southern men, for we of all people understand the symbolism of the ballot."[69] Yet, these White suffragists *would be allowed to exercise this privilege* granted them by the "generous men of other states." Most African American women in the region would not be so fortunate.[70]

Conclusion: Intractable as Well as Inhospitable

White Southern suffragists, with their elite cadre of leaders who shared many of the ideas of other Southerners of their race and class, offered no thorough-going indictment of their society. They did not challenge the idea that many within the region needed the "guardianship" of the more enlightened citizenry: they only objected to the idea that *they* needed such guidance and protection.[71] These suffragists were "radical" for their region only as advocates of reforms in laws and customs that would advance women's status in Southern society.

None of these reforms, however, were as threatening to the social order as woman suffrage; reforms short of suffrage could still be seen as evidence of male protection of women and children, secured through "indirect influence." The request for the vote, on the other hand, was interpreted as a challenge to the fundamentally hierarchical and paternalistic political structure of the region as well as to the White supremacy and the sovereignty of the states. However nicely the suffragists tried to put it, demanding the power to represent their own interests constituted an indirect accusation of failure that White Southern male politicians understood and resented.

The South was never, as Laura Clay hoped, fully "brought in" to the suffrage fold, even though the defection of four states from the otherwise solid South allowed the Nineteenth Amendment to be ratified. In rejecting woman suffrage, Southern politicians made it clear that they still found much about the old pattern of relations between the sexes quite attractive.

As for African American women of the South, it would take half a century and a mass movement before Congress adopted the Voting Rights Act of 1965, which allowed them to take full advantage of the right bestowed through the Nineteenth Amendment. Then, between 1972 and 1982, the South again proved to be intractable in the battle over the proposed Equal Rights Amendment, which fell short of ratification by three states. Once again, most "unratified states" were Southern states.[72]

After 1920, women still had a long way to go in their quest for equality in the South.

Notes

This is a revised and expanded version of an essay that appeared in Marjorie Spruill (Wheeler), ed. VOTES FOR WOMEN: The Woman Suffrage Movement in Tennessee, the South, and the Nation (Knoxville: University of Tennessee Press, 1995).

1. Clipping, Woman's Journal, Laura Clay Scrapbook, Laura Clay Papers, Special Collections and Archives, Margaret I. King Library, University of Kentucky.

2. Spruill (Wheeler), New Women of the New South: The Leaders of the Woman Suffrage Movement in the Southern States (Oxford University Press, 1993), 115–18.

3. Charles Reagan Wilson, Baptized in Blood: The Religion of the Lost Cause, 1865-1920 (Athens, Ga; University of Georgia Press, 1980); Gaines M. Foster, Ghosts of the Confederacy: Defeat, the Lost Cause, and the Emergence of the New South, 1865 to 1913 (New York: Oxford University Press, 1988); Karen L. Cox, Dixie's Daughters: The United Daughters of the Confederacy and the Preservation of Confederate Culture (Gainesville, Fla: Univ. Press of Florida, 2003).

4. Quotation from Albert Taylor Bledsoe, "The Mission of Woman," The Southern Review, October 1871, 923–43; Spruill (Wheeler), New Women of the New South, 8–13.

5. Ibid., 4-9, 13–19.

6. Quotation from anti-suffrage pamphlet, Clay Papers.

7. Spruill (Wheeler), New Women of the New South, 29–37.

8. Carrie Chapman Catt and Nettie Rogers Shuler, Woman Suffrage and Politics: The Inner Story of the Suffrage Movement (Seattle & London: University of Washington Press, 1923), 88–89.

9. Spruill (Wheeler), New Women of the New South, 38-71.

10. Belle Kearney, A Slaveholder's Daughter (Abbey Press, 1900); James P. Louis, "Sue Shelton White," in Notable American Women: A Biographical Dictionary Completing the Twentieth Century (Harvard University Press, 1971); Kate Gordon to Henry Blackwell, Oct. 1, 1907, Clay Papers.

11. Quotation from Kate Gordon to Catherine Waugh McCulloch, June 1, 1915, McCulloch Papers, Schlesinger Library, Harvard University; Desha Breckinridge to Madeline McDowell Breckinridge, May 3, 1913, Madeline McDowell Breckinridge Papers in the Breckinridge Family Papers, Manuscripts Division, Library of Congress, hereafter MMB Papers.

12. Spruill (Wheeler), New Women of the New South, 58-60.

13. Ibid.

14. Paul E. Fuller, Laura Clay and the Woman's Rights Movement

(Lexington, KY: University Press of Kentucky, 1992), 1-29.

15. Spruill (Wheeler), New Women of the New South, 61-62.

16. Ibid., 61-65; Quotation, Anna Howard Shaw, Story of a Pioneer, (New York: Harper & Bros., 1915), 309.

17. Spruill (Wheeler), New Women of the New South, 50-57, 65-71.

18. Madeline McDowell Breckinridge, "The Prospects for Woman Suffrage in the South," address to the NAWSA convention of 1911, MMB Papers.

19. Spruill (Wheeler), New Women of the New South, 65-71; Nellie Nugent Somerville, "Christian Citizenship," 1898, and Somerville, "Presidential Address to First Mississippi Woman Suffrage Association," March 28, Somerville-Howorth Family Papers, Schlesinger Library, Harvard University.

20. Sophonisba P. Breckinridge, Madeline McDowell Breckinridge: A Leader in the New South (Chicago, IL: Univ. of Chicago Press, 1921), 34–42, quot. 41–42.

21. Spruill (Wheeler), New Women of the New South, 66-67; Rebecca Felton, "The Subjection of Women and the Enfranchisement of Women," No. 2, "Rebecca Latimer Felton Papers" (n.d.), Special Collections Division, Hargrett Rare Book and Manuscript Library, University of Georgia; Josephine Bone Floyd, "Rebecca Latimer Felton: Champion of Women's Rights," Georgia Historical Quarterly 30, no. June 1946 (n.d.): 81–104; Josephine Bone Floyd, "Rebecca Latimer Felton: Political Independent," Georgia Historical Quarterly 30, no. March 1946 (n.d.): 14–34; Rebecca Latimer Felton, Country Life in Georgia in the Days of My Youth (Atlanta, Ga, 1919).

22. Madeline Breckinridge, "Public Schools and Southern Development" (n.d.), MMB Papers.

23. A. Elizabeth Taylor, "Last Phase of the Woman Suffrage Movement in Georgia," Georgia Historical Quarterly 43, March 1959: 11–28, quotation, 14.

24. Madeline Breckinridge, "Direct Versus Indirect Influence in Kentucky," written for the New York Evening Post, February 3, 1914, MMB Papers.

25. Spruill (Wheeler), New Women of the New South, 65-69

26. Jean Gordon, "New Louisiana Child Labor Law," Charities, January 26, 1908, 481.

27. M. Breckinridge, "Direct Versus Indirect Influence in Kentucky."

28. Melba Porter Hay, "Madeline McDowell Breckinridge: Kentucky Suffragist and Progressive Reformer," (Dissertation, University of Kentucky, 1980), 139–40.

29. Floyd, "Rebecca Latimer Felton," 86.

30. Nellie Nugent Somerville to the editor of a Greenville, Miss. newspaper, 16 May ?, Scrapbook, Somerville-Howorth Family Papers.

31. Pattie Ruffner Jacobs to the editor, *Birmingham Ledger*, Feb. 12, 1912, Jacobs Scrapbook, Pattie Ruffner Jacobs Papers, Birmingham Public Library, Birmingham, Alabama; "Sentimental Idea Hurts Suffrage," *Woman's Journal*, Apr. 12, 1913, Mary Johnston Papers, University of Virginia, Charlottesville.

32. Spruill (Wheeler), *New Women of the New South*, 74-78; Northern suffragists' reaction described in Anne Firor Scott, *The Southern Lady: From Pedestal to Politics: 1830-1930* (Chicago: Univ. of Chicago Press, 1970), 183, 184.

33. Mary Johnston, "Speech, Woman's Club Alumnae, May 31," [emphasis hers],1910-11 suffrage speeches, Johnston Papers.

34. Nellie Nugent Somerville, "Are Women Too Good to Vote?" clipping, ca 1914, Somerville-Howorth Family Papers.

35. Pattie Ruffner Jacobs, "Tradition Vs. Justice," speech at the 1920 NAWSA "Jubilee Convention" in Chicago, Clay Papers.

36. Pattie Ruffner Jacobs, "The Pulse of the South, How the South Really Feels About Woman Suffrage," clipping, Clay Papers; Mary Johnston, draft of a speech to be given in Philadelphia.

37. Spruill (Wheeler), *New Women of the New South*, 100–112; Marjorie Spruill (Wheeler), "Race, Reform, and Reaction at the Turn of the Century: Southern Suffragists, the NAWSA, and the 'Southern Strategy' in Context," in *Votes for Women: The Struggle for Suffrage Revisited*, ed. Jean H Baker (New York: Oxford Univ. Press, 2002), 102–17.

38. Spruill (Wheeler), *New Women of the New South*, 101.

39. Kearney, *A Slaveholder's Daughter*, 62–64, 92, and 97;

40. Felton, "The Subjection of Women."

41. M. Breckinridge to Miss Mary Winser, Jan. 1, 1912, Clay Papers; Historian Suzanne Lebsock states that the racism exhibited by Southern white suffragists should be considered in light of the extreme racism of anti-suffragists. White suffragists in Virginia, she wrote, "negotiated a middling course," neither "disavowing white supremacy" nor engaging in the "poisonous polemics" of the antis. Suzanne Lebsock, "Woman Suffrage and White Supremacy: A Virginia Case Study," in *Visible Women: New Essays on American Activism*, ed. Nancy A. Hewitt and Suzanne Lebsock (Urbana and Chicago: University of Illinois Press, 1993), 62–100; Spruill (Wheeler), *New Women of the New South*, chpt. 4, 100-32.

42. Mary Johnston to Lila Meade Valentine, Jan. 5, 1913, and Oct ? 1915, Lila Meade Valentine Papers, Virginia Historical Society, Richmond.

43. Glenda Elizabeth Gilmore, *Gender and Jim Crow: Women and the Politics of White Supremacy in North Carolina, 1896-1920* (University of North Carolina Press, 1996); Adele Logan Alexander, *Princess of the Hither Isles: A Black Suffragist's Story from the Jim Crow South* (Yale University Press, 2019); Adele Logan Alexander, "Adella Hunt Logan, the Tuskegee Woman's Club, and African Americans in the Suffrage Movement," in Marjorie Spruill (Wheeler), *Votes for Women!: The Woman Suffrage Movement in Tennessee, the South, and the Nation* (Knoxville: University of Tennessee Press, 1995): 71-104.

44. Spruill (Wheeler), *New Women of the New South*, 100–132; Spruill (Wheeler), "Race, Reform, and Reaction at the Turn of the Century.".

45. Spruill (Wheeler), *New Women of the New South*, 113-15.

46. Ibid., 116-120; Henry Blackwell, "What the South Can Do (1867)," in *Up from the Pedestal: Selected Writings in the History of American Feminism* (New York: Quadrangle Books, 1968), 253–

57; Henry Blackwell to Laura Clay, Nov. 21, 1885, Clay Papers; Fuller, *Laura Clay*, 54–56; A. Elizabeth Taylor, "The Woman Suffrage Movement in Mississippi, 1890–1920," *Journal of Mississippi History* 30, Feb. 1968 (1994): 1–34; Nellie Nugent Somerville, "President's Address, 1898, MWSA."

47. Alexander, "Adella Hunt Logan," 89; Spruill (Wheeler), *New Women of the New South*, 21, 118.

48. Ibid., 116-19.

49. Ibid.; Blackwell, "What the South Can Do (1867)"; Fuller, *Laura Clay*, 66–70; Belle Kearney, "Address to the 1903 NAWSA Convention," Belle Kearney Papers, Mississippi Department of Archives and History; Spruill (Wheeler), "Race, Reform, and Reaction"; Beverly Beeton, "How the West Was Won for Woman Suffrage," in this volume.

50. Spruill (Wheeler), *New Women of the New South*, 120.

51. Ibid., 120.

52. Ibid., 123.

53. Ibid.

54. Ibid., 125–32; Lebsock, "Virginia Women and White Supremacy."

55. For example, Mary Johnston wrote to Lila Meade Valentine that she was disgusted by Kate Gordon's racist "utterings" and refused the role of honorary vice-president of Gordon's Southern States Woman Suffrage Conference, but did so privately. Mary Johnston to Lila Meade Valentine, Jan. 5, 1913, Valentine Papers.

56. Spruill (Wheeler), *New Women of the New South*, 133–86.

57. Johnston quotation appears in Anne Goodwyn Jones, *Tomorrow Is Another Day: The Woman Writer in the South, 1859-1936* (Baton Rouge: Louisiana State University Press, 1981), 186.

58. Spruill (Wheeler), *New Women of the New South*, 135-41.

59. Ibid., 133-70.

60. Ibid., 154–57; See "Resolution adopted by the 1915 state convention of Tennessee suffragists, Jackson," Sue Shelton White Papers, Schlesinger Library, Harvard University.

61. Spruill (Wheeler), *New Women of the New South*, 156–80.

62. Somerville quoted in Kenneth R. Johnston, "Kate Gordon and the Woman Suffrage Movement in the South," *Journal of Southern History* 38, Aug. 1972 (n.d.): 381; Anne Dallas Dudley to Mrs. John South, KERA president, Jan. 2, 1919, Clay Papers.

63. Clipping n.d., "Democratic Party May Lose Support, "White Papers."

64. On Catt's "Winning Plan," see Robert Booth Fowler's essay in this volume; Carrie Chapman Catt to Southern presidents, Jan. 11, 1916, Clay Papers; Madeline Breckinridge, "Kentucky Chapter Woman Suffrage History: 1900-1930," MMB Papers.

65. Spruill (Wheeler), *New Women of the New South*, 172–80; Laura Clay to Kate Gordon, July 31, 1920, Clay Papers; Fuller, *Laura Clay*, 160.

66. *Richmond-Times Dispatch*, Aug. 19, 1920.

67. S. Breckinridge, *Madeline McDowell Breckinridge*, 236, 237.

68. Pattie Ruffner Jacobs, "Tradition Vs. Justice."

69. Ibid.

70. As predicted, after 1920 the restrictions that prevented black men from voting were used against black women. See essay by Rosalyn Terborg-Penn in this volume.

71. See for example, Jacobs, "Tradition Vs. Justice."

72. Marjorie J. Spruill, *Divided We Stand: The Battle Over Women's Rights and Family Values That Polarized American Politics* (Bloomsbury, 2017).

Mary Church Terrell (center), and her two sisters,
Annette (left) and Sarah Church

Ten

AFRICAN AMERICAN WOMEN AND THE WOMAN SUFFRAGE MOVEMENT

Rosalyn Terborg-Penn

Editor's Introduction: This essay by renowned historian Rosalyn Terborg-Penn, the pioneering scholar in the study of African American women in the suffrage movement, provides an overview of their involvement in the movement's long and complex history. African American suffragists played an active role in the fight for female enfranchisement despite many obstacles. These included obstacles placed in their path by other suffragists—White women—who were willing, in many cases, to win their own enfranchisement at the expense of leaving their African American sisters behind.

The women's rights movement and the movement for justice for African Americans had a close, albeit erratic, relationship throughout American history. Women—Black and White—played an active role in the fight to abolish slavery. Yet discrimination against women who took on a highly visible role in the fight led antislavery feminists to begin an enduring movement for women's rights. Just after the Civil War, supporters of the rights of Blacks and women worked together—for *universal* suffrage—in the American Equal Rights Association founded in 1866. However, they divided rancorously in 1869 over the exclusion of women from enfranchisement through the Fourteenth and Fifteenth Amendments. As Terborg-Penn reminds us, supporters of woman suffrage broke into two woman suffrage organizations over this issue, with some suffragists refusing to accept the idea that this was "the Negro's Hour" and that women must wait their turn.

The situation was drastically different in the last three decades of the woman suffrage movement when the historic connection between women's rights and the rights of African Americans became a distinct liability for advocates of *woman* suffrage. The 1890s and early 1900s was an era in which the vast majority of Southern Black men were disfranchised through legislation and constitutional amendments—unchallenged by the federal government. In addition, Jim Crow laws were adopted establishing segregation in nearly every aspect of life, resulting in one of the worst periods in the history of American race relations. At this time, many national suffrage leaders, working with White Southern suffragists, tried unsuccessfully to promote woman suffrage by saying that the enfranchisement of women—with educational requirements that would effectively limit the vote to White women— would actually help restore White supremacy in Southern politics. In the last decade of the suffrage movement, after disfranchisement had been completed, White suffragists insisted that woman suffrage and Black suffrage were *unrelated* issues. They countered anti-suffragists' claims that state or federal suffrage amendments threatened White supremacy by insisting that the same discriminatory provisions that kept Black men from voting would apply to Black women.

Victims of both racism and sexism and eager to fight against both, African American women were in a difficult position as relations between these two great social movements fluctuated. Not enfranchised along with the men of their race in the Reconstruction amendments, African American women faced a cruel dilemma when asked to wait patiently for their own enfranchisement. Their predicament worsened in the late nineteenth and early twentieth centuries. Black women who were eager to participate in the woman suffrage movement often found it difficult to do so, as White suffragists not only embraced racist tactics but excluded Black women from membership in suffrage organizations. When at last the long-awaited "woman's hour" seemed to be at hand, White suffragists deliberately avoided any action that might alarm White racists and endanger the suffrage cause—and *again* African American women were expected to understand.

As Terborg-Penn explains, African American women nevertheless played an active role in every stage of the suffrage movement from the antebellum period through the suffrage victory in 1920, working sometimes with White suffragists and sometimes in separate African American women's clubs. Among American suffragists, Black women were, perhaps, the most unwavering advocates of universal suffrage for all. Yet, as Terborg-Penn argues, they also understood and proclaimed publicly that the vote was essential for their own protection, the protection of their children, and the progress of their race.

African American suffragists did *not* understand or accept their exclusion from White suffrage organizations or the racist tactics employed by White suffragists. Neither did they accept the efforts of Southern state governments to exclude them from voting after the victory of the Nineteenth Amendment or the failure of White women's organizations to assist them in claiming that right. Though some African American women were able to register and vote even in the South, the vast majority remained disfranchised. Not until 1965 would Black women—and Black men—be fully enfranchised, after a new suffrage movement in which African American women *again* played a leading role. Only then was America, at last, a nation in which there was universal suffrage.

★   ★   ★   ★   ★

FRICAN AMERICAN WOMEN participated in the woman suffrage movement from the antebellum period through to the passage of the Nineteenth Amendment. Legal status, class, region of residence, gender, and racial identification determined the degree to which Black women could participate in the movement. Multiple forms of oppression, primarily slavery and then poverty, restricted many Black women from working to gain women's right to vote in the nineteenth century. Nevertheless, African American women resisted the many barriers put against their political participation. Similar categories bound all American women, and most African American men, all of whom were also disfranchised. However, during the seventy-two years of the movement, limitations on these groups were never as restricting as those set by the society for Black women.

Throughout the history of the movement, but particularly in the nineteenth century, Black women had little opportunity to participate in organized woman suffrage activities. During the antebellum period, only the relatively small number of legally free African American women were privileged enough to lobby for the right to vote. After emancipation during the post-Civil War years, impoverished Southern Black women seeking work, fleeing physical threats to their lives, and struggling with survival strategies for their families, could little afford to make the organized woman suffrage movement a priority. At this time, the large majority of Black women fell into this category. Nonetheless, there were always African American woman suffragists and as the century turned, more and more Black women, inside and outside of the South, began to flex their political muscles and demand the right to vote.

Although Blacks and Whites developed similar suffrage strategies and formed coalitions, differing experiences among the races and conflicts between the two groups resulted. The disfranchised all agreed that rational individuals could not argue against the ideas of freedom and justice for all adult citizens, though some educated White suffragists attempted to exclude immigrant women who did not speak English from qualifying to vote. Nonetheless, by the late nineteenth century an anti-Black woman suffrage strategy, more insidious than the anti-immigrant woman agenda, reinforced differences among African American and White woman suffragists, some of whom hoped to exclude Black women from gaining the right to vote. This anti-woman suffrage agenda further divided Black and White woman suffragists.

Class was another factor that influenced women's participation in the organized woman suffrage movement. Just as the majority of White women who actively participated in the organized movement were of the middle class, the majority of Black women suffragists appeared to have enjoyed higher status than the masses of women of their race. Because many of the activities of African American women participants were not recorded in the official histories of the movement, it is difficult to be sure that more middle-class Black women were suffragists than those of the working class. The changing status of African

American women during the duration of the movement—from slave to free, from rural to urban, from illiterate to literate—can be seen as factors which encouraged Black strategies to achieve women's enfranchisement. One thing is certain: for various reasons more and more Black women, like White women, joined the ranks of suffragists as the movement progressed in the twentieth century. This survey of African American women in the woman suffrage movement focuses on their reasons for supporting the "Votes for Women" campaign, but also on the obstacles they met along the way to enfranchisement.

Nineteenth-Century Black Woman Suffragists

There were two fundamental reasons why African Americans supported the woman suffrage movement during the nineteenth century. At mid-century their argument was based upon the belief, which was also held by White woman suffragists, that women were second-class citizens who needed the vote to improve their status in society. However, by the late nineteenth and early twentieth centuries, the rationale had grown to include the argument that Black women needed the vote in order to help uplift the race and to obtain their own rights. A discussion of the activities and views of Black female suffragists from the antebellum period to the turn of the century reveals that woman suffrage, to them, was a just and a practical cause.[1]

Although Black women participated throughout the nineteenth-century woman suffrage campaign, their views were seldom recorded during the antebellum period. During these years, most of the African Americans commonly associated with the leadership of the struggle were men. Nonetheless, several African American women were among the ranks of antebellum woman's rights advocates. The most renowned among them was Sojourner Truth, who attended several woman's rights meetings beginning with the Worcester, Massachusetts Convention of 1850. Ironically, she was quite unlike the other African American suffragists of her time. She was an emancipated slave who was illiterate and labored in various menial capacities for her keep. Her African American sisters in the movement were literate, privileged women who had been born free. Truth is known to the movement because the White leadership recorded her outspoken sentiments, often citing them as anomalous to those of the other women in the movement. In 1851, for example, at Akron, Ohio, Truth gave a remarkable address that made her famous in the annals of the movement, despite the attempts of some White feminists to thwart her efforts to be heard. From that time on, Truth's views on women's rights and woman suffrage, spoken in folk dialect, were highly publicized. At the New York City convention held in 1853, for example, Truth commented publicly about White prejudice against her, when she said: "I know that it feels a kind O'hissin' like to see a colored woman get up and tell you about things, and Woman's Rights."[2]

Unlike those of Sojourner Truth, the words of suffragists Harriet Forten Purvis and her sister, Margaretta Forten, were not recorded. Both women were founding members of the Philadelphia Female Anti-Slavery Society and daughters of the wealthy reformer James Forten, Sr. The sisters helped to lay the groundwork for the first National Woman's Rights Convention ever held, in October 1854. Another early Black female suffragist was abolitionist lecturer Sarah Remond from Salem, Massachusetts. She was honored in 1858, when she spoke at the Ninth National Woman's Rights Convention held at New York City, but her remarks were not recorded. According to the recollections of Susan B. Anthony, journalist and militant abolitionist Mary Ann Shadd Cary began her support of woman's rights during the late 1850s. However, it appears that none of her statements on woman suffrage during the antebellum period have survived.[3]

After the Civil War, these Black female abolitionists and feminists were joined by Hattie Purvis, who was Harriet Purvis's daughter, and by abolitionist and poet Frances Ellen Watkins Harper. Both women participated in the American Equal Rights Association (AERA). In an effort to campaign for universal suffrage, this organization of men and women was founded in 1866 during a woman's rights convention. Frances Harper spoke at the convention and also served on the financial committee, but there appears to be no record of her remarks. Aside from her participation as a committee member, during this period, little is known about her reasons for supporting woman suffrage. Nevertheless, during the years in which the AERA functioned, from 1866 through 1869, Black women served on committees and contributed financial as well as moral support.[4]

If Sojourner Truth is best remembered for her folk words of wisdom, Harriet and Hattie Purvis can be remembered for their consistent service in a variety of roles in the AERA. In 1866 Harriet and Black abolitionist William Still were elected to the Executive Committee. In 1867 she and Black abolitionist Charles Lenox Remond appeared as the Blacks elected to the Finance Committee. In 1868, Hattie Purvis was elected recording secretary, along with Henry Blackwell. Both were reelected the following year.[5]

By 1869, differences in ideology among suffragists in the AERA over the proposed Fifteenth Amendment split the membership. Although the association members all supported the goal of universal suffrage, they disagreed on the means by which this goal was to be achieved. Some felt that a just amendment should include all disfranchised Americans, despite widespread public opposition to woman suffrage. Others believed that universal suffrage would have to be achieved in stages and that the most politically advantageous means was to enfranchise Black men first, the campaign for which was called "Negro suffrage." As a result of this controversy, the AERA ceased to function. Elizabeth Cady Stanton, Susan B. Anthony, and their supporters abandoned the AERA and formed the National Woman Suffrage Association (NWSA) in May 1869 and divorced themselves from the "Negro suffrage" issue. Although men were allowed to participate in the NWSA, they were excluded from official positions. By November 1869, Lucy Stone and Henry Ward Beecher had led their followers into the American Woman Suffrage Association (AWSA), which supported the Fifteenth Amendment and allowed males to hold office in the AWSA.[6]

Black suffragists, both males and females, became involved in this ideological dispute. Mary Ann Cary, for example, disagreed with the final form of the Fifteenth Amendment because it did not enfranchise women. On the other hand, Frances Harper, although committed to woman suffrage, felt that it was politically expedient to fight first to enfranchise Black men despite the setback to the woman suffrage cause.[7] Divisions among female suffragists affected Black affiliation in the resulting suffrage associations. Hattie Purvis attended NWSA meetings, as did Cary. Harper affiliated with the AWSA. Sojourner Truth attended meetings of both groups.[8]

During the 1870s, the AWSA attracted several additional Black women. Among them was Caroline Remond Putman of the crusading Remond family of Salem, Massachusetts, whose members actively lectured against slavery. In 1870 she helped to found the Massachusetts Woman Suffrage Association under the

Mary Ann Shadd Cary
NATIONAL ARCHIVES OF CANADA

Frances Rollin, c. 1870 - 1879
NEW YORK PUBLIC LIBRARY

auspices of the AWSA.[9] Josephine St. Pierre Ruffin was another Massachusetts Black woman suffragist. She has been described as having played a leading role in every movement to emancipate Black women. Ruffin began her suffrage activities during 1875 as a member of the Massachusetts Woman Suffrage Association. A Bostonian, she affiliated with the group as a result of the welcome she received from Lucy Stone, Julia Ward Howe, and other pioneers in the Massachusetts movement.[10] Perhaps Ruffin's positive assessment of these prominent AWSA leaders gives clues as to why more African American women appear to have affiliated with the AWSA rather than the NWSA.

The first South Carolina delegate to a woman suffrage convention was a Black woman, Charlotte Rollin (known as Lottie) of Charleston. Along with her sisters, Frances, Louisa, and Kate, the Rollin sisters were influential in Reconstruction politics during the late 1860s and 1870s. Frances Rollin worked for and later married William J. Whipper who, as a delegate to the South Carolina Constitutional Convention of 1868, pleaded for the enfranchisement of women as well as Black men. Lottie Rollin worked for Black congressman Robert Brown Elliott. Rollin spoke on the floor of the South Carolina House of Representatives in 1869 to urge support of universal suffrage. By 1870, she chaired the founding meeting of the South Carolina Woman's Rights Association and was elected secretary. In 1871 her sister Louisa led a meeting at the state capital to promote woman suffrage. The following year Kate Rollin was elected treasurer of the association, and Lottie Rollin represented South Carolina as an ex-officio member of the Executive Committee of the AWSA, which met in New York City that year.[11]

Not until the 1870s do we find Black female arguments on behalf of woman suffrage preserved in written form—other than those attributed to Sojourner Truth. At this time, Lottie Rollin addressed the chairman of the South Carolina Woman's Rights Convention in 1870 and said: "We ask suffrage not as a favor, not as a privilege, but as a right based on the ground that we are human beings, and as such entitled to all human rights."[12] The Rollin rationale on behalf of woman suffrage reflected the contemporary rhetoric that women were second-class citizens who needed the vote to improve their status in society.

One strategy used by Blacks as well as Whites to obtain the ballot for women was an appeal for female enfranchisement based on the Fifteenth Amendment. In 1872, White suffragist Mary Olney Brown of Washington State wrote a letter to Frederick Douglass, editor of the Black newspaper, *The New National Era* (Washington). Offering an emotional plea for Black male support of the vote for Black women, Brown argued that the Fifteenth Amendment, which had enfranchised Black men in 1870, should be applied to the enfranchisement of women because it did not exclude them in the definition of citizenship. Douglass printed the letter, wherein Brown encouraged voting Black men to support her strategy. This appears to be the first in many efforts made by White suffragists to reestablish the political coalition they had severed with African American men.[13]

Brown's strategy to demand suffrage as woman's legal right, a strategy frequently employed in the 1870s, could very well have come from journalist Mary Ann Cary, who had argued on behalf of the ballot for Black women in the 1860s and became one of the few women during this period who successfully registered to vote. She did this in 1871 in the District of Columbia, although like Susan B. Anthony and others, Cary was prohibited from voting. Cary is an example of the women historian Ellen DuBois calls radical feminists, who emerged in the 1870s as independent suffragists.[14] Cary attended the NWSA Convention that met in Washington in January of 1871 while she was a student in the Howard University Law School, and supported the memorial that Victoria Woodhull presented before the House Judiciary Committee the previous December. Woodhull had argued, like Mary Olney Brown, that the proposed Sixteenth Amendment to enfranchise women was not necessary, for as citizens, women had the right to vote under the Fourteenth and Fifteenth Amendments. She appealed to Congress merely to pass a declaratory resolution to that effect since the Constitution made no distinction between citizens based on gender.[15]

In support of this strategy, Cary prepared a testimony for the Judiciary Committee of the House of Representatives about the need for Black women to vote in the District of Columbia. She noted that she was a taxpayer with the same obligations as the Black male taxpayers of the city. Cary felt, therefore, that suffrage should be her right just as it was theirs. She noted that many women of her race in the nation's capital supported the other women of the nation who demanded not only the vote, but the striking of the word "male" from the Constitution.[16]

Supporting her claim about Black female support for woman suffrage, Cary wrote the NWSA in 1876 on behalf of ninety-four Black women from the District of Columbia. Her letter requested that their names be enrolled in the July 4, 1876 centennial autograph book, as signers of the NWSA's Woman's Declaration of Rights. This declaration called for the immediate enfranchisement of American women.[17]

Cary and Mary Olney Brown were not alone in identifying woman suffrage as a potential source of strength to Black women during the Reconstruction years. Frances Harper argued similarly. In 1873, she attended the AWSA Convention at the Cooper Union in New York City. In making the closing speech, Harper declared that "as much as White women need the ballot, colored women need it more." She indicted what she called the "ignorant and often degraded men" who subjected Black women in the South to arbitrary legal authority. Acknowledging the progress already made by women of her race, Harper pleaded for equal rights and equal education for the African American women of the nation.[18]

The post-Civil War years were not only an era of change for White woman suffragists, they marked a time for expanding the rationale for woman suffrage among African American women. Even though Black women continued to express the original argument in support of woman suffrage—women are second-class citizens who need the vote—by the late nineteenth and early twentieth centuries, the rationale began to reflect more specifically needs of African American women. For example, in 1880 Cary organized the Colored Women's Progressive Franchise Association in the District of Columbia. Among the purposes of the group was what Cary called "an aggressive stand against the assumption that men only may begin and conduct industrial and other things." This idea was in keeping with the radical feminist belief that women, like men, should take leadership roles in developing industrial sectors in the economy. Cary even made plans to start a newspaper to support the rights and interests of women and to establish a joint stock company in which women were to have the controlling official power. There is no evidence, however, that she was ever able to accomplish these goals.[19]

Cary was not the only Black female journalist to favor woman suffrage in the 1880s. Gertrude Bustill Mossell of Philadelphia, like Cary, was from a prominent antebellum free-Negro family of reformers. Mossell initiated a woman's column in T. Thomas Fortune's first newspaper, *The New York Freeman*, a nationally oriented Black newspaper. In her first article, entitled "Woman Suffrage" published in 1885, she encouraged Blacks to read the *History of Woman Suffrage*, the *New Era*, the essays of John Stuart Mill, and other works about woman's rights to familiarize them with the woman suffrage movement and perhaps change the minds of those who opposed it. Mossell argued also that despite the anti-suffragists' charges to the contrary, most housewives supported woman suffrage.[20]

Other veteran suffragists continued their activities in the movement during the 1880s. Hattie Purvis was actively involved in the Pennsylvania Woman Suffrage

Mary McCurdy, 1897   Josephine St. Pierre Ruffin, 1902

Association. Frances Harper was a director of the Women's Congress, and by 1887 she was the Superintendent of Work Among Colored People for the Woman's Christian Temperance Union (WCTU), a national body quite supportive of woman suffrage. Josephine St. Pierre Ruffin was a member of the first board of the Massachusetts School Suffrage Association, which was founded in 1880.[21]

In the last decade of the nineteenth century, more and more African American women began to organize, raising their voices in support of woman suffrage. One of the reasons for this was the rising number of educated Blacks who emerged during the first generation out of slavery. With this new freedom, Black women, like White women, actively developed the women's club movement as a vehicle for change.

The first fifty-two delegates who met to organize the National Federation of Afro-American Women at Boston in August of 1895, were eager supporters of woman suffrage. The women cheered suffragist William Lloyd Garrison, Jr., who spoke of the need for political equality for women. Among the members of the Federation were veteran suffragists Frances Harper and Josephine Ruffin, who had made the initial call for an organization representative of African American women throughout the nation. Among the younger members destined to become prime movers among the Black woman suffragists of the twentieth century was Washington, D.C. educator Mary Church Terrell, a native of Memphis and an Oberlin graduate.[22]

In 1896 the National Federation of Afro-American Women merged with the National League of Colored Women to form the National Association of Colored Women (NACW). Mary Church Terrell was elected the first president. She and several other newly emerging Black female leaders included woman suffrage in their campaign to lead the nation's Black women toward self-help and racial uplift. Among this group was journalist Ida B. Wells-Barnett, who had been driven out of Memphis in 1892 because of her anti-lynching crusade. She later married, had a family, and settled in Chicago. Margaret Murray Washington, principal of the secondary school at Tuskegee Institute in Alabama and Booker T. Washington's wife, was also among this group. By 1900, Susan B. Anthony listed these three women among the prominent advocates of woman suffrage.[23]

A lesser-known Southern Black woman of the 1890s was Mary McCurdy, a temperance leader and advocate of woman suffrage whose views echoed the changing rationale for woman suffrage exemplified by racial and gender identification. She personified the growing number of Southern women, educated during Reconstruction, who sought political means to solve the social ills of Black communities. While living in Rome, Georgia, McCurdy was president of the local Black woman's temperance union and an official in the state temperance organization. She also edited the *National Presbyterian*, a temperance paper published in 1890. A firm believer in woman suffrage, McCurdy saw the franchise as the means to prohibit the liquor traffic, a major vehicle for political corruption. Not only did she blame White men for keeping the ballot from the women of the nation, she also blamed them for the political corruption in the South. McCurdy felt that the majority of African American men who had voted in the South after the Fifteenth Amendment enfranchised them had either been robbed of that right, or had allowed their ballot to be purchased. African American women, she predicted, would never allow their votes to be bought.[24]

While touring the South during the Reconstruction years, Frances Harper observed the results of political corruption. She echoed McCurdy's opinion when she expressed her sentiments against corruption, published in a poem of 1896. Harper spoke in dialect through "Aunt Chloe," who said:

> And this buying up each other
> Is something worse than mean.
> Though I think a heap of voting,
> I go for voting clean.[25]

Although White women complained about political corruption in the South and in immigrant communities in the Northeast, they were usually on the offensive with their criticism of others. African American women were always on the defensive, defending their race as well as criticizing the ills that kept many former slaves powerless. Mary Church Terrell responded to White women's criticism of the purchase of the "Negro vote" at the National American Woman Suffrage Association (NAWSA) meeting that she attended in Washington in 1904. By then a national figure, she felt that Black men were being unduly condemned for selling their votes and she said: "They never sold their vote til they found that it made no difference how they cast them." Terrell noted also that there were many cases of Black men who were tempted, yet never sold their right to the ballot. Furthermore, she suggested that the White suffragists should aid rather than merely condemn Black voters: "My sisters of the dominant race, stand up not only for the oppressed sex, but also for the oppressed race!"[26]

At the turn of the century, Terrell, like other Black suffragists before her, admonished America for violating the principle "government of the people, for the people and by the people," by denying women the right to the ballot. As a

"Woman to the Rescue," a pro-suffrage cartoon from *The Crisis*, May 1916
Woman Suffrage Media Collection

result of male-dominated politics, she asserted, women were held in subjugation by men, many of whom she called "illiterate, debauched, and vicious." [27] The Terrell rationale for support of woman suffrage included both themes—suffrage as the right of women as citizens and woman suffrage as a means to uplifting African Americans.

Twentieth-Century Black Woman Suffragists

By the first decade of the twentieth century, more Black women began to speak out about how important their right to vote could be to Black people as a whole and to Black women in particular. Yet, as growing numbers of African American women supported and joined the organized woman suffrage movement, their potential political influence stimulated the creation of greater obstacles blocking their attempts to achieve the right to vote.[28]

With the creation of the "colored" women's club movement, more and more resourceful women had a means of spreading the word about strategies for uplifting themselves and their race. Adella Hunt Logan was one of them. She was the only Alabama woman, Black or White, listed in 1900 by the NAWSA as a life member. A native of Georgia who joined the Tuskegee Institute faculty in 1883 as principal of the training school, Logan wrote one of the most comprehensive arguments in support of woman suffrage. In 1905, she argued similarly to Terrell: "Government of the people, for the people and by the people is but partially realized so long as woman has no vote."[29] She could not understand why women were treated as citizens in other aspects of American life, but not when it came to the exercise of the franchise. Her words were similar to those of Cary, who had indicted America for imposing taxation without representation upon the majority of women of the nation. Noting the suffrage victories for women in various Western states, Logan argued that as a result of woman suffrage in those states, civic affairs had improved.[30]

Logan rejected the argument of anti-suffragists who alleged that women did not need the ballot because they were not interested in politics. She opposed the view that woman suffrage would bring women into politics and, as a result, cause them to neglect the home. Logan went further and also dismissed the theory that exercising the franchise was a complicated process that women could not understand. She concluded, as did Terrell, that the right of suffrage was withheld from women for political reasons by those she called "ignorant and vicious men." Finally, like Cary, Truth, Harper and other Black women of the nineteenth century, Logan argued that if White women needed the vote in order to acquire advantages as well as protection of their rights, then Black women needed the ballot even more, because they carried the double burden of racism and sexism.[31] Numerous African American women followed in this tradition, formulating arguments that emphasized why Black women, specifically, needed the vote.

When given the opportunity, African American women exercised the right to vote. For instance, Black women voted in Colorado at the turn of the century. Their political activities were noted by Helen Woodbury, who in 1909 published a study of the equal suffrage movement in Colorado. She commented that Black women were interested in politics because in 1901 there was a "colored woman's" Republican club in Denver. In addition, she found that 1,373 Blacks voted in Denver during the 1906 election, of whom 45.2 percent were women. From Woodbury's overall statistics, she concluded that a larger percentage of Black women than White women voted in that Denver election.[32] Needless to say, reports like Woodbury's sent up red flags in front of those who feared the potential power of Black women voters, especially the power of Black club women.

Woodbury's findings are not surprising because, during the last quarter of the nineteenth century, the woman's club movement had expanded dramatically, usually with clubs developing membership and reform strategies along racially separate lines. Perhaps one reason for this separate development lay in the unique needs of Black women during the period. Native-born White women had no need to defend their dignity against widespread assumptions that they were wanton, immoral, and socially inferior. White women did not have the severe problems of racial discrimination that compounded Black women's plight in employment and education. Moreover, race consciousness was evident among African Americans in general as growing numbers of race-specific civil rights organizations, business groups, and self-help societies emerged at the century's end.[33]

Racism in the Suffrage Movement

Another reason for the development of racially separate women's groups was the exclusion of Black women from most White female clubs. Despite the differences between the two groups, there were some common causes and attempts at unity on local levels. Journalist Paula Giddings refers to the women who made these attempts as "radical interracialists"—Black women who were determined to enter the mainstream.[34] Nevertheless, doing so was not easy, for this was the era of "Jim Crow" nationwide. African American women were involved in temperance work, suffrage groups, and club work. The experiences of many of their leaders indicated the pervasiveness of White female prejudice and discrimination against Black females in women's groups, even those who were part of the woman suffrage coalition.[35]

Throughout the 1890s, Josephine St. Pierre Ruffin had challenged White women to unite with Blacks for the benefit of humanity, but her words went virtually unheeded outside of Massachusetts. She was discriminated against personally when attending the General Federation of Women's Clubs, which met in Wisconsin in 1900. Disillusioned by the incident, the Black woman's club she represented, The Woman's Era Club, made an official statement which included the view "that colored women should confine themselves to their clubs and the large field of work open to them there."[36]

At the same convention of the General Federation of Women's Clubs, Mary Church Terrell, representing the NACW, was refused permission to bring the group greetings on behalf of her association because the Southern clubs objected, threatening resignation. Despite this rebuff, Terrell was invited to speak before other White groups during the early years of the twentieth century. At the Minneapolis Convention of Women in 1900 she addressed the group not only about the needs of Black women, but also about the prejudice and lack of sympathy on the part of White women. Terrell indicted them for not extending a helping hand to African Americans whose aims were similar to their own. The same year, she made a similar speech at the NAWSA meeting in the District of Columbia.[37]

Ida B. Wells-Barnett reported how Fannie Barrier Williams, an African American club woman in Chicago, attempted to join the Chicago Woman's

Club in 1894. The all-White group split over the controversy created by those who wanted a Black member and those who did not. After fourteen months of controversy, Williams was admitted. At the turn of the century, Wells-Barnett noted that the issue was still significant in Illinois when the State Federation of Women's Clubs membership made it impossible for African American clubs to become members. Nonetheless, Black women's clubs were so numerous that by the second decade of the twentieth century a large federation of "colored" women's clubs was active in Black communities throughout Illinois. By 1914, Wells-Barnett helped to organize the Alpha Suffrage Club of African American women, who were influential later in electing a Black man to Congress, Oscar DePriest.[38]

The experiences of Ruffin, Terrell, Williams, and Wells-Barnett were not unique. During the same period, the woman suffrage campaign gained momentum, but the national leadership emulated the racial attitudes of White women's clubs around the nation. As historian Aileen Kraditor has observed, White supremacy was an influential factor in the strategy of the suffragists as the need developed for Southern support for a woman suffrage amendment. As early as the 1890s, Susan B. Anthony realized the potential to the woman suffrage cause in wooing Southern White women. She chose expedience over loyalty and justice when she asked veteran feminist Frederick Douglass not to attend the 1895 NAWSA Convention scheduled in Atlanta. Anthony explained to Wells-Barnett that Douglass's presence on the stage with the honored guests, his usual place at these conventions, would have offended the Southern hosts. Wells-Barnett, however, admonished Anthony for giving in to racial prejudice.[39]

By the 1903 NAWSA Convention in New Orleans, the board of officers prepared a statement endorsing the organization's position to allow states the right to develop their own woman suffrage positions, which was tantamount to an endorsement of White supremacy in most states, particularly in the South. The statement was signed by Susan B. Anthony, Carrie C. Catt, Anna Howard Shaw, Kate N. Gordon, Alice Stone Blackwell, Harriet Taylor Upton, Laura Clay, and Mary Coggeshall. During the convention week, Susan B. Anthony visited the Black Phillis Wheatley Club in New Orleans. In presenting flowers to Anthony on the occasion, Sylvanie Williams, president of the club, indicated that Black women were painfully aware of their "down trotten" [sic] position among White suffragists.[40]

Fear of offending Southern White suffragists in Atlanta and in New Orleans is one thing, but how can the prejudice against African American club women in Wisconsin, and in Chicago be explained? There was a nationwide, not just a Southern prejudice against African American women. It appears that White women outside of the South used Southern White women's overt prejudice as an excuse for the NAWSA's discriminatory policies, while hiding their own similar feelings about Black women, although they shared many of the Black women's goals for reform and women's political equity. African American woman suffragists were quite aware of their position, and they were determined to move beyond the attempts to keep them disfranchised.

Black suffragists knew that although those national suffrage leaders who courted Black support endorsed equal suffrage among the races while in African American circles, their public actions and statements to the mainstream society often contradicted their professed egalitarianism. For example, Alice Paul, organizer of the National Woman's Party (NWP) and the suffrage parade in front of the White House in 1913, had expressed her sympathy for Black woman's enfranchisement. Yet before the parade the leaders asked Wells-Barnett, who was representing the Alpha Suffrage Club, not to march with the White Chicago delegates. Again the rationale was fear of offending White Southern women. Terrell marched in the parade with African American women from Howard University, assembled in the section reserved for Black women—at the end of the line. By 1919, she confided her feelings about Paul to Walter White of the National Association for the Advancement of Colored People (NAACP). Both questioned Paul's loyalty to Black women, concluding that if she and other White suffragist leaders could get the amendment through without enfranchising African American women they would.[41]

Why this suspicion among African American leaders on the eve of the passage of the Nineteenth Amendment? By this time, nearly all the major White suffrage leaders had compromised their support of Black woman suffrage. For example, despite endorsing Black suffrage, Anna Howard Shaw had been accused of refusing to allow an African American delegate at the Louisville NAWSA convention of 1911 to propose an anti-discrimination resolution. As president of the NAWSA from 1910 to 1915, Shaw avoided offending White, Southern suffragists, and supported the states' rights position of the association.[42]

The strength of the states' rights strategy among Southern, White suffragists can be observed as early as the 1890s, when, they sought suffrage for White women through new state constitutions, which had been drafted to disenfranchise Black men. Historian Marjorie Spruill confirms that White suffragists believed votes for White women could be used as a way of countering the "Negro vote" in the South. The dynamics of this Southern woman suffrage strategy can be seen in looking at the similar positions of two leaders of the Southern movement. Laura Clay came from Kentucky, a state with a small Black population—which could hardly have affected the balance of political power in the state—whereas Kate Gordon came from Louisiana, a state where the Black population was very large, and had held considerable political influence in the state during the Reconstruction Era. By 1906, however, Clay had come to agree with Gordon that Southern suffragists should campaign for state suffrage amendments containing "Whites-only" clauses.[43]

African American leaders directed their displeasure upon Southern suffragists like Clay. For example, NAACP officials noted that at the Jubilee Convention of the NAWSA in 1919, Clay proposed "that certain sections [of the proposed amendment] be amended with particular reference to those parts that would permit the enfranchisement of Negro women in the South."[44] It appears that as the success of a non-restrictive woman suffrage amendment became apparent, some Southern leaders feared the potential threat to the status quo that an active and fast-growing Black woman suffrage movement would have in states such as Tennessee and Kentucky.

By 1919 a united front began to develop among African American suffragists nationwide, as Black women feared the growing alliance between national woman suffrage leaders and those who hoped to eliminate Blacks from the so-called Anthony Amendment being debated in Congress. As the amendment was debated in the Senate, several Southern senators attempted to alter it in ways that would either restrict the vote to White women, or restrict implementation to the states. For example, in 1918 Mississippi Senator John Sharp Williams proposed to amend the resolution to make it read, "The right of White citizens to vote shall not be denied."[45] However, the vote was laid on the table. Again in 1919, Mississippi Senator Pat Harrison attempted unsuccessfully to have the word "White" placed in the original amendment, while Louisiana Senator Edward J. Gay called for an amendment providing the states instead of the Congress the power to enforce it.[46]

Throughout the Congressional debates, the NAACP, representing Black and White supporters of enfranchising African American women, lobbied for the defeat of such efforts. In addition, the NACW took action by encouraging African American women in states where Black men still retained the franchise to pressure the NAWSA and the NWP to oppose any changes to the Anthony Amendment. In the meantime, NACW leaders knew that White woman suffragists, despite their reluctance to enfranchise Black women, needed the votes of Black men outside of the South. These African American women developed a strategy designed to expose the hypocrisy of the White suffrage leadership. In 1918, the leaders of the Northeastern Federation of Women's Clubs, which represented six thousand Black women from nine states, applied for NAWSA membership.[47] Carrie Chapman Catt, who was president of the NAWSA at the time, asked Ida Husted Harper, editor of the *History of Woman Suffrage* and a long-time friend of the late Susan B. Anthony, to discourage the Northeastern Federation from applying for membership. Both women felt NAWSA membership for the Black group would offend the White Southern organizations and hamper passage of the Anthony Amendment. Both Catt and Harper had argued in favor of Black woman suffrage in the past and apparently thought the Federation would understand their position and not be offended by their request.[48]

However, African American club women understood what White club women did not. Blacks were seeking more than NAWSA membership; they were seeking NAWSA support for the enfranchisement of African American women. Elizabeth C. Carter, president of the Federation, admonished Harper for her arrogance and patronizing testimony, which presumed that African American women were not politically sophisticated enough to use NAWSA membership as a strategy to gain the vote.[49] Fortunately amendments seeking to enfranchise White women only failed with the close of the Sixty-Fifth Congress and the Anthony Amendment was passed by Congress in June 1919. However, African Americans understood how vulnerable their women were as the amendment made the rounds in the states toward ratification.

By the summer of 1920, only one state was needed for ratification and President Wilson successfully appealed to the governor of Tennessee for a special legislative session to consider the amendment. Tennessee appeared to be the only hope, but even in this state the legislature could not resolve the stalemate. Once again, the White suffrage leaders realized that African Americans may be needed to break the deadlock. Alice Paul turned to the NAACP for help. At this point, NAACP leaders lent their support by urging Black voting men in Tennessee to lobby their state legislators to support the amendment, but not before taking the opportunity to remind Paul how White women had either worked against Black political leaders who were males, or ignored the plight of Black suffragists who were females. Nonetheless, these women had no compunction about asking Black people for their help.[50]

Fortunately for woman suffragists, the Tennessee deadlock ended positively for the Nineteenth Amendment, which was ratified in August 1920. Despite the White suffragists' record of discrimination, most African American leaders, both men and women, welcomed woman suffrage. Naively, they hoped that Black women could help uplift the standards of their race through exercising the franchise. Like many White woman suffragists, Blacks believed the vote to be the panacea to their social problems.

The Disfranchising of Black Women in the South

African American hopes for political equity were quickly dashed as the majority of Black women who still lived in the South were quickly disfranchised. In addition, the Black Republican women and men outside the South began to lose their political influence within a decade after the passage of the Nineteenth Amendment.

Disfranchisement had been predicted by several White Southern suffragists. Kentucky's Madeline McDowell Breckinridge, for one, considered herself a liberal on racial issues, but did not believe African American women should be voters until they could be properly educated. Breckinridge advocated educational requirements at the state level that would eliminate most potential Black voters. Nonetheless, she opposed the blatantly racist statements made by Southern suffragists like Louisiana's Kate Gordon and Mississippi's Belle Kearney. Of the two, Gordon opposed a federal amendment, saying it invited Northern intervention in the affairs of the states that would endanger White supremacy. However, by the eve of the Nineteenth Amendment's ratification, Kearney attempted to change Gordon's mind about opposing the amendment, arguing that the South need not fear Northern intervention on behalf of disfranchised Black women. Kearney had been convinced that Northerners were sympathetic with the South's "negro problem."[51] Indeed, she was correct.

African Americans, nonetheless, rallied nationwide to the woman suffrage victory. The enthusiastic responses of Black women may have seemed astonishing when one realizes that woman suffrage was a predominantly middle-class movement among native-born White women and that the Black middle class remained very small during the early twentieth century. Furthermore, the heyday of the woman suffrage movement embraced an era that historian Rayford Logan called "the nadir" in African American history, characterized by racial segregation, defamation of the character of Black women, and lynching of Black Americans, both men and women. It is a wonder that African American women dared to dream a White woman's dream—the right to enfranchisement.[52]

Apprehensions from discontented Black leaders about the inclusion of Black women as voters, especially in the South, had been evident throughout the second decade of the twentieth century. African American fears went beyond misgivings about White women in states like New York and Texas, where women gained the franchise before the ratification of the Nineteenth Amendment. In 1917, while the New York State woman suffrage referendum was pending in the legislature, Black suffragists in the state had complained of discrimination against their organizations by White suffragists during the state-wide convention at Saratoga. White suffrage leaders assured Black women that they were welcome in the movement. Although the majority of the African American delegates were conciliated, a vocal minority remained disillusioned. In 1918 the Black editors of the *Houston Observer* responded to Black disillusionment when they called upon the men and women of their race to register to vote in spite of the poll tax, which was designed especially to exclude Texas's African American voters.[53] Black women, nevertheless, were discriminated against. Six of them were refused the right to vote at Fort Worth on the grounds that the primaries were open to White Democrats only. Efforts to disfranchise Black women in Houston failed, however, when the women took legal action against the registrar who attempted to apply the Texas woman suffrage law to White women only. A similar attempt to disqualify African American women in Waxahachie, Texas failed also.[54]

After the ratification of the federal amendment, Black women registered in large numbers throughout the South, especially in Georgia and Louisiana, despite major obstacles placed against them by the White supremacists. In defense, African American women often turned to the NAACP for assistance. Field Secretary William Pickens was sent to investigate the numerous charges and recorded several incidents that he either witnessed personally or about which he received reports. In Columbia, South Carolina, for example, a requirement that a voter pay taxes on property valued at three hundred dollars or more was made mandatory for Black women. If they passed that test, the women were required to read from and to interpret the state or the federal constitutions. No such tests were required of White women.

Although the *Columbia State,* a local newspaper, reported disinterest in registering among African American women, Pickens testified to the contrary. By the end of the registration period, twenty Columbia Black women had signed an affidavit against the registrars who had disqualified them. In the surrounding Richland County, African American women were disqualified when they attempted to register to vote. As a result, several of them made plans to appeal the ruling.[55]

Many cases like these were handled by the NAACP, and after the registration periods ended in the South, its board of directors presented the evidence to Congress. The NAACP officials and others testified at a 1920 congressional hearing in support of the proposed Tinkham Bill that would have reduced representation in Congress from states where there was restriction of woman suffrage and thus protected African American women from disfranchisement. Belle Kearney's prediction was right, however. The North did not intervene in the Southern "negro problem." White supremacy prevailed, as Southern congressmen successfully claimed that Blacks were not disfranchised, just disinterested in voting. Despite the massive evidence produced by the NAACP, the Tinkham Bill failed to pass.[56]

White Southern apprehensions of a viable Black female electorate were not illusionary. "Colored women voter's leagues" were growing throughout the South, where the task of the leagues was to give Black women seeking to qualify to vote instructions for countering White opposition. Leagues could be found in Alabama, Georgia, Tennessee, and Texas. These groups were feared also by White supremacists because the women sought to qualify Black men as voters as well.[57]

African American women organize to vote in Georgia, 1920
SCHOMBURG CENTER, NEW YORK PUBLIC LIBRARY

During the November 1920 elections, Southern Whites also expected Black women to vote in larger numbers than White women. If this happened, they feared, the ballot would soon be returned to African American men. Black suffrage, it was believed, would also result in the return of the two-party system in the South, because African Americans would consistently vote Republican. These apprehensions were realized in Florida after the election. Black women in Jacksonville had registered and voted in greater numbers than White women. In reaction, the Woman Suffrage League of Jacksonville was reorganized into the Duval County League of Democratic Women Voters. The members were dedicated to maintain White supremacy and pledged to register White women voters.[58]

The inability of Congress and the NAACP to protect the rights of Black women voters led the women to seek help from national woman suffrage leaders. Not surprisingly, these attempts failed also. In 1919, anticipating victory, the NAWSA had changed its name to the League of Women Voters (LWV), a non-partisan organization designed to maintain women's political participation on national and local levels. At the 1921 national LWV convention held at Cleveland, African American women brought their complaints about disfranchisement before the LWV. The White Southern delegates at the convention threatened to walk out if the "negro problem" was debated. In typical League fashion, a compromise resulted, wherein African American women were allowed to speak before the body, but no action was taken by the organization.[59]

When the African American women suffragists sought assistance from the National Woman's Party, they were rebuffed totally. The NWP leadership position was that since Black women were discriminated against in the same ways as Black men, their problems were not woman's rights issues, but race issues. Therefore, the NWP felt no obligation to defend the right of African American women as voters.[60]

Abandonment by White women suffragists in 1920 really came as no surprise to most Black women leaders. The preceding decade of woman suffrage politics had reminded them of the assertions of Black woman suffrage supporters of the past. Frederick Douglass had declared in 1868 that Black women were victimized mainly because they were Blacks, not because they were women. Frances Ellen Watkins Harper answered in 1869 that for White women the priority in the struggle for human rights was sex, not race. By 1920 the situation had changed very little, and many African American suffragists had been thoroughly disillusioned by the racism of the White feminists they had encountered.[61]

A significant number of Black women and Black women's organizations had not only supported woman suffrage on the eve of the passage of the Nineteenth Amendment, but attempted to exercise their rights to vote in the elections immediately following the amendment's ratification in 1920. Unfortunately for them, African American women confronted racial discrimination in their efforts to support the amendment and to win the vote. Consequently, discontented Black feminists anticipated the disillusionment that their White counterparts encountered within a decade following amendment ratification, as women's votes did not become the panacea to social problems of the larger society.

Notes

1. Rosalyn Terborg-Penn, "Nineteenth Century Black Women and Woman Suffrage," *The Potomac Review* 7 (Spring/ Summer 1977): 13-24, 13.

2. Elizabeth Cady Stanton, Susan B. Anthony, and Matilda J. Gage, eds., *History of Woman Suffrage*, 6 vols., (New York, 1969), Vol. 1: 115, 546, 567, hereafter *HWS*.

3. Ibid., 386, 668; *HWS* 3: 72.

4. *HWS* 2: 168, 222.

5. Ibid., 191, 221, 378-79; *HWS* 3: 457.

6. *HWS* 2: 400, 406.

7. Speech to the Judiciary Committee, Mary Ann Shadd Cary Papers, Folder No. 2, Moorland-Spingarn Research Center, Howard University, Washington, D.C.; *HWS* 2: 215, 391-92; *HWS* 3: 346-47, 358.

8. See the proceedings for the NWSA and the AWSA for 1869 to 1876 in *HWS* 2.

9. *HWS* 3: 268-69.

10. *The Crisis*, 10 (August 1915), 188; Booker T. Washington, ed., *A New Negro for a New Century* (Chicago, 1900), 392.

11. *HWS* 3: 821, 827-28; Carole Ione, *Pride of Family: Four Generations of American Women of Color* (New York, 1991), 74-75; Joel Williamson, *After Slavery: The Negro in South Carolina During Reconstruction, 1861-1877* (New York, 1975), 338; Nearly three decades later, in *HWS* 4 (1900), Virginia D. Young, president of the South Carolina suffragists, dated the beginning of the suffrage movement in her state as 1890, the year her association was founded, completely ignoring the activities of the interracial woman's rights association founded twenty years before. Terborg-Penn, "Nineteenth Century Black Women and Woman Suffrage," 16.

12. *HWS* 3: 828.

13. Terborg-Penn, "Nineteenth Century Black Women and Woman Suffrage," 17.

14. Ellen Carol DuBois, *Feminism and Suffrage: The Emergence of an Independent Women's Movement in America, 1848-1869* (Ithaca, 1978), 201-02.

15. Speech of A.G. Riddle to the NWSA Anniversary Meeting, January 11, 1871, Washington, D.C., Cary Papers, Folder No. 7A.

16. Speech to the Judiciary Committee, Cary Papers, Folder No. 2.

17. *HWS* 3: 31, 72, 955.

18. *HWS* 3: 828, 833-834; Terborg-Penn, "Nineteenth Century Black Women and Woman Suffrage," 18.

19. Statement of Purpose, Colored Women's Progressive Franchise Association, Cary Papers, Folder No. 5.

20. Gertrude Mossell, "Woman Suffrage," *The New York Freeman*, December 26, 1885.

21. *HWS* 4, (reprint, New York, 1969), 898, 1104; F.E.W. Harper, "A Factor in Human Progress," *AME Church Review* 2 (1885), 14; *HWS*, 3: 273.

22. T. Thomas Fortune, "The New Afro-American Woman," *The New York Sun*, August 7, 1895; *The Woman's Era* (Boston), July 1896; Terborg-Penn, "Nineteenth Century Black Women and Woman Suffrage," 19.

23. Terborg-Penn, "Nineteenth Century Black Women and Woman Suffrage," 19.

24. M.A. McCurdy, "Duty of the State to the Negro," *Afro-American Encyclopedia*, ed. James T. Haley (Nashville, 1895), 141-45.

25. Frances E. Harper, *Sketches of Southern Life* (Philadelphia, 1896), 16.

26. Ida H. Harper, *History of Woman Suffrage*, vols. 5 and 6, (New York, 1900-1920), 105-06.

27. *HWS* 4: 358-59.

28. Rosalyn Terborg-Penn, "Discrimination Against Afro-American Women in the Woman's Movement, 1830-1920," 17-27, in *The Afro-American Woman: Struggles and Images*, Sharon Harley and Rosalyn Terborg-Penn, eds. (Port Washington, N.Y., 1978), 24-27.

29. Adella Logan, "Woman Suffrage," *The Colored American Magazine*, 9 (September 1905), 487.

30. Ibid., 488.

31. Ibid., 489.

32. Helen Laura Sumner Woodbury, *Equal Suffrage: The Results of an Investigation in Colorado Made for the Collegiate Equal Suffrage League of New York State* (New York, 1909), 70, 114-17.

33. Terborg-Penn, "Discrimination Against Afro-American Women," 21.

34. Paula Giddings, *When and Where I Enter: The Impact of Black Women on Race and Sex in America* (New York, 1984), 154.

35. Terborg-Penn, "Discrimination Against Afro-American Women," 21.

36. J.W. Gibson and W.H. Crogman, *Progress of a Race, Or the Remarkable Advancement of the Colored American* (Naperville, Ill., 1902, 1912), 216-20.

37. *Minneapolis Journal*, November 1900, Mary Church Terrell Papers, Manuscript Division, Library of Congress, Washington, D.C.; *HWS* 4: 358-59.

38. Ida B. Wells-Barnett, *Crusade for Justice: The Autobiography of Ida B. Wells-Barnett*, Alfreda Duster, ed. (Chicago, 1970), 345-47.

39. Aileen Kraditor, *The Ideas of the Woman Suffrage Movement, 1890-1920* (Garden City, N.Y., 1971), 213-14: Wells-Barnett, *Crusade for Justice*, 229-30.

40. *HWS* 5: 55, 59, 60 n. 1.

41. Walter White to Mary Church Terrell, March 14, 1919, Terrell Papers.

42. Terborg-Penn, "Discrimination Against Afro-American Women," 25.

43. Kraditor, 144-154; Marjorie Spruill (Wheeler), *New Women of the New South: The Leaders of the Woman Suffrage Movement in the Southern States*, (New York, 1993), 101-102, 104, 110, 113-125.

44. *The Crisis* 17 (June 1919), 103.

45. *HWS* 5: 640.

46. *HWS* 5: 645-46.

47. Terborg-Penn, "Discrimination Against Afro-American Women," 25-26; *New York World*, March 1, 1919, Suffrage File, NAACP Papers, Manuscript Division, Library of Congress, Washington, D.C.

48. Terborg-Penn, "Discrimination Against Afro-American Women," 26.

49. Elizabeth C. Carter to Ida Husted Harper, April 10, 1919, Suffrage File, NAACP Papers.

50. *HWS* 6: 617; Giddings, 164.

51. Spruill (Wheeler), *New Women of the New South*, 100-105, 143.

52. See Rayford W. Logan, *The Negro in the United States* (Princeton, 1957).

53. Rosalyn Terborg-Penn, "Afro-Americans in the Struggle for Woman Suffrage," Ph.D. diss., Howard University, 1977, 295-96.

54. Ibid, 301-02.

55. William Pickens, "The Woman Voter Hits the Color Line," *Nation* 3 (October 6, 1920): 372-73.

56. *Eleventh Annual Report of the NAACP for the Year 1920* (New York, 1921), 15, 25-30; Terborg-Penn, "Discontented Black Feminists," 267.

57. *The Crisis* 19 (November 1920), 23-25; *Negro Year Book*, 1921, 40.

58. Kenneth R. Johnson, "White Racial Attitudes as a Factor in the Arguments Against the Nineteenth Amendment," *Phylon* 31 (Spring 1970): 31-32, 35-37.

59. Giddings, 166.

60. Rosalyn Terborg-Penn, "Discontented Black Feminists: Prelude and Postscript to the Passage of the Nineteenth Amendment," 261-78, in *Decades of Discontent: The Women's Movement, 1920-1940*, edited by Lois Scharf and Joan M. Jenson (Westport, Conn., 1983), 267.

61. Ibid., 261, 267.

Eleven

THE INTERNATIONAL HISTORY OF THE U.S. SUFFRAGE MOVEMENT

Katherine M. Marino

Editor's Introduction: The woman suffrage movement in the United States did not occur in isolation. As historian Katherine M. Marino explains in this essay, it was part of a global struggle for women's rights.

While suffragists in the United States were engaged in their long battle, women were fighting for enfranchisement in many other countries. The first victory came in New Zealand in 1893, followed within a decade by Australia, Finland, and Norway. During World War I, the vote was extended to women in Denmark, Iceland, and Canada, and by the end of 1918, in many more countries on both sides of the conflict, in part as recognition of their wartime contributions. Suffragists in the United States finally persuaded President Woodrow Wilson to support a federal suffrage amendment in part by embarrassing him before the world, reminding him that he had declared the war a crusade to save democracy while half of American adults remained voteless.

Katherine Marino helps readers discover the connections between suffrage struggles worldwide. Suffragists from the United States both inspired, and were inspired, by their counterparts abroad with whom they collaborated, sometimes through formal international organizations and publications. Leading suffragists in the United States were, in many cases, prominent leaders in international organizations as well. Marino also points out that women from abroad—including immigrants and refugees—played important roles in promoting women's rights in the United States. African American women traveling abroad were inspired by the reception they received. Some used the world stage to expose racism in their home country, as well as calling out Anglo-American condescension and dominance in the international suffrage movement.

In its last two decades, the suffrage movement in the United States was influenced by the development of a more modern, militant spirit abroad. Socialism inspired many European women workers who, in turn, inspired many U.S. suffragists.

Marino also points out that after ratification of the Nineteenth Amendment, women from the United States continued to be involved in a global drive for women's rights. African American women who were denied their right to vote now joined other women of color in a new wave of international activism against racism and colonialism, and for women's political autonomy. Veterans of the U.S.

woman suffrage movement kept up the fight for women's rights, working with activists in Europe and Latin America. However, women's rights advocates from Latin America resisted the efforts of U.S. women to dominate the movement and took the lead in getting women's rights included as goals of the United Nations as well as winning the vote for women in their own countries.

After World War II, women gained the right to vote in newly decolonized nations such as India, Malaysia, and Iran. Latin American women and women from other areas of the Global South continued to be leaders in an increasingly successful international women's movement in which women's rights activists from the United States, notably First Lady Eleanor Roosevelt, also played important roles.

★　★　★　★　★

T HE HISTORY OF THE WOMAN SUFFRAGE MOVEMENT in the United States is usually told as a national one. It begins with the 1848 Seneca Falls convention; follows numerous state campaigns, court battles, and petitions to Congress; and culminates in the marches and protests that led to the Nineteenth Amendment. This narrative, however, overlooks how profoundly international the struggle was from the start. Suffragists from the United States and other parts of the world collaborated across national borders. They wrote to each other, shared strategies and encouragement, and spearheaded international organizations, conferences, and publications that in turn spread information and ideas. Many suffragists were *internationalist*, understanding the right to vote as a global goal.

Enlightenment concepts, socialism, and the abolitionist movement helped U.S. suffragists universalize women's rights long before Seneca Falls. They drew their inspiration not only from the American Revolution, but from the French and Haitian Revolutions, and later from the Mexican and Russian Revolutions. Many suffragists were immigrants who brought ideas from their homelands. Others capitalized on the Spanish-American War and the First World War to underscore contradictions between the United States' growing global power and its denial of woman suffrage. A number of women of color used the international stage to challenge U.S. claims to democracy, not only in terms of women's rights but also in terms of racism in the United States and in the suffrage movement itself. The complex international connections and strategies that suffragists cultivated reveal tensions in feminist organizing that reverberated in later movements and are instructive today.

These multiple, and sometimes conflicting, international strands worked in synergy, bolstering the suffrage cause and expanding the women's rights agenda. The resources that women shared with each other across national borders allowed suffrage movements to overcome political marginalization and hostility in their own countries.[1] A radical challenge to power, the U.S. movement for women's voting rights required transnational support to thrive.

Abolitionism and the Transnational Origins of Women's Rights

Although the American Revolution and U.S. circulation of Mary Wollstonecraft's *Vindication of the Rights of Woman* (1792) activated discussion of women's rights, it was the transatlantic crucible of abolitionism that truly galvanized the U.S. women's rights movement. The antislavery movement, which Frederick Douglass called "peculiarly woman's cause," provided broad ideals of "liberty" as well as key political strategies that suffragists would use for the next fifty years—the mass petition, public speaking, and the boycott.[2] Transatlantic networks of organizations, conferences, and publications drove abolitionism. Women in the United States looked to their British sisters, who in 1826 made the first formal demand for an immediate, rather than gradual, end to slavery.

Boston reformer and African American abolitionist Maria Stewart, one of the first U.S. women to publicly call for women's rights before a mixed-race and mixed-sex audience, embraced a diasporic vision of freedom when she asked in 1832, "How long shall the fair daughters of Africa be compelled to bury their minds and talents beneath a load of iron pots and kettles?"[3] Her vision of rights for African American women, specifically, in the face of economic marginalization, segregation, and slavery, drew upon universal rights that she found expressed not only in the U.S. Constitution and Declaration of Independence but in the French Declaration of the Rights of Man and the Haitian Revolution, the largest slave uprising, from 1791 to 1804.[4]

The hostility that Stewart and other female abolitionists faced for overstepping boundaries of female propriety by speaking out in public threw into sharp relief that, as U.S. abolitionist Angelina Grimké put it, "the manumission of the slave and the elevation of the woman" should be indivisible goals.[5] At the 1837 First Anti-Slavery Convention of American Women, an interracial group of two hundred women called for women's rights. When Quaker minister and abolitionist Lucretia Mott and other female delegates were excluded from the 1840 World Anti-Slavery Convention in London, Mott and Elizabeth Cady Stanton hatched the idea for a separate women's rights convention.

The resulting 1848 Seneca Falls Convention and its demands for women's rights were only possible because of abolitionists' groundwork and the broad meanings of emancipation flourishing in the United States and in Europe, where revolutions had broken out that year. Stanton's idea to include the right to vote in the convention's Declaration of Sentiments was directly inspired by calls for universal suffrage made by British Chartists, the first mass working-class movement in England.[6] Lucretia Mott explicitly connected the Declaration to the 1848 abolition of slavery in the French West Indies, opposition to the U.S. war with Mexico, and and defense of Native American rights. Mott and Stanton also found models in the matrilineal communities of the Seneca people, in which women held political power.[7] The right to vote proved to be the convention's most controversial demand, and abolitionist Frederick Douglass was one of its most avid proponents.

The right to vote became key to the many U.S. women's rights conventions that Seneca Falls set into motion, inspiring and drawing on the support of women in Europe and elsewhere, including immigrant women in the United States. In 1851, from Paris jail cells, revolutionary women's rights activists cheered U.S. women's activism. In March 1852, German immigrant and socialist Mathilde Anneke started the first women's rights journal in the United States published by a woman, the *Deutsche Frauen-Zeitung*. After the Prussian victory over Germany she had fled to the United States, where she became a friend of Stanton and Susan B. Anthony.[8] Polish-born immigrant and abolitionist Ernestine Rose expressed her global vision for suffrage in 1851: "We are not contending for the rights of women in New England, or of old England, but of the world."[9]

Sarah Parker Remond
THE PEABODY ESSEX MUSEUM

Such ideas resonated with Sarah Parker Remond, whose life reflects the overlapping transnational abolitionist and woman suffrage movements. In 1832 she helped found the first female antislavery group in Salem, Massachusetts. In 1859, while on an antislavery speaking tour in England, Remond reported, "I have been received here as a sister by White women for the first time in my life.... I have received a sympathy I never was offered before."[10] For Remond, transnational connections became a concrete way to escape racism in the United States. She settled permanently in Italy, where she became a physician. In 1866, Remond affixed her name to John Stuart Mill's petition to the British Parliament for woman suffrage.[11]

Internationalism was also key to African American abolitionist and suffragist Mary Ann Shadd Cary, who moved to Canada after the 1850 Fugitive Slave Act for fear it would endanger free Blacks like herself and enslaved people. She knit connections between her work for Black civil rights in Ontario, abolitionism, and the U.S. woman suffrage movement, founding one of the first suffrage organizations for Black women in the United States.[12]

Transnational Organizing and "Global Sisterhood"

Transnational connections initiated by the nineteenth-century abolitionist movement only grew in the following decades. After construction of the first transatlantic telegraph lines in the 1860s, communications, travel, and transnational print culture helped produce the first international organizations for women's rights that drew significantly on U.S. women. They included the World's Woman's Christian Temperance Union (WCTU), founded in 1884 by U.S. temperance leader Frances Willard; the International Council of Women (ICW), founded in 1888 by Stanton and Anthony; the International Woman Suffrage Alliance (IWSA), later renamed the International Alliance of Women, founded in 1904 and presided over by Carrie Chapman Catt (then president of the National American Woman Suffrage Association); and the Women's International League for Peace and Freedom (WILPF), founded in part by U.S. social settlement worker Jane Addams in 1915.[13]

Alongside each organization's particular focus—international arbitration, universal disarmament, temperance, married women's civil rights, anti-trafficking of women, equal pay for equal work, among others—a global goal of women's political equality drove them.[14] These organizations connected women across the lines of nation, culture, and language, and had overlapping memberships.[15] They hosted international conferences and they helped spearhead publications such as the IAW's *Jus Sufffragii* and the ICW's *Bulletin*, which shared information about suffrage organizing in Asia, Latin America, Europe, and other parts of the world.

Of the four, the WCTU inspired the most dramatic grassroots suffrage activism, becoming the largest women's organization in the world, with over forty national affiliates. Like members of the WCTU in the United States, WCTU members in many nations argued that women could use their vote to promote temperance and end men's alcohol-infused violence. The organization transformed the goal of woman suffrage into a clear and compelling one for large numbers of women.[16] Spearheading the first organized suffrage efforts in the White British colonies of South Africa, New Zealand, and South Australia, the WCTU was responsible for the world's first national suffrage victory in New Zealand in 1893, and in Australia in 1902.[17]

Although these groups spoke of "global sisterhood," their memberships were predominantly Anglo American and European, and their publications usually only published in French, English, and German, in spite of demands to expand beyond these languages from women in Spanish-speaking countries and other parts of the world.[18] These international groups generally marginalized or excluded women of color, and in the U.S. WCTU's case the organization segregated them.

These groups often reflected what historians have called "imperial feminism"—a belief that White, Western women will "uplift" women in "uncivilized" parts of the world.[19] This logic went hand in hand with some suffrage efforts. WCTU missionaries in Hawaii who sought to secure woman suffrage there in the 1890s, allied with White U.S. business and military interests, establishing imperial control over the island.[20] Suffragists also demanded the vote in the Philippines and Puerto Rico, U.S. imperial acquisitions from the 1898 Spanish-American War, both as part of a civilizing mission and to force discussion of a federal suffrage amendment in the United States.[21] Meanwhile, as they celebrated early suffrage victories within the western United States in the same period, most White suffragists overlooked the fact that these states denied the right to vote accorded native-born women to many Asian American, Mexican American, and Native American women.[22]

African American suffragists powerfully critiqued Anglo American dominance on the international stage and within the U.S. suffrage movement, even as they made important contributions to it. They also continued to connect global ideals of "freedom" with local women's rights issues, expanding the international agenda to address such goals as universal suffrage for men and women, anti-lynching laws, and education. Former abolitionist Frances Ellen Watkins Harper, a pivotal African American civil rights and women's rights leader, spoke at the 1888 founding of the ICW in Washington, D.C. and oversaw the formation of many "colored WCTU" groups that contributed to school suffrage victories in several states in the 1890s.[23] On a speaking tour in England, the anti-lynching activist Ida B. Wells-Barnett brought global attention to WCTU president Frances Willard's failure to defend African American men lynched on false rape accusations.[24] Wells-Barnett went on to found the most vital African American woman suffrage group in the country, the Alpha Suffrage Club in Chicago. At the 1913 suffrage march in Washington, D.C., Wells-Barnett refused to be relegated to the back of the procession reserved for African American women, and instead, marched with the Illinois delegation. In 1904, Mary Church Terrell, the first president of the National Association of Colored Women (NACW), spoke in fluent German at the International Council of Women (ICW) meeting in Berlin, pointing out that a global women's rights agenda must include attention to Black women's unequal access to many rights, including education and employment. Newspapers in Germany, France, Norway, and Austria lauded her speech.[25]

International Influences on the Modern Suffrage Movement

At the end of the nineteenth century, a more modern and militant suffrage internationalism emerged. A growing embrace of the term "feminism"—implying a movement that demanded women's full autonomy—along with working women's strong public presence, international socialism, and the Russian Revolution, contributed to the idea of a new womanhood breaking free from old constraints.[26]

International socialism had long upheld universal, direct, and equal suffrage as a demand, but in the 1890s, German socialist firebrand Clara Zetkin revived the goal, spearheading the inclusion of woman suffrage in the 1889 Second International in Paris. This gathering of socialist and labor parties from twenty countries in turn fostered vigorous women's movements in Germany, France, and elsewhere in Europe. In Finland, socialist feminists and the Social Democratic Party were critical to the country's woman suffrage victory in 1906, Europe's first.[27]

Socialism, and the growing numbers of working women it inspired, breathed new life into the U.S. suffrage movement. In 1909, women workers in New York demanded women's right to vote, launching what became International Women's

Teresa Villarreal

ARTE PÚBLICO PRESS,
UNIVERSITY OF HOUSTON

Day. Over the next six years, working women exploded in labor militancy, viewing the vote as a tool against unjust working conditions and for what Polish-born labor organizer and suffragist Rose Schneiderman called "bread and roses." The 1911 Triangle Shirtwaist Factory fire that claimed the lives of 145 workers, most of whom were young, immigrant women, made suffrage more urgent.[28] Collaborations with middle-class reformers helped spread many of the tactics that suffragists later employed on a wider scale; mass meetings, marches, and open-air street speaking.[29]

Immigrants and women from through-out the Americas were key to these efforts and to connecting suffrage to broad social justice goals. In cigar factories in Tampa, Florida, the Puerto Rican anti-imperialist, anarchist, and feminist Luisa Capetillo inspired African American, Cuban American, and Italian American women workers with calls for woman suffrage, and for free love, workers' rights, and vegetarianism.[30] From Texas, Mexican-born feminist Teresa Villarreal, who had fled the dictatorship of Porfirio Díaz, supported the Mexican Revolution, the Socialist Party, and woman suffrage. She and her sister Andrea Villarreal published the state's first feminist newspaper, *La Mujer Moderna* (*The Modern Woman*) in 1910, starting the publication *El Obrero* (*The Worker*) the same year.[31] In 1911, after the First Mexican Congress in Laredo, Texas, journalist Jovita Idár praised woman suffrage in *La Crónica* (*The Chronicle*), connecting it to her longstanding demands for Mexican American civil rights.[32]

Socialist, working-class suffrage militancy in England also galvanized the British Women's Social and Political Union (WSPU), founded in 1903 by Emmeline Pankhurst. This group broke away from the larger, more moderate National Union of Women's Suffrage Societies led by Millicent Garrett Fawcett and became the driving force in the British suffrage movement for nearly two decades, influencing militant activism around the world, including in China.[33]

After the U.S. suffragist Alice Paul, one of Pankhurst's followers, was arrested in London in 1912, she helped organize the 1913 suffrage march in Washington, D.C., and founded the Congressional Union for Woman Suffrage, later renamed the National Woman's Party (NWP). Paul and the NWP focused on a federal constitutional suffrage amendment. Its confrontational suffrage strategies of civil disobedience and picketing government buildings were inspired in large part by the WSPU, although Paul, a Quaker, rejected the violence of British activism. The NWP sash of purple, white, and yellow was modeled on the WSPU purple, white, and green one. Though U.S. suffragists generally called themselves "suffragists," a few even took on the British term "suffragette"—a term coined by the British *Daily Mail* as an epithet—to signal their radicalism.[34]

The First World War and a wave of suffrage legislation in Europe further accelerated the U.S. suffrage movement.[35] In the five years after

Jovita Idár at family printing press

GEORGIA STATE UNIVERSITY LIBRARY

1914, woman suffrage was adopted in Denmark, Iceland, Russia, Canada, Austria, Germany, Poland, and England. Although the NWP had already been picketing the White House for several months, it was only when they embarrassed President Woodrow Wilson in front of a visiting Russian delegation, whose wartime cooperation he was trying to secure, that the first six suffragists were arrested.[36] These women, jailed on charges of obstructing traffic, were immediately followed by a long line of U.S. women imprisoned for suffrage activism. The violence suffragists faced on the picket line for holding signs saying "Kaiser Wilson" amid rabid anti-German sentiment, and in jail with forced feedings during hunger strikes, became international news.[37]

International pressure, including the fact that women in Germany had been enfranchised before those in the United States, helped compel Wilson's January 1918 announcement of support for suffrage, as he promoted the United States as a beacon of democracy. By this time, the House of Representatives had already passed the suffrage amendment, but the Senate still voted against it. Wilson's endorsement was significant to U.S. and international public opinion. In Uruguay, suffragists utilized Wilson's support to push their legislators toward suffrage.[38]

Two more years of federal and state lobbying and organizing led to ratification of the Nineteenth Amendment in August 1920. For Crystal Eastman, a pacifist, enthusiast of the Russian Revolution, and cofounder of the American Civil Liberties Union (ACLU), this accomplishment represented not an end, but a new beginning—one with international significance: "Now [feminists] can say what they are really after," she announced, "and what they are after, in common with all the rest of the struggling world, is freedom."[39]

The International Afterlives of the U.S. Suffrage Movement

Struggles for women's voting rights did not end with ratification of the Nineteenth Amendment. Though African American women in other parts of the United States became voters, those living in the South faced the same obstacles— residency requirements, poll taxes, and literacy tests backed up by threatened or actual violence—that Southern states had adopted to counter the Fifteenth Amendment. It would take another major struggle for full enfranchisement—one that was a vital part of the civil rights movement in the 1960s—before Congress passed the Voting Rights Act of 1965 that made real the promises of the Fifteen and Nineteenth Amendments.[40]

For many African American women, deprival of their rights in the United States drove new transnational activism. In the 1920s and 1930s, they collaborated with women from Africa, the Caribbean, and around the globe in the International Council of Women of the Darker Races (1922) and in Pan Africanist and leftist organizing that connected demands for women's political autonomy with those for antiracism, anticolonialism, and Black nationalism, specifically viewing Black women's self-determination as critical to broad and transformative social justice.[41]

The involvement of women from the United States in European and Pan-American feminism was also an outgrowth of the U.S. suffrage movement. It reflected the differences in approach between the moderate and more radical U.S. suffragists that persisted beyond ratification of the Nineteenth Amendment in 1920. Carrie Chapman Catt was no longer the president of the National American Woman Suffrage Association (NAWSA)—which with the suffrage victory transformed itself into the League of Women Voters (LWV)—but she continued as president of the International Woman Suffrage Alliance (IWSA) until she retired in 1923. The National Woman's Party (NWP) continued under the leadership of Alice Paul who created an International Advisory Council to the NWP in 1925. Both the IWSA and the NWP aimed to support the efforts of suffragists in what the IWSA termed the "non-emancipated" countries where women still did not have the vote, and to aid in expanding women's rights in areas where woman suffrage had been established.[42]

However, divisions that had emerged between moderate and more radical suffragists only grew after the NWP introduced the Equal Rights Amendment (ERA) in 1923. Many progressive women's organizations and labor groups opposed the ERA for fear that requiring identical laws for women and men would eliminate hard-won labor legislation for working women. Nationally, the LWV took the lead in this opposition. Internationally, women's rights advocates were also divided over the issue of special legislation versus equal rights, and the IWSA had members on both sides. But in 1926, when the NWP applied for membership in the IWSA, and the LWV vigorously opposed it, the IWSA rejected the NWP application.[43]

The NWP thus turned its attention toward Latin America where a Pan-American feminist movement was growing. The IWSA was also interested in Latin America: between 1920 and 1923 Catt toured six countries in South America assessing the prospects for woman suffrage. And in 1922, the LWV hosted a Pan American Conference of Women in Baltimore, Maryland that brought a number of Latin American feminists to the United States. At the suggestion of the Latin American feminists, the Pan American Association for the Advancement of Women (PAAAW) emerged from the Baltimore conference and for a time played a role in knitting together leaders from throughout the Americas and providing a crucial apparatus for further development of a feminist movement in Latin America.

Many of the delegates from Latin America returned home and launched new feminist organizations in their own countries that were affiliated with the PAAAW. But Catt's negative assessment of the state of feminism and feminists in Latin America, along with her waning interest in the Pan American realm, alienated many Latin American suffragists. When NWP leaders became leaders of another new organization, the Inter-American Commission of Women (IACW), the NWP had more direct achievement in the Pan American arena.[44]

The IACW was created in 1928 by NWP members and Cuban feminists. It was the first intergovernmental organization that promoted women's rights in the world. Initially led by veteran NWP leader Doris Stevens, the commission forced international treaties for women's civil and political equal rights into Pan American and League of Nations congresses. These efforts led to League of Nations debates on married women's independent nationality rights and to a League of Nations sponsored commission on the legal status of women around the world.[45] In the Pan American realm, their efforts led to the passage of the Equal Nationality Treaty. Many countries in the Western Hemisphere ratified this treaty, including the United States in 1934, which led to a legislative act granting married women's equal nationality rights.[46]

Within the inter-American movement, however, a heterogeneous group of Latin American feminists also recognized continuing efforts of U.S. women to dominate, and developed a distinctive anti-imperialist, Pan-Hispanic feminism that included gaining the vote, but did not focus exclusively on suffrage. Asserting their own leadership over Pan-American feminism, they called for *derechos humanos*, which implied women's political, civil, social, and economic rights alongside anti-imperialism and anti-fascism. At the 1945 San Francisco meeting that created the United Nations (U.N.), Latin American female delegates, led by Brazilian feminist Bertha Lutz, drew on this movement to push women's rights into the U.N. Charter and proposed what became the U.N. Commission on the Status of Women. In the wake of these events, numerous Latin American countries passed woman suffrage.[47]

Women from the Global South continued to be pioneers on the international feminist stage in the postwar years, pushing for inclusion of women's rights in human rights treaties. Hansa Mehta from India, one of the two women on the

At this January 24, 1928, gathering of 200 women at the *Asociación de Reporteros* in Havana, Cuba, five U.S. National Woman's Party members joined suffragists from Cuba, Dominican Republic, Puerto Rico, and Costa Rica to successfully plan to inject women's rights into the 6th International Conference of American States meeting in Havana.

COURTESY OF THE SCHLESINGER LIBRARY, RADCLIFFE INSTITUTE, HARVARD UNIVERSITY

commission drafting the 1948 United Nations Universal Declaration of Human Rights with Eleanor Roosevelt, was responsible for Article 1 reading "All human beings are born free and equal" rather than "All men are born free and equal."[48]

After the Second World War, U.S. women's groups continued to connect with women throughout the world internationally, both through longstanding groups like the International Alliance of Women (IAW) and the Women's International League for Peace and Freedom (WILPF), as well as through new organs like the U.N. Commission on the Status of Women.

In the Cold War years, old tensions around feminist strategy were compounded by the Red Scare in the United States. In 1948, the Congress of American Women, a U.S. affiliate of the global leftist feminist group founded in 1946, the Women's International Democratic Federation (WIDF), was branded a communist front organization by the House Un-American Activities Committee, and it was dissolved in 1950. Meanwhile, the WIDF continued to be a major transnational feminist hub throughout the world, even after it was temporarily suspended from its consultative status with the United Nations. The WIDF merged demands for anticolonialism and antiracism with women's equality and political rights, and was linked to women's activism in decolonization struggles throughout Africa, Asia, the Middle East, and Latin America.[49]

In these years, suffrage for women spread throughout newly decolonized countries in India (1950), Malaysia (1957), Algeria (1962), Iran and Morocco (1963), Libya (1964), Bangladesh (1972) and elsewhere. In 1975, WIDF and the U.N.

Commission on the Status of Women were both responsible for the 1975 U.N. World Conference on Women in Mexico City. This conference sparked the United Nations Decade for Women from 1975 to 1985, a period that saw a profusion of new international feminist organizations, events, and activism.[50] One of its outcomes was the Convention on the Elimination of All Forms of Discrimination against Women (CEDAW), an international treaty on women's rights, adopted in 1979 by the U.N. General Assembly. Article 3 demands basic human rights and fundamental freedoms for women "on a basis of equality with men" in "political, social, economic, and cultural fields."[51] Since its institution in 1981, the treaty has been ratified by 189 countries, although not by the United States.

U.S. women's global activism, however, has never abated, and the transnational legacies of the suffrage movement are evident in U.S. women's ongoing quests for full citizenship today. Then, as now, fights for women's rights are connected to global movements for human rights—for immigrant, racial, labor, and feminist justice. The internationalist history of the woman suffrage movement shows us that activists and movements outside the United States, along with a broad range of diverse, international goals, were critical to organizing for that right deemed so quintessentially American—the right to vote. It reminds us how much we in the United States have to learn from feminist struggles around the world.

Notes

This article originally appeared as "The International History of the US Suffrage Movement" in the series, *19th Amendment and Women's Access to the Vote Across America*, edited by Tamara Gaskell and published online in 2019 by the U.S. National Park Service in cooperation with the National Conference of State Historic Preservation Officers.

1. Ellen Carol DuBois, "Woman Suffrage around the World," in *Suffrage and Beyond: International Feminist Perspectives*, ed. Caroline Daley and Melanie Nolan (New York: New York University Press, 1994), 254.

2. The full quote is "When the true history of the antislavery cause shall be written, women will occupy a large space in its pages; for the cause of the slave has been peculiarly woman's cause." Frederick Douglass, *Life and Times of Frederick Douglass* (Hartford, CT: Park Publishing, 1883), 570. On Wollstonecraft, see Estelle B. Freedman, *No Turning Back: The History of Feminism and the Future of Women* (New York: Ballantine Books, 2002), 51–52.

3. Maria W. Stewart, "Religion and the Pure Principles of Morality, the Sure Foundation on Which We Must Build. Productions from the Pen of Mrs. Maria W. Steward [sic], Widow of the Late James W. Steward, of Boston," reprinted in *Maria W. Stewart, America's First Black Woman Political Writer: Essays and Speeches*, ed. Marilyn Richardson (Bloomington: Indiana University Press, 1987), 38; Martha S. Jones, *All Bound Up Together: The Woman Question in African American Political Culture, 1830–1900* (Chapel Hill: University of North Carolina Press, 2007), 23–29.

4. On the significance of the Haitian Revolution to US abolitionists and debate about slavery, see Robin Blackburn, *The American Crucible: Slavery, Emancipation, and Human Rights* (London: Verso, 2011), and Manisha Sinha, *The Slave's Cause: A History of Abolition* (New Haven, CT: Yale University Press, 2016), 177–78, 245–50, 454–55. On female abolitionists' engagement with the Haitian Revolution, see Marlene L. Daut, *Tropics of Haiti: Race and Literary History of the Haitian Revolution in the Atlantic World, 1789–1865* (Liverpool: Liverpool University Press, 2015), and Carla L. Peterson, "Literary Transnationalism and Diasporic History: Frances Watkins Harper's 'Fancy Sketches,' 1859–60," in *Women's Rights and Transatlantic Slavery in the Era of Emancipation*, ed. Kathryn Kish Sklar and James Brewer Stewart (New Haven, CT: Yale University Press, 2007), 189–210.

5. Angelina Grimké to Sarah Douglass, February 25, 1838, quoted in Annelise Orleck, *Rethinking American Women's Activism* (New York: Routledge, 2016), 4; Sarah M. Grimké, "Letters on the Equality of the Sexes in Freedman (United States, 1837)," in *The Essential Feminist Reader*, ed. Estelle B. Freedman (New York: Modern Library, 2007), 47.

6. Ellen Carol DuBois, "Woman Suffrage and the Left: An International Socialist-Feminist Perspective," in *Woman Suffrage and Women's Rights*, ed. Ellen Carol DuBois (New York: New York University Press, 1998), 254.

7. Nancy A. Hewitt, "From Seneca Falls to Suffrage? Reimagining a 'Master' Narrative in U.S. Women's History," in *No Permanent Waves: Recasting Histories of U.S. Feminism*, ed. Nancy A. Hewitt (New Brunswick, NJ: Rutgers University Press, 2010), 24–25; Sally Roesch Wagner and Jeanne Shenandoah, *Sisters in Spirit: Haudenosaunee (Iroquois) Influence on Early American Feminists* (Summertown, TN: Native Voices, 2001).

8. Michaela Bank, *Women of Two Countries: German-American Women, Women's Rights and Nativism, 1848–1890* (New York: Berghahn Books, 2012), chap. 2. Her book also sheds light on the important work of German American suffragist Clara Neymann.

9. Quote from Freedman, *No Turning Back*, 54. Rose was instrumental in gaining married women's property rights in New York state. See Bonnie S. Anderson, *The Rabbi's Atheist Daughter: Ernestine Rose, International Feminist Pioneer* (New York: Oxford University Press, 2017). She also published on the 1853 anniversary of West Indian emancipation, "I go for the recognition of human rights, without distinction of sect, party, sex, or color." Quote from Ellen Carol DuBois, "Ernestine Rose's Jewish Origins and the Varieties of Euro-American Emancipation in 1848," in Sklar and Stewart, *Women's Rights and Transatlantic Slavery in the Era of Emancipation*, 280.

10. Sarah Parker Remond, "Lecture at the Lion Hotel, Warrington (1859)," in *Documenting First Wave Feminisms*, vol. 1, *Transnational Collaborations and Crosscurrents*, ed. Maureen Moynagh and Nancy Forestell (Toronto: University of Toronto Press, 2012), 46.

11. Kenneth Salzer, "Great Exhibitions: Ellen Craft on the British Abolitionist Stage," in *Transatlantic Women: Nineteenth-Century American Women Writers and Great Britain*, ed. Beth Lynne Lueck, Brigitte Bailey, and Lucinda L. Damon-Bach (Durham: University

of New Hampshire Press, 2012), 147; Angela Y. Davis, *Women, Race, and Class* (New York: Random House, 1981), 65; Sirpa Salenius, *An Abolitionist Abroad: Sarah Parker Remond in Cosmopolitan Europe* (Amherst: University of Massachusetts Press, 2016); Elizabeth Crawford, *Suffrage Centenary: A Brief History: The Diversity of the Suffrage Movement* (London: Fawcett Society, 2017), fawcettsociety.org.uk/Handlers/Download/ashx?IDMF=7f935e2e-7d93-4fd3-98e8-41e37b588674. On John Stuart Mill and Harriet Taylor see Freedman, *No Turning Back*, 52–54.

12. Rosalyn Terborg-Penn, *African American Women in the Struggle for the Vote, 1850–1920* (Bloomington: Indiana University Press, 1999), 39.

13. On the importance of the telegraph in materially connecting nineteenth-century women's rights reformers, see Margaret H. McFadden, *Golden Cables of Sympathy: The Transatlantic Sources of Nineteenth-Century Feminism* (Lexington: University Press of Kentucky, 1999), 1–3. On the ICW, IWSA, and WILPF, see Leila J. Rupp, *Worlds of Women: The Making of an International Women's Movement* (Princeton, NJ: Princeton University Press, 1998). On the founding of the ICW in 1888 by Stanton and Anthony, see Lisa Tetrault, *The Myth of Seneca Falls: Memory and the Women's Suffrage Movement, 1848–1898* (Chapel Hill: University of North Carolina Press, 2014), chap. 5. These groups were preceded by Swiss leader Marie Goegg-Pouchoulin's 1868 founding of one of the first international women's organizations, the International Association of Women (*Association internationale des femmes*), whose goal was to organize women of all classes so they could enjoy the same rights as men within their own countries. Although this group included women from the United States, it was short-lived. Bob Reinalda, *Routledge History of International Organizations: From 1815 to the Present Day* (New York: Routledge, 2009), 150. Women from the United States also played a role in the formation of the *Congrès International du Droit des Femmes* in Paris in 1878. However, at this conference, discussion of suffrage was banned. Rupp, *Worlds of Women*, 14. In these years, the NAWSA used these groups to connect with other movements internationally, but Elizabeth Cady Stanton also worked independently of these groups to carve out important transatlantic networks. See Sandra Stanley Holton, "'To Educate Women into Rebellion': Elizabeth Cady Stanton and the Creation of a Transatlantic Network of Radical Suffragists," *American Historical Review* 99, no. 4 (October 1994): 1112–36.

14. During the First World War, Addams and 1,150 other women from the United States and Europe gathered in The Hague to demand international peace and founded the WILPF; their declaration urged that "the exclusion of women from citizenship is contrary to the principles of civilization and human right" and as contrary to permanent peace. Jane Addams, Emily G. Balch, and Alice Hamilton, *Women at The Hague: The International Congress of Women and Its Results*, ed. Harriet Hyman Alonso (Urbana: University of Illinois Press, 2003), 64. The original resolutions from the women at The Hague were praised by President Wilson and may have shaped his Fourteen Points in 1918. Their internationalist position was unpopular in the United States at the time, and one of the leaders, Emily Greene Balch, later winner of the Nobel Peace Prize, was fired from her position as a professor at Wellesley College in 1918. Interconnected, international goals were what the IWSA had in mind when it announced in 1909, "We have been baptized in that spirit of the twentieth century which the world calls internationalism." Quoted in Nitza Berkovitch, *From Motherhood to Citizenship: Women's Rights and International Organizations* (Baltimore: Johns Hopkins University Press, 1999), 18.

15. The ICW claimed to represent four to five million women by 1907. The IWSA attained twenty-six national affiliates by 1913. Rupp, *Worlds of Women*, 22, 70. They also sprang from each other. Although Stanton and Anthony founded the ICW to promote suffrage, when the organization turned away from the vote soon after its creation, German suffragists Lida Gustava Heymann and Anita Augspurg helped found the IWSA with Catt, committed to "secur[ing] the enfranchisement of the women of all nations." Rupp, *Worlds of Women*, 21–22. Both the ICW and IWSA would inspire national suffrage organizing in Brazil, Argentina, Uruguay, and other countries in the world. Katherine Marino, *Feminism for the Americas: The Making of an International Human Rights Movement* (Chapel Hill: University of North Carolina Press,

2019), chap. 1.

16. DuBois, "Woman Suffrage around the World," 256.

17. Ian Tyrrell, *Woman's World, Woman's Empire: The Woman's Christian Temperance Union in International Perspective, 1880–1930* (Chapel Hill: University of North Carolina Press, 1991), chap. 10.

18. Marino, *Feminism for the Americas*, 24. These organizations increasingly included representatives from countries outside of Western Europe from the 1920s through '40s. Maire Sandell, *The Rise of Women's Transnational Activism: Identity and Sisterhood between the World Wars* (London: I. B. Tauris, 2015).

19. On imperial feminism in these groups, see Antoinette Burton, *Burdens of History: British Feminists, Indian Women, and Imperial Culture, 1865–1915* (Chapel Hill: University of North Carolina Press, 1994); Margot Badran, *Feminism, Islam, and Nation: Gender and the Making of Modern Egypt* (Princeton, NJ: Princeton University Press, 1995), 108–10, 232–38; Charlotte Weber, "Unveiling Scheherazade: Feminist Orientalism in the International Alliance of Women, 1911–1950," *Feminist Studies* 27, no. 1 (Spring 2001): 125–57.

20. These suffrage efforts were ultimately unsuccessful. Patricia Grimshaw, "'Settler Anxieties, Indigenous Peoples, and Women's Suffrage in the Colonies of Australia, New Zealand, and Hawai'i, 1888–1902," in *Women's Suffrage in Asia: Gender, Nationalism, and Democracy*, ed. Louise Edwards and Mina Roces (London: RoutledgeCurzon, 2004), 220–39; Rumi Yasutake, "Re-Franchising Women of Hawai'i, 1912–1920: The Politics of Gender, Sovereignty, Race, and Rank at the Crossroads of the Pacific," in *Gendering the Trans-Pacific World*, ed. Catherine Ceniza Choy and Judy Tzu-Chun Wu (Leiden: Brill, 2017), 114–39. As Ian Tyrrell has pointed out, the WCTU's promotion of a "benign American civilization" included the "benevolent assimilation" of Native Americans, overlooking the violence of Wounded Knee–the massacre that killed over 150 men, women, and children of the Lakota on the heels of the forced removal of thousands. Tyrrell, *Woman's World, Woman's Empire*, 181.

21. Allison L. Sneider, *Suffragists in an Imperial Age: U.S. Expansion and the Woman Question, 1870–1929* (New York: Oxford University Press, 2008).

22. Rosalyn Terborg-Penn also connects US imperial feminism in Puerto Rico and St. Thomas to racism within the suffrage movement in "Enfranchising Women of Color: Woman Suffragists as Agents of Imperialism," in *Nation, Empire, Colony: Historicizing Gender and Race*, ed. Ruth Roach Pierson and Nupur Chaudhuri (Bloomington: Indiana University Press, 1998), 41–56.

23. Terborg-Penn, *African American Women in the Struggle for the Vote*, 86; Noaquia N. Callahan, "A Rare Colored Bird: Mary Church Terrell, *Die Fortschritte der Farbigen Frauen*, and the International Council of Women's Congress in Berlin, Germany, 1904," *German Historical Institute Bulletin Supplement* 13 (2017): 97; Michelle M. Rief, "Thinking Locally, Acting Globally: The International Agenda of African American Clubwomen, 1880–1940," *Journal of African American History* 89, no. 3 (Summer 2004): 203–4. For more on Frances Ellen Watkins Harper, see Jones, *All Bound Up Together*, and the new edition of Harper's *Iola Leroy, Or, Shadows Uplifted*, ed. Koritha Mitchell (Ontario: Broadview Editions, 2018).

24. Patricia Ann Schecter, *Ida B. Wells-Barnett and American Reform, 1888–1930* (Chapel Hill: University of North Carolina Press, 2001), 110–11; Mia Bay, *To Tell the Truth Freely: The Life of Ida B. Wells* (New York: Hill and Wang, 2010), 185–89, 206–17. Also, as Callahan explains, Wells's pamphlet *The Reason Why the Colored American Is Not in the World's Colombian Exposition* (1893), which criticized the exclusion of African Americans from the Columbian Exposition, "sparked international debate about the limits of American citizenship when it came to race and gender." Callahan, "Rare Colored Bird," 100–102. On the work of the Alpha Suffrage Club, see Wanda A. Hendricks, "Ida B. Wells-Barnett and the Alpha Suffrage Club of Chicago," Chapter 17 in this volume; Susan Ware, *Why They Marched: Untold Stories of the Women Who Fought for the Right to Vote* (Cambridge, MA: Harvard University Press, 2019), Chapter 7.

25. Fluent in German, French, Latin, and Greek in addition to her native English, Terrell overheard German women talking about how eagerly they awaited "die Negierin" (the Negress). Later Terrell recounted, "I represented not only the colored woman in my own country but, since I was the only woman taking part in the International Congress who had a drop of African blood in her

veins, I represented the whole continent of Africa as well." Brittney C. Cooper, *Beyond Respectability: The Intellectual Thought of Race Women* (Urbana: University of Illinois Press, 2018), 78–80; Callahan, "Rare Colored Bird."

26. The term *feminisme* had first been used in its modern connotation by French suffragist Hubertine Auclert at the 1878 International Congress for the Rights of Women in Paris (*Congrès International du Droit des Femmes*), although that conference did not endorse woman suffrage itself. After 1882, she used the term in her newspaper *La citoyenne*. Sara L. Kimble, "Transatlantic Networks for Legal Feminism, 1888–1912," *German Historical Institute Bulletin Supplement* 13 (2017): 56; Karen Offen, *European Feminisms, 1700–1950: A Political History* (Stanford, CA: Stanford University Press, 2000), 19–20; Karen Offen, "On the French Origins of the Words Feminism and Feminist," *Feminist Issues* 8, no. 2 (June 1988): 45–51. For an excellent account of how the Russian Revolution infused modern suffragism, see Julia Mickenberg, "Suffragettes and Soviets: American Feminists and the Specter of Revolutionary Russia," *Journal of American History* 100, no. 4 (March 2014): 1021–51.

27. DuBois, "Woman Suffrage around the World," 265; Clara Zetkin, "From 'Women's Right to Vote,' 1907, A Resolution Introduced at the International Socialist Congress," in Moynagh and Forestell, *Documenting First Wave Feminisms*, 1:137–43.

28. Annelise Orleck, *Common Sense and a Little Fire: Women and Working-Class Politics in the United States, 1900–1965* (Chapel Hill: University of North Carolina Press, 1995), chap. 3. Women workers demanded maternity legislation, child care, protective labor laws, and equal representation in unions. DuBois, "Woman Suffrage and the Left," 259.

29. On collaborations with the WTUL see Orleck, *Common Sense and a Little Fire*. On the work of Stanton's daughter Harriot Stanton Blatch's suffrage organizing with working women in New York, see Ellen Carol DuBois, *Harriot Stanton Blatch and the Winning of Woman Suffrage* (New Haven, CT: Yale University Press, 1997).

30. Vicki L. Ruiz, "Class Acts: Latina Feminist Traditions, 1900–1930," *American Historical Review* 121, no. 1 (February 2016): 1–16; Nancy A. Hewitt, "In Pursuit of Power: The Political Economy of Women's Activism in Twentieth-Century Tampa," in *Visible Women: New Essays on Women's Activism*, ed. Nancy A. Hewitt and Suzanne Lebsock (Urbana: University of Illinois Press, 1993), 199–222.

31. Vicki L. Ruiz, *From Out of the Shadows: Mexican Women in Twentieth-Century America* (New York: Oxford University Press, 2008), 99. This was the first feminist newspaper in Texas. Leonor Villegas de Magnón, *The Rebel* (Houston: Arte Público Press, 1994), xv. For more on Teresa Villarreal and her sister Andrea, see Maylei Blackwell, *¡Chicana Power! Contested Histories of Feminism in the Chicano Movement* (Austin: University of Texas Press, 2011), 107–9; Emma Pérez, *The Decolonial Imaginary: Writing Chicanas into History* (Bloomington: Indiana University Press, 1999), 67–69; Nicolás Kanellos, "Envisioning and Re-visioning the Nation: Latino Intellectual Traditions," *American Latino Theme Study*, National Park Services website, home1.nps.gov/heritageinitiatives/latino/latinothemestudy/intellectual traditions.htm.

32. Jovita Idár, a journalist and civil rights leader from Laredo, Texas, founded the League of Mexican Women, which promoted woman suffrage, educated poor children, promoted the Spanish language, and spoke out against discrimination and violence against Mexican Americans. Gabriela González, "Jovita Idár: The Ideological Origins of a Transnational Advocate for La Raza," in *Texas Women: Their Histories, Their Lives*, ed. Elizabeth Haynes Turner, Stephanie Cole, and Rebecca Sharpless (Athens: University of Georgia Press, 2015), 225–48. For more on her and Villarreal, see Gabriela González, *Redeeming la Raza: Transborder Modernity, Race, Respectability, and Rights* (New York: Oxford University Press, 2018), 21, 24–26, 37, 41–42.

33. DuBois, "Woman Suffrage and the Left," 266. The working-class based suffrage movement of Lancashire textile workers in the 1890s helped inspire the militant tactics and public agitation of the middle-class women. Pankhurst's group was founded in Manchester and moved to London in 1906. On suffrage activism in China, see Louise Edwards, *Gender, Politics, and Democracy: Women's Suffrage in China* (Stanford, CA: Stanford University

Press, 2008) and Louise Edwards, "Chinese Women's Campaigns for Suffrage: Nationalism, Confucianism, and Political Agency," in Edwards and Roces, *Women's Suffrage in Asia*, 59–78.

34. Orleck, *Common Sense and a Little Fire*, 94. See "suffragette" in Cheris Kramarae and Paula A. Treichler, *A Feminist Dictionary* (Boston: Pandora Press, 1985), 435. See also Kenneth Florey, *Women's Suffrage Memorabilia: An Illustrated Historical Study* (Jefferson, NC: McFarland, 2013), 221 n32.

35. For an excellent history of the way the war accelerated the phenomenon of the "new woman" and suffrage debate, and on connections between women's war work and suffrage, see Lynn Dumenil, *The Second Line of Defense: American Women and World War I* (Chapel Hill: University of North Carolina Press, 2017), especially chap. 1.

36. Mickenberg, "Suffragettes and Soviets," 1021.

37. Nancy F. Cott, *The Grounding of Modern Feminism* (New Haven, CT: Yale University Press, 1987), 59.

38. Marino, *Feminism for the Americas*, 247 n35; Paulina Luisi, *Movimiento sufragista: Conferencia leída en el Augusteo de Buenos Aires, el 21 de febrero 1919, a pedido de la Unión Feminista Nacional Argentina* (Montevideo, Urug: Imp. "El Siglo Ilustrado," de Gregorio V. Mariño, 1919). In 1917, Uruguayans had already supported a constitution that included a mechanism for enacting woman suffrage, before a federal amendment was in the offing in the United States. As historian Francesca Miller has noted, this made Uruguay "in theory, the first of all Western Hemisphere nations to recognize female suffrage," though suffrage did not pass there until 1934. Francesca Miller, *Latin American Women and the Search for Social Justice* (Hanover, NH: University Press of New England, 1991), 98.

39. Quoted in Mickenberg, "Suffragettes and Soviets," 1048.

40. In addition, as Nancy Hewitt has written, "millions of Asian and Mexican Americans in the West and American Indians across the country were denied suffrage until the 1940s, and some waited until the Voting Rights Act and its extension in 1970 addressed the bilingual needs of Spanish-speaking citizens." Hewitt, "From Seneca Falls to Suffrage?," 11.

41. Rief, "Thinking Locally, Acting Globally," and Michelle M. Rief, "'Banded Close Together': An Afrocentric Study of African American Women's International Activism, 1850–1940, and the International Council of Women of the Darker Races" (PhD diss., Temple University, 2003); Keisha N. Blain, *Set the World on Fire: Black Nationalist Women and the Global Struggle for Freedom* (Philadelphia: University of Pennsylvania Press, 2018); Erik S. McDuffie, *Sojourning for Freedom: Black Women, American Communism, and the Making of Black Left Feminism* (Durham, NC: Duke University Press, 2011); Dayo Gore, *Radicalism at the Crossroads: African American Women Activists in the Cold War* (New York: New York University Press, 2011); Brandy Thomas Wells, "'She Pieced and Stitched and Quilted, Never Wavering nor Doubting': A Historical Tapestry of African American Women's Internationalism, 1890s–1960s" (PhD diss., Ohio State University, 2015); and Lisa G. Materson, "African American Women's Global Journeys and the Construction of Cross-Ethnic Racial Identity," *Women's Studies International Forum* 32, no. 1 (January–February 2009): 35–42.

42. Marino, *Feminism for the Americas*.

43. Rachel Adami, *Women and the Universal Declaration of Human Rights* (New York: Routledge, 2019).

44. Francisca de Haan, "Eugenie Cotton, Park Chong-ae, and Claudia Jones: Rethinking Transnational Feminism and International Politics," *Journal of Women's History* 25: 4 (Winter 2013): 174–89.

45. Jocelyn Olcott, *International Women's Year: The Greatest Consciousness-Raising Event in History* (New York: Oxford University Press, 2017); Kristen Ghodsee, *Second World, Second Sex: Socialist Women's Activism and Global Solidarity during the Cold War* (Duke University Press, 2018).

46. U.N. General Assembly, Convention on the Elimination of All Forms of Discrimination Against Women, 18 December 1979, United Nations, Treaty Series, vol. 1249, p. 13, available at: refworld.org/docid/3ae6b3970.html [accessed 19 December 2019].

Dr. Anna Howard Shaw served as president of the
National American Woman Suffrage Association for eleven years.

Twelve

THE SUFFRAGE RENAISSANCE:
A New Image for a New Century
1896—1910

Sara Hunter Graham

Editor's Introduction: One of the clearest and most fascinating examples in this volume of "rediscovering the woman suffrage movement" is this essay by historian Sara Hunter Graham, challenging long-accepted ideas about the woman suffrage movement at the turn of the century.

As the end of the nineteenth century approached, American suffragists were at last united in a single organization. The National Woman Suffrage Association and the American Woman Suffrage Association had come together to form the National American Woman Suffrage Association (NAWSA) in 1890. Susan B. Anthony quickly emerged as the organization's principal leader, serving as president from 1892 to 1900. Lucy Stone died in 1893, and Elizabeth Cady Stanton became somewhat estranged from the suffrage movement after the publication in 1895 of *The Woman's Bible* in which Stanton indicted Christianity for contributing to the subordination of women. Anthony, setting aside the militant tactics of the 1870s, now urged suffragists to avoid controversy and focus exclusively on gaining the vote. The NAWSA dedicated itself to building support throughout the nation and securing enough state victories that a federal amendment could be won.

The NAWSA leaders assisted suffragists throughout the nation in their efforts to obtain state suffrage amendments. The four thrilling victories in the Rocky Mountain states, however, stood out in contrast to countless defeats. The NAWSA's vigorous campaign in the South, an attempt to gain woman suffrage through the new state constitutions adopted during the 1890s, was unsuccessful. In fact, after the victories in Utah and Idaho in 1896, not a single state fell into the suffrage column until 1910.

The suffrage movement entered a stage that historian Eleanor Flexner in 1959—and suffrage historians ever since—describe as "the doldrums." As Flexner noted in her influential study, *Century of Struggle: The Woman's Rights Movement in the United States,* between 1896 and 1910 only six state referenda were held, and three of these were in Oregon. All of these failed, and the federal suffrage amendment "appeared moribund." Anthony retired from leadership, and her promising successor, Carrie Chapman Catt, rose to the presidency in 1900 only to be forced into retirement four years later due to the illness of her husband. Dr. Anna Howard Shaw, who served as NAWSA president from 1904 to 1915, is generally regarded by historians as an extraordinary orator—less talented as an administrator—who presided over a de-centralized and ineffective NAWSA.

In this essay, however, Sara Hunter Graham offers a revisionist view of this era. Rather than a period of indecision and inactivity, Graham sees the period from 1896 to 1910 as one of careful and successful rebuilding, in which the leaders of the NAWSA deliberately reshaped the image of their movement. They also expanded their ranks in ways that greatly enhanced the prestige and effectiveness of the suffrage movement, recruiting wealthy and socially prominent women as well as a new generation of energetic and talented college-educated women.

The leadership for this "suffrage renaissance" came largely from Carrie Chapman Catt who, before having to resign as president, strengthened the NAWSA in many ways. This included the introduction at the national level of the "society plan," tested earlier in Colorado, that brought women of wealth, prestige, and influence into the suffrage movement—and made it quite difficult for anti-suffragists to stigmatize suffragists as fanatics.

Graham also informs us that determination to create a new and more saleable image led NAWSA leaders to rewrite the history of the woman suffrage movement, de-emphasizing controversial aspects of its past and virtually canonizing early leaders, particularly Anthony. They emphasized the progress women had made in terms of educational, professional, and legal reforms and pictured suffrage as the next logical step. Through new rituals, symbols and rhetoric, they promoted solidarity throughout an enlarged and diverse constituency united only by the desire to gain the vote for women. They also, Graham concludes, brought women into the movement by creating a new political culture based on membership in a single-interest pressure group that was far more attractive to women than the male political culture of saloons and smoke-filled rooms.

Thus, writes Graham, "the visionary cause of the pioneers" was transformed into "an eminently safe program" acceptable to middle-class club women and the social elite—a development NAWSA leaders regarded as "a necessary precondition that would eventually win the vote." As we will see in subsequent essays, other women who were not of the nation's elite would also be an important part of the massive and diverse coalition amassing in support of woman suffrage in the first two decades of the twentieth century; but as Graham makes clear, the NAWSA's successful efforts to make the movement attractive to women with leisure, funds, and influence to contribute to the cause played a crucial role in the success of the woman suffrage movement.

★   ★   ★   ★   ★

SUFFRAGISM IN THE EARLY 1900S was burdened with an image arising from its history that was in many respects a hindrance to further progress. Suffragists' advocacy of divorce reform, experimental dress, and feminist interpretations of the Bible had given the nineteenth-century movement a reputation of radicalism that was exploited by the enemies of suffrage to dissuade more conventional women from participating in the movement. Consequently, during the years 1896 to 1910 suffragists made little tangible progress in state referenda or federal amendment campaigns. No new states were won for suffrage and, in Congress, the federal amendment lay dormant in committee, prompting one historian to label the period "the doldrums."[1]

Despite the poor record generated by state suffrage campaigns, however, the "doldrums" were in reality an important period of growth and renewal for the movement. So significant were these years of regeneration that the period might more appropriately be called "the suffrage renaissance." Aware of the movement's negative image but unwilling to disavow the contributions of the pioneers, the suffragists of the National American Woman Suffrage Association (NAWSA) sought to create a tradition that could reconcile their heroic and somewhat controversial past with the association's pragmatic plans for the future. Developing a reinterpreted, sanitized version of the past, coupled with a sincere celebration of the heroism of pioneer suffragists, NAWSA leaders forged a link between the heroic age of confrontational politics and the new organizational approach to reform that appealed to mainstream American women.

The Referendum of 1895: An Anti-suffrage Victory

A turning point for the woman suffrage movement came on election day, 1895, when the Massachusetts State Legislature held a mock, or nonbinding, suffrage referendum. The State Legislature had been besieged for years by both suffragists and their opponents to act on the issue. In an effort to determine public opinion on the question, the legislature ruled that both women and men would vote in the mock referendum. In a singularly odd twist, both suffragists and anti-suffragists opposed the contest. The former objected to the nonbinding status of the vote, while the latter expressed disgust at being forced to cast a vote in order to demonstrate their aversion to voting. Anti-suffragists resolved their dilemma, however, by clever strategy, good organization, and effective propaganda.[2]

The Massachusetts Association Opposed to Further Extension of the Suffrage to Women (MAOFESW), founded in 1882 by Mrs. Henry O. Houghton and revitalized several months before the November 1895 referendum, attempted to persuade women to abstain from voting on the issue. Arguing that a low female voter turnout would indicate the wishes of Massachusetts women far more convincingly than a large "no" vote, anti-suffragists solicited contributions from well-wishers and embarked on a house-to-house canvass of Boston in order to bring their message to the people. Aiding the MAOFESW workers was a group of prominent Boston men who formed the Man Suffrage Association (MSA). Boasting a membership that included two ex-governors of the state, the president of Harvard University, noted religious leaders, professors, business men and attorneys, the MSA raised over $3,600 in less than two months at a time when the combined expenditures of all suffrage advocates was a mere $1,300.[3]

In contrast to the wealthy and prestigious individuals that opposed woman suffrage, suffragists relied on reformers such as Henry Blackwell, his daughter Alice Stone Blackwell, Julia Ward Howe, and Thomas Wentworth Higginson for leadership and support. Blackwell and Higginson had served together in the abolition movement, and along with Julia Ward Howe, were among the pioneers of the nineteenth-century woman's rights crusade. In addition to the aging but able reformers, Senator George F. Hoar agreed to preside over the Suffrage Referendum State Committee, formed in July 1895, to coordinate the suffrage forces. Unfortunately, most suffragists continued their long-time practice of suspending suffrage work during the summer months. By the time the committee reassembled in October, its members faced a well-organized and active opposition. The anti-suffragists had used the summer to their advantage, circularizing each ward, publicizing their position in the press, and plastering walls and fences with huge placards bearing the message, "Men and Women, Vote No!"[4]

More effective than these publicity measures, however, was the anti-suffrage strategy that encouraged women to abstain from voting. On November 5, antis gleefully pointed to the low female turnout as proof that the vast majority of Massachusetts women did not want the vote. Of approximately 612,000 women eligible to register only 42,676 did so, and of those, only 23,065 actually cast a vote. Although women voters supported the measure 22,204 to 861, not a single female vote was cast in forty-four towns. Of the 273,946 male votes cast, a resounding 186,976 men voted against the measure.[5] By shifting attention away from the actual female vote in the mock referendum and emphasizing instead the percentage of the female population that stayed away from the polls, the anti-suffragists managed to interpret the referendum as an overwhelming victory for their position.

The 1895 referendum cast a long shadow: never again would suffragists call for a test of strength if that test was to include the disfranchised members of their own sex, and never again would anti-suffragists believe that the majority of women favored woman suffrage. Although suffrage leaders continued to maintain that a large latent sentiment for their reform existed, the strategic course that they pursued as the new century unfolded revealed a pragmatic acceptance of the weakness of their position. There was little doubt among suffragists that the majority of Americans accepted the idea of a separate domestic sphere for women. Moreover, in taking the position of defending the status quo and opposing any change in the status of women, the anti-suffragists had occupied the high ground in the coming battle for the vote.

During the Massachusetts referendum campaign, MAOFESW had demon-strated its ability to mobilize an influential constituency, utilize modern advertising methods, and raise large sums of money to finance their work. The suffragists, although dedicated to their cause, were unable to compete with the superior funding and efficiency of their opponents. Moreover, the anti-suffragists had effectively turned the referendum into a demonstration of indifference on the part of Massachusetts women, and had placed the suffrage forces in the defensive position of supporting a democratic reform that the majority of women did not desire. In the aftermath of the contest, many Massachusetts suffrage clubs lost members or disbanded completely, while MAOFESW and other anti-suffrage organizations grew in size and strength. The referendum of 1895, repeatedly cited in national periodicals and in anti-suffrage tracts as proof of female indifference to woman suffrage, shaped the opposition to suffrage for years to come.

More immediately, however, the 1895 Massachusetts referendum forced suffragists to reassess the strengths and weaknesses of their organization. The lesson of 1895 seemed to point toward a continuation of the NAWSA policy of educating the public to the benefits of woman suffrage, but with a new emphasis on effective organization and strong financial support. In addition, suffragists slowly began to recognize the need for a new public image. In response to anti-suffrage propaganda that characterized them as fanatics, and in an effort to attract a larger, more stable membership, suffragists in the first decade of the twentieth century attempted to win respect for their cause and legitimize their organization through a variety of tactics. Their efforts demonstrated a new awareness of the importance of public opinion and marked a turning point in the movement itself. Suffragism of old, shaped by the dedication of a few faithful friends, was to become the movement of the masses, and as such, had to be packaged in a form more attractive to a wider audience.

The Society Plan

Most suffragists believed that the greatest obstacle to woman suffrage was not anti-suffrage opposition or male recalcitrance but rather the indifference of American women. Doubtless many agreed with one anti-suffragist's diagnosis of the problem her opponents faced. "What [the suffrage movement] has to overcome," she explained, "is not an argument but a feeling."[6] Even when this "feeling" manifested itself in overt hostility to the movement, suffrage leaders remained convinced that their foremost task was to exorcise the demon of indifference by converting the apathetic masses to the idea of distaff democracy. And in an age that saw the proliferation of female associations and voluntary societies, it is not surprising that suffrage advocates turned to women's clubs for their organizational model and to society women for the talisman of respectability.

The active recruitment of prominent women by NAWSA officials was not an innovation at the turn of the century; pioneer suffragists had made repeated efforts along those lines throughout the Gilded Age. One of the first successful attempts, however, came in 1893, when Lucy Stone and Carrie Catt attempted to organize the prominent women of Denver, Colorado, according to the "society plan." Although the Colorado Equal Suffrage Association claimed a small but dedicated number of "respectable middle class women," Stone believed that an untapped reservoir of suffrage support existed among wealthy Denver clubwomen. Stone wrote to Den-

Carrie Chapman Catt, c. 1890

UNIVERSITY OF ROCHESTER

ver civic leader Mrs. John R. Hanna, imploring her to make Catt's acquaintance and help her protégée organize the city's leading citizens for suffrage. Hanna duly asked the young suffragist to dinner, and after a long discussion, the two embarked upon an ambitious plan to recruit the city's society women for woman suffrage. Within weeks of their initial meeting, the Denver Equal Suffrage League was formed, composed almost entirely of wealthy clubwomen and socialites. One of the League's first functions, a large public meeting ostensibly in honor of Catt, featured a long list of distinguished speakers from Denver's political and financial circles and was attended by what local suffragists considered the city's "best people." "A most marked result," wrote one Denver suffragist, "was that not one paper in Denver said a word of ridicule or even mild amusement concerning suffragists," and went on to attribute the press's favorable coverage to the presence for the first time of prominent citizens among the suffrage ranks.[7] Moreover, Catt's "society plan" was hailed as the crucial factor in the suffrage referendum in 1893, when Colorado joined Wyoming as the second woman suffrage state.

With her election to the NAWSA presidency in 1900, Catt laid plans to recruit prestigious women of wealth to the suffrage fold at the national level. Initially, most of the NAWSA leadership agreed with Catt's "society plan." Susan B. Anthony, for example, endorsed the idea, and urged NAWSA Corresponding Secretary Rachel Foster Avery to include in the annual convention program a list of all delegates and alternates in order to display prominently the names and addresses of prestigious converts to the cause.[8] Moreover, Catt asked Business Committee members to compile lists of influential clubwomen, ministers and politicians from which to solicit new members, and included well-heeled men as well as society women in her recruitment scheme. Suffragists also sought to win over influential labor and agricultural leaders, and drew up lists of union officials and Grangers for postal propaganda.[9]

In 1904, the Association acknowledged the "society plan" at the annual convention, when the official plan of work for the year recommended that suffragists become active in civic, charitable, or educational work in their communities.[10] Through local clubs and organizations, suffrage advocates could recruit wealthy women with both time and money to devote to the cause. Experience gained in club work could be turned to account in suffrage societies, enabling suffrage leaders to draw on a ready-made constituency already trained in parliamentary procedure, public speaking and fund-raising. Notably missing in the list of organizations to recruit, however, was the burgeoning Black women's club movement. The unspoken assumption of NAWSA leaders was that the "society plan" was for Whites only.

In addition to recruiting from White civic or charitable organizations, suffragists sought new members through parlor meetings, the traditional form of middle-class female assembly. Held in the privacy of the home, parlor meetings were deemed respectable by even the most modest Victorian women, and served to attract a conservative set that would have blanched at attending a public lecture or rally. One suffrage advocate described her role as a parlor meeting speaker in St. Paul:

> You had these little afternoon gatherings of women, maybe six or eight women. You had a cup of tea. A little social gathering. While we were drinking tea, I gave them a little talk and they asked questions about what was going on.... It was alot [sic] better, I thought at the time, than to have a lecture. Because a lot of them wouldn't go to a lecture. And it was what I could do.[11]

Occasionally, professional suffrage speakers would address parlor gatherings in the afternoon before a major nighttime suffrage rally. In this way advocates could reach both the timid and the bold; suffragists believed that through gradual education, encouragement, and attention to individual sensibilities, even the most timid souls could be transformed into "new women."

Although the days of ridicule experienced by nineteenth-century female reformers had passed, speaking in a public forum remained unthinkable for many women. Through the parlor meeting, elite women could gather in a non-threatening environment to discuss a wide range of topics. Woman suffrage, birth control, municipal reform, and labor conditions found their way into parlor conversations, along with the more traditional subjects of literature, history, and religion. Some women, like those who attended the Monday Club of Richburg, New York, combined the new with the old: on alternating weeks, club members turned their attention from New York history and bird-watching to the history of women and pro-suffrage arguments.[12] The growing interest in nontraditional subjects was reflected in other conservative women's groups like the General Federation of Women's Clubs (GFWC), an organization that refused to endorse woman suffrage until the second decade of the twentieth century. Evidence of this trend was demonstrated by the newly elected president of the GFWC when she informed the biennial convention that:

> Dante is dead. He has been dead for several centuries, and I think it is time that we dropped the study of his Inferno and turned our attention to our own.[13]

NAWSA headquarters in Warren, Ohio, c. 1900 was moved to a new
headquarters on Fifth Avenue in New York City, 1909,
thanks to wealthy patrons who supported suffrage.
FRANK CORBELL COLLECTION (LEFT) AND POSTCARD COLLECTION, LIBRARY OF CONGRESS

By concentrating their efforts on prosperous though conservative women, NAWSA suffragists sought to take advantage of the awakened interest in public affairs manifested by the GFWC and other women's organizations.

Initially, the "society plan" drew applause from many suffragists who had labored unsuccessfully to recruit new members in the past. Active recruitment in the woman suffrage state of Colorado, for example, drew influential women into the crusade and provided workers in non-suffrage states with ammunition with which to refute the negative stereotypes that had plagued the movement. One suffragist told congressmen at the 1904 Judiciary Hearing on Woman Suffrage that a leading anti-suffragist, when introduced to several prominent Colorado women, expressed admiration of their ability and dedication. "As social leaders, as philanthropists, as club women and church women, she had swallowed them whole and found them delicious," the suffragist testified. They only disagreed with her after she knew them also to be suffragists."[14]

While many society women limited their involvement in the suffrage crusade to timely financial support, others played a more important part in the movement. Wealthy New York socialite Mrs. Clarence Mackay, for example, organized her own suffrage league, contributed large sums to the cause, and recruited many of that state's most influential women into the suffrage camp.[15] Virginia's Equal Suffrage League included prominent Virginia writers Ellen Glasgow and Mary Johnston, as well as the great-granddaughters of Thomas Jefferson and George Mason.[16] Name recognition, handsome contributions, and social prestige were welcome boons to an organization that had borne the stigma of fanaticism for decades.

Though few NAWSA members questioned the strategy that brought such bounty, the "society plan" led a minority to protest. To some suffragists the "society plan" smacked of impropriety and elitism. "I could not help wondering what Lucy Stone would have thought to have seen the Special representative of the cause she gave her life to, promenading in low neck and arms bare to the shoulders at the Governor's reception," one elderly suffragist wrote in despair. "Mrs. [Evelyn H.] Belden worked bravely...according to her ideas of the right way—*the Society Way*—but there are some old workers who do not think that some of the methods tended to elevate the cause."[17] Others, like Harriot Stanton Blatch, chafed under the yoke of gradualism. Blatch characterized the suffrage movement at the turn of the century as "in a rut worn deep and ever deeper," and in 1907 founded the League of Self-Supporting Women in an effort to escape the tedium and elitism embodied in the NAWSA's "society plan."[18] New York Socialists like Ida Crouch Hazlett viewed with apprehension the new emphasis on upper-class status, and spoke out against mainstream suffragists' "snobbish truckling to the women of influence and social position."[19] So pronounced was the effort to woo socialites that one popular periodical labeled the suffrage crusade a "gilt-chair movement" in reference to suffragists' swank gatherings.[20]

Creating a Suffrage Tradition

Though the "gilt-chair movement" offended some, most suffragists believed that their newly won sense of respectability more than compensated for what little criticism the "society plan" generated. And in keeping with the new emphasis on image at the expense of ideological unity, NAWSA leaders took steps to legitimize their organization through the creation of a formal suffrage historical tradition. On a simple level, tradition may be used to legitimize events, groups, or causes by associating them with the rhetoric, rituals, or personalities of an historic past. A political party, for example, may employ tradition to establish a link between its heroic past and its present platform, as in the recurrent allusions to "The Great Emancipator" made by Republicans trolling for Black votes. Used in this way, tradition may represent a series of unspoken assumptions and loyalties, and serve as a symbol of organizational unity.

At a deeper level, however, tradition may mask the varied ideological perspectives of a diverse constituency with what one historian has called its "undefined universality."[21] The trappings of tradition allow leaders to de-emphasize conflicting opinions and ideals by focusing attention on non-controversial rituals and rhetoric. Moreover, the creation or reinterpretation of traditions may help to steer a group or movement away from an unsavory past or a discarded ideology without the discussion or disagreement engendered by the democratic process. A salient characteristic of tradition is that, for all its presumed foundation in the past, it can be manipulated with singular ease to suit the purposes of the present.

The chief components of the "new" suffrage tradition were a mixture of established, or genuine, rituals, and reinterpreted symbols, rhetoric, and practices that had been customized over time to suit the changing nature of the movement. One of the oldest and most important elements of suffrage tradition was an authorized history of women, with suffrage activism as its focal point. Suffragists had long insisted on the place of women in history. In this regard, nineteenth-century suffrage associations may be considered to have been the first American organizations to promote actively women's history as a discipline. The monumental *History of Woman Suffrage*, begun by Elizabeth Cady Stanton, Susan B. Anthony, and Matilda Joslyn Gage in 1881, was more than propaganda for the cause; to suffrage advocates it filled the void in history textbooks left by the omission of American women.[22] The multi-volume history was continued until the passage of the Nineteenth Amendment in 1920, and remains a testimony to the suffragists' conviction that the women's rights movement deserved a permanent place in history. One of Susan B. Anthony's last acts was to arrange for shipment of the unsold volumes, totaling over ten tons in weight, to NAWSA headquarters, from which the books were distributed to every major library in the country.[23]

The NAWSA showed a commitment to women's history by its efforts to disseminate works on or by women. Beginning in 1902, provisions were made to establish circulating suffrage libraries. These libraries gave women access to the major works on feminist theory and literature, as well as to biographies of famous women and histories of the women's rights movement. The 1903 NAWSA Plan of Work included the compilation of a catalog of woman suffrage literature, to be donated to libraries to encourage the use of such materials. Carrie Chapman Catt showed great enthusiasm for both the catalog and suffrage libraries, and urged each NAWSA suffrage league to appoint a committee on libraries to keep women's history before the public. "Perhaps someday we shall have in the Congressional Library in Washington a story of the work of women...," Catt mused to her friend Alice Stone Blackwell. "We must keep a careful record of our progress for the story is an important one."[24]

Many suffragists shared Catt's vision of the long-term significance of their cause, and despaired over the omission of women from traditional American histories of the period. "There never was another nation with as many parents as we have had," one suffragist wrote in disgust, "but they have all been fathers—Pilgrim Fathers, Plymouth Fathers, Forefathers, Revolutionary Fathers, City Fathers, Church Fathers—fathers of every description but no mothers!"[25] In response to such discontent, Pauline Steinem, chairman of NAWSA's Committee of Education, conducted a rudimentary investigation in 1909 of history and civics textbooks used in the public schools. Steinem wrote to four hundred school superintendents and twenty-six textbook publishing companies in an attempt to survey educators and publishers on the extent of female representation in history books. Although some responses pointed to a handful of famous women like Martha Washington and Betsy Ross who had found their way into the schoolbooks, most of those surveyed replied that they had never considered the problem at all. Steinem attributed lack of recognition to the "masculine point of view which has dominated civilization," and vehemently protested against the impression conveyed by textbooks "that this world has been made by men and for men."[26]

Steinem's findings, coupled with a growing frustration with "the masculine point of view" as it related to suffragism, led NAWSA officials to take their message directly into the schools in 1910. One plan of attack was the idea of suffrage debates to be held in classrooms across America. The NAWSA initially furnished a packet of debate material at a modest price, including citations for both pro- and anti-suffrage works, but by 1912 debaters could turn to the latest volume in the Debaters Handbook Series, *Selected Articles on Woman Suffrage*.[27] School debates offered an opportunity to educate the young on the role of women in history, as well as attracting free publicity for the movement. As one suffragist pointed out, "get the young people involved and you [also] catch mothers!"[28] The injection of women's history or woman suffrage into the schools, while applauded by suffrage advocates, outraged anti-suffragists. "The woman suffrage question has no place in the schools," one anti-suffrage press release maintained, and went on to insist that as long as parents were divided on the issue, school boards should refrain from tampering with textbooks.[29]

Evolution of American Women

Suffragists' efforts to place women's history, and particularly suffrage history, in classrooms and public libraries reflects the NAWSA's belief in the importance of suffrage recruitment. On the one hand, suffragists' enthusiasm for women's history could be interpreted as the natural desire for self-gratification and glory that a heroic history can bestow upon its participants. Legendary feats and heroine-worship can help to sustain an organization in the face of adversity, and so it was with the suffrage movement. But beyond its capacity to distract and sustain a troubled membership, suffragists used the idea of women's history to provide justification for their cause while simultaneously shaping that history to fit the needs of their movement. In a sense, the suffragists created a "great woman" history that ran parallel to the contemporary historical works that excluded them. And throughout that history runs the recurrent theme of the steady evolution of women toward a egalitarian, if distant, utopia.

Advocates of suffrage did not question the belief that women were subject to the forces of evolution and were making progress throughout the ages. This sense of progress marked the rhetoric of suffrage orators like Anna Howard Shaw, who made repeated references in her speeches to the gains that women had won through

Ida Husted Harper
LIBRARY OF CONGRESS

decades of sacrifice. Shaw told one audience:

> The real reformer does not judge of the reform from the day or of an hour, but traces its progress from the beginning, and no human being with the eye of faith can fail to see traversing the whole progress of our movement a divinity shaping our ends... and that divinity is the gospel of democracy.[30]

Others, like writer Ida Husted Harper, drew on the theory of female evolution in widely circulated articles and pamphlets. In a *North American Review* article, for example, Harper first traced the history of the franchise in America, and pointed out that religious, property, educational, and racial qualifications had all been abandoned for male Americans. She then cited the changing status of women from colonial times to the twentieth century that resulted from hard-won legal reforms and educational advancements. In the area of education Harper found the most conclusive evidence of progress: in 1902, for example, there were more girls than boys enrolled in high, normal, and manual-training schools, and over a third of all college students were female. Moreover, of the total number of college degrees conferred in 1902, almost half went to female graduates. Coupled with statistics on the dramatic rise in the number of women entering the professions, Harper's findings documented the evolution of American women to an audience eager to believe in progress.[31]

From an unenlightened past into a clean, well-lighted future, the women of an unwritten history were made to march, and their suffragist creators made the most of their progress. "Women [of the past] lived in a twilight life, a half-life apart, and looked out and saw men as shadows walking," wrote M. Carey Thomas, president of Bryn Mawr and ardent suffragist:

> Now women have won the right to higher education and to economic independence. The right to become citizens of the State is the next and inevitable consequence of education and work outside the home. We have gone so far; we must go farther. We cannot go back.[32]

If evolution of women and the inevitability of their progress provided the philosophical foundation of early women's history, accounts of educational, legal, and professional advances served as testimonials to the doctrine of female progress.

Women's history as seen by suffragists was comprised of a factual body shaped by an ideologically informed philosophy, or in other words, a content and meaning that were intricately entwined and mutually supportive.

History of this sort was important to the suffrage movement in several ways. First, NAWSA leaders drew from women's, and particularly suffrage, history a tradition of leadership handed down from pioneer suffragists and women's rights activists, canonized in the *History of Woman Suffrage* and hagiographic accounts of the movement's early workers, and imbued with the legacy of a century of heroic struggle. As the lineal successors of Anthony, Stanton, and Stone, twentieth-century leaders found legitimation for their position through the celebration of, and association with, what might be called the "founding mothers" of their organization.

The Creation of Consensus

For the NAWSA rank and file the reinterpreted suffrage tradition bridged the gap between the content and meaning of their history. NAWSA membership rolls contained the names of radical feminists, timid society women, socialists, moderates, and states' rights Southerners; the old adage that "politics makes strange bedfellows" was especially true of the suffrage movement at the turn of the century. Suffragist leaders used both genuine and reinterpreted traditions to bind this diverse constituency together and to create what may be called a movement psychology. Through ritual and pageantry, selected events and individuals were molded into a form of popular history that encapsulated both the pasteurized version of the past and a diluted dose of suffrage ideology.

Perhaps the most revered of all NAWSA traditions centered on the veneration of selected suffrage pioneers. Since the formation of the NAWSA in 1890, a generous part of every convention was dedicated to the movement's early adherents. This celebration of the pioneers took several forms, including memorials for deceased workers, greetings from those too old or too infirm to attend, and tributes from younger members who recognized the contributions of their predecessors. During her years as president, Susan B. Anthony often spoke of the pioneers' achievements, using the time between speakers to recognize informally members of the audience who had served the cause for years. Moreover, her stories of what one suffragist called "the cabbage and rotten-egg days" served to immerse converts in a kind of "living suffrage history," providing both role models and a heroic legacy to inspire the new recruits.[33] Formal recognition for the movement's early advocates was also included in convention programs in the form of "Evenings with the Pioneers," and in 1910, a "Decoration Day for our Heroines" became a permanent suffrage tradition.[34]

NAWSA leaders' interpretation of the suffrage pioneers, however, was strangely reticent about some of their predecessors' more controversial actions. Retaining the philosophy of female progress and the legend of heroism and self-sacrifice,

NAWSA leaders presented to their constituents a sanitized version of the past that robbed the pioneers of much of their color, complexity, and principles. Issues such as divorce reform, racial equality, and feminist religious reinterpretations were quietly dropped from the suffrage liturgy in an effort to pasteurize the pioneer experience. Most notable in this reinterpreted history of the movement was the disappearance from the suffrage canon of none other than Elizabeth Cady Stanton, one of the founders of the Seneca Falls Convention and, with Anthony, a dynamic force in the nineteenth-century suffrage crusade. Although both women worked together for decades and shared many of the same ideas and goals for the movement, Anthony's vision of the cause was more pragmatic and in some ways more limited than that of Stanton. For Anthony, the primary goal of the suffrage crusade was unity with other women's groups to form a broad-based constituency for the vote for women. As time passed, Anthony became convinced that rather than addressing working women's issues in order to bring them into the suffrage fold, it was easier to recruit elite women to the cause. Moreover, their advocacy of suffrage would provoke less hostility among the public and the press.

Stanton shared Anthony's vision of unity, but envisioned the movement as an open platform for any issue that concerned women. Rather than narrowing the focus of the NAWSA to elites, Stanton urged suffragists to "stir up a whole group of new victims from time to time, by turning our guns on new strongholds."[35] True to her word, she had over the years endorsed a variety of reforms considered radical for the time. Divorce reform, feminist revision of the Bible, dress reform, separation of church and state—all were subjects for her pen. Stanton's writings and speeches constantly put forward the notion that once women had the vote, they would use their ballots to enact an explicit political agenda including these and other reforms. Her radicalism can best be seen in her belief that all movements for freedom were linked inextricably, and that suffrage was part and parcel of that radical tradition. Stanton's radicalism, however, was on a collision course with the NAWSA's growing conservatism. By the time of her death in 1902, she was largely eclipsed in suffrage hagiography by the less-threatening image of her old friend Anthony. More importantly, the NAWSA's disavowal of Stanton signaled the narrowing of the movement's goals and constituency that was to be a crucial component of the twentieth-century campaign for the vote.[36]

Building a Suffrage Constituency

A second and equally important suffrage tradition, although similar in some respects to that of the pioneers, was in fact the creation of twentieth-century suffragists. Beginning in 1906, NAWSA conventions regularly featured "College Evenings," events designed to appeal to the young, well-educated recruits who increasingly flocked to suffrage functions. Active recruitment of college women was the brainchild of Boston suffragists Maud Wood Park and Inez Haynes Gillmore. While students at Radcliffe, Park and Gillmore had been initiated into the

Maud Wood Park, 1898
LIBRARY OF CONGRESS

The College Evening
OF THE
Fortieth Annual Convention
of the National American Woman
Suffrage Association

The College Evening will be held under the
auspices of the Council of the College Equal
Suffrage League, Saturday, October 17, at
8 o'clock. The subject of the evening will be
the claims of equal suffrage on college women

ADDRESSES WILL BE MADE BY

MRS. MAUD MAY WOOD PARK
Graduate of Radcliffe College
and Founder of the League

MISS SOPHRONISBA P. BRECKENRIDGE
Dean of Junior Women's College of
The University of Chicago

MISS CAROLINE LEXOW
Graduate of Barnard College and President of
the New York Branch of the League

MRS. FRANCES SQUIRE POTTER
Professor of English, in the
University of Minnesota

MISS RAY COSTELLOE OF OXFORD, ENGLAND
Graduate of Newnham College
On Equal Suffrage Among English
University Women

MISS M. CAREY THOMAS
President of Bryn Mawr College

College Days, 1908
LIBRARY OF CONGRESS

suffrage ranks by Massachusetts Woman Suffrage Association (MWSA) president Alice Stone Blackwell. With Blackwell's encouragement, Park and Gillmore founded the Massachusetts College Equal Suffrage League in 1900.[37] Their efforts were so successful that at the NAWSA annual convention in 1906, delegates overwhelmingly voted to establish a national College Equal Suffrage League.

The delegates' enthusiasm for the new organization was in part a result of the first of many NAWSA "College Evenings," held at the Lyric Theater in Baltimore on February 8, 1906. Susan B. Anthony, M. Carey Thomas, and Mary E. Garrett had conceived the idea of such an evening in the fall of 1905, when Anthony, worried that the suffrage convention would not be well received in conservative Baltimore, urged her two co-workers to do what they could "to make [the convention] respectable."[38] The three women planned the event both to involve new workers in the convention program and to "illustrate distinctly the new type of womanhood—the College Woman" as an integral part of their movement. Together they incorporated the disparate yet vital elements of heroism, respectability, and progress into a suffrage tradition that symbolized the new membership, methods, and image of twentieth-century suffragism.

The president of The Johns Hopkins University presided over the 1906 "College Evening," and area college women clad in cap and gown served as ushers for the event. With pioneer suffragists Clara Barton and Julia Ward Howe seated on the podium, an array of college presidents, professors, and deans spoke on the topic, "What has been accomplished for the higher education of women by Susan B. Anthony and other woman suffragists." One by one, the distinguished guests reminded the audience of the pioneers' achievements, and lauded their efforts to open the doors of higher education for women. "We are indebted to [the pioneer women]," Vassar historian Lucy M. Salmon told the audience, "for making it possible for us to spend our lives in fruitful work rather than in idle tears."[39] Others singled out Susan B. Anthony for special praise. "The women of today," one speaker maintained, "may well feel that it is Miss Anthony who has made life possible for them."[40] By linking the advancement of women's education to the pioneers, and in particular, to pioneer suffragists, College Evening dignitaries firmly bound a new generation of women to the historical continuum of the movement. Moreover, by presenting carefully selected early suffragists in a light that was clearly attractive to a college audience, College Evening speakers attributed to them an inflated influence on a development that was both respectable and popular.

In the years that followed the first College Evening, NAWSA leaders increasingly exploited this pioneer/college connection, and in doing so further steered clear of the radicalism of the movement's origins. According to Maud Wood Park, the purpose of the College Equal Suffrage League was to help college women "realize their debt to the women who worked so hard for them, and to make them understand that one way to pay that debt is to fight the battle in the quarter of the field in which it is still to be won, to make them realize the obligation of opportunity."[41] The "debt to the pioneers" became a kind of suffrage slogan, and was even adopted as the title of a 1907 Boston program to honor long-time suffrage workers. At that event, Park listed in her concluding remarks the names of women's rights activists including Frances Wright, Margaret Fuller, Ernestine Rose, and the Grimké sisters and the dates that they began their agitation, pointing out that many women's colleges were founded at the same time. "It seems to me," Park concluded, "that the so-called higher education, along with many other improvements in the standing of women, owes a heavy debt to the movement which advocated equal rights."[42] The debt to the pioneers would also resurface yearly at NAWSA conventions, as College Evening took its place beside such regular traditions as pioneer memorials and the president's address.

The Suffrage Saint

A third and final suffrage tradition grew out of both College Evening and pioneer memorials, and served as the touchstone of twentieth-century suffrage ideology, rhetoric, and ritual. The creation of this potent symbol occurred over a number of years, but reached fruition in March 1906, with the death of Susan B. Anthony. As past president of the NAWSA and as a representative of pioneer activism, Anthony had attained celebrity status within the movement long before her death. NAWSA conventions were carefully scheduled to coincide with the aging reformer's birthday, and convention-goers could count on lavish celebrations, emotional speeches, and a personal word or two from the celebrity herself. In addition to her appearances at the annual conventions, Anthony had travelled extensively for years and was well-known to suffragists throughout America, who increasingly viewed her as the living embodiment of their cause. Local fund-raisers often took the form of "Susan B. Anthony Day," and state suffrage convention badges and programs routinely bore her picture.[43] Such was her stature in the movement that during her later years she often witnessed her own apotheosis. In 1903, for example, while dining on bluefish and "diplomate pudding" with a Brooklyn, New York, suffrage league, she heard a series of speeches presented on the topic "Susan B. Anthony: Lessons and Inspirations from Her Life."[44]

Susan B. Anthony

Ida Husted Harper was in part responsible for Anthony's transformation from reviled fanatic to adored leader. Her two-volume biography of the reformer was published in 1898, and provided readers with the day-to-day occurrences of her subject's life in almost Boswellian detail. A third volume, added after Anthony's death, extended the work to more than sixteen hundred pages and included excerpts from over a hundred highly favorable editorials on Anthony that appeared after her death.[45] In addition to her work as a hagiographer, Harper proved to be unsurpassed as a nascent press agent. In keeping with the NAWSA's new emphasis on respectability, she composed an article in 1903 for *Pearson's Magazine* entitled "Miss Anthony at Home" that portrayed the aging suffragist as "domestic in every fiber of her body."[46] With an eye to her prospective female audience, Harper cloaked her subject in the rhetoric of domesticity with such "feminine" attributes as neatness, hospitality, self-sacrifice, patience, and loyalty. According to the article, "Aunt Susan" sat down at the breakfast table looking "like a lovely grandmother," to a meal "strictly of the feminine order." Later she embarked upon a day of womanly pursuits that included cooking, cleaning, and sewing. "Miss Anthony," concluded the article, "never has suggested ways for repairing the damages of society with one-half the skill she employed in teaching her nieces her wonderful method of darning rents in garments and household linens."[47] Through her literary efforts, Harper helped to replace the stereotypical image of masculinized fanatic with a non-threatening feminine heroine imbued with domestic virtues.

The sanctification of Susan B. Anthony, however, was not completed until her death in 1906. At the NAWSA convention of that year, the aging reformer appeared before her devoted disciples for the last time. Her health gone, she exhorted the delegates in a faltering voice to continue in the great work begun at Seneca Falls, and closed her remarks with the words, "Failure is impossible!" After the convention closed, she traveled to Washington to attend the annual Congressional Hearings but was too ill to leave her bed. Returning for the last time to her home in Rochester, New York, Anthony was attended by her niece and sister, and in her final hours, by Anna Howard Shaw. Profoundly shaken by the loss of her closest friend, Shaw would help to create the most enduring and vital of suffrage traditions: the suffrage saint.[48]

Like Harper, Anna Howard Shaw was uniquely fitted to the role of hagiographer. She met Anthony at a suffrage meeting in 1888, and a lifelong friendship had ensued. Shaw clearly worshipped the older woman. One of her favorite stories featured the seventy-year-old Anthony, wrapped in a dressing gown and talking until dawn, "foreseeing everything, forgetting nothing, and sweeping me with her in her flight toward our common goal until I...experienced an almost dizzy sense of exhilaration."[49] Such was Shaw's devotion that, in her 1915 autobiography, Anthony figures almost as prominently as does the author herself. As both president of the NAWSA and an Anthony disciple, Shaw hurried to Rochester when word came that the end was near. What followed would provide an important source of inspiration for the cult of personality that adopted Anthony as its patron saint.

Deathbed scenes were a popular literary device for turn-of-the-century novelists, and it is therefore not surprising that Shaw chose to record the scene she witnessed in both the periodical press and in her autobiography. Indeed, her vivid description of Anthony's pale visage and prophetic words lend credence to the expression, "life imitates art." Two passages in particular express the motif Shaw sought to capture. On the last afternoon of her life, Anthony suddenly began to recite the names of the women as this "final roll-call...seemed to file past her dying eyes that day in an endless, shadowy review," Shaw wrote, and she quoted Anthony as saying "I know the sacrifices they have made, but it has all been worth while!" With this benediction, Anthony lapsed into silence for a time, but rallied once more in order to assure Shaw that, after death, she would continue to be an active force in the woman suffrage movement. "Who knows?" Anthony speculated, "Perhaps I may be able to do more for the Cause after I am gone than while I am here."[50]

In a sense she was right. Anthony's vision (or Shaw's invention?) of "the shadowy review," coupled with her prophecy of a kind of mystic activism beyond the grave, suggests a type of secular sanctification well-known to readers of sentimental fiction of the period. The theme of suffrage saint was also conspicuous in a selection of poems written about Anthony and published after her death in Volume Three of Harper's biography. "She is not dead but more alive/ than in her fairest earthly days," one poet proclaimed, while another pictured her "with eyes that looked beyond the gates of death" and crowned by a "halo of her venerable age."[51] Perhaps the most explicit example of sanctification was by John Russell Hayes, who poetically recorded Anthony's entry into a supernatural suffrage procession:

And then my vision faded,
And a lordly melody rolled
As down celestial vistas
The saintly company strolled.
But the face of that latest comer
I longest kept in sight—
So ardent with consecration,
So lit with angelic light...
Crowned is she and sainted
In heavenly halls above
Who freely gave for her sisters
A life of boundless love.[52]

On March 15, 1906, the suffrage saint was buried in Rochester, New York. The mayor of Rochester, the president of Rochester University, and other local dignitaries were present, in addition to suffrage and temperance leaders, aging abolitionists, college women, friends, and family members. Despite a heavy snowfall, an estimated crowd of ten thousand assembled outside the church, pressing against the doors and windows in order to hear Anna Howard Shaw's eulogy. Touching briefly upon Anthony's "womanly attributes," she then described her subject's heroism and devotion to the cause. "There is no death for such as she," Shaw concluded, and predicted that "the ages will come to revere her name."[53] When the church doors were opened at the close of the service, crowds of mourners streamed past the body. One mourner in particular caught the attention of some reporters: an elderly Black woman, covered with snow and leaning heavily on a crutch, paused by the coffin and sobbed aloud into a frost-covered handkerchief. Other journalists chose to feature an aged Black man, also limping, who took as a *memento mori* a single leaf from the funeral wreath. The heroic eulogies, patriotic rhetoric and weeping Black spectators reminded some witnesses of another fallen emancipator. Describing the long line of mourners who filed past the body, one observer called them "the plain people, the people Susan B. Anthony and Abraham Lincoln loved." After the long procession had passed, a female honor guard from the university escorted the coffin past houses draped in black to the grave site where Shaw delivered the final words.[54]

In the days that followed, friends worked to ensure a lasting memory for their patron saint. Rochester educators named an elementary school after Susan B. Anthony, a local church commissioned a stained-glass window bearing her likeness, and women's clubs, temperance groups, and civic organizations honored her with memorials. Ida Husted Harper collected over a thousand editorials that eulogized Anthony, including one from the anti-suffrage *New York Times* lauding "the tender, womanly loveliness of the great reformer."[55]

Suffragists across the nation held memorial services similar to the one conducted by the Kentucky Equal Rights Association a week after Anthony's death. Mary Clay, a long-time suffragist and descendant of Henry Clay, "The Great Compromiser," presided over the service that took place in the Clay family home. In the center of the parlor draped in yellow satin and black crepe stood a large picture of Susan B. Anthony, flanked by a small candle in a pink candlestick, a souvenir from the suffrage leader's eightieth birthday celebration. On a nearby table was a smaller portrait of the reformer, surrounded by photographs of Lucy Stone, Elizabeth Cady Stanton, and Isabella Beecher Hooker. After a roll call of pioneer suffragists and a sketch of the reformer's work for women's rights, the assembly heard a series of elegies and a dramatic reading based on Anthony's final days. Following a rosary and benediction, the women sang "Nearer, My God, To Thee" and adjourned for refreshments.[56]

The nature of the Kentucky memorial service closely followed the form routinely employed by literary, church, or civic gatherings of women, but with a suffrage theme. Within this structure, songs, poems, and dramatic readings provided a thread of continuity between old forms and new meanings. The intimate atmosphere of the parlor meeting encouraged participation by women who would have shied away from speaking to a larger audience. Overtones of religious ritual endowed the service with both familiarity and stately respectability in accord with the tastes of the times. The parlor decor approached ecclesiastical parody with its makeshift altar and display of icons. In addition, the service followed a quasi-liturgical pattern, employing both poetic and prose readings and ending with the litany of the rosary and the benediction.

Kentucky suffragists also shaped the memorial service to suit the private agenda of their movement. Tradition played an important role: the veneration of the pioneers, the idea of a parallel women's history, and the philosophy of female progress were all incorporated into the ceremony. In her posthumous role, Susan B. Anthony became what no living woman could be: a universally shared symbol of the cause whose very name could conjure a constellation of images and sentiment. Across the nation clubwomen and suffragists met for similar services.[57] Within a decade Anthony had become, like Lincoln and Altgeld before her, part of the common mental property of Progressive Americans. Her picture was hung beside those of the Founding Fathers' in schoolrooms across America, her memory achieving a measure of the vague immortality accorded to the heroes of American democracy. In 1917, for example, Eugene V. Debs characterized her as "synonymous with the cause of human freedom and equal rights,...a moral heroine, an apostle of progress, a herald of the coming day."[58]

The Formation of a Female Political Culture

Mary Clay's memorial service, with its quaint sentimentality and solemn naiveté, summons up a lost world of women, conceived within the pages of popular fiction of the period, adorned with the trappings of Victorian respectability, and bound by parlor walls. Although trivial when compared to the larger course of world affairs, it reminds us that political participation for women at the turn of the century was not accomplished merely by the conversion of Congress or the ratification of an amendment. Instead, women entered the political arena through a lengthy process that included such seemingly apolitical institutions as historical biography, sentimental fiction and parlor meetings, as well as more familiar processes of state referenda campaigns, lobbyist activity, and direct political coercion. It would be unjust to downplay the early efforts of women's political organization. Given the high degree of female participation in Progressive Era movements like temperance, child-labor reform, and civic betterment crusades, the timid parlor meetings of the 1900 to 1910 period should be seen as the training ground for many Progressive activists.

Thus by 1910 the visionary cause of the pioneers had been transformed into an eminently safe program for middle-class club meetings. This stage of development, which first brought a wealthy, "respectable" class of women into comfortable participation in suffrage, was seen by NAWSA leaders as a necessary precondition of the movement that would eventually win the vote. For better or worse, these middle-class leaders could not conceive of conducting a successful campaign without the approval and the financial support of the social elite.

NAWSA benefactor Alva Vanderbilt Belmont often hosted gatherings of suffragists at Marble House, her opulent "summer house" in Newport, RI, 1914.

RECORDS OF THE NATIONAL WOMAN'S PARTY, LIBRARY OF CONGRESS

As tangible proof of the wisdom of their strategy, leaders of the NAWSA could point to a dramatic increase in support for their reform. Membership rolls soared from about 12,000 in 1906, the year of Anthony's death, to over 117,000 in 1910. After 1910, a widescale organizational scheme was put into effect, and a corps of dedicated organizers largely drawn from the ranks of college-educated women was active throughout the country. Moreover, by 1914 a professional lobby was at work to push the federal amendment through Congress. This expanded effort was fueled by an ample treasury; in 1916, for example, the NAWSA's operational budget stood at $100,000 annually. The suffrage political strategy, based on the precondition of a respectable image, had paid high dividends and was the foundation of their victory in 1920.

In a few years' time, NAWSA leaders had built a solid political base for suffrage by attracting into the movement large numbers of women who previously were uninvolved in politics. They had accomplished this by giving a political meaning to traditional forms of female assembly, organization, and entertainment. For the women involved, the familiar surroundings and rituals legitimized and demystified the alien world of political action. Anti-suffrage propaganda and the unflattering stereotype of nineteenth-century suffragists had hammered home the proposition that femininity and politics could never mix. In the first decade of the new century, however, a generation of women drew a different message from what they soon would call the "suffrage ideal." Women who had always been excluded from political participation were drawn, not to party affiliations, bosses, and smoke-filled rooms, but rather to a new kind of political activity: active membership in a reform or single-interest pressure group. Scholars who lament the decline of popular political participation in the Progressive Era fail to take into account this shift from party affiliation to interest group loyalty. In fact, movements like suffrage, temperance, child-labor reform, and other Progressive causes involved and included vast numbers of people who had had no part in the political process during the heyday of the parties, yet were involved in a popular politics of their own making.

In the first decade of the twentieth century, suffrage leaders set out to create a new image for their movement. Their basic goal was to forge a notion of women's history and female progress that could be accepted as consonant with the wider aspirations of mainstream society. In a sense they banished the radical past, turned their back on nonconformity, and in the process captured the support of quietly influential groups of women. Gone was the taint of extremism that suffragists believed had haunted the movement for decades; the parlor meeting had adopted "Aunt Susan" as its patron saint, and suffragism had come of age.

Notes

This article is drawn from the author's book, *Woman Suffrage and the New Democracy*, published posthumously by Yale University Press in 1996.

1. Eleanor Flexner, *Century of Struggle: The Woman's Rights Movement in the United States*, (1959; Cambridge, Mass., 1975), 256.
2. Ibid., 230.
3. James J. Kenneally, "Woman Suffrage and the Massachusetts Referendum of 1895," *The Historian* 30 (August, 1968): 620-623.
4. Susan B. Anthony and Ida Husted Harper, eds., *History of Woman Suffrage*, vol. 4 (1883-1900; reprint, New York, 1969), 735-737 (hereafter cited as *HWS*); and Kenneally, "Woman Suffrage and the Massachusetts Referendum of 1895," 625.
5. Ibid., 630. In *HWS*, Alice Stone Blackwell's account of the 1895 referendum emphasizes the positive aspects of the contest.
6. Priscilla Leonard, "The Ladies Battle," *Current Literature* 36 (April, 1904): 386-389.
7. Minnie Reynolds to Alice Stone Blackwell, December 12, 1930, National American Woman Suffrage Association Papers (hereafter cited as NAWSA), Reel 17, Library of Congress (hereafter cited as LC).
8. Susan B. Anthony to Rachel Foster Avery, January 22, 1900, Papers of Susan B. Anthony, Reel 1, LC.
9. Carrie Chapman Catt to Catherine Waugh McCullough, August 8, 1900, Dillon Collection, Box 9, Schlesinger Library, Radcliffe College, (hereafter cited as SL).
10. *Proceedings of the Thirty-Sixth Annual Convention of the National American Woman Suffrage Association, 1904*, 14-15; *Current Literature* 36 (April, 1904): 386-389.
11. Sherna Gluck, ed. *From Parlor To Prison: Five American Suffragists Talk About Their Lives* (New York, 1976); Calendar for 1912, NAWSA, Reel 48, LC.
12. Monday Club of Richburg, New York, Calendar for 1912, NAWSA, Reel 48, LC.
13. Quoted in Gluck, *From Parlor To Prison*, 12-13.
14. House Committee on the Judiciary Hearing on Woman Suffrage, February 16, 1904, Statement of Mary C.C. Bradford, Women's Rights Collection, Folder 42, SL.
15. Carrie Chapman Catt to Mrs. Millicent Garrett Fawcett, October 19, 1909, Carrie Chapman Catt Papers, Reel 3, LC.
16. See Dorothy Scura, "Ellen Glasgow and Women's Suffrage," *Research in Action* 6 (Spring 1982): 12-15. For Mary Johnston, see Elizabeth D. Coleman, "Penwoman of Virginia's Feminists," *Virginia Cavalcade* 6 (Winter 1956): 8-11; and Marjorie Spruill (Wheeler), "Mary Johnston, Suffragist," *Virginia Magazine of History and Biography* 100 (January 1992): 99-118.
17. Margaret Campbell to Henry B. Blackwell, May 14, 1900, NAWSA Reel 5, LC.
18. Harriot Stanton Blatch and Alma Lutz, *Challenging Years: The Memoirs of Harriot Stanton Blatch*, (New York, 1940), 91-92.
19. *New York Call*, March 11, 1917. Quoted in Mari Jo Buhle, *Women and American Socialism, 1870-1920* (Urbana, Ill., 1983), 225.
20. *Literary Digest* 36 (February 29, 1908): 290-292.
21. For a detailed discussion of tradition and its uses, see Eric Hobsbawm and Terence Ranger, eds., *The Invention of Tradition* (Cambridge, 1983), 1-12.
22. Ida Husted Harper, *History of Woman Suffrage* vol. 5 (Reprint, New York, 1969): 228.
23. *HWS* 5: 204-206. Anthony's interest in placing the work is documented in Ida Husted Harper, *The Life and Work of Susan B. Anthony*, 3 vols., (Indianapolis, 1898 and 1908), 1278-1279.
24. Carrie Chapman Catt to Alice Stone Blackwell, November 6, 1908, Carrie Chapman Catt Papers, Reel 2, LC.
25. Speech by Anna Howard Shaw, "The Fate of the Republic," (1892) Dillon Collection, Folder 499, SL. "That is where the weakness of every Republic lies," Shaw continued, "they have been fathered to death."
26. *HWS* 5: 263.
27. Edith M. Phelps, ed., *Selected Articles on Woman Suffrage*, Debaters Handbook Series, (Minneapolis, 1912).
28. Mary Gray Peck, Report of the Headquarters Secretary, quoted in *HWS* 5: 266-268.
29. Press Release, "Anti Suffrage News and Comment" (n.d.), issued by New York State Association Opposed Women's Suffrage, Folder 2, SL.

30. Speech by Anna Howard Shaw to the NAWSA Convention, April 14, 1910, Women's Rights Collection, Folder 514, SL.
31. Ida Husted Harper, "Why Women Cannot Vote in the United States," *North American Review* 179 (July, 1904): 30-35.
32. Pamphlet by M. Carey Thomas, "A New Fashioned Argument for Woman Suffrage," (October 17, 1908) Women's Rights Collection, Folder 730, SL.
33. Volume 5 of *HWS* devotes ample coverage to the pioneers in its chapters on the annual conventions. For the quotation, see *HWS* 5: 123.
34. Anna Howard Shaw, Letter to "Progress," (March, 1910) Dillon Collection, Box 22, SL. For examples of pioneer celebrations, see *HWS* 5: 30-31 and 219-220.
35. Ellen Carol DuBois, *Elizabeth Cady Stanton/Susan B. Anthony: Correspondence, Writings, Speeches* (New York, 1981), 226.
36. Not only were Stanton's more radical activities omitted from the suffrage pioneer tradition, but her role in founding the American women's rights movement was also forgotten. According to historian Ellen DuBois, Stanton's papers were not collected and she found no biographer until 1940. See DuBois, *Elizabeth Cady Stanton/Susan B. Anthony...*, 191-192.
37. Maud Wood Park, "The College Equal Suffrage League: Introductory notes," (1942), Women's Rights Collection, Folder 696, SL; *HWS* 5: 660-662.
38. *HWS* 5: 167; and Anna Howard Shaw, *The Story of a Pioneer* (New York, 1915), 221-223.
39. *HWS* 5: 170.
40. Ibid., 171.
41. Maud Wood Park, "Address to the 28th Annual Convention of NAWSA, College Night," February 8, 1906, Women's Rights Collection, Folder 855, SL.
42. Typescript of *Woman's Journal* article, "Debt to the Pioneers," March 30, 1907, Women's Rights Collection, Folder 855, SL. For examples of this theme, see *HWS* 5: 173 and 226.
43. *HWS* 5: 1373; *Life and Work of Susan B. Anthony*, 1355.
44. Program, Kings County Political Equality League, Brooklyn, New York, February 14, 1903, NAWSA, Reel 26, LC.
45. Harper, *The Life and Work of Susan B. Anthony*.

46. *Pearson's Magazine* March, 1903. Excerpts from this article also appear in Harper, *Life and Work of Susan B. Anthony*, 1298-1304.
47. Ibid., 1295-1304.
48. Ellen DuBois used the term "suffrage saint" in reference to Anthony in a conversation with the author in 1986.
49. Anna Howard Shaw, *The Story of a Pioneer*, 189-190.
50. Ibid., 232-234.
51. Harper, *Life and Work of Susan B. Anthony*, 1604 and 1606-1607.
52. Ibid., 1607-1610.
53. Anna Howard Shaw, "Address at Memorial Service for Susan B. Anthony," March 15, 1906, Dillon Collection, Box 22, SL.
54. Accounts of the Anthony funeral are drawn from Shaw, *Story of a Pioneer*, 235-238; and Harper, *Life and Work of Susan B. Anthony*, 1429-1444.
55. *New York Times*, March 18, 1906. Clipping in the Breckinridge Family Papers, Box 700, LC.
56. Notes from KERA Memorial Service for Susan B. Anthony by Mary Clay, March 22, 1906, NAWSA, Reel 5, LC.
57. For example, see Program, ERA Club Memorial Service for Susan B. Anthony, May 8, 1906, NAWSA, Reel 26, LC.; and Program, "A Meeting of Appreciation of the Life and Work of Susan B. Anthony," Interurban Political Equality Council of Greater New York, April 1, 1906, NAWSA, Reel 26, LC.
58. Eugene V. Debs, "Susan B. Anthony: Pioneer of Freedom," *Pearson's Magazine* (July, 1917). Copy in NAWSA, Reel 26, LC.

Jane Addams, c. 1896
By this time, the famed Progressive reformer had founded Hull House, a settlement house in a working-class immigrant neighborhood in Chicago, where she and other middle-class reformers lived along with the people they sought to aid. As Jane Addams explained later, they sought to "provide a center for a higher civic and social life, to institute and maintain educational and philanthropic enterprises, and to investigate and improve the conditions in the industrial districts in Chicago."– Addams, *Twenty Years at Hull-House.*

Thirteen

JANE ADDAMS, PROGRESSIVISM, AND WOMAN SUFFRAGE:

An Introduction to
"Why Women Should Vote"
Victoria Bissell Brown

"Why Women Should Vote"
Jane Addams

Editor's Introduction: In the passage that follows, historian Victoria Bissell Brown illuminates for us one of the most popular and influential pro-suffrage documents written during the long campaign for woman suffrage, Jane Addams's "Why Women Should Vote." Brown, author of *The Education of Jane Addams*, a biography of the revered Progressive reformer and suffragist, discusses the popularity of Addams's essay and analyzes it in the context of Progressive reform philosophy and pro-suffrage rhetoric.

An understanding of the Progressive movement and its relationship to woman suffrage as explained by one of the movement's luminaries is crucial to our understanding of the success of the woman suffrage movement. For of all the factors leading to the victory in 1920, the emergence around 1900 of this new era of reform—the "Progressive Era"—is one of the most important.

Progressivism, which energized American politics until World War I, began at the grassroots level and strongly affected American politics at all levels—including both major political parties. Indeed, in 1912, Progressives in the Republican Party bolted and formed the "Progressive Party" with Theodore Roosevelt as their candidate, after the Republicans chose to back President William Howard Taft for re-election. Roosevelt and Taft then lost to Woodrow Wilson, the Progressive politician nominated by the Democrats.

This reform zeal arose in response to the many ills that plagued American society in the last half of the nineteenth century as a result of massive industrialization, urbanization, and immigration. Progressives insisted that the hands-off, non-interventionist style of government demanded by conservatives, while appropriate, perhaps, for a rural, agrarian society, was no longer adequate in a new era in which an individual's pursuit of happiness brought him or her constantly into conflict with others, when large corporations ran roughshod over smaller businesses and exploited workers without restraint, and large numbers of people lived in close proximity in cities without adequate provision for sanitation, disease control, or recreation. Progressives demanded that government—from municipal to federal—*take action* on a variety of fronts, including (to name a few): regulating corporations to protect workers and consumers; safeguarding public health; banning child labor; establishing compulsory education, juvenile courts and public playgrounds; and reforming government to make it more responsible, accountable, and free of corruption.

The Progressive coalition included a diverse group of people determined to remedy the social evils produced by unrestrained capitalism but not always in agreement about solutions. In fact, Progressivism was riddled with contradictions. For example, Progressives generally supported democratic reforms including the secret ballot, the nomination of candidates by primaries rather than meetings in "smoke-filled rooms," and the direct election of United States Senators by the voters rather than the state legislatures. But some Progressives, believing that corrupt urban political machines were manipulating the "ignorant immigrant vote," favored undemocratic reforms such as literacy tests to eliminate the uneducated from the electorate. Most Progressives were middle class, and many patronizingly believed that the working class needed to be protected more than empowered: they believed that citizens like themselves should shape social policy out of a sense of noblesse oblige.

Progressivism aided the woman suffrage movement in several ways. New ideas about the functions of government were more in line with old ideas about woman's nature and abilities: a government that was expected to nurture and protect and arbitrate conflicts rather than focus exclusively on national defense and economic development might benefit from woman's presumably innate characteristics and domestic experience. In addition, public support for woman suffrage grew as a result of the widespread belief that women—if enfranchised—would support Progressive reforms because they were more moral, compassionate, and nurturing than men. People also assumed that woman suffrage would be a boon to Progressivism because hundreds of thousands of women were clearly demonstrating their support for Progressive reform as lobbyists and political activists. Indeed, many of these reform-minded women were converted to the suffrage movement out of frustration when politicians failed to take their lobbying seriously and/or opposed the reforms they supported. Like the women of the WCTU before them, women Progressives—and their male supporters—believed that they would be much more effective if women were able to vote rather than rely exclusively upon "indirect influence."

Suffragists recognized the advantages offered by this political climate. As the previous essay by Sara Hunter Graham demonstrates, early twentieth-century suffragists were eager to avoid the taint of radicalism, to counter the anti-suffragists' claim that suffrage was unwomanly, and to link their movement with popular ideas. Indeed, though suffragists never ceased to argue for woman suffrage on the grounds that it was *right* and *just* and due to them as citizens of the United States, they were at all times searching for ways to persuade politicians that enfranchising women was politically *expedient.*

In the Progressive Era, rather than arguing against the idea of separate spheres, suffragists typically proclaimed that woman suffrage was completely compatible with woman's traditional duties. They often argued that, as a result of industrialization and urbanization, women were no longer able to protect their homes and children without the vote! Some suffragists, either believing in women's innate differences from men or pandering to this popular supposition, insisted that women would *naturally* support the new nurturing role many believed government should adopt. As one widely used suffrage poster stated: "Women are by nature and training housekeepers. Let them help in the city housekeeping. They will introduce an occasional spring cleaning."

As Victoria Brown explains, Jane Addams's "Why Women Should Vote" is in some ways consistent with and in other ways different from the prevailing usage of Progressive ideology in pro-suffrage rhetoric. Addams's essay is extremely important as one of the strongest statements of the argument that changed conditions *require* women to vote in order to continue to fulfill their traditional functions. Publishing this powerful endorsement of woman suffrage as inextricably linked to Progressivism was of inestimable value to the suffrage cause—the seal of approval from America's best-loved Progressive.

Brown insists, however, that Addams—though a leading suffragist—was not necessarily typical of suffragists and did not focus her political energies primarily on this cause. In fact, she presented woman suffrage as of crucial importance primarily as an *implement* through which women could more effectively reach their political goals, a way for women to assert their political values while still fulfilling their traditional functions.

Brown defends Addams against charges that have been leveled against her by some historians, accusations that she pandered to popular ideas and prejudices. For example, Brown rejects the idea that Addams "grounded her suffrage reasoning in biological essentialism." Rather, Brown insists, Addams believed that whatever differences existed in the political values of men and women were attributable to women's *experience,* not innate habits or instincts. Furthermore, Addams did not employ the nativist, elitist, or racist arguments embraced by some suffragists. Brown insists that Addams was a woman of principle, and that this essay is a sincere statement of her Progressive reform philosophy—not mere suffrage propaganda.

Still, Brown concedes that Jane Addams was a brilliant strategist and a habitual diplomat, owing to her desire to avoid conflict and promote harmony. In this and other works, writes Brown, Addams astutely presented woman suffrage as inevitable given the new focus of government in the Progressive Era. Many a suffragist would follow her lead, presenting suffrage as something women were *compelled* to embrace given changed historical circumstances rather than the result of woman's desire for equality and power. "If there was any guile in Addams's pro-suffrage position," writes Brown, "this was surely it."

Yet Brown's emphasis here is on the sincerity of Addams's essay. The power of the essay, she argues, was in the neat fit between Addams's focus on the connection between suffrage and reform and the appeal of Progressivism. That the essay was so popular was a testimony to Addams's "unusual ability" to weave her Progressive concerns "into a pro-suffrage argument that appealed to mainstream sensibilities without bowing to mainstream prejudices."

IN THE YEARS between 1900 and 1915, close to two hundred articles appeared in popular American magazines concerning American woman suffrage. In the year 1910 alone, the interested American reader could sample some twenty-five articles on the subject. Perched at the top of this stack of articles for and against and about woman suffrage sits Jane Addams's editorial, "Why Women Should Vote," published in the January 1910 edition of *The Ladies' Home Journal*. Of all the popular articles on suffrage that appeared in these years, Addams's has probably been reprinted the most often, quoted the most regularly, cited the most frequently. The modern reader must ask, has this pro-suffrage essay received such attention over the years simply because it was written by the most famous woman of her day or because it best reflects the era's pro-suffrage ideology? Are the arguments Addams put forth in *The Ladies' Home Journal* unique to her or representative of the dozens of pro-suffrage articles Americans were reading in these years?

The answers to all of those questions are "yes." The article has, of course, received special attention because of Jane Addams's fame. But Addams's fame was due in no small part to her ability to craft popular articles that resonated with strong currents in public opinion while still marking out a unique philosophical position. Scholars have not always appreciated this particular talent in Jane Addams, nor have they always looked favorably on Addams's position in "Why Women Should Vote" that women "need this implement in order to preserve the home."

Back in the 1970s, when scholars of women were measuring every text by the single ideological yardstick of "liberal" feminism, Jane Addams's pro-suffrage argument appeared to fall short because she did not put the classical liberal emphasis on women's individual right to the vote. At that time, it was thought that her embrace of women's traditional domestic role in this *Ladies' Home Journal* essay, along with her focus on the social good women could perform with the vote, consti-tuted an accommodation to, even a pandering to, popular gender politics.[1] Current scholarship, however, allows for a new reading of "Why Women Should Vote." This scholarship reminds us that women's progress depends as much on "republican" commitments to the common good as on "liberal" rights and individual autonomy. Read in the light of contemporary research on female culture and moral values, Addams's assumption that women speak "in a different voice" appears to be more a positive assertion of the need for that particular ideological voice in politics than a capitulation to existing notions of women's innate moral nature.[2] Read, too, in light of the work of current historical research on women reformers in the Progressive Era, Jane Addams's focus on women's collective duty to reform (rather than their individual right to autonomy) in "Why Women Should Vote" appears to be more a reflection of the political climate unique to the Progressive Era, and more a function of the very particular emphasis Addams placed on economic democracy, than an accommodation to conservative nostalgia for selfless womanhood.[3]

Understanding "Why Women Should Vote" requires understanding that Jane Addams's central political goal was the legislative enactment of a Progressive social agenda, including protective labor legislation, health and welfare programs, educational reform, and legal equity for Blacks and immigrants. When she said that woman suffrage was an "implement" women needed to "preserve the home," she was saying that she regarded the achievement of the Progressive agenda as essential to the preservation of the homes of millions of poor and working-class Americans. Further, she was saying that woman suffrage was crucial to enacting that agenda because women occupied the homes that needed preserving and, therefore, were most likely to support Progressive reform. It was this set of assumptions that motivated her active support for woman suffrage and that shaped the arguments she crafted for woman suffrage.

Placed alongside the other pro-suffrage articles published at the time, "Why Women Should Vote" thus appears to be quite representative of the pro-reform, "Progressive" mood dominant in American political life in 1910. And in being representative of Progressives, Addams appears unique among suffrage leaders. Her devotion to improving the lives of the working class by creating an interdependent polity as responsive to domestic as to commercial needs meant that questions of women's particular situation were subordinated, in her writing, to questions of women's duty to demand expansion of the nation's entire political agenda. Whatever readers today may think of this approach, its popularity at the time may be detected in the fact that a year after this essay appeared in *The Ladies' Home Journal*, Addams was elected to a vice presidency in the National American Woman Suffrage Association (NAWSA).

Close inspection of "Why Women Should Vote" suggests that Jane Addams's popularity derived not only from her Progressive concern for economic and political democracy, but from her unusual ability to weave that concern with her own mediating temperament, diplomatic style, and genuine respect for domesticity into a pro-suffrage argument that appealed to mainstream sensibilities without bowing to mainstream prejudices. "Why Women Should Vote," is, first and foremost then, a statement of Jane Addams's Progressive reform philosophy. As such, the essay serves to inform our understanding of the ways in which woman suffrage and Progressivism were mutually reinforcing movements in the early twentieth century and the role Addams played in linking the success of one movement to the success of the other.

Jane Addams and Progressive Era Reform

When Jane Addams wrote "Why Women Should Vote" in 1910, she was fifty years old and enjoying a decade, 1905-1915, that would mark the peak of her power and influence in America. Four years before her pro-suffrage essay appeared in *The Ladies' Home Journal,* an article on Addams in *Current Literature* was published with the title, "The Only Saint America Has Produced." And in the year following her *Ladies' Home Journal* essay, when *The Independent* asked its readers to name "the most useful Americans," Addams was ranked second, behind Thomas Edison but ahead of Andrew Carnegie. Indeed, when *The Ladies' Home Journal* invited Addams to write "Why Women Should Vote," the magazine itself was on record in opposition to woman suffrage. Still, it gave Addams space to make a case for suffrage that was bound to be very appealing to *Journal* readers, and, three years later, hired her to write a monthly column on civic matters. The *Journal* introduced that column with the claim that "no woman in America today is so closely in touch with those great social and economic movements that are outside the home and yet vitally touch the home as Jane Addams."[4]

Addams had launched her reform career by opening, in 1889, the second, and by far the most famous, social settlement house in the United States, Hull House on Halstead Street in Chicago. The settlement began as one building, but by 1910 it comprised thirteen buildings encircling an entire square block of a working-class, immigrant neighborhood on Chicago's west side. Addams's settlement served as a meeting place for political activists, workers, students, immigrants, women's groups, unionists, artists and reformers, children and teenagers. It served as well as a catalyst for social legislation, political reform, social science theory, and labor organizing at the city, state, and national levels. Until her death in 1935, Jane Addams presided as the calm center of the storm that was Hull House, attracting extraordinarily gifted, innovative people around her and adroitly leading them in the development of all the sorts of social service programs and legislative agendas that have come to typify the "Progressive Era" of the 1890s and early 1900s.

Because of her close ties to the University of Chicago during that institution's glory years around the turn of the century, Addams is often called the founder of the academic discipline of social work. She was by nature more a sociologist than a social worker, however, and with the eye of a sociologist—and the voice of a kind and tactful but brutally honest aunt—she delivered thousands of speeches both in the United States and around the world, wrote over a dozen books, and published over five hundred articles for magazines and journals ranging from *The Ladies' Home*

Journal to the *Annals of the American Academy of Political and Social Sciences.* She was active with labor unions in strike mediation and labor legislation, was a founding member of the NAACP, served on the Chicago School Board, was the paid garbage inspector for her ward (the only paid position she ever held), staged unsuccessful political campaigns against corrupt ward bosses, worked on state programs for the criminal and the insane, was president of the National Conference of Charities and Corrections, and, as noted, served as a vice president of the National American Woman Suffrage Association from 1911 until 1914. Addams was a leading figure in Teddy Roosevelt's Progressive Party, becoming in 1912 the first American woman to give a nominating speech at a presidential political convention. In the course of her career, she traveled to every continent as a distinguished visitor, sat on countless boards and advisory committees, and counseled presidents, governors, mayors, senators, and congressmen as well as leaders of anarchist, socialist, feminist, immigrant, African American, and labor organizations.

Finally, Jane Addams was a peace activist who held out against supporting America's participation in World War I and formed, in protest, the Women's International League for Peace and Freedom. This unpopular political stance, the only political stance she ever adopted that was completely out of sync with her times, transformed Addams from a beloved American icon into public enemy number one. Almost fifteen years after the war was over, however, in 1931, Addams's on-going peace activism was vindicated when she became the first American woman to win the Nobel Peace Prize. But during the interim years, when she was vilified as a dangerous subversive, her critics published elaborate "spider web" charts on which they demonstrated that Jane Addams was the secret link connecting every reform and radical group in the country. Whatever we may now think of her critics' politics, we have to concede to the accuracy of their claim: Jane Addams was the secret link connecting every reform and radical group in the country in the years between 1890 and her death in 1935.[5]

The Appeal of Jane Addams

There were myriad reasons for Addams's enduring stature, not the least among them her ability to write about contentious public issues like woman suffrage in a persuasive but non-argumentative voice. Her argument for woman suffrage in *The Ladies' Home Journal* of 1910 is an excellent example of her unique stylistic ability to disarm opponents by gliding past fundamental disagreements, presuming shared goals, focusing almost entirely on the great good to be gained, and ignoring the position that was to be defeated. Though she herself would detest a military analogy, the contemporary reader cannot help but picture Addams striding untouched through battlefields where her comrades were engaged in bloody combat, always pointing to the hill that was to be captured and paying little heed to the enemy all around. Indeed, she was a master at occupying the enemy's ground. Her argument in "Why Women Should Vote" that the suffrage would help, not hurt, the home was not unusual; plenty of other suffragists made the same case. But other suffragists made this, and other arguments, in a contentious way, directly attacking the antis' claim that woman suffrage would destroy the home. Addams, by contrast, never once mentioned that opponents of woman suffrage claimed to be preserving the home. She simply refused to contend that point and thus rose above the fray. This was vintage Addams.

A non-confrontational style is not the only feature distinguishing Jane Addams's approach in "Why Women Should Vote." There is, as well, her targeted deployment of woman suffrage as part of the Progressive assault on Gilded Age greed in politics and the economy, and there is her careful derivation of female values from history and experience, not biology and intuition. But in order to appreciate fully Addams's idiosyncratic handling of these issues and their relationship to woman suffrage, it is perhaps useful to examine first some of the popular magazine articles on suffrage appearing contemporaneously with "Why Women Should Vote."

Popular Suffrage Arguments of the Day

A chronological survey of articles published between 1900 and 1915 makes several points quite clear: first, that pro-suffrage arguments were one half of an active, national debate with anti-suffrage arguments, and both sides in that debate were shaped by the other. Second, suffragists and anti-suffragists alike had, by 1900, moved away from the broad philosophical debates over women's "rights" and "female nature" that typified the latter half of the nineteenth century. The debate after 1900 centered on more prosaic discussions of whether the majority of women actually wanted the vote and whether women's votes would actually bring about the benefits to Progressive reform that suffragists claimed. It is here that another point comes clear, and that is the extent to which woman suffrage had become linked in the public mind with the Progressive movement for political and economic reform, but also the degree to which it was easier for conservatives to attack woman suffrage than to attack Progressive reform. Anti-suffragists never openly opposed woman suffrage on the grounds that women voters would enact reform; rather, they tried to argue that woman suffrage was irrelevant to reform. This development in the debate was partially rooted in the peculiarities of United States suffrage history, which was distinguished by women's state-by-state, city-by-city acquisition of voting rights. The discussion of suffrage in popular magazines was, thus, not occurring in a political vacuum; it was all being conducted while women were actually going to the polls and voting in an increasing number of states and in dozens of municipalities. As the aged reformer Julia Ward Howe pointed out in 1909, concrete events meant that the whole question of woman suffrage had become entirely practical.[6]

Given the gradual accretion of women's voting rights in the United States, it is hardly surprising to find that over a third of the fifty articles surveyed for this essay were devoted to descriptions of woman suffrage campaigns, debates over whether woman suffrage in Colorado or Wyoming or Idaho or Utah had achieved the Progressive benefits suffragists predicted, and arguments over whether women were actually going to the polls. By the first decade of the twentieth century, the time for philosophical debates about female nature and women's rights had pretty much passed.

This is not to say that the suffragists never mounted a principled argument for their position in popular magazines. On the contrary, the magazine evidence strongly supports the claim by historian Paula Baker that "the suffragists made every conceivable argument, from equal rights to home protection to the need for an intelligent electorate."[7] But what is interesting here is not that one pro-suffrage article would argue for equal rights while another would argue for home protection. The most striking characteristic of the popular pro-suffrage literature of the day is that within a single article could be found the whole array of justifications possible for woman suffrage.

So we find suffragists like Frank Parsons arguing on one page of *The Arena* in 1908 that "sex has nothing to do with the reasons on which the suffrage rests," and arguing two pages later that "women have a higher regard for principle than men...their gentleness, sympathy, refinement and incorruptibility are sadly needed in our politics." Or Rosamond Sutherland, another pro-suffrage writer, arguing in a 1910 issue of *North American Review* that "the emancipation of women is a natural evolution which can no more be stopped than the tides of the sea," while at the same time arguing that "woman is instinctively a home-maker," and the vote would not wash away that apparently non-evolving fact. Or the editors of *The Independent* asserting in 1915 that "partial suffrage—the suffrage of men alone—is a denial of democracy. Democracy will never be full and complete until every individual in the community has an equal right to determine how the affairs of the community shall be managed," and, in the same article, also asserting that "women, by the very nature of their being,...are experts on certain vital subjects.... Women have different qualities of mind from men. Men are...reasoning beings. Women are creatures of intuition."[8]

None of the authors of these articles worried about the inconsistencies now detectable in their positions; they slipped and slid easily from democratic principle to practical politics to biological determinism. As Julia Ward Howe said in 1909, "the fundamental argument for woman suffrage, of course, is its justice; and this would be enough were there no other. But a powerful argument can also be made for it from the standpoint of expediency."[9]

This "flexibility" in the pro-suffrage position allowed considerable room for volleying with the anti-suffragists. When the antis argued that women should rely on men for protection, not the ballot, the wealthy widow and suffrage militant Alva Belmont retorted that experience proved women could most definitely not rely on men for protection. When the antis argued that politics was a dirty, bloody battlefield that would soil and injure women, the suffrage movement's most prodigious publicist Ida Husted Harper said that politics should be a cooperative effort, not a bloody battle. And in mock sympathy for the adversarial mess she said men had made of civic life, the attorney and suffragist Florida Pier offered women's help with the cleanup. (This was the sort of help, said Pier, that any human being would offer to another who was in a "pickle.") When the antis said that women's domesticity had made them too narrow-minded to vote, the suffragists responded that the vote would expand women's horizons. When the antis said that the majority of women did not wish to vote, Sutherland responded that in matters of principle, numbers were irrelevant. When the antis said that ignorant, immoral, and immigrant women would vote, some suffragists retorted that citizens in a democracy should have more faith in the common folk and others argued that women would double the "respectable" vote and out-poll the already-enfranchised unfit men. Finally, and most importantly, when the antis—skirting the knotty question of biology—argued that woman's social function as a mother was far too demanding and far too important to afford them the time and energy for civic activities, the suffragists turned that argument right on its head, insisting that it was precisely because their maternal duties were so vital to national life that they needed a voice in government. "Woman has a right to this most effective means of transforming the social environment into greater fitness for herself and all her loved ones," wrote Frank Parsons in 1908.[10] This, as it turned out, was the suffragists' most unassailable argument. And it was this argument that Jane Addams made most eloquently in her pro-suffrage writings.

Jane Addams's Progressive Suffrage Argument

The Ladies' Home Journal essay was one of dozens of speeches and articles Addams penned on woman suffrage in the years between 1897 and 1920. Comparing the *Journal* piece to her other writings makes clear that "Why Women Should Vote" was typical of her approach to woman suffrage and illuminates how her approach was both similar to and different from that of the other popular arguments being made at the time. Addams's writings on woman suffrage are distinctive because they do not "make every conceivable argument"; she did not blend a biological argument with a human rights argument with an elitist argument with a utilitarian argument. Like the proverbial hedgehog, Addams knew one thing, she knew it well, and she repeated it often: "Only when all the people become the governing class can the collective resources and organizations [of the society] be consistently utilized for the common weal."[11] As has already been noted, in applying this overarching Progressive philosophy to the question of woman suffrage, Addams was unique among suffrage advocates. Unlike other suffrage leaders, Addams subordinated women's particular gender-based situation to the broader, class-based concerns of the Progressive program. In addition, she was uniquely consistent, single-minded, even redundant, in not mixing her fierce commitment to democracy and practical results with abstract liberalism. In "Pragmatism and Politics," written for *The Survey* in 1912, Addams declared:

> The American voter is not content with the 18th century formulae of liberty and equality, high-flown as they are, for they do not apply to the situation. Liberty has come to be a guarantee of equal opportunity to play our parts well in primary relations, and the elemental processes of birth, growth, nutrition, death are the great levellers that remind us of the essential equality of human life. No talk of liberty or equality "goes" that does not reckon with these.[12]

The pro-suffrage arguments Addams made must be viewed within the very particular political and historical context of the Progressive Era's assertion of collective over individual interests. Considered in terms of her outrage at Gilded-Age selfishness gone wild, Addams's focus on women's vote as a potential tool in the service of community interests makes all the sense in the world.

"Why Women Should Vote" requires no apology for its lack of attention to individual rights. In Jane Addams's world, individual rights had created the urban, industrial problems she and her neighbors battled every day. Her emphasis on the community good that housewives could enact with the vote does not make her a sellout to comfortable, bourgeois domesticity. Rather, it marks her as a fully engaged, Progressive Era reformer whose daily life was consumed with solving serious urban problems evident in every household in her neighborhood. From where Addams sat in Chicago's crowded, dirty Nineteenth Ward, living with other college-educated women who had joined her Hull-House settlement in order to use their privileges on behalf of the working poor, it was not gender per se that distinguished the disadvantaged in American society, it was class. And the remedy for that disadvantage was not, in Addams's experience, more individualism. Whatever "personal ambition" might have accomplished in the past, said Addams in 1912, "it is certainly too archaic to accomplish anything now. Our thoughts, at least for this generation, cannot be too much directed from mutual relationships and responsibilities."[13]

Contrary to what her critics have suggested, Addams did not focus on the collective utility of woman suffrage in order to take the sting out of female independence. Her focus derived honestly out of her political priorities; she was intent on eradicating the evils of economic inequality in American society and believed collective action was the only means to that end. She did not emphasize women's domestic role because she wished to placate the patriarchs or because she did not understand the power of patriarchy to manipulate women's traditional work to its own ends. She assigned great significance to female domesticity because her daily experience taught her that domesticity was no bourgeois ideal but a utilitarian reality for her working-class neighbors, and one that could be powerful if deployed in the political arena against America's individualistic patriarchs.

Addams never openly argued with the antis' claims that the mass of women were too weak or passive or uninterested to vote. Instead, she silently smothered those claims with her argument that the vote would make women stronger, more responsible, and more civic-minded. Note that the editorial for *The Ladies' Home Journal* is not titled "Why Women Should HAVE the Vote," but, rather, "Why Women Should Vote." She was not arguing constitutional principles here; she was talking about the pragmatic effect—on women and on men—of the act of voting.

Jane Addams, Biology, and Elitism

If all Jane Addams had cared about was the attractiveness of her pro-suffrage arguments to middle-class audiences, she would have done what so many of her peers in the movement did; she would have "made every conceivable argument." The fact that she did not, the fact that editorials like "Why Women Should Vote" made such a consistent and relatively narrow set of democratic and utilitarian arguments, deserves notice. Examination of her pro-suffrage language makes clear, for example, that Addams did not ground her suffrage reasoning in biological essentialism. Despite what some critics have charged, she did not claim that women were innately, "essentially," more moral than men.[14] Nor did she say that women were biologically destined for domesticity. In the opening paragraph of "Why Women Should Vote" Addams states that she regards women's domesticity as a product of history that could only be ended by "social change." She speaks of "tradition" in this and other pro-suffrage writings, and she speaks of women's "different experience." But this most careful of writers did not speak of biology determining women's nature or women's role. Yes, she does refer in *The Ladies' Home Journal* to "those affairs which naturally and historically belong to women," but readers familiar with Addams's phrasing as well as her psychology will agree that she used the word "naturally" in all sorts of arguments. It was, for her, a synonym for "logically," and served her need to sweep past opponents, leaving them with the burden of proving that she was not merely stating the obvious.

Back in the early 1970s, the historian Jill Conway claimed that Addams "accepted [the] idea of biologically determined masculine and feminine temperaments," and argued that Addams was incapable of "seeing men and women as moral equals."[15] But these claims are not supported by the language in Addams's own texts. Her argument in *The Ladies' Home Journal* against women influencing men's votes rests on the assumption that a man's "point of view" was "quite as honest and valuable" as a woman's. Indeed, in her first public address on woman suffrage in 1897, speaking before the Chicago Political Equality League, Addams stated:

> I am not one of those who believe—broadly speaking—that women are better than men. We have not wrecked railroads, nor corrupted Legislatures, nor done many unholy things that men have done; but then we must remember that we have not had the chance. But my

understanding of the matter is that woman should have the ballot because without this responsibility she cannot best develop her moral courage. As Mazzini once said...we have no right to call our country a country until every man has a vote, and surely no logical mind can stop at sex in granting suffrage.[16]

Seventeen years later, writing for the *Annals of the American Academy of Political and Social Science*, Addams would still claim, "good government is not a matter of sex when it means...defending little children."[17] She did believe, and recent historical research has borne Addams out on this, that women's daily experience made them more likely than men to place human welfare and aesthetics above concerns with profit—but she rooted that difference in nurture, not nature.[18]

The one possible exception to this general rule can be found in *The Ladies' Home Journal* for June of 1913 when Addams wrote an atypically ironic essay titled, "If Men Were Seeking the Franchise." There, in tones suggesting the influence of radical feminist philosopher Charlotte Perkins Gilman, Addams showed what women's objections to men voting would be if women controlled the government. Some of her arguments there—that men might not be good voters because they are "always so eager to make money," are "so reckless," think "so little of dust," and "are so fond of fighting...you always have been since you were little boys"—could be read as a biological, essentialist view of masculine and feminine nature. But it seems just as likely that Addams was trying to show the absurdity of essentialist claims. Certainly her concluding remarks for that article indicate that "such talk" was not serious, that "as far as the guardianship of the State is concerned there is no distinction between the powers of men and women save those which custom has made."[19] It would not be until the masculine carnage of World War I had seared her soul that Addams's language would begin to imply that female nature had any corner on morality. This was not her approach during the woman suffrage campaign.[20]

Just as she did not join other suffragists in making biological claims for women's right to the vote, so, too, Addams did not join the chorus of elitists, racists, and nativists who tried to argue that woman suffrage would double the "respectable," White, native-born vote more than it would expand the votes of the rabble. "Why Women Should Vote" is an excellent example of her view that working women and immigrant women and poor women not only needed the vote in order to protect their own interests and those of their families, but also wanted the vote in order to be responsible, active agents in their communities. By telling her largely White, largely middle-class readership that Scandinavian women were accustomed to the vote, that Jewish women had "covered markets" in Russia and Poland, and that Italian women saw no distinction between voting in school board elections to protect the education of older children and voting in state or federal elections to protect the milk drunk by younger children, Addams was slyly shaming those who had been surprised by the suffrage enthusiasm among these groups of women. True, she did romanticize her neighbors by implying that ethnic women's naivete gave them an organic grasp of political common sense, but in the context of the era's ethnocentric elitism, Addams's romanticism looks more like protection than pandering.

Had Addams been purely a strategist, she would have brushed past her working-class women's suffrage enthusiasm in the way she brushed past other potentially controversial points. But Addams calculated where to earn and where to spend her political capital. She ignored questions of women's individual rights precisely because she did not want to ignore the political aspirations of the women in her neighborhood. It was her concern for their collective need to improve their lives, rather than her concern for her own individual right to vote, that fueled Addams's suffrage energies in the first place. To say that she fashioned a palatable domestic argument for woman suffrage in order to make female voters less threatening completely overlooks the very real political risk she took by predicting that working-class, immigrant women would, as voters, actively demand services and legislative protections from federal, state, and municipal governments. This was hardly a neutral stance to take during the Progressive Era, and it speaks volumes about the class-oriented nature of Addams's political activism.

The Strategic Power of Addams's Argument

The modern feminist may well cringe at the link Addams made between women's traditional domestic duties and the vote. But that reaction should not blind us to the sincerity of her argument—or to the strategic value of her argument.

While it took political risks, Addams's "spin" on suffrage was also strategically brilliant. In her hands, suffrage advocates became steadfast defenders of women's right to care for home and family, not the destroyers of domesticity depicted in anti-suffrage lore. In her hands, the feminine powers of "persuasion" which anti-suffragists preferred in place of voting became dishonest tools of manipulation, just as unworthy of women as they were unfair to men. Finally, and most interestingly, in Addams's hands, it was historical inevitability that required women to move their caregiving into the public sector, not some feminist scheme to alter the course of history. With a curious but very characteristic mix of assertiveness and self-effacement, Addams trumpeted women's ability to rise to history's challenge while sliding right past the role women reformers like herself had played in changing history by placing women's traditional concerns on the political agenda.

In "Votes for Women and Other Votes," which appeared in *The Survey* in 1912, Addams expanded on the argument for historical inevitability implicit in "Why Women Should Vote" and downplayed the role of historical agents like herself. Addams claimed in this article that history is "merely a record of new human interests" becoming "the subjects of governmental action and the incorporation into government itself of those classes who represented new interests." As government became involved in commerce, merchants became voters; as

**Twelve Reasons
Why Women Should Vote**

1. BECAUSE those who obey the laws should help to choose those who make the laws.
2. BECAUSE laws affect women as much as men.
3. BECAUSE laws which affect WOMEN are now passed without consulting them.
4. BECAUSE laws affecting CHILDREN should include the woman's point of view as well as the man's.
5. BECAUSE laws affecting the HOME are voted on in every session of the Legislature.
6. BECAUSE women have experience which would be helpful to legislation.
7. BECAUSE to deprive women of the vote is to lower their position in common estimation.
8. BECAUSE having the vote would increase the sense of responsibility among women toward questions of public importance.
9. BECAUSE public spirited mothers make public spirited sons.
10. BECAUSE about 8,000,000 women in the United States are wage workers, and the conditions under which they work are controlled by law.
11. BECAUSE the objections against their having the vote are based on prejudice, not on reason.
12. BECAUSE to sum up all reasons in one—IT IS FOR THE COMMON GOOD OF ALL.

VOTES FOR WOMEN

NATIONAL WOMAN SUFFRAGE PUBLISHING CO., INC.
171 Madison Avenue.   New York City

Jane Addams, c. 1914
LIBRARY OF CONGRESS

Woman suffrage leaflet, c. 1915
SMITHSONIAN INSTITUTION

government became involved in industrial affairs, workers became voters. The campaign for woman suffrage, reasoned Addams, was the inevitable, sensible result of contemporary government's involvement with "the basic human interests with which women have been traditionally concerned." Thus skirting the female activism that had placed these "basic human interests" on the Progressive Era's political agenda, Addams argued that these new public duties had fallen to women simply through the natural unfolding of history. Pushing this argument even further, Addams claimed that women were only demanding a new household tool—the vote—"because they insist that they will not cease to perform their traditional duties, simply because these duties have been taken over by existing governments."[21]

If there was any guile in Addams's pro-suffrage position, this was surely it. According to her construction, the link between Progressive Era reforms and woman suffrage had arisen organically. Women's political activism was a result, not a cause, of the Progressive Era, and women's need for the vote was a result, not a cause, of historical change. Addams knew different, of course, but this approach satisfied her political and temperamental need to soothe the nerves of those dizzied by the explosion of Progressivism's government activism and women's connection to that activism. Rather than pandering to Americans' elitism or their nativism or their affection for biological essentialism, Addams instead insisted on democracy—economic, social, and legal—and then played to Americans' comfort with historical inevitability and with women's role as dutiful servants to posterity.

Conclusion

As one of America's most revered public figures, Jane Addams played an important role in the campaign for woman suffrage. Since her fame and stature did not reside in the woman suffrage movement, and since Americans perceived her as sincerely committed to the common good, her arguments for woman suffrage as a tool of reform carried special weight. It is doubtful that the majority of the readers of "Why Women Should Vote" in 1910 shared Addams's deep convictions about economic democracy, the dignity of immigrants and workers, or the historical (rather than biological) roots of female domesticity. But it is likely that they were sympathetic to her view that enfranchised women would strengthen contemporary efforts to clean up the factories and the cities, reduce poverty, and improve education and public health. And while Addams fashioned an emphasis on domesticity out of her desire to show the interdependence of the public and the private in modern life, it is also likely that readers found in Addams's domestic emphasis a comforting reassurance that woman suffrage would not destroy the traditional family. In this way, then, Addams maintained her own principles while still achieving popular appeal. The argument here is that Jane Addams's particular approach to woman suffrage, specifically her lack of attention to women's individual rights, arose less from political timidity about gender than from overriding, firm convictions about social and economic reform. As it happened, this focus on the link between suffrage and reform intersected sufficiently with the Progressive attitudes of many Americans to be attractive—despite the fact that Addams was more democratic in her goals than the majority of her readers.

Women's rights were always an avenue to matters of class for Addams; they were never the final destination on her political journey. "Why Women Should Vote" is just one piece of evidence that Addams's support for woman suffrage was rooted in her primary commitment to economic democracy, but it is a very strong piece of evidence. In addition, her writing in this essay, as in so many others, makes clear that, just as Addams always felt more comfortable privileging class issues over gender issues, so, too, she always felt more comfortable arguing for her causes in non-argumentative language. Over the course of her life, consciously and unconsciously, Addams trained the stream of her thinking to flow in elegantly diplomatic channels. Her personal recoil from conflict, coupled with her conviction that all conflict should be mediated, meant that she always presented her case in terms of ultimate harmony, not ultimate victory; this was no more or less true of her suffrage writings than of her writings about labor or militarism.

"Why Women Should Vote," like all of Jane Addams's contributions to the suffrage cause, is thus an exquisitely clever, carefully phrased, determinedly practical, democratic argument. One need not agree with it in order to appreciate its brilliance and its sincerity.

WHY WOMEN SHOULD VOTE

by Jane Addams, of Hull-House, Chicago

For many generations it has been believed that woman's place is within the walls of her home, and it is indeed impossible to imagine the time when her duty there shall be ended or to forecast any social change which shall release her from that paramount obligation.

This paper is an attempt to show that many women today are failing to discharge their duties to their own households properly simply because they do not perceive that as society grows more complicated it is necessary that woman shall extend her sense of responsibility to many things outside of her own home if she would continue to preserve the home in its entirety. One could illustrate in many ways. A woman's simplest duty, one would say, is to keep her house clean and wholesome and to feed her children properly. Yet if she lives in a tenement house, as so many of my neighbors do, she cannot fulfill these simple obligations by her own efforts because she is utterly dependent upon the city administration for the conditions which render decent living possible. Her basement will not be dry, her stairways will not be fireproof, her house will not be provided with sufficient windows to give light and air, nor will it be equipped with sanitary plumbing, unless the Public Works Department sends inspectors who constantly insist that these elementary decencies be provided. Women who live in the country sweep their own dooryards and may either feed the refuse of the table to a flock of chickens or allow it innocently to decay in the open air and sunshine. In a crowded city quarter, however, if the street is not cleaned by the city authorities no amount of private sweeping will keep the tenement free from grime; if the garbage is not properly collected and destroyed a tenement-house mother may see her children sicken and die of diseases from which she alone is powerless to shield them, although her tenderness and devotion are unbounded. She cannot even secure untainted meat for her household, she cannot provide fresh fruit, unless the meat has been inspected by city officials, and the decayed fruit, which is so often placed upon sale in the tenement districts, has been destroyed in the interests of public health. In short, if woman would keep on with her old business of caring for her house and rearing her children she will have to have some conscience in regard to public affairs lying quite outside of her immediate household. The individual conscience and devotion are no longer effective.

Chicago one spring had a spreading contagion of scarlet fever just at the time the school nurses had been discontinued because business men had pronounced them too expensive. If the women who sent their children to the schools had been sufficiently public-spirited and had been provided with an implement through which to express that public spirit they would have insisted that the schools be supplied with nurses in order that their own children might be protected from contagion. In other words, if women would effectively continue their old avocations they must take part in the slow upbuilding of that code of legislation which is alone sufficient to protect the home from the dangers incident to modern life. One might instance the many deaths of children from contagious diseases the germs of which had been carried in tailored clothing. Country doctors testify as to the outbreak of scarlet fever in remote neighborhoods each autumn, after the children have begun to wear the winter overcoats and cloaks which have been sent from infected city sweatshops. That their mothers mend their stockings and guard them from "taking cold" is not a sufficient protection when the tailoring of the family is done in a distant city under conditions which the mother cannot possibly control. The sanitary regulation of sweatshops by city officials is all that can be depended upon to prevent such needless destruction. Who shall say that women are not concerned in the enactment and enforcement of such legislation if they would preserve their homes?

Even women who take no part in public affairs in order that they may give themselves entirely to their own families, sometimes going so far as to despise those other women who are endeavoring to secure protective legislation, may illustrate this point. The Hull-House neighborhood was at one time suffering from a typhoid epidemic. A careful investigation was made by which we were able to establish a very close connection between the typhoid and a mode of plumbing which made it most probable that the infection had been carried by flies. Among the people who been exposed to the infection was a widow who had lived in the ward for a number of years, in a comfortable little house which she owned. Although the Italian immigrants were closing in all around her she was not willing to sell her property and to move away until she had finished the education of her children. In the mean time she held herself quite aloof from her Italian neighbors and could never be drawn into any of the public efforts to protect them by securing a better code of tenement-house sanitation. Her two daughters were sent to an Eastern college; one June, when one of them had graduated and the other still had two years before she took her degree, they came to the spotless little house and to their self-sacrificing mother for the summer's holiday. They both fell ill, not because their own home was not clean, not because their mother was not devoted, but because next door to them and also in the rear were wretched tenements, and because the mother's utmost efforts could not keep the infection out of her own house. One daughter died and one recovered but was an invalid for two years following. This is, perhaps, a fair illustration of the futility of the individual conscience when woman insists upon isolating her family from the rest of the community and its interests. The result is sure to be a pitiful failure.

One of the interesting experiences in the Chicago campaign for inducing the members of the Charter Convention to recommend municipal franchise for women in the provisions of the new charter was the unexpected enthusiasm and help which came from large groups of foreign-born women. The Scandinavian women represented in many Lutheran Church societies said quite simply that in the old country they had had the municipal franchise upon the same basis as men since the seventeenth century; all the women formerly living under the British Government, in England, Australia or Canada, pointed out that Chicago women were asking now for what the British women had long had. But the most unexpected response came from the foreign colonies in which women had never heard such problems discussed and took the prospect of the municipal ballot as a simple device—which it is—to aid them in their daily struggle with adverse city conditions. The Italian women said that the men engaged in railroad construction were away all summer and did not know anything about their household difficulties. Some of them came to Hull-House one day to talk over the possibility of a public wash-house. They do not like to wash in their own tenements, they have never seen a washing-tub until they came to America, and find it very difficult to use it in the restricted space of their little kitchens and to hang the clothes within the house to dry. They say that in the Italian villages the women all go to the streams together; in the town they go to the public wash-house; and washing, instead of being lonely and disagreeable, is made pleasant by cheerful conversation. It is asking a great deal of these women to change suddenly all their habits of living, and their contention that the tenement-house kitchen is too small for laundry-work is well taken. If women in Chicago knew the needs of the Italian colony they would realize that any change bringing cleanliness and fresh clothing into the Italian household would be a very sensible and hygienic measure. It is, perhaps, asking a great deal that the members of the City Council should understand this, but surely a comprehension of the needs of these women and efforts toward ameliorating their lot might be regarded as matters of municipal obligation on the part of voting women.

The same thing is true of the Jewish women in their desire for covered markets which have always been a municipal provision in Russia and Poland. The vegetables piled high upon the wagons standing in the open markets of Chicago become covered with dust and soot. It seems to these women a violation of the most rudimentary decencies and they sometimes say quite simply: "If women had anything to say about it they would change all that."

...The duty of a woman toward the schools which her children attend is so obvious that it is not necessary to dwell upon it. But even this simple obligation cannot be effectively carried out without some form of social organization as the mothers' school clubs and mothers' congresses testify, and to which the most conservative women belong because they feel the need of wider reading and discussion concerning the many problems of childhood. It is, therefore, perhaps natural that the public should have been more willing to accord a vote to women in school matters than in any other, and yet women have never been members of a Board of Education in sufficient numbers to influence largely actual school curriculi. If they had been kindergartens, domestic science courses and school playgrounds would be far more numerous than they are. More than one woman has been convinced of the need of the ballot by the futility of her efforts in persuading a business man that young children need nurture in something besides the three r's. Perhaps, too, only women realize the influence which the school might exert upon the home if a proper adaptation to actual needs were considered. An Italian girl who has had lessons in cooking at the public school will help her mother to connect the entire family with American food and household habits. That the mother has never baked bread in Italy—only mixed it in her own house and then taken it out to the village oven—makes it all the more necessary that her daughter should understand the complication of a cooking-stove. The same thing is true of the girl who learns to sew in the public school, and more than anything else, perhaps, of the girl who receives the first simple instruction in the care of little children, that skillful care which every tenement-house baby requires if he is to be pulled through his second summer. The only time, to my knowledge, that lessons in the care of children were given in the public schools of Chicago was one summer when the vacation schools were being managed by a volunteer body of women. The instruction was eagerly received by the Italian girls, who had been "little mothers" to younger children ever since they could remember.

As a result of this teaching I recall a young girl who carefully explained to her Italian mother that the reason the babies in Italy were so healthy and the babies in Chicago were so sickly was not, as her mother had always firmly insisted, because her babies in Italy had goat's milk and her babies in America had cow's milk, but because the milk in Italy was clean and the milk in Chicago was dirty.... She also informed her mother that the "City Hall wanted to fix up the milk so that it couldn't make the baby sick, but that they hadn't quite enough votes for it yet." The Italian mother believed what her child had been taught in the big school; it seemed to her quite as natural that the city should be concerned in providing pure milk for her younger children as it should provide big schools and teachers for her older children. She reached this naïve conclusion because she had never heard those arguments which make it seem reasonable that a woman should be given the school franchise but no other.

But women are also beginning to realize that children need attention outside of school hours; that much of the petty vice in cities is merely the love of pleasure gone wrong, the overrestrained boy or girl seeking improper recreation and excitement. It is obvious that a little study of the needs of children, a sympathetic understanding of the conditions under which they go astray, might save hundreds of them. Women traditionally have had an opportunity to observe the plays of children and the needs of youth, and yet in Chicago, at least, they had done singularly little in this vexed problem of juvenile delinquency until they helped to inaugurate the Juvenile Court movement a dozen years ago. The Juvenile Court Committee, made up largely of women, paid the salaries of the probation officers connected with the court for the first six years of its existence, and after the salaries were cared for by the county the same organization turned itself into a Juvenile Protective League, and through a score of paid officers are doing valiant service in minimizing some of the dangers of city life which boys and girls encounter....

The more extensively the modern city endeavors on the one hand to control and on the other hand to provide recreational facilities for its young people the more necessary it is that women should assist in their direction and extension. After all, a care for wholesome and innocent amusement is what women have for many years assumed. When the reaction comes on the part of taxpayers women's votes may be necessary to keep the city to its beneficent obligations toward its own young people.

...Ever since steam power has been applied to the processes of weaving and spinning woman's traditional work has been carried on largely outside of the home. The clothing and household linen are not only spun and woven, but also usually sewed, by machinery; the preparation of many foods has also passed into the factory and necessarily a certain number of women have been obliged to follow their work there, although it is doubtful, in spite of the large numbers of factory girls, whether women now are doing as large a proportion of the world's work as they used to do. Because many thousands of those working in factories and shops are girls between the ages of fourteen and twenty-two there is a necessity that older women should be interested in the conditions of industry. The very fact that these girls are not going to remain in industry permanently makes it more important that some one should see to it that they shall not be incapacitated for their future family life because they work for exhausting hours and under insanitary [sic] conditions.

If woman's sense of obligation had enlarged as the industrial conditions changed she might naturally and almost imperceptibly have inaugurated the movements for social amelioration in the line of factory legislation and shop sanitation. That she has not done so is doubtless due to the fact that her conscience is slow to recognize any obligation outside of her own family circle, and because she was so absorbed in her own household that she failed to see what the conditions outside actually were. It would be interesting to know how far the consciousness that she had no vote and could not change matters operated in this direction. After all, we see only those things to which our attention has been drawn, we feel responsibility for those things which are brought to us as matters of responsibility. If conscientious women were convinced that it was a civic duty to be informed in regard to these grave industrial affairs, and then to express the conclusions which they had reached by depositing a piece of paper in a ballot box, one cannot imagine that they would shirk simply because the action ran counter to old traditions.

To those of my readers who would admit that although woman has no right to shirk her old obligations, that all of these measures could be secured more easily through her influence upon the men of her family than through the direct use of the ballot; I should like to tell a little story. I have a friend in Chicago who is the mother of four sons and the grandmother of twelve grandsons who are voters. She is a woman of wealth, of secured social position, of sterling character and clear intelligence, and may, therefore, quite fairly be cited as a "woman of influence".... I happened to call at her house on the day that Mr. McKinley was elected President against Mr. Bryan for the first time. I found my friend much disturbed. She said somewhat bitterly that she had at last discovered what the much-vaunted influence of woman was worth; that she had implored each one of her sons and grandsons, had entered into endless arguments and moral appeals to induce one of them to represent her convictions by voting for Bryan! That, although sincerely devoted to her, each one had assured her that his convictions forced him to vote the Republican ticket.... I contended that a woman had no right to persuade a man to vote against his own convictions; that I respected the men of her family for following their own judgement regardless of the appeal which the honored head of the house had made to their chivalric devotion. To this she replied that she would agree with that point of view when a woman had the same opportunity as a man to register her convictions by vote. I believed then as I do now, that nothing is gained when independence of judgement is assailed by "influence," sentimental or otherwise, and that we test advancing civilization somewhat by our power to respect differences and by our tolerance of another's honest conviction.

This is, perhaps, the attitude of many busy women who would be glad to use the ballot to further public measures in which they are interested and for which they have been working for years. It offends the taste of such a woman to be obliged to use "indirect influence" when she is accustomed to well-bred, open action in other affairs, and she very much resents the time spent in persuading a voter to take her point of view, and possibly to give up his own, quite as honest and valuable as hers, although different because resulting from a totally different experience. Public-spirited women who wish to use the ballot, as I know them, do not wish to do the work of men nor to take over men's affairs. They simply want an opportunity to do their own work and to take care of those affairs which naturally and historically belong to women, but which are constantly being overlooked and slighted in our political institutions....

To turn the administration of our civic affairs wholly over to men may mean that the American city will continue to push forward in its commercial and industrial development, and continue to lag behind in those things which make a city healthful and beautiful. After all, woman's traditional function has been to make her dwelling-place both clean and fair. Is that dreariness in city life, that lack of domesticity which the humblest farm dwelling presents, due to a withdrawal of one of the naturally cooperating forces? If women have in any sense been responsible for the gentler side of life which softens and blurs some of its harsher conditions, may they not have a duty to perform in our American cities?

In closing, may I recapitulate that if woman would fulfill her traditional responsibility to her own children; if she would educate and protect from danger factory children who must find their recreation on the street; if she would bring the cultural forces to bear upon our materialistic civilization; and if she would do it all with the dignity and directness fitting one who carries on her immemorial duties, then she must bring herself to the use of the ballot—that latest implement for self government. May we not fairly say that American women need this implement in order to preserve the home?

Notes

The article, "Why Women Should Vote," was first published in *The Ladies Home Journal*, 27, (January 1910): 21-22.

1. For examples of this critical view of Addams, see: Jill Conway, "Women Reformers and American Culture, 1870-1930," *Journal of Social History* 5 (Winter, 1971-72): 164-177; Jill Conway, "Stereotypes of Femininity in a Theory of Sexual Evolution," *Victorian Studies* 14 (September, 1970): 47-62; Judith Lacerte, "If Only Jane Addams Had Been a Feminist," *Social Casework* 57 (December, 1976): 656-660; William O'Neill, *Everyone was Brave: A History of Feminism in America* (Chicago, 1971), 120; Aileen Kraditor, *The Ideas of the Woman Suffrage Movement* (New York, 1965).

2. Carol Gilligan, *In a Different Voice: Psychological Theory and Women's Development* (Cambridge, Mass., 1982); Joan Tronto, "Beyond Gender Difference Toward a Theory of Care," *Signs* 12 (Summer, 1987): 644-663; Jean Bethke Elshtain, "Antigone's Daughters," *Democracy* 2 (April, 1982): 46-59; Mary Dietz, "Context is All: Feminism and Theories of Citizenship," *Daedalus* (1987): 1-24; Kathleen B. Jones, "Citizenship in a Woman-Friendly Polity," *Signs* 15 (Summer, 1990).

3. Paula Baker, "The Domestication of Politics: Women and American Political Society, 1780-1920," *American Historical Review* 89 (June, 1984): 620-647. Kathyrn Kish Sklar, "Hull House in the 1890's: A Community of Women Reformers," *Signs* 10 (Summer, 1985): 658-677; and "The Historical Foundations of Women's Power in the Creation of the American Welfare State, 1830-1930," 43-93 and Eileen Boris, "The Power of Motherhood: Black and White Activist Women Redefine the 'Political,'" both in *Mothers of the New World: Maternalist Politics and the Origins of Welfare States*, Seth Koven and Sonya Michel, eds. (New York, 1993), 213-245.

4. "The Only Saint America Has Produced," *Current Literature* 40 (April, 1906); "The Most Useful Americans," *The Independent* 74 (May 1, 1913): 956-957; Editor's introduction to Addams's 1913 column, *The Ladies' Home Journal*, 30 (January, 1913): 25.

5. Allen F. Davis, *American Heroine: The Life and Legend of Jane Addams* (New York, 1973). Davis includes a copy of a "spider web" chart on p. 265.

6. Julia Ward Howe, "The Case for Woman Suffrage," *The Outlook* 91 (April 3, 1909): 780.

7. Baker, "The Domestication of Politics," 642.

8. Frank Parsons, "Shall Our Mothers, Wives and Sisters Be Our Equals or Our Subjects?" *The Arena* 40 (July, 1908): 92-94; Rosamond Sutherland, "The Appeal of Politics to Woman," *The North American Review* 191 (January, 1910): 82, 85; "The Justice and Desirability of Woman Suffrage," *The Independent* 82 (April 5, 1915): 3-4.

9. Howe, "The Case for Woman Suffrage," 781.

10. Alva P. Belmont, "Woman's Right to Govern Herself," *The North American Review* 190 (November, 1909): 664-674; Florida Pier, "The Delightfully Quaint Antis," *Harper's Weekly* 53 (December 11, 1909): 34; Harper, "Would Woman Suffrage Benefit the State, and Woman Herself?" 374; Sutherland, "The Appeal of Politics to Woman," 82; "Margaret vs. Bridget," *The Independent* 67 (1909): 1394; Parsons, "Shall Our Mothers, Wives and Sisters Be Our Equals or Our Subjects?" 93; Molly Warren, "The Housekeeper's Need of the Ballot," *The World Today* 12 (January-June, 1907): 418-421. For examples of anti-suffrage arguments in popular magazines in these years, see: "Concerning Woman's Suffrage," *The Outlook* 64 (March 10, 1900); Lyman Abbott, "Why Women Do Not Wish the Suffrage," *The Atlantic Monthly* 92 (September, 1903); Elizabeth McCracken, "The Women of America: Woman's Suffrage in Colorado," *The Outlook* 75 (November 28, 1903): 737-744; Annie Nathan Meyer, "Woman's Assumption of Sex Superiority," *North American Review* 178 (January, 1904): 103-109; Lyman Abbott, "The Assault on Womanhood," *The Outlook* 91 (April 3, 1909): 784-788; "Do Women Wish to Vote?" *The Outlook* 94 (February 19, 1910): 375-377; Molly Elliot Seawell, "The Ladies' Battle," *The Atlantic Monthly* 106 (September, 1910): 289-303; Jessie Atkinson McGriff, "Before the American Woman Votes," *The Ladies' Home Journal* 27 (April, 1910): 56.

11. Jane Addams, "Votes for Women and Other Votes," *The Survey* 29 (June 1, 1912): 368.

12. Jane Addams, "Pragmatism in Politics," *The Survey* 29 (October 5, 1912): 12.

13. Jane Addams, "A Modern Lear," *The Survey* 29 (November 2, 1912): 137.

14. Conway, "Women Reformers," and "Stereotypes of Femininity"; Davis, *American Heroine*, 187, 316.

15. Conway, "Women Reformers," 174, and "Stereotypes of Femininity," 58.

16. Jane Addams, "The Working Woman's Need of the Ballot," *The Woman's Journal* (November 20, 1897).

17. Jane Addams, "The Larger Aspects of the Woman's Movement," *Annals of the American Academy of Political and Social Science* 56 (November, 1914): 6.

18. See, for example, Maureen Flanagan, "Gender and Urban Political Reform: The City Club and the Woman's Club of Chicago in the Progressive Era," *American Historical Review* 95 (October, 1990): 1032-1050.

19. Jane Addams, "If Men Were Seeking the Franchise," *The Ladies' Home Journal* 30 (June, 1913): 21.

20. Jane Addams, "Women, War, and Suffrage," *The Survey* 35 (November 6, 1915): 148-149. This article indicates that Addams did not, in the years before 1920, rest her claims for women's role in international relations on biological essentialism.

21. Addams, "Votes for Women and Other Votes," 367-368.

"The New Woman —Wash Day." Suffrage opponents encouraged the idea that woman suffrage threatened to overturn traditional gender roles and the domestic division of labor in images like this from the 1890s.

Fourteen

"BETTER CITIZENS WITHOUT THE BALLOT":

American Anti-suffrage Women and Their Rationale During the Progressive Era

Manuela Thurner

Editor's Introduction: In this fascinating essay, Manuela Thurner discusses the women who organized to *oppose* woman suffrage, the anti-suffrage women popularly known as the "Antis." Thurner insists that these women are often misunderstood—when they are discussed at all—by historians who have accepted without sufficient examination the suffragists' characterization of their despised female adversaries as: "puppets of more powerful male forces"; selfish, pampered socialites, motivated by a desire to maintain their own highly privileged status; and reactionaries with an extremely narrow view of woman's proper role. Misunderstanding of the anti-suffrage women also stems from the fact that historians have at times generalized about anti-suffragists after studying only the writings of anti-suffrage men—who, in many cases, *were* reactionaries disturbed by the increasing public activity of women, or claimed that woman suffrage would "ruin women" and "destroy the home" out of fear that it would threaten their economic interests.

Thurner's own study, focusing particularly on Antis in the Northeast between 1900 and 1920 and based on the writings of anti-suffrage women and major Anti periodicals, avoids both of these pitfalls—and offers very different conclusions about anti-suffrage women. Thurner rejects the idea that the Antis were controlled by male anti-suffragists, and downplays the socio-economic differences between anti-suffragists and suffragists.

Most significantly, Thurner challenges prevailing assumptions about the *ideology* of the female anti-suffragists, who "portrayed themselves as very much in line with and in favor of turn-of-the-century Progressive reform and female activism." According to Thurner, the Antis *urged* women to play an active role in public affairs, but believed that this could best be done "without the ballot" by disinterested, nonpartisan women. They opposed woman's entry into politics believing that political activity—like participation in the woman suffrage movement itself—would diffuse women's energies and lessen their effectiveness by diverting them away from all-female clubs and organizations through which women had already proven to be very influential. And they argued (like some feminists and scholars today) that female separatism might be more effective in achieving reforms women desire than the dilution of women's efforts in gender-integrated political organizations.

Indeed, Thurner insists that this set of ideas regarding women's participation in public affairs was one of the reasons the Antis were initially successful and able to forestall the suffrage victory as long as they did. She implies that, had Progressive-Era Antis insisted on women remaining completely in the domestic sphere—like some suffrage opponents who denounced public activism on the part of women as unwomanly and ungodly—they might have been less convincing. This in itself is strong testimony concerning the degree of change that had taken place in the late nineteenth century in ideas about woman's sphere.

★ ★ ★ ★ ★

"WILL HISTORY REMEMBER the heroines of feminism...? It will not." Thus anti-suffragist Florence R. Hall expressed her optimism about her opponents' fate in the September 1915 issue of *The Woman's Protest*, the official publication of the National Association Opposed to Woman Suffrage (NAOWS).[1] Seventy-five years after the passage of the Nineteenth Amendment, and after three decades of feminist scholarship, which has produced a huge body of literature on exactly those "heroines of feminism," Hall's assertion sounds peculiar, if not outright absurd. Yet, in the fall of 1915, this assessment on the part of an anti-suffrage woman was by no means far-fetched or unrealistic. The "Antis"—as the female anti-suffragists came to be known—accurately predicted victories for their cause in the November state suffrage referenda of New York, New Jersey, Massachusetts, and Pennsylvania. Coming, as they did, after a host of preceding suffrage defeats throughout the country, the Antis' triumphs in those four Eastern states constituted their latest and most promising success. That very same year, they could also point to the fact that suffrage amendments had been lost in twenty state legislatures. It was not until New York State finally adopted woman suffrage in November of 1917 and the House of Representatives voted in favor of a federal amendment, in the year following, that signs of disillusion and resignation began to show within the ranks of the organized anti-suffragists. Ultimately defeated in 1920 when Tennessee cast the necessary thirty-sixth vote to ratify the Nineteenth Amendment, anti-suffragists disappeared from the public stage—and from the subsequent historical record. Now, it was the suffragists' turn to invoke the dictum that "[v]ictorious movements record their history, vanquished ones rarely do."[2]

Historians and the Anti-suffrage Movement

Feminist scholarship has indeed recounted women's collective endeavors and triumphs more extensively than the manifold conflicts and tensions among women of different ethnic, racial, religious, political, and class backgrounds. Women's historians all too often uncritically adopt feminist perspectives and judgments when they set out to write women into history. In the historiography of the woman suffrage movement, this point of view has led to various misconceptions about the women who opposed their own enfranchisement. Reiterating the assessments of prominent suffragists, later historians of the suffrage movement have dismissed the female antis as insignificant and have elaborated instead on the male liquor, business, political, and Southern states' rights interests as the more important and potent anti-suffrage forces.[3] The small body of secondary literature focusing on the anti-suffragists does little to modify these interpretations or to dispel the myths. While minutely exploring the organizational history and makeup of the more important anti-suffrage associations, it does not, surprisingly, take much care to investigate more fully those women's motivations for opposing their enfranchisement.[4]

The majority of scholars have accepted the "woman's place is in the home" argument as the fundamental and most frequently invoked rationale of the Antis. For the most part, historians have depicted the opponents of woman suffrage as late Victorians who, married with children, were not ready or willing to accommodate themselves to the individualistic tendencies and altered social and gender relations of the modern era, and whose adherence to an ideology of domesticity was doomed to failure in an era of widespread Progressive reform and public activism. However, an analysis of the female anti-suffragists' major periodicals and writings of the first two decades of the twentieth century, the most active and successful phase of the organized Antis' short history, reveals the relative insignificance of this argument. Instead, the Antis not only actually but also ideologically ventured considerably beyond the domestic sphere in their effort to forestall women's enfranchisement. They, in fact, portrayed themselves as very much in line with and in favor of turn-of-the-century Progressive reform and female activism. This may not only help to explain the fact that the Antis were able to prolong the suffrage fight considerably; it also promises an analysis of their arguments in terms that are of relevance to current debates about women's relationship to the public and political realms.

Women as Anti-suffrage Theorists and Activists

The organized anti-suffrage movement started in 1882 with the founding of the Massachusetts Association Opposed to the Further Extension of Suffrage to Women (MAOFESW). By 1900, there were female anti-suffrage associations in New York, Illinois, California, South Dakota, Washington, and Oregon. In 1911, the National Association Opposed to Woman Suffrage (NAOWS) opened its headquarters in New York City, from which it moved to Washington, D.C. in 1917. Due to the NAOWS's vigorous recruitment efforts, twenty-five state associations with combined membership estimated at 200,000 subscribed to the anti-suffrage cause by 1915.[5] Yet it is of minor significance to recollect the exact founding dates, membership figures, and organizational structures of the twenty-odd anti-suffrage associations (the data offered on those counts by both contemporary observers and historians are incomplete and often contradictory) or to remember the names of the participating states (which varied from year to year). The crucial point is to realize that the movement was commonly understood to be founded, staffed, and led by women. Although men's anti-suffrage organizations existed, they did not issue their own periodicals or engage in the kind of sustained publicity work that became the hallmark of the older and more seasoned female organizations. In keeping with their avowed philosophy to steer clear of politics and to concentrate instead on educating the public about their beliefs, female antis occasionally voiced their resolve to "leav[e] the political end entirely to men."[6] Yet, in practice, it was usually representatives of female anti-suffrage organizations who appeared before congressional committees or other political forums to speak out against women's enfranchisement.

Women also came to be the most prolific theorists of the anti-suffrage movement. Not only did the bulk of articles and essays in the anti-suffrage periodical press stem from the pen of female contributors; women also authored the more elaborate treatises and tracts delineating a rationale for opposing women's enfranchisement. When Helen Kendrick Johnson's *Woman and the Republic* was first published in 1897, reviews across the nation were full of praise. *The St. Paul Pioneer-Press* termed it the "most temperate, concise, and well-conducted argument against woman suffrage which has yet appeared in book form."[7] One newspaper declared: "If the woman suffrage movement is ever to be finally defeated, it will be by women themselves, and by arguments and considerations like those so ably stated in this remarkable book."[8] Heartened by the press's generally favorable attitude towards their cause, other female anti-suffragists followed in Johnson's footsteps. Virginian Molly Elliot Seawell's *The Ladies' Battle* (1911); journalist Ida Tarbell's *The Business of Being a Woman* (1912); Grace Duffield Goodwin's *Anti-Suffrage: Ten Good Reasons* (1915), a booklet written by the president of the Washington, D.C. anti-suffrage association; and Annie Riley Hale's *The Eden Sphinx* (1916) were other well-received books that more or less forcefully advanced a coherent rationale for opposing women's enfranchisement.[9] Though none of these works achieved the popularity or critical acclaim of Johnson's treatise, their mere existence and wide circulation nevertheless testified to the fact that women not only worked but wrote to thwart their own enfranchisement.

Who were these women? In addressing this question, one encounters a host of stereotypes and clichés that have been transmitted through the suffragist record. "A little band of rich, ultra society women," "the candied fruit of a generation characterized by 'frenzied finance,'" "butterflies of fashion" who "move in a limited though most unimpeachable circle" were only a few of many unflattering epithets the suffragists held in store for their opponents.[10] Some sociologists and historians have in fact argued that the female anti-suffragists were mostly upper-class women whose primary motivation for their vehement opposition to the ballot was their fear of a decline in status. According to this interpretation, the Antis were most of all wary of the democraticizing tendencies of suffragist politics and thus eager to safeguard their class privileges.[11]

However, the class-related differences between the proponents and the opponents of women's enfranchisement should not be overemphasized. To be sure, many of the female Antis came from old and well-established families whose names were often known well beyond their native states' boundaries for the social, political, and economic clout they had carried for decades or even centuries. It is also true that the organized leadership's particular makeup did not facilitate or encourage the participation of women of non-White, non-Protestant backgrounds. African American, immigrant, and working-class women may very well have harbored anti-suffrage sentiments, but they were not represented in the movement's front ranks or on the editorial boards of the anti-suffrage periodicals. Yet the suffrage movement, too, especially in its later phase, counted a fair number of socially prominent women among its activists and, moreover, had its own share of elitist, nativist, and racist rhetoric.

Most importantly, a college education, professional employment, and a life without a husband and children were not infallible indicators of a woman's pro-suffrage stance. Indeed, most anti-suffragists would have had no difficulty in embracing the label of the "New Woman" as appropriate designation for themselves. Alike in many biographical particulars, pro- and anti-suffrage women shared above all one crucial conviction: both groups declared themselves to be deeply committed to women's public activism and social reform.

The Anti-suffragist as "New Woman"

In March 1909, *The Anti-Suffragist*, a publication of the New York State Association Opposed to Woman Suffrage (NYSAOWS), reprinted a comment by well-known suffragist Florence Kelley, general secretary of the National Consumers League, in which she branded the Antis as "shirks," "lazy, comfortable, sheltered creatures, caring nothing for the miseries of the poor."[12] Few other accusations could have struck more to the heart of the anti-suffrage women's self-definition and could have provoked a more indignant reaction. Addressing the Judiciary Committee of the House of Representatives in 1914, Massachusetts Anti Mrs. Henry Preston (Sarah C.) White took pains to refute such claims. Listing a long catalog of the MAOFESW members' and leaders' manifold philanthropic, charitable, educational, and civic activities, White asserted that the anti-suffragists, all widely publicized stereotypes to the contrary, were "disinterested, public-spirited citizens who give their time and service to questions of public service without the hope of political reward or preference."[13]

Similar assertions resounded throughout the anti-suffrage literature of the first two decades of the twentieth century. In a prefatory chapter to a collection of anti-suffrage essays by Massachusetts women, published on the occasion of the defeat of the state's 1915 suffrage referendum, Mrs. John (Katharine Torbert) Balch, then president of the MAOFESW, emphasized that its members represented a fair cross section of the population, comprising women of every "class or type." Even more importantly, she asserted that she "could fill pages with the record" of the Antis' "public welfare activities."[14] As if to underscore that claim, every one of the seventeen anti-suffrage essays following Balch's introduction was prefaced by a roster of the various public activities of their respective authors—activities that included work in educational associations, municipal, health, consumer, and trade union leagues, women's clubs, settlement houses, state boards of charity, prison, playground, and child reform organizations.[15]

The public activities or the professional experiences of an anti-suffrage woman were often cited as if they conferred upon her the very legitimacy and authority to speak out in opposition to women's enfranchisement and to make her opinion one of particular interest and value to the female population of America. When addressing themselves to the public, whether in the form of legislative committees or a more general audience, Antis emphatically underscored their public commitment and thus took pains to dissociate themselves from the image of sheltered, domestic creatures foisted upon them by their opponents. Yet references to civic activities did more than boost the Antis' stature in public. The anti-suffragists' involvement in all kinds of reform and associational endeavors was reflected by and shaped the rationale of the women opposed to their enfranchisement. I want to argue that the arguments turn-of-the-century Antis most frequently invoked against women's enfranchisement had less to do with woman's place in the home than with her appropriate role in the public realm.

A Woman's Place Is in Public

Just as the Antis rejected their image as idle, elitist, "bridge-playing" socialites,[16] they steadfastly sought to refute the suffragists' assertions that the domestic sphere was the only one they allegedly considered appropriate for women. They continually pointed out that they did *not* "make a fetish of the home as a place, nor of woman in the home, merely because she happens to be there."[17] On the contrary. Turn-of-the-century anti-suffrage leaders constantly urged women to leave the household to engage in a multitude of extra-domestic activities. In what came to be the unofficial creed of NAOWS, reiterated time and again in *The Woman's Protest*, president Mrs. Arthur M. (Josephine) Dodge stated at the organization's fourth annual meeting in January 1916:

> We believe that women according to their leisure, opportunities, and experience should take part increasingly in civic and municipal affairs as they always have done in charitable, philanthropic and educational activities and we believe that this can best be done without the ballot by women, as a non-partisan body of disinterested workers.[18]

Another Anti put it even more forcefully: "Do not mistake me. No woman should spend all her time at home. Public needs and social duties must be attended to."[19] In an attempt to clarify the Antis' position on this issue, Mrs. J.B. Gilfillan, president of the Minnesota Association Opposed to Woman Suffrage, announced that:

Anti-Suffragists are opposed to women in political life, opposed to women in politics. This is often interpreted to mean opposition to women in public life, which is a profound mistake. We believe in women in all the usual phases of public life, except political life. Wherever woman's influence, counsel or work is needed by the community, there you will find her, so far with little thought of political beliefs.... The pedestals they are said to stand upon move them into all the demands of the community.[20]

In keeping with their own public activism and visibility, anti-suffrage leaders, speakers, and authors thus saw women's legitimate sphere of action not reduced to or circumscribed by domestic concerns. Rather, they stimulated women to venture beyond the home dutifully to shoulder their responsibilities in the public realm of reform and civic activities.

Given their obvious advocacy of women's presence in public life, both in theory and in practice, the question becomes *why* the anti-suffragists shied away so vehemently from the political realm. What explains the resolute stance of New York journalist Jeanette L. Gilder who wrote: "Give woman everything she wants, but not the ballot. Open every field of learning, every avenue of industry to her, but keep her out of politics"?[21] What made the vote so unpalatable to those women who otherwise embraced a host of public duties and responsibilities?

Anti-suffragists of the Progressive Era provided two answers. Some, by far the minority among them, argued that women were already overburdened, "with the demands of society, the calls of charity, the church, and philanthropy constantly increasing."[22] They thus could not possibly take on other, i.e. political duties, which would include not only casting the ballot, but also serving on juries or running for office. A further diffusion of women's energies would not increase their positive effect on society, as the suffragists argued, but entail a lessening of female influence as women would be forced to sacrifice quality for quantity in their attempt to add another weighty task to their already packed agenda.

More often, however, the Antis' rejection of the vote reflected not so much their dread of overwork and exhaustion, as it was based on a more sophisticated and recommendable rationale. "For me, the vital argument against suffrage for women is that it would hamper them in their more effective work in social and political lines," social worker Mary Ella Swift wrote in the lead article of a 1913 issue of *The Woman's Protest*.[23] Most Antis would certainly have agreed with this observation. Swift and other anti-suffragists insisted that political beliefs and the ballot would not only be of little value to the female reformer, but would in fact constitute a serious handicap in her work for the social good. Since casting the ballot would necessitate a woman's alignment with a political party, to become a voter would rob her of her political neutrality and non-partisanship. This in turn would diminish her influence with legislative or other governmental authorities that had so far been responsive to women's requests on the very grounds of their political disinterestedness.[24] Standing "apart from and beyond party politics," unenfranchised women, the Antis argued, were especially effective in addressing social problems and bringing about much-needed reform legislation.[25] "Outside the political machinery," *The Anti-Suffragist* announced in its December 1908 issue, "there is a world ... where all reform begins."[26] "The more reform movements are separated from politics the better for them," the journal declared again in April 1912.[27]

It was largely for this reason that the powerful umbrella organization of the nation's myriad female literary and educational groups, the General Federation of Women's Clubs, did not officially endorse woman suffrage until 1914. When it did, this came as a serious blow to the Antis. For years, they had tried to prevent this development by insisting that the collective work of the women's clubs was "more potent" than women's individual exercise of political privileges, which would only splinter female solidarity along party lines.[28] Likewise, the Antis considered trade unions, not political organizations, the better representatives of working women's interests and the more effective agents in providing good working conditions and propagating fair labor legislation.[29] To alleviate and remedy all kinds of social ills, concerning all classes and segments of society, anti-suffragists preferred nonpartisan to partisan bodies, and politically neutral women to male voters whose reform intentions they found to be inevitably compromised by their affiliations to a political party.

Far from supposedly urging women to stay in or retreat into a narrowly circumscribed domestic realm and to "shirk" their public responsibilities, the female anti-suffragists advanced arguments that derived from and reflected their sincere efforts to discharge those responsibilities with the best possible results. In their opinion, it was the advocates of woman suffrage who egotistically dodged all civic obligations, attending suffrage meetings instead of "giv[ing] hours, days, thought and energy to quiet, persistent, unheralded work toward the amelioration of the condition of women, children, and the unfortunate."[30] When the suffragists announced that they would stop contributing to civic and philanthropic causes until they were given the vote, the Antis uttered a collective cry of indignation. Taking this as further example of the suffragists' selfishness and unscrupulousness, they grasped the opportunity to portray themselves as the truly reform-oriented and caring social force of the two.

Nonpartisan Women, Society, and the State

The fight for woman suffrage, at least during the Progressive Era, was not a conflict between women who were active in public and those who advocated that a woman's place was in the home. Rather, it was two different notions of women's relationship to the public and the political realm that were at odds in the debates concerning women's enfranchisement. In an essay entitled "Woman's Civic Work Better Done Without Suffrage," Anti Elizabeth McCracken summarized the controversy's underlying issue as follows:

[O]ur position, as Anti-Suffragists, is not negative, but positive. We are not so much opposing the policy of the Suffragists as we are presenting a policy of our own. The Suffragists have one conception of the relation of women to good government—and we Anti-Suffragists have another— which seems to us better. Just as fervently as the Suffragists, do the Anti-Suffragists desire to be citizens, and intend to be citizens.... We Anti-Suffragists feel that we not only can be and are citizens without the ballot, but that we shall remain better citizens without it than with it.[31]

Mrs. Andrew J. (Alice N.) George, a principal secretary of both the Massachusetts and the National Association Opposed to Woman Suffrage, also asserted that "[w]oman's citizenship is as real as man's. The question we must answer is one of social efficiency."[32] Thus, the issue at stake was not, as many historians have argued implicitly or explicitly, one of anti-suffragists pitting their private female sphere of domestic concerns against a male public sphere of political affairs in a vestigial Victorian scenario. Rather, in the social and political context of the Progressive Era, Antis tried to hold on to what they considered to be a distinctive female public realm, different from the male realm of politics in its functions, but equal or even superior in its societal ramifications.

In order to bring women's positive influence to bear even more successfully upon public life, anti-suffragists believed that the boundaries between men's and women's public activities should not be erased, but rendered even more distinct. Such was the gist of a lecture Mrs. Barclay Hazard held before the New York State Federation of Women's Clubs in 1907:

[W]e must accept partisanship, political trickery and office-seeking as necessary evils inseparable from modern conditions, and the question arises what can be done to palliate the situation. To our minds, the solution has been found by the entrance of women into public life. Standing in an absolutely independent position, freed from all party affiliations, untrammeled by any political obligations, the intelligent, self-sacrificing women of to-day are serving the State (though many of them hardly realize it) as a third party whose disinterestedness none can doubt.[33]

The successful continuation of women's disinterested work, "untainted by political ambition" and motives, would only be ensured, according to the anti-suffragists, by keeping men and women in their separate public spheres and by recognizing their respective promises as well as limitations.[34]

In the eyes of the anti-suffragists, the vote threatened to divest women of their public power. By forcibly redirecting women's attention and energies to politics, the proponents of women's enfranchisement were about to undermine the non-partisan foundation of the all-female clubs, societies, and associations, i.e., women's citadels of public power. Seeing the suffragists' demand for the vote as an indication of their willingness to sacrifice women's social activism in the arena of male electoral politics, the Antis were upset by this apparent denial of the efficiency and validity of women's public influence as manifested through channels other than electoral politics. Women's strength in the public sphere, the Antis argued, could be more fully developed if they remembered their difference, not their sameness with male political actors. What was at stake for the Antis in the debates about woman suffrage was not women's domesticity, but women's effectiveness as non-voting, yet public-spirited citizens and agents of social change.

In order to show that their claims about the reform successes and social efficiency of unenfranchised women were not just sheer hypotheses or wishful thinking on their part, the Antis cited a variety of evidence in their favor. Their preferred strategy was to enlist the testimony of a host of female social workers, reformers, and activists who maintained that they would have never accomplished what they did if they had been entitled to cast the ballot and thereby been asked to abdicate their political neutrality. Furthermore, the anti-suffragists buttressed their assertions with "empirical evidence" from the states that had already granted the franchise to their female populations. Charts unfavorably comparing the reform legislation as well as the laws pertaining to women in Colorado, the Antis' exemplary suffrage state, to those of the Eastern non-suffrage states filled the pages of the anti-suffrage periodicals.[35] Such legal documentation also constituted the basis for Minnie Bronson's influential anti-suffrage tract, "The Wage-Earning Woman and the State," reprinted annually in the early 1910s, which tried to disprove contentions about working women's need for the ballot.[36] Finally, the Antis cited statistical as well as impressionistic evidence to announce the numerical decline of women's civic and reform associations in the suffrage states.

The years during World War I seemed to be an especially propitious time for the Antis to advance their argument of the efficiency of politically neutral women carrying out disinterested relief service in the name of peace and patriotism. While some suffragists proclaimed that they ranked their efforts to win the vote above the country's commitment to win the war, the Antis instead never tired of highlighting their self-sacrificing and loyal stance towards the nation. In fact, they channeled much of their associational, human, and financial resources into war relief work, which was extensively documented in the war-year issues of *The Woman's Protest*. Asserting that the "importance of nonpolitical women to the state [was] greater than ever before," the anti-suffragists saw the global conflict as an opportunity to put an end to allegations about their idleness and to demonstrate the validity and relevance, not to mention the patriotic implications, of their rationale against

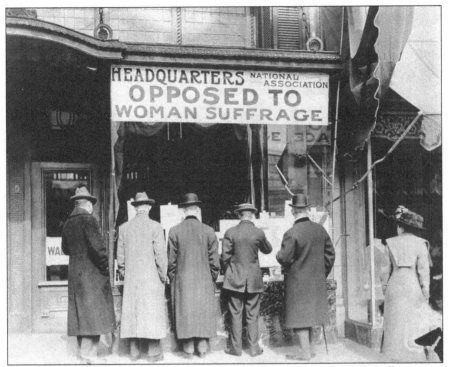

Headquarters of the National Association Opposed to Woman Suffrage
in New York City

women's enfranchisement.[37] Ironically, what had looked like a perfect opportunity
to underscore the logic of the Anti position turned out to be one of the major
determining factors in their ultimate defeat. In recognition of the invaluable aid
and service women had rendered to their country during this time of crisis, many
formerly undecided legislators finally acceded to the Nineteenth Amendment,
granting women the vote in 1920.

Anti-suffragism, Female Activism, and Progressive Reform

The emergence, in the 1890s and the first two decades of the 1900s, of an anti-
suffrage rationale that centered on the public activities rather than the domestic
"nature" and destiny of American women reflected and drew upon certain
historical developments and circumstances that made the argument both timely
and persuasive. This is not to say that *all* female or, for that matter, male, opponents
of women's suffrage espoused the reasoning outlined in this essay. Nor do I want to
argue that this has been the dominant anti-suffrage rationale ever since women
first demanded their enfranchisement. Rather, it was an argument particularly
suited to the Progressive Era. In that particular period of American history, which
was characterized by a near-universal preoccupation with reform and enthusiasm
for progress, women gained new visibility and clout. Women founded and

WHY WE DO NOT APPROVE
— OF —
WOMAN SUFFRAGE

BECAUSE: We feel that the ballot makes absolutely no difference in the economic status of woman. Whether she votes or not, her charities, great and small, will continue, professions will extend diplomas to her intelligence, and trade will grant recompense to her ability. As for the protection of the ballot to working women, it will protect them no farther than it protects men who, in spite of their voting power, find themselves unable to cope with labor conditions by legislation and form themselves into unions outside of law and law making.

BECAUSE: Our hospital Boards, our social and civic service work, our child welfare committees and countless other clubs and industries for the general welfare and uplift need women who can give non-partisan and unselfish service, the worth of which service would be greatly lessened by political affiliations.

BECAUSE: Behind law there must always be force to make it effective. If legislation was shaped by a majority of women over men we should soon have, not government, but chaos.

BECAUSE: It is an attested fact that politics degrade women more than women purify politics.

BECAUSE: We believe that American men would speedily remedy all conditions needing reform if urged with half the force now brought to bear in favor of suffrage.

BECAUSE: We believe that the interests of all women are as safe in the hands of men as in those of other women.

BECAUSE: Thorough investigation of the laws of suffrage states shows that non-suffrage states have by far the better and more humane laws, and that all laws are more strictly enforced than in suffrage states.

BECAUSE: We believe that if franchise for women would better general conditions, there would be some evidence of that betterment in states where it has been exercised for twenty and up to forty-four years.

BECAUSE: Women make little use of suffrage when it is given them. School suffrage has been a lamentable failure, the women vote averaging scarcely two per cent in any state.

BECAUSE: The energies of women are engrossed by their present duties and interests, from which men cannot relieve them, and there is great need of better performance of their present work rather than diversion to new fields of activity.

BECAUSE: The suffrage movement develops sex hatred which is a menace to society.

BECAUSE: Of the alliance of suffrage with socialism which advocates free love and institutional life for children.

BECAUSE: The greatest menace to the morals of today lies in the efforts of suffragists to convince the world that vice is predominant. In the mad rush for the ballot and the consequent advertisement of immorality, reverence has been dethroned and reticence annihilated. It is high time for the right thinking, purity-loving women to arise and undo the terrific impress made on the public mind by the preachments of these pursuers of vice.

BECAUSE: The great majority of intelligent, refined and educated women do not want enfranchisement. They realize no sense of injustice such as expressed by the small minority of suffragists. They have all the rights and freedom they desire, and consider their present trusts most sacred and important. They feel that the duties which naturally must ever revert to their sex are such that none but themselves can perform and that political responsibilities could not be borne by them without the sacrifice of the highest interests of their families and of society.

 Nebraska Association Opposed to Woman Suffrage.

Anti-suffrage leaflet, c. 1914

participated in a variety of associations, organizations, clubs, and societies; they entered many educational institutions that had formerly been the exclusive preserve of men; and they were newly visible in the public as clerical workers, department store employees, professionals, and social reformers.[38] Contrary to common historical wisdom, the female Antis were not opposed to but actively involved in such and similar developments. Their associational and sometimes (semi-)professional experiences did not only provide them with the expertise and the know-how to establish an organized anti-suffrage movement; they also became an integral part of their anti-suffrage rationale. Far from divorcing themselves from the activist and reformist traditions and tendencies of the past and the present, the anti-suffrage women eagerly stressed their indebtedness to nineteenth-century female reformers and emphasized their firm commitment to the reform agenda of the Progressive Era.

As a matter of fact, early twentieth-century Antis cited the female notables of the preceding century as fitting exemplars of women whose fame and reputation rested upon a host of extraordinary achievements, all of which had been possible without the ballot. The Antis were not at a loss to find distinguished nineteenth-century women who had combined public activism with a resolute anti-suffrage stance. English relief worker Octavia Hill was occasionally introduced as the prototypical woman whose distinctive and invaluable contribution was not that of a "politician," but of "a disinterested factor working to render public service uncolored by political motives."[39] Closer to home, educators Catharine Beecher, Emma Willard, and Civil War nurse Dorothea Dix, "the Florence Nightingale of this country," led the throng of influential women whom the American Antis took to be their sisters in spirit and action as well as the truly progressive forces in society.[40]

Claiming to be the rightful descendants of this distinctively female tradition of public activism, the anti-suffragists aligned themselves with the "true woman" ideology that they saw as the driving force behind all major reform achievements of the nineteenth and early twentieth centuries.[41] Anti Lilian Bayard Taylor Kiliani cited the entrance of women into institutions of higher education, industry, and the professions as well as the profusion of female reform associations and movements as irrefutable proof of how much women were able to achieve, "without going to the polls or becoming involved in party politics."[42] Helen Kendrick Johnson, in particular, made it her avowed objective to wrest praise for women's progress and manifold accomplishments from the suffragists. She asserted that "'Movement' and 'Progress' [were] not synonymous terms," but with regard to woman suffrage virtually irreconcilable opposites. In her *Woman and the Republic,* she argued that wherever advocates of woman suffrage had meddled in matters of major national concern—be it abolitionism, temperance, or woman's rights—they had only caused delays, dissensions, and serious disturbances, which had frustrated a more prompt and efficient approach to these affairs.[43]

Aware that "next to being unpopular, to be unprogressive, is the worst thing that can be said of an American, male or female,"[44] Antis were especially sensitive to criticism of that kind and went to great lengths to refute allegations about their aversion to change. New York Anti Annie Nathan Meyer, one of the driving forces behind the foundation of Barnard College and an associate editor of the anti-suffrage, anti-feminist, anti-socialist *The Woman's Patriot*, was especially insistent in refuting the widespread assumption that the "movement to obtain the ballot for women is identical with and not to be separated from all other movements for women's progress." In the spring of 1910, she indignantly wrote:

Anti-suffragist Annie Nathan Meyer. She and her sister, Maud Nathan, were leaders of opposite sides of the woman suffrage movement.

THE BARNARD ARCHIVES AND SPECIAL COLLECTIONS

The suffragists have battled for suffrage the past forty years in America—on the whole with rather conspicuous unsuccess. Some of them—fewer by far than is claimed—also incidentally battled for other reform, but never without the help and enthusiasm of convinced anti-suffragists…. The women who really blazed the paths of education and reform in this country were either outspoken antisuffragists or at best lukewarm suffragists who were too busy doing their work to bother about imaginary wrongs. This confusion of the suffrage movement with every movement that made for advance goes merrily on, and few take the trouble to stop it.[45]

Turning the tables on the suffragists, the Antis characterized the votes-for-women movement as "fifty years behind the time," calling it a "movement backward towards men and mastodons, the miocene hipparion and eocene anchitherium."[46] In comparison, the average female anti-suffragist was seen as standing "in the very front rank of progress for she [was] a preventive philanthropist," she was "the newest new woman…at work at home and in public."[47]

Because it allowed them to combine their rejection of women's enfranchisement with an unequivocal affirmation of the ideas of social progress and women's advancement, such reasoning understandably attracted many women to the anti-suffrage cause. The appeal of this particular argumentation could largely be explained by the fact that it built on and embraced several assumptions that were shared by most women—and men—during the Progressive Era, regardless of their stance on the question of suffrage.

In fact, agreement on women's public influence and the need for social reform often brought opponents and proponents of woman suffrage alike together in their common concern for the public good. In 1891, Annie Nathan Meyer edited a book called *Woman's Work in America,* a collection of essays on women's manifold contributions to education, literature, journalism, medicine, ministry, law, industry, philanthropy, and the state.[48] Ironically, and significantly, most of the contributors to this volume, which was compiled by an ardent anti-suffragist, professed to be in favor of women's enfranchisement; the preface, for example, was written by well-known Bostonian suffragist Julia Ward Howe.

Suffragists were in fact willing to acknowledge the successes and positive changes in social work that women had wrought without the vote. In an essay entitled "The Legislative Influence of Unenfranchised Women," historian and activist Mary Ritter Beard conceded that "other influences than those of the ballot box operate on" legislators and state representatives.[49] Elaborating on this point, Beard in 1915 published her *Woman's Work in Municipalities,* an impressive compendium of the various types of women's activities on the local and communal levels—paying no heed to those women's opinion on the suffrage issue.[50]

While anti-suffragists most probably wholeheartedly welcomed Beard's observations, they could not assent to her suggestion that women's influence would reach even further if they were given the vote. For the Antis, it was the very fact of their disfranchisement and concomitant disinterestedness that had made women such efficient reformers. Looking back on women's multitudinous accomplishments over the past decades, they saw no reason to believe that the continuing success and expansion of women's charitable, philanthropic, and civic reform activities depended on the ballot. It was at this crucial juncture where anti- and pro-suffrage women's opinions took different turns. While the demand for the vote, in some instances, served as a unifying cause for many women of different backgrounds and interests, it became the divisive issue for many female activists who otherwise found themselves in general accord on matters concerning women's prominent role in turn-of-the-century social reform.[51] Agreeing on social reform as the desirable objective of women's public involvement, Antis and suffragists differed on which way was the better and more efficient to that end.

Conclusion

Such findings not only correct or modify traditional accounts concerning the female anti-suffragists' makeup and motives, but also carry with them implications that are relevant to larger debates in the field of women's history. It would not be an exaggeration to claim that women's involvement in reform associations, institutions, and movements is probably the most widely studied area of American women's history. Much of the secondary literature has focused on the

"O SAVE US, SENATORS, FROM OURSELVES!"

Cover of *Harper's Weekly,*
February 23, 1907

question of whether or to what extent women's manifold organizational activities foreshadowed and/or constituted the necessary prerequisites of suffragism and feminism. For the most part, historians have tried to establish a continuum between early- and mid-nineteenth-century women's participation in a variety of reform movements and turn-of-the-century women's espousal of suffrage and feminist principles. Earlier abolitionist, moral reform, temperance, and other largely single-sex reform societies have been seen as consciousness-raising training-grounds for later avid suffragists. Similarly, historians have argued that nineteenth-century women's activism gave them an incentive to expand their sphere of influence and provided them with a rationale to demand the vote to that end.[52]

The example of the female anti-suffragists, however, calls for a more complex interpretation. As their case demonstrates, women's public activities have not always been put to feminist ends nor have they necessarily bred ideas critical of the patriarchal organization of the state as women, so the story goes, came to realize their powerlessness and ineffectiveness in the political arena.[53] The Antis, as discussed in this essay, opposed women's enfranchisement not in spite of, but *because of* their involvement and experiences in a huge number of extra-domestic organizations, which they came to look upon as their bulwarks of public power and influence. The majority of organized Antis were women who occupied many public positions and offices and who brought their experiences and expertise in the public realm to bear on their anti-suffrage labor. While they saw suffragism and feminism as dangerous to the progress of society, they, at the same time, had no difficulty proclaiming their affinities with various pioneering women activists of the nineteenth century, or welcoming every possible development that they perceived as furthering women's progress. Both the Antis' own activism and their interpretations of women's historical and social mission combined to generate strong anti-feminist, defined as anti-suffrage, beliefs and convictions.

Yet, strangely and ironically, anti-suffrage women have something to tell the late twentieth-century feminist historian and theorist. Although the turn-of-the-century Antis' own definition of politics as a male, partisan enterprise was a very narrow one, which did not encompass their reform activities, this fact should not and cannot prevent us from regarding women's public activism in the realm of social reform legislation as highly political. Recent feminist scholarship has expanded traditional definition of politics so as to incorporate many areas, activities, and actors that have generally been excluded by political theory. Some scholars have even gone so far as to suggest that there were times, the Progressive Era prominent among them, when women's distinctive contributions to society had more far-reaching social and political implications than men's exercise of their voting privileges.[54] Emphasizing the integrity and importance of a distinctively female tradition of public activism and asserting that women's citizenship did not, for its valuation, depend on the vote, the turn-of-the-century anti-suffrage women styled themselves as champions and defenders of an area and of ideas that are of increasing interest to feminist political theorists who are trying to introduce an "alternative concept of public life" deriving its force from non-electoral, non-partisan forms of political participation.[55] Once historians and political theorists start to examine more closely the workings and the concerns of the female public culture of the past to gain insights for the present and the future, they cannot afford to ignore the voices of the women who opposed woman suffrage.

Notes

This essay is a revised version of an article originally published in the *Journal of Women's History* 5, no. 1 (Spring 1993), 33-60, and appears here with the permission of the journal.

1. Florence R. Hall, "Disinterested, Appealing to All Humanity," *The Woman's Protest* 7, no. 5 (September 1915), 6.

2. Carrie Chapman Catt and Nettie Rogers Shuler, *Woman Suffrage and Politics: The Inner Story of the Suffrage Movement* (1923; reprint, Seattle, 1969), 132.

3. See Eleanor Flexner, *Century of Struggle: The Woman's Rights Movement in the United States* (Cambridge, 1968), 294-305; Alan P. Grimes, *The Puritan Ethic and Woman Suffrage* (New York, 1967), 78-98; Aileen S. Kraditor, *The Ideas of the Woman Suffrage Movement, 1890-1920* (New York, 1965), 14-42; William L. O'Neill, *Feminism in America: A History* (New Brunswick, 1989), 55-64; and Carl N. Degler, *At Odds: Women and the Family in America from the Revolution to the Present* (New York, 1980), 349-355.

4. See, Jane Jerome Camhi, "Women Against Women: American Anti-Suffragism, 1880-1920," Ph.D. diss., Tufts University, 1973; Thomas J. Jablonsky, "Duty, Nature, and Stability: The Female Anti-Suffragists in the U.S., 1894-1920," Ph.D. diss., University of Southern California, 1978; See also Mara Mayor, "Fears and Fantasies of the Anti-Suffragists," *Connecticut Review* 7, no. 2 (April 1974): 64-74; Catherine Cole Mambretti, "The Battle Against the Ballot: Illinois Woman Antisuffragists," *Chicago History* 9, no. 3 (Fall 1980): 168-177; and Louise L. Stevenson, "Women Antisuffragists in the 1915 Massachusetts Campaign," *New England Quarterly* 52, no. 1 (March 1979): 80-93.

5. For more information see, Camhi, "Women Against Women," and Jablonsky, "Duty, Nature, and Stability."

6. *The Woman's Protest* 7, no. 1 (May 1915): 16.

7. *The St. Paul Pioneer-Press*, cited in Helen Kendrick Johnson, *Woman and the Republic: A Survey of the Woman-Suffrage*

Movement in the United States and a Discussion of the Claims and Arguments of Its Foremost Advocates (1897; New York, 1913), 364, 367, 368.

8. *The Brooklyn Standard-Union*, quoted in Rossiter Johnson, *Helen Kendrick Johnson: The Story of Her Varied Activities* (New York, 1917), 51.

9. Molly Elliot Seawell, *The Ladies' Battle* (New York, 1911); Ida Tarbell, *The Business of Being a Woman* (New York, 1912); Grace Duffield Goodwin, *Anti-Suffrage: Ten Good Reasons* (New York, 1915); and Annie Riley Hale, *The Eden Sphinx* (New York, 1916).

10. Quotes are taken from *The Woman's Standard* (May 1906): 3, ibid. (February 1905): 1, cited in Jablonsky, "Duty, Nature, and Stability," 10; *The Woman's Protest* 8, no. 5 (March 1916): 13; and Susan B. Anthony and Ida Husted Harper, *History of Woman Suffrage* 4 (New York, 1969), 716.

11. Susan E. Marshall, "In Defense of Separate Spheres: Class and Status Politics in the Antisuffrage Movement," *Social Forces* 65, no. 2 (December 1986): 327-351; and Susan E. Marshall and Anthony M. Orum, "Opposition Then and Now: Countering Feminism in the Twentieth Century," in *Research in Politics and Society: A Research Annual; Vol. 2: Women and Politics: Activism, Attitudes and Office-Holding*, eds. Gwen Moore and Glenna Spitze (Greenwich, Conn., 1986), 23.

12. Florence Kelley, quoted in *The Anti-Suffragist* 1, no. 3 (March 1909): 2.

13. Mrs. Henry White, "Who Are the Anti-Suffragists—And Why," *The Woman's Protest* 4, no. 6 (April 1914): 5, 6.

14. See Mrs. John Balch, "Who the Massachusetts Anti-Suffragists Are," in *Anti-Suffrage Essays by Massachusetts Women*, ed. Ernest Bernbaum (Boston: Forum Publications, 1916), 21-23.

15. That this self-representation on the part of the Antis did indeed correspond with their actual experiences and

employments is corroborated by a look at the 1914-1915 edition of the *Woman's Who's Who of America*. In this biographical dictionary of American and Canadian women who "are leading in or contributing to women's larger participation in the good causes and higher endeavors of our time," one finds a great number of women who, while actively engaged in a host of leagues, clubs, societies, and voluntary organizations, declared themselves opposed to or undecided with regard to woman suffrage; see John William Leonard, ed., *Women's Who's Who of America: A Biographical Dictionary of Contemporary Women of the United States and Canada, 1914-1915* (New York, 1914), 22.

16. Laura Fay-Smith, quoted in Marshall, "In Defense of Separate Spheres," 341.

17. *The Woman's Protest* 5, no. 6 (October 1914): 14.

18. Mrs. Arthur M. Dodge, "The Report of the President," *The Woman's Protest* 8, no. 3 (January 1916): 6.

19. Mrs. Charles Burton Gulick, "The Imperative Demand Upon Women in the Home," in *Anti-Suffrage Essays by Massachusetts Women*, 133.

20. Mrs. J.B. Gilfillan, "Work and the Home," *The Woman's Protest* 7, no. 1 (May 1915): 17.

21. Jeanette L. Gilder, "Why I am Opposed to Woman Suffrage," pamphlet, 1894, MAOFESW, Mudd Library, Yale University (hereafter cited as Mudd).

22. Quoted in Kraditor, *The Ideas of the Woman Suffrage Movement*, 27-28; also *The Anti-Suffragist* 1, no. 1 (July 1908): 4; and Emily Bissell, "A Talk to Women on the Suffrage Question," pamphlet, 1909, 2, NYSAOWS, Mudd.

23. Mary Ella Swift, "Suffrage for Women a Handicap in Civic Work," *The Woman's Protest* 3, no. 4 (August 1913): 3.

24. See *The Anti-Suffragist* 1, no. 2 (December 1908): 11, 13; 2, no. 1 (September 1909): 5; 3, no. 3 (March 1911): 3; 3, no. 4 (June 1911): 8; 4 no. 2 (April 1912): 2; *The Woman's Protest* 1, no. 4 (August 1912): 12; 6, no. 3 (January 1915): 9; and 7, no. 5 (September 1915): 19. See also the contributions of Mrs. A.J. George, Monica Foley, Dorothy Godfrey Wayman, and Margaret C. Robinson in *Anti-Suffrage Essays by Massachusetts Women*.

25. *The Anti-Suffragist* 1, no. 2 (December 1908): 11.

26. *The Anti-Suffragist* 1, no. 2 (December 1908): 13.

27. *The Anti-Suffragist* 4, no. 2 (April 1912): 2.

28. Anon., "Women's Clubs More Potent Than the Ballot," *The Woman's Protest* 5, no. 3 (July 1914): 5.

29. See Anon., "Working Women and Suffrage," *The Anti-Suffragist* 2, no. 2 (December 1909): 1; and Adeline Knapp, "Do Working Women Need the Ballot?—An Address to the Senate and Assembly Judiciary Committee of the New York Legislature," NAOWS, Mudd.

30. Anon., "Missing the Opportunities," *The Woman's Protest* 1, no. 5 (September 1912): 4.

31. Elizabeth McCracken, "Woman's Civic Work Better Done Without Suffrage," *The Woman's Protest* 4, no. 3 (Jan 1914): 16.

32. Mrs. A.J. George, "Efficiency the Real Test of Woman Suffrage," *The Woman's Protest* 8, no. 6 (April 1916): 5.

33. Mrs. Barclay Hazard, "How Women Can Best Serve the State" (Chicago: Illinois Association Opposed to the Extension of Suffrage to Women; reprinted by courtesy of the NYSAOWS, n.d.), 2, Mudd.

34. *The Woman's Protest* 2, no. 2 (December 1912): 6; see also Annah Robinson Watson, "The Attitude of Southern Women on the Suffrage Question," *The Arena* 11 (February 1895): 366.

35. See Eliza D. Armstrong, "Non-Partisan Woman Wins Where Voters Fail," *The Woman's Protest* 4, no. 3 (December 1913): 21; Mrs. Rowland G. Hazard, "Some Reasons Why We Oppose Suffrage; Its Effect on the State," pamphlet, 1911, Rhode Island Association Opposed to Woman's Suffrage, Mudd; Ellen Mudge Burrill, "Some Practical Aspects of the Question"; and Catherine Robinson, "Massachusetts Compared With Suffrage States," in *Anti-Suffrage Essays by Massachusetts Women*, 43-52, 62-66.

36. Minnie Bronson, "The Wage-Earning Woman and the State," 1912, 1913, 1914, NAOWS, Mudd.

37. *The Woman's Protest* 7, no. 4 (August 1915): 7-8.

38. For an excellent overview of this period, see Sara M. Evans, *Born for Liberty: A History of Women in America* (New York, 1989), 145-173.

39. Mrs. Arthur M. Dodge, "Woman Suffrage Opposed to Woman's Rights," in *Women in Public Life*, ed. James P. Lichtenberger, *The Annals of the American Academy of Political and Social Science* 56 (November 1914), 104.

40. *The Woman's Protest* 8, no. 5 (March 1916): 19.

41. Mrs. Herbert Lyman, "The Anti-Suffrage Ideal," in *Anti-Suffrage Essays by Massachusetts Women*, 121; *The Woman's Protest* 5, no. 2 (June 1914): 10.

42. Lilian Bayard Taylor Kiliani, "Women Without Ballot Do Greater Work," *The Woman's Protest* 3, no. 2 (June 1913): 8.

43. See especially the introduction and the chapter on "Woman Suffrage and Philanthropy" in Johnson, *Woman and the Republic*, 5-9, 104-155; quotation on 104.

44. Mrs. Robert McVickar, "What is an Anti-Suffragist?," undated pamphlet, NAOWS, Mudd.

45. Annie Nathan Meyer, "Miss Johnston and Woman Suffrage," *The Bookman* 31 (May 1910): 314.

46. Alice Hill Chittenden, "The Inexpediency of Granting the Suffrage to American Women—An Address at the Tenth Biennial of the General Federation of Women's Clubs, Cincinnati, May 14, 1910," pamphlet, NAOWS, Mudd; "A Movement Toward Mastodons," *The Woman's Protest* 4, no. 1 (November 1913): 14.

47. Margaret H. Freeman, "The Voice of the Majority," *The Anti-Suffragist* 2, no. 1 (September 1909): 3; and Margaret Doane Gardiner, "A Mining Experiment," *The Anti-Suffragist* 3, no. 1 (September 1910): 3.

48. Annie Nathan Meyer, ed., *Woman's Work in America* (New York, 1972).

49. Mary Ritter Beard, "The Legislative Influence of Un-enfranchised Women," in *Women in Public Life*, 54, 60.

50. Mary Ritter Beard, *Woman's Work in Municipalities* (1915; New York, 1972).

51. See Lucy Jeanne Price, "Lessons Learned From the Campaign," *The Woman's Protest* 8, no. 1 (November 1915): 5-6.

52. See especially Keith Melder, "Ladies Bountiful: Organized Women's Benevolence in Early Nineteenth-Century America," *New York History* 48, no. 3 (July 1967): 231-255; Alice Rossi, "Social Roots of the Woman's Movement in America," in *The Feminist Papers*, ed. Alice Rossi, (New York, 1973), 241-281; Barbara Berg, *The Remembered Gate: Origins of American Feminism. The Woman and the City*, 1800-1860 (New York, 1978); and Lori Ginzberg, "'Moral Suasion is Moral Balderdash': Women, Politics, and Social Activism in the 1850s," *Journal of American History* 73, no. 3 (December 1986): 601-622.

53. Studies that have acknowledged the anti-feminist potential of women's associations include: Mary Ryan, "The Power of Women's Networks: A Case Study of Female Moral Reform in Antebellum America," *Feminist Studies* 5, no. 1 (Spring 1979): 66-85; Nancy Cott, *The Bonds of Womanhood: "Woman's Sphere" in New England, 1780-1835* (New Haven, 1977); and Nancy A. Hewitt, *Women's Activism and Social Change: Rochester, N.Y., 1822-1872* (Ithaca, 1984).

54. See Estelle Freedman, "Separatism As Strategy: Female Institution Building and American Feminism, 1870-1930," *Feminist Studies* 5, no. 3 (Fall 1979): 512-529; Paula Baker, "The Domestication of Politics: Women and American Political Society, 1780-1920," *American Historical Review* 89, no.2 (June 1984): 620-647; idem., *The Moral Frameworks of Public Life: Gender, Politics, and the State in Rural New York, 1870-1930* (New York, 1991); and Maureen A. Flanagan, "Gender and Urban Political Reform: The City Club and the Woman's City Club of Chicago in the Progressive Era," *American Historical Review* 95 (October 1990): 1032-1050.

55. Sara M. Evans, "Women's History and Political Theory: Towards a Feminist Approach to Public Life," in *Visible Women: New Essays on American Activism*, Nancy A. Hewitt and Suzanne Lebsock, eds. (Urbana, 1993), 121.

Fifteen

WORKING WOMEN, CLASS RELATIONS, AND SUFFRAGE MILITANCE:

Harriot Stanton Blatch and the
New York Woman Suffrage Movement,
1894—1909

Ellen Carol DuBois

Editor's Introduction: Rediscovering the woman suffrage movement means revising a number of widely held but inaccurate ideas about the movement and its history. One of these misconceptions is that the woman suffrage movement in America was a "middle-class movement." Though it is true that many suffragists and suffrage leaders were middle-class, characterizing the movement as such, as Ellen Carol DuBois explains, "homogenizes" the movement. It distorts the picture by ignoring the presence in, and the contributions to, the suffrage movement of women from both ends of the economic scale.

As DuBois makes clear in this essay, elite women and working-class women were increasingly involved in the suffrage movement around the turn of the century. And in New York, a coalition of these women headed by Harriot Stanton Blatch, Elizabeth Cady Stanton's daughter, created a new tradition of class relations among women—one on which, writes DuBois, a "thriving, modern woman suffrage movement could be built." DuBois, author of *Harriot Stanton Blatch and the Winning of Woman Suffrage*, describes Blatch as a born politician with the "combination of suffrage convictions and class awareness to lead New York suffragists through that transition." After a fascinating discussion of the attitudes of the wealthy suffragists who became prominent in the movement in the 1890s, DuBois explains how Blatch rejected the pattern of class relations favored by many elite suffragists and pointed the way to a new and far more productive working relationship between women from both ends of the socioeconomic spectrum that would transform and invigorate the entire suffrage campaign.

Though from an elite background, Blatch rejected the maternalistic attitudes toward working-class women held by many elite suffragists who presumed that working-class women should defer to their leadership in return for their protection. And she emphatically denounced the idea endorsed by some suffrage leaders in the

1890s (including Elizabeth Cady Stanton) that suffragists should call for woman suffrage with an educational qualification that would curtail the number of working-class women who would be enfranchised. A college-educated woman with B.A. and M.A. degrees from Vassar, Blatch's view of work as the key to women's independence, dignity, and freedom was similar to that of her contemporary, the feminist intellectual, Charlotte Perkins Gilman. Indeed, Blatch saw working-class women more as exemplars for women like herself rather than "victims to be succored."

Blatch, like Jane Addams, was convinced that working-class women not only understood their own interests but needed the vote in order to represent those interests and support reform. Impressed by the successful efforts of some British suffragists to organize across class lines (Blatch had married an Englishman and lived in Great Britain from 1882 to 1902), and by the partnership created between working-class and wealthy women in the Women's Trade Union League, she was also convinced that working-class women were able co-workers in the fight for woman suffrage.

Blatch urged established suffrage societies "to recognize the importance of the vote to wage-earning women and the importance of wage-earning women to winning the vote." However, writes DuBois, when existing groups failed to respond, Blatch formed her own society, the "Equality League of Self-Supporting Women." This organization, which harnessed the talents of educated professionals and the power and political sagacity of trade-union women, provided the medium for introducing a new and aggressive—indeed militant—style of activism into the suffrage movement.

Indeed, DuBois helps us rediscover the suffrage movement in yet another very important way as she demonstrates that the militant tactics embraced by American suffragists in the twentieth century were not entirely imported, but partly home grown—a contribution of working-class suffragists. Their involvement in the movement "broaden[ed] the class basis and the outlook of American suffragism" and thus prepared the way for American women "to respond to the heroism of the British militants."

Following a 1907 visit to New York by a leader of the British militants, Blatch and other "new" suffrage leaders introduced their tactics into the American movement. Some New York suffragists even adopted the name "suffragette"—a term embraced by the British militants, but generally shunned by moderate or conservative American suffragists precisely because it associated them with the British militants and was used by American anti-suffragists to belittle or denigrate suffrage advocates. But the embrace of the term by some New York suffragists—as well as their participation in public demonstrations—suggested just how willing these suffragists had become to part with genteel tradition.

Militant tactics, including parades and open-air (as opposed to parlor) meetings, and other such attention-getting tactics, would soon be embraced by the mainstream suffrage movement all over the nation (though the NAWSA continued to shun picketing and civil disobedience). These tactics proved to be extremely important to the cause, as they made it impossible for the press to continue to ignore the movement as they seemed determined to do. And, as Blatch shrewdly comprehended, participation in these public acts by women who had been taught to shun publicity was in itself good for the cause, in that it forced a re-examination of assumptions about definitions of femininity and cemented the participants' commitment to the cause.

★   ★   ★   ★   ★

T HE POLITICS of Harriot Stanton Blatch illuminates the origin and nature of the woman suffrage movement in the Progressive Era. Blatch was the daughter of Elizabeth Cady Stanton, the founding mother of political feminism. Beginning in the early twentieth century, she was a leader in her own right, initially in New York, later nationally. As early as 1903, when politics was still considered something that disreputable men did, like spitting tobacco, Blatch proclaimed: "There are born politicians just as there are born artists, writers, painters. I confess that I should be a politician, that I am not interested in machine politics, but that the devotion to the public cause...rather than the individual, appeals to me."[1]

Just as her zest for politics marked Blatch as a new kind of suffragist, so did her efforts to fuse women of different classes into a revitalized suffrage movement. Blatch's emphasis on class was by no means unique; she shared it with other women reformers of her generation. Many historians have treated the theme of class by labeling the organized women's reform movement in the early twentieth century "middle-class." By contrast, I have tried to keep open the question of the class character of women's reform in the Progressive Era by rigorously avoiding the term. Characterizing the early twentieth-century suffrage movement as "middle-class" obscures its most striking element, the new interest in the vote among women at both ends of the class structure. Furthermore, it tends to homogenize the movement. The very term "middle-class" is contradictory, alternatively characterized as people who are not poor, and people who work for a living. By contrast, I have emphasized distinctions between classes and organized my analysis around the relations between them.

Class Complexities and Progressive Era Suffragism

No doubt there is some distortion in this framework, particularly for suffragists who worked in occupations like teaching. But there is far greater distortion in using the term "middle class" to describe women like Blatch or Carrie Chapman Catt or Jane Addams. For example, it makes more sense to characterize an unmarried woman with an independent income who was not under financial compulsion to work for her living as "elite," rather than "middle class." The question is not just one of social stratification, but of the place of women in a whole system of class relations. For these new style suffragists, as for contemporary feminists who write about them, the complex relationship between paid labor, marital status, and women's place in the class structure was a fundamental puzzle. The concept of "middle class" emerged among early twentieth-century reformers, but may ultimately prove more useful in describing a set of relations between classes that was coming into being in those years, than in designating a segment of the social structure.

Blatch, examined as a political strategist and a critic of class relations, is important less as a unique figure than as a representative leader, through whose career the historical forces transforming twentieth-century suffragism can be traced. The scope of her leadership offers clues to the larger movement: She was one of the first to open up suffrage campaigns to working-class women, even as she worked closely with wealthy and influential upper-class women; she pioneered militant street tactics and backroom political lobbying at the same time. Blatch's political evolution reveals close ties between other stirrings among American women in the Progressive Era and the rejuvenated suffrage movement. Many of her ideas paralleled Charlotte Perkins Gilman's influential reformulation of women's emancipation in economic terms. Many of Blatch's innovations as a suffragist drew on her prior experience in the Women's Trade Union League. Overall, Blatch's activities suggest that early twentieth-century changes in the American suffrage movement, often traced to the example of militant British suffragettes, had deep, indigenous roots. Among them were the growth of trade unionism among working-class women and professionalism among the elite, changing relations between these classes, and the growing involvement of women of all sorts in political reform.

Wealthy Women and Suffragism in the 1890s

The suffrage revival began in New York in 1893-1894, as part of a general political reform movement. In the 1890s New York's political reformers were largely upper-class men concerned about political "corruption" which they blamed partly on city Democratic machines and the bosses who ran them, partly on the masses of voting men, ignorant, immigrant, and ripe for political manipulation. Their concern about political corruption and about the consequences of uncontrolled political democracy became the focus of New York's 1894 constitutional convention, which addressed itself largely to "governmental procedures: the rules for filling offices, locating authority and organizing the different branches."[2]

The New York woman suffrage movement, led by Susan B. Anthony, recognized a great opportunity in the constitutional convention of 1894. Focusing on political corruption, Anthony and her allies argued that women were the political reformers' best allies. For while men were already voters and vulnerable to the ethic of partisan loyalty—indeed a man without a party affiliation in the

1890s was damned close to unsexed—everyone knew that women were naturally nonpartisan. Enfranchising women was therefore the solution to the power of party bosses. Suffragists began by trying to get women elected to the constitutional convention itself. Failing this, they worked to convince the convention delegates to include woman suffrage among the proposed amendments.[3]

Anthony planned a house-to-house canvass to collect signatures on a mammoth woman suffrage petition. For the $50,000 she wanted to fund this effort, she approached wealthy women in New York City, including physician Mary Putnam Jacobi, society

Harriot Stanton Blatch, 1911
LIBRARY OF CONGRESS

leader Catherine Palmer (Mrs. Robert) Abbe, social reformer Josephine Shaw Lowell, and philanthropist Olivia (Mrs. Russell) Sage. Several of them were already associated with efforts for the amelioration of working-class women, notably in the recently formed Consumers League, and Anthony had reason to think they might be ready to advocate woman suffrage.[4]

The elite women were interested in woman suffrage, but they had their own ideas about how to work for it. Instead of funding Anthony's campaign, they formed their own organization. At parlor meetings in the homes of wealthy women, they tried to strike a genteel note, emphasizing that enfranchisement would *not* take women out of their proper sphere and would *not* increase the political power of the lower classes. Eighty-year-old Elizabeth Stanton, observing the campaign from her armchair, thought that "men and women of the conservative stamp of the Sages can aid us greatly at this stage of our movement."[5]

Why did wealthy women first take an active and prominent part in the suffrage movement in the 1890s? In part they shared the perspective of men of their class that the influence of the wealthy in government had to be strengthened; they believed that with the vote they could increase the political power of their class. In a representative argument before the constitutional convention, Jacobi proposed woman suffrage as a response to "the shifting of political power from privileged classes to the masses of men." The disfranchisement of women contributed to this shift because it made all women, "no matter how well born, how well educated, how intelligent, how rich, how serviceable to the State," the political inferiors of all men, "no matter how base-born, how poverty stricken, how ignorant, how vicious, how brutal." Olivia Sage presented woman suffrage as an antidote to the growing and dangerous "idleness" of elite women, who had forgotten their responsibility to set the moral tone for society.[6]

Yet, the new elite converts also supported woman suffrage on the grounds of changes taking place in women's status, especially within their own class. Jacobi argued that the educational advancement of elite women "and the new activities into which they have been led by it—in the work of charities, in the professions, and in the direction of public education—naturally and logically tend toward the same result, their political equality." She argued that elite women, who had aided the community through organized charity and benevolent activities, should have the same "opportunity to serve the State nobly." Sage was willing to advocate woman suffrage because of women's recent "strides...in the acquirement of business methods, in the management of their affairs, in the effective interest they have evinced in civic affairs."[7]

Suffragists like Jacobi and Sage characteristically conflated their class perspective with the role they saw for themselves as women, contending for political leadership not so much on the grounds of their wealth, as of their womanliness. Women, they argued, had the characteristics needed in politics—benevolence, morality, selflessness, and industry; conveniently, they believed that elite women most fully embodied these virtues. Indeed, they liked to believe that women like themselves were elite *because* they were virtuous, not because they were wealthy. The confusion of class and gender coincided with a more general elite ideology that identified the fundamental division in American society not between rich and poor, but between industrious and idle, virtuous and vicious, community-minded and selfish. On these grounds Sage found the purposeless leisure of wealthy women dangerous to the body politic. She believed firmly that the elite, women included, should provide moral—and ultimately political—leadership, but it was important to her that they earn the right to lead.[8]

The problem for elite suffragists was that woman suffrage meant the enfranchisement of working-class, as well as elite, women. Jacobi described a prominent woman who "had interested herself nobly and effectively in public affairs,...but preferred not to claim the right [of suffrage] for herself, lest its concession entail the enfranchisement of ignorant and irresponsible women." An elite anti-suffrage organization committed to such views was active in the 1894 campaign as well, led by women of the same class, with many of the same beliefs, as the pro-suffrage movement. As Stanton wrote, "The fashionable women are about equally divided between two camps." The antis included prominent society figures Abby Hamlin (Mrs. Lyman) Abbott and Josephine Jewell (Mrs. Arthur) Dodge, as well as Annie Nathan Meyer, founder of Barnard College and member of the Consumers League. Like the elite suffragists, upperclass antis wanted to insure greater elite influence in politics; but they argued that woman suffrage would decrease elite influence, rather than enhance it.[9]

Elite suffragists' willingness to support woman suffrage rested on their confidence that their class would provide political leadership for all women once they had the vote. Because they expected working-class women to defer to them, they believed that class relations among women would be more cooperative and less antagonistic than among men. Elite women, Jacobi argued before the 1894 convention, would "so guide ignorant women voters that they could be made to counterbalance, when necessary, the votes of ignorant and interested men." Such suffragists assumed that working-class women were too weak, timid, and disorganized to make their own demands. Since early in the nineteenth century, elite women had claimed social and religious authority on the grounds of their responsibility for the women and children of the poor. They had begun to adapt this tradition to the new conditions of an industrial age, notably in the Consumers League, formed in response to the pleas of women wage earners for improvement in their working conditions. In fact, elite antis also asserted that they spoke for working-class women, but they contended that working-class women neither needed nor wanted the vote.[10]

From an exclusively elite perspective, the anti-suffrage argument was more consistent than the pro-suffrage one; woman suffrage undoubtedly meant greater political democracy, which the political reform movement of the 1890s most fundamentally feared. Elite suffragists found themselves organizing their own arguments around weak refutations of the antis' objections.[11] The ideological weakness had political implications. Woman suffrage got no serious hearing in the constitutional convention, and the 1894 constitutional revisions designed to "clean up government" ignored women's plea for political equality.

The episode revealed dilemmas, especially with respect to class relations among women, that a successful suffrage movement would have to address. Elite women had begun to aspire to political roles that led them to support woman suffrage, and the resources they commanded would be crucial to the future success of suffrage efforts. But their attraction to woman suffrage rested on a portrait of working-class women and a system of class relations that had become problematic to a modern industrial society. Could elite women sponsor the entrance of working-class women into politics without risking their influence over them, and perhaps their position of leadership? Might not working-class women assume a newly active, politically autonomous role? The tradition of class relations among women had to be transformed before a thriving and modern woman suffrage movement could be built. Harriot Stanton Blatch had the combination of suffrage convictions and class awareness to lead New York suffragists through that transition.

Bringing Working Women Into Suffragism

The 1894 campaign, which confronted suffragists with the issue of class, also drew Blatch actively into the American woman suffrage movement. She had come back from England, where she had lived for many years, to receive a master's degree from Vassar College for her study of the English rural poor. A powerful orator, she was "immediately pressed into service...speaking every day" at parlor suffrage meetings, often to replace her aged mother.[12] Like her mother, Blatch was comfortable in upper-class circles; she had married into a wealthy British family. She generally shared the elite perspective of the campaign, assuming that "educated women" would lead their sex. But she disliked the implication that politics could ever become too democratic and, virtually alone among the suffragists, criticized all "those little anti-republican things I hear so often here in America, this talk of the quality of votes." And while other elite suffragists discussed working-class women as domestic servants and shop clerks, Blatch understood the centrality of industrial workers, although her knowledge of them was still primarily academic.[13]

Blatch's disagreements with the elite suffrage framework were highlighted a few months after the constitutional convention in an extraordinary public debate with her mother. In *The Woman's Journal*, Stanton urged that the suffrage movement incorporate an educational restriction into its demand, to respond to "the greatest block in the way of woman's enfranchisement...the fear of the 'ignorant vote' being doubled." Her justification for this position, so at odds with the principles of a lifetime, was that the enfranchisement of "educated women" best supplied "the imperative need at the time...woman's influence in public life." From England, Blatch wrote a powerful dissent. Challenging the authority of her venerated mother was a dramatic act that—perhaps deliberately—marked the end of her political daughterhood. She defended both the need and the capacity of the working class to engage in democratic politics. On important questions, "for example...the housing of the poor," their opinion was more informed than that of the elite. She also argued that since "the conditions of the poor are so much harder...every working man needs the suffrage more than I do." And finally, she insisted on the claims of a group her mother had ignored, working women.[14]

The debate between mother and daughter elegantly symbolizes the degree to which class threatened the continued vitality of the republican tradition of suffragism. Blatch was able to adapt the republican faith to modern class relations, while Stanton was not, partly because of Blatch's participation in the British social democratic movement known as Fabianism. As a Fabian, Blatch had gained an appreciation for the political intelligence and power of the working class very rare among elite reformers in the United States. When she insisted that the spirit of democracy was more alive in England than in the United States, she was undoubtedly thinking of the development of a working-class political movement there.[15]

Over the next few years, Blatch explored basic assumptions of the woman suffrage faith she had inherited in the context of modern class relations. In the process, like other women reformers of her era, such as Charlotte Perkins Gilman, Florence Kelley, Jane Addams, and numerous settlement house residents and supporters of organized labor, she focused on the relation of women and work. She emphasized the productive labor that women performed, both as it contributed to the larger social good and as it created the conditions of freedom and equality for women themselves.

Women had always worked, she insisted. The new factor was the shift of women's work from the home to the factory and the office, and from the status of unpaid to paid labor. Sometimes she stressed that women's unpaid domestic labor made an important contribution to society; at other times she stressed that such unpaid work was not valued, but always she emphasized the historical development that was taking women's labor out of the home and into the commercial economy. The question for modern society was not whether women should work, but under what conditions, and with what consequences for their own lives.[16]

Although Blatch was troubled by the wages and working conditions of the laboring poor, her emphasis on work as a means to emancipation led her to regard wage-earning women less as victims to be succored, than as exemplars to their sex. She vigorously denied that women ideally hovered somewhere above the world of work. She had no respect for the "handful of rich women who have no employment other than organizing servants, social functions and charities." Upper-class women, she believed, should also "work," should make an individualized contribution to the public good, and where possible should have the value of their labor recognized by being paid for it.[17] As a member of the first generation of college-educated women she believed that education and professional achievement, rather than wealth and refinement, fitted a woman for social leadership.

Turning away from nineteenth-century definitions of the unity of women that emphasized their place in the home, their motherhood, and their exclusion from the economy, and emphasizing instead the unity that productive work provided for all women, Blatch rewrote feminism in its essentially modern form, around

A New York City suffrage parade, c. 1912
SCHLESINGER LIBRARY, RADCLIFFE INSTITUTE, HARVARD UNIVERSITY

work. She tended to see women's work, including homemaking and child rearing, as a mammoth portion of the world's productive labor, which women collectively accomplished. Thus she retained the concept of "women's work" for the sex as a whole, while vigorously discarding it on the individual level, explicitly challenging the notion that all women had the same tastes and talents.[18]

Her approach to "women's work" led Blatch to believe that the interconnection of women's labor fundamentally shaped relations among them. Here were the most critical aspects of her thought. Much as she admired professional women, she insisted that they recognize the degree to which their success rested on the labor of other women, who cared for their homes and their children. "Whatever merit [their homes] possess," Blatch wrote, "is largely due to the fact that the actress when on the stage, the doctor when by her patient's side, the writer when at her desk, has a Bridget to do the homebuilding for her." The problem was that the professional woman's labor brought her so much more freedom than the housemaid's labor brought her. "Side by side with the marked improvement in the condition of the well-to-do or educated woman," Blatch observed, "our century shows little or no progress in the condition of the woman of the people." Like her friend Gilman, Blatch urged that professional standards of work—good pay, an emphasis on expertise, the assumption of a lifelong career—be extended to the nurserymaid and the dressmaker, as well as to the lawyer and the journalist. Until such time, the "movement for the emancipation of women [would] remain…a well-dressed movement."[19]

But professional training and better wages alone would not give labor an emancipatory power in the lives of working-class women. Blatch recognized the core of the problem of women's work, especially for working-class women: "How can the duties of mother and wage earner be reconciled?" She believed that wage-earning women had the same desire as professional women to continue to enjoy careers and independence after marriage. "It may be perverse in lowly wage earners to show individuality as if they were rich," Blatch wrote, "but apparently we shall have to accept the fact that all women do not prefer domestic work to all other kinds." But the problem of balancing a career and a homelife was "insoluble—under present conditions—for the women of the people." "The pivotal question for women," she wrote, "is how to organize their work as home-builders and race-builders, how to get that work paid for not in so called protection, but in the currency of the state."[20]

As the female labor force grew in the late nineteenth century, so did the number of married women workers and demands that they be driven from the labor force. The suffrage movement had traditionally avoided the conflict between work and motherhood by pinning the demand for economic equality on the existence of unmarried women, who had no men to support them. Blatch confronted the problem of work and motherhood more directly. In a 1905 article, she drew from the utopian ideas of William Morris to recommend that married women work in small, worker-owned manufacturing shops where they could have more control over their hours and could bring their children with them. Elsewhere, she argued that the workplace should be reorganized around women's needs, rather than assume the male worker's standards, but she did not specify what that would mean. She never solved the riddle of work and children for women—nor have we—but she knew that the solution could not be to force women to choose between the two nor to banish mothers from the labor force.[21]

Blatch's vision of women in industrial society was democratic—all must work and all must be recognized and rewarded for their work—but it was not an egalitarian approach nor one that recognized most working women's material concerns. According to Blatch, women worked for psychological and ethical reasons, as much as for monetary ones. "As human beings we must have work," she wrote; "we rust out if we have not an opportunity to function on something." She emphasized the common promises and problems work raised in women's lives, not the differences in how they worked, how much individual choice they had, and especially in how much they were paid. She was relatively unconcerned with the way work enabled women to earn their livings. No doubt, her own experience partially explains this. As a young woman fresh out of college in the 1870s, she had dared to imagine that her desire for meaningful work and a role in the world need not deprive her of marriage and motherhood, and it did not. Despite her marriage, the birth of two children, and the death of one, she never interrupted her political and intellectual labors. But she also never earned her own living, depending instead on the income from her husband's family's business. In later years, she joked about the fact that she was the only "parasite" in the organization of self-supporting women she headed.[22]

But the contradictions in her analysis of the problem of work and women reflected more than her personal situation. There were two problems of work and women: the long-standing exploitation of laboring women of the working classes and the newly expanding place of paid labor in the lives of all women in bourgeois society. While the two processes were not the same, they were related, and women thinkers and activists of the Progressive period struggled to understand how. As more women worked for pay and outside of the home, how would the meaning of "womanhood" change? What would be the difference between "woman" and "man" when as many women as men were paid workers? And what would be the class differences between women if all of them worked? Indeed, would there be any difference between the classes at all, once the woman of leisure no longer existed? Virtually all the efforts to link the gender and class problems of work for woman were incomplete.

Blatch rethought the principles of political equality in the light of her emphasis on women's work. At an 1898 congressional hearing, Blatch hailed "the most convincing argument upon which our future claims must rest—the growing recognition of the economic value of the work of women."[23] Whereas her mother had based her suffragism on the nineteenth-century argument for natural rights and on the individual, Blatch based hers on women's economic contribution and their significance as a group.

The contradictions in Blatch's approach to women and work also emerged in her attempts to link work and the vote. On the one hand, she approached women's political rights as she did their economic emancipation, democratically: Just as all sorts of women must work, all needed the vote. Wealthy women needed the vote because they were taxpayers and had the right to see that their money was not squandered; women industrial workers needed it because their jobs and factories were subject to laws, which they had the right to shape. On the other hand, she recognized the strategic centrality of the enormous class of industrial workers, whose economic role was so important and whose political power was potentially so great. "It is the women of the industrial class," she explained, "the wage-earners, reckoned by the hundreds of thousands,...the women whose work has been submitted to a money test, who have been the means of bringing about the altered attitude of public opinion toward woman's work in every sphere of life."[24]

New York City and Political Reform

Blatch returned to New York for several extended visits after 1894, and she moved back for good in 1902. She had two purposes. Elizabeth Stanton was dying, and Blatch had come to be with her. Blatch also intended to take a leading role in the New York City suffrage movement. On her deathbed in 1902, Stanton asked Anthony to aid Blatch. However, hampered by Anthony's determination to keep control of the movement, Blatch was not able to make her bid for suffrage leadership until Anthony died, four years later.[25]

Meanwhile, Blatch was excited by other reform efforts, which were beginning to provide the resources for a new kind of suffrage movement. During the first years of the twentieth century two movements contributed to Blatch's political education—a broadened, less socially exclusive campaign against political corruption and a democratized movement for the welfare of working women. By 1907, her combined experience in these two movements enabled her to put her ideas about women and work into practice within the suffrage movement itself.

Women had become more active in the campaign against political corruption after 1894. In New York City Josephine Shaw Lowell and Mary Putnam Jacobi formed the Woman's Municipal League, which concentrated on educating the public about corruption, in particular the links between the police and organized prostitution. Women were conspicuous in the reform campaigns of Seth Low, who was elected mayor in 1901.[26]

By the early 1900s, moreover, the spirit of political reform in New York City had spread beyond the elite. A left wing of the political reform movement had developed that charged that "Wall Street" was more responsible for political corruption than "the Bowery." Women were active in this wing, and there were women's political organizations with links to the Democratic party and the labor movement, a Women's Henry George Society, and a female wing of William Randolph Hearst's Independence League. The non-elite women in these groups were as politically enthusiastic as the members of the Woman's Municipal League, and considerably less ambivalent about enlarging the electorate. Many of them strongly supported woman suffrage. Beginning in 1905, a group of them organized an Equal Rights League to sponsor mock polling places for women to register their political opinions on election day.[27]

Through the 1900s Blatch dutifully attended suffrage meetings, and without much excitement advocated the municipal suffrage for propertied women favored by the New York movement's leaders after their 1894 defeat. Like many other politically minded women, however, she found her enthusiasm caught by the movement for municipal political reform. She supported Low for mayor in 1901 and believed that his victory demonstrated "how strong woman's power really was when it was aroused." By 1903 she suggested to the National American Woman Suffrage Association (NAWSA) that it set aside agitation for the vote, so that "the women of the organization should use it for one year, nationally and locally, to pursue and punish corruption in politics." She supported the increasing attention given to "the laboring man" in reform political coalitions, but she pointedly observed that "the working woman was never considered."[28]

However, working-class women were emerging as active factors in other women's reform organizations. The crucial arena for this development was the Women's Trade Union League (WTUL), formed in 1902 by a coalition of working-class and elite women to draw wage-earning women into trade unions. The New York chapter was formed in 1905, and Blatch was one of the first elite women to join. The WTUL represented a significant move away from the tradition of elite, ameliorative sisterhood at work in the 1894 campaign for woman suffrage. Like the Consumers League, it had been formed in response to the request of women wage earners for aid from elite women, but it was an organization of both classes working together. Blatch had never been attracted to the strictly ameliorative tradition of women's reform, and the shift toward a partnership of upper-class and working-class women paralleled her own thinking about the relation between the classes and the role of work in women's lives. She and other elite women in the WTUL found themselves laboring not for working-class women, but with them, and toward a goal of forming unions that did not merely "uplift" working-class women, but empowered them. Instead of being working-class women's protectors, they were their "allies." Instead of speaking on behalf of poor women, they began to hear them speak for themselves. Within the organization wage earners were frequently in conflict with allies. Nonetheless, the league provided them an arena to articulate a working-class feminism related to, but distinct from, that of elite women.[29]

Rose Schneiderman speaking
at a union rally, c. 1910s

BROWN BROTHERS, JEWISH WOMEN ARCHIVES

Although prominent as a suffragist, Blatch participated in the WTUL on its own terms, rather than as a colonizer for suffrage. She and two other members assigned to the millinery trade conducted investigations into conditions and organized mass meetings to interest women workers in unions. She sat on the Executive Council from 1906 through 1909 and was often called on to stand in for President Mary Dreier. Her academic knowledge of "the industrial woman" was replaced by direct knowledge of wage-earning women and their working conditions. She was impressed with what she saw of trade unionism, especially its unrelenting "militance." Perhaps most important, she developed working relations with politically sophisticated working-class women, notably Leonora O'Reilly and Rose Schneiderman. Increasingly she believed that the organized power of labor and the enfranchisement of women were closely allied.[30]

Working-class feminists in the league were drawn to ideas like Blatch's—to conceptions of dignity and equality for women in the workplace and to the ethic of self-support and lifelong independence; they wanted to upgrade the condition of wage-earning women so that they, too, could enjoy personal independence on the basis of their labor. On the one hand, they understood why most working-class women would want to leave their hateful jobs upon marriage; on the other, they knew that women as a group, if not the individual worker, were a permanent factor in the modern labor force. Mary Kenney O'Sullivan of Boston, one of the league's founders, believed that "self support" was a goal for working-class women, but that only trade unions would give the masses of working women the "courage, independence, and self respect" they needed to improve their conditions. She expected "women of opportunity" to help in organizing women workers, because they "owed much to workers who give them a large part of what they have and enjoy," and because "the time has passed when women of opportunity can be self respecting and work *for* others."[31]

Initially, the demand for the vote was less important to such working-class feminists than to the allies. Still, as they began to participate in the organized women's movement on a more equal basis, wage-earning women began to receive serious attention within the woman suffrage movement as well. Beginning about 1905, advocates of trade unionism and the vote for women linked the demands. At the 1906 suffrage convention WTUL member Gertrude Barnum pointed out that "our hope as suffragists lies with these strong working women." Kelley and

Addams wrote about the working woman's need for the vote to improve her own conditions. In New York, Blatch called on the established suffrage societies to recognize the importance of the vote to wage-earning women and the importance of wage-earning women to winning the vote. When she realized that existing groups could not adapt to the new challenges, she moved to form her own society.[32]

The Equality League of Self-Supporting Women

In January 1907 Blatch declared the formation of a new suffrage organization, the Equality League of Self-Supporting Women. The *New York Times* reported that the two hundred women present at the first meeting included "doctors, lawyers, milliners and shirtmakers."[33] Blatch's decision to establish a suffrage organization that emphasized female "Self-support"—lifelong economic independence—grew out of her ideas about work as the basis of women's claim on the state, the leadership role that she envisioned for educated professionals, and her discovery of the power and political capacity of trade-union women. The Equality League provided the medium for introducing a new and aggressive style of activism into the suffrage movement—a version of the "militance" Blatch admired among trade unionists.

Initially, Blatch envisioned the Equality League of Self-Supporting Women as the political wing of the Women's Trade Union League. All the industrial workers she recruited were WTUL activists, including O'Reilly, the Equality League's first vice president, and Schneiderman, its most popular speaker. To welcome working-class women, the Equality League virtually abolished membership fees; the policy had the added advantage of allowing Blatch to claim every woman who ever attended a league meeting in her estimate of its membership. She also claimed the members of the several trade unions affiliated with the Equality League, such as the bookbinders, overall makers, and cap makers, so that when she went before the New York legislature to demand the vote, she could say that the Equality League represented thousands of wage-earning women.[34]

Blatch wanted the Equality League to connect industrial workers, not with "club women" (her phrase), but with educated, professional workers, who should, she thought, replace benevolent ladies as the leaders of their sex. Such professionals—college educated and often women pioneers in their professions—formed the bulk of the Equality League's active membership. Many were lawyers, for instance, Ida Rauh, Helen Hoy, Madeleine Doty, Jessie Ashley, Adelma Burd, and Bertha Rembaugh. Others were social welfare workers, for instance the Equality League's treasurer, Kate Claghorn, a tenement housing inspector and the highest paid female employee of the New York City government. Blatch's own daughter, Nora, the first woman graduate civil engineer in the United States, worked in the New York City Department of Public Works. Many of these women had inherited incomes and did not work out of economic need, but out of a desire to give serious, public substance to their lives and to make an impact on society. Many of them expressed the determination to maintain economic independence after they married.[35]

Although Blatch brought together trade-union women and college-educated professionals in the Equality League, there were tensions between the classes. The first correspondence between O'Reilly and Barnard graduate Caroline Lexow was full of class suspicion and mutual recrimination. More generally, there were real differences in how and why the two classes of working women demanded the vote. Trade-union feminists wanted the vote so that women industrial workers would have power over the labor laws that directly affected their working lives. Many of the college-educated self-supporters were the designers and administrators of this labor legislation. Several of them were, or aspired to be, government employees, and political power affected their jobs through party patronage. The occupation that might have bridged the differences was teaching. As in other cities, women teachers in New York organized for greater power and equal pay. The Equality League frequently offered aid, but the New York teachers' leaders were relatively conservative and kept their distance from the suffrage movement.[36]

Blatch's special contribution was her understanding of the bonds and common interests uniting industrial and professional women workers. The industrial women admired the professional ethic, if not the striving careerism, of the educated working women, and the professionals admired the matter-of-fact way wage-earning women went out to work. The fate of the professional woman was closely tied to that of the industrial worker; the cultural regard in which all working women were held affected both. Blatch dramatized that tie when she was refused service at a restaurant because she was unescorted by a man (that is, because she was eating with a woman). The management claimed that its policy aimed to protect "respectable" women, like Blatch, from "objectionable" women, like the common woman worker who went about on her own, whose morals were therefore questionable. Blatch rejected the division between respectable women and working women, pointing out that "there are five million women earning their livelihood in this country, and it seems strange that feudal customs should still exist here."[37]

The dilemma of economically dependent married women was crucial to the future of both classes of working women. Blatch believed that if work was to free women, they could not leave it for dependence on men in marriage. The professional and working-class members of the Equality League shared this belief, one of the distinguishing convictions of their new approach to suffragism. In 1908, Blatch and Mary Dreier chaired a debate about the housewife, sponsored by the WTUL and attended by many Equality League members. Charlotte Perkins Gilman took the Equality League position, that the unemployed wife was a "parasite" on her husband, and that all women, married as well as unmarried, should work, "like every other self-respecting being." Anna Howard Shaw argued that women's domestic labor was valuable, even if unpaid, and that the husband was dependent on his wife. A large audience attended, and although they "warmly applauded" Gilman, they preferred Shaw's sentimental construction of the economics of marriage.[38]

A month after the Equality League was formed, Blatch arranged for trade-union women to testify before the New York legislature on behalf of woman suffrage, the first working-class women ever to do so. The New York Woman Suffrage Association was still concentrating on the limited, property-based form of municipal suffrage; in lethargic testimony its leaders admitted that they had "no new arguments to present." Everyone at the hearing agreed that the antis had the better of the argument. The Equality League testimony the next day was in sharp contrast. Clara Silver and Mary Duffy, WTUL activists and organizers in the garment industry, supported full suffrage for all New York women. The very presence of these women before the legislature, and their dignity and intelligence, countered the antis' dire predictions about enfranchising the unfit. Both linked suffrage to their trade-union efforts: While they struggled for equality in unions and in industry, "the state" undermined them, by teaching the lesson of female inferiority to male unionists and bosses. "To be left out by the State just sets up a prejudice against us," Silver explained. "Bosses think and women come to think themselves that they don't count for so much as men."[39]

The formation of the Equality League and its appearance before the New York legislature awakened enthusiasm. Lillie Devereux Blake, whose own suffrage group had tried "one whole Winter…to [interest] the working women" but found that they were "so overworked and so poor that they can do little for us," congratulated Blatch on her apparent success. Helen Marot, organizing secretary for the New York WTUL, praised the Equality League for "realizing the increasing necessity of including working women in the suffrage movement." Blatch, O'Reilly, and Schneiderman were the star speakers at the 1907 New York suffrage convention. "We realize that probably it will not be the educated workers, the college women, the men's association for equal suffrage, but the people who are fighting for industrial freedom who will be our vital force at the finish," proclaimed the newsletter of the NAWSA.[40]

Militance for American Suffragists

The unique class character of the Equality League encouraged the development of a new style of agitation, more radical than anything practiced in the suffrage movement since…since Elizabeth Stanton's prime. The immediate source of the change was the Women's Social and Political Union of England (WSPU), led by Blatch's comrade from her Fabian days, Emmeline Pankhurst. Members of the WSPU were just beginning to be arrested for their suffrage protests. At the end of the Equality League's first year, Blatch invited one of the first WSPU prisoners, Anne Cobden-Sanderson, daughter of Richard Cobden, to the United States to tell about her experiences, scoring a coup for the Equality League. By emphasizing Cobden-Sanderson's connection with the British Labour party and distributing free platform tickets to trade-union leaders, Blatch was able to get an overflow crowd at Cooper Union, Manhattan's labor temple, two-thirds of them men, many of them trade unionists.[41]

A crowd gathers to hear speeches from a group of New York suffragists who admired the British militants and adopted the name "American Suffragettes."
LIBRARY OF CONGRESS

The Equality League's meeting for Cobden-Sanderson offered American audiences their first account of the new radicalism of English suffragists, or as they were beginning to be called, suffragettes. Cobden-Sanderson emphasized the suffragettes' working-class origins. She attributed the revival of the British suffrage movement to Lancashire factory workers; the heroic figure in her account was the working-class suffragette, Annie Kenney, while Christabel Pankhurst, later canonized as the Joan of Arc of British militancy went unnamed. After women factory workers were arrested for trying to see the prime minister, Cobden-Sanderson and other privileged women, who felt they "had not so much to lose as [the workers] had," decided to join them and get arrested. She spent almost two months in jail, living the life of a common prisoner and coming to a new awareness of the poor and suffering women she saw there. Her simple but moving account conveyed the transcendent impact of the experience.[42]

Cobden-Sanderson's visit to New York catalyzed a great outburst of suffrage energy; in its wake, Blatch and a handful of other new leaders introduced the WSPU tactics into the American movement, and the word suffragette became as common in New York as in London. The "militants" became an increasingly distinct wing of the movement in New York and other American cities. But it would be too simple to say that the British example caused the new, more militant phase in the American movement. The developments that were broadening the class basis and the outlook of American suffragism had prepared American women to respond to the heroism of the British militants.[43]

The development of militance in the American suffrage movement was marked by new aggressive tactics practiced by the WSPU, especially open-air meetings and outdoor parades. At this stage in the development of British militance American suffragists generally admired the heroism of the WSPU martyrs. Therefore, although the press emphasized dissent within the suffrage movement—it always organized its coverage of suffrage around female rivalries of some sort—the new militant activities were well received throughout the movement. And, conversely, even the most daring American suffragettes believed in an American exceptionalism that made it unnecessary to contemplate going to prison, to suffer as did the British militants.[44]

Despite Blatch's later claims, she did not actually introduce the new tactics in New York City. The first open-air meetings were organized immediately after the Cobden-Sanderson visit by a group called the American Suffragettes. Initiated by Bettina Borrmann Wells, a visiting member of the WSPU, most of the American Suffragettes' membership came from the Equal Rights League, the left-wing municipal reform group that had organized mock polling places in New York since 1905. Feminist egalitarians with radical cultural leanings, its members were actresses, artists, writers, teachers, and social welfare workers—less wealthy versions of the professional self-supporters in the Equality League. Their local leader was a librarian, Maud Malone, whose role in encouraging new suffrage tactics was almost as important as, although less recognized than, Blatch's own.[45]

The American Suffragettes held their first open-air meeting in Madison Square on New Year's Eve, 1907. After that they met in the open at least once a week. Six weeks later, they announced they would hold New York's first all-woman parade. Denied a police permit, they determined to march anyway. The twenty-three women in the "parade" were many times outnumbered by the onlookers, mostly working-class men. In a public school to which they adjourned to make speeches, the American Suffragettes told a sympathetic audience that "the woman who works is the underdog of the world"; thus she needed the vote to defend herself. Socialists and working women rose from the floor to support them. Two years later the Equality League organized a much more successful suffrage parade in New York. Several hundred suffragettes, organized by occupation, marched from Fifty-ninth Street to Union Square. O'Reilly, the featured speaker, made "a tearful plea on behalf of the working girl that drew the first big demonstration of applause from the street crowd."[46]

Perhaps because the American Suffragettes were so active in New York City, Blatch held the Equality League's first open-air meetings in May 1908 upstate. Accompanied by Maud Malone, she organized an inventive "trolley car campaign" between Syracuse and Albany, using the interurban trolleys to go from town to town. The audiences expressed the complex class character of the suffrage movement at that moment. In Syracuse Blatch had her wealthy friend Dora Hazard arrange a meeting among the workers at her husband's factory. She also held a successful outdoor meeting in Troy, home of the Laundry Workers'

Union, one of the oldest and most militant independent women's trade unions in the country. Albany was an anti-suffrage stronghold, and its mayor tried to prevent the meeting; but Blatch outwitted him. The highlight of the tour was in Poughkeepsie, where Blatch and Inez Milholland, then a student at Vassar College, organized a legendary meeting. Since Vassar's male president forbade any woman suffrage activities on college grounds, Blatch and Milholland defiantly announced they would meet students in a cemetery. Charlotte Perkins Gilman, who was extremely popular among college women, spoke, but it was the passionate trade-union feminist, Rose Schneiderman, who was the star.[47]

Blatch believed that the first function of militant tactics was to gain much-needed publicity for the movement. The mainstream press had long ignored suffrage activities. If an occasional meeting was reported, it was usually buried in a small back-page article, focusing on the absurdity and incompetence of women's efforts to organize a political campaign. Gilded Age suffragists themselves accepted the Victorian convention that respectable women did not court public attention. The Equality League's emphasis on the importance of paid labor for women of all classes struck at the heart of that convention. Blatch understood "the value of publicity or rather the harm of the lack of it." She encouraged open-air meetings and trolley car campaigns because they generated much publicity, which no longer held the conventional horror for her followers.[48]

Militant tactics broke through the "press boycott" by violating standards of respectable femininity, making the cause newsworthy, and embracing the subsequent ridicule and attention. "We…believe in standing on street corners and fighting our way to recognition, forcing the men to think about us," an *American Suffragette* manifesto proclaimed. "We glory…that we are theatrical." The militant pursuit of publicity was an instant success: Newspaper coverage increased immediately; by 1908 even the sneering *New York Times* reported regularly on suffrage. The more outrageous or controversial the event, the more prominent the coverage. Blatch was often pictured and quoted.[49]

The new methods had a second function; they intensified women's commitment to the movement. Militants expected that overstepping the boundary of respectability would etch suffrage beliefs on women's souls, beyond retraction or modification. Blatch caught the psychology of this process. "Society has taught women self sacrifice and now this force is to be drawn upon in the arduous campaign for their own emancipation," she wrote. "The new methods of agitation, in that they are difficult and disagreeable, lay hold of the imagination and devotion of women, wherein lies the strength of the new appeal, the certainty of victory." Borrmann Wells spoke of the "divine spirit of self-sacrifice" which underlay the suffragette's transgressions against respectability and was the source of the "true inwardness of the movement."[50]

If suffrage militants had a general goal beyond getting the vote, it was to challenge existing standards of femininity. "We must eliminate that abominable

Margaret Hinchey, head of the Laundry Workers Union of N.Y., leads union women in parade, 1914. LIBRARY OF CONGRESS

word ladylike from our vocabularies," Borrmann Wells proclaimed. "We must get out and fight." The new definition of femininity the militants were evolving drew, on the one hand, on traditionally male behaviors, like aggression, fighting, provocation, and rebelliousness. Blatch was particularly drawn to the "virile" world of politics, which she characterized as a male "sport" she was sure she could master. On the other hand, they undertook a spirited defense of female sexuality, denying that it need be forfeited by women who participated vigorously in public life. "Women are no longer to be considered little tootsey wootseys who have nothing to do but look pretty," suffragette Lydia Commander declared. "They are determined to take an active part in the community and look pretty too." A member of a slightly older generation, Blatch never adopted the modern sexual ethic of the new woman, but she constantly emphasized the fact that women had distinct concerns that had to be accommodated in politics and industry. These two notes—the difference of the sexes and the repressed ability of women for manly activities—existed side by side in the thought of all the suffrage insurgents.[51]

The militant methods, taking suffrage out of the parlors and into the streets, indicated the new significance of working-class women in several ways. Blatch pointed out that the new methods—open-air meetings, newspaper publicity—suited a movement whose members had little money and therefore could not afford to rent halls or publish a newspaper. As a style of protest, "militance" was an import from the labor movement; WTUL organizers had been speaking from street corners for several years. And disrespect for the standards of ladylike respectability showed at least an impatience with rigid standards of class distinction, at most the influence of class-conscious wage-earning women.[52]

Working-class feminists were eager to speak from the militants' platform, as were many Socialists. A Socialist cadre, Dr. Anna Mercy, organized a branch of the

American Suffragettes on the Lower East Side, which issued the first suffrage leaflets ever published in Yiddish. Militants also prepared propaganda in German and Italian and, in general, pursued working-class audiences. "Our relation to the State will be determined by the vote of the average man," Blatch asserted. "None but the converted...will come to us. We must seek on the highways the unconverted."[53]

Shoulder to Shoulder for Woman Suffrage

However, it would be a mistake to confuse the suffragettes' radicalism with the radicalism of a working-class movement. The ultimate goal of the suffragettes was not a single-class movement, but a universal one, "the union of women of all shades of political thought and of all ranks of society on the single issue of their political enfranchisement." While the Equality League's 1907 hearing before the state legislature highlighted trade-union suffragists, at the 1908 hearing the league also featured elite speakers, in effect de-emphasizing the working-class perspective.[54] Militants could neither repudiate the Socialist support they were attracting, and alienate working-class women, nor associate too closely with Socialists and lose access to the wealthy. Blatch—who actually became a Socialist after the suffrage was won—would not arrange for the Socialist party leader Morris Hillquit to join other pro-suffrage speakers at the 1908 legislative hearing. Similarly, the American Suffragettes allowed individual Socialists on their platform but barred Socialist propaganda. Speaking for Socialist women who found the "idea of a 'radical' suffrage movement...very alluring," Josephine Conger Kaneko admitted that the suffragettes left her confused.[55]

Moreover, the militant challenge to femininity and the emphasis on publicity introduced a distinctly elite bias; a society matron on an open-air platform made page one while a working girl did not, because society women were obliged by conventions and could outrage by flouting them. In their very desire to redefine femininity, the militants were anxious to stake their claim to it, and it was upper-class women who determined femininity. In Elizabeth Robin's drama about the rise of militance in the British suffrage movement, *The Convert*, the heroine of the title was a beautiful aristocratic woman who became radical when she realized the emptiness of her ladylike existence and the contempt for women obscured by gentlemen's chivalrous gestures. The Equality League brought *The Convert* to New York in 1908 as its first large fund-raising effort; working-class women, as well as elite women, made up the audience. Malone was one of the few militants to recognize and to protest against excessive solicitousness for the elite convert. She resigned from the American Suffragettes when she concluded that they had become interested in attracting "a well-dressed crowd, not the rabble."[56]

Blatch's perspective and associations had always been fundamentally elite. The most well connected of the new militant leaders, she played a major role in bringing the new suffrage propaganda to the attention of upper-class women. She presided over street meetings in fashionable neighborhoods, where reporters commented on the "smart" crowds and described the speakers' outfits in society-page detail. Blatch's first important ally from New York's social leaders (the "Four Hundred") was Katherine Duer Mackay, wife of the founder of the International Telephone and Telegraph Company and a famous society beauty. Mackay's suffragism was very ladylike, but other members of her set who followed her into the movement were more drawn to militancy. Alva Belmont, a veritable mistress of flamboyance, began her suffrage career as Mackay's protégée. The elitist subtext of militance was a minor theme in 1908 and 1909. But by 1910 becoming a suffragette was proving "fashionable," and upper-class women began to identify with the new suffrage style in significant numbers. By the time suffragette militance became a national movement, its working-class origins and trade-union associations had been submerged, and it was in the hands of women of wealth.[57]

From the beginning, though, class was the contradiction at the suffrage movement's heart. In the campaign of 1894, elite women began to pursue more power for themselves by advocating the suffrage in the name of all women. When Cobden-Sanderson spoke for the Equality League at Cooper Union in 1907, she criticized "idle women of wealth" as the enemies of woman suffrage, and she was wildly applauded. But what did her charge mean? Were all rich women under indictment, or only those who stayed aloof from social responsibility and political activism? Were the militants calling for working-class leadership of the suffrage movement or for cultural changes in bourgeois definitions of womanhood? This ambiguity paralleled the mixed meanings in Blatch's emphasis on working women; it coincided with an implicit tension between the older, elite women's reform traditions and the newer trade-union politics they had helped to usher in; and it was related to a lurking confusion about whether feminism's object was the superfluity of wealthy women or the exploitation of the poor. It would continue to plague suffragism in its final decade, and feminism afterwards, into our own time.

Notes

This essay is an abridged version of the essay by the same title that appeared in the *Journal of American History*, 74 (1987), 34-58, and is printed here with the permission of the journal. The author wishes to thank the Papers of Elizabeth Cady Stanton and Susan B. Anthony, University of Massachusetts, Amherst, for providing generous research assistance.

1. "Mrs. Blatch's Address," clipping, 1903, Women's Club of Orange, N.J., Scrapbooks, v. 4 (New Jersey Historical Society, Trenton). Thanks to Gail Malmgreen for this citation.

2. Richard L. McCormick, *From Realignment to Reform: Political Change in New York State, 1893-1910*, (Ithaca, 1979), 53.

3. Susan B. Anthony and Ida Husted Harper, eds., *History of Woman Suffrage* (Rochester, 1902), 4: 847-52; New York State Woman Suffrage Party, *Record of the New York Campaign of 1894* (New York, 1895); Ida Husted Harper, *The Life and Work of Susan B. Anthony* 3 vols. (Indianapolis, 1898-1908), 2: 758-76, esp. 759.

4. Mary Putnam Jacobi, "Report of the Volunteer Committee in New York City," in *Record of the New York Campaign*, 217-20; Maud Nathan, *The Story of an Epoch-Making Movement* (Garden City, 1926); William Rhinelander Stewart, ed., *The Philanthropic Work of Josephine Shaw Lowell* (New York, 1911), 334-56.

5. *New York Times*, April 14, 1894, 2; ibid., April 15, 1894, 5 Suffrage scrapbooks, Mrs. Robert Abbe Collection (Manuscript

Division, New York Public Library). Theodore Stanton and Harriot Stanton Blatch, eds., *Elizabeth Cady Stanton As Revealed in Her Letters, Diary and Reminiscences*, 2 vols. (New York, 1922), 2: 299.

6. Mary Putnam Jacobi, "Address Delivered at the New York City Hearing," in *Record of the New York Campaign*, 17-26; Olivia Slocum Sage, "Opportunities and Responsibilities of Leisured Women," *North American Review*, 181 (Nov. 1905): 712-21.

7. Ibid.

8. Ibid.

9. Jacobi, "Report of the Volunteer Committee," 217; Stanton and Blatch, eds., *Elizabeth Cady Stanton*, 2: 305; *New York Times*, May 3, 1894, 9.

10. Jacobi, "Address Delivered at the New York City Hearing," 22; *New York Times*, April 12, 1894, 5.

11. *Woman's Journal*, May 12, 1894, 147.

12. Ibid., May 19, 1894. The study, patterned after Charles Booth and Mary Booth's investigation of the London poor, on which Blatch worked, was published as Harriot Stanton Blatch, "Another View of Village Life," *Westminster Review*, 140 (Sept. 1893): 318-24.

13. Stanton and Blatch, *Elizabeth Cady Stanton*, 11, 304: unidentified clipping, April 25, 1894, Scrapbook 20, Susan B.

Anthony Collection (Manuscript Division, Library of Congress); New York Times, April 25, 1894, 5; ibid., May 3, 1894, 9; New York Sun, April 15, 1894, n.p.

14. Woman's Journal, Nov. 3, 1894, 348-49; ibid., Dec. 22, 1894, 402; Ibid., Jan. 5, 1895, 1. Blatch wrote that her mother's position "pained" her but there is no evidence of any personal conflict between them at this time. Ibid., Dec. 22, 1894, 402.

15. Harriot Stanton Blatch and Alma Lutz, Challenging Years: The Memoirs of Harriot Stanton Blatch (New York, 1940), 77. Woman's Journal, Jan. 18, 1896, 18.

16. Woman's Journal, May 12, 1900, 146-47. Along with Blatch and Charlotte Perkins Gilman, Florence Kelley and Jane Addams were the most important figures to focus on women and class. See Charlotte Perkins Gilman, Women and Economics: A Study of the Economic Relation between Men and Women as a Factor in Social Evolution (Boston, 1898).

17. Harriot Stanton Blatch, "Specialization of Function in Women: Gunton's Magazine 10 (May 1896): 349-56, esp. 350.

18. Ibid.

19. Ibid, 354-55.

20. Blatch, "Specialization of Function in Women," 350, 353.

21. Harriot Stanton Blatch, "Weaving in a Westchester Farmhouse," International Studio, 26 (Oct. 1905): 102-5: Woman's Journal, Jan. 21, 1905; Ibid., Dec. 31, 1904, 423.

22. Blatch, "Weaving in a Westchester Farmhouse," 104; Blatch and Lutz, Challenging Years, 70-86; Rhoda Barney Jenkins interview by Ellen Carol DuBois, June 10, 1982 (in DuBois's possession); Ellen DuBois, "Spanning Two Centuries: The Autobiography of Nora Stanton Barney," History Workshop, no. 22 (Fall 1986), 131-52, esp. 149.

23. HWS 4: 311.

24. "Mrs. Blatch's Address," Women's Club of Orange, N.J., Scrapbooks; HWS 4: 311.

25. Harriot Stanton Blatch to Susan B. Anthony, Sept. 26, 1902, in Epistolary Autobiography, Theodore Stanton Collection (Douglass College Library, Rutgers University, New Brunswick, N.J.).

26. Oswald Garrison Villard, "Women in New York Municipal Campaign," Woman's Journal, March 8, 1902.

27. New York Times, Jan. 14, 1901, 7.

28. HWS 4: 861; Ida Husted Harper, ed., History of Woman Suffrage, (New York, 1922), 6: 454; New York Times, March 2, 1902, 8; Woman's Tribune, April 25, 1903, 49.

29. Minutes, March 29, 1906, reel 1, New York WTUL Papers (New York State Labor Library, New York).

30. Nancy Schrom Dye, As Equals and As Sisters: Feminism, the Labor Movement, and the Women's Trade Union of New York (Columbia, 1980), 63; Minutes, April 26, Aug. 23, 1906, New York WTUL Papers; New York Times, April 11, 1907, 8.

31. Mary Kenney O'Sullivan, "The Need of Organization among Working Women (1905)," Margaret Dreier Robins Papers (University of Florida Library, Gainesville).

32. Woman's Journal, March 17, 1906, 43; Kelley, Woman Suffrage; Jane Addams, Utilization of Women in Government, in Jane Addams: A Centennial Reader (New York, 1960), 117-18; Woman's Journal, Dec. 31, 1904, 423; "Mrs. Blatch's Address," Women's Club of Orange, N.J., Scrapbooks.

33. New York Times, Jan. 3, 1907, 6; Woman's Journal, Jan. 12, 1907, 8.

34. Progress, June 1907. Carrie Chapman Catt to Millicent Garrett Fawcett, Oct. 19, 1909, container 5, Papers of Carrie Chapman Catt (Manuscript Division, Library of Congress).

35. Woman's Journal, Aug. 17, 1907, 129. On Nora Blatch (who later called herself Nora Stanton Barney), see DuBois, "'Spanning Two Centuries,'" 131-52. Those self-supporters who, I believe, had independent incomes include Nora Blatch, Caroline Lexow, Lavinia Dock, Ida Rauh, Gertrude Barnum, Elizabeth Finnegan, and Alice Clark.

36. Caroline Lexow to Leonora O'Reilly, Jan. 3, 1908, reel 4, Leonora O'Reilly Papers (Schlesinger Library, Radcliffe College, Cambridge, Mass.); O'Reilly to Lexow, Jan. 5, 1908, ibid; Robert Doherty, "Tempest on the Hudson: The Struggle for Equal Pay for Equal Work in the New York City Public Schools, 1907-1911," Harvard Educational Quarterly 19 (Winter 1979): 413-39. The role of teachers in the twentieth-century suffrage movement is a promising area for research. For information on teachers' organizations in the Buffalo New York, suffrage movement, I am indebted to Eve S. Faber, Swarthmore College, "Suffrage in

Buffalo, 1898-1913" (unpublished paper in DuBois's possession).

37. New York Times, June 6, 1907, 1.

38. On self-support for women after marriage, see New York World, July 26, 1908, 3; and Lydia Kingsmill Commander, "The Self Supporting Woman and the Family," American Journal of Sociology, 14 (March 1909), 752-57. On the debate, see New York Times, Jan. 7, 1909, 9.

39. New York Times, Feb. 6. 1907, 6.; Harriot Stanton Blatch, ed., Two Speeches by Industrial Women (New York, 1907), esp. 8.

40. Woman's Tribune, Feb. 9, 1907, 12; Minutes, April 27, 1909, New York WTUL Papers; Progress, Nov. 1907.

41. Blatch and Lutz, Challenging Years, 100-101; Progress, Jan. 1908.

42. Woman's Journal, Dec. 28, 1907, 205, 206-7.

43. By 1908, there was a racehorse named "Suffragette," New York Evening Telegram, Sept. 16, 1908. Blatch noted that once she left England in the late 1890s, she and Emmeline Pankhurst did not communicate until 1907, after they had both taken their respective countries' suffrage movements in newly militant directions. Blatch to Christabel Pankhurst, in Christabel Pankhurst, Unshackled: How We Won the Vote (London, 1959), 30.

44. The first American arrests were not until 1917. For American suffragists' early response to the WSPU, see Woman's Journal, May 30, 1908, 87. Even Carrie Chapman Catt praised the British militants at first. Woman's Journal, Dec. 12, 1908, 199. For an example of divisive coverage by the mainstream press, see "Suffragist or Suffragettes," New York Times, Feb. 29, 1908, 6.

45. On Bettina Borrmann Wells, see A.J.R., ed., Suffrage Annual and Women's Who's Who (London, 1913), 390. Thanks to David Doughan of the Fawcett Library for this reference. The American Suffragettes found a predecessor and benefactor in seventy-five-year-old Lady Cook, formerly Tennessee Claflin, in 1909 the wife of a titled Englishman. "Our Cook Day," American Suffragette I (Nov. 1909): 1.

46. On the first open air meeting, see New York Times, Jan. 1, 1908, 16. On the parade, see ibid., Feb. 17, 1908, 7; there is also an account in Dorr, What Eight Million Women Want, 298-99; New York Evening Journal, May 21, 1910.

47. Equality League of Self-Supporting Women, Report for Year 1908-1909 (New York, 1909), 2; Blatch and Lutz, Challenging Years, 107-9. On Vassar, see also New York American, June 10, 1908.

48. Harriot Stanton Blatch, "Radical Move in Two Years," clipping, Nov. 8, 1908, suffrage scrapbooks, Abbe Collection. Blatch "starred" in a pro-suffrage movie, What Eight Million Women Want, produced in 1912. Kay Sloan, "Sexual Warfare in the Silent Cinema: Comedies and Melodramas of Woman Suffragism," American Quarterly 33 (Fall 1981): 412-36. She was also very interested in the propaganda possibilities of commercial radio, according to Lee de Forest, a pioneer of the industry who was briefly married to her daughter. Lee de Forest, Father of Radio: The Autobiography of Lee de Forest (Chicago, 1950), 248-49.

49. Mary Tyng, "Self Denial Week," American Suffragette, 1 (Aug. 1909); New York Herald, Dec. 19, 1908.

50. Blatch, "Radical Move in Two Years"; Mrs. B. Borrmann Wells, "The Militant Movement for Woman Suffrage," Independent, April 23, 1908, 901-3.

51. "Suffragettes Bar Word Ladylike," clipping, Jan. 13, 1909, Suffrage scrapbooks, Abbe Collection; Blatch and Lutz, Challenging Years, 91-242; New York Herald, March 8, 1908.

52. Blatch and Lutz, Challenging Years, 107; Dye, As Equals and As Sisters, 47.

53. Woman's Journal, May 30, 1908, 87; Blatch, "Radical Move in Two Years."

54. Borrmann Wells, "Militant Movement for Woman Suffrage," 901, Woman's Journal, Feb. 29, 1908, 34.

55. New York Times, Feb. 11, 1908, 6; [Josephine C. Kaneko], "To Join, or Not to Join," Socialist Woman, 1 (May 1908): 6.

56. On The Convert, see Equality League, Report for 1908-1909, 4; Jane Marcus, "Introduction," in The Convert (London, 1980), v-xvi; New York Call, Dec. 9, 1908, 6; and Minutes, Dec. 22, 1908, New York WTUL Papers.

57. New York Times, May 14, 1909, 5. On Mackay and her Equal Franchise Society, see New York Times, Feb. 21, 1909, part 5, 2. On Blatch's relation to Mackay, see Blatch and Lutz, Challenging Years, 118.

Sixteen

A POLITICS OF COALITION:
Socialist Women and the
California Suffrage Movement,
1900—1911

Sherry J. Katz

Editor's Introduction: In this study of the California suffrage movement, Sherry J. Katz illustrates the increasing diversity of the early twentieth-century suffrage movement as she highlights the contributions of socialist women to the successful California suffrage campaign of 1911. Socialist women, Katz explains, had an unusual degree of prominence and influence among California's suffragists. Though socialist women were active in state suffrage movements elsewhere, "mainstream suffragists" in the Northeast, Midwest, and South tended to marginalize or shun socialist women—even before World War I when socialists were persecuted for alleged disloyalty and subversiveness.

Socialist women had been active in the first attempt to gain a state suffrage amendment in California, the failed referendum of 1896. As the state's suffrage movement revived in the early 1900s, socialist women contributed to the revival. Particularly after 1907, writes Katz, California socialist women made a deliberate effort to broaden the perspective and the constituency of what they perceived to be a "bourgeois movement." From middle-class or stable working-class families, often well-educated and employed in professional or clerical positions, these socialist suffragists proved to be crucial intermediaries between the middle-class and elite suffragists and the working class. They were highly effective in recruiting working-class women into the movement and winning support from the labor movement and working-class men. After the success of California's state suffrage campaign in 1911—the second in a new round of twentieth-century victories that helped breathe new life into the national suffrage movement—mainstream suffragists in the state freely acknowledged the crucial role of the socialist suffragists.

Like the working-class suffragists in New York described by Ellen Carol DuBois, these suffragists introduced new arguments and modern tactics that contributed to the success of the suffrage movement. Though many of the arguments used by the socialists were similar to those of other suffragists, including the idea that women's "social housekeeping" talents would be useful in politics, the socialist suffragists emphasized that women were entitled to political rights because of their economic contributions. "The heart of their argument," writes Katz, was "the idea that women's labor, inside and outside the home, had always contributed to 'social wealth' and that women, as social producers, deserved the ballot." California's socialist women employed some of the modern tactics used to attract publicity by working-class suffragists and their allies in New York, but they also invented new tactics—from door-to-door canvassing to the use of electric signs—that would become common during the movement's last decade. Significantly, the socialist suffragists' innovative tactics included printing campaign literature and conducting suffrage rallies in foreign languages, indicating a desire to attract the support of new immigrants. Yet even these women were affected by the racism that was so common among White suffragists in the early twentieth century.

The 1911 campaign seemed to socialist women to be a fulfillment of their dream of a cross-class sisterhood, writes Katz. After the victory, however, the level of unity and cooperation that marked the state suffrage campaign declined to a degree. Still, socialist and "mainstream" women's groups continued to work together and to achieve much. Indeed, Katz concludes, "socialist women's influence on the legislative proposals advocated by mainstream women's groups helps explain why California was at the forefront of social welfare legislation for women during the Progressive Era."

★　★　★　★　★

DURING THE EARLY TWENTIETH CENTURY the woman suffrage movement experienced a revitalization and expansion, becoming for the first time a mass coalition utilizing militant tactics and modern methods. The California suffrage campaign provides an illuminating case study of the political and social diversity of this mass movement, and sheds light on the process and success of coalition-building. Although socialist women in many regions of the country joined suffrage organizations or campaigned for suffrage through the Socialist Party, California socialist women achieved an apparently unprecedented level of integration, leadership, and influence. Their prominence depended, in part, on California's congenial political and social context, and on an effective strategy that socialist women devised to forge an influential left-wing constituency within the larger movement.

This case study demonstrates the critical role that socialists played in expanding the boundaries of the suffrage coalition, contributions less visible in states where they participated as individuals or achieved less prominence as an organized subgroup. By spearheading efforts to recruit wage-earning women, win the support of organized labor, and court the working-class vote, socialist women broadened the suffrage movement's base. In providing leadership and strategies for class-bridging, they emphasized new arguments for women's enfranchisement and introduced modern methods of suffrage agitation, including militant and flamboyant street tactics. Socialist women's vigorous grassroots campaigns in urban, working-class communities, especially in Los Angeles, proved critical to the success of California's 1911 suffrage referendum. Socialist women made California, along with New York, a center of working-class coalition building and experimentation in militant strategies that influenced the trajectory of both state and national campaigns after 1911.

Socialism and Woman Suffrage: Linkages and Chasms

From 1890 to 1920, powerful international socialist and feminist movements helped to reinvigorate the woman suffrage demand and to create mass, militant, and modern suffrage movements. In the United States, the activism of both independent feminists sympathetic to socialism and female members of the Socialist Party of America helped to transform the suffrage movement into a broad and diverse coalition in the early twentieth century. Although the Second Socialist International instructed socialist women in 1907 to reject collaboration with mainstream suffragists and to conduct separate campaigns under party auspices, only party leaders in New York City adopted this policy. Everywhere else, Socialist Party women and independent left suffragists joined mainstream organizations, and, where feasible, built their own groups to represent working-class interests in the larger suffrage movement. Often working in close collaboration, they spearheaded the recruitment of working-class women, gained the support of organized labor, and introduced a new level of tactical militance. They played particularly forceful and effective roles in suffrage campaigns in the Western states, as well as in Wisconsin, and New York.[1]

Despite their vital contributions to the revitalization and expansion of the suffrage movement, socialists often faced marginalization by mainstream suffragists seeking to distance themselves from radical and working-class politics. Attempts to downplay the socialist contribution were most pronounced in the industrial Northeast and Midwest, where the predominantly native-born, elite leadership feared association with the immigrant masses, and after the onset of World War I, when socialism became identified with disloyalty and subversion. In the Southern states, social conservatism prompted the suffragists with socialist and trade union sympathies to avoid making public connections between radicalism and the suffrage cause.[2]

California's Fertile Ground for Political Experimentation

California socialist women achieved an apparently unprecedented level of integration, leadership, and influence in the suffrage coalition. The construction of their substantial left-wing presence depended, in part, on the fertile ground of the state's political climate and social context. During the late nineteenth century, the state provided space for the growth of numerous indigenous protest movements, such as Bellamy Nationalism and Populism, that sought to combat the harsh consequences of corporate capitalism. California's speedy economic development, accompanied by glaring economic inequalities, nurtured an openness to radical ideas and political alternatives. This climate of political experimentation gave rise to a sizeable and well-organized socialist women's movement that flourished in California from the 1890s until World War I. Beginning in the 1890s, several generations of radical women active in suffrage and temperance crusades found in socialism the basis for an egalitarian society guaranteeing women's freedom. In the early 1900s, local activists built a network of autonomous socialist women's clubs, under the umbrella of the Woman's Socialist Union of California (WSU), and worked within both the male-dominated socialist movement and the mainstream woman's movement.[3]

The Woman's Socialist Union represented hundreds of the most active socialist-feminists in the state. A number of like-minded radical women remained independent, but developed close ties to their sisters in the WSU. Information gathered on thirty-five state and local leaders of the WSU suggests a social portrait of the leadership cadre of the socialist women's movement. Most were born in the United States in the 1860s and 1870s, attained either stable working-class or middle-class status, and came to the socialist women's movement through participation in

Votes for Women

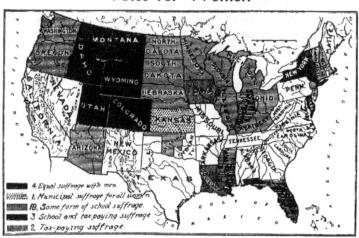

Equal Suffrage Map of the United States, 1908

Men and women vote on equal terms for all officers, even for presidential electors, in four of the United States. In twenty-seven other states, women have partial suffrage.

California women have no votes

Copies of this map may be obtained at California Equal Suffrage Headquarters
2419 California Street, San Francisco

Price one cent each

In 1908 only four states allowed women the vote.

the woman and left movements of the 1890s. Many of these activists had been raised in Protestant households, had married and borne one or two children, and were surrounded by socialist family members. Relatively well educated, these women worked in professional or clerical occupations, particularly in teaching and newspaper work, for at least part of their adult lives. They were joined by a number of veteran activists born in the United States between the 1820s and the 1840s who had had formative political experiences in abolitionism, early women's rights, and spiritualism. A younger generation of women born in the United States in 1880s and 1890s joined the socialist women's movement around 1910.[4]

The same climate of openness to political alternatives that nurtured a vigorous socialist women's movement also enabled socialists to establish a strong presence within California's suffrage movement from its inception. In fact, prominent radical women founded the suffrage movement in Northern California in the 1870s and in Southern California a decade later. A favorable social context undergirded their leadership and eased their early efforts to expand the movement's base of support along the lines of class and culture. In Southern California, socialist women and their working-class allies largely shared the native-born, Protestant backgrounds of mainstream suffragists, which meant that radicalism did not suffer from association with "foreignness." In Northern California, where Northern European immigrants and their children comprised a majority of the urban working class, socialism appeared somewhat more threatening to mainstream suffragists. As the suffrage demand moved from the margins to the center of organized White womanhood's political agenda in the late 1880s and 1890s, socialist women remained at the forefront of the movement, especially in the southern part of the state.[5]

Cross-Class Coalition Building, 1900—1910

The founding of the Woman's Socialist Union in 1902 coincided with, and contributed to, the revival of the state suffrage movement and the creation of a diverse suffrage coalition. After the defeat of a state suffrage amendment in 1896, suffrage activism declined as many demoralized participants left the movement. But during the first decade of the century, California women, like their counterparts across the nation, created new voluntary associations and social movements, through which they exerted an enormous collective influence on public policy and pursued woman suffrage. As the membership of mainstream suffrage clubs associated with the California Equal Suffrage Association (CESA) expanded from 100 to over 50,000, White clubwomen, college-educated reformers, working-class labor activists, African American clubwomen, as well as socialists, established their own organizations dedicated to the suffrage cause.[6] The demand for suffrage unified women in the early twentieth century because it encompassed their sense of commonality as well as their differences. Disfranchisement was a powerful symbol of women's socially constructed unity and an indicator of their common oppression in male-dominated society. Conceptualized as a tool of group interests, as well as a means of individual self-expression, the ballot also came to be understood as a means of achieving the goals considered important to different subgroups of women. The demand for suffrage constituted a "capacious umbrella" under which a large diversity of women, organizations, and beliefs, could temporarily stand. A genuine mass movement for women's enfranchisement emerged for the first time, one that embodied the widest spectrum of ideas and opinion, as well as participants, in its long history.[7]

As the suffrage coalition expanded after 1900, socialist women increased their numbers and their visibility as a distinctive left-wing entity within the movement. By 1907, WSU leader Josephine Cole celebrated the fact that every "Socialist woman [she knew] in this part of the country [was] a suffragist and almost every one of them [was] in a suffrage club." While Cole may have exaggerated, many WSU activists, female party members, and independent socialist-feminists joined mainstream suffrage groups. Although neither local suffrage clubs nor the CESA maintained good records, we know from scattered newspaper accounts that at least thirty-six socialists led local suffrage organizations and that most of them also served as delegates to or officers of the CESA. At least one socialist, and more often two or three, held important posts on the CESA's executive committee from 1903 to 1911. Under WSU guidance, socialist women exerted a strong, collective presence at state and local CESA conventions and in the Pacific Coast's suffrage press.[8]

Although few in-depth analyses of state suffrage movements are now available, in no other state did socialist women appear to gain so much prominence within the mainstream suffrage movement. Socialist women became leaders of the CESA based on their own dedication and commitment and because mainstream suffragists welcomed and acknowledged the participation of the left. This openness developed from the history of radical women's leadership in California suffrage, the context of political experimentation in California politics, and the public support offered by the state Socialist Party after its founding in 1902. Prominent suffragist Sarah M. Severance maintained in 1910 that "Socialists have [long] been our consistent friends" and she thanked them for their "just attitude" and "consistent record on woman's suffrage."[9]

Equally important in helping socialist women become "an acknowledged factor" in the state suffrage movement from 1902 to 1911 was the dual strategy of autonomous collaboration and full integration they devised to expand their influence. Rooted in their experience as participants in multiple and overlapping movements, dual strategy allowed them to collaborate with mainstream suffragists without losing their independent identity and separate base of power. "One woman lifting up her voice is not so well listened to as when she represents a body of women," WSU president Ethel Whitehead reasoned. The leaders of the WSU believed that socialist women's voices would carry greater weight when associated with independent organizations of radical suffragists.[10]

Socialist women self-consciously attempted to expand the boundaries of the suffrage coalition as leaders of the CESA and local mainstream organizations who remained based in, and coordinated their actions with, the WSU and other independent socialist suffrage groups. They believed that their "special mission... in the woman-suffrage field" involved enlarging the movement's constituency and political vision. The WSU leaders made the recruitment and integration of working-class women a major priority, arguing that no group was "better fitted" for the task. Socialist women also dedicated themselves to providing an "entering wedge" for the "Socialist thought" that would undergird a "more progressive, more democratic" movement. They hoped to convince non-socialists that women's emancipation depended upon economic independence, as well as political rights, and that such independence could be achieved only through a major restructuring of class relations and social resources. Likewise they sought to demonstrate that the social problems female reformers frequently attacked—child labor, prostitution, and poverty—could be eliminated only if women used their ballots to undermine capitalism. They envisioned the construction of an inclusive woman's movement dedicated to the emancipation of both women and the working class.[11]

In WSU affiliates, socialist women refined their arguments for enfranchisement. Many of their arguments paralleled those utilized by their non-socialist comrades. Both "sameness" and "difference" arguments appeared often in early twentieth-century suffrage literature. Suffragists argued that to the extent women were the same as men they deserved the ballot as a matter of justice, and to the extent they possessed special qualities, they needed a direct means of affecting public decision making.[12] Members of the WSU asserted that women deserved the ballot based on their inherent equality with men and their right to represent themselves. Most WSU activists also maintained that women's distinctive qualities—their socially constructed moral, maternal, and altruistic sensibilities—were desperately needed in the public sphere where male competitiveness and self-interest had been unable to combat the harsh social consequences of capitalist development. In combining these two strands of suffrage thought, Josephine Cole insisted that "possession of the ballot" would allow woman "the opportunity to alter many existing conditions which bear cruelty upon her, to her own injury and that of the race, but which...receive little attention from male legislators, be they Socialist or otherwise."[13]

Socialists also generated several new and distinctive arguments for suffrage shaped by their understandings of modern transformations in women's labor and the relation of women's work to women's emancipation. As socialist women pioneered these arguments in California, other members of a new generation of suffrage activists, many of them middle-class, college-educated reformers influenced by and sympathetic to radicalism, popularized them in New York and introduced them to the National American Woman Suffrage Association. Proponents of these new arguments drew upon the contributions of Charlotte Perkins Gilman, the most influential feminist theorist of their time, who insisted that gender equality depended

Charlotte Perkins Gilman, 1900

FRANCES B. JOHNSTON

upon women's economic independence achieved through wage labor outside the home and the socialization of housework and child rearing. Interestingly, Gilman developed her "sexuo-economic" theory of social relations in the early 1890s when she began her public career as a member of California's emerging socialist-feminist community.[14]

Socialist women proposed that women's economic contributions entitled them to political rights. The heart of their argument rested on the idea that women's labor, inside and outside the home, had always contributed to "social wealth" and that women, as social producers, deserved the ballot. But they highlighted the ways in which women's increasing involvement in the paid labor force provided a new rationale for suffrage. As women's "field of labor" shifted from the home to the factory, they became, in the words of Josephine Cole, permanent "financial factor[s]" who would "necessarily" be regarded as independent human beings and citizens rather than as "helpless dependents." Indeed the WSU's Jennie Arnott believed that because women's paid employment "forced their recognition as social units," it had "done more than any one thing to make the voters of the country see their need of the ballot." Ultimately, this wage-earners' suffragism not only provided a new rationale for women's entitlement to political rights, but helped socialist women draw working-class women into the suffrage coalition.[15]

A strong identification with working-class women undergirded socialist women's distinctive emphasis on wage-earning women's need of the ballot. Suffrage would provide wage-earning women with an important tool for their own advancement and self-protection, as well as for the empowerment of working-class communities. "That army of women who labor with their hands," WSU leader Mary Garbutt reminded her fellow suffragists, are the ones "whose hard experiences in life, long hours, poor pay and unsanitary conditions...really demand...the ballot for their protection against such untoward conditions."[16]

Wage-earning women never assumed the same importance in the arguments and literature of most mainstream suffragists in California. Socialist and trade-union activists generated most of the materials utilized by suffrage forces to attract such women. In this regard, independent socialist-feminist Alice Locke Park, a longtime ally of the WSU, played a key role as a prominent leader of the CESA's literature committee from 1906 to 1911. She issued several CESA leaflets directed towards working-class and wage-earning women, highlighted socialist and trade union endorsements, and helped her colleagues in the WSU and union movement produce their own literature.[17]

Park's work on the literature committee was only part of an intensive effort on the part of socialist women, networked through the WSU, to broaden the arguments and constituency of the suffrage movement. At CESA conventions in 1906 and 1907, substantial and well-organized socialist delegations, in concert with Progressive suffragists sympathetic to working women, advocated the recruitment of wage-earning women, outreach to working-class communities, and efforts to obtain greater support from organized labor. The 1906 convention featured a discussion devoted to securing the "interest and co-operation of the wage-earning women" led by WSU leader Anna Ferry Smith, a veteran feminist labor activist, and several other socialist and trade union women. They advised suffragists to meet with the leaders of women's unions, as the Los Angeles county suffrage organization had recently done. In 1907, a proposal drafted by the socialist-dominated resolutions committee pledged the CESA to widen the "scope of the suffrage movement by enlisting in its service the tremendous force of the women who work for wages and bringing to bear the pressure which organized labor can exert." The resolution invited trade union women to join the suffrage movement, stressing that their "struggle for better economic conditions" was hampered by their lack of political power.[18]

The approval of this resolution solidified the commitment of mainstream suffragists to working-class recruitment. Pragmatism, as well as socialist organizing within the CESA, underlay this strategic shift. Suffrage leaders saw in the rise of Progressivism a political climate conducive to social reform and women's enfranchisement. But they also believed that a suffrage victory depended on a new and enlarged base of suffrage activists, the backing of male-dominated institutions, better organization, and coordinated legislative lobbying. Whether sympathetic to organized labor or not, mainstream suffragists understood by 1906 that unions had become a powerful force in state politics and that the passage of a constitutional amendment depended on working-class votes.[19]

The success of working-class outreach and integration differed by city and region. Social context and socialist leadership proved critical factors in coalition-building efforts. In Southern California, and particularly in Los Angeles, relative ethnic homogeneity among Whites and longstanding socialist leadership within organized womanhood facilitated class-bridging. But even as mainstream suffragists relied on their socialist comrades and supported the recruitment of wage-earning women, they felt uneasy in working-class environs. Socialist sympathizer Helen Bary recalled that elite and middle-class suffragists in Los Angeles thought her "very brave" to visit the Labor Temple, located in a downtown working-class district. In general, mainstream suffragists left the work of class-bridging to socialist women and their labor-identified allies.[20]

From 1906 to 1911, the Los Angeles WSU, a member of the local suffrage coalition, began to sponsor class-bridging activities in the form of meetings, conferences,

Frances Nacke Noel (right)
HUNTINGTON LIBRARY

and actions that brought mainstream suffragists and union women together. In 1908, Socialist Party member and WSU supporter Frances Nacke Noel emerged as the most prominent and effective organizer of class-bridging efforts. Under Noel's guidance, the California branch of the Woman's International Union Label League, an organization that promoted the consumption of union-made goods, became an important champion of female unionization, protective labor legislation, and woman suffrage.[21]

Label League activists drawn from the WSU's and the Socialist Party helped the organization become the grassroots, working-class component of the suffrage coalition in Southern California from 1908 to 1911. In Los Angeles, San Diego, and elsewhere, socialist women arranged joint meetings for label leaguers and mainstream suffragists in which they shared their thoughts on suffrage strategies and social reform proposals. In the winter of 1910, Los Angeles' Label League, Votes for Women Club, and WSU also collaborated on a Christmas benefit for the wives and children of local striking workers.[22] These activities culminated in the short-lived Woman's Conference of Los Angeles County, which Noel and her socialist comrades envisioned as a permanent cross-class umbrella organization devoted to advancing the welfare of women and children, particularly those from the laboring classes. Called by the Label League and women's unions, the conference attracted over one hundred delegates to its first meeting in January 1911, many of them from mainstream women's organizations. After demanding that the legislature place a constitutional amendment for woman suffrage on the ballot, the conference conducted investigations of housing, industrial working conditions, and protective labor legislation. The conference disbanded in March 1911 as many of its constituent groups found a more pressing collaborative venture in the upcoming suffrage amendment campaign.[23]

Modern Methods and Militant Tactics in the 1911 Campaign

In February 1911, shortly after the California legislature voted to place a suffrage amendment on the October ballot, CESA leaders approved a plan to coordinate suffrage activism during the campaign that lay ahead. Led by Elizabeth Lowe Watson, a longtime socialist ally, the CESA called for collaboration among the thousands of suffragists in the state, including members of the California Federation of Women's Clubs (CFWC), the Woman's Christian Temperance Union (WCTU), women's trade unions, socialist organizations, and independent suffrage groups. The commitment to cooperation among diverse "kinds of suffrag[ists]," and the inclusion of radical and trade union organizations, rested on the preceding decade of socialist leadership and class-bridging efforts in the state association, as well as on the practical notion that a broad and well-organized suffrage coalition had the best chance of success. Although the Cooperative Council faced difficulty in "dove-tailing" precinct work and nurturing "new methods of propaganda and [an] exchange of talent" on the state level, regional coordinating bodies, especially in Southern California, facilitated cooperation among the many groups that comprised the suffrage coalition in 1911.[24]

Across California, and particularly in the southern part of the state, socialist women pioneered some of the most innovative tactics of the first state-level campaign to demonstrate the modern, militant, and often flamboyant methods characteristic of the suffrage movement's final decade. California suffragists perfected door-to-door canvassing and precinct organization, engaged in street speaking and car campaigning, coordinated press work, designed "modern" literature for mass distribution featuring concise arguments and catchy slogans, developed billboard ads and electric signs, staged plays and pageants, and held outdoor meetings and rallies. Socialist women helped to make press work and door-to-door canvassing—two modern tools of organization first introduced in the 1890s—more systematic and widespread. But they contributed most by experimenting with new styles of protest. Suffrage militance involved taking suffrage agitation aggressively into the streets. First employed to gain working-class support, militant methods became an effective means of acquiring widespread publicity because they challenged the bourgeois notions of female respectability that had mitigated against women's vigorous participation in public life. First in New York and then in California, socialists and working-class feminists helped popularize and expand the use of these militant methods nationwide.[25]

As the CESA formulated its plans for the suffrage campaign, WSU leaders prepared to mobilize their troops and the

California Suffrage Poster designed by Bertha Boye, 1911

HOMBRES Y MUJERES

¿Quien Dio Al Hombre El Derecho De Votar Y Cuando?

¿Quien Dara a Las Mujeres el Derecho de Votar?

Votese por Dar la Mujer de California el Derecho de Votar

EN LA ELECCION DEL 10 DE OCTUBRE, 1911

Leaflet in Spanish from the
1911 California campaign

SOPHIA SMITH COLLECTION

state Socialist Party. They were overjoyed by the party's pledge to work actively for suffrage, a commitment they had attempted to secure for nearly a decade, and formed a State Woman's Committee to coordinate the party's effort. Committee chairs Mary Garbutt and Georgia Kotsch quickly realized, however, that the state party's commitment consisted primarily of generous use of its weekly newspaper, the *California Social-Democrat*. While few party locals developed sustained campaigns, socialist women in all regions stepped up their suffrage activism in mainstream organizations and autonomous groups. Through WSU branches, socialist suffrage clubs, wage-earners' suffrage leagues, and Socialist Party locals, they worked to gain the support of organized labor and working-class voters, often collaborating with mainstream suffrage organizations and regional coordinating committees in which their comrades exercised influence.[26]

In Los Angeles County, socialist women played a highly visible role in the regional campaign that achieved the greatest success in constructing a diverse, cross-class coalition. As the campaign began, socialist women occupied leadership positions in all of the county's major suffrage organizations—the Political Equality League, the Votes for Women Club, and the WCTU. Although socialists and other labor-identified suffragists secured commitments for outreach to immigrant and working-class communities, these organizations remained focused on gaining the support of middle-class women and men.[27] In order to conduct an intensive campaign among the county's working-class population, WSU veterans and their allies founded two new suffrage groups: the Socialist Suffrage Club (SSC) and the Wage Earners' Suffrage League (WESL). Delegates from the SSC, WESL, and several mainstream groups represented the socialist/labor forces on the county's Equal Suffrage Central Committee, which loosely coordinated the overall campaign and facilitated an extraordinary interchange of personnel among its constituent groups.[28]

Under the direction of Mary Garbutt, Ethel Whitehead, and Frances Noel, the SSC and the WESL developed distinctive, but complementary, niches in the campaign. The Socialist Suffrage Club, founded in March 1911 and led by WSU veterans, organized public meetings and conducted house-to-house canvasses in working-class communities throughout the county.[29] The WESL, initiated by Frances Noel in May 1911, attracted labor as well as socialist activists, especially working-class homemakers from the label leagues and members of the garment workers union. Modeled after a similar organization founded by elite labor reformer Maud Younger in San Francisco in 1908, the WESL focused on mobilizing the support of the county's trade unions. The WESL maintained a visible presence at the Labor Temple, distributed literature to union members, and brought street speaking and outdoor meetings to neighborhoods in which union members resided. Both groups sought to empower working-class women, as well as to gain the support of working-class men.[30]

Maud Younger, c.1919
LIBRARY OF CONGRESS

The actions of the SSC and the WESL reveal both the breadth and the limits of socialist women's conceptions of community and coalition, and the boundaries that circumscribed their political vision. Although their efforts focused on the predominantly White and native-born sector of Los Angeles' working-class community and labor movement, socialists campaigned in immigrant communities. In August, Noel promoted the suffrage cause in German at one of the first foreign-language meetings in the county. Similar meetings may have been held at the party's Jewish, Hungarian, Finnish, Latvian, and Mexican branches, and socialists probably distributed more foreign-language materials than any other sector of the county suffrage coalition. But many socialist women excluded Asian immigrants from their conception of the working class, despite a theoretical commitment to international solidarity. Socialists active in the labor movement internalized the hostility towards Asians that had ironically helped to unify California's White workers since the 1860s. Although their own suffrage materials were implicitly inclusive, socialist women widely distributed Maud Younger's "Why Wage-Earning Women Should Vote," first reproduced by Alice Park for the CESA in 1908, which decried the fact that native-born "Mongolians" (men) could vote and (White) women could not. In addition, socialist women apparently failed to challenge the exclusion of African American suffragists from mainstream suffrage groups and the county coordinating committee, even though their party had a small African American branch. Although socialist women clearly included ethnic and immigrant Euro-Americans and Latinos in their "imagined communities," the constructions of racial difference shared by most White reformers in California during the Progressive Era impoverished the vision of female solidarity they possessed and the diversity of the suffrage coalition they worked to build.[31]

Through the SSC and the WESL, socialist suffragists experimented with modern methods of suffrage organization, many of which challenged the Victorian notion that respectable women should not seek public attention. An extensive use of the socialist and labor press reflected the suffrage movement's growing emphasis on the importance of systematic and sustained publicity. Leaders of the SSC and the WESL coordinated the publication of a steady stream of suffrage propaganda in the *Citizen*, the newspaper of the Los Angeles labor movement, and the *California Social-Democrat*. The September 29, 1911 "Votes for Women" issue of the *Citizen* featured seventeen articles on the subject.[32]

In July and September, the SSC organized forty neighborhood suffrage meetings held in socialist halls throughout the city, in order to reach systematically a predominantly White, native-born working-class population that comprised more than fifty percent of the residents of all but one of Los Angeles' wards, and more than seventy percent in East Side wards.[33] The SSC also conducted a house-to-house canvass that sent pairs of socialist suffragists into selected precincts in order to speak personally with female homemakers and registered male voters about the suffrage cause. The club's canvass appears to have dovetailed with that of the Political Equality League (PEL), the largest and most powerful suffrage organization in the county. While the PEL focused on the middle-class and elite West Side, socialists concentrated on the precincts with large populations of working people and socialist voters (primarily in central and eastern Los Angeles). Although canvassing has not been regarded by historians as a particularly militant method of suffrage organizing, WSU leaders Ethel Whitehead and Georgia Kotsch argued that it was an effective strategy in part because of the curiosity and interest that women's presence in the streets engendered about their new public roles. Kotsch reported that many women treated her as an "amusing creature" and welcomed the "break" from the "monotony [of] their lives" that her presence offered. Whitehead, who encountered more hostility, relished the excitement of "assailing the enemy on his own doorstep," as the embodiment of the modern woman fully engaged in public life.[34]

The WESL focused on gaining grassroots labor support through equally modern methods. The WESL sent a circular letter to hundreds of labor organizations in the county and throughout the state. The San Francisco WESL, the key working-class suffrage organization in the Bay Area, published the letter in the newspaper of the San Francisco Labor Council and mailed it to local unions that could not be personally contacted. Maud Younger believed that the letter "brought endorsements that otherwise might not have been forthcoming," increased agitation among new converts, and garnered attention in the press. An innovative tear-off informed the WESL that the targeted organization had endorsed the suffrage amendment.[35]

As part of their effort to mobilize working-class support, socialist women pioneered the use of the most aggressively militant street tactics employed by California suffragists. Street tactics were certainly familiar to socialist women, since most had participated in the street demonstrations common to American labor and socialist protest. Socialist leaders of the CESA, including Alice Park and Jennie Arnott, had also been impressed with the militance of British suffragists since 1908.[36]

The WESL sponsored the first open-air meeting of the Southern California campaign on July 13 in Hollenbeck Park, located in an ethnically mixed, working-class neighborhood on Los Angeles' East Side. This move showed daring, not only because open-air meetings had not been part of conventional suffrage organizing, but also because the WESL had to find a way to circumvent a city ordinance prohibiting political speeches in public parks. Instead of speaking, the hundred suffrage supporters in attendance sang their arguments for the ballot and informally discussed the issue around picnic tables where coffee and doughnuts were served. Excellent press coverage in papers across the state emphasized the innovativeness of the outdoor gathering and the courage displayed in challenging local police. Good coverage, in turn, encouraged many suffrage groups to sponsor outdoor meetings in other areas of the county and state.[37]

The WESL also "broke the way for street speaking, going into the highways and byways to talk to the men who would not come to [them]." During the last three weeks of the campaign, the league conducted daily street speaking in working-class wards of central and eastern Los Angeles. Before street meetings held near the Labor Temple, WESL speakers would drive about the neighborhood "with votes for women banners flying in the breeze" in order to draw a larger crowd.[38] Many mainstream suffragists in Los Angeles and elsewhere found the courage to speak on the streets with the example and encouragement of socialists. Alice Park reported that by September street speaking had become so popular that many suffragists were engaging in it who had "no idea three months ago they would ever do such a thing."[39]

Victory and Its Aftermath

The broad, militant, and well-organized suffrage campaign, waged in the context of popular enthusiasm for "direct democracy" and Progressive reform, resulted in the enfranchisement of California women on October 10, 1911. But the suffrage amendment remained one of the most contested of all ballot measures in 1911, approved by the state's voters by a narrow margin of 3,587 out of 246,487 votes cast. The amendment won in Southern California and in most of the rural regions of the state, but it lost in San Francisco and Oakland. A complex set of demographic and political factors contributed to these regional differences. In San Francisco, a largely

Teacher Emma Tom Leung (left) and Clara Elizabeth Chan Lee of Oakland, California register to vote in 1911 as their husbands look on. They became the first Chinese American women to become eligible to vote in the United States.
OAKLAND TRIBUNE

German and Irish Catholic population associated woman suffrage with temperance activists and moral reformers who appeared to threaten their traditional social customs. The union movement remained ambivalent or opposed, Progressive political forces failed to make suffrage a priority, and a well-organized opposition funded by liquor interests campaigned vigorously against the amendment. Although mainstream suffragists went after the working-class and immigrant vote, an undercurrent of nativism and anti-union sentiment informed their campaign and strained relations with working-class suffragists. In the southern cities and rural counties, the population tended to be native-born and Protestant, and hence theoretically more favorable to temperance and suffrage. In Los Angeles, Progressive reformers, organized labor, and a popular Socialist Party endorsed suffrage with more fervor. And the opposition, aligned with the anti-reform and anti-union Merchants and Manufacturers Association, may have actually increased support for the amendment among both working-class and middle-class voters. The suffrage coalition, with socialist women serving as an important class-bridging force, more successfully united women from divergent backgrounds.[40]

It is difficult to assess the precise impact of socialist women on the outcome of the suffrage campaign. In many cities, their contributions cannot be separated from those of their non-socialist sisters, although they no doubt took the lead in agitating in working-class communities and in the streets.[41] In Los Angeles, however, socialist women clearly made a difference, playing a major role in securing a victory for suffrage in working-class neighborhoods and therefore in the city overall. Of Los Angeles' seven assembly districts, five supported the amendment, and four of those contained working-class majorities. Contemporary accounts suggest that working-class precincts provided greater margins of victory than the middle-class and elite precincts that favored the amendment. The voters most likely to reject the amendment lived on the "respectable, stylish West Side" and in the downtown neighborhoods that housed the city's most transient and impoverished residents. The precinct surrounding the Labor Temple, in which many union members lived, carried the amendment by a two-to-one margin.[42]

Mainstream suffragists freely acknowledged the critical importance of working-class and socialist support and praised socialist suffragists for their activism. The *Western Woman Voter*, the organ of the West Coast suffrage movement, credited the victory in Southern California to the fact that "the labor unions and the Socialists there...[had] actively lined up in favor of the amendment." Progressive suffragist Helen Bary considered the campaign to get out the labor and socialist vote conducted by the WESL and the SSC more "productive" than the "whole elaborate campaign" devised by mainstream groups to gain support among the elite and middle classes.[43]

For socialist women, the 1911 campaign seemed to represent the fulfillment of their "dream of solidarity among women," of a sisterhood that crossed the boundaries of class, political ideology, and organizational affiliation. Tensions between mainstream and socialist activists surfaced periodically in the post-suffrage period, however, especially during partisan elections. But overall, enfranchisement contributed to greater collaboration among socialist and mainstream women on a wider variety of political projects, rather than to a fragmentation of the woman's movement. Socialist women, in alliance with a small group of labor-oriented Progressive clubwomen, continued to comprise a left-wing of the woman's movement from 1911 to 1917. During this period, radical women became the leading proponents of labor legislation and unionization, the most outspoken advocates of a redistributive social welfare state, and the earliest supporters of birth control. In fact, socialist women's influence on the legislative proposals advocated by mainstream women's groups helps explain why California was at the forefront of social welfare legislation for women during the Progressive Era. Socialist women's activism appears to offer an important reason why California devised better protection for women workers than most other states and debated more comprehensive and less oppressive mothers' pension programs than were considered elsewhere.[44]

The activism of Josephine Cole and her comrades highlights the ways in which socialist women reinvigorated and expanded the suffrage movement in the early twentieth-century United States. An influential sector of California's suffrage coalition, socialist women broadened its boundaries by recruiting working-class women, emphasizing new arguments, and introducing militant methods. They also demonstrated a fruitful strategy for coalition-building, one that made them a distinctive and independent tendency within the larger movement. Their grassroots activism in working-class communities contributed to a critical suffrage victory that, following on the heels of the successful Washington State campaign in 1910, ignited expectations nationwide. As the California campaign served to emphasize the importance of collaborative and class-bridging efforts, innovative methods, and working-class support, the socialist suffragists of the state helped shape the course of the national suffrage movement.

Notes

1. Ellen Carol Dubois, "Woman Suffrage and the Left: An International Socialist-Feminist Perspective," *New Left Review,* no. 186 (March/April 1991), 29-45; Mari Jo Buhle, *Women and American Socialism, 1870-1920* (Urbana, 1981), chpt. 6; Nancy F. Cott, *The Grounding of Modern Feminism* (New Haven, 1987), chpt. 1.; John D. Buenker, "The Politics of Mutual Frustration: Socialists and Suffragists in New York and Wisconsin," in Sally M. Miller, *Flawed Liberation: Socialism and Feminism* (Westport, Conn., 1981), 113-144.

2. Buhle, *Socialism,* 231-238; Buenker, "Politics," 113-144; Marjorie Spruill (Wheeler), *New Women of the New South: The Leaders of the Woman Suffrage Movement in the Southern States* (New York, 1993), 74-75, 184.

3. Michael Kazin, "The Great Exception Revisited: Organized Labor and Politics in San Francisco and Los Angeles, 1870-1940," *Pacific Historical Review* 55 (August 1986), 381-388; Sherry Jeanne Katz, "Dual Commitments: Feminism, Socialism, and Women's Political Activism in California, 1890-1920," (Ph.D. diss., University of California, Los Angeles, 1991), chpts. 1-3.

4. Katz, "Dual Commitments," 106-112; and Sherry Katz, "Socialist Women and Progressive Reform," in William Deverell and Tom Sitton, eds., *California Progressivism Revisited* (Berkeley, 1994), 119.

5. Gayle Ann Gullett, "Feminism, Politics, and Voluntary Groups: Organized Womanhood in California, 1886-1896," (Ph.D. diss., University of California, Riverside, 1983), esp. 19-21, 144-150, 176-184, 196-201, 297-313; Susan L. Englander, "The San Francisco Wage Earners' Suffrage League: Class Conflict and Class Coalition in the California Woman Suffrage Movement, 1907-1912," (M.A. thesis, San Francisco State University, 1989), 54-80; Katz, "Dual Commitments," 54-69.

6. Donald Waller Rodes, "The California Woman Suffrage Campaign of 1911," (M.A. thesis, California State University, Hayward, 1974), 10-11, 23-31; Ronald Schaffer, "The Problem of Consciousness in the Woman Suffrage Movement: A California Perspective," *Pacific Historical Review* 45 (Nov. 1976), 469-493; Douglas Flamming, "African-Americans and the Politics of Race in Progressive-Era Los Angeles," in Deverell and Sitton, eds., *California Progressivism,* 206-208; Bess Marjory Munn, "Activity of the Suffragette," *Citizen* (Los Angeles), Sept. 29, 1911.

7. Nancy F. Cott, "Feminist Theory and Feminist Movements: The Past Before Us," in Juliet Mitchell and Ann Oakley, eds., *What Is Feminism?* (New York, 1986), 52-54.

8. Josephine R. Cole, "In Defense of Woman Suffrage," *Common Sense* (Los Angeles), March 30, 1907; Katz, "Dual Commitments," 259-277.

9. Katz, "Dual Commitments," 263-264; n. 47-48, 317-320; "For Political Equality," *People's Paper* (Los Angeles), September 24, 1910.

10. M[ary] E. G[arbutt], "Notes from the Convention of the Socialist Women's Union of California," *Los Angeles Socialist,* Oct. 4, 1902; Ethel Whitehead, "Woman and the Socialist Movement," *People's Paper,* Oct. 28, 1910; Ethel Whitehead, "The Woman's Movement in California," *Progressive Woman* 2 (May 1909), 7.

11. Josephine R. Cole, "Women's Unions," *Appeal to Reason,* June 13, 1903; report by M[ary] E. G[arbutt], *Los Angeles Socialist,* Jan. 3, 1903; Josephine R. Cole, "A Reply to Mrs. Corbin," *Los Angeles Socialist,* June 20, 1903; Agnes Halpin Downing, "Woman's Needs," *Socialist Woman* 1 (March 1908), 2; Whitehead, "Woman and the Socialist Movement."

12. Cott, "Feminist Theory," 50-54; Cott, *Grounding,* 19-21, 29-30.

13. Sallie E. Bowman, "Why Women Should Have the Ballot," *Citizen,* March 5, 1909; Georgia Kotsch, "The Mission of the Socialist Woman," *Progressive Woman* 5 (Aug. 11), 13-14; J[osephine] R. Cole, "Political Power for Women," *Los Angeles Socialist,* April 4, 1903.

14. Ellen Carol DuBois, "Working Women, Class Relations, and Suffrage Militance: Harriot Stanton Blatch and the New York Woman Suffrage Movement," in this volume; Cott, *Grounding,* 24-25, 41-42; Ann J. Lane, *To "Herland" and Beyond: The Life and Works of Charlotte Perkins Gilman* (New York, 1990), chpts. 6-10.

15. Josephine R. Cole, "The Economic Cause of Woman's Advancement," *Yellow Ribbon* 1 (Feb. 1907), 1-3; Jennie Arnott, "Forces Which Are Working For Suffrage," *Yellow Ribbon* 1 (Jan. 1907), 1.

16. [Mary Garbutt], *Los Angeles Socialist,* Feb. 28, 1903.

17. Alice Park, "The Ballot," *Yellow Ribbon* 1 (Oct. 1906), 3; CESA leaflet, "Woman Suffrage Endorsed by California Conventions," [1906], box 4, Keith-McHenry-Pond Family Papers, Bancroft Library, University of California, Berkeley; "California Literature," *Woman's Journal,* April 29, 1911; [Alice] Park to [Agnes] Downing, March 8, 1911, box 3, Alice Locke Park Collection, Huntington Library, (hereafter cited as Park Coll., HL.)

18. M[able] C[raft] D[eering], "Annual Convention of California Equal Suffrage Association," *Yellow Ribbon* 1 (Nov. 1906), 1-2; *San Francisco Call,* Oct. 6, 1907; CESA convention program, *Western Woman* 1 (Oct. 1907), 12.

19. Report of the San Francisco Equal Suffrage League, *Yellow Ribbon* 1 (Dec. 1906), 1; Rodes, "Woman Suffrage Campaign," 23-57; Englander, "San Francisco Wage Earners' League," 81-86.

20. Helen Valeska Bary, "Labor Administration and Social Security: A Woman's Life," interview by Jacqueline K. Parker, 1972-1973, Regional Oral History Office, Bancroft Library, 1974, 20-21, (hereafter cited as Bary OH, BL).

21. Georgia Kotsch, "State Conference of the Women's Socialist Union," *World,* May 22, 1909; Mary E. Garbutt to Mrs. [Mary] Wilshire, May 20, 1909, in *Wilshire's Magazine* 13 (Aug. 1909), 18; Katz, "Dual Commitments," 273, n. 70, 329-330, 578-580, n. 28, 614-615.

22. "San Diego Women Study Laws for Women," *Citizen,* March 4, 1910; "The Union Label and Votes For Women," *Citizen,* Dec. 9, 1910; "Christmas for Strikers' Children," *People's Paper,* Dec. 23, 1910.

23. See recruitment letters and Noel's "The Woman's Conference of Los Angeles County: It's Aim and Object," folder 12, box 4, Frances Noel Papers, Department of Special Collections, University Research Library, UCLA, (hereafter cited as Noel Papers, UCLA); "Council of Women Formed," *Citizen,* Jan. 20, 1911; "Woman's Conference of L.A. County," *Citizen,* Feb. 24, 1911.

24. Elizabeth Lowe Watson, "To the Members of the California Equal Suffrage Association and friends who favor Votes for Women, throughout the State of California," March 2, 1911, box 227, John Randolph Haynes Papers, Special Collections, University Research Library, UCLA (hereafter cited as Haynes Papers, UCLA); "Denver Woman Will Conduct Local Battle," San Francisco Call, Sept. 19, 1911; list, Equal Suffrage Campaign Committee, n.d., [1911], box 10, Elizabeth Morrison (Boynton) Harbert Collection, Huntington Library (hereafter cited as Harbert Coll., HL).

25. Buhle, Socialism, 230; Cott, Grounding, 24-29; DuBois, "Woman Suffrage and the Left," 35-41; DuBois, "Suffrage Militance," 52-58.

26. "Official Bulletin of the Socialist Party of California," California Social-Democrat (Los Angeles), Sept. 9, 1911; State Woman's Committee, "Suffrage Amendment Must Be Carried at the Polls," California Social-Democrat, July 22, 1911; Agnes H. Downing, "Woman Suffrage In California," Progressive Woman 5 (Sept. 1911), 1; Katz, "Dual Commitments," 279-296.

27. Katz, "Dual Commitments," 287-288, n. 106, 346-347; Bary, OH, BL, 17-22, 24; Helen V. Bary to Adella M. Parker, Nov. 23, 1911, box 3, Park Coll., HL.

28. Downing, "Woman Suffrage in California"; list, Equal Suffrage Central Committee, [1911], and Lloyd Galpin to "Dear Madam," Aug. 30, 1911, box 10, Harbert Coll., HL; California Social-Democrat, Sept. 9, 1911.

29. "Socialists Open Woman Suffrage Campaign," Citizen, June 2, 1911; Ethel Whitehead, "The Socialists' Fight," California Social-Democrat, Sept. 9, 1911.

30. "Wage-Earners' Suffrage Rally," Citizen, June 2, 1911; WESL circular letter, "To All Union Men of California," [1911] and Estelle Lawton Lindsey, "The Wage-Earners Suffrage League Plans Great Educational Campaign," Los Angeles Record, n.d., folders 7 and 14, box 1, Noel Papers, UCLA.

31. "Next Municipal Election May Be Open to Women," n.p., n.d., Woman's Suffrage Scrapbook, compiled by Mrs. M.A. Holmes, Pasadena Historical Society, Pasadena, California (hereafter cited as Suffrage Scrapbook, PHS); Leonard Pitt, "Red Flag Over City Hall? The Socialist Labor Ticket in the Los Angeles Mayoral Election of 1911," (Paper delivered at AHA Convention, 1989), n. 12, 29; Bary, OH, 20-22; Bary to Parker, Nov. 23, 1911, box 3, Park Coll., HL; "Report on Publicity of the Political Equality League of Southern California," box 227, Haynes Papers, UCLA; Kazin, "Great Exception," 378-380, 384, 389-392; and Maud Younger, "Why Wage-Earning Women Should Vote," folder 1, box 1, Noel Papers, UCLA; Flamming, "Politics of Race," 207-210.

32. On the increased use of publicity among suffragists, see DuBois, "Suffrage Militance."

33. People's Paper, July 1, 1911; Citizen, July 14, Sept. 8, 1911; Whitehead, "The Socialists' Fight"; California Social-Democrat, July 22, Sept. 9, 1911; Downing, "Woman Suffrage in California"; Pitt, "Red Flag?" 14-18.

34. "Workers are Wanted," People's Paper, July 1, 1911; report from Mary Garbutt, Citizen, July 21, 1911; Woman's Journal, April 15, June 17, 1911; Whitehead, "The Socialists' Fight"; Georgia Kotsch, "Through Battle's Smoke," Citizen, Oct. 20, 1911.

35. Citizen, July 28, 1911; WESL circular letter; "Wage Earners' Suffrage League," Labor Clarion (San Francisco), Sept. 1, 1911; Maud Younger to [Frances] Noel, Oct. 24, 1911, Knox Mellon Collection (a collection of Frances Nacke Noel materials held privately by historian Knox Mellon, hereafter cited as Mellon Coll.)

36. Woman's Journal, Oct. 10, 1908; Sofia M. Loebinger to Alice Park, Aug. 4, 1909 and Alice Park, American Suffragette, n.p., n.d., box 2, Park Coll., HL.

37. "Suffrage Battle Hymn Swells in City Park," Los Angeles Herald, July 14, 1911; "Musical Pleas for Votes By Women Thwart Police," San Francisco Call, July 15, 1911; 1911 clippings, Suffrage Scrapbook, PHS; Woman's Journal, Aug. 26, 1911.

38. "Behold the Advent of the Woman Orator," Los Angeles Tribune, Aug. 20, 1911; Citizen, Sept. 15, 1911; [Frances Noel] to E[thel] Duppy Turner], Oct. 19, 1911, Mellon Coll.; "Suffrage Message Carried to Men in Territory Before Neglected," n.p., n.d., Suffrage Scrapbook, PHS.

39. Letter from Elizabeth Lowe Watson, Woman's Journal, Aug. 12, 1911; Alice Park, "The California Campaign," Western Woman Voter 1 (Oct.-Nov. 1911).

40. Katz, "Dual Commitments," 277-297, n. 140, 356-358.

41. Ibid., 283-287.

42. Pitt, "Red Flag?" 19-20; California Social-Democrat, Oct. 14, 1911; Bary OH, BL, 18-24, esp. 24; "At Los Angeles," Progressive Woman 5 (Dec. 1911), 5; Citizen, Oct. 13, 1911.

43. Western Woman Voter 1 (Oct.-Nov. 1911), 1; Bary to Parker, Nov. 23, 1911, box 3, Park Coll., HL.

44. Bary to Parker, Nov. 23, 1911, box 3, Park Coll., HL; Katz, "Dual Commitments," 299-301; Katz, "Socialist Women and Progressive Reform," 117-143.

Ida B. Wells-Barnett and her children, 1909.
From left: Charles Aked; Ida B. Wells, Jr.; Alfreda Marguerita;
and Herman Kohlsaat

Seventeen

IDA B. WELLS-BARNETT AND THE ALPHA SUFFRAGE CLUB OF CHICAGO

Wanda A. Hendricks

Editor's Introduction: Wanda A. Hendricks's article on Ida B. Wells-Barnett and the first African American woman suffrage club in Chicago, like the articles by Ellen DuBois and Sherry Katz that precede it, underscores the diversity of the suffrage movement in the early twentieth century. Though Black women encountered much discrimination from White suffragists, they were active participants in the movement nonetheless. One of the most famous of the African American suffragists was the indomitable Ida B. Wells-Barnett, under whose leadership Black women in Chicago not only worked for suffrage but played a significant role in the city's politics.

Beginning with her refusal to move from the "ladies car" to the "colored car" on a train in Mississippi in 1884, Ida B. Wells-Barnett did not allow anyone to deny her or her race their rights without a challenge—and the National American Woman Suffrage Association (NAWSA) was no exception. The famous incident Hendricks describes below, in which Wells-Barnett refused to obey the NAWSA's instructions to march with an all-Black contingent at the end of the 1913 suffrage parade in Washington, D.C. rather than with the Illinois delegation, would have come as no surprise to those who knew her. She was well known for her opposition to accommodation and gradualism and for her fearless advocacy of justice and equality.

Wells-Barnett was convinced that the vote was crucial for Black Americans— including as a weapon in the crusade against lynching to which she devoted much of her life—and thus she fought *against* the disfranchisement of African American men and *for* the enfranchisement of African American women. And through the Alpha Suffrage Club, the first and most important of several Black suffrage clubs in Chicago, she helped African American women and Chicago politicians realize that Black women could play a decisive role in city elections.

The fact that in 1913 Illinois gave women the right to vote in presidential and municipal elections (the first state east of the Mississippi River to do so), meant that Illinois suffragists had the opportunity to be politically active and influential— even while working for *full* suffrage. As Wanda Hendricks clearly demonstrates, these African American suffragists took full advantage of this opportunity. The women of the Alpha Suffrage Club worked hard and successfully to get more Black women and men to register and vote in Chicago elections, thus encouraging African Americans to run for office. Their support was a decisive factor in the election of Oscar DePriest, the first Black alderman in Chicago's history, who later (1928) made history as the first Northern Black to be elected to Congress and the first Black congressman since the disfranchisement of Southern Blacks in the 1890s.

★　★　★　★　★

IDA BELL WELLS-BARNETT played an important role in the municipal politics of Chicago during the second decade of the twentieth century. She sought civic representation for the masses of Black women and men who fled the South seeking economic, social, and political opportunity. In defense of the rights of African Americans and women, she had by 1915 formed the largest Black women's suffrage club in Illinois, defied the National American Woman Suffrage Association's ban on allowing African American women to march under their state banners alongside their White counterparts at the landmark 1913 suffrage parade in Washington, and played a crucial role in the election of the first African American alderman in Chicago.

Like most African Americans growing up in the Jim Crow South, Wells's early life was wrought with strife and conflict. She was the eldest of eight children, born in Holly Springs, Mississippi, on July 16, 1862 to a former slave from Virginia named Lizzie Warrenton and Jim Wells, the son of his master.[1] Despite the ravages of segregated Mississippi, the Wells educated their children at Shaw University in Holly Springs, later renamed Rust College. A community activist, Jim Wells became a trustee at Shaw while Lizzie Wells accompanied her children to classes so that she could learn to read and write.[2]

In 1878, the yellow fever epidemic that swept through the area drastically changed Ida Wells's life. Her father, mother, and a nine-month-old sibling, died in the epidemic, leaving sixteen-year-old Ida to care for the other children.[3] Financially responsible for the family, she passed the teachers' exam for the county schools and gained employment at a school six miles from her home that paid a monthly salary of $25. A year later, invited by her mother's sister in Memphis, Tennessee, Wells left Holly Springs. She took the two younger girls with her and left a sister and two brothers with relatives. Another brother had died several years earlier of spinal meningitis.[4]

Post-Reconstruction Memphis, like much of the South, began a program built on the usurpation of African American rights. With the aid of the Supreme Court, Southern states implemented a pervasive system of Jim Crow rules. The Court, in a series of cases, had by 1883 upheld the right of Southern states to enforce laws that violated the civil rights gained by African Americans in the post-Civil War era.

Deeply disturbed over the events leading to the restoration of White supremacy, Wells challenged the legality of the system. In May 1884, twenty-two-year-old Wells boarded a train owned by Chesapeake and Ohio Railroad and chose a seat in the "ladies" coach. Though informed by the conductor that as a Black woman she could not sit in the car reserved for White females, Wells stood her ground and refused to move to the all-Black Jim Crow car. Rather than allow Wells to remain seated, the conductor attempted forcefully to remove her. In retaliation, she bit his hand. Refusing to be outdone, the conductor sought the aid of the baggage man who assisted in dragging Wells from the coach.

Seeking justice, Wells hired a lawyer, and sued the railroad. Though she was initially victorious, the settlement of $500 was bittersweet. The state supreme court reversed the ruling of the lower court. Though disappointed, she understood that hers' "was the first case in which a colored plaintiff in the South had appealed to a state court since the repeal of the Civil Rights Bill by the United States Supreme Court," and if she had won, it "would have set a precedent which others would doubtless have followed."[5] The case and its subsequent reversal served as a springboard for her career to fight racism and discrimination. Over the years Wells pushed the system to its limit by persistently defending her rights as an African American woman. She advocated protest, demanded equality, and sought redress for crimes committed against the race.

One of the media Wells used to publicize her message was the newspaper. Before she reached thirty years of age, she had been co-owner of the *Memphis Free Speech and Headlight* and contributed articles to local and national publications such as the *Memphis Watchman* and the *Living Way,* the *New York Age,* and the *Indianapolis World.*[6] Many of the articles centered on the lynchings of African American men. The deaths of three colleagues, Thomas Moss, Calvin McDowell, and Henry Stewart by a lynch mob on March 9, 1892 in Memphis prompted these writings.

The three successfully managed the People's Grocery in a heavily populated Black section just outside Memphis. Accompanied by a police deputy, a competing White grocery store owner whose business was failing, harassed two of the African American owners. In the ensuing altercation, McDowell knocked the White grocer down and confiscated his gun. Stewart and McDowell were charged with assault and battery and arrested. McDowell later posted bond and they were released. The following Saturday night, the White grocer accompanied by a mob of White men entered the back door of People's Grocery. Fear compelled the African American men inside to fire several shots. Three of the White men were wounded. Chaos erupted when several Black men were dragged from their homes and questioned or incarcerated. Eventually, Moss, McDowell, and Stewart were indicted and thrown in jail. During the night they were removed from the county jail, shot, mutilated, and hanged.[7]

The African American community responded in several ways. The *Free Speech* ran an editorial that indicted the entire White community for the deaths of the three men and encouraged Blacks to leave the city. Pushed by fear, many Black Memphis residents heeded the call of the *Free Speech* and migrated to Oklahoma. So many departed that Black ridership on the City Railway Company's trains rapidly deteriorated. Reduced profits for the owners of the railway company and other businesses heavily trafficked by African Americans resulted. Concern over the massive out-migration forced mainstream White newspapers to discourage such moves and declare Oklahoma to be a major disappointment and plagued by hardships.

Wells refused to bow to pressure from White business owners to join them in their efforts to terminate the movement. Lost profits, she believed, were such a small price to pay for the lives of three responsible citizens. She even visited several Black churches and urged members "to keep on staying off the [railway] cars." Too, she quietly "rejoiced" when many more Blacks sought refuge in Oklahoma.[8]

Wells also decided to do her own investigation of the murders. The fates of Moss, McDowell, and Stewart forced her to question the rationale of White mob action and rethink her own ideas about the reasons for lynchings. Like most Americans, Black and White, she had been heavily influenced by White myths that suggested that lynchings happened to accused rapists; that is, Black men raping White women. The men brutally murdered in Memphis, however, did not fall into that category. They were outstanding community citizens whose only crime involved competing with a White grocer. The realization compelled Wells to examine previous lynching cases. After extensive research, she concluded that more often than not, the cry of rape masqueraded as a legitimate device for White men to eliminate African American competitors.

Subsequently, she wrote a scathing editorial: "Eight Negroes lynched since last issue of the *Free Speech.* Three were charged with killing White men and five with raping White women. Nobody in this section believes the old thread-bare lie that Negro men assault White women. If Southern men are not careful they will overreach themselves and a conclusion will be reached which will be very damaging to the moral reputation of their women."[9] The editorial attacked Southern White male honor and suggested that White women could be attracted to Black men. And, it infuriated the White community.

Fortunately, when the editorial appeared, Wells was en route to Philadelphia to attend the African Methodist Episcopal General Church Conference. Warnings from an enraged White mob persuaded the co-owner of the paper to flee. The mob destroyed the newspaper office and in their rage threatened Wells's life should she dare return to Memphis. Exiled from her home, she went to New York, joined the staff of the *New York Age* and continued her exposé on lynchings.[10]

Ida B. Wells had met the editor of the *New York Age,* Timothy Thomas Fortune, in the summer of 1888 and maintained her contact with him. When Fortune called for the formation of the National Afro-American League, she supported him. Through

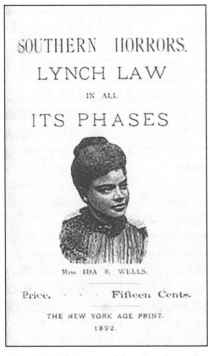

Ida B. Wells' pamphlet, *Southern Horrors,*written in 1892, and her portrait, 1893
LIBRARY OF CONGRESS & NATIONAL PORTRAIT MUSEUM

the *Age* and the encouragement of Fortune, Americans were alerted to the inherent problems of disfranchisement, lynching, inequitable distribution of educational funding, the convict lease system, and Jim Crow.[11]

Wells's research on lynching culminated in the pamphlet *Southern Horrors: Lynch Law In All Its Phases*. Published in October 1892, Wells prefaced it with "Somebody must show that the Afro-American race is sinned against [rather] than sinning, and it seems to have fallen upon me to do so." She was determined to prove that Blacks were not a "bestial race" and to "arouse the conscience of the American people to a demand for justice to every citizen."[12]

Creating the Alpha Suffrage Club

By the time Wells married newspaper publisher and attorney Ferdinand Barnett in 1895, she had visited England twice, caused an uproar at the Columbian Exposition of 1893 held in Chicago by publishing and handing out the pamphlet *The Reason Why The Colored American is not in the World's Columbian Exposition,* and become an active club woman by establishing the Ida B. Wells Club. Marriage to Barnett brought part ownership in his newspaper, the *Conservator,* two step-children and four of her own. Domestic duties as a wife and mother did not deter Wells from public life. She joined the National Association of Colored Women, organized in 1896, actively pursued the suffrage cause for both disenfranchised African American men and all women, and heeded the call for the development of the National Association for the Advancement of Colored People (NAACP) in the aftermath of the 1908 Springfield, Illinois, race riot. She also continued her exposés on lynching. In 1910 she wrote "How Enfranchisement Stops Lynching," for *Original Rights Magazine*.[13]

The Barnetts resided on the South Side of Chicago in the Second Ward. By the second decade of the twentieth century, the largest majority of African Americans in the city also lived in the area. In 1910 African Americans comprised twenty-five percent of the 42,801 population in the Ward and by 1915 represented nearly forty percent of the 63,342 residents.[14] Voting-age women in the ward developed a keen interest in the electoral process, particularly because of the pending female suffrage bill in the state legislature. They founded several suffrage clubs, developed voter education classes and held mass rallies.[15]

One of the most important and the first African American suffrage club in the city was the Alpha Suffrage Club. Wells-Barnett and a White colleague, Belle Squire, established the organization in January 1913.[16] Ida B. Wells-Barnett used the Suffrage Club as a basis to demonstrate the significance of the ballot to the masses of Black women in Chicago. During her early years in Chicago she toured the state for the Women's State Central Committee encouraging women to organize and develop political knowledge. She found on one of these trips that "in only a few instances did I see any of my own people." From this she concluded that "if the White women were backward in political matters, our own women were even more so."[17]

Lacking the skills to understand the political process, Wells-Barnett concluded, hindered African American women from full participation in civic matters. The necessity for the suffrage club took on new urgency when it became clear "that we were likely to have a restricted suffrage, and the White women of the organization [Women's Suffrage Association] were working like beavers to bring it about."[18]

To generate interest in the Suffrage Club and the ballot, she pooled her meager resources, organized meetings and insisted that the club hold membership in national, state, and local organizations such as the National Federation of Colored Women, the State Federation of Colored Women's Club, the Illinois Federation of Colored Women's Clubs and the City Federation of Colored Women's Clubs. The Club's goals included showing Black women how to use their "vote for the advantage of ourselves and our race" and acting as a liaison to the city, state, and national organizations. Within less than three years of its founding two hundred women claimed membership. Ida B. Wells-Barnett was elected president.[19]

Racism in the Suffrage Movement

One of Wells-Barnett's first official duties as president was to attend the March 1913 parade sponsored by the National American Woman Suffrage Association in the nation's capital. Carrying banners representing almost every state in the union, the parade marchers highlighted the demand for universal female enfranchisement.

But because of racist attitudes, African American
women were relegated to
the back of the line
regardless of state resi-
dency. Sixty-five enthusiastic delegates from Illinois prepared for the
march along Pennsylva-
nia Avenue. As they lined
up, Grace Wilbur Trout,
president of the Illinois
Equal Suffrage Associa-

Ida B. Wells-Barnett at 1913 NAWSA suffrage parade
Chicago Daily Tribune

tion and chairperson of the Illinois delegation, informed the Illinois group that the
NAWSA advised them "to keep our delegation entirely white" because many
women, especially those from the South, resented the presence of a Black woman in
the Illinois ranks. They would not march, Trout concluded, if Wells-Barnett remained
in the Illinois line. They expected her to march with the Black women's contingent at
the end of the procession.

Fear of antagonizing Southern White women, whose support was worth more to
the NAWSA's cause than that of African American women, prompted state
colleagues to deny Wells-Barnett's opportunity to march with them. Viewing Black
women as a threat to White supremacy, White Southern women rejected the
legitimacy of Black female state delegates marching with White state delegates.
Historian Steven Buechler argues that the NAWSA became the vehicle for Southern
White women to "maximize White women's votes, minimize Black women's votes,
and leave restrictions on Black male voters intact." The desire of Southern White
suffragists to assure the public and their state legislatures that African American
suffrage and woman suffrage were unconnected pushed them to devise the Jim
Crow strategy and to petition for the assistance of the NAWSA.[20] The NAWSA's
acquiescence made it blatantly clear that the organization took advantage of the
racist agenda, especially when it proved expedient. Ida B. Wells-Barnett's inclusion
in the state delegation in the 1913 parade threatened to impede that tactic by stripping
away the veil of Jim Crow and opening the door to other African American women.

When Trout pleaded with Wells-Barnett to march with the Black delegates at the
back of the procession, she refused; she insisted that "the Southern women have
tried to evade the question time and again by giving some excuse or other every
time it has been brought up. If the Illinois women do not take a stand now in this
great democratic parade then the colored women are lost."[21] But, Wells-Barnett's
plea fell on deaf ears just as an earlier appeal from Virginia Brooks, a White woman
from West Hammond, had. If "[w]e have come down here to march for equal
rights," then, "[i]t would be autocratic to exclude men or women of any color,"

Brooks told the contingent. Furthermore, she continued, "I think that we should allow Mrs. Barnett to walk in our delegation. If the women of other states lack moral courage, we should show them that we are not afraid of public opinion. We should stand by our principles. If we do not the parade will be a farce."[22] The state delegates refused to reconsider and acquiesced to the demands of Southern White women. Black women could march only if they maintained a very low profile and stayed in their place—at the back of the line.

Angry at the blatant disregard for her right as a woman and an Illinois resident to take part, Wells-Barnett told delegates that "I shall not march at all unless I can march under the Illinois banner" because "[w]hen I was asked to come down here I was asked to march with the other women of our state, and I intend to do so or not take part in the parade at all." One member of the group retorted "If I were a colored woman, I should be willing to march with the other women of my race." Wells-Barnett replied "there is a difference,…which you probably do not see…. I shall not march with the colored women. Either I go with you or not at all. I am not taking this stand because I personally wish for recognition. I am doing it for the future benefit of my whole race."[23]

After this debate Wells-Barnett disappeared from the parade site. Illinois delegates probably assumed that she had relented and decided to march with the Black contingent. But, as the delegates began marching down Pennsylvania Avenue, she quietly stepped out from the crowd of spectators and joined the only White Illinois colleagues sympathetic to her cause, Belle Squires and Virginia Brooks. So important was the event that a photograph of her, flanked by Squires and Brooks, appeared in The Chicago Daily Tribune giving the event and its participants local and national exposure.[24] As the marchers proceeded, Southerners did not defect. This may be in part because they did not learn of Wells-Barnett's inclusion until after the parade ended. At any rate, the press coverage reassured many Black women of their own tenuous place in the suffrage movement and probably convinced many Whites, despite the NAWSA's insistence, that the "Negro question" and female suffrage were not separate issues.

The staunch refusal by Wells-Barnett to march with the Black contingent impeded the White female prerogative of discriminating against African American women on racial grounds while simultaneously embracing them along gender lines. Racial xenophobia rather than gender inclusion guided their principles. The endorsement of Jim Crow segregation blinded White participants to the fact that unlike the requirement for their African American counterpart, they did not have to separate their Whiteness from their femaleness. Indeed, they could embrace the White, middle-class, nativist, racist sentiments prevalent during the Progressive Era under the guise of expediency. Ultimately, White women could express the desire for the enfranchisement of women while ignoring African American women.

But, Wells-Barnett frustrated their plans. She defined the battle for African American women by intertwining her state citizenship, her African American-ness, and her femaleness. She affirmed African American women's place in the fight for the ballot by confronting White women. For women and for the race, she rejected the notion that she did not belong among her state delegates.

Electing a Black Man as Alderman

On May 7 of that same year, the Illinois Senate passed the Presidential and Municipal Suffrage Bill and on June 11 the House approved the measure. Before the month ended, the legislature ratified the bill that granted partial suffrage to female citizens twenty-one years or older. Illinois became the first state east of the Mississippi River to enfranchise its women.[25] More importantly, for the first time in the city's history, African American females could cast their ballots in the race for alderman of the Second Ward. Mobilizing their forces quickly and instituting a large grassroots campaign, Black women became powerful political allies to voting-age African American men.

The Alpha Suffrage Club increased its activism in communities with large percentages of African Americans, especially since the aldermanic primary was less than a year away. Under Wells-Barnett's leadership, the Club implemented a block system to canvass neighborhoods. In addition, once-a-week meeting sessions were established as learning centers on the rights and duties of citizens. Women worked as clerks in the voter registration process and provided the necessary civic education.[26]

In the 1914 aldermanic primary the club endorsed the Independent candidate, William Randolph Cowan, a prominent Black real estate businessman, against the incumbent machine candidate, Hugh Norris.[27] While Black politicians championed the new gender-integrated electorate, several other ward men challenged female entry into their domain. As members of the Alpha Suffrage Club marshalled their forces and canvassed the Black community, registering women for the February 1914 primary, some men "jeered at them and told them they ought to be at home taking care of the babies." Other male hecklers accused them of "trying to take the place of men and wear the trousers."[28] The jeers made an impact on these Victorian ladies. Discouraged and unsure of their own place in politics, many of the women questioned the legitimacy of their role in the faction-riddled arena. Reassuring members that their efforts were important, Wells-Barnett refused to allow Black women to bow to male pressure. She urged each of the workers to return to the neighborhoods and continue registering women. Under her tutelage, most of the women stuck by their convictions, continued the registration efforts, and, in the process realized the importance of their participation in politics.

Some 7,290 female and 16,327 male potential voters registered during this campaign.[29] Though the club was not solely responsible for the number of registrants, it does suggest that the members aroused considerable interest and probably increased the potential number of African American voters. Ida B. Wells-Barnett proudly proclaimed that due to the impressive demonstration of women, "our men politicians were surprised," especially "because not one of them even our ministers, had said one word to influence women to take advantage of the suffrage opportunity Illinois had given to her daughters."[30]

The Black weekly, the *Chicago Defender*, captured the sentiments of many women in its sensational headlines for February 21, 1914: "Women To Show Loyalty By Casting First Ballot For Cowan For Alderman"; "Second Ward Women Determine to Use Their Power to Better Themselves and Strengthen the Race"; "Asserted Men Needed Their Assistance"; and "Garbage Question, Children's Playgrounds, Ventilation in Public Places, Supervision of 'Movies' Important Matters to Them." The paper triumphantly predicted that Black women would become "the balance of power" in the aldermanic campaign and would "see their first vote make race history in Chicago."[31]

On primary day, almost 3,000 women cast ballots in the Second Ward. Still, William Cowan lost the election. Though disappointed with the outcome, the Suffrage Club women consoled themselves with the knowledge that they had played a significant role in attracting forty-five percent of the women who voted for Cowan to the polls. For the *Defender*, this showed that Black women understood better than the men the interconnection between duty and politics because "they were actuated by principal in politics just as they are in everything else." Moreover, the newspaper article stated that "The women's vote was a revelation to everyone, and after analysis shows them still actuated by the sense of duty to do more" and that because of female votes "Traitorous leaders are to be relegated to the background and citizens of strength and character are to take their places." The *Defender* vigorously promoted both Victorian ideals and female access to the electoral process.[32]

The female vote even compelled another weekly, the *Broad Ax*, to acknowledge that "Cowan and his followers woke things up…for he received 2,700 votes more than one thousand of that number being cast by the ladies." The vote "plainly brought to the front one thing and that is that within the next two or four years at the longest a high class popular solid Colored man of affairs can and will be elected to the city council from that ward." For if only three hundred of the Black votes to Norris had been transferred to Cowan, the paper concluded, "nothing could have prevented him from breaking into the city council."[33]

The Alpha Suffrage Club's role generated the most attention. Within a few days after Cowan's defeat, two members of the Republican Party visited the Alpha Suffrage Club. A Black Republican and contractor, Oscar DePriest, joined the president of the ward organization, Samuel Ettelson, in an appeal for the women to campaign and vote for the machine candidate in the next election.[34] The two men urged the women not to support an Independent candidate for alderman as they had in the Cowan primary, because if they did so, the Black vote would split and the Democratic candidate might win. In turn, the Republican Party "having realized that there was now a demand for a colored man, would itself nominate one at the next vacancy." The next vacancy, they were told would probably be in

1915. In November, 1914, George Harding, a Second Ward alderman, was elected state senator. Keeping its promise, the organization pushed DePriest to the forefront by endorsing him as their Black candidate for alderman.[35]

Despite the Chicago political machine's endorsement of DePriest, his candidacy was contested. As a matter of fact, his nomination opened the door for other African American candidates seeking the coveted post of alderman. For the first time in Chicago's political history, three Black candidates campaigned for alderman in the primary. Joining DePriest were Louis Anderson, a former journalist from Washington, D.C., and Charles Griffin, an insurance and real estate broker.[36]

With battle lines drawn, the candidates began seeking votes. One of the first forums for the three politicians was at the Alpha Suffrage Club's headquarters. They presented their political platform and entertained questions. The Club decided to "endorse" the Republican ticket and "our young giant Oscar DePriest for alderman of the Second Ward." They pledged "to leave no stone unturned" for his election because "we realize that in no other way can we safeguard our own rights than by holding up the hands of those who fight our battles."[37]

On February 27, 1915, DePriest won the Republican primary. After the victory DePriest appealed to those who did not vote for him. "[A]s all good Republicans," he wrote, I hope that they "give me in my coming fight for election their heartiest loyalty and support."[38] But despite his plea dissenters lingered. For example, Edward Wright, disgruntled over DePriest's victory and his own failed bids for alderman, requested that the Political Equality League endorse William Cowan as an independent candidate against DePriest. As a member of the League and on behalf of the Alpha Suffrage Club, Wells-Barnett recoiled from the appeal. She argued that this scheme was conjured up by "this nameless white man" who "had not been prompted by the desire to secure a better man for nomination. It simply was to get two colored men to fight against each other, and the result would be that neither one of them would secure the place." The League agreed and the Wright-Cowan challenge ended.[39]

The contest between DePriest and three White candidates drew thousands of African Americans in the Second Ward to the polls to cast their ballots. When the votes were tabulated, DePriest was the clear winner—and became the first Black alderman of Chicago. The final count was: DePriest, 10,599 (Republican); Al Russell, 6,893 (Democrat); Simon P. Gary, 3,697 (Progressive); Samuel Block, 433 (Socialist).[40]

Oscar DePriest's victory inspired public discussion of the significance of the female electorate. The woman's vote was a decisive factor and without it, DePriest would not have been the first Black alderman. Women's ballots accounted for more than one third of the ballots cast for DePriest. The nearly 4,000 remaining votes went to the other candidates.[41] More than one third of the total votes cast came from women.

DePriest acknowledged his debt to Second Ward women. Soon after the election, he asserted in the national Black journal, *The Crisis*, "I favor extension of the right of suffrage to women" because the women in Chicago "cast as intelligent a vote as the men." Although there was a certain degree of "timidity" during "the first campaign in which women voted in Chicago," women educated themselves. And in the 1914 and 1915 campaigns, "the work of the women was as earnest and the interest as keen as that of the men and in some instances the partisanship was almost bitter." Moreover, DePriest asserted that during

the campaign of 1915 when colored men were primary candidates for alderman, the women of the race seemed to realize fully what was expected of them, and, with the men, rolled up a very large and significant vote for the colored candidates; and they were consistent at the election, contributing to a plurality of over 3,000 votes for the successful colored candidate in a field of five. Personally, I am more than thankful for their work and as electors believe they have every necessary qualification that the men possess.[42]

The Legacy

A year after the election, the Alpha Club elected new officers and continued its suffrage work. Ida B. Wells-Barnett retained the presidency.[43] In addition to the Second Ward, the Club also canvassed the Sixth, Fourteenth, and Thirtieth Wards in Chicago because each had high concentrations of African Americans. The lure of jobs opened by America's involvement in World War I and the fear of the continued deterioration

of race relations in the South prompted a mass exodus from Southern states to large urban areas like Chicago. By 1920, the Second Ward African American population was 47,647 or sixty-nine percent of the residents. Voting-age women accounted for 17,144, while men numbered 19,894.[44] This united force challenged political leaders, elected African Americans to the aldermanic post, and commanded some of the spoils from patronage politics.

Little is known about the Alpha Suffrage Club during those late teen years. It is likely that African American women in the Second Ward and other heavily populated Black wards continued canvassing and voting in large numbers, in part because of the preceding labor by Suffrage Club members. Despite the passage of the Nineteenth

Ida B. Wells-Barnett, c. 1917-1919, wearing "Martyred Negro Soldiers" button
UNIVERSITY OF CHICAGO LIBRARY

Amendment in 1920 granting suffrage to all women, the political necessity of a united African American constituency remained. For that reason Wells-Barnett continued to press for Black women to vote by making speeches and canvassing throughout Chicago and the state. In 1930 she ran for the Illinois Senate as an Independent candidate. Though she lost, her zeal for political involvement continued.[45]

The year after her political bid for the senate Wells-Barnett died of a kidney disease.[46] She left a legacy of activism in social and civic endeavors. Courageously, she exposed the horrors of lynching to a national audience, inspired the growth of the Black female club movement in the state, encouraged African Americans to become a part of the political process, and inspired hundreds of women to enter into the public domain of politics.

Notes

1. Alfreda Duster, ed. *Crusade For Justice: The Autobiography of Ida B. Wells* (Chicago, 1970), 7-8; See also Neil R. McMillen, *Dark Journey: Black Mississippians In The Age of Jim Crow* (Urbana, 1989) for discussion of African American life in Mississippi in the post-Civil War era.
2. Duster, *Crusade*, 8-9.
3. Ibid., 9-17; Monroe A. Majors, *Noted Negro Women Their Triumphs And Activities* (Chicago, 1893; reprint ed., Nashville, Tenn., 1971), 187-188.
4. Duster, *Crusade*, 15-18.
5. Ibid., xvii, 18-20; Mildred Thompson, "Ida B. Wells-Barnett: An Exploratory Study of An American Black Woman, 1893-1930," (Ph.D. diss., George Washington University, 1979), 26-28.
6. Duster, *Crusade*, 22-24, 69, 71; Thompson, "Ida B. Wells Barnett: An Exploratory Study of An American Black Woman, 1893-1930," 29-31; Majors, *Noted Negro Women*, 189.
7. Duster, *Crusade*, 47-51; Ida B. Wells, *Southern Horrors: Lynch Law In all Its Phases* (New York, 1892; reprint ed., New York, 1969), 18-19; David M. Tucker, "Miss Ida B. Wells and Memphis Lynching," *Phylon* 32 (1971): 115-116.
8. Duster, *Crusade*, 53-58.
9. Ibid., 65-66.
10. Ibid., 61-67.
11. Ibid., 71, 77; Thompson "Ida B. Wells Barnett: An Exploratory Study of An American Black Woman, 1893-1930," 36-37, 58; Emma Lou Thornbrough, "The National Afro-American League, 1887-1908," *Journal of Southern History* 27 (1961): 504.
12. Wells, *Southern Horrors*, preface.
13. Duster, *Crusade*, xxiii, 239, 321-327; Ida B. Wells, *The Reason Why The Colored American is Not in the World's Columbian Exposition* (Chicago, 1893); Elizabeth Lindsay Davis, *The Story of The Illinois Federation of Colored Women's Clubs* (Chicago, 1922), 26-28, 56; Ida B. Wells-Barnett, "How Enfranchisement Stops Lynching," *Original Rights Magazine* (June 1910), 42-53.
14. *Thirteenth Census Of The United States, 1910: Population*, v. 2: The breakdown of the population was Native White, native parentage = 11,642; Native White, foreign or mixed = 11,225; Foreign-Born White = 9,118; Negro = 10,709; Indian, Chinese, Japanese, and all other = 107. Yearly census data for the area was kept by the *Chicago Daily News*. Corrections and updates can be found in James Langland, M.A. Compiler, *The Chicago Daily News Almanac And Year-Book For 1916* (Chicago, 1916), 585, 586. Also see Allan H. Spear, *Black Chicago: The Making Of A Negro Ghetto 1890-1920* (Chicago, 1967) 15 and 122 for population data from 1915.
15. *Chicago Defender*, February 21, 1914; Also see listing in Ford S. Black, *Black's Blue Book Directory Of Chicago's Active Colored People And Guide To Their Activities* (Chicago, Ill., 1916), 55, Illinois State Historical Library, Springfield, Ill.
16. Katherine E. Williams, "The Alpha Suffrage Club," *The Half Century Magazine* (September 1916): 12.
17. Duster, *Crusade*, 244-245.
18. Ibid., 345.
19. Williams, "The Alpha Suffrage Club," 12; *Alpha Suffrage Record*, 18 March 1914 [1915], Ida B. Wells-Barnett Papers, University of Chicago. Other officers included: Mary Jackson, Viola Hill, Vera Wesley Green, Sadie L. Adams, and K.J. Bills. There is not an "official" roster of members.
20. Carrie Chapman Catt and Nettie Rogers Shuler, *Woman Suffrage and Politics: The Inner Story of the Suffrage Movement* (1923; reprint, Seattle, 1969), 241-242; Rosalyn Terborg-Penn, "Discrimination Against Afro-American Women in the Woman's Movement, 1830-1920," in *The Afro-American Woman: Struggles And Images*, eds. Sharon Harley and Rosalyn Terborg-Penn (New York, 1978), 24-25; Aileen S. Kraditor, *The Ideas of the Woman Suffrage Movement, 1890-1920* (1965; reprint New York, 1981), 212-218; Steven Buechler, *The Transformation of The Woman Suffrage Movement: The Case of Illinois, 1850-1920* (New Jersey, 1986), 149-150, 226; Adade Mitchell Wheeler, "Conflict in the Illinois Woman Suffrage Movement of 1913," *Journal of the Illinois State Historical Society* 76 (Summer 1983): 106; Marjorie Spruill (Wheeler), *New Women Of The New South: The Leaders of the Woman Suffrage Movement in the Southern States* (New York, 1993); *The Chicago Daily Tribune*, March 3 and 4, 1913.
21. *The Chicago Daily Tribune*, March 4, 1913.
22. Ibid.
23. Ibid.
24. Ibid.
25. John D. Buenker, "Illinois and the Four Progressive-Era Amendments to the United States Constitution," *Illinois Historical Journal* 80 (Winter 1987): 210-227; Wheeler, "Conflict in the Illinois Woman Suffrage Movement of 1913," 65-114; Anne Firor Scott and Andrew MacKay Scott, *One Half the People: The Fight for Woman Suffrage* (1975; reprint, Urbana, Ill., 1982), 116-121.
26. Williams, "The Alpha Suffrage Club," 12.
27. *Broad Ax*, January 17, 1914; Gosnell, *Negro Politicians*, 74.
28. Duster, *Crusade*, 346.
29. *The Chicago Daily News Almanac And Year-Book For 1915* (Chicago, 1914), 632, Chicago Municipal Library, Chicago, Ill.; Also, the *Chicago Defender*, February 21, 1914, mentions the Alpha Political Club and Josephine Crawford as active in the political process as well.
30. Duster, *Crusade*, 346.
31. *Chicago Defender*, February 21, 1914.
32. Spear, *Black Chicago*, 81-82; *Chicago Defender*, March 28, 1914.
33. *The Chicago Daily News Almanac And Year-Book For 1915*, 632. Spear, *Black Chicago*, 123; *Chicago Defender*, February 21, 1914; *Broad Ax*, February 28, 1914.
34. Duster, *Crusade*, 346.
35. Duster, *Crusade*, 346-348; Gosnell, *Negro Politicians*, 170.
36. Gosnell, *Negro Politicians*, 30, 70, 104-105; Pinderhughes, *Race and Ethnicity*, 77-78.
37. *Suffrage Record*, March 18, 1914 [1915].
38. *Chicago Defender*, February 27, 1915; *The Chicago Daily News Almanac And Year-Book For 1916* (Chicago, 1916), 567.
39. Duster, *Crusade*, 348.
40. *The Chicago Daily News Almanac And Year-Book For 1916*, 567, 591; Gosnell, *Negro Politicians*, 171.
41. *The Chicago Daily News Almanac And Year-Book For 1916*, 567, 591; Gosnell, *Negro Politicians*, 171.
42. Oscar DePriest, "Chicago and Woman's Suffrage," *The Crisis* 10 (August 1915): 179.
43. Williams, "The Alpha Suffrage Club," 12. Other officers were: Sadie L. Adams, E.D. Wyatt, J.E. Hughes, W.N. Mills, and Laura Beasley.
44. *Fourteenth Census of the United States*, 274.
45. See Wanda Hendricks, "Ida Bell Wells-Barnett," In Darlene Clark Hine, ed. *Black Women In America: An Historical Encyclopedia*, v. 2, s.v. (New York, 1993), 1245.
46. Ibid., 1246.

Alice Paul celebrating the victory of the ratification of the
Nineteenth Amendment, 1920

Eighteen

ALICE PAUL AND THE TRIUMPH OF MILITANCY

Linda G. Ford

Editor's Introduction: As historian Linda G. Ford so clearly illustrates in this article, the spirit of militancy that had been evident in the early stages of the woman suffrage movement was rekindled near its end. This militant spirit inspired women to bold and dramatic acts that made it impossible for the public or the politicians to ignore the movement or fail to perceive the determination of suffragists to bring the long battle to a victorious conclusion.

As the movement entered its last decade, a new mood was developing among American suffragists: there was a growing impatience with the slow progress and a sense that victory should have come long ago. Indeed, to a generation of women who had come of age in an era of greater educational and employment opportunities for women and who witnessed the political activism of women in the Progressive Era, the denial of the vote to women seemed like an anachronism that must be swiftly rejected—along with the concept of separate spheres upon which that denial was based. This new generation of suffragists, together with many veterans of the movement who had buried one revered suffrage leader after another while politicians still denied them their rights, were responsible for the new wave of suffrage militancy. Militant tactics, as we have seen, were increasingly evident, including in the states of New York and California. Suffrage militants were incensed that women were forced to plead and cajole and to devise arguments as to why woman suffrage was good for society. Equal suffrage was their right, they declared, and they would *take* it.

Alice Paul soon emerged as the leader of the American militants. Paul had returned from Great Britain in 1910, but for two years devoted herself to the completion of her doctoral degree, earning a Ph.D. in sociology from the University of Pennsylvania. During her three years in Great Britain (where she was a caseworker for a settlement house), Paul had been inspired by Emmeline Pankhurst and the militant Women's Social and Political Union (WSPU). Radicalized by participation in the bold and defiant British suffrage movement, Paul was disturbed by the relative docility of the National American Woman Suffrage Association (NAWSA) under President Anna Howard Shaw, and appalled that the entire energies of American suffragists were absorbed by state suffrage campaigns while the federal amendment remained on the back burner.

Working at first through the NAWSA's Congressional Committee and later the NAWSA-affiliated Congressional Union (CU), Paul tried to refocus the attention of suffragists on the federal amendment and revitalize—and publicize—the national suffrage movement. Paul masterminded the dramatic suffrage parade in 1913 during Woodrow Wilson's inauguration, a grand and dramatic display of the strength of the national movement that became even more sensational when the largely hostile crowd attacked the marchers—provoking massive press coverage and a Congressional investigation, commanding the attention of the nation.

As explained in this essay by Linda Ford and the subsequent essay by Robert Booth Fowler, Alice Paul and the CU soon parted company with the NAWSA (in 1914), largely over the issue of tactics. Influenced by the strategy of the British suffragists, Paul introduced her famous plan of holding the party in power responsible for the failure to enfranchise women. Rather than beg for enfranchisement, Paul sought to direct the full power of the women already enfranchised in Western states against President Wilson and the Democrats (who had a majority in Congress), hoping to force the president and his party to abandon their traditional insistence on states' rights and to secure the passage of the federal woman suffrage amendment. Paul's approach violated the NAWSA's traditional nonpartisan strategy, and led to a new schism in suffrage ranks. For the rest of the movement's history, the NAWSA and the militants would be involved in a public dispute over strategy and tactics.

It is interesting to note that one point of disagreement between the two groups was the *name* of the federal amendment. Soon after the CU became an independent organization, its members began referring to the proposed amendment as "The Susan B. Anthony Amendment"—over the objections of the NAWSA and some CU members, including Harriot Stanton Blatch, who believed it was inappropriate to single out any one of the nineteenth-century pioneers for this recognition.

The CU continued to exist as a separate organization and was renamed the National Woman's Party (NWP) when it merged with its Western affiliate (the Woman's Party) in 1917. As Ford describes, the NWP gradually but steadily became more militant, engaging in acts of non-violent civil disobedience that provoked a stern—even violent—response from the Wilson administration. But the harsh and unjust treatment the suffragists received only cemented their determination. Women became the first in the United States to picket the White House, a form of protest that lasted nearly three years before the Nineteenth Amendment was ratified. During this time hundreds of suffragists were arrested illegally and jailed, with some organizing hunger strikes while in jail, and facing forced feedings by prison officials. These actions, and more, continued to focus the public's and the politicians' attention on woman suffrage.

Militancy, Ford insists, was a success. Not only did suffrage militancy successfully focus attention on woman suffrage and reawaken the "slumbering issue of a national woman suffrage amendment," it "made the government and politicians acutely aware of women's potential political power." Though reviled by many politicians—and suffragists—the militants "created a situation in which something had to be done." The violent reaction to their uncompromising demand for political equality solidified their determination to win the vote and also to wipe out all vestiges of discrimination against American women. It was this group that drafted and introduced the Equal Rights Amendment in 1923—an amendment they called the "Lucretia Mott Amendment."

★　★　★　★　★

THE STRONG, FEMINIST MILITANCY of the National Woman's Party (NWP) evolved as a logical response to the intransigence of male-centered government in the first decades of this century. Feminist militancy, which I define as the readiness to resist governmental authorities and break the law for the cause of women's rights, developed gradually from men's (non)reaction to women's political claims to equal citizenship. Woman militants for suffrage were not shy about critiquing the male monopoly on power, and, in turn, male authorities responded to the perceived threat, describing the suffragists as "unnatural, iron-jawed" females—even "revolutionaries." Militant suffragists were *feminist* revolutionaries, "striking the blow" themselves to secure drastic political change for women, and with that, change in women's social role, status and image.

Women's New Independence

In the early twentieth century, angry women—potential militants—were beginning actively to change their lives. Time and time again, in autobiographies of women of this period, there emerges a strong sense of impatient resentment and desire for independence. A growing number of women wanted independence from the nineteenth-century concept of a stiffly corseted, rigidly role-stereotyped woman. These women wanted freedom from centuries of having to depend on men for identity, sustenance, and decision-making.

In the twentieth century, cultural and economic change would slowly make a difference in the social role a woman could play. Virginia Woolf wrote that if a woman had the means to support herself, all sorts of possibilities arose; she might even be able to do something with her anger. The American feminist theorist Charlotte Perkins Gilman echoed Woolf, arguing that the time had come for women to be completely independent, especially economically, of men. In the early twentieth-century, women were a rapidly growing presence in the labor force, in offices and factories, and even in "male" professions such as law and medicine. In addition, these women's expectations were growing.[1]

In the United States, the women who joined Alice Paul in a new militant suffrage movement were, as Paul put it, not of any particular class, but shared a "feeling of loyalty to our own sex and an enthusiasm to have every degradation that was put upon our sex removed." *The Suffragist*, the militants' weekly journal, was decidedly feminist in tone and subject matter. These new suffrage leaders saw revolutionary social implications in their struggle for political rights, and they were not the only ones to see them. A 1916 *New York Times* editorial called the "threat of sex vs. sex" carried out by the suffragists:

> political blackmail...an ugly portent, whose possibilities of damage are not limited to politics, but may extend to other parts of the social structure. These [women] leaders have justified to the extent of their powers the worst that has ever been said about the danger of giving votes to women.

That same year a Georgia woman wrote Western suffrage leader Anne Martin: "A female creature, queer and quaint, Who longs to be just what she ain't/ We cannot efface—we can't forget her—We love her still—the stiller the better."[2] Suffrage militants were not at all within the bounds of proper womanhood.

American and English Suffragists

"Improper" woman suffragists revealed their impatience with passive roles in both England and the United States. There was a very direct relation between the arch-militant Women's Social and Political Union (WSPU) of England and the National Woman's Party of the United States. Women who were very important to the woman suffrage movement had long traveled the Atlantic to inspire and inform each other. Many of them advocated a new sort of independence for women featuring a determination to act—strike their own blows—to take matters into their own hands. The feminism of mid-nineteenth century reformer Elizabeth Cady Stanton was directly inspired by English women like Mary Wollstonecraft, author of the 1792 *A Vindication of the Rights of Woman*, and Frances Wright, who spoke out for women's rights when she came to America in the 1820s. *The Revolution*, published by Stanton and feminist reformer Susan B. Anthony, kept close track of the English scene.[3]

By 1887 the American/English Women's Franchise League included among its members the British Emmeline Pankhurst, along with Stanton and her daughter, Harriot Stanton Blatch (who had married an Englishman). Both the Pankhursts and the Stantons advocated a certain aggressive style of seeking reform. According to both Emmeline and her daughter Christabel Pankhurst, when Susan B. Anthony visited London in 1901, she was a great inspiration for British feminists. Realizing that Anthony would die without gaining the franchise for women, Christabel Pankhurst decided that "deeds, not words" should be the motto of the WSPU's organized fight for woman suffrage.[4]

American graduate student Alice Paul was "extremely thrilled" when she joined the parliamentary deputations of the WSPU while in England. Alice Paul, like her

Alice Paul in academic robes, 1913
LIBRARY OF CONGRESS

Alice Paul started *The Suffragist* in
1913 along with NAWSA's
Congressional Union.

idol Susan B. Anthony before her, had a feminist philosophy that demanded full equality for women and a belief that moral principles should be committed to action. Paul was born in 1885 in the Quaker community of Moorestown, New Jersey, and was brought up with the Quaker maxim that women were equal before God and were entitled, even obliged, to address social problems. Paul had a serious-minded childhood, during which she developed a strong sense of right and wrong, and the belief that any life without a cause was empty. For Paul, although trained as a social worker, that cause would single-mindedly be women's rights.

Although not without hesitation and much trepidation, Paul first became involved in women's rights advocacy in England by interrupting the speeches of Foreign Secretary Edward Grey and Home Secretary Winston Churchill. In addition, she went to Scotland to organize and rabble-rouse—traveling with fellow American Lucy Burns and Emmeline Pankhurst herself. It was while working with the WSPU in England that Paul and Burns first felt a "blazing" feminist anger, both at the rough treatment they received at the hands of male police and jailers—including forced feeding in jail—*and* at the continued indifference of male political authorities.[5]

Their militant experiences in England gave Paul and Burns a notoriety of sorts and a credibility with American suffragists upon their return to the United States in 1910. Their English experiences also left Paul and Burns with a lasting adulation for the Pankhursts and the WSPU, although they never did use the Pankhurst's "violent" tactics such as destroying property. After their deputations to Parliament were repeatedly dispersed with violence, and after suffering harsh jail terms, the women of the WSPU reasoned that the violent actions against them demonstrated that property—not human life—was most important to the English government. The British authorities unleashed a tremendously hostile counterattack and in the process spurred a large portion of public opinion to shift to the WSPU side. Only World War I would put an end to the war between the WSPU and the British government.[6] What Alice Paul learned from her participation in the British movement was a resentment of male domination, a desire for full equality, and a determination to organize women to act aggressively on their demands—to *take* their rights.

A Militant Approach in America

The fame they gained in England culminated in an invitation for Alice Paul and Lucy Burns to speak to the National American Woman Suffrage Association (NAWSA) in 1910. Two years later, through the auspices of social reform paragon Jane Addams, Paul and Burns were asked to chair a "congressional committee" for the NAWSA that would work for a federal woman suffrage amendment in Washington. The two young militants brought a new excitement—an aggressive spirit—to what had become a lethargic woman suffrage movement in America.

The flamboyance of the militants' new committee was directed toward overcoming indifference to women's issues in the United States. In time, their concerted militant actions generated hostility and violence—directed at them as "unnatural" women. How would a movement to energize the campaign for the middle-class, Progressive reform of woman suffrage come to be considered a dangerously militant, antigovernment conspiracy? The coming of World War I certainly helped shape events, but Woman's Party policy—a direct reaction to government non-action—went through gradual, increasingly militant stages, leading to the women's arrest and imprisonment.

The Congressional Committee was defiant and aggressive from the beginning. That brand of impatient, militant feminism, coupled with competition over NAWSA-held suffrage territory and money, soon offended the NAWSA's deliberately moderate leaders. The Congressional Committee evolved into the Congressional Union (CU), a more independent and stronger group. The CU approach of strong feminism and militant-spirited strategies—obviously influenced by the British—became a liability and an embarrassment to a NAWSA leadership determined not to erode the legislative and public support they had painstakingly won for suffrage. NAWSA officers were sure that the aggressive CU was doing damage by pushing too hard, alienating President Woodrow Wilson and antagonizing the public with their incessant, unladylike lobbying. The CU promoted militancy, an aggressive, unapologetically egalitarian, militant style, which the more moderate NAWSA members could not countenance. In 1914, Paul and Burns' group was expelled from the NAWSA for being "too British."[7]

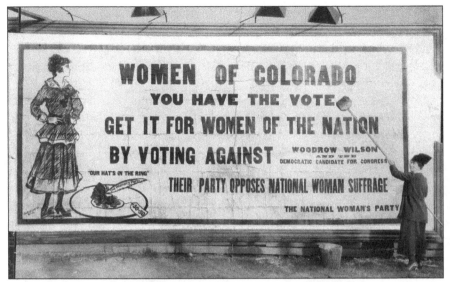

A billboard in Denver goes up in 1916, part of the NWP's strategy to harness the voting power of Western women to pressure the national Democratic Party to support a woman suffrage amendment.

LIBRARY OF CONGRESS

As an independent organization, the CU used increasingly militant methods between 1914 and 1917, trying to force the Wilson administration to secure the passage of woman suffrage. They began with "heckling" Wilson—interrupting speeches and asking pointed questions—and combined that with strenuous speaking and petitioning campaigns for suffrage. A small but dedicated new suffrage organization, the CU was particularly well-known for the British-inspired tactic of organizing women voters in the West to vote against recalcitrant Democrats in 1914 and again in 1916. In the 1916 elections, under a strict "party responsibility" policy, the Democrats were held responsible for non-action on the newly formed Western Woman's Party's one and only plank, "the enfranchisement of the women of America through a Federal Amendment." Through the efforts of traveling organizers and helped by their own increasingly popular journal, *The Suffragist*, the militants did their best to convince women in the Western states, many of whom had had the vote for years, to vote "Republican, Socialist, Prohibitionist or Progressive—anything but Democratic." Although studies have shown that the Woman's Party did affect those elections with their appeals to Western women to "help their sisters in the East," the Wilson administration was not impressed enough to pass the suffrage amendment. However, a few years later, Wilson *was* persuaded to favor woman suffrage due to a shift in public opinion. Unquestionably this change of heart was influenced by the NWP pressure and propaganda, yet personally Wilson remained "repelled" by women who, by speaking in public, "reversed the social order."[8]

Organizing the National Woman's Party

When the assertive policy of holding the party in power responsible did not secure woman suffrage, the Woman's Party began overt acts of militancy in defiance of authority and the law. This group of militant women decided in March of 1917 that in order to further a united, politically powerful campaign, they needed to merge the Western campaign's Woman's Party with the Washington-based CU, and to call themselves the National Woman's Party (NWP). The militants' tactics, including their shrewd use of women's existing political power and their obvious courage and iron-willed determination, continued to reflect their belief that women were worthy of political power. Increasingly resentful of the men who held power over them, NWP suffragists used progressively more militant actions against an unyielding government. At the same time, they sharpened their feminist critique. They slowly shifted from just insisting on a greater democracy that included women, to a condemnation of an oppressive, "autocratic," patriarchal society, including their effort to show that the "women's" militancy—picketing and civil disobedience—was different from and highly superior to, the current manifestation of "men's" militancy—war. Paradoxically, the NWP used the weapon of nonviolence very effectively to illustrate their enormous strength as women. Furious that the war-harried Wilson decided to receive no more NWP suffragist delegations, the militant women, in the first stage of their open militancy, began a perpetual delegation of White House pickets in January 1917, continuing almost daily pickets even after the United States entered the war in April.

The first stage of outright militancy was characterized by beautifully staged and deliberately peaceful, nonviolent demonstrations—consisting of banner-holding suffragists arranged outside the White House—protesting the Wilson government's inaction on suffrage. The NWP's suffrage strategy is a classic example of nonviolent resistance against a government, with the intent to defy and coerce authorities to act. A typical NWP banner mocked the president by using his own lofty moral rhetoric. One example of this was the use of Wilson's war message: "We shall fight for the things which we have always held nearest our hearts—for democracy, for the right of those who submit to authority to have a voice in their own government."[9] The peaceful and perfectly legal picketing method was adopted from several sources, including labor activists as well as the British militant suffragists. The tactic also in part reflected Alice Paul's adherence to a tradition of Quaker civil disobedience. To some NWP leaders, such demonstrations were particularly appropriate for women, "peace-loving by nature," to show that "woman's" militancy was brave and defiant, but peaceful, whereas "male" militancy, in 1917, was violent and destructive. Paul said it was clear that "women were the peace-loving half of the world and that by giving power to women we would diminish the possibilities of war."[10] Whether they thought women naturally more peaceful or not, all NWP pickets demanded that Wilson act on woman suffrage immediately, and give women a voice in decisions on war.

Suffragists Arrested

The first mob attacks, arrests, and jailings began the second stage of open militancy in June 1917. The government began to regard the women as more than a nuisance when the pickets raised new banners that were sharply critical of the Wilson government, proclaiming that America, fighting a war for freedom in Europe, was not as democratic as "free Russia," which had enfranchised its women. Banners lambasted "Kaiser Wilson" and his "dictatorial and oppressive" policies toward women. The Wilson administration's violent reaction, including jailing many of the protesters and exposing them to harsh treatment and terrible conditions, brought the NWP to the third stage of open militancy—the October demands for political prisoner status in the face of what the women called "administration terrorism" against their members.

The abusive treatment meted out to the NWP demonstrators was suffered by rich and poor, old and young suffragists alike. Co-leaders Alice Paul and Lucy Burns—both from very comfortable backgrounds, highly educated and progressive "New Women" professionals (one an educator, the other a social worker/scholar) initially attracted other impatient feminists of similar backgrounds. The core membership of the NWP in the suffrage period, 1912-1920, tended to be of two types: the state and local officers, either mature (over forty) social reformer/ clubwomen, inspired to greater militancy; or speaker/organizers, young college-educated "New Women," with very liberal, modern ideas of women's equality and economic independence. There was, therefore, conflict within the NWP over race and class issues and over how inclusive their "united sisterhood" should be. But to all NWP suffrage leaders and organizers, the defiant stance against the Wilson administration, as part of the battle against sexism, always came first.

Other groups of antigovernment dissenters directed their protests directly against war itself, or against the capitalist system which made a war of "imperialist

Police arrest suffrage pickets, Washington, D.C., 1917
WOMAN SUFFRAGE MEDIA COLLECTION

aggression" possible. The antigovernment, feminist demonstrators of the NWP also wanted to change the system, but their vision was one in which women should be included, not just in government, but in full equality in all aspects of American society. Some NWP feminists stressed women's "superior" qualities, evolved over centuries of being "other directed," but many others stressed that all women must be given the opportunity to participate fully in their culture, whatever qualities they did or did not possess.[11] National Woman's Party feminists shared a radical vision of completely equal opportunity, and were not willing to wait for their goal. In fact, they were more than willing to act, to fight against their opponent, the Wilson government.

Political Prisoners

The government started jailing militant suffragists in June 1917. But the sentences were not more than a few days in length until mid-August and the "Kaiser" banners, when sixty-day sentences at Occoquan Workhouse in Virginia began to be meted out. By mid-September, sympathetic socialist women began to be more apparent among the arrested, including newspaper writer Peggy Baird Johns, one of the first to suggest demanding political prisoner status. The women at Occoquan, including Lucy Burns, readily assented to the plan, agreeing that they were not "traffic obstructors," as charged, but in reality, political offenders. The women drafted a letter to the district commissioners in Washington demanding political prisoner privileges and protesting their unjust and erratic sentences that ranged from a suspended sentence to sixty days for the same offense.[12] Their letter went unanswered, but the women continued to demand recognition as political prisoners.

Helena Hill Weed jailed
for picketing in 1917
LIBRARY OF CONGRESS

Government and prison authorities had little patience for the women's demands and showed their growing irritation in late October by giving Alice Paul a seven-month sentence for picketing. Paul was placed in a psychopathic ward and force-fed after she decided to go on a hunger strike along with socialist Rose Winslow. Alice Paul and Winslow decided to go on hunger strikes in order to get political prisoner status "in accordance with the plan started by the sixty-day group"—the group led by Peggy Baird Johns and arrested back in September. Paul had not wanted other NWP suffragists to hunger strike, but only wanted to take the sacrifice on herself. As she wrote national board member Dora Lewis, "Things took a more serious turn than I had planned, but it's happened rather well because we'll have ammunition against the Administration, and the more harsh and repressive

Dora Lewis arriving at NWP Headquarters after five days of a hunger strike in prison in 1918. Lewis, a member of a prominent Philadelphia family, was the oldest suffragist to be imprisoned, and endured repeated jail sentences, a hunger strike, forcible feeding, and during the "night of terror," was knocked unconscious. Still, she persisted in supporting the cause.

Doris Stevens, *Jailed for Freedom*, Library of Congress

they seem the better."[13] The administration's reaction to her hunger strike was to forcibly feed her in order to "save" her. Lewis protested to District Commissioner Gwynne Gardener, insisting that Paul and the other prisoners be given political offender status as "government enemies."[14]

The Night of Terror and Forced Feedings

On November 14, thirty-three NWP women, arrested for picketing the White House in protest against the treatment of Alice Paul, suffered Superintendent Raymond Whittaker's infamous "night of terror." The terror began immediately when two soldiers attacked the picketing Boston matron Agnes Morey, jabbing her broken, splintered banner pole between her eyes. Philadelphia grandmother Dora Lewis, always in the forefront, was knocked about by three youths. All the arrested suffrage militants regarded themselves as political prisoners of the Wilson administration, and were quite willing to undergo whatever was necessary to have prison and government authorities recognize them as such. After the women were taken to Occoquan Workhouse, their demands for political offender status were not even delivered to prison superintendent Whittaker before his men seized Lewis. The guards seemed in a frenzy of rage. After Louisiana suffragist Alice Cosu was clubbed into her cell, Whittaker told her that "in her work she could stand anything." Cosu later wrote that she "was completely unnerved....I was sick all

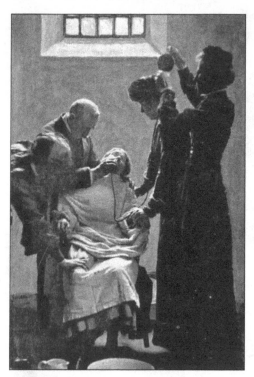

This image shows a suffragist being force fed; taken from U.K. suffragist Sylvia Pankhurst's book, *The Suffragette: The History of the Women's Militant Suffrage Movement, 1905–1910.*

night long from this treatment." When the other women suspected Cosu had had a heart attack, their cries to Whittaker's guards for help were ignored. NWP vice president Lucy Burns, a vocal leader at Occoquan, was singled out for especially rough treatment. When she resisted being hauled away, she was beaten and then eventually had her wrists handcuffed high on her cell door. A young suffrage organizer, Julia Emory, stood in the same position as Burns in sympathy. Dorothy Day (founder of the Catholic Workers' Movement) said she "naturally... tried to pull away" from the guards, so they responded by pinching her arms, twisting her wrists, then wrestling her down over an iron bench, bruising her back and shoulders. One man had his hand at her throat. By morning, Day was "in an hysterical and sick condition." No one treated Day's or anyone else's injuries; they were not even allowed to use a toilet. This was true although most of the women reported later they were at least bruised and shaken, and felt "terrorized."[15]

Their night of terror ended, but the women did not relinquish their insistence on being considered Wilson's political prisoners. The only practical resistance seemed to be to use the hunger strike, just as the British had, to secure public sympathy and move the government to act on woman suffrage. But the hunger strike had its own horrors. It was met by the counterforce of "forcible feeding," ostensibly done to save lives, but a harsh and cruel procedure. Feeding was done with tubing forced down the mouth or nostrils, and the suffragists faced it stoically but with dread. Rose Winslow, who experienced forcible feeding three times a day during her imprisonment, smuggled out notes saying:

> I had a nervous time of it, gasping a long time afterward, and my stomach rejecting during the process.... The poor soul who fed me got liberally besprinkled during the process. I heard myself making the most hideous sounds.... One feels so forsaken when one lies prone and people shove a

pipe down one's stomach.... Yesterday was a bad day for me in feeding. I was vomiting continually during the process. The tube had developed an irritation somewhere that is painful.... The same doctor feeds both Alice Paul and me. Don't let them tell you we take this well.... We think of the coming feeding all day. It is horrible.

Besides using forcible feeding, doctors and matrons tried to "persuade, bully and threaten" the women out of "sticking to their purpose, hunger striking to gain political offender status." But on November 23, 1917, Judge Edmund Waddill decided the suffragists had been illegally committed to Occoquan, and should be remanded to the District Jail; all were released on November 27 and 28.[16]

The Wilson Administration Versus the Militants

The violence of the night of November 14, 1917, and the trauma of forcible feedings that NWP suffragists endured, were all endured for a cause about which they were deadly serious. The women insisted that the Wilson government was oppressing and discriminating against American women, while hypocritically fighting a war for democracy in Europe. The government considered the suffragists' on-going, defiant presence near the White House to be a threat to national security, and therefore did not stop mob abuse of the pickets and freely arrested demonstrators for "obstructing traffic."

In March of 1918, the Federal Court of Appeals decided that the women arrested in 1917, some serving several months in jail, had been tried and imprisoned under no existing law.[17] The pickets had been caught up in a wave of war hysteria. (They might arguably have been tried under the Sedition Act on expressing "scurrilous" opinions of the administration, but that act was not passed until May of 1918.) The militant suffragists were deprived of their civil liberties in the same way numerous others would soon be, from high school teachers and ministers with antiwar opinions to radical socialists. The suffragists had been arrested for obstructing traffic, a misdemeanor, but their lengthy sentences were far from appropriate punishment for such a crime. The sentences backfired as a deterrent however, since the jail experience thoroughly radicalized the suffragists in terms of their feminism and sense of solidarity with all women, as well as in terms of their disillusionment with the government, leading to still further acts of militancy.

In the highest circles of government, NWP suffragists had made themselves very unpopular since their 1914 presidential heckling. Between 1914 and 1917 President Wilson had become more and more respectful and attentive to the moderate NAWSA, as he became more convinced that NWP women were unreasonable radicals. In October of 1917 he had written NAWSA President Carrie Chapman Catt, saying that he realized her group should not be associated with the militants, who had "laid themselves open to serious criticism." Wilson was convinced "the treatment of the woman picketeers [sic] has been grossly exaggerated" and there had been "an extraordinary

WE DEMAND
THAT THE
AMERICAN GOVERNMENT GIV
ALICE PAUL
A POLITICAL OFFENDER.
THE PRIVILEGES RUSSIA GAVE MIYUKOF

Lucy G. Branham, an organizer for the NWP, protesting treatment of jailed suffragists. LIBRARY OF CONGRESS

amount of lying about the thing." He also wrote his secretary, Joseph Tumulty, on November 16, stating that the United States had no political prisoners, but the militant suffragists "offended against an ordinance of the District and are undergoing the punishment appropriate in the circumstances."[18] Wilson apparently thought that the misdemeanor of disobeying a traffic regulation required a punishment of harsh treatment at the workhouse with some sentenced to six months or more.

The Wilson administration had also tried to thwart the militants in other ways besides imprisonment. The NWP militancy was designed to reach the public through the media; its effectiveness depended on public support, sympathy and outrage. Therefore, the administration thought press control of the suffragists' activities might be an effective curb. In July of 1917, Tumulty suggested to the president a press blackout of NWP stories. Wilson thought that "bare, colorless chronicles" might be better, but many papers, particularly the Washington *Times, Star,* and *Post,* eventually adopted a policy of rarely covering NWP activities, or covering them in an unfavorable light.[19] The NWP organizers testified time and again that the lack of coverage by the press became a problem. Also, after the June "Russian" banner appeared, contrasting Russia's franchise for women with "democratic" America's lack of one, the government's brand-new Secret Service kept tabs on the NWP all across the country. Western NWP leader Anne Martin was especially plagued by agents in October and November of 1917, with several of them usually in attendance at her suffrage rallies; she even found one listening at her hotel door. One reason for such vigilance may have been Martin's proclivity for making statements like "Russia fears the world war is only a capitalistic war" because the United States' "democracy" jails its women. In Los Angeles, a government agent informed her that she would not hold a meeting. In response, she told him America had guarantees of freedom of speech and assembly, and he could come arrest her if she said something "seditious." Martin wrote to NWP activist Pauline Clarke: "The hand of the administration is certainly reaching out after us. The prison story gets the women and they fear it." Martin argued strongly that criticizing

Wilson's blocking of woman suffrage was not treason.[20] Obviously, the Wilson government disagreed.

A week after the "night of terror," the *New York Tribune* accused the NWP of having incriminating links with radical socialists and "anarchists." From 1917 to 1919 the militants would be accused of "bolshevism," charges they would usually not even bother to answer. The Wilson administration and the public considered the NWP's feminist views and their militant actions "radical," and many (leftist) political radicals agreed. The socialist *Liberator* reported in early 1918, "Alice Paul and her young army of militants are one of the leading radical forces in American politics in the near future."[21] Beginning in 1917, socialist women joined the NWP in droves to demonstrate against the Wilson government. "Laboring women,"

Virginia Arnold holding the infamous banner that enraged soldiers and sailors who attacked the NWP pickets in August 1917

NATIONAL WOMAN'S PARTY RECORDS, LIBRARY OF CONGRESS

particularly Connecticut munitions workers protesting their lack of suffrage as workers and as women, also joined the fray.[22] Obviously, many NWP members did not wholeheartedly embrace the anticapitalist stance of the socialists, but at least for a time they were united with socialists in feeling left out of American society and in their grievances against the Wilson government for suppressing their rights to free speech, and for sustaining a war in which they felt they had had no say.

Fighting Hypocrisy

The violence that NWP suffragists suffered at the hands of the Wilson administration, beyond showing that the government perceived the NWP as a threat to national security along with other dissenters, served to radicalize further and to disillusion the largely middle-class and relatively sheltered woman suffragists. The jail experience made the NWP feel alienated from their own government. However, it strengthened their radical feminism and identification with other women; for some of them this identification extended even to the poor and Black women in prison. The suffragists all recoiled in disbelief from the way in which the government had had them punished, simply for fighting for women's rights. In essence, the Woman's Party suffragists were angry at the hypocrisy of the Wilson government in fighting for democracy in Europe while denying American women the right to vote—or even the right to free speech.

When Alice Paul and Lucy Burns first founded the NWP, they staunchly believed, as good Progressive reformers, in the promise of American democracy. They also expected a superior generosity of American men as compared to the unyielding British political system and brutish "bobbies" who had put down the Pankhurst rebellion. By 1917 the NWP saw the promise of American liberty as empty. Upon being released after the November terrors, Paul asked how "people fail to see our fight as part of the great American struggle for democracy? We are bearing on the American tradition, living up to the American spirit."[23]

It would be difficult for women jailed by their society for exercising their rights of free speech to look upon that society in the same way ever again. Perhaps because they were middle-class reformers, the NWP suffragists reacted to their brutal treatment with incredulity and anger. The Occoquan prisoners felt desolate, alienated, and very bitter. New York suffragist, Kathryn Lincoln, who participated

In 1917, the day after the police announced that future suffrage pickets would be given a limit of six months in prison, Alice Paul led a picket line with a banner reading: "The time has come to conquer or submit for there is but one choice – we have made it." Paul is followed by Dora Lewis leaving the National Woman Party's headquarters.

LIBRARY OF CONGRESS

in the hunger strike, said the days in jail were "an eternity." She would throw herself on her bed sobbing, feeling that she was "gradually losing my hold upon life." Buffalo newspaper columnist Ada Davenport Kendall testified that Occoquan was "a place of chicanery, sinister horror, brutality and dread" from which "no one could come out without just resentment against any government which could maintain such an institution."[24] These women reformers had come to a conclusion similar to that of socialists and other radical dissidents—that there was no justice, no real democracy in America in 1917.

The NWP suffragists blamed the government, and Wilson in particular, for their harsh treatment, for the suppression of their rights, and for their continued political powerlessness as women. As Boston NWP leader Agnes Morey wrote: "So far as democracy and liberalism goes it is for men—that politicians speak—women are outside their cosmos."[25] Inasmuch as the government ignored their claims as women, the militants felt their grievance as feminists more pointedly. Perceived common oppression increased the "bonds of sisterhood." Many imprisoned suffragists saw life in prison as a microcosm, in extreme form, of women's situation in American society. They experienced utter powerlessness and violent attacks at the hands of male authorities.

In prison, the women saw more clearly the particular injustice of women's vulnerable position vis-à-vis men, a view amplified by a new knowledge of the condition of their fellow women, especially Black women, prisoners. As Estelle Freedman wrote in *Their Sisters' Keepers,* under the control of male jail keepers, woman prisoners represent "an extreme case of sexual powerlessness," symbolizing the constraints placed on all women by authoritarian institutions. Many of the guards at Occoquan seemed to carry out their duties with relish. Linda Gordon, author of *Woman's Body, Woman's Right: A Social History of Birth Control in America,* has argued that guards were "hostile and violent" to women imprisoned for working for birth control, because they seemed to "violate every male fantasy about what women should be like."[26] Militant suffragists were regarded as unnatural members of their sex by those outside the prison, from the mobs in the streets to the President of the United States. They were also perceived as unwomanly within prison walls and treated accordingly.

For most Woman's Party activists, harsh treatment by prison guards did not dampen their feminist ardor, but only intensified it. As Texas suffragist Lucille Shields explained: "In jail as one empty hour succeeds another, you realize more keenly the years that women have struggled to be free and the tasks that they have been forced to leave undone for lack of power to do them." Or note Massachusetts NWP leader Katharine Fisher's statement: "In prison or out, American women are not free....Disfranchisement is the prison of women's power and spirit." If disillusion and anger at injustice was one effect of jail, inspiration and renewed faith in their fellow women and in their cause, was another. Although, as mentioned above, she had at first despaired in prison, Kathryn Lincoln testified upon her

Watchfire outside of the White House was maintained by
National Woman's Party pickets, 1919.

NATIONAL ARCHIVES

release in late November 1917: "Prison bars mean only freedom....The cause of
women must advance."[27] Many of the released prisoners insisted the government
had not daunted their spirit, and their continued militancy made that clear.

In spite of physical injury and illness, and of deeply felt disillusion and anger,
most suffrage prisoners came out of jail renewed in purpose. As middle-class
Progressive reformers, which most of them were, they had first believed in the
process of American democracy, although they went well beyond the bounds of
Progressive reformism with their militancy. When the Wilson government
cracked down on the pickets, unleashing mob and police attacks and leaving the
imprisoned suffragists to the vagaries of Occoquan Superintendent Whittaker
and his guards, the radical suffragists' militancy and determination only
increased. As established feminist radicals in 1918 and 1919, they would persist
with demonstrations pointedly critical of the Wilson administration and would
continue to be jailed.

More Militant Action

The National Woman's Party did not shrink from further acts of militancy
when woman suffrage was still not won in 1918. In January, President Wilson
finally endorsed woman suffrage by federal action and the House passed the
suffrage amendment. According to the NWP all this political progress was made
as a direct result of the Woman's Party's actions.[28] But by the fall of 1918, the
Senate had not yet passed the amendment, lacking two votes. This necessitated
further militancy by the NWP. Picketing and arrests began again. In early 1919,

Doris Stevens (center) standing with Alice Paul (right). Stevens was imprisoned many times and wrote *Jailed for Freedom*, documenting suffragists' experiences.
LIBRARY OF CONGRESS

the demonstrations were intent upon forcing the Wilson administration's hand. With World War I over, Wilson was triumphant on the world stage; but to frustrated suffrage militants, the battle was not yet won. The NWP kept "watchfires" burning in front of the White House, fueling the flames with Wilson's hypocritical words as well as with his effigy. In February 1919, a "welcome party" of protesting NWP women met Wilson in Boston, upon his return from the peace talks in Europe. Using nonviolent resistance against the Boston police, a line of silent pickets held banners calling for the president's aid. Women also gathered on Boston Common and burned the parts of Wilson's Boston speech that spoke of democracy and liberty. Additionally a group of Woman's Party luminaries—women who had been (as NWP leader Doris Stevens wrote) "jailed for freedom"—toured on a "Prison Special" train, wearing replicas of their prison uniforms and taking the cause to cities throughout the country.[29] The men of the Senate remained unmoved.

What turned out to be the NWP's last militant protest provoked the harshest response from authorities and bystanders yet. It was held outside the New York Metropolitan Opera House in March of 1919. On March 3, Congress had adjourned without a Senate vote. When President Wilson stopped in New York to speak at the Opera House, Alice Paul planned to burn immediately a copy of anything he said about democracy. Bearing banners protesting Wilson's "autocracy" at home, a picket line of twenty-five women marched toward the Opera House, but were soon met by two hundred policemen in close formation. The police were joined by a crowd made up of mostly soldiers and sailors, rushed the pickets, and the ensuing battle went on for hours. Doris Stevens, a participant, wrote:

Not a word was spoken by a single officer of the 200 policemen in the attack to indicate the nature of our offense. Clubs were raised and lowered and the women beaten back with such cruelty as none of us had ever witnessed before.... Women were knocked down and trampled under foot, some of them almost unconscious, others bleeding from the hands and face; arms were bruised and twisted; pocket-books were snatched and wrist-watches stolen.

Called a "bunch of cannibals and Bolsheviks" by the police, the militants were charged with "disorderly conduct" and "assaulting the police," and arrested, but then released.[30]

Until victory was finally achieved, the NWP moved from one action to another, continually keeping the pressure on the authorities. By late spring 1919, victory was finally in sight for the militant suffragists. In May, the House passed the amendment again, and in June, Wilson secured the last Senate votes for passage. After another long and arduous lobbying campaign, including picketing the Republican convention, the Susan B. Anthony Woman Suffrage Amendment was finally ratified by a sufficient number of states in August 1920. The National Woman's Party took full credit for the victory, saying the Wilson administration had "yielded under the gunfire" of the NWP.[31]

The Woman's Party was certainly instrumental in moving the "center" of the woman suffrage movement toward greater activity by its own radical actions. The militants demanded attention for the cause of woman suffrage and got it. They reawakened the slumbering issue of a national woman suffrage amendment, revitalized the entire movement and made the government and politicians acutely aware of women's potential political power. The militants' stubborn protests, however reviled they may have been, created a situation in which something had to be done. Each act of open militancy was followed by government action: feminist militancy worked.

In the process, feminist militancy—which insisted on the vital importance of a woman's right to participate in the political life of her society—transformed the suffragists themselves. Feminist militancy was a tactic, but it was also a state of mind. Doris Stevens wrote that the militants' campaign compelled women to "stop being such good and willing slaves." In June of 1919 Alice Paul declared that, "Freedom has come not as a gift but as a triumph, and it is therefore a spiritual as well as a political freedom which women receive."[32]

And the NWP emphasized that winning suffrage was only the first step in "woman's emancipation." As The Suffragist observed just after the victory: "The ballot is the symbol of a new status in human society, it is the greatest possible single step forward in the progress of women, but it does not in itself complete their freedom." For the members of the NWP, then, the struggle did not end with gaining the vote. They knew there was much more to do to secure women's equality in all facets of American society. In a press release just after the ratification was announced, Alice Paul stated her determination to use the vote as "the tool with which [women] must end completely all discriminations against them." "Our victory," she said, "cannot be a signal for rest."[33] Thus began the fight for the Equal Rights Amendment, spearheaded by the NWP, and first introduced in Congress only three years after ratification of the Nineteenth Amendment.[34]

Notes

This essay is drawn largely from Linda Ford's *Iron-Jawed Angels: The Suffrage Militancy of the National Woman's Party, 1912-1920* (Lanham, Md.: University Press of America, Inc., 1991), and appears here with the permission of the publisher.

1. See George Dangerfield, *The Strange Death of Liberal England* (London, 1936); Marian Ramelson, *Petticoat Rebellion: A Century of Struggle for Women's Rights* (London, 1967); Charlotte Perkins Gilman, *Women and Economics* (Boston, 1900).

2. *New York Times*, July 14, 1916, 10; Nelly Gordon to Anne Martin, Feb. 4, 1916, Reel 23 of the National Woman's Party Papers, Suffrage Series, on microfilm, Microfilming Corporation of America, 1981, hereafter referred to as NWPP.

3. On militancy in the American suffrage movement before Alice Paul, see Ellen DuBois, "Taking the Law into Our Own Hands: Bradwell, Minor, and Suffrage Militancy in the 1870s," and "Working Women, Class Relations, and Suffrage Militance: Harriot Stanton Blatch and the New York Woman Suffrage Movement, 1894-1909," in this volume.

4. Harriot Stanton Blatch and Alma Lutz, *Challenging Years: The Memoirs of Harriot Stanton Blatch* (New York, 1940), 73; Emmeline Pankhurst, *My Own Story*, (New York, 1917), 19-30, 33-40; Andrew Rosen, *Rise Up, Women! The Militant Campaign of the WSPU, 1903-1914* (London, 1974), 80-85; Katharine Anthony, *Susan B. Anthony: Her Personal History and Her Era* (Garden City, N.Y., 1954), 366, 484.

5. Katharine Anthony, *Susan B. Anthony*, Amelia Fry, interview with Alice Paul in 1972-73, "Woman Suffrage and the Equal Rights Amendment," Bancroft Library Suffragists Oral History Project, University of California at Berkeley; Sylvia Pankhurst, *The Suffragettes: The History of the Women's Militant Suffrage Movement, 1905-1910* (New York, 1912), 416-417.

6. Pankhurst, extended accounts in *My Own Story*; Rosen, *Rise Up!*, 80-85.

7. See NAWSA's Mary Ware Dennett to Paul, Oct. 30, 1913, Reel 5, NWPP; Robert Gallagher's interview with Alice Paul, "I Was Arrested, Of Course," *American Heritage*, Feb. 1974, 17-24; 92-94; *New York Times*, Jan. 5, 1914, 3. On the "too British" accusation, see Shaw to Burns, Nov. 29, 1913, Reel 5, NWPP.

8. Inez Irwin, *Alice Paul and the National Woman's Party*, (1921: Fairfax, Va., 1964), 158-160; Sidney Bland, "'Never Quite as Committed as We'd Like': The Suffrage Militancy of Lucy Burns," *Journal of Long Island History*, (Summer/Fall 1981): 12-13; Meredith Snapp, "Defeat the Democrats: The Congressional Union for Woman Suffrage in Arizona, 1914 and 1916," *Journal of the West*, (1975): 131-138; Edwin A. Weinstein, *Woodrow Wilson; A Medical and Psychological Biography* (Princeton, 1981), 83.

9. Banner is quoted in Irwin, *Paul and the NWP*, 214.

10. Fry interview with Paul, 551.

11. NWP activist Rheta Childe Dorr wrote for *The Suffragist* (April 1920, 36) that if women voted as a group on social and political problems, improvements would occur. However, Mabel Vernon argued that women had a right to vote, no matter their views or qualities. Fry interview with Vernon, "Mabel Vernon: Speaker for Suffrage and Petitioner for Peace," Bancroft Project 1976, 164.

12. See Sherna Gluck, ed., *Parlor to Prison: Five American Suffragists Talk About Their Lives* (New York, 1976), 228, 242-243; Doris Stevens, *Jailed For Freedom* (1920: New York, 1976), 177.

13. Alice Paul to Dora Lewis, Nov. 1917, Reel 53, NWPP.

14. Dora Lewis to Gwynne Gardener, Nov. 7, 1917, Reel 52, NWPP.

15. Papers of Camilla Whitcomb, Schlesinger Library, Radcliffe, n.d., *Worcester Telegram* article; Cosu affidavit, Nov. 28, 1917, Reel 53; Emory affidavit, Nov. 1917, Reel 53; Burns's Nov. 1917 statement, Reel 52; Day affidavit, Nov. 28, 1917, Reel 53; Nolan affidavit, Nov. 23, 1917, Reel 52, NWPP.

16. Rose Winslow quotation from Doris Stevens, *Jailed for Freedom*, (1920: Troutdale, Ore., 1995), 118-119; Day, *The Long Loneliness*, (New York, 1952), 89-90; NWP Press Release, Nov. 27, 1917, Reel 92, NWPP.

17. In 1918 and 1919 the NWP protesters would receive sentences of up to fifteen days, first for holding public meetings without a permit and climbing on a public statue, and then for building fires. Stevens, *Jailed*, 229; Irwin, *Paul and the NWP*, 273, 418.

18. Wilson to Catt, Oct. 13, 1917, Reel 210; Wilson to Tumulty, Nov. 12, 1917; Wilson to "WFJ, Secretary," Nov. 16, 1917, Reel 210, Wilson Papers, Library of Congress.

19. A. Brisbane to Joseph Tumulty, July 20, 1917; Tumulty to Wilson, July 21, 1917; Wilson to Tumulty, July 21, 1917, Reel 210, Wilson Papers.

20. Author's interview with Rebecca Hourwich Reyher, April 23, 1983; Anne Martin to Pauline Clarke, Oct. 31, 1917, Reel 51 and Nov. 19, 1917, Reel 51; Martin to a Eugene, Oregon editor, Nov. 1, 1917, Reel 51, NWPP.

21. *New York Tribune*, Nov. 22, 23, 1917, Reel 95, NWPP; *Suffragist*, March 2, 1918.

22. See NWP Press Releases, Jan. 19 and 23, 1918, Reel 92, NWPP.

23. NWP Press Release, Nov. 27, 1917, Reel 91, NWPP.

24. Lincoln affidavit, Nov. 28, 1917, Reel 53; Kendall affidavit, Nov. 2, 1920, Reel 83, NWPP.

25. Morey to Mabel Vernon, May 3, 1917, Reel 42, NWPP.

26. *Their Sisters' Keepers: Woman's Prison Reform in America, 1830-1930* (Ann Arbor, 1981), 1; Gordon, *Woman's Body, Woman's Right: A Social History of Birth Control in America* (New York, 1974), 233.

27. Shields, NWP Press Release, Jan. 18, 1919, Reel 92, NWPP; Stevens, *Jailed*, 156; Lincoln affidavit, Nov. 28, 1917, Reel 53, NWPP.

28. Irwin, *Paul and the NWP*, 344-345, 349; Stevens, *Jailed*, 248.

29. Stevens, *Jailed*.

30. Stevens, *Jailed*, 331-332; *New York Times*, March 5, 1919, 3, 10; *Suffragist*, March 15, 1919, 4-5.

31. *Suffragist*, June 4, 1919, 10-11; Sept. 1920, 191; NWP Press Release, March 20, 1920, Reel 92, NWPP.

32. Stevens, "Militant Campaign," Stevens Papers, Schlesinger Library, Radcliffe, Cambridge, Mass.; *Suffragist*, March 29, 1919, 8.

33. NWP Press Release, 1920, in Folder 24, Anna Kelton Wiley Papers, Radcliffe.

34. *The Suffragist*, Sept. 1920, 191.

Carrie Chapman Catt, 1909
National American Woman Suffrage President
1900-1904 and 1915-1920

Nineteen

CARRIE CHAPMAN CATT, STRATEGIST

Robert Booth Fowler

Editor's Introduction: Political scientist Robert Booth Fowler discusses the strategic decisions made by Carrie Chapman Catt, president of the National American Woman Suffrage Association (NAWSA). Catt's decisions were of vital importance for the woman suffrage movement, and as president of the NAWSA twice—from 1900 to 1904 and from 1915 to 1920—she had a major influence on the strategy pursued by the organization in both periods. In this essay, a chapter from his book *Carrie Catt: Feminist Politician,* Fowler focuses primarily on Catt's second presidency, analyzing her decisions that he claims were crucial to the success of the federal suffrage amendment in 1920.

Fowler emphasizes that, though Catt cared deeply about other reforms and political issues, during the last years of the suffrage battle she focused her energies on woman suffrage alone. Like Susan B. Anthony with whom she had worked closely in the 1890s, Catt was determined not to allow other issues to divide suffragists, dispel their energy, or alienate potential supporters. Continuing the strategy of making woman suffrage appear respectable and in keeping with widely shared American values and goals, she was particularly eager to distance the movement from unpopular causes or radical tactics that could undermine the steady growth in support for woman suffrage between 1910 and 1920. This strategy disappointed many within the movement as well as would-be allies outside the movement. Fowler insists, however, that Catt's pragmatism was strategically sound, even if it seems—then and now—cynical or unethical. As a single-issue campaign, the woman suffrage movement was more efficient, united, and less vulnerable to its critics.

A dramatic example of Catt's implementation of this policy was her decision to put aside her own strong antiwar sentiments and shun an alliance between the woman suffrage and peace movements during World War I. As public opinion shifted rapidly from an insistence upon American neutrality to an overwhelming prowar fervor that tolerated no dissent, Catt aligned the NAWSA and its leaders first with "preparedness" and then the war effort. Though some suffragists, notably peace advocate Jane Addams, were dismayed by this turn of events, Fowler argues that this decision saved Catt and the NAWSA from the extreme hostility and loss of influence that Addams and other peace advocates endured during the war, and aided the suffrage cause significantly with Wilson and the public—creating the impression that women deserved the vote as a reward for war service.

A second example of Catt's pragmatic strategy discussed by Fowler is "The Plan" that Catt devised soon after she returned to the NAWSA presidency late in 1915. "The Plan" was approved by NAWSA members at an "Emergency Convention" in Atlantic City in September 1916. Often called "The Winning Plan," this strategy was designed to centralize authority within the massive but disorganized NAWSA, and coordinate the efforts of suffragists nationwide in a final campaign that would at last secure the adoption of the federal amendment. It is interesting to note that, as Fowler observes, this decision does not seem at all controversial today; indeed, both Catt and Alice Paul are celebrated for their role in finally returning the suffrage movement to an emphasis on the federal approach to winning woman suffrage. Yet in 1916, this decision was far more controversial than Catt's alignment of the suffrage movement with the war effort.

Catt's "Winning Plan," was a significant departure from the policy of her predecessor Anna Howard Shaw, whose highly decentralized administration had given scant attention to the federal amendment. Shaw was influenced to an extent by Southern suffragists including Laura Clay and Kate Gordon who served for years as self-appointed "watch-dogs" for the South on the NAWSA Executive Board and who opposed suffrage by federal amendment. Catt, however, had no difficulty finding other Southern women to work with such as Madeline McDowell Breckinridge, Pattie Ruffner Jacobs, Anne Dallas Dudley, and Minnie Fisher Cunningham who, frustrated by repeated rejections of state suffrage initiatives in the South, enthusiastically supported the federal amendment. As Fowler explains, Catt believed that the state approach would never enfranchise *all* American women, and that the national approach was more in keeping with "women's dignity," allowing suffragists to bypass at least some of the state-by-state pleading that, even back in the 1870s, Elizabeth Cady Stanton and Susan B. Anthony rejected as demeaning.

Fowler also analyzes Catt's dealings with the militant suffragists, emphasizing that while Catt agreed with Paul on the need to refocus on the federal amendment, she objected strenuously to the tactics employed by Alice Paul and the National Woman's Party and believed that Paul lacked the "pragmatic sense" essential in a leader. Catt was particularly critical of Paul and the NWP for engaging in partisanship and picketing, believing that they were alienating Democrats in Congress whose votes were so desperately needed—not to mention President Wilson himself. Catt was convinced that the NAWSA's lobbying campaign directed by Maud Wood Park and Helen Gardener between 1917 and 1919—dignified, diplomatic, non-partisan, non-threatening and nicknamed by the press the "Front Door Lobby"—was the only way of persuading Congressmen to approve the federal amendment.

Historians *still* debate this issue—the strategic effectiveness of both Paul and Catt's tactics—as we try to explain why the woman suffrage amendment was finally adopted and assess the relative contributions of the NAWSA and the NWP to that victory. Most would agree with Fowler that both groups played a positive role and that "the Woman's Party's tactical radicalism helped enormously to legitimate the NAWSA."

Catt's "Winning Plan" was clearly a major factor in the final victory. Historian Eleanor Flexner described Catt as bringing "order out of chaos and victory out of apparent stagnation," and a genius at uniting all of the disparate elements within the massive NAWSA into a "potent political force." Instead of allowing suffragists in the various states to adopt whatever policy they wished and launch campaigns as they chose, Catt assigned a role to each state and demanded that state suffrage leaders adhere to an over-arching national strategy. As Maud Wood Park later explained in her 1960 autobiography *Front Door Lobby*, Catt divided the states into four categories and "assigned a particular form of legislative work" to each. First, she directed suffrage organizations in the equal suffrage states and in Illinois (which had presidential and municipal suffrage) to obtain from their legislatures resolutions requesting that Congress approve the federal amendment and send it to the states. Second, Catt identified several states including the key state of New York where she believed there was a good chance of winning a state suffrage amendment, and urged workers from those states to prepare at once for a new campaign. Third, she advised the remaining states to try for presidential suffrage, as this could be granted by legislatures without having to be approved by the voters in referenda. Last, Catt advised suffragists in the Southern, one-party states to try for "primary suffrage," which could also be granted by the legislatures. Much to the disappointment of suffragists in states such as Kentucky, in which local women were far more optimistic than Catt about the chances of successful state amendment campaigns, the NAWSA president demanded that they defer to her judgment, and play their assigned part in "The Plan."

Catt's plan, then, did not abandon state campaigns, but coordinated them with unprecedented care to insure that a series of victories would together build momentum for the federal amendment, and that defeats in states she considered "hopeless" would be avoided. The Plan was not announced to the public. Swearing everyone to secrecy, Maud Wood Park recalled Catt explained that these initiatives would be launched at the beginning of legislative sessions the following January (1917), catching the opposition off-guard, and requiring the anti-suffragists to fight on "many fronts at once." Catt presented a "compact" to be signed by suffragists representing at least thirty-six states—the number needed for ratification. As the signing ceremony ended, wrote Park, "I felt like Moses on the mountain top after the Promised Land had been shown to him and he knew the long years of wandering in the Wilderness were soon to end. For the first time I saw our goal as possible of attainment in the near future." Park concluded:

Often since then, remembering how hard it was at best to win our vote in the Congress and the subsequent ratification by thirty-six states, I have speculated as to what would have happened if Mrs. Catt's plan had not been presented on that sultry afternoon in 1916. Undoubtedly a woman suffrage amendment would have been adopted at some time, even if Mrs. Catt had never been born; but, if success had not come when it did, the cause might easily have been caught in a period of postwar reaction, and victory postponed for another half-century. That women all over the United States were able to vote in 1920 is due, I believe, to the carrying out of the plan prepared and presented by an incomparable leader.

★   ★   ★   ★   ★

ANYONE WHO KNOWS the story of the struggle for the enfranchisement of women in the 1915-1920 period knows that Carrie Catt's strategic decisions were of fateful importance. Their pragmatic wisdom is clear, though their ethical wisdom is now, as it was then, a good deal more controversial.

Catt's Progressive agenda was wide-ranging, and suffrage for her was in large part a *means* to realize other reform objectives. Nevertheless, during the suffrage fight Catt focused all her energies on that issue. Her conscious strategy was to allow no other cause to enter the NAWSA's agenda: "As a matter of fact we do not care a ginger snap about anything but that Federal Amendment."[1] She did not object when the NAWSA Convention adopted all sorts of resolutions favoring a number of this or that measures to assist women in economic, professional, and legal realms. But she insisted that the NAWSA would be doing nothing about them. She did not think it could and at the same time promote women's enfranchisement: "we cannot…until the Federal Amendment is through, spare any force for the support of any bill…we haven't the power to do anything but merely pass a resolution. It is of no avail."[2]

Catt made sure her wishes were followed as she fashioned her version of that very contemporary phenomenon, the single-issue pressure group. Her rationale was simple, one goal would mobilize women and the NAWSA's resources in a focused direction. It was efficient and—equally valuable—it freed the NAWSA of the conflicts and attacks that involvement with other causes inevitably generated.

This was not a self-evident strategic choice, however, and it drew opponents. On the one hand, some earlier feminist leaders, such as Elizabeth Cady Stanton, objected to this approach as too narrow. On the other, some groups, especially the WCTU, the Anti-Saloon League, and, later, peace groups sought alliance with Catt and the NAWSA and were not happy when they did not get it. But Catt pushed all such complaints aside, arguing that even hints of such links were a formula for disaster.[3]

Woman Suffrage and World War I

A remarkable illustration of Carrie Catt's willingness to pursue this strategy—even at the cost of compromise with other of her values—came in her much disputed strategic moves before and during World War I. All her life, Catt proudly identified with efforts to end war. In the decades after 1920 this became her principal field of public activity. However, when the First World War began in Europe, Catt was caught between her antiwar inclinations and her suspicion that suffragist peace activity could adversely affect the struggle for women's enfranchisement. Catt calculated even before the United States became a direct belligerent in the Great War that the situation was out of control and suffragists' efforts would be a costly venture for nothing. Concerned women, led by Jane Addams, might try, but the unleashed forces of war could not be stopped by their necessarily "puny effort." She doubted that anything could stop "these men in whom the furious beast" had been unchained.[4] Trying to stop them was "like throwing a violet at a stone wall." "There is no power on earth that is going to stop that war until there has been perhaps the most terrible battle that the world has ever seen."[5]

At first Catt tried to have it both ways. While accounts differ as to whom credit belongs for initiating organized opposition to the war among women, in 1914 Catt and Addams worked together in this cause. In general, Catt worked behind the scenes lest she create the kind of backlash toward suffrage that so worried her. She specifically refused to accept a public leadership post. On the other hand, Catt did

U.S. delegates to the Women's Peace Conference in The Hague, aboard the *MS Noordam*, April 1915. Jane Addams is third from left.
LIBRARY OF CONGRESS

not avoid public appearances altogether, and her participation with Addams and others undoubtedly lent peace forces prestige without which its modest endeavor might have collapsed even sooner than it did. Catt did, for example, go to the White House on several occasions in 1914 to urge American neutrality to Woodrow Wilson and to Secretary of State William Jennings Bryan. She felt that she took a great risk in such public actions. That risk certainly did not diminish when Catt continued, albeit as quietly as possible, to support Addams when she founded the Woman's Peace Party.[6]

Nonetheless, Catt's heart was not in the Woman's Peace Party or any other part of the active but tiny women's peace movement in the United States from 1914 to 1917. She insisted she had to be concerned about votes for women above all else. She observed with dismay the barrage of attacks on her and woman suffrage by anti-suffragist publications once war broke out in Europe. She feared that if she were more active in the peace cause she might confirm their propaganda that the woman's movement was a harbor for pacifists at best and for disloyal American women at worst. Most of the main organs of the anti-suffragists were early on the bandwagon of United States preparedness and outspoken hostility to Germany and they ridiculed every effort of peace groups and every peace plan. Such ideas, they challenged, were dangerous and had a large part in encouraging the weakness that led to war in the first place. Moreover, as time went on, anti-suffragists lost the distinction between pacifist "disloyalty" and outright support for Germany and the Kaiser. It all became rather ugly and the charges specifically toward Catt were as ugly as the rest.[7]

As war approached for the United States, Catt moved with the tide. She had no intention of allowing enemies of her crusade to get away with their antiwar, pro-German charges and thus damage it. In February 1917, Catt convened the NAWSA, recognizing that war for the United States was imminent. It was necessary for the NAWSA to get its house in order because "The future of our movement depends upon the right action being taken now."[8] What Catt wanted was a willingness on the part of the NAWSA to support national war readiness. She got it, successfully steering past both extremist doves and hawks. In her terms the convention was a great success also because it attracted favorable publicity from the growing prowar segments in American society and brought the NAWSA into contact with such influential government notables as Secretary of War Newton Baker and Secretary of the Navy Josephus Daniels.

When the United States did declare war on Germany and the contest she had long expected (and dreaded) began in earnest, Catt quickly offered her personal endorsement; she made sure that the NAWSA was in line with national war policy in every way; and she repudiated suffragists who disagreed, notably Montana Congresswoman Jeannette Rankin, who voted against the war.[9]

These actions led to Catt's ejection from the Woman's Peace Party and a good many hard feelings between her and its small cohort of pacifists. Her decision could not have come as a surprise to them, but it still led to some bitter denunciations. They did not really bother her because she had absolutely no hesitation about paying this price. For her, opposition to the war, once the United States had entered it, was courting martyrdom and taking the suffrage movement down in the process. And so Carrie Catt began her war work, publicly working to get women involved in the Red Cross, canteen service, food production, and the like. She campaigned in Liberty Loan drives, and she accepted appointment to the Woman's Committee of the Council of National Defense (under Anna Howard Shaw's leadership).[10]

These activities, especially service on the Woman's Committee of the Council of National Defense, were not easy. Catt hated war and now she found herself busy supporting one, albeit one she eventually con-

Dr. Anna Howard Shaw receiving the Distinguished Service Medal from Secretary of War Newton D. Baker, May 1919, in recognition of her coordination of women's contributions during World War I.
LIBRARY OF CONGRESS

vinced herself was legitimate. Equally difficult was the treatment Catt, along with the other members of the committee (especially Shaw), received from the male leaders of the Council of National Defense and assorted government agencies. They found themselves, once again, treated as second-class citizens, bossed, patronized, or ignored. The situation was often acutely frustrating, but Catt remained convinced that working for the war was vital to the suffrage cause.[11]

There clearly were a great many enemies waiting to pounce. Once the United States entered the war, they crossed the already thin line between criticism of suffragists and wild, even frenzied accusations. Without any shame, critics called suffragists disloyal and pro-German. "Woman suffrage is proving of more potent assistance to the Kaiser than his wonderful army." In addition, anti-suffragists repeatedly tried to tar them with the brush of socialism, bolshevism, and just about anything that might make suffragists seem anti-American in what became a time of unpleasant xenophobia.[12]

Once again, the anti-suffragists singled out Catt for special charges and smears. How intensely the anti-suffragists, now garbed in the most patriotic of uniforms, hated Catt is difficult to comprehend unless one actually reads the flood of denunciatory articles on her in their press during World War I. In their portrait Catt was a knowing opponent of the war, a virtual traitor who continued to criticize her government in disgusting fashion during wartime. Her work for the war was a sham, hiding her conspiratorial actions for woman suffrage, and often for the Germans. In at least one article deportation was suggested as the way to deal with Catt.[13]

It is only in this context that Catt's own strategy can be understood. And it is only in this context, despite the loud cries of the anti-suffragists, that its success can be understood. For, despite the cries of the anti-suffragists, Catt's strategy regarding World War I worked. All over the country she gained praise as a patriot actively behind the war effort. Though publicly abused, Catt and the NAWSA escaped the almost unbelievable hostility that befell some others, Jane Addams in particular, which undercut their political influence for a time. When charges of disloyalty and other ugly words flew, Catt could and did reply with her war record and that of the NAWSA.

It would be wrong, however, to portray Catt's strategic purposes in World War I, as only defensive. She looked in this direction, but she also realized that there was another, much more positive side to her strategy. Patriotic service could create "opportunity" for the cause of women's enfranchisement. It could greatly increase the respectability of suffragists and their cause, and thus advance the cause, which is exactly what happened both with the public at large and with many Washington decision-makers including Woodrow Wilson. It happened in part because Catt made sure every contribution by the NAWSA and prominent members of the NAWSA received as much publicity as possible. The not very subtle point was that the vote for women was American, was patriotic. Meanwhile, Catt sought to foster the impression that women, while they gave their service freely, nonetheless deserved something in return, and that something of course, was the vote.[14]

Catt did not hesitate to make sure that people got the point that suffragist war service deserved repayment with enfranchisement. In fact, Catt relentlessly kept up the pressure for woman suffrage throughout the war. A frequent argument was that women's enfranchisement was needed "as a war measure."[15] Her argument that, if it was to fight a war for democracy, the United States should advance democracy at home by making women full citizens was effective—just how effective is indicated by the outrage it provoked from anti-suffragists. They stormed at Catt, accusing her of being a monomaniac, pursuing her cause at all costs, and thus threatening American democracy when such divisive matters ought to be laid aside in the name of wartime unity.[16]

Catt paid no attention. Just as she spurned those who expected her peace concern would lead her to oppose the war, so she rejected those who urged she drop the cause of the vote during the war. For her the central issue never changed.

Overall, Catt was proud of her strategy during the Great War, though she hoped it would never be required again and dreamed that once women got the vote they might well end all wars. But questions were raised then—and have been since. Shouldn't she of all people have known the shortsightedness of her strategy? After all, from her own perspective, war corrupted progressive impulses in history. Some historians agree, regarding World War I.[17] But this analysis does not apply to votes for women. World War I hardly killed the chance for enfranchisement.

The uneasiness over Catt's strategy mostly derives from a sense that it was cynical. Cynical it was, but Catt did not see it this way. She never had any interest in a politics of purity in the impure world. To her the fact was that she could not stop the war, but the NAWSA's opposition to war could seriously delay women's enfranchisement. And her belief was that she was called to help women. Her devotion in subsequent decades of her public life to the cause of world peace was not an act of expiation. It was rather a resumption of the peace mission, which she had never lost sight of. But it was a long-range goal and she had no intention of losing momentum for women's enfranchisement because of it.

The Winning Plan

Much less controversial in retrospect, but much more so at the time, was the adoption of "The Plan," in 1916, to push for congressional passage of the Anthony Amendment to the United States Constitution, giving women the right to vote. Catt had long looked toward the Anthony Amendment as a way of overcoming the slow and cumbersome process of achieving women's enfranchisement state-by-state.[18] But by 1915-1916, she was sure it was absolutely necessary to concentrate NAWSA resources on this strategy, a major shift in NAWSA focus.

"The Plan" was adopted in 1916 at an emergency meeting of the NAWSA which Catt had called at Atlantic City, New Jersey.[19] Catt was by

Cartoon illustrating the choices of strategy Carrie Chapman Catt confronted as she again became NAWSA president in 1915.

then president of the NAWSA, and she reflected dissatisfaction with the NAWSA's drift during Shaw's long reign towards (unsuccessful) campaigning for the extension of suffrage at the state level, including support for the Shafroth-Palmer constitutional amendment intended to encourage opportunities for state electorates to vote on woman suffrage. The Shafroth-Palmer proposal would have required any state to hold a vote on woman suffrage where eight percent of the voters in the previous presidential election petitioned for such a referendum.

The drift during the Shaw years towards action on the state level was the result of several factors. One was fealty to those in the NAWSA, including Catt, who had been struggling for success state-by-state. Another was the necessity of placating Southern members of the NAWSA who were states' rights oriented and strongly against the Anthony Amendment. A third was anger at Alice Paul and her supporters, who were committed exclusively to the federal strategy—a knee-jerk resistance on the NAWSA's part to whatever Paul and her faction favored.[20]

But by 1916 Catt was convinced that reversal of strategy was essential. She based her strategic judgment on what she thought was the practical situation. The old approach now seemed what Catt frankly called "negative—not positive."[21] It simply was not working, certainly not fast enough. No doubt, the memory of the loss of the suffrage referendum in New York State in 1915 was a painful factor in this assessment. As she looked ahead, moreover, Catt increasingly doubted the state approach alone could ever work. Its chances in many states were nearly hopeless. State election laws and constitutional provisions often made state constitutional revision almost impossible. Even worse, Catt doubted whether there was a majority of men in many states who would soon vote for women's enfranchisement if they got the chance. She continued to be haunted by "the others," the "groups of recently naturalized and even unnationalized foreigners, Indians, Negroes, large numbers of illiterates, ne'er-do-wells, and drunken loafers," who she felt resisted women's enfranchisement.[22] Catt also worried that even if she was wrong, and some states did begin to approve enfranchisement, this might represent a victory of distinctly mixed blessings. Concern with national enfranchisement might decline in every state that granted women the vote. Valuable energy and talent might be lost to the NAWSA; and "disintegration" would increase.[23] Thus, from every angle it seemed imperative to Catt to redirect attention to the national effort to obtain congressional passage of the Anthony Amendment.

Catt's expectation was that Congress would prove more cooperative than many of the resistant states. She understood that this was a gamble and intended to keep some pressure on the states while hoping that suffrage states and those with strong pro-suffrage forces would help by pressuring Congress. Pressure from the states was needed, after all, to impress Congress that there was popular support for woman suffrage. Moreover, the states could not be ignored because, when Congress finally capitulated, the Anthony Amendment would need approval by three-fourths of the state legislatures. Yet Catt was convinced emphasis had to shift to the federal level. Victory there would lead to victory everywhere.[24]

Catt also argued that the national approach best fit her long-run ideal for women. It acknowledged women's dignity, she insisted, because it took them seriously. It made the issue of woman suffrage a national matter, as it should be, and it left behind the image of women pleading state-by-state for something that was basic to democracy and human rights.[25]

At the Atlantic City convention Catt pushed her strategy through largely on the force of her personal and political leadership. In a mood for strong leadership and attracted by her effective plea for her strategic gamble, the convention swung behind "The Plan" with an enthusiasm that overcame earlier positions and earlier doubts.[26]

Undoubtedly, Catt was aided in her coup by the decision of Anna Howard Shaw to back her plan fully (except for moving the national headquarters [from New York] to Washington). While Shaw had lost much respect within the NAWSA during her presidency, she was still, second only to Catt, the most formidable force to be reckoned with. Her enthusiasm for "The Plan" was strong. She helped arrange the special Atlantic City meeting, in fact, and thereafter repeatedly backed its decisions, probably in part because she thought it would undermine the appeal of the Woman's Party.[27]

On the other hand, there were costs. There were personal costs: Catt drove herself night and day as she built support within the NAWSA for her shift in strategy. There were organizational costs: there was serious opposition to "The Plan" from significant Southern voices in the NAWSA. Kate Gordon, of Louisiana, and Laura Clay, of Kentucky, both prominent during the Shaw presidency, argued that suffrage could (and should) have appeal in the South only if it did not remind Southerners of earlier national attempts to change the South at the behest of federal edicts. And they feared that if a national effort were successful in this instance a similar attempt to dictate to the South on the subject of race might follow.

Moreover opponents of several stripes felt that Catt bulldozed her plan through in Atlantic City with precious little concern for them or for a diverse NAWSA. From their perspective, they were quite right. But Catt wanted action in response to the strategic imperative at hand. They had had their way for a long time; now their day was over. Indeed, Catt believed it should have ended long before, since an honest evaluation would have revealed that the "littleness of the view, which our states' rights' plan has stimulated for a hundred years, is the greatest enemy of woman suffrage."[28]

Privately, Catt had arranged to resign if "The Plan" was not adopted by the NAWSA. She insisted there just was no point in continuing the struggle in the old, humiliating, and ineffective fashion. This issue went beyond compromise or temporizing. But Catt won in Atlantic City and she used "The Plan" as her vehicle towards victory, defending it as she went.[29]

Dealing with Divisiveness

Catt's strategic analysis is further illuminated by her attitude towards and dealings with "the Militants" in the later suffrage movement. The first major sign of division in the suffrage crusade occurred in 1907 when Harriot Stanton Blatch, daughter of Elizabeth Cady Stanton, turned against the NAWSA. Influenced by the more active and more militant movement in Great Britain, Blatch founded a more radical

organization in 1907, which became the Women's Political Union in 1910. While Blatch's tiny splinter movement played a minor role, it was a harbinger of the future.

A far more serious split in the suffrage forces became apparent in 1913 with the emergence of the remarkable Alice Paul. Paul's first serious work for votes for women began in England, where she associated with the British militants and went to prison for her militancy.[30] With this background, the young Alice Paul arrived in Washington in 1913 and went to work for the NAWSA's Congressional Committee. Through the force of her charismatic personality, Paul soon transformed the committee. She changed

Alice Paul, 1915
LIBRARY OF CONGRESS

it from the inactive, sleepy arena it had been under Anna Howard Shaw's regime into a permanent committee that was a busy lobbying center determined to push the Susan B. Anthony Amendment through Congress. In spite of the changes, Paul became dissatisfied with the unwieldy committee, linked as it was to the "conservative" NAWSA and its multileveled strategies. As an alternative, Paul set up the Congressional Union to concentrate exclusively on the Anthony Amendment, ignoring state efforts for suffrage and efforts to get Congress to encourage enfranchisement of women by the states. At first Paul acted within the NAWSA and with the approval of President Shaw, but Paul's focus and her sometimes brash style soon aroused opposition within NAWSA circles. Moreover, as the Congressional Union took on the unmistakable appearance of a separate and independent organization, still others within the NAWSA became uncomfortable. Aware of the criticisms by the end of 1913, Paul defended herself by claiming that the Congressional Union existed only to assist the Congressional Committee.

In reality, however, the Congressional Union was an almost separate organization—empire, critics charged—which used NAWSA stationery to raise money and recruit membership while not accepting direction from the NAWSA board. Indeed, as Anna Howard Shaw eventually argued, it pursued policies never approved by the NAWSA. Not surprisingly, the NAWSA board sought to force Paul to do its bidding. The result was that in 1914 Paul was asked to resign as head of the Congressional Committee. She did so and she soon took the Congressional Union with her, feeling very much that she had been rejected and forced to secede. While in later years Paul conceded that she had erred in not communicating along the way with the NAWSA leadership, she doubted at the time that compromise was possible—and it was not, in fact.[31]

Dr. Anna Howard Shaw, 1914
LIBRARY OF CONGRESS

Paul did not act alone. She had support from others who had tired of the NAWSA's largely fruitless pursuit of votes for women via state referenda. They wanted to get the Anthony constitutional amendment passed, and they wanted to move fast. Among them were Blatch, whose Women's Political Union fused with the Congressional Union in 1916, and Alva Belmont, who contributed a great deal of her considerable wealth to the cause. By 1916 the Woman's Party had emerged, with Anne Martin as first chair. Martin was a former NAWSA board member from Nevada who, like a number of others from Western states where woman suffrage was a reality, was impatient with the slow progress of the NAWSA towards national enfranchisement of women. Finally, in 1917 the National Woman's Party was founded with Alice Paul as its acknowledged leader.[32]

It was Anna Howard Shaw who took the role of chief and consistent opponent and who rallied those within the NAWSA seeking to control Paul. Shaw detested Paul. "I wish something would happen to Miss Paul," she wrote, and one senses she did not mean something pleasant.[33] But her larger complaint went to Paul's followers, who were "blank fools"[34] and who, Shaw insisted, hurt the suffrage cause by their divisiveness, disloyalty, and tactical militance.

Shaw blamed herself for not attacking Paul's tendency to go her own way from the first, stopping her before she was in a position to make a cause célèbre out of the affair. Shaw suspected that would have ended the entire affair, since in her judgment it was not at bottom a fight over tactics or policy but a matter of willful ambition on the part of Paul and her coworker Lucy Burns.[35]

Alice Stone Blackwell

Shaw's opinion was widely shared among other suffragists. One of the most important, and most hostile, was Alice Stone Blackwell, [editor of *The Woman's Journal* and daughter of Lucy Stone and Henry Blackwell], who was still denouncing the Woman's Party in the late 1920s. She would not forgive them for the divisions she felt they had brought to the suffrage cause, and she thought it incredible that they blithely took credit for the passage of the Anthony Amendment. And yet even Blackwell acknowledged their appeal. They might be "pestiferous," but they had "cleverness and enthusiasm"—which made them continually "dangerous."[36]

In 1913 and 1914, while Catt shared Shaw's doubts about the organizational loyalty of the Paul group, Catt did not join President Shaw in her assault on them.[37] Nor did she share the antagonism that some in the NAWSA felt toward Paul and her allies because they wished to push Congress to adopt the Anthony Amendment. Indeed, Catt favored the same approach. This fact explains why informed critics of the NAWSA did not single out Catt nearly as much as they did Shaw as a major cause of the split.[38]

1915 was a decisive year in Catt's relations with the Alice Paul group, by then gone from the NAWSA. On the one hand, Catt made efforts to heal the wounds between the NAWSA and Paul. She met with Paul, despite Shaw's intense disapproval and fear,[39] though to no good result.[40] And she moved rapidly, upon her election to the presidency of the NAWSA in 1915, towards adoption of a national strategy for women's enfranchisement (which Paul had supported with no success within the NAWSA), a goal she accomplished when "The Plan" was approved in 1916.

By then, however, the split was too deep, too personal, and too institutionalized for the two groups to get back together. Moreover, new conflicts arose that sealed a split between Catt and her NAWSA and Paul and her associates. As a consequence, while all of Catt's contacts with Woman's Party supporters did not dissolve,[41] Catt made her decision. Alice Paul and her group—soon to be the National Woman's Party—were a destructive influence on the cause, and the NAWSA must keep free from them. While never denying that they sometimes were "doing some good work," Catt concluded that there was a fundamental split and all suffragists had to choose: "No one can carry water on both shoulders."[42] At the same time Catt unrealistically hoped to avoid open warfare. A choice had to be made but that did not mean each group should continually waste energy "battling each other when they should be more concerned to help the big cause on."[43]

The source of conflict between Catt and Paul concerned tactics, and whether Paul and her allies had a realistic understanding of practical politics. The question

Alva Belmont (left) c. 1914 and Anne Martin, c. 1916, joined Alice Paul to establish the National Woman's Party. Martin became the party's first chair.

LIBRARY OF CONGRESS

Catt asked of any strategy or tactic was: will it help the cause, will it maximize votes in referenda and in Congress? In Catt's judgment this pragmatic sense was missing among people such as Alice Paul. A "sharp tongue," radical pronouncements, radical actions did not produce votes. They were the products of those who chose self-indulgence over practicality.[44]

In the suffrage fight two tactics of the Paul group drew Catt's opposition, partisanship and picketing. The militants' eagerness to abandon nonpartisan-ship, enter the world of party and electoral politics, and campaign against political enemies appealed to some women activists more than nonpartisanship did.[45] Catt claimed to appreciate the appeal of activism by recognizing that nonpartisanship "lacks the avenger's satisfaction."[46] She could also agree with those such as Rose Young who thought more in terms of positive action and wondered if using a "big stick" such as electoral politics might not speed progress by striking fear into politicians.[47]

But Catt thought this was a dangerous idea, a judgment undoubtedly encouraged by her natural suspicion of partisan politics in every situation. Catt insisted, first, that alliances for or against a political party invariably proved costly in terms of independence. In this case, she feared that suffrage would be swallowed up by other party concerns and the compromising, self-promoting ethic of all parties. Second, even if one were to enter party politics to the extent of endorsing candidates—which was too much involvement to begin with—the endorsements had to cross party lines or else one would find oneself saddled with a partisan label and the bitter opposition of at least one political party.

Catt's position was faithful to the long-time gospel of the women's movement, especially the ideas of Susan B. Anthony. Had there been a party prepared to endorse "Freedom to Women" on its banner, Anthony and, later, Catt would have rallied to it. In the meantime, Catt was prepared to follow Anthony's classic advice to appeal to both parties and to serve as "a balance of power" when possible, never accepting a marriage to one party or a crusade against another.[48] It was incredible to her that Paul and her allies sought to go after all Democrats in the 1914 and 1916 elections, blaming Democratic President Wilson and all congressional Democrats for the failure of Congress to pass the Anthony Amendment. The policy of nonpartisanship failed to distinguish between Democrats who favored suffrage and those who did not. Moreover, it was bound to alienate desperately needed Democrats in Congress where the Anthony Amendment had to gain a two-thirds majority if it were to start its way to final enactment.

It was also bound to alienate President Wilson, whose support was needed, especially to persuade reluctant Southern Democrats in Congress to give their support. Nor was it the way to promote success in state referenda. As she wrote Jane Addams, any crusade against the Democrats was "exceedingly distasteful to most of us because it committed the stupendous stupidity of making an anti-democratic campaign when the suffrage question was pending in eleven states and depending for success upon Democratic votes."[49]

Instead, Catt preferred to work closely with friends in both parties while exerting pressure in all legal (but nonelectoral) ways on senators, members of the House, and the president. She gave full support to Maud Wood Park's direct lobbying work on Capitol Hill and kept in close lobbying touch with Park's "Front Door" effort, the joint strategy sessions, and "machinations," which were (and are) part of the game there. She worked the White House personally, convinced that dignified lobbying was the way to get results.[50]

Yet Catt did not object only because she considered entering partisan, electoral politics a strategic mistake. The Woman's Party's strategy also offended her ideals. It was natural for her to skate away from playing partisan electoral politics. Such a strategy clashed with her nonpartisan ideal for a democracy and activated her substantial ambivalence about politics in general and party politics in particular. The Woman's Party was guilty of a tactical blunder, in her mind, but it also seriously offended Catt's dream for a politics without politics. Catt fought for her perspective with all her energy, challenging Charles A. Beard when he defended the Woman's Party's partisanship in that bosom of Progressivism, the *New Republic*. And she fought back against other critics. A lot was at stake for her that went beyond strategy, though her replies invariably stressed her claim that only her approach would work—and was working. And Catt had the considerable satisfaction (if that is the word) of watching the radicals' adventures into partisan electoral politics fail in both 1914 and 1916.[51]

Nonpartisanship remained a fixed star in her belief, but by 1918 Catt became open to the idea of bringing women's muscle to bear on congressional opponents of women's enfranchisement through the electoral process. Her impatience with the manifest dilatoriness of Congress from 1915 to 1917 had grown. She began to issue unmistakable warnings that votes for women was an idea that would "not perish," but "the party which opposed it may," and she told the 1917 convention to expect to take action against individual senators who were up for re-election in 1918 if they opposed woman suffrage.[52] When the 1918 campaign came, Catt led the NAWSA into a carefully circumscribed, nonpartisan battle to defeat four recalcitrant senators (three Republicans and one Democrat), and was delighted by the defeat of one of them in November. Of course—though not for the first time—this move reflected the adoption of a part of Paul's strategy, yet it did so only within Catt's nonpartisan strategic constraints, which, she asserted once again, preserved the NAWSA's freedom while advancing its effectiveness.[53]

A far more rigid position was adopted by the head of the NAWSA towards the other major "radical" tactic of the Woman's Party, the aggressive picketing of the president which began in 1917. Women picketers caused a sensation and, in many circles including within the NAWSA, they created a scandal. Nor were the Woman's Party picketers necessarily modest and sedate. As time went on they became more aggressive in pursuit of their mission, refusing to cooperate when police arrested them.[54]

Once again the issue here was not solely a matter of strategic effectiveness. Catt put it this way. So did her opponents. Interminable arguments followed over whether militant picketing and what became civil disobedience were, or ever could be, effective. Catt was convinced that suffrage was past its strictly agitational phase. What it needed now was male support, and especially the support of the male who was president of the United States. Picketing could not accomplish this goal. It was better to work mostly on education, particularly during the war, as that would produce more male acquiescence or support.[55]

Though Catt and everybody else treated the matter in these terms, the enormous national controversy over a few picketers suggested much more was at stake. The fight over the picketers actually involved an intense and significant dispute over the definition of a good woman. Were women pushing for suffrage always to be proper ladies and law-abiding citizens? Or was it appropriate for free women in control of their lives to break convention and law in pursuit of the vote? Most of the leadership and members of the NAWSA were outraged at the tactics of the picketers, in part because they seemed brash and unfeminine—and thus were detrimental to their cause.

Carrie Chapman Catt, however, was not among those who joined the assault on the picketers as unladylike women. Given Catt's resentment over undignified treatment of women, indeed their daily humiliation, it is no surprise that she had more than a sneaking sympathy with the picketers' tactical militance—especially when they were safely located in Great Britain. At home the problem for Catt, as always, concerned their political effectiveness.[56] She knew the public reaction would be negative—as it was. She also observed the picketers' negative effects on Congress.

Carrie Chapman Catt on April 6, 1916 christening the *Golden Flyer*. Alice Burke and Nell Richardson are in the car about to began a journey across the United States to promote women's right to vote.   LIBRARY OF CONGRESS

As a result, Catt publicly appealed in 1917 for the Woman's Party to stop damaging the chances for passage of the Anthony constitutional amendment by its picketing. She privately wrote Alice Paul deploring the "futile annoyance to the members of Congress."[57] She worried too about picketing as "an insult to President Wilson," which could alienate his needed support. (She tried to compensate by quietly notifying the White House of planned embarrassments to Wilson, which her friends in the Woman's Party leaked to her.) Finally, Catt saw only unfortunate effects on the state level also, since she was certain that "the picket party" had hurt the 1917 New York campaign for the enfranchisement of women.[58]

Everywhere she heard opponents denouncing the picketing. They charged it showed the danger of women in politics and the foolishness of granting women the vote. They insisted that to give women the ballot while they were picketing would reward tactics that should have no place in American politics. At another, lower level, anti-suffragists consciously used the uproar over the picketers as an opportunity to denounce the suffragists as exemplars of "fanaticism," and as "freaks" and "spoiled" children undeserving of suffrage. Moreover, intent on destroying all suffragists through public disapproval of the picketers, they worked as hard as they could to collapse any distinction between them and Catt and the NAWSA. Over and over they asserted that Catt and the NAWSA were in league with the militants, equally deserving of popular condemnation.[59]

Throughout much of 1917 and thereafter, Catt tried to repair the continuing damage she believed the picketers caused the movement. Her private assistance to the White House was an illustration of this, but mostly Catt did her work in public. She succeeded in getting the NAWSA to disavow the picketing tactic and she led the NAWSA to publish its objections in some 350 newspapers across the country. She spoke out personally, arguing that all suffragists should not be judged by what she correctly insisted was a tiny minority. She was especially anxious to establish that suffragists were not against Wilson (and thus not unpatriotic) in what was wartime.

Catt's course offended (and still does) those who contended that Catt should have embraced the picketers as fellow participants in the struggle who were determined to get action quickly. Such judgments did not impress Catt. Her constant refrain was that one had to be practical, to make trade-offs, and to ask about the consequences of tactics. Catt thought she, and not the Woman's Party, recognized how to play politics. And those who did not know its rules had to be neutralized because, though naive, they could hurt the work of those who did. The danger was always that the Woman's Party might become the tail that wagged the suffrage dog, that the work of two million women might be lost in the actions of a group that never was larger than 50,000.[60]

Pragmatism was not the only root of Catt's objections to the picketers, however. She may not have found their "unladylike" activities offensive to her ideal of womanhood, but their actions did clash with her ideal of the kind of politics she wanted suffragists to model for society at large. When Carrie Catt looked at the Woman's Party, she saw individuals who had already proven themselves "untrustworthy and extremely disloyal."[61] They operated by churning up dark forces of emotion and conflict, not at all the kind of politics she wanted anything to do with. After all, Catt was to devote almost as many years of her life to world peace as to woman suffrage. She could not see how promoting "warfare" in any realm for any reason was acceptable. In this Catt's thought was identical to that of Jane Addams and many other Progressives. Conflict was their enemy. It could not and did not facilitate a harmonious democracy or a peaceful world. In effect, Catt's complaint was that the militants were merely reflecting the world in their tactical moves. They did not represent change and were not reformers at all. They had surrendered to the world and were trying to beat men at their own game.

Of course, Catt respected toughness and employed military language often enough that she had no business being too self-righteous in condemning the Woman's Party. Moreover, all along she suspected that emotional appeals could at times be more effective than rational ones. Yet none of these things were quite to the point in Catt's calculations. To her, the Woman's Party gloried in confrontation and seemed to operate under the illusion that conflictual emotionalism was somehow laudatory. It would not work, nor, she thought, should it work if the woman suffrage movement was to herald the new politics of Catt's Progressive dreams.[62]

Another factor that alienated Catt from the radicals was clashing temperaments. It cannot be neatly separated from more straightforward issues. We know Catt loved order and organization; that inclination automatically recoiled from the milieu of Alice Paul and the Woman's Party, which Catt believed housed a good many unconventional souls, organizational arrangements, and, of course, tactics. Even the NAWSA sometimes attracted what Catt saw as strange people, but Catt was pleased that they rarely stayed long. She felt they were welcome in the Woman's Party, where disorder was a way of life.

Catt misunderstood how the Woman's Party actually functioned. It may have been unconventional in many ways, but it was not disorganized. In practice Alice Paul commanded it in a remote but far tighter fashion than Catt ever dreamed of doing with the NAWSA. Moreover, the picketers were extremely disciplined generally. But to Catt the Woman's Party was another part of America out of control in a country already blighted by too many other instances of the same thing.[63]

Eventually Peck and Catt conceded that both the NAWSA and the Woman's Party had contributed to the success of the suffrage crusade. While it was true that "an icy gulf existed" between the two groups, "the two organizations worked side by side" in effect.[64] Each had done so by compensating for the limitations of the other. The limitations of the NAWSA spurred the creation of the Woman's Party as a home for militants who could not work for suffrage elsewhere and provided a base for the development of more radical and experimental tactics and strategies. For instance, the Woman's Party and its predecessors created the idea of the suffrage parade and it argued for the federal amendment strategy, both of which Catt's NAWSA adopted. Above all, the Woman's Party's tactical radicalism helped enormously to legitimate the NAWSA: it turned the NAWSA into a respectable vehicle for reform and increased its effectiveness both in attracting women and the public at large. Catt went a bit far in later years when she pretended that "there was no serious quarrel between the two." She was more convincing in her perception that each organization had nothing to apologize for in its respective endeavors.[65] By her lights neither organization was flawless, neither was totally "right," and neither deserved full credit for the adoption of the suffrage amendment.[66]

Conclusion

In reflecting on Carrie Catt as a strategist, we can see how much strategy mattered to her and how much she was involved in its formation and defense. Thinking strategically was natural to her, integral to Catt's very being. No one can have a sense of her as a politician, or recognize her as one, without understanding that strategy was foremost on her mind. This is what it means to say she had an intensely political mind. She had goals, of course, and they meant a lot to her, but she never visualized them apart from strategy. It was not just that she did not approve of "unrealistic" or "unstrategic" idealists. She was totally different from such people just as, in turn, her Progressive form of idealism prevented her from being merely another politician.

Her single-minded pursuit of woman suffrage led Catt to be flexible in strategy and tactics, so flexible indeed that she sometimes seemed to compromise far too much, as in her response to World War I or her tolerance of racism. But she insisted that being practical in this fashion was being moral. It was not the whole of morality, but without it moral idealism was more a self-righteous pose than a relevant program to change the world.

Notes

This essay was originally published as "Strategy," Chapter Nine of Robert Booth Fowler's *Carrie Catt: Feminist Politician* (Boston: Northeastern University Press, 1986), and appears here with the permission of the publisher.

1. C.C. Catt to Ethel M. Smith (Aug. 3, 1917), Carrie Chapman Catt Papers, Library of Congress, Washington, D.C., (hereafter designated as Catt Papers), box 8.

2. C.C. Catt in "Proceedings," 1919 NAWSA Convention, 418, National American Woman Suffrage Association Papers, Library of Congress, Washington, D.C. (hereafter designated as NAWSA Papers), box 84.

3. As they often were. See, for example, Abigail Duniway to Alice Stone Blackwell (Dec. 12, 1913), NAWSA Papers, box 10.

4. C.C. Catt to Jane Addams (Dec. 14, 1914), Catt Papers, box 4; Loretta E. Zimmerman, "Alice Paul and the National Woman's Party," Ph.D. diss., Tulane University, 1964, 245.

5. C.C. Catt to Jane Addams (Nov. 12, 1915), Catt Papers, box 4.

6. Robert E. Riegel, *American Women: A Story of Social Change*, (Rutherford, N.J., 1970), 290; Marie Louise Degen, *The History of the Woman's Peace Party* (1939: New York, 1974), 36, 30; Mercedes M. Randall, *Improper Bostonian: Emily Greene Balch* (New York, 1964), 162, 138; Barbara J. Steinson, *American Women's Activism in World War I* (New York, 1982), chpts. 1 and 3; also see Steinson for "Minutes of the Peace Parade Committee" (Aug. 12, 1914), 10; William L. O'Neill, *Everyone Was Brave: The Rise and Fall of Feminism in America* (Chicago, 1969), 174.

7. "The Flag," *Woman's Protest* 9 (Oct. 1916): 3; "The Suffragist Peace Fiasco," *Woman's Protest* 7 (July 1915): 6-7; "Peace of Politics," *Woman's Protest* 6 (March 1915): 4; "For Woman's Service or Woman Suffrage?" *Woman's Protest* 10 (March 1917): 8; Alice Hill Chittendon, "Our Duty to the State," *Woman's Protest* 10 (April 1917): 3; "Questions for Mrs. Catt To Answer," *Woman's Protest* 11 (Sept. 1917): 16; Grace D. Goodwin, *Anti-Suffrage: Ten Good Reasons* (New York, 1912), 142.

8. C.C. Catt to Executive Council, (Feb. 5, 1917), NAWSA Papers, box 82.

9. Ida Husted Harper, *History of Woman Suffrage*, (New York, 1922), vol. 5: 722-730 and 517; C.C. Catt, "Organized Womanhood," *Woman Voter* 8 (April 1917): 9; J. Stanley Lemons, "The New Woman in the New Era: The Woman Movement From the Great War to the Great Depression," Ph.D. diss., University of Missouri, 1967, 27-28.

10. Steinson, *American Women's Activism*, 237-240 and 308-312; "Third Liberty Loan Drive," *Woman Citizen* (March 30, 1918): 355; also see Mary Summer Boyd, "The Menace to War Workers," *Woman Citizen* 1 (June 9, 1917): 31, for a characteristic expression of concern for mobilized women.

11. "Mrs. Catt Urges Big Drive For More Food," *Woman's Journal* 48 (April 14, 1917): 85-86; Lemons, "The New Woman," 26; Mary G. Peck, *Carrie Chapman Catt* (New York, 1944), 270-272; Ida Tarbell, *All In The Days Work* (New York, 1939), 320-327; David Howard Katz, "Carrie Chapman Catt and the Struggle for Peace," Ph.D. diss., Syracuse University, 1973, 41, 44-45; Steinson, *American Women's Activism*, 313-315.

12. Margaret Robinson, "Woman Suffrage and Pacifism," *Woman Patriot* 1 (April 27, 1918): 3; Margaret Robinson, "Germany's Strongest Allies," *Woman Patriot* 1 (July 6, 1918): 4; "Woman's Suffrage To Please Germans Is Now Urged By Suffrage Leaders," *Woman Patriot* 1 (Sept. 14, 1918): 1; "Is Suffrage Pro-German?" *Woman Patriot* 1 (Oct. 26, 1918): 3; "How Pro-Germans and Pacifists Carried Suffrage In New York," *Woman's Protest* 11 (Nov. 1917): 4-5.

13. "Mrs. Catt and the Schwimmer Peace Plan," *Woman's Protest* 11 (Oct. 1917): 10-11; "Suffragists Have No Part in This War," *Woman Patriot* 1 (July 13, 1918): 4; "Mrs. Catt's Defamation of Her Country," *Woman Patriot* 4 (June 19, 1920): 6; "War Record of Mrs. Carrie Chapman Catt," *Woman Patriot* 1 (Nov. 16, 1918): 3, 5; "Unscrupulous Suffrage Leaders Playing Politics Without Stint Limit with Council of Defense," *Woman Patriot* 1 (Oct. 12, 1918): 1; "Mrs. Catt Again Attacks the Government," *Woman Patriot* 3 (Dec. 27, 1919): 3.

14. C.C. Catt to Maud Wood Park (April 13, 1918), Catt Papers, box P80-5453; *HWS* 5: 736; Steinson, *American Women's Activism*, 319-320.

15. C.C. Catt, speech, "Woman Suffrage As A War Measure," *Woman Citizen* 3 (June 1918), and other speeches on the same theme, see NAWSA Papers, box 83.

16. "Suffrage As A War Measure," *Remonstrance* (Oct. 1917): 7; "Is Suffrage A War Measure?" *Woman Patriot* 1 (Sept. 28, 1918): 4; "Suffrage vs. Patriotism," *Woman's Protest* 11 (May 1917): 5.

17. Richard Hofstadter, *The Age of Reform: From Bryan to F.D.R.* (1955; New York, 1960), 275.

18. For example, C.C. Catt, statement, Committee on Judiciary, House of Representatives (1904), 19, Catt Collection, Box 1, folder 13, Sophia Smith Library, Smith College.

19. "The Plan" was in Catt's "Report: Campaign and Survey Committee" (1916), NAWSA Papers, box 82.

20. David Morgan, *Suffragists and Democrats: The Politics of Woman Suffrage in America* (East Lansing, Mich., 1972), chpts. 6 and 7.

21. C.C. Catt, "Report: Campaign and Survey Committee" (1916), 32, NAWSA Papers, box 82.

22. Ibid., 1-2 and passim; C.C. Catt, editor, *Woman Suffrage by Federal Constitutional Amendment* (New York, 1917), 6-7, 35, and passim; C.C. Catt, speech, "The Crisis" (Sept. 7, 1916), "Suffrage: U.S." Catt Collection, Box 6, folder 117.

23. C.C. Catt, "Report: Campaign and Survey Committee" (1916), 34-35, NAWSA Papers, box 82.

24. Morgan, *Suffragists and Democrats*, 112; C.C. Catt to Ida H. Harper (Oct. 14, 1921), Catt Papers, box 5; Inez Haynes Irwin, *Angels and Amazons: A Hundred Years of American Women*, (1933; New York, 1974), 372; Mari Jo Buhle and Paul Buhle, eds. *The Concise History of Woman Suffrage* (Urbana, Ill., 1978), 38; also see Alice Blackwell's report on Catt's calculations in the Blackwell Papers, Library of Congress, box 36.

25. C.C. Catt, *An Address to the Legislature of the United States* (New York, 1919), 19-22; C.C. Catt, An Address to the Congress of the United States (New York, 1917), 8, 17, 19.

26. See "Handbook" and "Proceedings," 1916 Convention.

27. See, for example, Anna Howard Shaw to C.C. Catt, (July 1916 [two letters], Sept. 1916, and Jan. 4, 1916, NAWSA Papers, box 27.

28. C.C. Catt to Sue White (May 16, 1918), Sue White Collection, Box 2, folder 21, Schlesinger Library, Radcliffe College; Aileen S. Kraditor, *Ideas of the Woman Suffrage Movement: 1890-1920*, (New York, 1965), 173; Paul E. Fuller, *Laura Clay and the Woman's Rights Movement*, (Lexington, 1975), chpt. 9, and the 1919 NAWSA Convention "Proceedings," 13-27, NAWSA Papers, box 84; also Dewey W. Grantham, *Southern Progressivism: The Reconciliation of Progress and Tradition*, (Knoxville, 1983), 200-217.

29. C.C. Catt, *An Address to the Legislature*, 1-23.

30. Amelia R. Fry, interviewer, *Conversations with Alice Paul: Woman Suffrage and the Equal Rights Amendment*, (Berkeley, 1976), section I, Schlesinger Library, Radcliffe College.

31. Ibid., 96 and 106-107.

32. Robert McHenry, *Liberty's Women*, (Springfield, Mass., 1980), 28, 37-38, 272, 319-320; Zimmerman, "Alice Paul and the National Woman's Party," 40; Caroline Katzenstein, *Lifting the Curtain*, (Philadelphia, 1955), 165-200; Inez Haynes Irwin, *The Story of the Woman's Party*, (1921; New York, 1971), 12 and Part 1, chpt. 5; HWS 5: 380-381; Penelope P.B. Huse, "Appeals to Congress," in NAWSA, *Victory: How Women Won It*, (New York, 1940), 103; Anna H. Shaw, "Tells of the Stand of the Union," *Woman's Journal* 45 (Feb. 14, 1914): 54; also see *Woman's Journal* throughout 1913 and 1914 (vols. 44-45) on the Congressional Union; Andrew Sinclair, *The Better Half: The Emancipation of the American Woman*, (New York, 1965), 300-304; Irwin, *Angels and Amazons*, 357; Carrie Chapman Catt and Nettie Rogers Shuler, *Woman Suffrage and Politics: The Inner Story of the Suffrage Movement*, (1923; Seattle, 1970), 255; Inez H. Irwin to Maud Wood Park (March 14, 1921), NAWSA Papers, box 17.
33. Anna Howard Shaw to Harriet Laidlaw (Aug. 16, 1917), Laidlaw Collection, Box 8, folder 137, Schlesinger Library, Radcliffe College.
34. Ibid.
35. See, for example, Anna H. Shaw to Rosamond Danielson (March 11, 1914) and Anna H. Shaw to C.C. Catt (Oct. 14, 1916, and March 12, 1916), all in NAWSA Papers, box 27.
36. Alice Stone Blackwell to C.C. Catt (Sept. 4, 1929), Blackwell Papers, box 12; by the 1930s, however, Blackwell and Alice Paul were corresponding fairly regularly; see NAWSA Papers, box 23.
37. Fry, *Conversations with Alice Paul*, 96-98.
38. Zimmerman, "Alice Paul and the National Woman's Party," chpt. 3 and, 65; Sinclair, *Better Half*, 303-304; C.C. Catt to Harriet Laidlaw (May 23, 1912), Laidlaw Collection, Box 7, folder 101; Fry, *Conversations with Alice Paul*, 324.
39. Anna Howard Shaw to Harriet Laidlaw (June 5, 1915), Laidlaw Collection, Box 7, folder 101.
40. Paul claimed that Catt announced no compromise was possible; Fry, *Conversations with Alice Paul*, 202-203.
41. For example, Sue White to C.C. Catt (April 27, 1918; May 9, 1918; and May 16, 1918), Sue White Collection, Box 2, folder 21.
42. C.C. Catt to Mrs. Leslie Warner (April 24, 1918), Sue White Collection, Box 2, folder 21; C.C. Catt to Maud Wood Park (Dec. 11, 1918), Carrie Chapman Catt Collection, Box 4, folder 33, Schlesinger Library, Radcliffe College.
43. C.C. Catt to Sue White (July 20, 1918), Sue White Collection, Box 2, folder 21.
44. C.C. Catt to Clara Hyde (May 29, 1911), Catt Papers, box 6; Eleanor Flexner, *Century of Struggle: The Woman's Rights Movement in the United States*, (1959; New York, 1973), 287; C.C. Catt, "Their First Convention" (1920), Catt Papers, box P80-5456; Sinclair, *Better Half*, 330.
45. C.C. Catt to Sue White (May 6, 1918), Sue White Collection, Box 2, folder 21.
46. Catt, "Report: Campaign and Survey Committee" (1916), 30.
47. Rose Young to C.C. Catt (Aug. 8, 1916), Blackwell Papers, box 36.
48. Susan B. Anthony to Alice Stone Blackwell (June 14, 1872), Blackwell Papers, box 9, in which she enunciates the classic position that Catt followed.
49. C.C. Catt to Jane Addams (Jan. 4, 1915), Catt Papers, box 4.
50. C.C. Catt to Joseph Tumulty (Jan. 19, 1917), Catt Papers, box 9; Catt and Shuler, *Woman Suffrage and Politics*, chpt. 11; HWS 5: 714; C.C. Catt to Joseph Tumulty (May 3, 1918), Catt Papers, box 9; C.C. Catt, statement (May 21, 1915), Catt Papers, box P80-5459; Morgan, *Suffragists and Democrats*, chpts. 9 and 10; Grace Sample McClure to Alda Wilson (March 20, 1947), Catt Papers, box 9; Maud Wood Park, *Front Door Lobby* (Boston, 1960), is the fullest account.

51. C.C. Catt, "The Suffrage Platform," *Woman's Journal* 46 (June 12, 1915): 184; C.C. Catt, "If We Win in New York," *Woman's Journal* 46 (Oct. 30, 1915): 345; C.C. Catt, "Opening of the Convention," *Woman Citizen* 2 (Dec. 15, 1917): 54.
52. C.C. Catt, "Opening of the Convention," 54.
53. C.C. Catt, "What Every Senator Knows," *Woman Citizen* 2 (March 2, 1918): 263; C.C. Catt to Maud Wood Park (April 18, 1933), Catt Papers, box 7; Catt and Shuler, *Woman Suffrage and Politics*, 327-328.
54. Fry, *Conversations with Alice Paul*, 209-241.
55. C.C. Catt, "Why We Did Not Picket the White House," *Good Housekeeping* 66 (March 1918): 32.
56. C.C. Catt to Mary G. Peck (April 20, 1913), quoted in Peck, *Carrie Chapman Catt*, 210.
57. C.C. Catt to Alice Paul, quoted in Zimmerman, "Alice Paul and the National Woman's Party," 238-239.
58. C.C. Catt, "Excuses Only," *Woman Citizen* 1 (Aug. 11, 1917): 179.
59. "Militant Methods In Action," *Woman's Protest* 10 (Nov. 1916): 5-6; "Organized Obtrusion for a Campaign of Clamor," *Woman's Protest* 9 (July 1916): 3; "Pickets Determine to Persecute President," *Woman Patriot* 1 (Aug. 3, 1918): 1; "Recent Militant Freaks," *Remonstrance* (Oct. 1913): 1; "More Proof that 'Pickets and Conservative' Suffragists Have a 'Mutual Working Agreement,'" *Woman Patriot* 2 (Jan. 4, 1918): 8; "Do American Suffragists Favor Militancy?" *Woman Patriot* 4 (Dec. 1913): 12; "Picketing and 'Pestering,'" *Woman Patriot* 1 (Aug. 24, 1918): 8.
60. See, for example, C.C. Catt, "Pickets Are Behind the Times," *Woman Citizen* 1 (Nov. 1917): 470; Zimmerman, "Alice Paul and the National Woman's Party," 243; 50,000 is undoubtedly too high a figure for the Woman's Party; so is two million for NAWSA. But the proportions are roughly correct.
61. C.C. Catt to Sue White (May 6, 1918), Sue White Collection, Box 2, folder 21.
62. C.C. Catt to Millicent G. Fawcett (Oct. 19, 1909), Catt Papers, box 5; C.C. Catt to E. Garrison (Aug. 1, 1914), quoted in Riegel, *American Feminists*, 178; "Mrs. Catt's International Address," *Woman's Journal* 39 (June 27, 1908): 101-103; C.C. Catt, "Their First Convention" (1920), Catt Papers, box P80-5456; Harriot Stanton Blatch and Alma Lutz, *Challenging Years: The Memoirs of Harriot Stanton Blatch*, (New York, 1940), 129, 203.
63. Susan D. Becker, *The Origins of the Equal Rights Amendment: American Feminism Between the Wars*, (Westport, Conn., 1981), 89; C.C. Catt to Millicent G. Fawcett (Oct., 19, 1909), Catt Papers, box 5; Shaw, "Tells of the Stand of the Union," *Woman's Journal* 45 (Feb. 14, 1914): 54; Zimmerman, "Alice Paul and the National Woman's Party," 97.
64. Mary G. Peck, "Changing the Mind of a Nation: The Story of Carrie Chapman Catt," *World Tomorrow* 13 (Sept. 1930): 358-361.
65. C.C. Catt to Eileen Morrissey (March 4, 1933), Catt Papers, box P80-5458; on NAWSA borrowings, see, for example, Rheta Childe Dorr, *A Woman of Fifty*, (New York, 1924), 222.
66. Others agree: Morgan, *Suffragists and Democrats*, 186; Blatch and Lutz, *Challenging Years*, 131, 199; Buhle, *Concise History*, 38; Irwin, *Angels and Amazons*, 392-393; Sinclair, *Better Half*, 304.

Twenty

MINNIE FISHER CUNNINGHAM'S BACK DOOR LOBBY IN TEXAS:
Political Maneuvering in a One-Party State

Judith N. McArthur

Editor's Introduction: In this essay, Judith McArthur tells the fascinating story of the Texas suffragists who, shrewdly exploiting a rift within the state's Democratic Party, achieved something that had long seemed impossible: they made it politically expedient to support woman suffrage in a Southern state. In keeping with Carrie Chapman Catt's "Winning Plan," Texas suffragists in 1918 sought and won primary suffrage, the right to vote in the state-wide elections through which the political parties selected their candidates—an important gain in a one-party state. More significantly, this victory was a major breakthrough in the virtually "Solid South," setting the stage for ratification in Texas, which became one of the few Southern states to approve the Nineteenth Amendment. If the South had remained solidly opposed to ratification, the amendment would have failed.

This victory did not come easily. Texas suffragists were opposed by anti-suffrage forces that were powerful and entrenched, and amply funded by the liquor industry. Their implacable enemy, Governor James E. Ferguson, a well-known "wet" (opponent of prohibition), had led the anti-suffrage forces at the 1916 National Democratic Convention. Driven from office in 1917 in a scandal, he was down but not out—and he was determined to return to office.

Texas suffrage leader Minnie Fisher Cunningham and her supporters, however, outfoxed even the wily Ferguson, beating him at his own game of political maneuvering. By 1918, suffragists had long since learned that, if they were to win, they would have to convince politicians that it was in their interest to support woman suffrage. But this was particularly difficult to accomplish in the South where there was such hostility to woman suffrage and (in most Southern states) no two-party competition to exploit. Yet Cunningham and her associates found a way to convince politicians it was expedient to assist them by skillfully playing one faction within the Democratic Party against another, and making it clear that women voters would support a politician who welcomed them into the political fold. Cunningham and the Texas suffragists also demonstrated their ability—and willingness—to exploit ethnic tensions and war-time anxieties and cater to racial prejudice, as did the male politicians. But in the process, they prevented the re-election of James Ferguson, who, if victorious, would have been in office at the time of the ratification campaign and, in all likelihood, prevented Texas from ratifying the Nineteenth Amendment.

This essay is a vivid reminder of the fact that suffragists did not win the battle in 1920 by appealing to politicians' sense of justice alone. As McArthur clearly illustrates, "front door lobbying" was aided and abetted by "back door lobbying." To win, suffragists found it necessary to master the intricacies of partisan politics and, at times, embrace demagogic tactics—as unsavory as it might seem. Some suffragists found political maneuvering distasteful; others found it exciting. Some, including Minnie Fisher Cunningham, found that they were quite good at it.

Impressed with her success in Texas, Carrie Chapman Catt called Cunningham to Washington to be the Secretary for the NAWSA's Congressional Committee headed by Maud Wood Park. Thus Cunningham became part of the core group of suffragist-politicians that successfully lobbied Congress for the passage of the Nineteenth Amendment.

★   ★   ★   ★   ★

I N THE SPRING OF 1893, thirty-nine women and nine men met in Dallas to form the Texas Equal Rights Association, the state's first suffrage organization. One of the most outspoken feminists in the small group, Dr. Grace Danforth, M.D., warned that hard work and justice alone would probably not bring success. "Every concession of right or suffrage that has ever been made to the people has proceeded from the need of the powers that be for the votes of the people," she pointed out. Danforth then made a perceptive prediction: "The Republican party needed the votes of the negroes and the negroes were enfranchised. It will not be long until some party will need the votes of the women, and then we will be granted the right of suffrage."[1]

Grace Danforth's observation was optimistic as well as cynical, for in the 1890s it appeared that Southern Democrats might be receptive to votes for women— White women—as the "solution" to Negro suffrage that the Republican Party had imposed after the Civil War. As Southern legislatures pondered ways to restore White supremacy, the National American Woman Suffrage Association (NAWSA) created a special Southern Committee to launch an organizing effort in the former Confederacy. Money from the Southern Committee helped bring the Texas Equal Rights Association and other Southern suffrage societies into being, but their aspirations were thwarted as state legislatures and local vigilantes invented ways to reestablish White supremacy without sacrificing patriarchy. Legal restrictions— especially the poll tax (which Texas approved in 1902) and the literacy test—now supplanted violence, fraud, and intimidation in disfranchising the majority of Blacks. Many lower-class Whites who had been attracted to the Populist Party's challenge to conservative Democratic rule in the 1890s were also winnowed out of the electorate in the process.[2]

The result was one-party government that, in combination with deeply rooted cultural obstacles, made the South barren ground for suffragists. Anti-feminism, negrophobia, and the gospel of states' rights created formidable obstacles to the suffrage movement. The lack of viable Republican opposition in most of the Southern states made it impossible for suffragists to exploit party competition, a strategy that helped advance the cause in the North. Consequently, most suffrage campaigns below the Mason-Dixon line met repeated failure. None of the Southern states gave women full suffrage, and the opposition of their Senators and Congressmen killed, year after year, the federal bill that eventually became the Nineteenth Amendment. When it finally passed in 1919, seventy percent of Southern congressional representatives voted in opposition.[3]

Minnie Fisher Cunningham, 1900
LIBRARY OF CONGRESS

By that time, however, Southern suffragists had won three partial victories that were to have important consequences nationally: the right to vote in primary elections in Arkansas (1917) and Texas (1918); and in presidential elections in Tennessee (1919). The NAWSA still needed to persuade thirty-six state legislatures to ratify the amendment, and some of those votes would have to be found in the South. Southern Democratic opponents of ratification, led by Governor Ruffin Pleasant of Louisiana, called upon the thirteen Southern state legislatures to unite to defeat the amendment, and several of them passed rejection resolutions.[4] The three partial-suffrage states, however, helped clinch the victory in just fourteen months by providing the only ratifying votes from the former Confederacy.

What accounts for these isolated successes in the most anti-suffrage region in the country? In the case of Texas, the victory was the result of skillful political maneuvering by state suffrage leaders, who found a way to exploit political rivalry even in the absence of a two-party system. The women and their male allies left a paper trail that clearly contradicts the legislators' public professions that primary suffrage was a reward for women's patriotic work on the homefront during World War I. Although Grace Danforth did not live to see it, the supposedly impossible came to pass in a one-party Southern state: women were enfranchised because politicians needed their votes.

In 1918 the Texas Democratic Party was temporarily rent by issues that divided it into bitterly feuding factions. The president of the Texas Equal Suffrage

Association shrewdly exploited the rift by back door lobbying; she invited collusion with a group of legislators who had self-interested motives for helping the cause. Facing a hotly contested primary election that it appeared likely to lose, the Progressive-prohibitionist wing of the party made a quiet bargain with suffrage leaders. It pushed a bill permitting women to vote in primary elections through the legislature in return for a promise that they would turn out en masse to vote for its gubernatorial candidate.

Early Failures

Until 1918 the Texas suffrage movement shared the same history of discouragement and defeat as its counterparts in the rest of the South. Like the other Southern societies that the NAWSA helped establish in the 1890s, the Texas Equal Rights Association had a short, unproductive life. Still tainted in Southern eyes by its abolitionist origins, woman suffrage evoked little positive response among women whose conservative culture idealized retiring, refined ladyhood "protected" by chivalrous manhood. One by one, the Southern suffrage associations disbanded, lapsed into dormancy, or ceased to be more than sporadically active. Unsuccessful in recruiting members and raising money, the Texas Equal Rights Association had stopped holding meetings by 1896. Another organizing attempt in 1903 produced the Texas Woman Suffrage Association that expired in all but name two years later when its president moved to New York.

In the 1910s, as increasing numbers of women were drawn into the Progressive movement and discovered the ballot's potential usefulness as a weapon for social reform, the Southern suffrage movement was reborn and revitalized. New associations were founded and dormant ones like the Texas Woman Suffrage Association revived; it was reactivated in 1913 and within three years had eighty local affiliates.[5] Yet the second generation of Southern suffrage leaders, enthusiastic, hard-working, and backed by state associations that now counted membership in the thousands, faced the familiar pattern of defeat as they lobbied state legislatures for constitutional amendments to enfranchise women. The experience of the Texas organization, which changed its name to Texas Equal Suffrage Association (TESA) in 1916, was typical: constitutional amendments were voted down decisively in the biennial legislative sessions of 1915 and 1917. The margin of defeat was even larger in 1917 than in 1915, and alternative bills for primary and presidential suffrage failed to come to a vote.[6]

Discouraging results like these in every part of the nation helped convince NAWSA president Carrie Chapman Catt to devise a new strategy, the famous "Winning Plan" adopted in 1916. Thereafter the NAWSA gave priority to securing a federal amendment and continued state work selectively, mounting campaigns only where there was a strong likelihood of success. State presidents in the unpromising South were instructed to focus on partial enfranchisement—primary or presidential suffrage.[7] Legislators could grant these partial measures as amendments to existing election laws without the public referenda required for constitutional amendments, which had often been expensive failures. And since "white primary" laws restricted Black participation, primary suffrage would circumvent the conservative argument that woman suffrage would bring huge numbers of Black women to the polls. (This reality unfortunately proved no obstacle to anti-suffragists determined to manipulate debate on the "negro problem.") When Texas suffragists failed again in 1917, it appeared that the state would remain part of the "Solid South" against woman suffrage.

Suffragists Versus Governor Ferguson

In the months that followed, the governor of Texas, James E. Ferguson, and the president of the TESA, Minnie Fisher Cunningham of Galveston, emerged as protagonists in a political drama that unexpectedly made Texas women voters. Both were strong personalities and they first clashed publicly at the Democratic National Convention in 1916 in St. Louis, where suffragists were demonstrating for a plank supporting suffrage by federal amendment. The convention's compromise endorsement of suffrage on a state-by-state basis merely stiffened the conservatives' determination to keep it out of their own states. Governor Ferguson, leading the Texas delegation, infuriated the women by presenting the dissenting minority report in a theatrical speech studded with injunctions about "woman's place." A member of the Resolutions Committee who defended the suffrage plank was howled down by the Texas delegation. Minnie Fisher Cunningham, who had a flair for political theater herself, retorted by leading the state suffrage delegation in a counter demonstration: the Texas suffragists carried a Lone Star Flag draped with mourning that Cunningham improvised by cutting up a black crepe dress.[8]

Both Cunningham and Ferguson shared a common allegiance to the Democratic party, but their political supporters came from different ends of the socio-economic spectrum. Suffragists were disproportionately urban women from the middle and upper classes, the wives and daughters of professional men. Minnie Fisher Cunningham, who in 1901 had become one of the first women to earn a pharmacy degree from the University of Texas, was married to an attorney and belonged to the selective Woman's Wednesday Club of Galveston and the Woman's Health Protective Association, a citywide coalition of activists and reformers. Although Cunningham's interest in suffrage far exceeded her rather nominal involvement in voluntary associations, many TESA women were active in club-inspired civic work and often at odds with entrenched political interests over social reform issues.[9]

Governor Ferguson had started out as a struggling farm youth, but after several years of drifting and manual labor he had studied law, married well, and opened a bank. He had promoted himself for governor as a successful self-made businessman and a populist who sympathized with farmers' problems, especially the high rate of tenancy (in excess of fifty percent) and the poor quality of rural schools. Ferguson's studied platform image of folksy but shrewd "Farmer Jim" won him a large following among native-born rural Whites. He made education a focal point of his populism, denouncing the University of Texas as an elitist institution where rich men's sons were educated with the tax dollars of struggling farmers and workers. When he tried to purge the university of half a dozen professors whose politics he disliked and vetoed its appropriation in 1917, organized women were prominent in the coalition that rallied to its defense. An Austin suffragist, fuming in her diary, expressed the common opinion of elite women: the governor was "an ignorant, common personage." Stronger adjectives tempted her, "—but not having the vocabulary of a sea captain…I can't express what I think of Jim Ferguson." [10]

Elite women particularly disliked Ferguson because he enjoyed strong support among opponents of prohibition, including the state's substantial populations of German, Czech, and Mexican immigrants. Prohibition had been the dominant political issue in Texas for a decade, splitting the Democratic party into "wet" and "dry" camps. More than a moral question or a social problem, prohibition took center stage as an issue of political corruption and the power of special interests. Since most organized women sympathized with the drys, anti-prohibitionism went hand in hand with anti-suffragism. The politically strong brewing interests helped fund the "Texas Business Men's Association," a powerful and underhanded lobbying organization that distributed anti-suffrage and anti-prohibition boilerplate to hundreds of county newspapers. Brewery money, raised by a sixty-cents-per-barrel-sold assessment, and the organized ethnic vote helped put Ferguson in office and regularly elected anti-prohibition, anti-suffrage majorities in the Texas Legislature. [11]

Consequently, Cunningham and the TESA rejoiced when the governor's enemies began scrutinizing his questionable administrative expenditures and flexible ethics in the summer of 1917. Suffrage activity was put on hold while they quietly assisted the legislative investigation against Ferguson and publicized his misdeeds. [12] When he was impeached in August 1917 on multiple counts of misusing public funds and barred from again seeking public office, the Democratic Party was left bitterly divided in Texas and the political future unpredictable.

A New Governor Hesitates

Governor Ferguson's departure elevated the young lieutenant governor, William P. Hobby, to the governorship. A thirty-nine-year-old newspaper publisher nurtured in the party's conservative inner circle, Hobby, like Ferguson, had been elected as an anti-prohibitionist; the influential conservatives who backed him also opposed woman suffrage. Hobby himself took no public stand on the issue, but Cunningham knew from his response to a legislative questionnaire sent out by her predecessor that he was privately receptive. This and the post-impeachment political climate encouraged her to seek the NAWSA's approval for another attempt to secure primary suffrage. The revelations of the legislative investigation had lent credence to the demand for the woman's ballot to "clean house" in political affairs.

"It has been a full six weeks since I have found any man with the temerity to look us in the eye and say he opposed women's voting in the face of the outrageous condition that has been proven to prevail in our state government," Cunningham reported to Carrie Chapman Catt that fall.[13]

Cunningham pinned her hopes on the near certainty that Hobby would have to call the Thirty-fifth Legislature back into special session to deal with problems caused by the Ferguson impeachment and mobilization for the First World War. But she had no illusions that women could succeed solely on the claim of morality and political housecleaning unless they could make these issues seem more compelling than in the past. The fact that the state constitution disfranchised men in uniform while permitting resident aliens, many of whom were German-born, to vote after applying for their preliminary citizenship papers seemed to Cunningham to open a window of opportunity for a suffrage bill. Women's votes could be presented as a way of compensating for those of husbands and brothers in the army, offsetting the ballots of unnaturalized aliens, who were known to be "wet" and pro-Ferguson and suspected of being disloyal. The TESA hoped to arouse public sentiment against the fact that "enemy aliens" could vote, while loyal American women were disfranchised. If the legislators held a fourth special session, Cunningham told Catt, "Perhaps we can prove to them that they need us even if they do not want us!"[14]

Cunningham could not make the case to the legislators, however, unless Hobby summoned them back to Austin, and he deliberately delayed. War mobilization was inflaming the divisive prohibition question, and a special session would make it a front-page issue. Hobby would have to run for the gubernatorial nomination in his own right in the July 1918 primary and feared that any position he took on the liquor question would cost votes. It would be safer not to convene another session until after the election, by which time Congress would probably have passed a prohibition amendment and resolved the issue. Governor Hobby took the same approach to suffrage, putting off the TESA representatives as they repeatedly tried to extract a promise that primary suffrage would be part of the agenda of any special session.[15]

Pressure from the Progressive spokesmen in the party, and increasing public and War Department concern over reports of free-flowing liquor and open prostitution near Texas's numerous army training camps and military airfields, eventually persuaded Hobby to capitulate and call the special session. Popular sentiment was increasing for prohibition as a war measure, and Hobby himself was beginning to think it might be justifiable.[16] But he remained immovable on woman suffrage; there was no reason to think that it would pass the same legislature that had already rejected three different bills, and endorsement would cost him votes among the anti-prohibitionists. His message to the legislature did not mention suffrage or even amending the election laws, which would have opened the door for a primary suffrage bill. Since a special session could not consider any measures except those submitted by the governor, the TESA's options once again appeared to have been foreclosed.

Minnie Fisher Cunningham
AUSTIN PUBLIC LIBRARY

Leaflet from the woman suffrage
campaign in Texas
AUSTIN PUBLIC LIBRARY

The Back Door Lobby

A potential friend had failed the Texas suffragists, but a confirmed enemy would inadvertently be their salvation. The impeached James Ferguson had declared himself a candidate for governor in 1918, contending that the legal ban against him was invalid because he had resigned from office before the senate voted for conviction. A peerless stump speaker, Ferguson had the backing of the powerful brewing interests, and he stood a good chance of winning a plurality in the primary. His political resurrection worried the Progressive-prohibitionist wing of the Democratic Party, who knew he would get the wet vote, especially the manipulated Hispanic portion of it along the Mexican border, where political bosses ruled. James Ferguson's candidacy also worried the old-line conservatives, who shared Ferguson's aversion to prohibition and woman suffrage but feared his strong appeal to tenant farmers and the working class. When the suffragists called on Governor Hobby late in January 1918, Cunningham reported, "We found him somewhat exercised over Mr. Ferguson's activity, and we left him more so. We had nothing cheerful to tell him along that line."[17]

However, Cunningham was an astute politician, and as Ferguson's star rose she quietly began to negotiate a back door approach to suffrage. She knew that Representative Charles Metcalfe of San Angelo, a friend of the TESA, was actively supporting Hobby's campaign and that he had a son in the army. Before the date for the special session had even been announced, Cunningham asked Metcalfe by letter to help persuade Hobby to submit a primary suffrage bill. She offered two reasons: the necessity to support the troops overseas by electing a loyal American government and not one chosen by "a solid pro-German vote"; and the very real possibility that a divided vote among the prohibitionists would allow Ferguson to win the governor's race by a plurality. She hinted broadly that it would be in Hobby's own best interest to submit the suffrage bill: "A large number of new and grateful voters would be his salvation, I should think!"[18]

Representative Metcalfe ignored the reference to the "German menace" and took the hint, as Cunningham had hoped, about the real danger to his candidate. The prohibitionists had lost the gubernatorial election in 1910 by fielding multiple candidates who split the dry vote. They had lost again in 1914 (to Ferguson) by offering a weak candidate with doubtful prohibition credentials (like Hobby) who had failed to rally the drys. Several prohibitionists had already announced their interest in running for governor, and as Ferguson's campaign gathered momentum, it appeared that the Progressives were once again poised to snatch defeat from the jaws of victory. Metcalfe asked Cunningham if she could truly guarantee to deliver the woman vote for Hobby. He cautioned her to keep their discussion confidential:

> Please write me at once saying how the women of the state to your knowledge would vote in the Governors [sic] race if they have the ballot: not officially—but so I can use your letter if I wish to do so, not for publication, but as I see fit otherwise. It seems to me very probable if you know they will vote right, that…a bill may be passed….

He added bluntly that success would also depend on the suffragists' maintaining a low profile, that he did not want to be pestered by "the old maids and *masterful* women, or *militants*. They get in the way & tire me and the others."[19]

Immediately, Cunningham furnished the "unofficial" letter for Metcalfe to circulate. In it she explained that at the last TESA board meeting the suffrage leaders had passed a resolution to support Hobby's candidacy if he submitted their primary suffrage bill with a recommendation for passage. Some of the other candidates were strong friends of suffrage, but their chances of winning were slim. It was better strategy to back the incumbent and persuade him to adopt suffrage convictions. Knowing full well what cards the other political players were holding, Cunningham laid her aces on the table:

> …vote in hand we will quite naturally concentrate on the man who enfranchised us. And with the Pro's divided, with the purchasable, corrupt, ignorant, pro-German vote going to Ferguson, whomsoever the women of Texas concentrate on in the July primaries, that man is just as good as elected. But without us, it is Ferguson with a plurality,…[20]

Representative Metcalfe had worked with the suffragists long enough to know that they had amassed complete political profiles of every representative and senator. He asked Cunningham for a breakdown of legislators according to their views on suffrage—supportive, opposed, or undecided—for his "confidential use" so that he could begin "all the lining up possible" before the lawmakers assembled in Austin at the end of February.[21] Although Metcalfe felt certain that women's ballots could offset the wet vote that Hobby would lose by supporting suffrage, the young acting governor was not inclined to take the risk. His promise to support dry zones around the military cantonment towns, which he could justify to wets by pleading pressure from the War Department, prompted the dry candidates to withdraw and throw him their support. Expecting to draw votes from both sides with his "win the war" platform, Hobby avoided the controversial suffrage issue like a virus. When the suffragists urged him to reconsider, he replied that he would ask to have the election laws brought up *only* if presented with a petition signed by a majority of both houses of the legislature.

It was a clever response: whether they succeeded or failed, he would be absolved of responsibility. If Hobby anticipated failure he underestimated the determination of women like Nonie B. Mahoney, of the TESA's Dallas chapter, who helped staff the special suffrage headquarters set up during the called session. An anti-suffrage Dallas representative told Mahoney that he would not believe women really wanted the vote unless five thousand of his townswomen petitioned for it; four days later Mahoney lugged a suitcase to the speaker's rostrum and presented the petition—with *ten* thousand signatures. When the suffragists had succeeded "after many hours of labor" in collecting signatures from two-thirds of the legislators, prompting the necessary action from Hobby's office at last, Metcalfe and several co-sponsors immediately introduced a primary suffrage amendment.[22]

Since the deadline for paying the poll tax had passed, Metcalfe and company were careful to specify that women would be exempted for the current year. Fear of Ferguson pushed wet anti-suffrage conservatives into a reluctant alliance with the Progressive-prohibitionist faction, and the bill moved through the legislature quickly. Within four days after it was introduced on March 12 the bill had been passed to its third reading and cleared the House with seventy-one percent of the vote. Less than a week later, the Senate gave it an even larger majority.[23] Governor Hobby signed the bill on March 26, four months before the primary election.

Sidestepping the "Negro Problem"

As Cunningham had foreseen, woman suffrage passed in Texas in 1918 because it was a subtle and effective way of outflanking Ferguson.[24] Restricting women to primary suffrage secured the benefit of their votes without subjecting legislators to accusations of betraying the White race. A provision requiring each woman to fill out her registration blank in her own hand was added as a de facto literacy test to keep out the "illiterate negro women and the Mexican women along the border" who would be likely to vote for Ferguson. Minnie Fisher Cunningham was personally opposed to this restriction but conceded that it was necessary to appease influential conservatives like the senate's Rienzi M. Johnston. Editor and part owner of the *Houston Post*, Johnston was Hobby's political and journalistic mentor and a spokesman for the party's conservative wing. The edition of the *Post* that announced the bill's passage carried Johnston's dire warning that allowing Black women to vote would bring Black men into the primaries and put an end to the state's political sovereignty. The paper refrained from mentioning that Johnston, like other conservatives torn between personal conviction and political necessity, had quietly cast an affirmative vote.[25]

Like other Southern suffragists of this era, Cunningham countered that the "negro problem" was a smoke screen; the majority of Blacks had long been disfranchised. In Texas some 100,000 Black men had voted in the 1890s; by the early twentieth century the poll tax and the White primary had reduced the number to about 5,000. Anti-suffragists nevertheless thundered about the danger of "placing the ballot in the hands of 300,000 negro women and prostitutes." Rienzi Johnston claimed that 10,000 Northern women were prodding the federal government to enforce the Fifteenth Amendment in the South.[26]

The TESA's decision not to admit African American members needs to be judged within this context. Perpetually on the defensive and unable to puncture this emotional negrophobic rhetoric with logic and facts, Cunningham and her followers had no realistic hope of succeeding unless they distanced themselves from Black women. Consequently, the suffrage leadership was taken aback when, in the midst of the post-victory registration campaign to enroll the new women voters, a Black women's club applied for TESA membership. In the letters they exchanged pondering the dilemma none of the White suffragists expressed any personal objection to admitting the Black women; the issue was their enemies' potential reaction. What the legislature had given it could take away, and conservatives would have raised an angry cry that they had been right all along: Black women were flocking to the polls.

Ultimately, the TESA officers made the politically expedient decision. Minnie Fisher Cunningham followed Carrie Chapman Catt's advice to tell the Black women "that you will be able to get the vote for women more easily if they do not embarrass you by asking for membership." On her own, she added resourcefully that since the application was without precedent it would require a convention vote and the next convention would not meet until 1919, by which time she hoped that the federal amendment enfranchising all women would have passed.[27]

Suffragists Keep Their Promise

The more immediate concern for Cunningham was fulfilling her part of the political bargain that had brought the suffragists' victory. Representative Metcalfe urged a massive registration campaign, reminding her of the danger that many women would not want to vote, and some country women would even vote for

Ferguson. "I hope tho [sic] to be vindicated in my statements that they *will vote* and for the *right men*," Metcalfe reminded Cunningham. The NAWSA was equally concerned. If Ferguson regained control of the statehouse, Texas would vote against ratifying the federal suffrage amendment that was almost certain to pass within the next year. Carrie Chapman Catt quietly diverted a thousand dollars to the Texas suffragists, with instructions to use it to get out the anti-Ferguson vote.[28]

Characteristically, Cunningham had an inspiration of her own: a woman candidate on the ticket to help draw women to the polls. At its convention in May, the TESA unanimously adopted a resolution urging Annie Webb Blanton, a professor of English at North Texas State Normal College to run for state superintendent of public instruction. Since public education was conceded to be woman's domain and several other states had already elected female superintendents, a woman candidate was unlikely to arouse significant male criticism. In Blanton the suffragists also had a proven candidate: she had just completed a term as the first woman president of the Texas State Teachers' Association. As a professional, she could also be expected to appeal strongly to educated urban women, the ones most likely to vote for Hobby.[29]

Once Blanton had been persuaded to make the race, Cunningham channeled all of the TESA's energy and resources into signing up as many women as possible during the seventeen-day registration period that had been substituted for the poll tax. Local equal franchise societies transformed themselves into precinct committees and "suffrage schools" that taught women how to mark ballots. "Women's Hobby Clubs" chauffeured women without transportation to the courthouse and volunteered as hostesses at the registration booths; in the larger cities suffragists persuaded officials to authorize registration substations in popular department stores, permitting women the easy option of registering while they did their errands. "Hobby Club" women stood on downtown street corners to hand out campaign literature and urge registration; they distributed yellow badges, signifying intention to vote, for women to pin on their street clothes.[30]

The suffragists astutely linked registration and voting to war patriotism, stressing women's "duty" to take the place of their absent husbands and brothers at the polls, and urged every woman to turn out in defense of her home and not be a "slacker." Since some 100,000 men were away in the army, it was possible that a large female turnout might decide the election, which added news interest to the registration drive. The large metropolitan newspapers published running tallies of local registrations and speculated that between seventy-five to ninety percent of these women would vote for Hobby. Some 386,000 women ultimately signed up, and Cunningham exulted that "the registration figures are enough to make Ferguson sick."[31]

Faced with an apparent groundswell of female support for Hobby, "Farmer Jim" worked to divide women along rural-urban lines, appealing to country women to vote against "an aristocracy that doesn't care anything more about you than a hog does for a side-pocket." He urged farm wives not to be influenced by the "pink tea and poodle dog nursing women" of the cities.[32] Ferguson was justly feared for the effectiveness of such rhetoric, and suffragists met it with action. Although residents of towns under 10,000 in population were not legally required to register, suffragists organized Hobby Clubs and registration drives in country precincts to draw out rural women. While Ferguson mounted a populist assault, suffrage leaders countered with a cross-class appeal for gender solidarity by presenting Hobby as the "woman's" candidate.

First, they emphasized how much Hobby's tenure in office had benefitted the female sex. Speakers stressed that a Ferguson victory would mean the repeal of primary suffrage: "If your first vote is not cast for the man who made it possible for you to have a vote, you may never cast a second vote." To engage women who had not actively sought suffrage, they promoted the connection between the candidate and the unprecedented reform legislation or "Hobby laws" passed during the special session: liquor and prostitution outlawed within ten miles of military training camps; the age of consent for girls raised from fifteen to eighteen years of age; and statutory prohibition for the entire state. All were reforms for which women's voluntary associations had lobbied. Campaign flyers addressed "To the Women of Texas" stressed women's indebtedness to Hobby for the realization of their legislative goals. One signed by five women's organizations, including the Woman's Christian Temperance Union, the Federation of Women's Clubs, and the Congress of Mothers, exhorted women to elect "by an OVERWHELMING MAJORITY OUR SPLENDID YOUNG GOVERNOR who speaks through deeds rather than words."[33]

Second, the suffragists made political capital from the old tradition of separate spheres and cultural assumptions about female moral superiority, appealing to women across divisions of class and geography to help save the state. Governor Hobby and his advisors were accusing Ferguson of ties to the German-American Alliance, which had admitted during a United States Senate investigation to having taken an "interest" in his 1914 gubernatorial race. There was also the matter of $156,000 that Ferguson had once borrowed to cover a business debt from friends whose names he refused to reveal; speculation ranged from the brewing interests to the Kaiser himself. The suffragists helped the Hobby forces invert Ferguson's populism and define the contest as a struggle against brewery-manipulated, special-interest politics by urging women to stand together for good government and morality. The cards they distributed for Hobby proclaimed him to be "The Man Whom Good Women Want."[34]

Ferguson on the Defensive

So successful were Cunningham and the suffrage leadership in mobilizing vocal female support for Hobby and helping shape public debate that they made the unimaginable happen in a Southern state: it actually became politically expedient to be *for* suffrage rather than against it. The once reluctant Hobby began to cultivate his new female constituency and to embrace the pro-woman image that the suffragists had manufactured for him. He urged women to help make Texas safe for democracy by going to the polls and even promised to recommend a constitutional amendment for full suffrage to the next legislature.[35]

Noting the direction of the prevailing political wind, Ferguson abruptly switched tactics and made his own pitch for the female vote. He claimed he had never opposed the *principle* of suffrage for women, only the idea of forcing them to become voters without their consent. His weekly paper, the *Ferguson Forum*, played up the occasional endorsement from a prominent woman, the formation of women's Ferguson clubs, and supportive letters from female readers. By June the *Ferguson Forum* was regularly running long pieces supposedly by "Sally Jane Spottswood," represented as a school teacher in mythical Pine Hollow, Texas, who addressed women directly. Lauding Ferguson as "the proven friend of every mother in the state," she urged country women to register. "Follow your intuition and you can't go wrong," Sally Jane exhorted. "Intuitively you will vote for Ferguson!"[36]

The Ferguson camp repeatedly tried to make an issue of the fact that Hobby's recently acquired enthusiasm for woman suffrage and prohibition was an eleventh-hour conversion for political advantage. The claim that Hobby had given women the vote was "sheer political buncombe," Ferguson jeered. He offered a new hat to any woman who could show that the governor had ever done anything to assist suffrage except sign the bill. A two-part article in the *Ferguson Forum* by "One Who Was There" described how the primary suffrage bill had passed without any assistance from "our young Christian governor and reformed anti-prohibitionist for political reasons." "After this year they are going to charge you good women $1.75 [in poll taxes] to vote," Ferguson pointed out, "but this year you can vote for Hobby for free. Instead of wanting to do something for the women, he wants you to do something for him."[37]

The charge was perfectly true, but it failed to stick. The superheated passions of wartime provided the suffragists with the same kind of political cover that their enemies had so long exploited with the "negro problem." Now the "German menace" made women's enfranchisement appear not only necessary but patriotic. The Progressives who had persuaded Hobby to change his position on the liquor issue had astutely predicted that it could be pulled off with "a show of patriotism" that would smother charges of "flopping to the pros overnight." The same strategy worked for suffrage, as Southern-bred Woodrow Wilson had already demonstrated by taking up the NAWSA's claim that women deserved the vote as a reward for their war work. Using the TESA's variation of this rationale, Hobby, who turned out to be better than anticipated on the hustings, claimed that women had been admitted to the primaries "to offset the votes of those whose carcasses are in this country but whose souls are in Germany." Former governor Tom Campbell hit the campaign trail declaring that "every slacker and every pro-German will vote for James E. Ferguson for Governor and it is up to the good women of this State to kill those votes."[38]

Women Clench Hobby's Victory

When the ballots were counted, both Hobby and Annie Webb Blanton won enormous victories. "'Hurrah for the women!'" R.M. Dudley, who had won nomination to the state senate, wrote jubilantly to Cunningham. "We probably would have elected Hobby anyway, but we know the women clenched it and nailed it down." Governor Hobby's total was more than twice as large as Ferguson's; Blanton won nearly 70,000 more votes than the incumbent superintendent of public instruction and a minor third candidate combined and carried every county except one. About the voters themselves, only anecdotal evidence exists. A Hobby chairman in East Texas, a Ferguson stronghold, reported during registration that many women were saying that they planned to vote for Hobby even though their husbands supported Ferguson. They may well have done so. Ferguson had predicted that he would win only twenty percent of the urban women but that eighty percent of the country women would support him; afterward he admitted that women had apparently voted ten to one for Hobby. Analysis of the election returns for San Antonio, where the newspaper published the candidates' total votes by precinct as well as a numerical breakdown of men and women registered in each precinct, indicates that at least eighty percent of women voters cast their ballots for Hobby for governor and eighty-six percent voted for Blanton as superintendent of public instruction.[39]

This impressive show of "voting right" notwithstanding, Cunningham soon discovered that her allies of convenience had not altered their underlying convictions. Rienzi Johnston's *Houston Post*, for years the anti-suffrage foil of the Progressive *Houston Chronicle*, had done a sharp editorial about-face after the suffrage bill passed. During the registration campaign it monitored the rising totals in a regular front page feature, urging the city toward a goal of 15,000 enrolled women. Rienzi Johnston abruptly ceased agitating the race issue and became so indifferent to the Black women who signed up that the *Post* did not even bother to tally them beyond round numbers. In the end, Black women made up less than eight percent of the female registrants in Houston, home to the state's largest Black community, and surrounding Harris County. The *Post* celebrated Hobby's victory by declaring that "the hand that rocks the cradle is the hand that rules the ballot box."[40] But when Cunningham asked Hobby for a resolution endorsing the federal suffrage amendment on the eve of the state Democratic convention six weeks later, he declined because his mentor, Johnston (who would be acting governor later that month while Hobby was out of the state), was adamantly opposed.

Minnie Fisher Cunningham "still feeling a little pert," as she later said, from the election victory, promptly declared that she would organize a women's floor fight for the resolution and was reproached for threatening to embarrass a young governor with "a fine political future." "If he doesn't support this amendment, he doesn't *have* any future," Cunningham retorted. Weeks before, Cunningham had been named to chair the convention as a reward for the women's campaign, but on the opening day she coolly rose and declined the honor. Her only purpose as a delegate was to secure endorsement for the federal suffrage amendment, she announced, and she reserved the right to speak on the subject if the committee report was unsatisfactory. "We really did organize a fine floor fight; it's a pity we didn't have to have it," she recollected forty years later. "We would have shown them something in termagants they had never seen." The opposition backed down and the convention endorsed the federal amendment, virtually guaranteeing the NAWSA a vote for ratification when the Nineteenth Amendment passed the following summer.[41]

Only two years earlier, in 1916, Cunningham and two other TESA suffragists had appeared before the state Democratic convention to ask for suffrage and been rebuffed; James Ferguson, fresh from his performance in St. Louis, had been in control. Nothing then seemed less likely than that the suffragists' implacable enemy would soon be their means to victory. As historian Aileen Kraditor noted long ago, political considerations often override personal convictions when legislators vote, and a reform movement has the best chance of succeeding if its leadership is "politically sophisticated" and has "something to offer the potential ally,... something to trade." The lack of such opportunities in the one-party South, she pointed out, doomed suffragists there to failure.[42] In 1918 Texas suffragists unexpectedly found themselves possessed of precisely those essentials for success: [intra-] party competition, something to trade, and a leader politically shrewd enough to recognize it.

Prudently, Cunningham and her inner circle kept the details of their legislative bargain to themselves. Political trading did not fit the self-image suffragists projected as earnest pleaders for simple justice, a "front door lobby" that shunned back room deals and politicking. It appeared that hardworking women had persevered until fair-minded men had seen the light of reason, when in fact temporary political expediency camouflaged in patriotic rhetoric had secured the suffrage victory. Years later, in a letter to one of her closest associates, Cunningham neatly summed up in words what they had earlier demonstrated in deed: "At the moment, we were the smartest group of politicians in the state."[43]

Notes

1. Grace Danforth, "Struggling for Freedom," *Dallas Morning News*, May 11, 1893. On the founding of the Texas Equal Rights Association, see Ruthe Winegarten and Judith N. McArthur, eds., *Citizens at Last: The Woman Suffrage Movement in Texas* (Austin, Tex., 1987), 87-93.

2. Marjorie Spruill (Wheeler), *New Women of the New South: The Leaders of the Woman Suffrage Movement in the Southern States* (New York, 1993), 13-14, 113-116; *Proceedings of the Twenty-sixth Annual Convention of the National American Woman Suffrage Association, February 15-20, 1894*, edited by Harriet Taylor Upton (Warren, Ohio, [1894]), 47-49.

3. On the "Solid South" see Carrie Chapman Catt and Nettie Rogers Shuler, *Woman Suffrage and Politics: The Inner Story of the Suffrage Movement* (1926; reprint, Seattle, 1969), 323-26; Eleanor Flexner, *Century of Struggle: The Woman's Rights Movement in the United States* (1959; reprint, New York, 1974), 302-305; and David Morgan, *Suffragists and Democrats: The Politics of Woman Suffrage in America* (East Lansing, 1972), 122-23, 155-56, 165-77. Anne Firor Scott, *The Southern Lady: From Pedestal to Politics, 1830-1930* (Chicago, 1970), chpt. 7, and Spruill (Wheeler), *New Women of the New South*, chpt. 1, analyze the difficulties of Southern suffragists.

4. Spruill (Wheeler), *New Women of the New South*, 37. Kentucky, which was not part of the former Confederacy, is sometimes mentioned as the fourth Southern state that ratified.

5. For the history of the Texas suffrage movement, see A. Elizabeth Taylor, "The Woman Suffrage Movement in Texas" *Journal of Southern History*, 27 (May 1951): 194-215.

63 percent of the Texas House of Representatives voted for the amendment in 1915; 59 percent did in 1917. In both sessions the amendment failed to come to a vote in the Senate. Calculated from tallies in Taylor, "The Woman Suffrage Movement in Texas," 208-212.

Spruill (Wheeler), New Women of the New South, 160-62.

Catt and Shuler, Woman Suffrage and Politics, 255-56; Jane Y. McCallum, "Activities of Women in Texas Politics," in Texas Democracy: A Centennial History of Politics and Personalities of the Democratic Party, 1836-1936, 2 vols., Frank Carter Adams, ed. (Austin, 1937), 1: 470-74; Dallas Times-Herald, June 16, 1916; Maud Wood Park, Front Door Lobby, Edna Lamprey Stantial, ed., (Boston, 1960), 14-15.

Elizabeth Hayes Turner, "'White-Gloved Ladies' and 'New Women' in the Texas Woman Suffrage Movement," in Southern Women: Histories and Identities, Virginia Bernhard et al, eds. (Columbia, Mo., 1992), 129-156.

). Lewis L. Gould, Progressives and Prohibitionists: Texas Democrats in the Wilson Era (Austin, 1973), 130-32, 185-221, and Gould, "The University Becomes Politicized: The War with Jim Ferguson," Southwestern Historical Quarterly, 86 (Oct. 1982): 255-6; Janet Humphrey, ed., A Texas Suffragist: Diaries and Writings of Jane Y. McCallum (Austin, 1988), quotations 64, 80-81.

1. "Brewing Propaganda," New Republic, Aug. 21, 1915, 62-64; Anti-Saloon League, The Brewers and Texas Politics, 2 vols. (San Antonio, 1916), 1: 109-112. Catt and Shuler, Woman Suffrage and Politics, list Texas as one of the eight states where the "organized German-liquor vote was hurled against woman suffrage referenda campaigns with the unerring accuracy claimed for it," 148.

2. See Judith N. McArthur, "Motherhood and Reform in the New South: Texas Women's Political Culture in the Progressive Era," (Ph.D. diss., University of Texas at Austin, 1992), 479-490.

3. Minnie Fisher Cunningham to Carrie Chapman Catt, Sept. 6, 1917, box 1, folder 8, Minnie Fisher Cunningham Papers, Houston Metropolitan Research Center, Houston Public Library.

4. Cunningham to Catt, July 31 (quotation), Aug. 27, 1917, ibid.

5. Hobby to Thomas B. Love, Oct. 22, Nov. 16, Dec. 31, 1917; Feb. 9, 1918, Thomas B. Love Papers, Dallas Historical Society. Cunningham to Hortense Ward, Sept. 27, 1917; Ward to Cunningham, Dec. 7, 22, 1917, box 13, folder 193, Cunningham Papers; Cunningham to Carrie Chapman Catt, Jan. 25, 1918, box 1, folder 9, ibid.

6. Gould, Progressives and Prohibitionists, 227-33; Hobby to Thomas B. Love, Dec. 31, 1917; Feb. 9, 1918, Love Papers.

7. Cunningham to Tom Finty, Jan. 28, 1918, box 4, folder 3, Jane McCallum Family Papers (Part I), Austin History Center, Austin Public Library.

8. Cunningham to C.B. Metcalfe, Jan. 28, 1918, box 14, folder 13, Cunningham Papers.

9. Metcalfe to Cunningham, Feb. 10, 1918, ibid.

10. Cunningham to Metcalfe, Feb. 13, 1918, ibid.

11. Metcalfe to Cunningham, Feb. 18, 13, 1918, ibid.

12. McCallum, "Activities of Women in Texas Politics," 481.

3. Texas Legislature, House Journal, 35th Leg., 4th Called Sess., (Austin, 1918), 264, 328-36. Final vote appears in Senate Journal, 455. Only the previous summer sentiment against suffrage had been so strong that Cunningham had not dared to attempt a second try at bringing a primary suffrage bill to a vote before the third special session ended. See Cunningham to Hortense Ward, Sept. 5, 1917, box 13, folder 193, Cunningham Papers.

14. The primary suffrage bill was only one of several election law changes passed during the special session in an attempt to keep Ferguson from winning. See Robert Maxwell, "Texas in the Progressive Era," in Texas: A Sesquicentennial Celebration (Austin, 1984), 191-92; Gould, Progressives and Prohibitionists, 234; and Austin American, March 19, 24, 1918.

25. Austin American, March 21, 1918 (quotation); Cunningham to Catt, March 25, 1918, box 1, folder 9, Cunningham Papers; Houston Post, March 21, 1918; Farm and Ranch, April 6, 1918.

26. Alwyn Barr, Black Texans: A History of Negroes in Texas, 1528-1971 (Austin, 1981), 79-80; Houston Post, April 11, 1915, March 21, 1918.

27. Mrs. E. Sampson to Mrs. [Maud Wood] Park, June 1918; Belle C. Critchett to Edith Hinkle League, July 1, 1918; League to Ruth White, July 8, 1918, and White to League, July 12, 1918; Catt to League July 17, 1918; Cunningham to Sampson, Aug. 31, 1918. All in box 3, folder 4, McCallum Papers, (Part I).

28. Metcalfe to Cunningham, April 12, 1918, box 14, folder 213, Cunningham Papers; "Minutes of Special Meeting of Executive Board of the Leslie Woman Suffrage Commission, Inc., Held June 20, 1918," Mrs. Percy V. Pennybacker Papers, Center for American History, University of Texas at Austin; Carrie Chapman Catt to Minnie Fisher Cunningham, June 20, 1918, box 18, folder 5, McCallum Papers (Part II).

29. Debbie Mauldin Cottrell, Pioneer Woman Educator: The Progressive Spirit of Annie Webb Blanton (College Station, Tex., 1993), 53-55.

30. Austin American, Dallas Morning News, Fort Worth Star-Telegram, Houston Post, and San Antonio Express, June 26 through July 12, 1918,.

31. McCallum, "Activities of Women in Texas Politics," 482; Cunningham to T.N. Jones, July 13, 1918, box 3, folder 4, McCallum Papers (Part I).

32. Dallas Morning News, July 27, 1918, July 19, 1918.

33. Humphrey, ed., A Texas Suffragist, 18, "To the Women of Texas," campaign flyer, box 19, folder 279, Cunningham Papers.

34. Home and State, June 1, 1918; "Vote for HOBBY for Governor," box 15, folder 234, Cunningham Papers.

35. Austin American, May 30, 1918.

36. "Extract from speech by James E. Ferguson, at City Auditorium, Houston, Texas, May 22, 1918—stenographic report by J.A. Lord," typescript, box 15, folder 227, Cunningham Papers; Ferguson Forum, March 28, April 25, 1918; July 11, 1918, June 20, 1918.

37. Dallas Morning News, June 27, 1918, July 19, 1918; Ferguson Forum, April 18, 1918, May 21, 1918.

38. M.M. Crane to Hobby, Feb. 2, 1918, box 3N98, folder 4, Martin McNulty Crane Papers, Center for American History, University of Texas at Austin; Thomas B. Love to Hobby, Jan. 26, 1918, Love Papers; Dallas Morning News, July 3, 1918, June 30, 1918.

39. R.M. Dudley to Cunningham, July 31, 1918, box 14, folder 206, Cunningham Papers; Seth Shepard McKay, Texas Politics, 1906-1944 (Lubbock, Tex., 1952), 82; Cottrell, Pioneer Woman Educator, 61; Blanton to Anna Pennybacker, Aug. 9, 1918, Pennybacker Papers; M.M. Crane to Walter Crawford, July 12, 1918, box 3N98, Crane Papers; Ferguson Forum, July 18, Aug. 1, 1918; McArthur, "Motherhood and Reform in the New South," 554-556; Hobby received 461,479 votes to Ferguson's 217,012. Ferguson carried only 22 counties of 245, including 6 of the 9 "German" counties in the central part of the state.

40. Houston Post, July 4, 9, 12, 13, 29 (quotation), 1918. In Harris County black women were allowed to register at a separate table in the courthouse after the NAACP filed a protest. The Houston Post, on July 13, 1918, reported a final total of 14,400 white and 1,200 Negro women who registered. The 1920 census recorded 25,528 Negroes age 21 and over in the county; 1,200 is less than ten percent of the female half. Newspaper reports indicate in Texas black women were permitted to register in some counties, turned away in others, and in still others permitted to register but told that they would not be allowed to vote.

41. "Spanning the Old to the New South," Texas Observer, Nov. 21, 1958 (Cunningham quotations).

42. McCallum, "Activities of Women in Texas Politics," 206; Gould, Progressives and Prohibitionists, 170-73; Aileen S. Kraditor, "Tactical Problems of the Woman Suffrage Movement in the South," Louisiana Studies, 4 (Winter 1966): 295, 300 (quotations).

43. Cunningham to Jane Y. McCallum, April 5 [ca. 1939], box 7, folder 3, McCallum Papers (Part I).

Nina Pinckard, a Confederate veteran, and Josephine Pearson at the Anti-ratification Headquarters, Hermitage Hotel, Nashville. The caption, handwritten by Pearson on the original photograph, reflects Southern antis' equation of the fight against the federal woman suffrage amendment with the Confederates' unsuccessful battle to protect states' rights during the Civil War. The caption reads verbatim:

"'Truth Crushed to the Earth will rise again"—is illustrated in this lovely picture of Mrs. Jas. S. Pinckard, president general of the Southern Woman's League for the Rejection of the Susan B. Anthony Amendment, who as grand-niece of John C. Calhoun-unfurls the Confederate flag as emblematic of Southerners' States Rights fight for the defeat of the Federal Amendment; to her left sits the Veteran who 'fought and bled' for Tennessee's States Rights; standing to his left, holding the flag of the Union, is Miss Josephine A. Pearson, Pres. Of the Tenn. Division of the Southern Women's Rejection League for the Rejection of the Susan B. Anthony Amendment, who led the fight in Tennessee which became the Battle Ground of the Nation, August 1920."

Twenty-One

ARMAGEDDON IN TENNESSEE:
The Final Battle Over the
Nineteenth Amendment

Anastatia Sims

Editor's Introduction: In 1917, with the adoption of a suffrage amendment by the influential state of New York, the suffrage bandwagon seemed to be gaining momentum. As the list of "suffrage states" grew and the numbers of Congressmen accountable to women voters rose, the prospects for passage of the federal suffrage amendment brightened. In 1918 President Wilson finally endorsed the measure and urged Democrats on Capitol Hill to give it their support. To the great delight of the suffragists, the House of Representatives approved the amendment in January 1918. But, despite a personal plea from Wilson, the Senate failed to give it the two-thirds vote required for adoption. Before Congress met again, the National American Woman Suffrage Association and the National Woman's Party—joined by national political leaders well aware of the electoral votes now controlled by suffrage states—sought desperately to gain the two votes yet needed for Senate approval. In May of 1919, the House of Representatives again overwhelmingly approved the amendment, and this time the Senate concurred. On June 4, 1919, the Congress of the United States finally approved the woman suffrage amendment.

Even as they celebrated, however, suffragists were all too aware of the challenge that remained: getting three-fourths of the states (thirty-six) to ratify the amendment. The task did indeed prove to be difficult, and seemed to grow more difficult as it neared completion. As historian Anastatia Sims tells us in this dramatic and colorful essay, the battle for the thirty-sixth state was a virtual "Armageddon," in which suffragists fought opponents whose determination and willingness to resort to any means necessary to defeat the amendment astounded even seasoned veterans of the suffrage movement including Carrie Chapman Catt.

By mid-June 1920, a year after Congress had sent the amendment to the states for approval, thirty-five states had ratified. Needing only one more state, suffragists were extremely frustrated when Delaware unexpectedly defeated the amendment—the only state north of the Mason-Dixon line to do so—and no other state was slated to hold a legislative session before the November 1920 presidential election. Polls of the Republican-dominated legislatures in Connecticut and

Vermont indicated that they would ratify if called into special session, but the anti-suffrage, anti-Prohibition governors of the two states refused to do so—despite frantic efforts by local and national suffragists to persuade them. Woodrow Wilson was able to convince Democratic governors in North Carolina and Tennessee to call special sessions, but North Carolina legislators defeated the amendment—and urged Tennessee to follow their example. Wilson exhorted these predominantly Democratic legislatures to ratify for the sake of the national Democratic Party, but North Carolina anti-suffrage legislators declared that "they were not going to sacrifice their honor upon the fickle altar of supposed political expediency" and urged their counterparts in Tennessee to "fight to the last ditch, and then some." The Tennessee anti-suffragists did exactly that.

As both sides mobilized for the fight, writes Sims, suffragists had reason to be encouraged. In keeping with Catt's "Winning Plan," Tennessee suffragists had persuaded these legislators to enact presidential and municipal suffrage for women in 1919, and many powerful political leaders, businessmen, and newspaper editors were pro-suffrage. However, as Catt warned, the anti-suffragists would spare no tactic or expense to dissuade legislators from supporting the amendment.

Anti-suffragists made use of anti-feminist arguments now nauseatingly familiar to the suffragists, including the idea that woman suffrage would ruin women and destroy the home. And familiar corporate opponents—particularly the liquor industry—were clearly operating in Tennessee. Sims describes the liquor industry, allied with the railroads and the cotton textile industry, as playing a leading role in the struggle.

That this final battle took place in the South clearly added to the difficulties of the suffragists, as anti-suffragists used race and states' rights arguments lavishly to arouse public sentiment against the amendment. Since the 1890s, Southern suffragists had struggled against anti-suffragists who denounced the suffrage movement as anathema to Southern values including White supremacy, state sovereignty, and reverence for traditional womanhood, and the antis now presented the fight over ratification as a battle to save "Southern Civilization." Earlier in the year, when Mississippi rejected the amendment, the Jackson *Clarion-Ledger* proclaimed (inaccurately) that "the vile old thing is as dead as its author [Susan B. Anthony], the old advocate of social equality and intermarriage of the races, and Mississippi will never be annoyed with it again." The leader of the Tennessee Division of the Southern Women's League for the Rejection of the Susan B. Anthony Amendment, Josephine Pearson, declared to her followers that Tennessee "could not fail in this most crucial test of Southern rights and honor, when Tennessee became the pivotal battle-ground of the Nation!" Ironically, two Southern suffragists and former NAWSA officers, Laura Clay and Kate Gordon, agreeing that the federal amendment was a threat to states' rights, actually came to Nashville and lobbied against ratification—though Clay hated being associated with the antis.

Leaders from both sides of the suffrage battle flocked to the state to assist their allies in Tennessee. Anti-suffrage leaders including Anne Pleasant, the wife of the Louisiana governor who had attempted to unite the South against the amendment, was there, for example, as was Charlotte Rowe of the National Association Opposed to Woman Suffrage. From the NAWSA, Marjorie Shuler, and finally President Carrie Chapman Catt herself, came to Nashville to assist Tennessee suffrage leaders, including Nashville socialite and former NAWSA Vice President Anne Dallas Dudley who had played a leading role in the NAWSA's lobbying of Congress. Alice Paul of the NWP did not come, but lobbied actively from a distance and dispatched capable assistants to the state. This was a wise decision: leading Tennessee Democrats greatly resented the NWP's campaign against their party and the picketing of President Wilson, and NWP orators on a 1917 speaking tour in the state had difficulty even obtaining a lecture hall. However, Paul was well represented by Sue Shelton White, formerly editor of the NWP's national organ *The Suffragist* and chair of the NWP in Tennessee, who worked well with all suffrage factions.

As the long, hot, summer progressed, suffragists struggled to retain their supporters and win new ones, but the anti-suffragists nearly succeeded in their dogged and unscrupulous fight to block ratification. It is amazing but true, as Sims explains, that after the seventy-two-year-long struggle for woman suffrage, the outcome was determined by an elderly mother in the Tennessee mountains who instructed her son (from an anti-suffrage district) to vote for woman suffrage if it became necessary. May her name live in the annals of the movement: Febb King Ensminger Burn, mother of twenty-four-year-old Harry Burn whose vote for ratification saved the woman suffrage amendment from defeat.

The anti-suffragists believed that, had they been able to prevent ratification of the suffrage amendment until after the November 1920 national elections, this "fad" that Wilson had promoted as a war measure would lose momentum and they might be able to block it permanently. They may have been right. As Catt and Shuler reported in *Woman Suffrage and Politics*, there was only one other ratification between that of Tennessee and the November election: in September, the Connecticut legislature was called into session to make provisions for registering women and took the occasion to ratify the Nineteenth Amendment—against the instructions of their anti-suffrage governor. This put the Nineteenth Amendment on firmer ground—since, as Sims describes below, anti-suffragists were *still* contesting the validity of Tennessee's ratification. However, the Connecticut legislature would not have had the *opportunity* to ratify had it not been for Tennessee's action. Without Tennessee's ratification, it is possible that in the conservative climate of the 1920s, the amendment would have failed—a scenario that seems more plausible after the failure of the Equal Rights Amendment in more recent times.

Suffragists, however, celebrated August 26, 1920, the day Tennessee's ratification reached Washington and was signed by the Secretary of State, as the day of their great victory. As the news spread, bells rang and whistles blew, and politicians of many stamps offered congratulations and attempted to take credit for enfranchising women. Carrie Chapman Catt returned to Washington to a giant victory celebration, and went on to New York for another. Alice Paul sewed the last star—the thirty-sixth—on a suffrage banner and hung it from the balcony of the NWP headquarters in Washington. In Seneca Falls a flag was draped over the tablet that marked the site where it had all begun.

★ ★ ★ ★ ★

I N JUNE 1919 Congress passed the Nineteenth Amendment and sent it on to the states. By the summer of 1920 thirty-five states had ratified it. If suffragists could win the approval of just one more state, they would, at long last, achieve their goal. When the Delaware legislature unexpectedly defeated the amendment in early June, women pinned their hopes on Tennessee. During a steamy Southern summer, Nashville, the "Athens of the South," became the site of one of the most fiercely fought contests in American political history. For the amendment's friends and foes alike it was Armageddon—the final battle in the long, bitter struggle that had, in the words of one observer, pitted "powers that pray" against "powers that prey."[1]

Suffragists were by no means certain of victory. Tennessee, like the rest of the South, had a history of hostility toward women's rights. In 1908, for example, Governor Malcolm R. Patterson offered this comment on woman suffrage: "Let the women pray and the men vote."[2] Twelve years later many Tennesseans—male and female alike—still agreed with the governor. Woman's place was at home, in church, in the schoolroom or even in the factory—but not at the polls.

At the same time, there appeared to be reasons for cautious optimism. In 1919, just two months before Congress submitted the Nineteenth Amendment to the states, the Tennessee General Assembly had passed a law giving women the right to vote in presidential and municipal elections, and the same men would consider the amendment. The state Democratic party had endorsed woman suffrage, and so had most of the state's major newspapers.

As suffragists knew from past experience, however, appearances could be deceiving, and close examination revealed a grim picture in Tennessee. The first obstacle was a section of the state constitution that prohibited ratification by a legislature elected before Congress submitted an amendment to the states. (Members of the current legislature had been elected in 1918.) When the United States Supreme Court handed down a decision that nullified that provision, suffragists immediately began clamoring for a special session. Sue Shelton White, chair of the National Woman's Party (NWP) in Tennessee, requested the session in a letter to Governor Albert H. Roberts on June 19. Two days later, Catherine Talty Kenny and Kate Burch Warner of the Tennessee Equal Suffrage Association (an affiliate of the National American Woman Suffrage Association) led a delegation of women who urged the governor to call the session in time for women to vote in the state primaries August 5. At the request of the Tennessee League of Women Voters and the NAWSA, pro-suffrage politicians from Tennessee and elsewhere wrote the governor. The United States attorney general, the state attorney general and other prominent jurists assured Roberts that such a session would be legal. Even President Woodrow Wilson bowed to the suffragists' pleas, and telegraphed his support.[3]

But the governor stalled. During his campaign two years earlier Roberts had spoken out against woman suffrage. According to Catherine Kenny, he had signed the presidential and municipal suffrage bill only because he believed it was unconstitutional. Subsequently, he had blocked women's attempts to

Sue Shelton White
LIBRARY OF CONGRESS

expand their political power further when he refused to call a special session to give women the right to vote in party primaries.[4]

Roberts had good reason to want to keep women out of politics. There were persistent rumors that his highly paid private secretary, who had been working for him on the state payroll since 1915, was a woman of questionable reputation. He was firmly allied with the "wet" [anti-prohibition] wing of the Democratic Party, and his advisers were hostile to votes for women. As a candidate, he was unlikely to appeal to women voters.[5]

And it was his appeal as a candidate that was foremost in A.H. Roberts's mind in the summer of 1920. He was embroiled in a bitter fight for renomination. He confronted challengers within his own party, as well as strong Republican opposition. His tax reform program had alienated farmers, while his support for management during the strikes of 1919 turned industrial workers against him. Opponents accused him of raising taxes and increasing the state's debt.[6]

With his political career hanging in the balance, Governor Roberts faced a seemingly impossible choice. If he endorsed woman suffrage, perhaps women would forgive his other transgressions, and maybe their support would offset disillusioned farmers and workers. On the other hand, if women voted (as suffragists predicted they would) on moral issues alone, he might be ensuring his own defeat. Whatever women did, Roberts was under increasing pressure from his own party. Democratic leaders at the national level, including President Wilson himself, were staking the party's honor (and chances for victory in the November elections) on their ability to ratify the Nineteenth Amendment and enfranchise women who, they presumed, would then express their gratitude by voting the Democratic ticket. Uncertain of his own chances for reelection, Roberts could not afford to repudiate the national platform. Within Tennessee, however, he drew his support from men likely to oppose votes for women. If he followed Wilson's lead, he risked offending some of his staunchest friends. Finally, however, the governor capitulated. On June 25 he announced that he would convene the legislature later in the summer—*after* the Democratic primary August 5.

The Battle Begins

The governor's announcement set off one of the most heated political fights ever witnessed in Tennessee, a state hardly known for political tranquility. Professor Edwin Mims observed that "The Battle of Nashville in 1864 was a five o'clock tea in comparison with this one." Writing fifty years after the fact, journalist Joe Hatcher described the special session as "the bitterest, bare-fisted, name-calling, back-biting session in the state's history." The stakes were high, and both sides were hard at work long before the session opened.[7]

Suffragists initiated their campaign by recruiting a Men's Ratification Committee composed of some of the most prominent men in the state. With former governor Tom Rye as chair, the committee included newspaper publishers (George Fort Milton of the *Chattanooga News*, Edward B. Stahlman of the *Nashville Banner* and Luke Lea of the *Nashville Tennessean*), politicians (speaker of the Tennessee house Seth Walker, Memphis political boss Edward H. Crump, United States Senator Kenneth D. McKellar, former Republican Governor Ben Hooper, and Republican gubernatorial candidate Alfred A. Taylor) and businessmen (Guilford Dudley, among others). It was an eclectic coalition, representing diverse political factions and economic interests. Such strange bedfellows were unlikely to rest easily together. Before the end of the summer, some of the men who had allowed themselves to be named to the Ratification Committee had joined the opposition, and the committee itself played only a limited role in the campaign.[8]

Suffragists expected that in Tennessee, as elsewhere, they would lead the fight to win votes for women. Accordingly Abby Crawford Milton, president of the Tennessee League of Women Voters, appointed a Women's Ratification Committee, with Catherine Kenny as chair. To their dismay, Governor Roberts decided to form his own Women's Ratification Committee. He named as its head Kate Warner, "a lady of culture and refinement," and a lady who, unlike Milton and Kenny, was firmly aligned with the Roberts camp.[9] Abby Milton's husband edited the *Chattanooga News,* which had endorsed Roberts's rival for the Democratic gubernatorial nomination. Catherine Kenny was a friend of Luke Lea, publisher of the anti-Roberts, pro-suffrage *Nashville Tennessean,* and arch-rival of Major Edward B. Stahlman, one of Roberts's strongest supporters. Factionalism was the keynote of Tennessee politics; factionalism had earlier torn apart the suffrage movement in Tennessee. "You know we Tennesseans and Kentuckians are rather strong on 'feuds,'" Catherine Kenny wrote the NAWSA president Carrie Chapman Catt. "Sorter [sic] drunk it in with our mother's milk." Now factionalism jeopardized the ratification of the Nineteenth Amendment.

Anne Dallas Dudley
LIBRARY OF CONGRESS

"I don't believe there's a ghost of a chance of ratification in either Tennessee or North Carolina," Catt told Nashville suffragist Anne Dallas Dudley on July 12. "Tennessee has always been torn by factions in all men's and women's work, and it was these factions which defeated us in Delaware."[10]

The existence of two "official" women's ratification committees implied that there was disagreement among the suffragists themselves (and, in fact, the two groups were not always in harmony). Suffrage leaders recognized that the appearance of disunity could seriously damage their cause. The NAWSA's representative in Nashville, Marjorie Shuler, negotiated a compromise, persuading Governor Roberts, the League of Women Voters, and the NAWSA to recognize both committees. Through letters, telegrams, and telephone calls Shuler kept in close touch with Carrie Chapman Catt in New York. In mid-July, Catt decided the situation required her personal attention. She arrived in Nashville on July 17, expecting to stay only a few days. Instead, she remained more than a month.[11]

Upon her arrival Catt told reporters, "I have no definite plan of action for my stay in Nashville." At least one reporter knew better. After describing her "pleasing personality," "kindly but animated face," and "soft, musical voice," he added, "yet there is about her expression something that strongly suggests that she can be firm when the occasion requires, and, if need be, aggressive."[12] Catt had worked for suffrage for thirty years. She was an intelligent woman, and a shrewd politician. She came to Tennessee determined to win the final victory.

Catt had been coordinating the campaign from New York long before she set foot in Nashville. In June she instructed Tennessee suffragists to begin polling the legislators

National Woman's Party Headquarters in Nashville, Tenn. where the
campaign for ratification of the suffrage amendment was centered.
LIBRARY OF CONGRESS

to determine how they would vote on the amendment. They should not rely on
hearsay, she warned; they should accept only the word of "bona fide" suffrage
workers. She urged volunteers to get firm commitments, but cautioned them that
these might not be binding. At the same time the women undertook to poll the
legislators, they conducted another survey to find out which lawmakers might be
susceptible to bribes. Catt was a seasoned politician, with few illusions about the
political process. "[N]o matter how well the women may work or how effective their
results may be," she wrote Catherine Kenny, "ratification in Tennessee will go through
the work and actions of men, and the great motive that will finally put it through will
be political and nothing else. We have long since recovered from our previous faith in
the action of men based upon a love of justice. That is an animal that doesn't exist."[13]

The Anti-suffragists

While suffragists organized, their opponents also went into action. On the same
day that Carrie Chapman Catt arrived in Nashville, Josephine Anderson Pearson,
an educator from east Tennessee who had been tapped to lead the fight against suffrage in 1917, was entertaining guests in her mountain home when she received a
telegram summoning her to Nashville to fight the *"invasion by foreign forces."* She
caught the train to the capital city that afternoon. That night she checked into the

cheapest room available at the Hermitage Hotel, and reserved assembly rooms on the mezzanine and the first floor for the Tennessee branch of the Southern Women's Rejection League (full name: Southern Women's League for the Rejection of the Susan B. Anthony Amendment). For the next six weeks the Hermitage Hotel would be her home, and anti-suffrage headquarters.[14]

Although the anti-suffragists (or antis) criticized suffragists for bringing in "foreign forces" they did not hesitate to call in their own reinforcements. Mrs. James Pinckard of Alabama, Mrs. Ruffin Pleasant of Louisiana, and Miss Charlotte Rowe of New York were among the women who came to Nashville to fight the Nine-teenth Amendment. These women were not really outsiders, Josephine Pearson declared, because "Tennessee considers no influence as 'outside' that is Southern, or invited to this state by united Southern sentiment for the preservation of our state constitution and white civilization."[15] Like the suffragists, female anti-suffragists recognized that this confrontation was crucial, and, like the suffragists, they believed they acted for the good of women and of society.

"A few women representatives of the National Association Opposed to Woman Suffrage are in Nashville," Marjorie Shuler reported in early August, "but far more deadly is the corps of men who have quietly stolen into the state and whose work is evident in the wavering of certain legislators and in the organization of a Tennessee Constitutional League." The League, a subsidiary of the American Constitutional League and the anti-suffrage counterpart to the Men's Ratification Committee, was dedicated to the defeat of the Susan B. Anthony Amendment. It included "prominent lawyers and business men," men who would use their wealth and influence in their attempt to block ratification in Tennessee.[16]

Suffragists faced formidable adversaries. They believed that "sinister forces" were working against them, and they set out to discredit their opponents. In late July, Carrie Chapman Catt and Abby Crawford Milton embarked on a statewide speaking tour, to convince the public that the "whiskey lobby, manufacturers' lobby, and the railroad lobby" were united against "the women of Tennessee."[17] After the fight was over, Catt declared: "Never in the history of politics has there been such a nefarious lobby as labored to block ratification in Nashville." Other participants and observers agreed with Catt's assessment. George Fort Milton described the antis as "insidious," and "a well-organized and unscrupulous opposition." The *Christian Science Monitor* compared the anti lobbyists to "a horde of locusts," and characterized the battle over ratification as "justice against vested influence." Writing four months after the suffragists had won, Abby Crawford Milton insisted that the devil himself had been at work in Tennessee in the summer of 1920, collaborating with the antis to keep the ballot from women.[18]

"Nefarious." "Insidious." "Unscrupulous." These are strong words, even when hurled in the wake of a feverish political contest. Were the suffragists prone to hyperbole, or were their accusations on target? Certainly by 1920 the suffragists were skilled publicists for their own cause, and they recognized the advantages of portraying themselves as defenseless women fighting ruthless political machines and heartless corporate giants. The portrait was an effective piece of public relations. It was also rooted in fact. Across the nation distillers, brewers, and manufacturers (particularly those who employed large numbers of women and children) subsidized campaigns against state suffrage referenda and against the federal woman suffrage amendment, although they worked, for the most part, in secrecy. A Senate investigation of the United States Brewers' Association in 1918 revealed that that organization had actively tried to defeat woman suffrage in several states.[19] In some states textile manufacturers joined with liquor interests. Walter Clark, Chief Justice of the North Carolina Supreme Court, believed that "the Whiskey Interests and the Cotton Mill owners of the South" underwrote anti-suffrage campaigns. Clark was one of the South's leading Progressive reformers, but his son, David, edited the *Southern Textile Bulletin*, mouthpiece of the region's cotton industry.[20]

These forces had been evident on the political scene in Tennessee for years, and it is likely that they were in Nashville in the summer of 1920. Prohibition had been the central issue of Tennessee politics during the first fifteen years of the twentieth century, and distillers and brewers had mobilized to protect their businesses. The Manufacturers' Association was also active politically, opposing bills to regulate child labor, set minimum wages, and establish employers' responsibility for workers' safety on the job. Finally, the Louisville and Nashville Railroad (L&N) had been involved in Tennessee politics since the 1880s. The L&N's generosity in distributing free passes to legislators in 1913 (while the General Assembly was considering a railroad bill) led to an Interstate Commerce Committee investigation in 1916. Woman suffrage—with its promise to deliver women's votes for the enforcement of Prohibition, regulation of child labor, and reforms to end political corruption—threatened vital interests of all three of these powerful lobbies.[21]

Suffragists charged that these groups "paid the bills" for the antis in 1920. There is no concrete evidence to confirm or refute their accusations. We do know that some of the men who led the fight against the Nineteenth Amendment in Tennessee were affiliated with the businesses that had opposed woman suffrage elsewhere. For example, John Vertrees, one of the best-known opponents of suffrage, was also associated with the liquor industry. Although he denied being part of the "whiskey ring," he represented at least one executive of George A. Dickel and Company in both personal and business matters, and was closely identified with liquor interests.[22] Garnett Andrews, one of the founding members of the Tennessee Constitutional League, was involved with several knitting and hosiery mills, and, according to John Trotwood Moore, was "one of the most prominent representatives of the knitting industry in the South."[23] Mr. and Mrs. George A. Washington both participated in the fight against woman suffrage; Mr. Washington was a director of the L&N.[24]

Finally there was Edward Bushrod Stahlman, "the Major," publisher of the *Nashville Banner* and one of the most colorful (and powerful) figures in Tennessee politics. Stahlman had come to the United States from Germany before the Civil War. He got a job with the L&N in 1863, and worked his way up to a vice presidency. In 1884 he led a successful attempt to abolish the state railroad commission, established only two years earlier. During that debate Stahlman not only presented the L&N's case to the General Assembly, he also attempted to curry favor with Nashville newspapers. His attempts failed. By the time the fight was over, all the papers in the capital city were hostile to the railroad, a situation that could weaken the L&N in future legislative contests. In 1885, Stahlman bought the Banner. He left the L&N in 1890 to become commissioner of the Southern Railway and Steamship Association, a post he held until 1895. After that he devoted his attention to his family, the *Banner,* and Tennessee politics.[25] Although he officially severed his ties with the railroad industry, his critics (notably Luke Lea) suspected that he continued to represent the L&N's interests in Nashville. In 1914 Lea's *Nashville Tennessean* ran an editorial cartoon with the following caption: "Tennessee is governed by [Republican Governor Ben] Hooper; Hooper is manipulated by Stahlman; Stahlman is dominated by L&N; find the real ruler of Tennessee."[26] Stahlman dismissed Lea's accusation as "a malicious lie"; nevertheless, some Tennesseans continued to regard the *Banner* publisher as an agent of the L&N. In the summer of 1920, Stahlman waffled on woman suffrage. After being named to the Men's Ratification Committee, he changed his mind, and, through the pages of the *Banner* as well as in public addresses, became an outspoken opponent of votes for women.[27]

The influential men who fought the Nineteenth Amendment may have acted from conviction instead of (or in addition to) self-interest. Many antis sincerely believed that women had no business in politics, and that enfranchising them would only create problems. But connections between prominent antis and liquor, textile, and railroad companies convinced the suffragists that these men represented larger interests. Events like Stahlman's change of heart and what Marjorie Shuler described as "the wavering of certain legislators" persuaded the women that their enemies were employing underhanded tactics. As the special session drew near, more and more lawmakers who had pledged themselves to suffrage switched sides. Two days before the legislature was to meet, suffragists lost one of their most valuable allies, Seth Walker, Speaker of the House of Representatives. Just a week earlier, a newspaper had announced that Walker was firmly committed to ratification. He had even promised to introduce the resolution. His defection, according to *The Suffragist,* official journal of the NWP, was a "sure indication of the strength of the opposition forces at work."[28] Support for the amendment eroded steadily. By the time the session opened, suffragists who earlier in the summer had been confident of victory were worried. "All that we can say at this writing," reported the NAWSA's *Woman Citizen,* "is that the signs are favorable, but that the opposition is massed as it was never massed before." Before the final vote on the amendment, every single legislator who the suffragists had identified as bribable moved from the pro column to the anti list.[29]

The Battle Intensifies

At the same time that both sides worked behind the scenes to influence lawmakers, they also waged massive publicity campaigns to sway public opinion. Anti-suffragists took the offensive with assertions that representatives and senators who voted for the amendment would violate their oath of office. Attempting to circumvent the Supreme Court decision, they maintained that legislators pledged to uphold the state constitution as it was written, not as it was interpreted by the United States Supreme Court. Suffragists countered with numerous opinions from legal authorities within Tennessee and throughout the United States.[30]

Anti-suffragists also relied on arguments that had been used ever since the idea of woman suffrage was introduced in 1848. They predicted that female enfranchisement would result in nothing less than the end of civilization. It would destroy the home and the family. Wives would divorce their husbands when they disagreed about politics. Mothers, preoccupied with their new status as voters, would neglect their children. Women would become "masculinized" and men "feminized." One anti-suffrage leaflet warned men: "A Vote for Federal Suffrage is a Vote for Organized Female Nagging Forever."[31]

Suffragists quickly responded to the anti attack. They affirmed their loyalty to domesticity and motherhood. A widely circulated photograph showed Anne Dallas Dudley, a Tennessee suffrage activist with an impeccable pedigree, reading to her children. Suffragists argued that circumstances of modern life required housewives to get involved in politics, because politics affected family life. The vote would not make women forsake their home duties, suffragists insisted. Instead, it would enable them to fulfill their domestic obligations more effectively.[32]

At the beginning of the campaign, Carrie Chapman Catt warned Tennessee suffragists that "The anti suffragists will flood Tennessee with the most outrageous literature it has ever been your lot to read.... It will be extremely harmful, and the 'nigger question' will be put forth in ways to arouse the greatest possible prejudice."[33] Catt was right. For many Southern opponents of suffrage, the central issue in 1920 was race. Josephine Pearson identified "three deadly principles" in the Nineteenth Amendment: "1st, surrender of state sovereignty. 2nd, Negro woman suffrage. 3rd, Race equality."[34] A leaflet addressed to the "Men of the South" reminded voters of the similarity between the Fifteenth and Nineteenth Amendments, and predicted that ratification would lead to "another period of Reconstruction horrors," when African American men and "female carpetbaggers" would rule. Anti leaders informed White Southerners that Congress had three "force bills" ready for consideration, bills similar to those used during Reconstruction.[35] A broadside entitled "Woman Suffrage, A Menace to the South" warned that the Nineteenth Amendment would destroy state sovereignty and increase the number of African American voters in the South because it would enable Black women to vote.[36] Anti-suffrage propaganda quoted feminists and African American leaders who favored social equality between Blacks and Whites, and concluded that woman suffrage would lead to interracial marriage. Again and again Southern antis declared that woman suffrage would result in the downfall of White supremacy, which, they implied, would leave White Southern women vulnerable to assaults by Black men. According to Mrs. Ruffin Pleasant of Louisiana, "the passage of the Nineteenth Amendment would embolden both the negro [sic] woman and the negro man to give us even greater trouble than they are doing now."[37]

To counter the anti assault, suffragists pledged to uphold White supremacy, and argued that the same measures that disfranchised African American men would also disqualify African American women. Privately, some suffragists defended the contributions Black women could make to politics. Because of the presidential and municipal suffrage bill enacted in 1919, African American women had already begun to vote in Tennessee. In January, 1920, Catherine Kenny told Carrie Chapman Catt that the record of Black women voters in Nashville was "one of which every Southern suffragist may not only feel proud but hopeful for the future." In July she repeated her endorsement: "[I]n every instance...they voted with the best White women thereby eliminating any political prejudice." After the ratification fight was over, Kenny wrote in the Tennessee chapter of the History of Woman Suffrage that African American woman suffrage "was anything but the 'bugaboo' politicians had tried to show it would be and in some instances it was a contributing factor to good government." In Tennessee, as in other Southern states, Black women had joined in the campaign for woman suffrage, working in segregated organizations.[38]

The special session was scheduled to open on Monday, August 9. Lawmakers began arriving in Nashville on Saturday, and they, along with suffragists and antis, converged on the Hermitage Hotel. There were others at the Hermitage, too, "mysterious men," whom the suffragists did not recognize, but who clearly had a stake in the outcome of the vote. Suffragists observed these unidentified men escorting legislators to a room on the eighth floor, a room where liquor flowed freely. By late in the evening, Carrie Chapman Catt recalled, "legislators, both suffrage and anti-suffrage men, were reeling through the hall in a state of advanced intoxication." Horrified suffragists asked officials to enforce the Prohibition laws. They were told that this was the "Tennessee way," and that "in Tennessee, whiskey and legislation go hand in hand."[39]

Armageddon: The Final Showdown

The legislature convened at noon on Monday, August 9. The Senate was solidly pro-suffrage. The ratification resolution was introduced on August 10, and referred to the committee on constitutional amendments the following day. On Friday, August 13, the committee recommended its adoption. "National woman's suffrage is at hand," the majority report stated; "it may be delayed but it cannot be defeated, and we covet for Tennessee the signal honor of being the thirty-sixth and last State necessary to consummate this great reform." That same day, the Senate passed the resolution by a vote of 25 to 4.[40]

With the question settled in the Senate, suffragists and their opponents focused their attention on the House. The antis immediately invoked a number of delaying tactics, and continued their efforts to win over lawmakers. Each side accused the other of foul play. Carrie Chapman Catt claimed that anti-suffrage men tapped phones, listened at transoms, and intercepted telegrams in order to anticipate the suffragists' plans. According to Catt, they used liquor, loans, bribes, promises of high office and "every other device which old hands at illicit politics could conceive or remember"[41] to get legislators to vote their way. On August 12 a newspaper reported that "Nashville looks like a real oasis in the dry desert. Moonshine corn whiskey is flowing freely."[42]

The suffragists, meanwhile, allegedly employed tactics that were more subtle but no less persuasive. "Automobile rides, hugs, kisses, even the absurdity of powdering the members' noses and rouging their cheeks in the assembly hall were frequently witnessed," *The Lookout* of Chattanooga told its readers. The suffragists were testing the boundaries of ladylike behavior with their aggressive tactics, the journal implied, and *The Lookout* clearly disapproved. According to *The Lookout's* vigilant observer, one suffragist—"a very pretty lady"—eager to convert a dubious legislator "grabbed his tie…and held him in a grip that one would suppose invincible." As the woman kept talking, the man pulled a knife out of his pocket, cut himself loose, and walked away, leaving the startled suffragist holding the remnants of his tie. "Just keep it," he remarked as he strolled away.[43]

In the House, as in the Senate, a ratification resolution had been introduced on August 10. But day after day passed; the House took no action. On August 17, the committee on constitutional convention and amendments issued a favorable report. Dismissing the arguments that ratification would be unconstitutional or a violation of the oath of office, the committee agreed with its Senate counterpart that it would be "an honor" for Tennessee to be the final state to ratify the amendment, "giving to our mothers, wives, daughters, sisters and sweethearts a precious right which they have so long been unjustly denied."[44]

The debate began. In an impassioned speech, Seth Walker urged his colleagues to vote against the ratification resolution on states' rights grounds. He also defended his reputation. He resented the charge that he had changed his mind on the issue because of pressure from "a certain railroad," he declared. But, as Marjorie Shuler noted, he "made no specific denial." Speaking for the suffragists, Joe Hanover of Memphis condemned the interference of antis from other states, and denounced the tactics of Tennessee's own anti-suffragists. "What is a greater crime," he demanded, "than for certain newspapers connected with the opposition to threaten you as they have been doing for the last ten days?" The debate continued for several hours, but the House adjourned without voting.[45]

That night was a long one for suffragists. They patrolled the corridors of the Hermitage Hotel and stationed sentries at the train station to prevent the untimely departure of any of the men still pledged to support them. They met in Carrie Chapman Catt's room for yet another strategy session. But this time even Catt had exhausted her political resources. "There is one more thing we can do—only one," she said. "We can pray." [46] After all the careful organization, the years of winning over public opinion, the arduous task of wooing legislators, the women were still left to pray while the men voted.

The galleries were packed when House Speaker Seth Walker called the session to order on August 18. The atmosphere was tense; both sides knew the vote was too close to call. An anti motion to table the ratification resolution ended in a tie. [47] It was a victory for suffragists, but the real test lay ahead.

"The hour has come!" Seth Walker shouted. The roll call began. There were two votes for, followed by four against. The seventh name on the list was Harry Burn. At twenty-four, he was the youngest man in the legislature, a Republican from McMinn County in east Tennessee. Suffrage polls listed him as undecided. He had voted with the antis on the motion to table. Although Burn had promised suffrage leaders he would vote with them if they needed his vote to ratify, suffragists feared he would continue to side with the antis. They knew that political leaders in his home district opposed the Nineteenth Amendment. But they did not know that in his pocket was a letter from his mother telling him to "be a good boy" and vote for ratification. When his name was called, Harry Burn voted yes. [48]

It took a few moments for the suffragists to absorb what had happened, but before the roll call was over they realized that Harry Burn had given them the last vote they needed. The antis realized it, too. As soon as the clerk announced the vote—49 to 47—Seth Walker changed his vote from no to aye, and introduced a motion to reconsider. (Under House rules, only a representative voting with the winning side could move to reconsider). That parliamentary maneuver did not diminish the suffragists' joy. "Emancipated at last!" some exclaimed. That night, Carrie Chapman Catt sent a telegram to North Carolina suffragist Gertrude Weil: "The thirty-sixth state is won." [49]

The story should have ended there, but it continued. For two days Walker refused to bring up the motion to reconsider, while he and the antis tried to round up enough votes to defeat the measure on the second vote. They sent telegrams to pro-suffrage representatives, reproaching them for their votes. Two legislators, T.O. Simpson and S.F. Stovall, complained that they "were called up every half hour day and night so that they had no sleep." Assemblyman Simpson received threats that he would lose his teaching job if he did not change sides. But the pro-suffrage majority held firm. Late on the night of August 20, thirty-eight anti-suffrage representatives fled to Decatur, Alabama, on an L&N train ("very suitably indeed in their choice of conveyance" was Marjorie Shuler's caustic comment). Members of the "Red Rose Brigade" (named after the anti-suffrage emblem, the red rose;

Harry Burn   Febb King Ensminger Burn

suffragists adopted the yellow rose) hoped that their absence would break the quorum, and prevent further action on the amendment.[50]

Meanwhile, antis appealed to public opinion. On August 19, they held a mass meeting at Ryman Auditorium "to save the South." E.B. Stahlman was the featured speaker. Antis organized similar rallies throughout the state later in the month. Observers disagreed on the response to the meetings. "Indignation Spreads Over Whole State" declared a headline in the anti-suffrage *Chattanooga Daily Times,* while the pro-suffrage *Nashville Tennessean* reported "Little Interest Manifested in Mass Meetings."[51] Antis all over the nation condemned the Tennessee legislators who voted with the suffragists. Martin Lee Calhoun of Selma, Alabama, compared them to "assassins of the night who have stabbed the heart of the South and its traditions to the core."[52]

Antis directed much of their outrage at Harry Burn. Josephine Pearson labelled him a "traitor to manhood's honor," while anti newspapers reported that Joe Hanover paid him $10,000 to change his vote.[53] In response to the antis' attacks on his integrity, Burn inserted a personal statement in the House journal, explaining that he cast his vote for morality, justice, his mother, and the glory of the Republican party. Charges of bribery did not stick to Harry Burn, but they persisted against the antis. In September, a grand jury investigated the activities of lobbyists during the campaign. It returned no indictments against either side.[54]

House custom gave the representative who introduced a motion to reconsider three days to bring the motion before the floor; after that, any member could call the question. Pro-suffrage legislators were determined to resolve the issue once and for all on August 21; if Walker did not call for a vote on his motion, they would. The legislature convened, with all the suffrage men in their places, and women occupying the desks of the absent members, sitting in silent protest against the retreat of the Red Rose Brigade. Fifty-eight members of the legislature were present that morning—forty-nine suffrage men and nine antis. T.K. Riddick, one of the amendment's strongest supporters, moved to reconsider the ratification resolution. Speaker Walker ruled him out of order. There was no quorum, he said. Besides, he announced, just that morning antis had won an injunction to prohibit the governor from certifying Tennessee's ratification. Riddick appealed the Speaker's decision to the members of the House. They

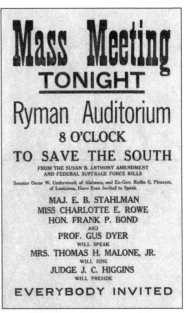

Mass Meeting

TONIGHT

Ryman Auditorium

8 O'CLOCK

TO SAVE THE SOUTH

FROM THE SUSAN B. ANTHONY AMENDMENT
AND FEDERAL SUFFRAGE FORCE BILLS

Senator Oscar W. Underwood, of Alabama, and Ex-Gov. Ruffin G. Pleasant, of Louisiana, Have Been Invited to Speak

MAJ. E. B. STAHLMAN
MISS CHARLOTTE E. ROWE
HON. FRANK P. BOND
AND
PROF. GUS DYER
WILL SPEAK
MRS. THOMAS H. MALONE, JR.
WILL SING
JUDGE J. C. HIGGINS
WILL PRESIDE

EVERYBODY INVITED

TENNESSEE STATE LIBRARY AND ARCHIVES

voted 49 to 8 to overturn Walker's ruling (Walker abstained) then went on to table the motion to reconsider. Walker's procedural ploy had failed.[55]

On August 23, the Tennessee Supreme Court overturned the injunction against the governor. Governor Roberts signed the certificate of ratification on August 24 and sent it on to Washington. On the morning of August 26, Secretary of State Bainbridge Colby issued a proclamation declaring the Nineteenth Amendment ratified and part of the United States Constitution.[56]

Still the antis refused to surrender. When members of the Red Rose Brigade returned to the House August 31, they moved to expunge the activities of August 21 from the record. The motion carried, largely because pro-suffrage members refused to vote. "I consider that the Nineteenth Amendment has been legally adopted," one stated, "and that any other action by this House would be a farce." Having erased August 21 from history, anti legislators went on to reconsider the Nineteenth Amendment, and vote it down. Most pro-suffrage representatives were recorded as present and not voting.[57]

Anne Dallas Dudley found it highly amusing. "Tennessee enacted a little farce to add to the gayety [sic] of the nation today," she wired Carrie Chapman Catt. A day later she was not laughing. "Find out from Washington if action yesterday seriously injures our case," her next telegram read. "Lawyers here differ. Must know at once."[58] She had no reason to worry. Ratification was secure, despite Tennessee's attempt to rescind its approval, and despite Seth Walker's ongoing efforts to prevent the amendment from taking effect. In September, he and other antis went first to Washington, to persuade Secretary of State Colby that Tennessee's ratification was unconstitutional (the Secretary was not convinced) then on to Connecticut, where the legislature was considering ratification. There, as well, too few men heeded their pleas. Connecticut ratified in mid-September, and American women's right to vote was at last assured.[59]

Aftermath

The antis were no more gracious in defeat than they had been during the battle. Unable to stop woman suffrage, in the fall of 1920 they encouraged women voters to vote against the men who had enfranchised them. In Tennessee, they set their sights on Harry Burn and A.H. Roberts. Roberts was particularly vulnerable. Already unpopular because of his tax program and hostility to organized labor, he had alienated his political allies with his stand on suffrage. The special session of the General Assembly, after acceding to his request to ratify the Nineteenth Amendment by the narrowest of margins, proceeded to turn down every other proposal he submitted. E.B. Stahlman's *Nashville Banner,* which had supported him in the Democratic primary, now turned against him. The *Chattanooga Daily Times* even demanded that he be removed from the ticket.[60]

Suffragists rallied to the aid of their champions. Abby Crawford Milton traveled around the state, defending Burn and organizing women for Roberts. In Nashville, Catherine Kenny appealed to working women to support the governor. Still, suffragists recognized that Roberts's campaign was in serious trouble. In early October, a member of the women's committee of the state Democratic Party turned to Carrie Chapman Catt for help. "This is private and confidential and TNT," she began. "The Antis have concentrated their campaign against Governor Roberts and intend to defeat him at any cost." She pleaded with Catt to use her influence to raise money for the governor's campaign, and concluded: "If I knew anyway to make this appeal stronger I would do it. I shall feel forever disgraced if Roberts is repudiated. This is a woman's fight and we can't afford to lose."[61]

But they did lose. "Election Returns Prove Strength of Anti-Suffragists" proclaimed the *Woman Patriot,* official newspaper of the National Association Opposed to Woman Suffrage. Harry Burn won reelection, but A.H. Roberts went down to defeat, and Republican presidential candidate Warren G. Harding carried Tennessee. Female anti-suffragists—women who had not wanted the vote in the first place—now claimed that they had used the franchise to drive their enemies from office.[62] Democratic politicians blamed women for the defeat as well—Black women, who, they said, had turned out in large numbers and voted Republican. The day after the election, Edward H. Crump of Memphis wrote: "I was never so certain in all my life as I was that with woman suffrage and no poll tax provision it would be harmful to the Democratic party in Tennessee."[63]

The outcome of the election troubled suffragists, and they, too, cast about for scapegoats. Catherine Kenny attributed Roberts's loss to labor, farmers, and the Democrats themselves. The state party made only feeble attempts to turn out White women's votes, she reported, while Republicans actively recruited Black female voters. She conceded, too, that the governor was an unattractive candidate. "He was pathetic," she told Carrie Chapman Catt, and unable to overcome the scandals that had tainted his reputation.[64]

Woman suffrage undoubtedly played a crucial role in Roberts' loss. The large turnout of both men and women in Republican east Tennessee meant a strong anti-Democratic vote.[65] The governor's half-hearted support of suffrage, along with the rumors surrounding him and his secretary, alienated potential women voters. Most important, when he called the special session and endorsed ratification of the Nineteenth Amendment, he turned many

Catherine Talty Kenny
LIBRARY OF CONGRESS

of his own allies against him. Roberts was an unpopular incumbent facing a beloved Republican opponent. When powerful friends like E.B. Stahlman deserted him because of his stand on woman suffrage, Roberts' candidacy was doomed.

Suffragists had staked their honor on a Roberts victory, and his loss hurt them. In January 1921, Catherine Kenny forecast a cold political season for women voters. "I believe the effect of our successful fight here in Tennessee will be to nullify any real power or influence of the women in either party," she told Carrie Chapman Catt. The newly elected legislators—"about 70% [sic] new men, inexperienced, and not even up to the usual poor standard"—seemed uniformly hostile to any measures of interest to women. Antis continued their efforts to dilute women's political strength. They introduced a bill to abolish primaries. Since women had little influence within party organizations, if the proposal succeeded it would, in the words of Abby Crawford Milton, "about disfranchise the women of Tennessee." Although the General Assembly voted to retain the primary, women's political prospects remained bleak. "Just now in Sunny Tennessee, we are certainly 'dead ones,'" Kenny concluded.[66]

Woman suffrage had, for the moment, failed to live up to its promise. But Kenny, Milton, and other suffragists never abandoned their faith in their cause and, in spite of their disappointments, they continued to believe that the prize was worth the price. "I shall never be as thrilled by the turn of any event as I was at that moment when the roll call that settled the citizenship of American women was heard," Abby Crawford Milton declared. "It seemed too dramatic to happen in real life, with the real thrill of history making, not the excitement of the stage or movies. Personally, I had rather have had a share in the battle for woman suffrage than any other world event."[67] It was, indeed, an historic occasion. The women and men who secured the ratification of the Nineteenth Amendment acknowledged the truth of the message suffragists had been spreading since 1848: that women and men *were* equal, with the same rights, privileges, and responsibilities. In that hot Nashville August, suffragists faced their Armageddon and emerged victorious; "powers that pray" vanquished "powers that prey." They demonstrated once and for all that, when it came to politics, women were capable of far more than prayer, and they moved the nation one step closer to realizing its ideal of equality.

Notes

This essay is drawn from, "'Powers That Pray and Powers That Prey': Tennessee and the Fight for Woman Suffrage," *Tennessee Historical Quarterly* 50(4), 1991, and is reprinted with permission of the journal.

1. "Why?," newspaper clipping, *Nashville Tennessean*, Aug. 22, 1920, Harry T. Burn Scrapbook, Manuscripts Department, Special Collections, University of Tennessee Library, Knoxville; [For further information on the ratification struggle in Tennessee, including reprints of many of the pro- and anti-suffrage documents mentioned in this article, see Marjorie Spruill (Wheeler), ed. *Votes for Women! The Woman Suffrage Movement in Tennessee, the South, and the Nation,* (Knoxville, 1995)].

2. Quoted in Wilma Dykeman, *Tennessee Women, Past and Present,* Narrative by Wilma Dykeman with selected additional material edited by Carol Lynn Yellin (Memphis, Nashville, 1977), 25.

3. Carrie Chapman Catt and Nettie Rogers Shuler, *Woman Suffrage and Politics: The Inner Story of the Suffrage Movement* (New York, 1923), 424-28; Sue Shelton White to Gov. Albert H. Roberts, June 19, 1920, box 26, folder 4, Albert H. Roberts Papers, Tennessee State Library and Archives, Nashville (hereafter cited as TSLA); "Special Session in Tennessee!" *The Suffragist* 8 (July 1920): 121-22; Catherine Talty Kenny to Rose Young, June 21, 1920, box 1, folder 13; Charles Evans Hughes to Mary Garrett Hay, June 25, 1920, box 1, folder 10; Catherine Kenny to Carrie Chapman Catt, July 11, 1920, box 1, folder 14, all in Carrie Chapman Catt Papers, TSLA; "What's The Matter With Tennessee?" *Woman Citizen* 5 (July 3, 1920): 125.

4. Catherine T. Kenny to Ida Husted Harper, Dec. 16, 1919, box 1, folder 13; Catherine T. Kenny to Carrie Chapman Catt, Jan. 5, 1920, box 1, folder 13; Catherine T. Kenny to Mrs. Shuler, June 28, 1920, box 1, folder 14; Catt Papers; Albert H. Roberts, March 11, 1920, box 36, folder 1, Roberts Papers.

5. Catherine T. Kenny to Mrs. Shuler, June 28, 1920; Sue Shelton White, "The Tennessee Campaign at Close Range," *The Suffragist* 8 (Aug. 1920): 164; Gary W. Reichard, "The Defeat of Governor Roberts," *Tennessee Historical Quarterly* 30 (1971): 94-110.

6. Reichard, "Defeat of Governor Roberts"; "How Leading Democratic Newspapers Size Up Gov. Roberts and His Administration," (Nashville, [1920]), pamphlet, TSLA. See also Kenneth S. Braden, "The Wizard of Overton: Governor A.H. Roberts," *Tennessee Historical Quarterly* 43 (1984): 273-94.

7. Edwin Mims, *The Advancing South: Stories of Progress and Reaction* (1926; reprint, Port Washington, N.Y., 1969), 238; Joe Hatcher, "1920: Amendment and a Perfect 36," *Nashville Tennessean,* March 26, 1972, Vertical File—Woman Suffrage, TSLA.

8. Taylor, *Woman Suffrage Movement in Tennessee,* 108, n. 140.

9. Albert H. Roberts to Carrie Chapman Catt, July 10, 1920, box 1, folder 18, Catt Papers.

10. Catherine T. Kenny to Carrie Chapman Catt, July 11, 1920; Carrie Chapman Catt to Mrs. Guilford Dudley, July 12, 1920, box 1, folder 6, Catt Papers.

11. Catt and Shuler, *Woman Suffrage and Politics,* 432-33; Taylor, *Woman Suffrage Movement in Tennessee,* 109.

12. "Mrs. Carrie C. Catt Arrives in City," clipping, n.p., n.d., Vertical File—Woman Suffrage, TSLA.

13. Carrie Chapman Catt to Mrs. John M. [Catherine Talty] Kenny, June 29, 1920, box 1, folder 6, Catt Papers; Catt and Shuler, *Woman Suffrage and Politics,* 435-37; "Tennessee—The 36th," *The Suffragist* 9 (Sept. 1920): 199.

14. Josephine Anderson Pearson, "My Story!" 1, 19, box 1, folder 17, Josephine Anderson Pearson Papers, TSLA.

15. "Antis Gather New Strength," clipping, *Chattanooga Daily Times,* Aug. 9, 1920, box 2, folder 6, Catt Papers.

16. Marjorie Shuler, "Outside Influences Fight Suffrage in Tennessee," clipping, *Public Ledger,* Philadelphia, Pa., Aug. 8, 1920, box 2, folder 4; "Anti-suffrage Faction Busy," clipping, *Chattanooga Daily Times,* July 30, 1920, box 2, folder 5, both in Catt Papers.

17. Ida Husted Harper, ed., *History of Woman Suffrage,* (New York, 1922), vol. 6: 620; NAWSA, *VICTORY: How Women Won It: A Centennial Symposium, 1840-1940* (New York, 1940), 149.

18. HWS 6: 621 n.; G.F. Milton, "Editorial Correspondence," clipping, *Chattanooga News,* Aug. 19, 1920, Burn Scrapbook; "Winning the Vote in Tennessee," clipping, *Christian Science Monitor,* Sept. 4, 1920, Burn Scrapbook; Abby Crawford Milton to Carrie Chapman Catt, Jan. 13, 1921.

19. Catt and Shuler, *Woman Suffrage and Politics,* 135-38.

20. Walter Clark to Henry Watterson, April 12, 1919, in Aubrey Lee Brooks and Hugh Talmage Lefler, eds., *The Papers of Walter Clark* (Chapel Hill, 1950) 2: 396. See also David Morgan, *Suffragists and Democrats: The Politics of Woman Suffrage in America* (East Lansing, Mich., 1972), 157-77, and Jane Jerome Camhi, "Women Against Women: American Antisuffragism, 1880-1920," (Ph.D. diss., Tufts University, 1974), 183-94.

21. See Joe Michael Shahan, "Reform and Politics in Tennessee, 1906-1914," (Ph.D. diss., Vanderbilt University, 1981); Paul E. Isaac, *Prohibition and Politics: Turbulent Decades in Tennessee 1885-1920* (Knoxville, 1965); and Maury Klein, *History of the Louisville and Nashville Railroad* (New York, 1972), 368-94.

22. Paul E. Isaac, historian of the prohibition movement in Tennessee, identified Vertrees as "an attorney for liquor concerns"; see Isaac, *Prohibition and Politics,* 46.

23. John Trotwood Moore, *Tennessee: The Volunteer State 1769-1923* (Chicago, Nashville, 1923), 4: 650-51.

24. "Speaker Walker Lauded From Many States," *Woman Patriot* 4 (Aug. 28, 1920): 1.

25. Will T. Hale and Dixon C. Merritt, *A History of Tennessee and Tennesseans: The Leaders and Representative Men in Commerce, Industry and Modern Activities* (Chicago, New York, 1913) 2: 1401-02; Dumas Malone, ed., *Dictionary of American Biography* (New York, 1936) 9: 493-94; *National Cyclopedia of American Biography* (New York, 1898) 8: 224; Klein, *History of the Louisville and Nashville Railroad,* 376-78.

26. "The Power Behind the Throne," clipping, *Nashville Tennessean,* July 11, 1914, box 1, folder 3, Edwin A. Price Scrapbook, TSLA.

27. Clipping, *Nashville Banner,* July 11, 1914, box 1, folder 3, Price Scrapbook; Catt and Shuler, *Woman Suffrage and Politics,* 443.

28. Marjorie Shuler, "From the Tennessee Firing Line," *Woman Citizen* 5 (Aug. 28, 1920): 331; "Tennessee—The 36th," 200.

29. Quotation, "The Crisis," *Woman Citizen* 5 (Aug. 14, 1920): 277; Catt and Shuler, *Woman Suffrage and Politics,* 441, 446.

30. "Supreme Law of Tennessee Prohibits Ratification," broadside, box 1, folder 4; "Foster V. Brown, Champion of Suffrage, Declares That Ratification is Violation," broadside, box 1, folder 4; "The Federal Suffrage Amendment WILL NEVER BE RATIFIED If The People of Tennessee Guard Their Rights," broadside, box 1, folder 4; "Can The Present Legislature Act?" pamphlet, box 1, folder 5; Josephine A. Pearson to "Dear Sir or Madam," box 1, folder 7, all in Pearson Papers; "Vertrees Says There is No Excuse for Ratification," *Woman Patriot* 4 (Aug. 7, 1920): 1-2; Shuler, "Outside Influences Fight Suffrage in Tennessee"; "History of the Bitter Struggle to Ratify Suffrage," clipping, *Nashville Tennessean,* Aug. 29, 1920, Burn Scrapbook; Catherine T. Kenny to Carrie Chapman Catt, July 11, 1920; Catt and Shuler, *Woman Suffrage and Politics,* 434-36, 440; NAWSA, *VICTORY: How Women Won It,* 149.

31. "America When Feminized," broadside, box 1, folder 4, Pearson Papers. For other examples see broadsides in box 1, folder 4, and pamphlets in box 1, folder 3, Pearson Papers.

32. The photograph of Mrs. Dudley and her children is reprinted in John Egerton, *Nashville: The Faces of Two Centuries,* (Nashville, 1979), 184.

33. Carrie Chapman Catt to Mrs. John M. [Catherine T.] Kenny, June 29, 1920, box 1, folder 6, Catt Papers.

34. Josephine Pearson to "Dear [blank]," form letter, Aug. 9, 1920, box 1, folder 18, Pearson Papers.

35. "Beware!" broadside, box 1, folder 4. See also "That Deadly Parallel," "Can Anybody Terrorize Tennessee Manhood," and other leaflets and broadsides, folders 3, 4, and 5; "Three Federal Suffrage Force Bills in Congress," press release, May 15, 1920, *Woman Patriot,* all in Pearson Papers.

36. "Woman Suffrage, A Menace to the South. A Protest Against Its Imposition Through Federal Authority," pamphlet, box 1, folder 3, Pearson Papers.

37. Quotation from "Statement of Mrs. R.C. Pleasant, Leader of Anti-Federal Suffrage Ratification Forces of Louisiana," Burn Scrapbook.

38. Catherine T. Kenny to Carrie Chapman Catt, Jan. 5, 1920; Kenny to Catt, July 11, 1920; *HWS* 6: 606.

39. Catt and Shuler, *Woman Suffrage and Politics,* 442.

40. *House and Senate Journals of the Extraordinary Session of the Sixty-First General Assembly of the State of Tennessee,* (Nashville, 1920), 254, 263, 292-96; quotation, 293.

41. *HWS* 6: 621 n.; Catt and Shuler, *Woman Suffrage and Politics,* 445-46.

42. "Tennessee Likely To Vote Suffrage in Next Few Days," clipping, Aug. 12, 1920, n.p., box 2, folder 7, Catt Papers.

43. "The People Against the Politicians," *The Lookout: A Journal of Southern Society* 25 (Aug. 24, 1920): 1, box 1, folder 8, Pearson Papers. Carol Lynn Yellin identified the suffragist and the solon as Anne Dallas Dudley and Senator Lon McFarland; see Carol Lynn Yellin, "Countdown in Tennessee, 1920" *American Heritage* 30 (1978): 29-30.

44. *House Journal,* 33, 86-88; quotation, 87.

45. Quotations, Marjorie Shuler, "From the Tennessee Firing Line," 331. See also "Winning the Vote In Tennessee"; *House Journal,* 89; *HWS* 6: 623; Catt and Shuler, *Woman Suffrage and Politics,* 447.

46. Catt and Shuler, *Woman Suffrage and Politics,* 447.

47. *House Journal,* 91; Catt and Shuler, *Woman Suffrage and Politics,* 448-49.

48. Shuler, "From the Tennessee Firing Line," 331; Catt and Shuler, *Woman Suffrage and Politics,* 449; *HWS* 6: 623; "Suffrage Amendment Adopted By House," clipping, *Nashville Tennessean,* Aug. 19, 1920; G.F. Milton, "Burn Vote Was Influenced By His Mother's Views," clipping, *Chattanooga News,* Aug. 19, 1920; "Burn Changed Vote On Advice of His Mother," clipping, *Nashville Tennessean,* Aug. 20, 1920; Zoe Beckley, "Mother Proud of Boy Who Cinched Suffrage Victory," clipping, *Memphis Press,* Aug. 31, 1920; all in Burn Scrapbook.

49. Quotations from "Shouts of Joy and Groans of Dismay Greet News of Action of Legislature on Suffrage," clipping, *Knoxville Journal and Tribune,* Aug. 19, 1920, Burn Scrapbook, and telegram, Carrie Chapman Catt to Gertrude Weil, box 3, folder 4, Catt Papers; *House Journal,* 92-94; Catt and Shuler, *Woman Suffrage and Politics,* 449; "History of Bitter Struggle to Ratify Suffrage."

50. Quotations, Shuler, "On The Tennessee Firing Line," 332, 334. See also "Suffragists Inspired With House Victory," clipping, *Chattanooga News,* Aug. 20, 1920, Burn Scrapbook; Pearson, "My Story!" n.p.; *HWS* 6: 624; Catt and Shuler, *Woman Suffrage and Politics,* 450-54.

51. "MASS MEETING *TONIGHT* TO SAVE THE SOUTH," broadside, box 1, folder 2, Catt Papers; "Indignation Spreads Over Whole State," *Chattanooga Daily Times,* Aug. 26, 1920; "Little Interest Manifested in Mass Meetings," clipping, *Nashville Tennessean,* Aug. 29, 1920, box 1, folder 2, Price Scrapbook.

52. Martin Lee Calhoun, "God of Our Fathers Spare Us Yet!" *Woman Patriot* 4 (Sept. 11, 1920): 3.

53. Pearson, "My Story!" 13; "Burn Strongly Denies Charges" and "Nashville Papers Publish Affidavits Alleging Burn Was Approached on Subject," clippings, *Knoxville Sentinel,* Aug. 19, 1920, Burn Scrapbook; "The Truth About The Tennessee Campaign," *Woman Patriot* 4 (Sept. 11, 1920):6.

54. *House Journal,* 94-95; telegram, Carrie Chapman Catt to Frank J. Shuler, Aug. 20, 1920, box 3, folder 4, Catt Papers; "Reconsideration of Ratification Comes Up Today," clipping, *Nashville Tennessean,* Aug. 20, 1920, Burn Scrapbook; *HWS* 6, 621.

55. Catt and Shuler, *Woman Suffrage and Politics,* 450, 453-54; *House Journal,* 117-21; *HWS* 6: 624.

56. *HWS* 6: 624-25; Catt and Shuler, *Woman Suffrage and Politics,* 454-55.

57. *House Journal,* 130-35; quotation, 136-37.

58. Telegram, Anne Dallas Dudley to Carrie Chapman Catt, Aug. 31, 1920; telegram, Anne Dallas Dudley to Carrie Chapman Catt, Sept. 1, 1920, box 3, folder 5, Catt Papers.

59. Catt and Shuler, *Woman Suffrage and Politics,* 459-60.

60. "Anti-Suffrage Party Declares Bitter War," clipping, n.p., July 21 [1920], box 2, folder 4, Catt Papers; A.H. Roberts to Carrie Chapman Catt, Sept. 13, 1920, box 1, folder 18, Catt Papers; "Tennessee Antis Wage Campaign Against Roberts," *Woman Patriot* 4 (Oct. 16, 1920): 1-2; "The Truth About The Tennessee Campaign," 6; Braden, "The Wizard of Overton," 287-91; Reichard, "Defeat of Governor Roberts," 106-08.

61. Ellis Meredith to Carrie Chapman Catt, Oct. 5, 1920, box 1, folder 15, Catt Papers. See also Catherine T. Kenny to Carrie Chapman Catt, Sept. 10, 1920; Abby Crawford Milton to Carrie Chapman Catt, Sept. 1, 1920, box 1, folder 16, Catt Papers.

62. "Election Returns Prove Strength of Anti-Suffragists," *Woman Patriot* 4 (Nov. 6, 1920): 1; "Governors Who Forced Ratification Defeated," *Woman Patriot* 4 (Nov. 13, 1920): 6.

63. Edward H. Crump to Hill McAlister, Nov. 5, 1920, box 9, folder 5, Hill McAlister Papers, TSLA.

64. Catherine Talty Kenny to Carrie Chapman Catt, Nov. 16, 1920, box 1, folder 14, Catt Papers; "Where the Suffrage Issue Counted," *Woman Citizen* 5 (Nov. 20, 1920): 682.

65. Reichard, "Defeat of Governor Roberts," 108-09.

66. Catherine T. Kenny to Carrie Chapman Catt, Jan. 21, 1921, box 1, folder 14; Abby Crawford Milton to Carrie Chapman Catt, Feb. 5, 1921, box 1, folder 17, both in Catt Papers.

67. Abby Crawford Milton to Carrie Chapman Catt, Feb. 5, 1921, box 1, folder 17, Catt Papers.

Twenty-Two

ACROSS THE GREAT DIVIDE:
Women in Politics Before and After 1920

Nancy F. Cott

Editor's Introduction: In this thought-provoking essay, eminent historian Nancy F. Cott challenges widespread assumptions concerning women and politics "across the Great Divide." The passage of the Nineteenth Amendment in 1920 was unquestionably one of the great turning points in American history. However, as Cott argues, "too great a focus on the achievement of the Nineteenth Amendment obscures the similarities in women's political behavior before and after it and the relation of that behavior to broader political and social context."

In the immediate aftermath of the suffrage victory, political analysts and historians posited theories concerning the impact of the Nineteenth Amendment on American politics and women's political behavior that remained unchallenged for many decades. The often-told story went something like this: despite suffragists' claims that women would transform politics, many failed to vote, and those who voted did not vote as a "bloc." As a result, politicians quickly lost their new-found respect for women voters, and women were relegated to a minor role in party politics. Furthermore, the massive and cohesive women's movement, having lost—by winning—the issue that held it together, disintegrated, with many former suffragists becoming politically apathetic and the few that remained active locked in bitter combat with one another over the Equal Rights Amendment introduced in 1923. Such theories implied that woman suffrage was a failure, or, at best, a great victory that led (ironically) to a decline in women's political activism.

As Cott acknowledges, these widespread perceptions are correct in part. No significant "gender gap" emerged in the immediate aftermath of the Nineteenth Amendment. The massive National American Woman Suffrage Association (NAWSA) converted itself into the League of Women Voters (LWV), but the LWV retained only a small percentage of the giant suffrage organization's membership. The National Woman's Party (NWP), which continued under the same name, introduced the Equal Rights Amendment (ERA), hoping to wipe out all remaining legal discrimination against women. But this proposal alarmed the LWV and many women reformers who insisted that who insisted that working women desperately needed the laws that "discriminated" in their *favor*—the "protective legislation" for women that had been a primary accomplishment of the Progressive Era and that was under attack in the conservative climate of the 1920s.

However, as Cott explains (and readers of *One Woman, One Vote* are by now well aware), the woman suffrage movement was never a "unity"; there was diversity and factiousness in the women's movement *before* and *after* 1920. From the debate in the 1860s over whether or not to support the Fifteenth Amendment, to the dispute over the picketing of the White House as the movement neared an end, suffragists disagreed fervently over tactics—even as they agreed upon a goal. Furthermore, the suffrage coalition included women of diverse racial, ethnic, religious, regional, and class backgrounds, as well as party identifications, who could not reasonably be expected to fall into a solid "bloc" after enfranchisement. Indeed, as Cott suggests, those who lamented—or merely pointed out—the fact that enfranchised womanhood failed to "bloc vote" were quite unrealistic. Given the natural divisions among women (as among men), Cott considers the idea of a "woman's bloc" as an imaginary construct, "an interpretive fiction rather than a realistic expectation." Furthermore, re-examining the pronouncements of the suffragists on this subject, Cott makes it clear that "even when maintaining that women would exercise civic duties differently from men, suffragists rarely if ever portrayed a future voting 'bloc' of women." They spoke of issues about which they expected women voters to be concerned, such as children's health, political corruption, and the liquor traffic, but they "rarely specified by what means, exactly, the injection of women's votes into the polity was to bring about change."

Cott also objects strongly to the suggestion that 1920 ushered in a great decline in women's political and social activism. On the issue of voter turnout, she points out that women's political participation can only be understood when studied in the context of overall voter turnout—which *declined* in the 1920s. She also explains that both before and after 1920, women were involved in a range of political activities besides voting or even party politics. Cott is particularly disdainful, however, of the idea that women's participation in voluntary organizations declined sharply after 1920, and suggests that to measure women's political activity, as many have done, by comparing the size of the NAWSA and the dissimilar League of Women Voters is absurd. For a more accurate picture, Cott insists, one must examine (as she does in this essay) the broad range of women's voluntary associations from the Parents and Teachers Associations (PTA) to the Daughters of the American Revolution (DAR) to the American Birth Control League. Indeed, writes Cott, the years between the two world wars were marked by an extremely high level of political activity on the part of women, though they often were engaged in organizations with conflicting—or directly competing—agendas. The disagreement among feminists over the ERA in the 1920s was only one of many areas in which female activists of all persuasions exercised their right to pursue their diverse political goals. Indeed, it might be argued that, with its success, the Nineteenth Amendment freed women to disagree among themselves, as well as to work for a wide variety of causes other than suffrage, whether individually, in women's groups, or in mixed-gender organizations.

Cott's reminder about the diversity among politically active women before and after 1920 not only sets the record straight, but, combined with her point about the impossibility of a woman's bloc, it clearly demonstrates (in her words) "the unique power of disenfranchisement to bring diverse women into coalition." Millions of American women who became suffragists agreed on one point if nothing else: they were weary of a social and political system based on the idea of separate spheres and wanted full recognition of their individuality, equality, and right to participate fully and directly in making the laws under which they lived.

★   ★   ★   ★   ★

THE NINETEENTH AMENDMENT is the most obvious benchmark in the history of women in politics in the United States. To neglect the political watershed of 1920 when assessing the history of women's politics would be obtuse, since the sex barrier to the ballot was eliminated then and also the decades-long campaign for the vote, which had mobilized millions of women, ended. Yet too great a focus on the achievement of the Nineteenth Amendment obscures the similarities in women's political behavior before and after it and the relation of that behavior to broader political and social context.

There were striking continuities in women's political choices and actions on both sides of 1920. After women gained the ballot, they continued to engage in a range of politics broader than simply electoral activity. While it may be impossible to compare the influence women as a group had in politics before and after the Nineteenth Amendment, it is possible to consider more carefully suffragists' promises and their results. Women's voting must be put in the context of men's voting—that is, in the context of popular political participation in the period. Perhaps most important, the organizational and political roles of women's voluntary associations—which, far from declining, multiplied in membership—must be considered within rather than outside of politics.

The Suffrage Coalition — A Woman's Bloc?

Although historians have long presented the campaign for suffrage as a unity, in contrast to the disunity among women's groups of the 1920s, there is reason to see disunity among politically active women as typical of both the 1910s and 1920s. For instance, suffragists were opposed by female anti-suffragists; White suffragists raised racial bars to Blacks. In other matters great and small, from the conflicts between clubwomen and entertainers over the status and standards of dance halls to standoffs between pacifists and preparedness advocates during World War I, there were strategic, ideological, class-based and race-based differences among groups of women that were acted out in the public arena before as well as after 1920. From 1869 on, within the suffrage movement itself there were successive deep divisions over strategy and method. Intense internal conflicts over leadership, finances, and tactics so racked the National American Woman Suffrage Association (NAWSA) in 1911 that longtime suffragist, the Reverend Olympia Brown, called her colleagues' "shallow false talk of love excellence harmony &c &c ...so false that it makes me vomit."[1] The bitter split between the National American Woman Suffrage Association and the Congressional Union (CU) leaderships beginning in 1913 was the latest but not the only such cleavage.

The way that suffragists built coalitions during the 1910s acknowledged that women had variant and perhaps clashing loyalties. Suffrage leaders purposely addressed defined groups (mothers, wage-earners, Black women, White women, professionals) with specifically designed instrumental appeals, tacitly acknowledging that not all women shared the same definition of self-interest. Even nonvoting women took on partisan affiliations, which mattered: In the final years of the suffrage campaign Maud Wood Park, head of Congressional lobbying for the NAWSA, was so aware of Republican and Democratic partisan loyalties clashing within her own Congressional Committee that she preferred to meet with its members individually. The women were so "inclined to be suspicious" of one another that full meetings of the committee were unproductive. Though distressed by the division, Park took it for granted that "party women could not be expected to free themselves from the prevailing currents of thought."[2]

Even when maintaining that women would exercise civic duties differently from men, suffragists rarely if ever portrayed a future voting "bloc" of women. It is striking that the one time that a small minority of suffragists *did* attempt to marshal women's votes into a voting bloc, they were condemned by the majority of their colleagues. That was in 1914 and 1916, when the Congressional Union (predecessor of the National Woman's Party) campaigned among enfranchised women of the Western states to defeat all Democrats. They intended to "punish the party in power" in Washington for failure to adopt a constitutional amendment for woman suffrage. Their effort to make women's power at the polls count on a single issue inspired horrified rejection from mainstream suffragist leaders and little agreement from women voters. Alice Paul, architect of the CU plan, had a definite conception of a single-issue feminist bloc—not a generalized "woman bloc"—operating in a two-party system to swing the balance: "To count in an election you do not have to be the biggest Party; you have to be simply an independent Party that will stand for one object and that cannot be diverted from that object."[3]

Very likely the CU strategy failed to evoke support from the bulk of suffragists not only because of its approach but because of its object—to unseat all Democrats, whether they as individuals supported woman suffrage or not. There was the thorn on the rose of any such proposal: a woman's bloc, to cohere and have an impact, had to make a single issue its clear priority, while candidates' positions on so-called women's issues would not stand alone but would combine with their positions on other questions that concerned women. The NAWSA's judgment that the CU was misguided gave more evidence that women had differing priorities

Women casting their ballots in New York City
LIBRARY OF CONGRESS

and tactics; perceiving that division, suffragists were unlikely to imagine women voting as one. When the National Woman's Party moved on to militant demonstrations, which the NAWSA also deplored, Maud Wood Park found nothing more exasperating than having to answer Congressmen's questions: "'Why don't you women get together? You can't expect us to vote for you if you can't agree among yourselves.'" She pointed out as "mildly" as possible "that men, even within the same party, were not without their differences. But sauce for the gander was rarely accepted as sauce for the goose." Lest we assume that suffragists were too naive to recognize the coalition nature of their association, they remind us, as Harriot Stanton Blatch reminded a colleague in 1918, "altho [sic] all sorts and conditions of women were united for suffrage…they are not at one in their attitude towards other questions in life."[4]

Suffragists spoke of issues—safeguarding children's health, eliminating political corruption, ending the liquor traffic, improving the economic leverage of women wage-earners—but rarely addressed exactly how or for whom women's votes would be collected, whether electing women to office was a high priority, or whether women's votes were adjuncts or substitutes for the established practice of lobbying and educational work by women's voluntary associations. As much as suffragists talked about women's inclinations, duties, and contributions, they rarely specified by what means, exactly, the injection of women's votes into the polity was to bring about change. Suffragists usually made very general or else modest claims, and (interestingly) rarely touched on the subject of women in political office. True, there were some overarching retorts such as Anna Howard Shaw's to an anti-suffragist who objected that voting women would have little time for charity, "Thank God, there will not be so much need of charity and philanthropy!" There was rhetoric—equally vague— regarding women's inclination against war, such as the Congressional Union's claim that "A government responsible to all women, as well as all men, will be less likely to go to war, without real necessity." There were particular anticipations of women's efficacy, such as Florence Kelley's that "the enfranchisement of women is indispensable to the solution of the child labor problem." Typically, however, suffragists' proposals and predictions in the 1910s were locally relevant: it was claimed at the New York Woman Suffrage Party's 1910 convention, for instance, that women's votes would help to alleviate the evils of inadequate inspection of milk, high prices, overcrowded classrooms, crime, prostitution, and child labor; the ballot would enable women to preside as associate justices in children's court and women's night court. During the 1915 New York campaign, Carrie Chapman Catt even warned suffragist speakers against promising "what women will do with the vote."[5]

The idea that women's votes would line up in one direction certainly existed in an implicit imprecise form, in the views of both suffragists and their opponents. As prospective voters, women were often expected to punish candidates who did not show deference to women's organizations' aims and to embrace those who supported Prohibition and social legislation. There was some evidence in the 1910s (mainly from Scandinavia) that women were "conservative" voters and some claims (from New York City) that women swelled the "radical" vote. When Washington, Oregon, and Arizona each adopted Prohibition shortly after adopting woman suffrage, women's votes were presumed to have turned the tide. Since the Western states that enfranchised women early did not have extensive industries employing women and children, they gave little evidence whether women's ballots would decisively protect such vulnerable wage-earners. Shortly after New York women got the right to vote, however, four state legislators who had opposed minimum-wage legislation for women, child-labor laws, and other social legislation were unseated. Two of the four were replaced with assembly*women*. In Columbus, Ohio, in 1919, after women received municipal suffrage, their organizing and voter-registration work through voluntary associations succeeded in dumping the city boss who had been mayor for sixteen years, despite his organization's labeling them a "shrieking sisterhood." However, most big-city machine politicians had dropped objections to woman suffrage by the late 1910s after observing and reasoning that enfranchised women had *not* shown a habit of voting together to oppose existing political organizations. Claims about the impact of women's votes were so speculative and contradictory by 1919, in fact, that social scientists William Ogburn and Inez Goltra, after studying "how women vote," could conclude only that there might be some significant sex differences *or* that "the enfranchisement of women will have no other effect than approximately to double the number of votes previously cast." With more evidence, a 1923 study drew the similarly ambivalent conclusion that women neither "merely vote the same as men" nor vote "with marked independence."[6]

Voter Turnout

The unspoken notion that adding women to the electorate should transform politics did prompt some suffragists to be disappointed at the lack of outcome in the 1920s, but they were not the only ones looking dourly at the scene. Both popular journalists and political scientists expressed a mood of skepticism, if not downright cynicism, about mass political participation. Social scientists stressed the irrational motivations driving individual political behavior, the inability of the mass public to make objective judgments in popular government, and the likelihood that politicians would manipulate these failings.[7] Observers' discouragement about democratic participation found corroboration in the deepening decline in voter participation, a trend continuous from 1896 and intensifying from the 1910s to the 1920s. Mean national turnout in the presidential election years 1920, 1924, and 1928 was just over half of the eligible electorate, as compared to an average of almost eighty percent in the late nineteenth century. In the off-year elections between 1922 and 1930, little more than a third of the electorate voted, whereas nearly two-thirds, on the average, had voted in the off-years between 1876 and 1896.[8]

The meaning of the decline in voter turnout is not absolutely clear, in great part because of the debatable meaning of early twentieth-century Progressive reform— that is, whether its intents and/or effects were democratic or elitist. In light of such reforms as direct election of senators, direct primaries, the initiative, referendum and recall, it seems ironic, even tragic, that the Progressive Era should have ushered in the decade of the lowest voter participation ever. But if Progressive reforms intended to keep the reins of the state in the hands of the expert or the economically powerful few—as some reforms more than others indicate—then the decline in voter turnout fulfilled rather than undid that aim. Voting "reforms" included the continuing disfranchisement of Blacks and Populist or Republican Whites in the South by means of poll taxes, literacy tests, and other bars to registration and balloting; more complicated and rigorous residency and registration requirements in Northern states which limited immigrant voting; and, at the municipal level, replacement of district voting with at-large elections, which predestined minority interest-group candidates to fail.

While Progressive reformers embraced the salutary aim to eliminate corrupt influence-peddling and substitute neutral and informed standards, their emphasis on expert presence and management in the state also diverted control away from the populace, to an elite of professional and business-managerial experts. The results could be seen institutionalized in the 1920s in various forms, from city-manager rule in municipalities, to federal and state commissions, to such quasi-governmental institutions as the National Bureau of Economic Research. "It is a misfortune for the woman's movement," mordantly commented Suzanne La Follette, a feminist and pacifist of anti-statist leanings, in 1926, "that it has succeeded in securing political rights for women at the very period when political rights are worth less than they have been at any time since the eighteenth century." The most persuasive explanations of downsliding voter turnout from 1896 to the 1920s also have to do with the entrenchment of the Democratic Party's hold on the South and the Republican Party's domination of the North and West (and thus of the national government) to the extent that the interest of voters in partisan contest, and voter sense of efficacy, collapsed. The portrait of increasingly dispirited voters does not account for the vigor of third parties during the period, but it does account for the overall trend.[9]

Analyses in the 1920s pinned much of the blame for the contemporary drop in voter turnout on newly eligible women. Just before the presidential election in 1924, journalists and political scientists turned the spotlight on the "failure" of women to flock to the polls, although dependable data on voting behavior were very scarce.[10] Votes were not counted by sex except in the state of Illinois. In the 1920 national elections, slightly less than half of the eligible women in Illinois cast a ballot, while three-quarters of the eligible men did. Early discussions based on that evidence generalized only downward, on the reasoning that Illinois women were more likely than most to vote since they had had the ballot since 1913.

Women's voting participation actually varied greatly from place to place, group to group, and issue to issue. Fewer women than men voted, but the difference in their voting behavior was not as stark as initial extrapolations from the Illinois data established. Analysis via regression techniques have now made it clear that the 1920s low in turnout was not due to women's behavior alone, but also to male voters' sinking interest. Hull House leader Jane Addams was on the mark when to a magazine's 1924 question, "Is Woman Suffrage Failing?" she responded that the question ought to be "is suffrage failing?"[11]

Voting Women and Their Organizations

As Addams noted, the context in which to look at women's voting behavior in the 1920s is that of declining voter participation overall. A few vigorous female voices, such as that of former National Woman's Party leader Anne Martin of Nevada, urged women to enter the electoral arena in force and move directly to claim "woman's share, woman's *half* in man-controlled government."[12] The much more general trend—and one deplored by Martin as merely "indirect influence"—was women's reliance on voluntary associations rather than the electoral arena for

League of Women Voters members encouraging voter registration, August 1920.

political efficacy. Since the early nineteenth century, women had influenced what took place in electoral and legislative halls from outside, not only by seeking suffrage but by inquiring about a range of health, safety, moral, and welfare issues. They had built a tradition of exercising political influence (one admittedly hard to measure), which continued vigorously once the vote was gained. Women's organizations' lobbying route should be seen as pioneering in the modern mode of exerting political force—that is, interest-group politics. This voluntarist mode, with its use of lobbying to effect political influence, and the kinds of interests pursued (i.e., health, safety, moral, and welfare issues), prevailed in women's political participation both before and after 1920.[13]

From recent histories one might gain the impression that women's voluntary organizations waned after 1920, but nothing is further from the truth. In her 1933 history of women, author and former NWP suffragist Inez Haynes Irwin observed that women were, if anything, *over*organized in voluntary associations during the 1920s and 1930s. She closed her book with a staggering list, from professional to civic to patriotic to social welfare to charitable to ethnic and religious women's organizations.[14] Although historians often cite as evidence of decimation in activism the contrast between the two million women in the NAWSA in the 1910s and the tiny fraction of that membership—probably five percent—who joined in the NAWSA's successor group, the National League of Women Voters (LWV), the two figures are not really comparable. The two organizations differed widely in form and intent: the first was a federation that pursued one specific goal, made few demands on its local members, imposed no homogeneity upon affiliates, and used all volunteer labor; the subsequent organization stated many aims (including civic reform, citizenship education, international peace, and women's rights), made strenuous demands on its local members, attempted standardized national procedure, and employed professional staff.

Quickly evolving into a "good government" rather than a feminist organization, its premise being to ready women for political life, the LWV found itself, ironically, competing with women's partisan activity as much as preparing women for it. When all women became fair game for party organizations, Republican and Democratic women's divisions vied with the nonpartisan League for the time and loyalty of women interested in politics. Some leading NAWSA suffragists went directly into party organizations instead of into the League. Lillian Feickert, for example, a prominent New Jersey suffragist who was named vice-chairman of the Republican state committee in 1920, built the New Jersey Women's Republican Club on the grassroots model of the New Jersey Woman Suffrage Association. Feickert claimed that three-quarters of the suffragists joined; by the spring of 1922 the club claimed 60,000 members. Women's divisions in state and national party committees should be seen, as logically as the League, as successor organizations to the NAWSA.[15]

More generally, where one large or vital pre-1920 women's organization declined or ended, more than one other arose to take its space, if not its exact task. While the General Federation of Women's Clubs seemed to decline in vigor (although not clearly in membership), the National Congress of Parents and Teachers Associations (PTA) rose into a mass membership whose local units took up efforts similar to those of many unnamed women's clubs of the earlier generation, working to establish playgrounds, libraries, and health clinics, as well as lobbying at the national level, on issues from film standards to international peace. More than quintupling during the 1920s, the membership of the PTA reached over a million and a half by 1931. Its color bar led (in effect) to the founding in 1926 of a National Colored Parent-Teachers Association, which had at least the cooperation of the older group.[16]

The two national organizations that had labored most avidly on behalf of wage-earning women in the pre-World War I era did show drastic reductions in membership and resources in the 1920s. These were the National Consumers League (NCL)—not strictly but for the most part a women's group—and the National Women's Trade Union League (WTUL). Although both had set out auspicious programs in 1919, neither gained members nor momentum, their experience more like that of labor unions than of women's associations. Both the WTUL's and the NCL's efforts had informed public consciousness to the extent that unions themselves and agencies of government took up the concerns raised by those voluntary associations. As pressure from women's voluntary organizations was instrumental in making local public health and school departments assume some responsibilities for sanitation and for children's safety, and in inducing states to institute social welfare and protective labor legislation and the federal government to establish pure food and drug laws, likewise it was pressure from the WTUL and NCL (and other women's groups) that led to establishing the Women's Bureau in the United States Department of Labor. The Women's Bureau's mandate was to investigate the conditions and protect the interests of wage-earning women; it also took on the WTUL's aim to educate the public, and, in alliance with the WTUL, staunchly defended sex-based protective legislation.[17]

The WTUL's intention to raise the trade-union consciousness of industrially employed women as well as sweeten their lives through association was seized by Industrial Clubs formed by the YWCA. In 1926, the YWCA stopped requiring that members be Protestant Christians, and membership grew; by 1930 the organization boasted over 600,000 members, 55,000 volunteer advisors, and a dispersed professional staff of almost 3,500. The YWCA Industrial Clubs educated and helped to organize both Black and White women workers in Southern textile mills, and brought them to testify before legislatures about industrial conditions. These clubs also served as recruitment grounds for summer schools for women workers. The summer schools themselves, founded during the 1920s by labor reformers and academics, formed a sequel to the WTUL cross-class efforts earlier in the century.[18]

The YWCA was also instrumental in bringing together white-collar women workers. The founding in 1919 of the National Federation of Business and Professional Women's Clubs (BPW) resulted from a conference of businesswomen called by the YWCA during World War I. Lena Madesin Phillips, a Kentucky-born lawyer who was drafted from her wartime YWCA position to become the first executive secretary of the National Federation, warmed to the subject of encouraging business and professional women's teamwork, courage, risk-taking, and self-reliance. The slogan the federation used to develop hundreds of local educational fundraising efforts during the 1920s, "at least a high school education for every business girl," indicated its orientation toward ordinary white-collar workers. Lawyers, teachers, and independent entrepreneurs also formed an important part of its membership. The clubs affiliated with the federation (required to have three-quarters of their members actively employed) numbered 1,100 by 1931, including about 56,000 individuals. Scores of new associations of women professionals were also founded between 1915 and 1930, as were two more federations of such clubs, called Zonta International and Quota International.[19]

The alliance with professionals—social workers, social researchers, college and university professors—so noticeably important in efforts on behalf of women workers and in the YWCA in the 1920s was also apparent in the birth control movement. In 1919 Margaret Sanger, leader in the American Birth Control League, left behind her former socialist politics, along with her purposeful lawbreaking and agitation in working-class communities and her emphasis on women's control of their own bodies. Sanger thenceforward emphasized eugenic reasoning about better babies. The American Birth Control League organized and educated the public and lobbied for the legalization of birth control on the

First Convention of the Montana Federation of Negro Women's Clubs,
Butte, Montana, August 3, 1921

premise of allowing "doctors only" to provide information and methods. Women who saw the virtues of that approach and volunteered their time for birth control in the 1920s were mainly middle-class matrons, more socially and politically conservative than the birth control advocates of the 1910s, and also more numerous. The American Birth Control League claimed over 37,000 members in 1926, almost ninety percent female. Fewer women followed the approach of civil libertarian Mary Ware Dennett, founder of the Voluntary Parenthood League, which stood on First Amendment rights and aimed to decriminalize birth control by removing it from federal obscenity statutes.[20]

While major women's organizations founded earlier, such as the Woman's Christian Temperance Union (WCTU), persisted, a host of organizations that women could and did join in the 1920s were new ones, founded during or after World War I. The American Association of University Women (AAUW), whose members had to be graduates of accredited collegiate institutions, evolved from the Association of Collegiate Alumnae into a truly national operation in 1921 under the new name and a decade later had 36,818 members in 551 branches. Black collegiate alumnae, excluded by the spirit if not the letter of the AAUW, founded their own national association in 1924, not only to promote mutual benefit, educational standards, and scholarship among their own race, but also to work toward "better conditions of contact" between White and Black college women. In 1932 it had eight branches and almost 300 members.[21]

Group consciousness among minority-group women was a major source of new organizations. Both Jewish women and Catholic women founded numerous voluntary associations during the 1920s and 1930s.[22] Black women continued the National Association of Colored Women (NACW), the organizational hub that had been central to Black suffragist efforts and had linked Black clubwomen in communities across the nation. Its umbrella covered between 150,000 and 200,000 members in forty-one states in the mid-1920s. Many of its leaders also pursued their aims of racial uplift through male-dominated Black organizations, especially the NAACP, the Urban League, and the Commission on Interracial Cooperation. All through the decade, Black women campaigned vigorously against lynching and for the federal anti-lynching bill languishing in the Southern-dominated United States Senate— their numbers far beyond Ida B. Wells-Barnett's lone crusade in an earlier generation. Despite (or, perhaps, because of) the way that the NACW had brought women into political activism, its numbers declined by the end of the decade to about 50,000. Civil rights and welfare organizations of men and women were conducting the kinds of activities the NACW had begun, and they had more benefit of White financial support. Lacking resources, in 1930 the NACW cut its departments from thirty-eight to two: the home, and women in industry. But five years later Mary McLeod Bethune, a former president of the NACW and longtime laborer in the Black struggle for freedom, led the way in establishing a new national clearinghouse, the National Council of Negro Women. She was emphatic that neither organizations dominated by Black men nor by White women had given Black women sufficient voice.[23]

Other new organizations women joined in the 1920s were patriotic, security-minded societies formed in the wake of World War I, including the American War Mothers and the American Legion Auxiliary, which grew from an initial 131,000 to over 400,000 members after ten years. The American Legion Auxiliary often worked in concert with the longer-established Daughters of the American Revolution (DAR), which more than doubled in size between 1910 and 1932, reaching 2,463 chapters and almost 170,000 members by the latter date. During the 1920s and 1930s these women's organizations—loudly anti-communist and enthusiastic in red-baiting—advocated military preparedness.[24] They positioned themselves against women's peace organizations, for international peace was *the* major item of concern among organized women in the 1920s.

In an unprecedented tide of public concern, a range of peace groups from the conservative and nationalistic American Peace Society, through Protestant church agencies, to the left-wing pacifist War Resisters League formed during and after the war. In the 1920s they proposed competing alternatives, including the League of Nations, the World Court, international arbitration conferences, disarmament, and noncooperation with the military. Women could follow a number of avenues instigated and dominated by men; they appeared in all the peace societies, but clustered in their own organizations. Two groups were founded in 1919: the Women's International League for Peace and Freedom, whose American section included such luminaries of social reform as Jane Addams, Lillian Wald, and Alice Hamilton, and the much smaller, more extremely nonresistant Women's Peace Society. The foundings of the Women's Peace Union of the Western Hemisphere, and the Women's Committee for World Disarmament, followed in 1921. In addition, the major women's organizations—the LWV, the AAUW, the WCTU, the BPW, and the PTA—all put international peace prominently on their agendas. In 1925 Carrie Chapman Catt, the former general of NAWSA, assembled from the memberships of the major women's organizations with peace departments the National Committee on the Cause and Cure of War (NCCCW). That collectivity met annually for many years and formed a basis for peace lobbying; it claimed cumulative membership over five million at the start and eight million—or one out of five adult women in the United States—by the 1930s.[25]

The Politics of Women's Voluntary Associations

The level of organization among American women after 1920 thus appears to compare very favorably to that before, even considering that voluntary memberships would have to increase by slightly more than a fifth to keep up with the growth in the adult female population. The number of women in organizations is compelling although memberships in the various organizations could and often did overlap, as had been no less true of the pre-war generation. Repeated foundings and aggregate memberships make it clear that women were still joining women's organizations, as they had for generations. By their very constitution of specialized memberships (professional women, religious women, mothers, women of a particular political bent) and purposes (birth control, education, anti-lynching, peace, and so on), such organizations were as likely to sustain or even to rigidify the differentiations and diversities among women according to racial, ethnic, class, and political grounds, however, as to make women feel a common cause. The more purposive and specialized a women's organization was, the more likely it was to be instrumentally allied with professional expertise and involved with the bureaucratic machinery of institutions, commissions, and conferences that developed rapidly in and outside government during the 1920s. It was also more likely to be working in concert with male-dominated organizations pursuing similar purposes. These women's organizations were not purporting to emanate from or to operate in a separate sphere, as had many of their forebears in the nineteenth century. Consequently, there was an omnipresent potential for the groups working on issues not peculiar to women—peace, for example—to self-destruct by routing their members toward male-dominated organizations that had more funds and thus seemed more effective (as it happened with the NACW).

Carrying on the voluntarist legacy of pre-war (unenfranchised) women's groups, women's organizations in the 1920s and 1930s had the benefit of the ballot and the ethos that women were full citizens. Such organizations benefitted from the much increased rate of high school and college education among women and the lower birth rate, which together meant that there were many more women knowledgeable about social issues and not entirely occupied with child care. At the same time, three-quarters of all adult women were not gainfully employed. These factors created the pool of enfranchised women who peopled voluntary associations in the

First Board of the LWV at the Chicago Victory Convention, February 1920. First row, from left; Maud Wood Park, Grace Wilbur Trout; Carrie Chapman Catt. Standing, from left; Katharine Ludington, Marie Stuart Edwards, Della Dortch, Edna Fischel Gellhorn, Mabeth Hurd Paige, Euphemia "Effie" Comstock Simmons, Pattie Ruffner Jacobs. LIBRARY OF CONGRESS

era between the two world wars, very probably the highest proportion of women so engaged in the whole history of American women.

Not all women's organizations entered politics, but most of the national organizations did. They adopted the mode of pressure politics rather than fielding their own candidates: that is, they aimed to educate the public and lobbied for specific bills as they had during the suffrage campaign. As the first president of the LWV, Maud Wood Park took the lead in 1920 in forming among ten women's organizations a Capitol Hill lobbying clearinghouse, the Women's Joint Congressional Committee (WJCC). The National League of Women Voters, the General Federation of Women's Clubs, the Woman's Christian Temperance Union, the National Congress of Parents and Teachers, the National Federation of Business and Professional Women's Clubs, were all charter members. The WJCC promised to establish a lobbying committee on behalf of any item that at least five of its constituent members wished to forward, and it immediately started working on two different attempts, one for federal funds for maternity and infancy health protection (realized in 1921 in the Sheppard-Towner Act), the other for removal of citizenship discrimination against American women who married aliens (partially realized in the Cable Act of 1922).

Describing the WJCC in 1924, by which time it included twenty-one organizations, Mary Anderson, Director of the United States Women's Bureau, asserted with pride that "American women are organized, highly organized, and by the millions. They are organized to carry out programs of social and political action." She called the WJCC the "cooperative mouthpiece" of American women, conveying its members' opinions to Washington and bringing back to them news of legislators' doings. Women's organizations operated from motives and resources different from those of men's chambers of commerce, fraternal organizations, manufacturers' associations and so on, in Anderson's view. Where men's pressure groups relied on economic power in politics and looked for commercial or financial advantage or professional gain, women's organizations were working without self-interest, for the public good, for social welfare, on largely volunteer talent, relying on their influence on public opinion and "upon their voting strength for their success."[26] Anderson's commentary highlighted how far women leaders such as she persisted in assumptions formed before suffrage about women citizens' salutary disinterestedness. It also, unintentionally, explained why women's organizations (lobby as they might, and did) commanded only a weak position. Women could marshal only votes (in an era of widespread voter resignation) and public opinion. Men had the economic clout.

Voluntary Conflicts

The considerable unity of method among women's organizations contrasted with the diversity—often acrimony—among their specific goals.[27] Although women formed groups of probably greater number and variety in the 1920s than ever before, that did not necessarily mean they could work together nor could any particular group claim—without being countered—to speak politically for women. Differences among women's groups were at least as characteristic as their techniques of pressure politics. The controversy over the Equal Rights Amendment in the 1920s is well known: when the National Woman's Party had introduced into Congress in December 1923 an amendment to the Constitution reading "Men and women shall have equal rights throughout the United States and every place subject to its jurisdiction," it was immediately—and for decades after—opposed by the LWV and most other major women's organizations, which supported sex-based protective labor legislation, presumed to be put at risk by an ERA.[28] What is not so well recognized are the other equally important divisions among politically active women, and the fact that these divisions might cross-cut. Partisan loyalty has been wrongly slighted in historians' assessments of women's political behavior in the 1920s: women loyal to one party not only conflicted with women loyal to another, but also, importantly, partisan women conflicted with women who wanted to organize nonpartisan alliances.[29]

On the peace issue—where at first glance women seemed most wholeheartedly united—women's groups urging disarmament were opposed by patriotic women's organizations who boosted military preparedness. To counter the antimilitarist impact that the Women's International League for Peace and Freedom (WILPF) was making, the DAR and allied groups in 1924 formed a National Patriotic

Council. When WILPF speakers testified in Congress in 1928 against the naval building program, for instance, members of the DAR and the Dames of the Loyal Legion were also present, and Mrs. Noble Newport Potts, president of the National Patriotic Council, outspokenly warned the House Naval Affairs Committee Chairman about Dorothy Detzer, executive secretary of the WILPF, "That's a dangerous woman you've been talking to!" In that particular instance WILPF and other antimilitarists had the desired effect, and the House Committee, deluged by adverse mail, cut their authorization from seventy-one to sixteen naval vessels. Still, confidence that antimilitarism was "women's" stance was shattered.[30]

The impact that women activists made on one side or another of the pacifism/militarism question proved, ironically, the absence rather than the substance of gender solidarity. Right-wing women's confrontation and red-baiting of women pacifists and antimilitarists also led Carrie Chapman Catt, who intended to be moderate and mainstream, to leave out the WILPF and the Women's Peace Union when she organized the National Committee on the Cause and Cure of War. Regardless, ultra-patriotic women's organizations tarred Catt with the same brush that they used on the pacifists.[31]

On Prohibition—generally presumed in the 1910s to command women's support—the late 1920s revealed another crevasse. Pauline Morton Sabin recalled being motivated to found the Women's Organization for National Prohibition Reform (WONPR) when she heard Ella Boole, president of the WCTU, announce to the Congress, "I represent the women of America!" Sabin felt, "Well, lady, here's one woman you don't represent." A New Yorker born to wealth and elite social position, Sabin was president of the Women's National Republican Club, an active Republican fund-raiser and director of Eastern women's activities for the Coolidge and Hoover presidential campaigns. Sabin first brought together women of her own class and acquaintance, but after she launched her organization formally in Chicago in 1929 with a national advisory council of 125 women from twenty-six states, it gathered much broader middle-class membership. Its numbers grew to 300,000 by mid-1931 and doubled that a year later, vastly exceeding the membership of the longer-established men's Association Against the Prohibition Amendment and surpassing the membership claimed by the WCTU. The WONPR actively challenged the stereotype that women supported Prohibition. For instance, it disputed the WCTU's public assurance that the three million women under the aegis of the General Federation of Women's Clubs endorsed the Eighteenth Amendment. After WONPR leaders dared the GFWC to poll its membership on Prohibition—emphasizing that WONPR members also belonged to GFWC clubs—the WCTU no longer made that assertion.[32]

The Fiction of a Woman's Bloc

"The woman 'bloc' does not tend to become more and more solidified but tends to become more and more disintegrated," journalist William Hard observed in 1923.[33] The quantity of evidence that women arrayed themselves on opposing political sides (even if they used gender-dependent justifications to do

Rally of the Women's Organization for National Prohibition Reform, 1932
HAGLEY MUSEUM AND LIBRARY

so) calls into question the very possibility of a woman bloc. Given the divisions among women and given the nature of the political system, a women's voting bloc—or, even the possibility of a lobbying bloc representing *all* women—must be considered an interpretive fiction rather than a realistic expectation, useful perhaps to some minds, but requiring a willing suspension of disbelief.

In the 1920s most politically active women (and the LWV as an organization) eschewed the notion of a women's voting bloc in favor of women's diverse individuality. In her early leadership of the LWV, Carrie Chapman Catt made clear that it was not a woman's party intending to mobilize women's votes but a group dedicated to guiding women into the male-dominated political process and parties where change could be effected from the inside. Only a very few spokeswomen pointedly disagreed: Anne Martin, for instance, excoriated the decision to "train women for citizenship," saying that it handed women over to the Republican and Democratic parties "exactly where men political leaders wanted them, bound, gagged, divided, and delivered." The head of the Republican Women's Division believed, however, that voting women "do not want to differ from men on lines of sex distinction" and predicted that women would never vote for female candidates because of their sex alone but would choose the most qualified individuals. Grace Abbott, head of the Children's Bureau, said that women's voting record by 1925 showed that they were "trying hard to vote as citizens rather than as women, measuring a party or candidate in terms of their judgment on general community needs." Cornelia Bryce Pinchot, a leading Pennsylvania Republican, believed that women should enter politics to improve the position of their sex; nonetheless, as a candidate for Congress she found it counterproductive to isolate women as such in politics. She wanted to be listened to as an individual with views on many issues. Freda Kirchwey, influential left-leaning writer for *The Nation*, emphasized that "women are going to vote according to the dictates of class interest and personal interest as well as sex interest." To urge women otherwise, she contended, was to make them "forget they are human beings."[34]

Such remarks suggest that feminist impulses might scuttle the notion of a woman's bloc as reasonably as champion it. The fiction that women were unified in the political arena laid a foundation for feminist action, but also involved risks—most pointedly, the risks of denying women's diversity and individuality or prescribing a "woman's sphere" in politics. As much as suffragist rhetoric had stressed women's need to represent themselves and women's duty to become voters because their interests and expertise differed from men's, it had also stressed that women and men were equally citizens and individuals in relation to the state. A *New York Times* editorialist heard the suffragists' clarion to be that "women are people—human beings sharing certain fundamental human interests, aspirations, and duties with men." That very important strand of suffragist rationale was renewed in the 1910s along with rationales stressing women's differences from men; it justified and anticipated women's integration into men's political associations rather than the formation of a woman bloc.[35]

There were also strategically defensive reasons why most women active in politics did not pursue nor speak of their goals in terms of mobilizing a woman bloc. The notion of a woman bloc was portrayed as the deployment of destructive sex antagonism and was condemned in the harshest terms by mainstream male politicians as well as by right-wing ideologues. Once when the fledgling LWV did try to marshal a women's voting bloc—in New York in 1920, trying to unseat Republican Senator James Wadsworth, an intransigent opponent of woman suffrage whose wife headed the National Association Opposed to Woman Suffrage—the organization was violently condemned by New York's Republican governor as *"a menace to our free institutions and to representative government."* In the two-party system, Governor Nathan Miller said, "there is no proper place for a *league of women voters,* precisely as I should say there was no proper place for a *league of men voters.*" His attack differed only in degree rather than in kind from the blast of *The Woman Patriot,* a right-wing hyper-patriotic "news"-sheet published during the 1920s by former anti-suffragists, which trumpeted that women's organizations on Capitol Hill formed an "interlocking lobby dictatorship" bent on "organizing women for class and sex war." *The New York Times,* too, censured the forming of a political organization by women, claiming that such formation presupposed that women were "a class, a group, something apart,…a class which apparently hates and distrusts men." In *The New York Times'* editorialist's view, such thinking not only signaled a "revival of sex-antagonism" but even amounted to a "socialist" theory, of "a world divided into hostile classes."[36]

Anne Martin of Nevada, in the front passenger seat, on the campaign trail, 1920
NEVADA HISTORICAL SOCIETY

Although rarely proposed or envisioned by women leaders as desirable or likely, the notion of a woman bloc was denigrated, repressed and ridiculed by defenders of "politics as usual" as fiercely as if it threatened them. Although the woman bloc could only have been an interpretive fiction, it was, curiously, a large enough looming specter for male politicians to slay it again and again. Those who have imagined that women entering politics in the 1920s should have or could have constituted a bloc of women voters similar to the coalition formed on behalf of woman suffrage have underestimated how profoundly at cross purposes to the existing party system such a proposition really was. Yet how else could women lobbyists, without economic resources to speak of (as Mary Anderson admitted) swing any weight? Women leaders in the political arena faced a classic double bind: damned outright for attempting to form a woman bloc, damned (in effect) by male politicians' indifference or scorn for failing to form one. There was the dilemma for women who intended to make it clear that politics was no longer a man's world.

Conclusion

An improved view across the great divide of 1920 clarifies the accomplishments of women in American politics and the limits to those accomplishments. A more continuous view highlights not only the immense organizational implications of women's lack of the ballot until the early twentieth century but also the unique power of disenfranchisement to bring diverse women into coalition. By taking fuller account of women's political efforts (including voluntary associations and lobbying as well as candidacies and voting), and by acknowledging that political efforts by various subsets of women may be mutually counterpoised, we might move the focus of inquiry after 1920 from the "woman bloc" to the possibility of a feminist bloc—the latter admittedly a grouping by politics and ideology rather than by sex.

Notes

This is a revised version of Cott's article by the same title that appeared in Women, Politics, and of Change, Louise A. Tilly and Patricia Gurin, eds., published by the Russell Sage Foundation, 1990 and is printed here with permission of the Russell Sage Foundation.

1. Olympia Brown to Catharine Waugh McCulloch, June 25, 1911, folder 236, Dillon Collection, Schlesinger Library, Radcliffe College; Rosalyn Terborg-Penn, "African American Women and the Woman Suffrage Movement," in this volume, One Woman, One Vote; Gayle Gullett, "City Mothers, City Daughters, and the Limits of Female Political Power in San Francisco, 1913," in Barbara J. Harris and JoAnn McNamara, eds., Women and the Structure of Society (Durham, N.C., 1984), 149-159; Barbara Steinson, American Women's Activism in World War I (New York, 1982).

2. Maud Wood Park, Front Door Lobby, Edna Stantial, ed. (Boston, 1960), 179-80.

3. Paul's statement, from 1916, is quoted in Inez Haynes Irwin, The Story of the Woman's Party (New York, 1921), 151. On the CU, see Eleanor Flexner, Century of Stuggle (New York, 1968), 261-70, 275-77, 282-89; Nancy F. Cott, The Grounding of Modern Feminism (New Haven, 1987), 53-59; Christine A. Lunardini, From Equal Suffrage to Equal Rights: Alice Paul and the National Woman's Party, 1913-1928 (New York, 1986).

4. Park, Front Door Lobby, 23; Harriot Stanton Blatch to Anne Martin, May 14, [1918], Anne Martin Collection, Bancroft Library, University of California, Berkeley; On the mixed nature of the suffrage coalition, see Cott, Grounding, 24-33.

5. Quotations from Shaw, CU, and Kelley cited by Aileen S. Kraditor, The Ideas of the Woman Suffrage Movement, 1890-1920 (New York, 1971), 50; Ronald Schaffer, "The New York City Woman Suffrage Party, 1910-1919," New York History, 43 (1962): 273;" Catt quotation, Doris Daniels, "Building a Winning Coalition: The Suffrage Fight in New York State," New York History, 60 (1979): 71.

6. J. Stanley Lemons, The Woman Citizen: Social Feminism in the 1920s (Urbana, Ill., 1973), 92-93; John D. Buenker, "The Urban Political Machine and Woman Suffrage," The Historian, 33 (1970-71): 264-79; William Ogburn and Inez Goltra, "How Women Vote: A Study of An Election in Portland, Oregon," Political Science Quarterly, 34 (1919): 413-33; Stuart A. Rice and Malcolm M. Willey, "American Women's Ineffective Use of the Vote," Current History, 20 (1924): 641-47.

7. See Edward A. Purcell, Jr. The Crisis of Democratic Theory (Lexington, Ky., 1973), 95-114, on political scientists.

8. Walter Dean Burnham, "The Changing Shape of the American Political Universe," American Political Science Review, 59 (1965): 10; see also E.E. Schnattsneider, The Semisovereign People (Hinsdale, Ill., 1960).

9. See Schattsneider, SemiSovereign; Burnham, "Changing Shape"; Samuel P. Hays "The Politics of Reform in Municipal Government in the Progressive Era," Pacific Northwest Quarterly, 55 (1964): 157-69; James Weinstein, The Corporate Ideal in the Liberal State, 1900-1918 (Boston, 1968), esp. 92-116; J. Morgan Kousser, The Shaping of Southern Politics (New Haven, 1974); David W. Eakins, "The Origins of Corporate Liberal Policy Research, 1916-1922: The Political Economic Expert and the Decline of Public Debate," in Jerry Israel, ed., Building the Organizational Society: Essays on Associational Activities in Modern America (New York, 1972), 163-179, 288-291. Quotation from Suzanne LaFollette, Concerning Women (New York, 1926), 268.

10. Susan C. Bourque and Jean Grossholz, "Politics an Unnatural Practice: Political Science Looks at Female Participation," Politics and Society, (1974): 225-266, very effectively shows that early 1920s analyses of female non-voting—especially Charles Meriam and Harold Gosnell, NonVoting: Causes and Methods of Control (Chicago, 1923) were still being repeated in political science texts of the 1960s.

11. Addams quoted in "Is Woman Suffrage Failing?" Woman Citizen, n.s. 8 (April 19, 1924): 14-16. Early analyses are Stuart A. Rice and Malcolm M. Willey, "American Women's Ineffective Use of the Vote," Current History, 20 (1924): 641-47, and Hugh L. Keenleyside, "The American Political Revolution of 1924," Current History, 21 (1925): 833-40; see also Meriam and Gosnell, Non-Voting. Recent treatments are Paul Kleppner, "Were Women to Blame? Female Suffrage and Voter Turnout," Journal of Interdisciplinary History, 12 (1982): 621-643, and Sara Alpern and Dale Baum, "Female Ballots: The Impact of the Nineteenth Amendment," Journal of Interdisciplinary History, 16 (1985): 43-67.

12. Anne Martin, "Woman's Vote and Woman's Chains," Sunset Magazine, April 1922, 14; see also Anne Martin, "Feminists and Future Political Action," Nation, 115 (Feb. 18, 1925): 165-166; Frances Kellor, "Women in British and American Politics," Current History, 17 (Feb. 1923): 831-35.

13. Viz. Edward B. Logan, "Lobbying," Annals AAPSS, 144 supplement, (1929), 32; Dorothy Johnson, "Organized Women as Lobbyists in the 1920s," Capitol Studies, 1 (1972): 41-58; Paula Baker, "The Domestication of Politics: Women and American Political Society, 1780-1920," American Historical Review, 89 (1984): 620-48, Anne Firor Scott, Making the Invisible Woman Visible (Urbana, Ill., 1984), 259-294, have stressed the voluntarist political tradition among women in the nineteenth century, but its continuity after 1920 has received little attention, except very recently in the N.J. study by Felice D. Gordon, After Winning: The Legacy of the New Jersey Suffragists, 1920-1947, (New Brunswick, N.J., 1986).

14. Inez Haynes Irwin, Angels and Amazons (Garden City, N.Y., 1934), 408-11 and Appendix.

15. The League had branches in 45 states in 1931, with total membership probably under 100,000; see Sophonisba Breckinridge, Women in the Twentieth Century: A Study of their Political, Social and Economic Activities (New York, 1933), 66-68. On the LWV program, Lemons, Woman Citizen, 49-55; on Feickert, Gordon, After Winning, 79.

16. On GFWC, see Margaret Gibbons Wilson, American Woman in Transition: The Urban Influence 1870-1920 (Westport, Conn., 1979), 98, 100-101, 107 n. 26; William P. O'Neill, Everyone Was Brave: A History of Feminism in America (Chicago, 1969), 256-62; Breckinridge, Women, 39; on Parent-Teacher Associations, 53-54, 79-80.

17. Allis Wolfe, "Women, Consumerism, and the National Consumers League in the Progressive Era, 1900-23," Labor History, 16 (1975): 378-92; Nancy Schrom Dye, As Equals and As Sisters: Feminism, Unionism, and the Women's Trade Union League of N.Y. (Columbia, Mo., 1980); Lemons, Woman Citizen, 25-30, 122-23; O'Neill, Everyone, 231-49.

18. Breckinridge, Women, 56-57; Alice Kessler-Harris, Out to Work: A History of Wage-Earning Women in the U.S. (New York, 1982), 243-45; Theresa Wolfson, "Trade Union Activities of Women," Annals AAPSS, 143 (1929): 130-131; Mary Frederickson, "The Southern Summer School for Women Workers," Southern Exposure, 4 (1977): 70-75; Mary Frederickson, "'I know which side I'm on': Southern Women in the Labor Movement in the Twentieth Century," in Ruth Milkman, ed., Women, Work and Protest (Boston, 1985), 169-171; Dolores Janiewski, Sisterhood Denied: Race, Gender and Class in a New South Community (Philadelphia, 1985), 83, 151; Rita Heller, "The Bryn Mawr Workers' Summer School, 1921-1933: A Surprising Alliance," History of Higher Education Annual, (1981), 110-31.

19. Lemons, Woman Citizen, 58-59 n.8; Breckinridge, Women, 63-64.

20. See Linda Gordon, Woman's Body, Woman's Right (New York,

1976), 295-98; Joan Jensen, "The Evolution of Margaret Sanger's Family *Limitation Pamphlet*, 1914-21," *Signs* 6 (1981): 548-67; Ellen Chesler, *Woman of Valor* (New York, 1992).

21. Breckinridge, *Women*, 54-55, 79.

22. Breckinridge, *Women*, 49-51, 58-59; June Sochen, *Consecrate Each Day: The Public Lives of Jewish American Women 1880-1980* (Albany, 1981); Norma Fain Pratt, "Transitions in Judaism: The Jewish American Woman Through the 1930s," in Janet James, ed., *Women in American Religion* (Philadelphia, 1978), 222.

23. Breckinridge, *Women*, 77-79; Rosalyn Terborg-Penn, "Discontented Black Feminists: Prelude and Postscript to the Passage of the Nineteenth Amendment," in Lois Scharf and Joan Jensen, eds., *Decades of Discontent* (Westport, Conn., 1983), 269-70, 272-73; Paula Giddings, *When and Where I Enter: The Impact of Black Women on Race and Sex in America* (New York, 1984), 177, 183-185, 203-204. On Southern white women's anti-lynching efforts, see Jacqueline Dowd Hall, *Revolt Against Chivalry: Jessie Daniel Ames and the Women's Campaign against Lynching* (New York, 1979).

24. Breckinridge, *Women*, 43-49, 58.

25. Charles De Benedetti, *Origins of the Modern American Peace Movement, 1915-1929* (Millwood, N.Y., 1978), esp. 90-97; Charles Chatfield, *For Peace and Justice: Pacifism in America, 1914-1941* (Knoxville, Tenn., 1971); Florence Brewer Boeckel, "Women in International Affairs," *Annals AAPSS*, 143 (1929): 231-32; Joan Jensen, "All Pink Sisters: the War Department and the Feminist Movement in the 1920s," in Scharf and Jensen, eds., *Decades of Discontent*; Breckinridge, *Women*, 85-87.

26. [Mary Anderson,] "Organized Women and their Program," typescript, c. 1924, folder 84, Mary Anderson Collection, Schlesinger Library.

27. See Kay Lehman Schlozman, "Representing Women in Washington: Sisterhood and Pressure Politics," in Tilly and Gurin, eds., *Women, Politics, and Change*, 339-382.

28. In 1943 the NWP changed the wording of the ERA to its current reading. On the controversy between women's organizations over the ERA see O'Neill, *Everyone*, 274-94; William Chafe, *The American Woman: Her Changing Political, Social and Economic Roles, 1920-1970* (New York, 1972), 112-32; Lemons, *Woman Citizen*, 184-99; Sheila Rothman, *Woman's Proper Place* (New York, 1978), 153-65; Kessler-Harris, *Out to Work*, 205-12; Susan Becker, *The Origins of the Equal Rights Amendment: American Feminism between the Wars* (Westport, Conn., 1981), 121-51; Lunardini, *From Equal Suffrage*; Cott, *Grounding*, 115-42.

29. Partisan/nonpartisan controversies bulked large in the first year or two of the LWV; see Lemons, *Woman Citizen*, 49-53, and Gordon, *After Winning*, 34-39.

30. Carrie Foster-Hayes, "The Women and the Warriors: Dorothy Detzer and the WILPF," Ph.D. diss., University of Denver, 1984, 318-21.

31. See Jensen, "All Pink Sisters," and Cott, *Grounding*, 244-61.

32. David Kyvig, "Women Against Prohibition," *American Quarterly*, 28 (1976): 465-82, and *Repealing National Prohibition* (Chicago, 1979), 118-127.

33. William Hard, quoted in "What the American Man Thinks," *Woman Citizen*, Sept. 8, 1923, cited by O'Neill, *Everyone*, 264.

34. On Catt, see Lemons, *Woman Citizen*, 90-91; Anne Martin, "Feminists," 185; on Pinchot, John Furlow, "Cornelia Bryce Pinchot: Feminism in the Post-Suffrage Era," *Pennsylvania History*, 95 (1976): 329-346; all other quotations are cited from Alpern and Baum, "Female Ballots," 60-62.

35. *New York Times*, Nov. 30, 1918, 16. See Cott, *Grounding*, 29-30, 37-38.

36. Lemons, *Woman Citizen*, 98-100; "Are Women a Menace?" *Nation*, 112 (Feb. 9, 1921): 198; "The Interlocking Lobby Dictatorship," *The Woman Patriot*, 6 (Dec. 1, 1922); "Organizing Women for Class and Sex War," *The Woman Patriot*, 7 (April 15, 1923); *New York Times*, Nov. 30, 1918, 16.

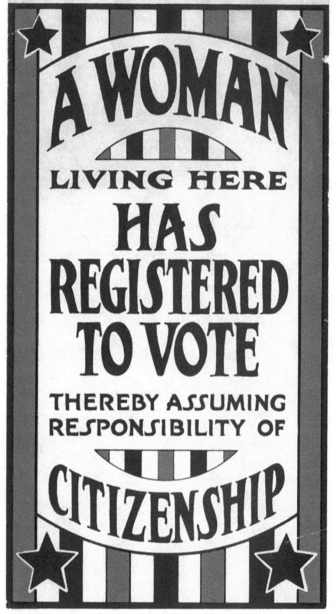

In 1920, fliers like this were widely displayed in windows
of homes to honor new women voters and to encourage
other women to register to vote.

Twenty-Three

A CENTURY OF WOMAN SUFFRAGE

Marjorie J. Spruill

Editor's Introduction: The ratification of the Nineteenth Amendment on August 26, 1920 was one of the most important events in the history of the United States—not only because it added more than twenty-seven million new voters to the electorate. It empowered women to participate in the making of the laws that governed them. Implicitly, it recognized women as individuals entitled to direct influence, rather than female auxiliaries to male decision makers, reliant on indirect influence. Ratification of the Nineteenth Amendment was also a crucial step toward women gaining access to power through elected office and full equality in the laws of the land, though over the past century those ongoing battles have proven to be as long and as frustrating as the suffrage battle itself.

The success of the Nineteenth Amendment was both a reflection of changing attitudes about women and gender roles and a factor that encouraged further change. Henceforth, women who organized to advocate for or against a political issue would be backed by the weight of their votes.

One hundred years after women were enfranchised through the Nineteenth Amendment, the women's vote is recognized as massive and highly influential in the outcomes of elections. Politicians are keenly aware that women turn out to vote at a higher rate than men and that there are significant differences in the voting patterns of the sexes. In the 2012, 2016, and 2020 presidential elections, women outvoted men by millions of ballots and were more likely than men to vote for the Democratic candidate—trends that were first noticeable in the 1980 election. However, these two trends were slow to appear. It took many decades for women to vote at the same rate as men, or for the "gender gap" to emerge.

In 1920, and for many years thereafter, there were cultural obstacles as well as deliberately constructed barriers that kept many women away from the polls. The deeply entrenched ideas about gender roles that led so many to oppose woman suffrage did not immediately disappear upon ratification of the Nineteenth Amendment. Despite the fact that the enfranchisement of women led election officials to relocate polling places from saloons and livery stables to schools, libraries, and city halls, the idea that politics was a nasty and complicated business, inappropriate for respectable women, was slow to die. As a result, many women shied away from politics and voting.

At the same time, many women who were eager to vote were kept away from the polls. In the Southern states, the majority of African American women were prevented from voting through an array of laws and policies adopted by state governments determined to preserve White supremacy in politics. While turnout among White women increased gradually after 1920, turnout among African American women increased dramatically only after Congress passed the Voting Rights Act of 1965. Meanwhile, federal policy regarding immigration and naturalization also kept many women who were living in the United States and its territories—women who were then barred from becoming citizens—from becoming voters.

For much of the first century of woman suffrage, women who chose to vote and were permitted to do so, voted like similarly situated men. Despite persistent assumptions that gender would shape their political preferences, women voters tended to make their voting choices in much the same way as men, influenced by their class, race, ethnicity, religion, and region, as well as the party preferences of their families and communities. It would take another major voting rights movement, followed closely by a new wave of the women's rights movement, for women to turn out to vote at higher rates than men and for the gender gap to develop.

Yet, even as women became more politically active, they were as divided as ever in their ideas about what was best for women, families, and society. The new wave of the American women's rights movement profoundly altered American society as feminists succeeded in changing many laws and customs to correspond to new realities of women's lives and broke down barriers that had long prevented women from full and equal participation in society and politics. But the movement's success inspired a new wave of activism by socially conservative women deeply invested in traditional ideas about women's nature and social roles and determined to roll back feminist gains. The competition for influence between the two groups heightened women's political activism as both sides sought to apply the weight of their votes.

As the centennial of the Nineteenth Amendment approached, the "woman's vote" was widely recognized as large and influential, though divided. Women turned out to vote at higher rates than men and were active in both parties and a wide range of political organizations. But despite important gains, women remained severely under-represented in elected office, especially at the highest levels of government, and they were more determined than ever to change that.

Ironically, the approaching celebration of women's long struggle to gain the vote coincided with major efforts to suppress voting, especially voting by people of color. There was a new appreciation of the fact that voting rights are not only hard to win but, once gained, must be defended. Over the years, women, especially African American women, had emerged as leaders in registering and mobilizing voters, and in 2020 those efforts would have national impact as women of color led successful campaigns against voter suppression.

In 2020, women were determined that their votes were counted and their voices were heard. After a century of voting, they were determined to gain their share of political power. In 2018 and 2020, women ran for office in record numbers and record numbers of them won, many of them women of color. As the first century of woman suffrage came to an end, there were more women in Congress than ever before. And for the first time in U.S. history, a woman—a woman of color—was elected Vice President of the United States.

★　　★　　★　　★　　★

THE IMMEDIATE AFTERMATH of ratification of the Nineteenth Amendment was a time of great excitement and high anxiety. Former suffragists went right to work to leverage the power of their votes, eager to capitalize on their victory. In towns and cities across the nation, the League of Women Voters (LWV), successor to the National American Woman Suffrage Association (NAWSA), ran "citizenship schools" to educate the new voters about procedures for registering and voting. With so little time between the August 1920 ratification of the Nineteenth Amendment and the November elections, there was no time to lose. The LWV sponsored registration drives, conducted house-to-house canvassing, and provided information to prospective voters. State fairs in many places featured mock voting booths where women could practice filling out ballots or pulling voting machine levers; in some cities, civic-minded merchants featured department store windows with women mannequins standing in line to vote.1 The Nineteenth Amendment had enfranchised more than twenty-seven million women. Previously, women had voted in fifteen states, but now women would have full voting rights in every state, including the ten states that had refused to ratify the amendment. Politicians were understandably anxious about this tremendous expansion of the electorate and quickly sprang into action to court women's votes.

Democrats and Republicans were singing the same tune: one political cartoonist, paraphrasing a popular song, portrayed a donkey and an elephant singing in unison, "How Dear to My Heart are the Sweet Lady Voters, the Coming Election Reveals Them to View," with the caption, "Strange to Say, the Feeling Seems to Be Unanimous." The Democratic Party doubled the size of its national committees to include a woman as well as a man from each state. The Republican Party created a "Women's Division" to attract and integrate women into the party. Both parties seated far more women as convention delegates. And both claimed credit for having "given" women the vote. Democrats reminded women voters that the Nineteenth Amendment had been adopted under the Woodrow Wilson administration. Republicans replied that it had won congressional approval only because of overwhelming support from the GOP, and that twenty-nine of the thirty-six ratifying states were controlled by Republicans.[2]

Great Expectations

Politicians speculated endlessly about the strength and nature of the women's vote. Many people assumed that women would vote similarly, differently from men, and that a "woman's bloc" would emerge. They believed that owing to woman's nature and responsibilities as wives and mothers, women had common sensibilities, needs, and concerns, and required different political appeals. Some politicians worried that women did not have a man's concept of party loyalty and never would: they predicted the parties would have to scramble to attract women voters, asserting that party labels meant nothing to women, but instead, issues such as health, education, maternity, and infant protection were paramount. Republican and Democratic Party leaders were rattled by the creation of the non-partisan League of Women Voters and feared women might eschew party politics and create a party of their own. Moreover, politicians were keenly aware that many proponents as well as opponents of women's enfranchisement had predicted woman suffrage would clean up politics. Who knew what that might mean? And what if they chose to run for office themselves?[3]

Some women did just that. The number of women announcing their candidacy increased steadily throughout the decade, especially at the state and local levels. Between 1920 and 1923, at least twenty-two women won races for mayor in towns from Washington to Georgia. By 1929, there were 149 women serving in state legislatures in 38 states, and by 1931, only Louisiana had failed to elect a female legislator. At the federal level, party nominations for seats in Congress were so coveted that male politicians were rarely willing to sacrifice them. A few women, including former suffrage leader Ruth Hanna McCormick of Illinois, were elected to Congress, but most women who served in Congress in the 1920s filled seats previously held by their late husbands. Women's primary gains at the federal level were to appointed positions. By 1929, women had entered nearly every aspect of the U.S. government, many of them reformers seeking to carry out their reform objectives.[4]

Many politicians expected that since the suffrage movement had ridden to victory on the wave of the Progressive Movement, former suffragists would press hard for reform. They did not disappoint. Maud Wood Park, formerly the coordinator of the National American Woman Suffrage Association's (NAWSA) "Front Door Lobby" and in 1920, the first national president of the League of Women Voters (LWV), presented the Democratic and Republican conventions with what the LWV called "The First Woman's Platform." The fifteen planks endorsed restrictions on child labor, a minimum wage for working women, government programs to aid pregnant women and children, and improvements in public health and education, as well as other reforms. The Democratic Party and the Republican Party endorsed several of the LWV's recommended planks, and Republican presidential nominee Warren Harding—who won the 1920 presidential election in part because of women's votes—endorsed them all.[5]

In Washington, the LWV took the lead in organizing the Women's Joint Congressional Committee (WJCC), representing ten major women's groups that collectively claimed ten million members. The WJCC included a variety of organizations that had worked for woman suffrage, among them the General Federation of Women's Clubs (GFWC), the Women's Trade Union League (WTUL),

Leaders of the National LWV display the "First Woman's Platform" that the new organization promoted at the 1920 Democratic Convention. Seated: (left) Della Dortch, Marie Stuart Edwards. Standing: (from left) Mary McDowell, Adah Bush, Pattie Ruffner Jacobs, Maud Wood Park, Effie Simmons, Mabeth Hurd Paige

the Woman's Christian Temperance Union (WCTU), and the Daughters of the American Revolution (DAR). The WJCC's purpose was to coordinate lobbying efforts, and as a result, measures it backed passed with surprising regularity. Each year from 1921 to 1924, the WJCC made gains regarding consumer protection and protection of women and children, including passage of a child labor amendment. Congress seemed to view the WJCC as the lobbyist for an energized womanhood, backed by an amorphous feminine threat the strength of which was yet to be determined—the women's vote.[6]

The most dramatic victory came right away. In 1921, Congress passed the Sheppard-Towner Maternity and Infancy Protection Act, which appropriated money for states to run maternal and infant care clinics. This was an effort to curb the United States' appallingly high infant mortality rates. Significantly, it was the first bill providing federal funds for a social welfare purpose. Privately, many politicians who voted for the Sheppard-Towner Act regarded it as outrageous government overreach, but they feared being punished at the polls. One supporter observed, "If the members could have voted in the cloakroom it would have been killed." Instead, the progressive measure passed by overwhelming margins with bipartisan support. One historian called it "the first major dividend of the full enfranchisement of women."[7]

Former suffragists also sought to use their votes to expand women's rights at the state and federal levels. In many states, women led successful campaigns for women to have the right to serve on juries. By 1922, twenty state legislatures had complied. At the national level, women reformers were eager to establish "independent citizenship" for married women, and again, Congress was responsive. At their urging, Congress passed The Cable Act of 1922, repealing a previous immigration law that had denied an American woman her U.S. citizenship—and thus her right to vote—if she married an "alien," a law that had not applied to male U.S. citizens who married foreign women. With all these victories, some historians called the early twenties a "honeymoon" for women reformers.[8]

By the end of the 1920s, however, former suffragists were keenly disappointed as it became clear that many women did not vote. Though no separate records were kept and there were no exit polls, in the early 1920s voter turnout was low generally and most contemporaries blamed the newly enfranchised women. Twenty-first century political scientists confirm that in 1920 only one third of women turned out to vote. Former adversaries gloated that perhaps women had not wanted to vote after all and those who did vote did not all favor reform. But the "failure" to vote as a bloc should not have been surprising.[9]

In retrospect, a "woman's bloc" was an imaginative construct. Political scientists assert that women vote much like others in their immediate communities: factors including class, race, ethnicity, region, and religion—all of which influence party preferences—shape their political opinions. And though women's shared experiences and concerns do have some impact on their voting preferences, gender identity affects their vote far less than these other factors.[10]

Furthermore, given the great diversity of the suffrage movement at its height, it was unreasonable and unrealistic to expect that once enfranchised, all former supporters of woman suffrage would have the same political goals. To win a federal woman suffrage amendment, suffragists had to bring into the movement women of diverse backgrounds, ethnicities, and ideologies who agreed with one another on a single goal: gaining the right to vote. The ratification of the Nineteenth Amendment freed women to disagree and to use their new political power however they saw fit.[11]

And they did. Women pursued their political goals through both the Democratic and Republican parties, as well as through a great variety of voluntary organizations across the political spectrum that, at times, pitted them against one another. Some, like Ruth Hanna McCormick, urged women to enter the political arena solely through the parties. McCormick was a staunch Republican, as were Mary Church Terrell and Hallie Q. Brown, who worked to turn out the African American vote for "the party of Lincoln." McCormick hired Terrell to head the Colored Division of her campaign when she ran for the Senate in 1929. Nannie Burroughs was a cofounder and first president of the National League of Republican Colored Women, established in 1924. Throughout the 1920s, Burroughs traveled as a representative of the Republican Party's national speakers bureau.[12]

In turn, Emily Newell Blair, a Missouri writer not previously affiliated with a party, in 1920 became head of the Democrat's new Women's Division and traveled the country, giving hundreds of speeches urging women to become Democrats. In 1923, the party rewarded Blair by making her a Vice Chairman of the Democratic National Committee, a position she held throughout the decade. Social reformer Belle Moskowitz, considered one of the most powerful women in the Democratic party, was said to be the "right arm" of Al Smith, the New York mayor Democrats nominated for president in 1928.[13]

Miss NANNIE H. BURROUGHS
PRESIDENT NAT'L LEAGUE
OF REP. COLORED WOMEN
LIBRARY OF CONGRESS

Some worried that the non-partisan LWV was competing with the parties for women's time. Carrie Chapman Catt insisted women should join the LWV *and* a political party, saying, "We are not going to be such quitters to stay on the outside and let all the reactionaries have it their way." In her view, woman suffrage was only one round in the fight for women's progress; having won the vote, women should work through the parties to advance the women's movement. Catt emphasized that the LWV was not a party, but it should show parties the way forward on this and other issues. "If the League of Women Voters hasn't the power and the vision to see what is coming, and what ought to come, and to be five years ahead of the political parties," she insisted, "then our work is of no value."[14]

Anne Martin, a former University of Nevada history professor who had been jailed for working for suffrage both in the United Kingdom and the United States, the leader of the successful Nevada suffrage campaign in 1914, was one of those urging women to enter partisan politics in force. The daughter of a Nevada state senator, Martin ran unsuccessfully for the U.S. Senate in 1918 and 1920. She discouraged women's continued reliance on nonpartisan voluntary organizations for political efficacy. However, after ratification of the Nineteenth Amendment, large numbers of women continued to be involved in women's groups, old and new, inspired by the belief that their lobbying efforts were now backed by the power of women's votes. The decades following women's enfranchisement saw a remarkably high level of political activity on the part of women, often in organizations with conflicting or competing agendas. For instance, many women were active in pacifist groups while others were involved in organizations advocating military preparedness.[15]

In the 1920s, some groups that had been part of the suffrage coalition continued to work for progressive reform; others moved sharply to the right—even attacking women reformers as dangerous radicals. For example, the DAR, which had joined the WJCC and backed the Sheppard-Towner Act, changed dramatically during the

Even before drafting a constitutional amendment to establish women's equality, fifty prominent members of the National Woman's Party met with President Warren Harding in April 1921 asking for his support in passing an "Equal Rights Bill" for women in the next Congress.

RECORDS OF THE NATIONAL WOMAN'S PARTY, LIBRARY OF CONGRESS

1920s. By the end of the decade, the DAR denounced the Sheppard-Towner Act as Bolshevism and joined far-right organizations in red-baiting, even accusing many Progressive reformers of being communist sympathizers.[16]

The Equal Rights Amendment

Even former suffragists who agreed on the need to press forward on women's rights and to advance the status of women in America were divided about the best way to do so. One of the most passionate and public disputes between political activists in the 1920s was the fight between the League of Women Voters (LWV) and its Women's Joint Congressional Committee (WJCC) allies on one side of the fight, and the National Woman's Party (NWP) on the other side. The battle, as intense as the conflicts between the National American Woman Suffrage Association (NAWSA) and the NWP in the previous decade, was over the NWP's bold new proposal, the Equal Rights Amendment (ERA).[17]

After ratification of the Nineteenth Amendment, the NWP, still led by Alice Paul, chose as its new goal the establishment of complete equality for women and removal of the legal disabilities they still faced. Unlike most former suffragists, NWP members embraced the term "feminist," a term originating in Europe that caught on in the United States after 1910 among women interested not only in better treatment of women by society but women's equality and autonomy.[18] NWP surveys of state and federal statutes identified over a thousand state laws that restricted women's activities and discriminated against them regarding property ownership, inheritance, guardianship of children, and ability to serve on juries and as elected or appointed offices. In 1923, the NWP proposed an additional constitutional amendment calling for equal rights for men and women throughout the United States and its jurisdictions. Unveiling the Equal Rights Amendment at ceremonies at Seneca Falls, and initially calling it the "Lucretia Mott Amendment," the NWP presented the ERA as a means of fulfilling suffragists' unfinished goals. It was introduced in Congress in December 1923 by Susan B. Anthony's nephew, Daniel Anthony.[19]

If added to the U.S. Constitution, the ERA would prohibit sex-specific legislation. For that reason, the LWV and its allies, including labor unions, bitterly opposed it. They viewed the ERA as a threat to hard-won protective legislation such as minimum wage and maximum hour laws—strongly opposed by conservatives—that reformers had been able to gain for women but not for men. To a certain extent, the ERA was a partisan issue; some business-friendly Republicans—including many NWP members—favored the ERA *because* it would end protective legislation. Democrats—including many women reformers—were generally opposed.[20]

Florence Kelley, a member of the NWP's National Council who was also head of the National Consumers Union, parted ways with the NWP over the ERA; she insisted women workers in hazardous occupations that employed mostly women needed special legislation that would be wiped out if the ERA was adopted, and that the privileged NWP members were blind to the needs of women industrial workers. Throughout the 1920s and for decades thereafter, the LWV and its allies strenuously opposed the ERA, which got nowhere in Congress. Meanwhile, the NWP vigorously opposed protective legislation for women, and when courts struck down minimum wage and maximum hour laws, the NWP celebrated it as a victory. These very public battles over how best to aid women and advance the cause of

After "unveiling" the ERA at Seneca Falls, New York, in July 1923, Alice Paul (right) and Anita Pollitzer visited Susan B. Anthony's gravesite in nearby Rochester.
<small>LIBRARY OF CONGRESS</small>

women's rights thoroughly undermined the idea that women were united in their political goals.[21]

Woman Suffrage a Failure?

By the mid-1920s, politicians recognized that there was no unified "woman's vote" to fear. In Washington, D.C., the honeymoon for women reformers was over. Congress became far less receptive to the Women's Joint Congressional Committee (WJCC) and much of the reformers' attention had to shift to a rear-guard action to defend gains already made. The Supreme Court undercut reformers' previous victories in rulings against a federal child labor law and a minimum wage for women, and the child labor bill failed when it was not ratified by a sufficient number of states. The women's campaign to gain jury service, so successful in the early 1920s, ground to a halt, and in some states the League of Women Voters (LWV) had to fight to prevent cutbacks in women's jury participation. At the end of the decade, the Sheppard-Towner Act—which symbolized politicians' desire to court women voters right after ratification of the Nineteenth Amendment when there was great uncertainty about its impact—was not renewed, and it expired in June 1929.[22]

By 1925, observers were already assessing the impact of woman suffrage. It was common for newspapers and popular magazines to question its success, such as *Harper's* 1925 article, "Are Women a Failure in Politics?" and *The Century's* 1924 essay, "Is Woman Suffrage a Failure?" Some claimed that this tremendous innovation in American politics had made little difference, and that woman suffrage had failed to live up to its promise to improve society. Others suggested that suffragists had promised too much and raised expectations too high, especially near the end of the long movement.[23]

The tenth anniversary of the Nineteenth Amendment brought a groundswell of such articles, some from former suffragists expressing their disappointment about the results of woman suffrage and others who rose in its defense. Alice Paul, who always insisted that woman suffrage was a woman's right no matter what she chose to do with it, roundly rejected the question. She countered, "Why not ask if this country is better off because men have voted for the last four years, the last forty years or a hundred years?" Carrie Chapman Catt also shrugged off assertions that woman suffrage had failed, but for a different reason: She insisted that no adequate appraisal of its impact could be made after just ten years and that women's influence had grown even though no woman's bloc had appeared.[24]

For decades thereafter, many scholars who analyzed the effects of woman suffrage concluded that with low turnout and no bloc vote, woman suffrage had little impact. As one eminent historian writing in the 1950s put it, "women's suffrage had few consequences, good or evil," and though millions of women voted and some held office, "the new electorate caused scarcely a ripple in American political life."[25] Others, however, including historians who deplored the conservative turn in the United States in the 1920s, offered a more positive assessment of women's impact on politics after 1920. They credited women reformers for keeping progressive ideas alive through an era of retrenchment until the 1930s when many of the policies they had supported in the 1920s were carried out and on a much larger scale.[26] Frances Perkins, the former suffragist appointed in 1933 as Secretary of Labor by President Franklin Roosevelt—making her the first woman to serve in a Presidential Cabinet—was instrumental in the development and implementation of the New Deal's fair labor laws, including the forty-hour work week, abolishing child labor under age sixteen, the nation's first minimum wage, and Social Security.[27]

Newer research on the impact of the Nineteenth Amendment, which focused more on state and local results of women's voting than on the impact on national politics, also found positive results. Scholars have suggested that woman suffrage led to increases in spending on charities and hospitals as well as on social programs and public education. Moreover, across the nation—even in the South—women used "the weight of their votes" effectively, lobbying state legislators for policy changes and threatening them with defeat if their demands were ignored. Furthermore, scholars have pointed out that the establishment of woman suffrage opened paths toward office-holding and party activism.[28]

An Incomplete Victory

Recent research not only questions the idea that woman suffrage had little impact, it also emphasizes the tremendous obstacles to women's participation in elections and the impact of voter suppression, which continues to be a problem in the United States.[29] There were many reasons, cultural and political, for the low voter turnout in the 1920s and for the subsequent slow rate of increase. Any analysis of the impact of the Nineteenth Amendment that fails to take these factors into account is as incomplete as the 1920 suffrage victory itself.

In their 1923 book, *Woman Suffrage and Politics: The Inner Story of the Suffrage Movement*, Carrie Chapman Catt and Nettie Rogers Shuler noted that victory had "been virtually wrung from hesitant and often resentful leaders." Even after ratification, some of those resentful politicians refused to surrender. A small, hardcore faction of anti-suffragists continued to challenge the validity of the Nineteenth Amendment, taking the issue all the way to the Supreme Court. In one court case, the American Constitutional League (ACL) argued that forcing states that had not ratified the amendment to allow women to vote was a violation of the states' constitutional rights, stating as an aside that the almost identical Fifteenth Amendment, a product of military force during a time "when civil war overrode all constitutional guarantees," was thus, a dead letter. In 1922, the Supreme Court ruled against the ACL, finally putting the challenges to rest.[30]

Still, the resentment of political leaders in the states that refused to ratify the Nineteenth Amendment was evident in the sluggish way it was implemented.

Georgia and Mississippi did not allow any women to vote in 1920, refusing to hold the special legislative sessions necessary to set up the mechanism for female participation in the November 1920 elections. Florida did so only under court order.[31]

Even for many White women who were free to vote if they wished, it took a while to get past the norms against women's participation in politics in the states where political leaders had resisted woman suffrage "to the last ditch, and then some," comparing themselves to their ancestors who had fought for the Confederacy. Southern anti-suffragists had denigrated suffragists as unfeminine as well as ungrateful. After 1920, many White men—and women—continued to see politics as a dirty business outside the sphere of a respectable woman. However, far more significant for understanding Southern women's relatively low voter turnout—as well as the grim politics of the "Solid South" in the four decades following adoption of the Nineteenth Amendment—were the successful efforts to suppress the vote conducted by conservative White officials in Southern states.[32]

Obstacles to the African American Vote

Unlike many countries that initially enfranchised White women while denying the vote to women of color or indigenous people, the United States did extend the franchise to *all* women citizens in 1920.[33] However, states erected many obstacles, including residency requirements, educational or literacy tests, and poll taxes that deprived vast numbers of women—especially women of color and the poor—of their voting rights. And for a half century, the federal government did little to stop this flagrant voter suppression. The effect on African Americans was devastating.

Outside the South, Black women registered and voted. For instance, members of Ida B. Wells-Barnett's Alpha Suffrage Club in Chicago had been voting since 1913 when Illinois extended the vote to women in presidential and municipal elections, and they were influential in city politics. In the early 1920s, the Republican Party still valued and courted African American votes, for example engaging Mary Church Terrell as its director of "Work Among Colored Women in the East." However, when the Nineteenth Amendment took effect, the vast majority of African American women lived in the Southern states. And though they sought to register and vote in large numbers, most were blocked by state governments that quickly applied the same or similar measures used for decades to deprive Black men of the vote.[34]

Recent scholarship emphasizes the heroic efforts of African American women as they tried to register and vote in the South and the tremendous resistance they encountered. At first, some state election officials were caught off guard and registered African American women. For instance, in North Carolina approximately one thousand Black women registered in Charlotte, Greensboro, Asheville, Salisbury, Southport, New Bern, and elsewhere. In Atlanta, Georgia, 6,400 African American women registered. Often, these results were the product of collective efforts to

The White Women of Kentucky
cannot afford to fail to vote. The Negro
women are registering in large numbers and
will vote SOLIDLY for the Republican ticket
thus making
A Negro Vote of 150,000
and theirs will be the deciding vote in this election if the
White Women Do Not Register and Vote The Straight Democratic Ticket
STAMP Under The ROOSTER
VOTE THIS WAY (X) UNDER THE ROOSTER

A broadside urging "The White Women of Kentucky" to vote and offset the
Republican bloc of African Americans who had already registered for the vote
LIBRARY OF CONGRESS

mobilize voters. Since there was safety in numbers, sometimes large groups of
African American women appeared together to confront hostile registrars.[35]

Soon, on their own or under orders from government officials, White registrars
began taking action to rebuff these applicants. In Columbia, South Carolina,
twenty-eight Black women reported that the local registrar required them to take
literacy tests that were different from the one mandated by the state. The African
American women protested that "white women were not required to go through
this illegal routine."[36]

The high turnout of African American women registering to vote in many places
alarmed White politicians, especially when it exceeded the turnout by White
women. In either case, the White press rallied to protect White supremacy, raising
bogus alarms about the threat of "Negro domination." A Fulton County, Georgia
newspaper stated that "the registration of negro women has been at least ten to one
heavier than the registration of White women." The registrar also reported there
were "automobiles hauling negro women to the courthouse Tuesday morning
when he closed the books." In Americus, Georgia, the registrar would personally
"hide the book or himself" when African American women approached his office.[37]

The fact that many African American women were initially successful—before
registrars figured out just how to exclude them—inspired some Black men,
including servicemen returning from the war in Europe, to renew efforts to claim
the vote. This, in turn, fueled the fears of White Southern politicians about the
survival of White supremacy and the Democratic Party's dominance of the region.

As a result, they not only applied to African American women the legal barriers used to deter Black male voters, at times they resorted to intimidation and violence.[38]

After reports of heavy Black registration in Jacksonville, Florida, White supremacists organized in opposition. A Republican campaign official reported that a thousand members of a revived Ku Klux Klan paraded the streets just days before the November 1920 election. In the town of Ocoee, Florida, African Americans' attempts to vote led to a pogrom in which a mob organized by the Klan attacked the Black community, killing many and leaving the town in ashes.[39]

At the same time, Mary McLeod Bethune, founder of Daytona Normal and Industrial Institute for Negro Girls in Daytona Beach, Florida and a member of the Equal Suffrage League, an offshoot of the National Association of Colored Women (NACW), led a group of one hundred African American women and men to the polls. Beforehand, she had knocked on doors to raise funds to pay for poll taxes and held special night classes on how to pass the tests required to register. When the Klan heard about Bethune's activities, they threatened to burn down her school on the night before the election. Determined to vote, Bethune met the Klan at the front

Leaders of the Southeastern Federation of Colored Women's Clubs. Front row, left to right; Margaret Murray Washington, Mary McLeod Bethune, Lucy Craft Laney, Mary Jackson McCrorey. Second row, left to right; Janie Porter Barrett, M.L. Crosthwaite, Charlotte Hawkins Brown, Eugenia Burns Hope

MOORLAND-SPINGARN RESEARCH CENTER, MANUSCRIPT DIVISION, HOWARD UNIVERSITY, WASHINGTON, D.C.

of the campus "with arms folded and head held high." The Klan members backed down, and though Bethune and her group were forced to wait all day before being allowed to cast their ballots, they voted. That year, Bethune helped create the Southeastern Federation of Colored Women's Clubs, which galvanized African American women across the region to fight to vote. Not long thereafter, she became president of the NACW.[40]

After the November 1920 election, African American women worked with the National Association for the Advancement of Colored People (NAACP) to gather evidence documenting the flagrant violation of the Nineteenth and Fifteenth Amendments to present to Congress. In December 1920, NAACP leaders testified at a hearing on the Tinkham Bill proposed by Massachusetts Congressman George H. Tinkham. The bill called for reducing the size of Congressional delegations from Southern states that were preventing African Americans from voting—punishment mandated by the Fourteenth Amendment. Former suffragist Mary B. Talbert, then president of the National Association of Colored Women (NACW) and a NAACP vice president, was one of those who testified. Archibald Henry Grimké also testified; a nephew of women's rights and antislavery pioneers, Sarah and Angelina Grimké, he was a former U.S. consul to the Dominican Republic, in 1920 serving as the head of the District of Columbia branch of the NAACP. Despite this, White Southern Democrats still insisted that African Americans in their states were simply not interested in voting and Congress refused to intervene.[41]

African American women then appealed to the League of Women Voters (LWV) and the National Woman's Party (NWP) for assistance, but without success. When they brought their complaints about disfranchisement to the LWV national convention in Cleveland, Ohio in 1921, White women delegates from the South threatened to walk out if the "Negro problem" was debated. In a compromise, the LWV allowed the African American women to present their case, but in the end, the organization took no action other than forming a "Special Committee on Negro Problems" to study the issue. Prominent White LWV members, including Minnie Fisher Cunningham of Texas and Adele Clark of Virginia, served as chairs of the committee, but it accomplished nothing, largely because too few White Southern LWV members were willing to serve on it, some resenting the committee's very existence.[42]

As the 1921 conference of the NWP approached, African American women wishing to appeal for support were denied a hearing. In response, a delegation of sixty women from Black women's organizations in fourteen states appeared at Alice Paul's office a few days before the conference, demanding an interview. They presented Paul with verified evidence of African American women being denied the vote, along with a "memorial" praising pioneers of the woman suffrage movement who believed not only "in the inherent rights of women, but of humanity at large, and gave themselves to the fight against slavery in the United States." The African American delegation also praised the NWP for being "in the forefront of the organizations that have undergone all the pains of travail to bring into existence the Nineteenth Amendment." Then they stated:

> We can not then believe that you will permit this amendment to be so distorted in its interpretation that it shall lose its power and effectiveness. Five million women in the United States can not be denied their rights without all the women of the United States feeling the effect of that denial. No women are free until all are free.[43]

The African American delegation requested that Paul use her influence "to have the convention of the National Woman's Party appoint a special committee to ask Congress for an investigation of the violations of the Susan B. Anthony Amendment in the election of 1920." Paul replied that since the discriminatory laws in the South applied to both sexes, this was a racial problem rather than a gender problem and therefore, outside the NWP's mission. Freda Kirchwey, a White NWP member and an associate editor of *The Nation*, bitterly protested this incident in her journal, calling Paul's rebuff "of the representatives of the colored women" a "tragic chapter" of the NWP's story. Meanwhile, both the LWV and NWP were actively assisting women in other countries in gaining the vote, particularly in Europe and Latin American, and in some cases, in U.S. overseas territories.[44]

Women Left Without the Vote

Though African American women, as American citizens, were enfranchised by the Nineteenth Amendment, many Native American women and immigrant women were ineligible to vote because they lacked citizenship status. In 1920, this was the case for at least one third of Native American adults who were considered wards of the U.S. government. After Congress passed the Indian Citizenship Act of 1924, all Native Americans could become citizens with full voting rights. Still, especially in the West, many faced barriers that were similar to those used to suppress the African American vote in the South.[45]

Zitkála-Šá, "Red Bird," 1898
GERTRUDE STANTON KÄSEBIER

One of those most influential in advocating for the Indian Citizenship Act was Native American suffragist Zitkála-Šá (Red Bird), a Yankton Dakota Sioux writer, educator, musician, and activist, also known as Gertrude Simmons Bonnin. A member of the Society of American Indians since 1913, she promoted suffrage for women and Native Americans, traveling nationwide giving speeches as well as writing to legislators and testifying at congressional hearings. Like the African American women who sought Alice Paul's aid in 1921, Zitkála-Šá appealed to the National Woman's Party (NWP) without success. However, at Zitkála-Šá's urging, the General Federation of Women's Clubs (GFWC) created a Department of Indian Welfare and hired her to travel the country as an investigator and speaker, urging White women to use their votes to enfranchise Native people. In 1926, Zitkála-Šá co-founded and began serving as president of the National Council of American Indians, working to expand and protect Native Americans' voting rights and other civil rights.[46]

Asian American women born in the United States were enfranchised in 1920, but those who had been born abroad were ineligible to become U.S. citizens and vote, no matter how long they had lived in the United States. Mabel Ping-Hua Lee, Ph.D., who as a young woman had worked for suffrage, even leading a New York City suffrage parade, hoped that her support for suffrage—and that of other Chinese American women—might help change U.S. policy toward Asians. But in 1924, Congress passed the Johnson-Reed Immigration Act that further restricted immigration from China and broadened the policy to apply to all Asian countries.[47]

These anti-Asian policies did not begin to change until the 1940s, after China fought as an ally of the United States in World War II. The first major change came in 1943 when Chinese immigrants were allowed to naturalize. Laws allowing Japanese, Filipino, and East Indian immigrants to become citizens with full voting rights soon followed.

Mabel Ping-Hua Lee
RECORDS OF THE INS/
NATIONAL ARCHIVES

Woman Suffrage in U.S. Territories

The Nineteenth Amendment did not mention the U.S. territories when it prohibited the states from denying the vote to American citizens "on account of sex." Thus, the issue of women's enfranchisement had to be resolved territory by territory and in different ways, depending upon local circumstances and each territory's unique and evolving relationship with the U.S. government. In 1920, the United States possessed six territories: Alaska, purchased in 1867; Hawai'i, annexed in 1898; the Philippines, Puerto Rico, and Guam that came under U.S. control in 1898 after war with Spain; and the U.S. Virgin Islands, purchased from Denmark in 1916.[48]

In some cases, the "organic acts" —laws passed by Congress to organize each territorial government—left decisions about suffrage requirements to the territorial legislatures. In other cases, Congress expressly forbid the territorial legislature from enfranchising women. This occurred despite the efforts of Susan B. Anthony and other mainland suffragists who fought to keep the word "male" out of the various organic acts and territorial constitutions that Congress devised—efforts reminiscent of their unsuccessful quest to keep the word "male" out of the Fourteenth Amendment. Thus, policies regarding women's eligibility to vote in the territories changed gradually as suffragists secured the vote by a different means in each U.S. territory. In each case, women played an active role in their own enfranchisement, and in some instances sought and received support from mainland suffragists.[49]

Alaska

By 1920, one U.S. territory, Alaska, had already settled the issue. In 1912, Congress authorized Alaska to form a territorial legislature and empowered the legislature to extend the right to vote to women, if it so chose. Alaska legislators were ready, having been lobbied extensively by Alaskan women who were aided by the National American Woman Suffrage Association (NAWSA).[50]

The first bill they passed extended the vote to women citizens on the same basis as men. However, indigenous women of the territory remained disfranchised. Few Alaska Natives were citizens: territorial law allowed citizenship only for Alaska Natives willing to go through a complicated process to prove abandonment of tribal relationships and customs. Even after Congress passed the Indian Citizenship Act of 1924, Alaska's indigenous people continued to face obstacles. In 1925, the Alaska legislature passed the Alaska Voters Literacy Act to prevent voting by people who did not read or speak English, further limiting the numbers of Alaska Natives able to vote. Alaska became a state in 1949.[51]

Hawai'i

A U.S. territory since 1898, Hawai'i had a government organized by Congress, much like other U.S. territories destined for eventual statehood. However, despite Hawai'i's long history of women leaders—the last Hawai'ian monarch, deposed in a revolt instigated by Americans, had been Queen Lili'uokalani—the U.S. Congress *still* prohibited Hawai'i from enfranchising women. Susan B. Anthony was furious and called on all other suffragists to "raise your voices in protest against the impending crime of this Nation upon the Islands it has clutched from other folks." And Carrie Chapman Catt demanded that Congress omit the word male, arguing that "the declared intention of the United States in annexing the Hawai'ian Islands [was] to give them the benefits of the most advanced civilization."[52]

Thus, by 1920 Hawai'ian women had been working for years to remove that ban on their enfranchisement. Mainland suffragists saw an opportunity to promote woman suffrage by federal action by assisting the suffrage effort in Hawai'i, so they provided aid and encouragement. In 1912, Catt met with suffragists in both Hawai'i and the Philippines while on a world tour as president of the International Woman Suffrage Association (IWSA). When Catt arrived in Honolulu, she knew little about Hawai'ian culture and was surprised to be greeted by Native Hawai'ian women who were the officers of the Women's Equal Suffrage Association of Hawai'i (WESAH). The leader, Wilhelmina Kekelaokalaninul Widemann Dowsett, was a Native Hawai'ian whose father was a German planter and her mother a Native Hawai'ian of the chiefess rank. Catt was impressed by the Hawai'ian suffragists and in 1918 returned to the islands to provide assistance and encouragement.[53]

Queen Lili'uokalani, 1891
HAWAI'I STATE ARCHIVES

Congress's Hawai'ian Organic Act of 1900 had enfranchised male citizens as long as they were literate in English or Hawai'ian, but excluded foreign-born Asians, a group ineligible for citizenship under U.S. law until 1943. Thus, Native Hawai'ian men constituted the majority of voters. Native Hawai'ian women were the principal force in the islands' woman suffrage movement, joined by a smaller number of "white-settler" women.[54]

At the urging of the WESAH, in 1915 the territorial legislature requested that its delegate to the U.S. House of Representatives, Prince Kūhiō, beseech Congress to amend the Organic Act for Hawai'i to extend suffrage to women. Congress took no action, but in 1918 under pressure from mainland suffragists, Congress relegated to the territorial legislature the authority to decide the issue. Hawai'ian suffragists

Wilhelmine Kekelaokalaninul Widemann Dowsett, 1918
HAWAI'I STATE ARCHIVES

assumed their legislature would enfranchise them. However, for two years the legislature delayed a decision as they debated how and when to extend the vote to women, and what restrictions should be applied.[55]

In 1919, after the Hawai'ian Senate approved the woman suffrage bill, but the Hawai'ian House of Representatives resisted, Wilhelmina Dowsett organized a protest with more than five hundred women of all ages and nationalities who marched to the state capitol, demanding enfranchisement, but to no avail. After several more demonstrations, Dowsett and her associates began lobbying the U.S. Congress directly all the while confidently preparing women across the islands for the time when they would finally win the vote.[56]

When the Nineteenth Amendment was ratified in 1920, it was taken as granting suffrage to women who were citizens of Hawai'i. Thus, when Hawai'i became a state in 1949, Hawai'ian women had been voting for twenty-nine years.[57]

Philippines

The path to woman suffrage was much more challenging in the Philippines and Puerto Rico, territories that had not been designated as on track to become states and where residents were not considered citizens of the United States. The U.S. Supreme Court's decision in the Insular Cases (1901) declared that the Philippines and Puerto Rico were not *part of* the United States, but rather *belonged* to the United States. The women and men of these "appurtenant territories" were, correspondingly, deemed subjects, not citizens of the republic.[58]

Many, if not most Filipinas, did not wish to become U.S. citizens, but supported Philippine independence. After Spain ceded the Philippines, along with Puerto Rico and Guam, to the United States in 1898, Filipino nationalist forces kept up a costly fight for independence, which was defeated by U.S. military forces in 1902. Proclaiming its intent to "civilize" the Filipinos and prepare them for self-government, Congress then established a territorial government with a Governor General and an upper house appointed by the U.S. Congress and a lower house to be elected by male Filipino voters. However, suffrage was severely restricted by literacy, property, and language requirements, to the point that less than two percent of the total population—men and women—were able to vote.[59]

The United States governed the Philippines like a colony until granting the country independence in 1946. Many Filipinas sought to participate in the limited self-government granted to male residents, simultaneously participating in campaigns for woman suffrage and independence. For example, Filipina suffragist Clemencia López traveled for two years in the United States seeking to build support for Philippine independence, and at one point testifying before Congress. In 1902, when addressing the New England Woman Suffrage Association in Boston, López declared, "I believe that we are both striving for much the same object—you for the right to take part in national life; we for the right to have a national life to take part in."[60]

The first woman suffrage bill in the territory was put forth in the Philippine Assembly in 1907, encouraged by Pura Villanueva Kalaw, a women's rights pioneer and founder of the *Asociacion Feminista Ilonga* (Association of Ilonga Feminists) created in 1906. Throughout the decade a core group of Filipina women's rights supporters, including Kalaw, López, and Sofia Reyes de Veyra, pushed for women's enfranchisement through several different organizations.[61]

Clemencia López

After meeting with Carrie Chapman Catt in 1912, they established the Society for the Advancement of Women (SAW), later renamed *Club Damas de Manila* or Women's Club of Manila (CDM), to take up the suffrage cause.[62] In 1917, de Veyra worked with mainland suffragists after coming to Washington, D.C. with her husband who was the Resident Commissioner of the Philippines to the House of Representatives. Upon returning home, de Veyra continued her work for woman suffrage together with other educated clubwomen and writers, allied with Rosario Lam and other working women.[63]

The Filipino women's fight for woman suffrage continued through the 1920s and into the 1930s. In 1922, María Paz Guanzón, M.D., organized *Liga Nacional de Damas Filipinas* (National League of Filipino Women), to work for suffrage, as well as for better working conditions in factories and for Philippine independence.[64]

Oddly, Filipinas won the vote, then lost it, then regained it, which meant they had to reassemble a suffrage movement after briefly attaining their goal. In 1933, the Philippine Legislature passed a law granting women suffrage, but in 1934 the U.S. Congress passed an act establishing the Philippine Commonwealth, which did not secure woman's suffrage, and the previous Philippine legislation was swept away before it took effect.[65]

The new constitution that Filipinos adopted called for a plebiscite of women voters to determine if they wanted to be enfranchised. In 1937, Filipina women overwhelmingly reaffirmed their desire for the vote, and the vote was granted. Still, suffrage in the Philippines was limited to a privileged few; at the end of the American period only fourteen percent of Filipinos could vote. Universal adult suffrage did not exist until 1946 when the Philippine Republic was established.[66]

Puerto Rico

It took almost as long for women to win the vote in Puerto Rico where, as in the Philippines, residents were initially considered subjects rather than citizens of the

First Lady Florence Harding (center) welcomes to the White House the wives of a Philippine delegation seeking independence, presented by Sofia Reyes de Veyra, second from right, 1922.
LIBRARY OF CONGRESS

United States. In 1917, Congress granted Puerto Ricans citizenship—some claimed so that the men could be called to serve in World War I—but left it as an "unincorporated territory" of the United States, not slated for future statehood. Beginning in 1900, Puerto Ricans were governed by a presidentially appointed upper house and a lower house of representatives consisting of members elected by male residents of the territory. The territorial government had the authority to set the requirements for voting but did not enfranchise women.[67]

Ana Roqué de Duprey, an educator, writer, and journalist was one of the territory's earliest women's rights advocates and suffragists. She began publishing the territory's first feminist newspaper, *La Mujer*, in 1894, and helped found the University of Puerto Rico in 1903. Duprey also enlisted others in the cause of woman suffrage, including many of the teachers who graduated from the university. In 1917, Puerto Ricans gained U.S. citizenship, but since women were still unable to vote, Duprey helped establish one of the first suffrage organizations in her country, the *Liga Femínea Puertorriqueña* (Puerto Rican Feminist League).[68]

Another Puerto Rican advocate of women's enfranchisement was Luisa Capetillo, a leading labor organizer, writer, and anarchist who worked for gender equality and

Luisa Capetillo   Milagros Benet de Mewton

class emancipation throughout her life. Capetillo believed in the inseparable tie between class struggle and woman suffrage. She promoted the woman's vote as a part of her work for radical reform in Puerto Rico, and at times, in Florida where she worked with Hispanic U.S. labor leaders while employed as a *lectora* (a reader hired by the workers to inform and entertain them) in cigar factories. In 1911, Capetillo published Puerto Rico's earliest feminist treatise in which she promoted radical ideas such as equal education for all and "free love." She is also remembered for being among the first women to wear pants in public, an act of defiance for which she was arrested more than once. Capetillo's radicalism set her apart from most Puerto Rican suffragists, as did her advocacy of suffrage for all. Many working-class Puerto Rican women supported suffrage, often through the Socialist Party, which began pressing for woman suffrage when it was founded in 1915. Women workers' strong support for suffrage made conservative male lawmakers fear that enfranchising women would strengthen socialism in Puerto Rico.[69]

Middle-class and upper-class suffragists in Puerto Rico organized separately. One of the most prominent, Milagros Benet de Mewton, a teacher and activist, was born to a liberal, intellectual family with family members who were elected officials and politically influential. In 1917, de Mewton became active in the *Liga Femínea Puertorriqueña*, later renamed *La Liga Social Sufragista* (Suffragist Social League) to reflect an expansion of goals beyond suffrage to include a woman's right to hold public office.[70]

After 1920, both working-class and middle-class suffragists sought to get the Nineteenth Amendment applied in Puerto Rico. Within a few weeks after the amendment was ratified, Genara Pagán, a labor activist, tested the political waters in Puerto Rico by seeking to register to vote. When denied, she filed a complaint that led the governor of Puerto Rico to request a ruling from the U.S. federal government, which stated the Nineteenth Amendment had no bearing on the case of Puerto Rican women. De Mewton and several other women filed lawsuits challenging the right of the Puerto Rican officials to refuse to register women on the grounds that they were U.S. citizens, but the territorial supreme court ruled against them in each case. They also pressed the territorial legislature to enfranchise women, but suffrage bills failed repeatedly.[71]

Puerto Rican suffragists also traveled to Washington, D.C. seeking support. De Mewton personally lobbied Presidents Calvin Coolidge and Herbert Hoover for woman suffrage. In addition, Puerto Rican suffragists sought support from mainland women's rights advocates, including the National Woman's Party (NWP), which took up their cause and successfully lobbied Congress on their behalf. In 1928, the U.S. House passed a bill enfranchising all Puerto Rican women and the Senate was about to do the same, when the Puerto Rican legislature pre-empted universal suffrage for Puerto Rican women by passing a bill extending voting rights only to women who were literate. The U.S. Congress did not intervene and thus, in 1929, only a minority of Puerto Rican women who could read and write gained the vote. Finally, in 1935 the Puerto Rican legislature allowed *all* women in the territory to vote.[72]

Virgin Islands

Another U.S. territory where women had to fight for woman suffrage long after 1920 was the U.S. Virgin Islands (St. Croix, St. John, St. Thomas, and several smaller islands). At the time the Nineteenth Amendment was ratified, the Virgin Islands had only recently become part of the United States, purchased from Denmark in 1917. The islands were administered by the U.S. Navy until 1931. After that, civilian governors appointed by the U.S. president administered the islands. In 1932, the U.S. Congress granted U.S. citizenship to all Virgin Islanders, however, women were not allowed to vote.[73]

Gaining women's enfranchisement took years of strategic activism by women of the Islands, with teachers at the heart of the struggle. The St. Thomas Teachers Association, a network of teachers, students, and working women founded by Edith Williams, known as the "Mother of Education" for her lifelong work on behalf of students in St. Thomas, played a crucial role. Williams was one of the founding members of the Suffragist League, established in 1932 by St. Thomas entrepreneur Ella Gifft. Other suffragists included Anna Vessup and Eulalie Stevens; like Williams, they were teachers who had spent time in African American communities on the mainland United States and had witnessed the use of judicial power in relationship to voting rights.[74]

In 1935, these Virgin Islands suffragists seized a promising opportunity presented by the appointment of Federal Judge Albert Levitt to St. Thomas District Court. Levitt was married to Elsie Hill, a former chair of the National Woman's Party who

Virgin Islands suffrage leaders
Edith WIlliams, Anna Vessup, and Eulalie Stevens, 1930s.
LIBRARY OF CONGRESS

soon joined the local women's groups and became a key advocate for the women of St. Thomas, helping them acquire a lawyer. After Edith Williams applied to become a registered voter, twenty-three more women also filed, but the St. Thomas electoral board rejected their applications. Hill, Stevens, and Vessup then filed a petition, seeking a court order to be added as voters. A few days later, Judge Levitt issued a judgment, ruling that the three women were "herewith adjudged to be duly and properly qualified voters," and allowing all women of the Virgin Islands to vote in local elections. In 1936, the Organic Act of the Virgin Islands established a "civil government" for the territorial domain and prohibited "any discrimination in qualification [for voting rights] be made or based upon difference in race, color, sex, or religious belief."[75]

Guam

The United States acquired the small, western Pacific island of Guam in 1898 at the outbreak of the Spanish-American War in a bloodless takeover of the territory. As part of its strategy to overtake the Philippines from Spain, the United States considered Guam to be a strategic acquisition. It was not until 1950 that the U.S. government passed the Guam Organic Act, which established a government in Guam. The Act also declared those born in Guam to be U.S. citizens. Subsequent amendments to the Guam Organic Act applied several U.S. constitutional amendments to Guam, including the Nineteenth Amendment. However,

Guamanians still cannot vote for U.S. president, and similar to other U.S. territories, they have no voting representatives in Congress.[76]

Samoa

American Samoa became a U.S. territory in 1900 after establishing treaties with local island chiefs, Great Britain, and Germany. Acquired for strategic purposes, Samoa was administered by the U.S. Navy until transferred to the U.S. Department of the Interior in 1951. American Samoans are still not citizens of the United States and people born in the territory are considered U.S. nationals. The Nineteenth Amendment and many other provisions of the U.S. Constitution do not apply in American Samoa, but the American Samoan Constitution, established in 1967, enfranchised "every person" age eighteen and older. In 1977, for the first time Samoans elected their own governor and legislature. In 1981, American Samoans elected the territory's first delegate to the U.S. House of Representatives, however, this is a nonvoting position, except in congressional committees where the delegate is a member.[77]

Gaining the vote in all of these overseas territories was a limited victory. As of 2020, residents *still* cannot vote in presidential elections and are allowed only one, non-voting representative in the House of Representatives.

Washington, D.C.

Strange but true, women (and men) with full U.S. citizenship but living in the nation's capital, Washington, D.C., have faced—and still face as of 2020—a struggle for full enfranchisement. For a brief period after Congress established the city in 1790, residents could vote as residents of Maryland or Virginia. But when Congress adopted the District of Columbia Organic Act of 1801, it took full control of governing the city and as a result, residents lost their right to vote in federal elections.[78]

In 1961, the Twenty-third Amendment to the U.S. Constitution extended the right to vote in presidential elections to D.C. residents. Still, until 1973 when they were permitted to elect their own city officials, they were governed by Congress. In 1971, Congress began allowing D.C. residents to elect a non-voting "Delegate to the United States House of Representatives." As of 2020, the District is led by two African American women; Muriel Bowser who has served the district as mayor since 2015, and Eleanor Holmes Norton, a nationally prominent civil rights and women's rights leader, who has served as the district's delegate to Congress since 1991. Both support a goal long held by many D.C. residents—statehood.[79]

Some who oppose the District of Columbia becoming a state, insist it would require amending the U.S. Constitution. Every year since 1991, Delegate Norton has proposed a congressional bill that would by-pass this formidable obstacle. While not eliminating the "seat of government" that the Constitution called for, the bill would shrink the national capital to a small complex of federal buildings and allow the rest of the district to become the 51st state. The name proposed for the new state, "State of Washington, Douglass Commonwealth," would maintain the "D.C." abbreviation while paying homage to the famous African American leader and long-time D.C. resident, Frederick Douglass. If adopted, the 700,000 Americans living in the District of Columbia would gain full voting rights and representation in the House and the Senate. However, the bill faces formidable obstacles owing to partisanship. Since most D.C. residents are Democrats, Republicans strongly oppose it.[80]

The Voting Rights Movement of the 1960s

For a half century after ratification of the Nineteenth Amendment, the woman's vote gradually increased, but the two major trends that were much discussed in the 1920s continued: a lower turnout of women voters compared to men, and the absence of a woman's voting bloc. Women continued to vote much like the men in their families and communities. It was rare for either women or men to engage in crossover voting, breaking with their parties even temporarily. During rare instances of re-alignment, including African Americans' shift from the Republican to the Democratic Party during the New Deal in the 1930s, and White Southerners' shift from the Democratic to the Republican Party in the 1960s through the 1980s, women moved in the same direction as similarly situated men.[81]

The wholesale suppression of the African American vote in the South continued with little change. However, in the 1960s and 1970s, major political and social movements led to changes in women's voting patterns that had major consequences for the nation. In the 1960s, a mass movement for voting rights in which African American women played leading roles compelled the federal government to remove the barriers that so thoroughly suppressed the African American vote in the South. Leaders in the movement for voting rights included remarkable women such as Ella Josephine Baker, Septima Poinsette Clark, and Fannie Lou Hamer.

Ella Baker, born in Virginia and reared in North Carolina, grew up determined to work for social justice, in part from hearing her grandmother's stories about being enslaved. After college, Baker moved to New York City where she began her career as an activist for race, gender, and economic justice. After working as a field secretary for the National Association for the Advancement of Colored People (NAACP), she helped Martin Luther King, Jr. organize a new organization, the Southern Christian Leadership Conference (SCLC) and ran a voter registration campaign called the Crusade for Citizenship.[82]

After African American students began spontaneous sit-ins and demanding service in restaurants and stores, Baker left the SCLC to guide this emerging youth movement, helping to establish the Student Nonviolent Coordinating Committee (SNCC). In 1960, Baker brought the students together at Shaw University in Raleigh, North Carolina, and invited Vanderbilt University theology student,

James Lawson, to address them on the philosophy and strategy of promoting justice through non-violent direct action. Lawson had been influenced by Mahatma Gandhi, who as a young man visiting London was inspired by the courage and methods of the militant suffragists. Their example aided him in developing his non-violent mass movement through which India had won independence.[83]

The SNCC was also devoted to registering voters, and in 1964 it helped create Freedom Summer in which brave volunteers—White and Black young people from across the United States—spread out in towns and rural areas through the state, encouraging and assisting people eager to become voters. Baker worked largely behind the scenes for more than five decades, inspiring and guiding other civil rights activists, particularly young people. She always insisted that voting was a key to freedom.[84]

South Carolinian Septima Poinsette Clark was an educator who became an organizer with the NAACP and the SCLC, pioneering the link between education and political organizing aimed at gaining the right to vote. Her own experiences with racism fueled her activism, and she was a major advocate for teachers, working with Thurgood Marshall for equal pay for Black teachers in South Carolina. She left the state after the South Carolina legislature prohibited state

Septima Clark (center) poses with Rosa Parks (left) and Parks's mother, Leona Mc-Cauley, a rural teacher, in 1956 at the Highlander Folk School in Tennessee, known for its work in developing leadership training for civil rights leaders.

employees from involvement in civil rights organizations, and soon became the director of education and teaching for the SCLC. Eventually, Clark was responsible for establishing nearly 900 adult "citizenship schools" throughout the South, which focused on empowering and enfranchising African Americans. The schools made it possible for many African Americans in the South, especially previously uneducated people in rural areas, to navigate the challenges to voting that Southern states had adopted to suppress the Black vote, including literacy tests and "understanding" tests that required interpreting portions of the Constitution.[85]

Fannie Lou Hamer, who grew up in poverty in rural Mississippi, the youngest of twenty children, became a courageous and inspiring advocate for voting rights for African Americans and an advocate of economic and gender justice. After eighteen years working as a sharecropper and timekeeper on a Sunflower County plantation, in 1962 she attended her first mass meeting where representatives of the SNCC and the SCLC emphasized the importance of voting.[86]

Inspired by the speeches, Hamer volunteered to be part of a group going to the county courthouse to register to vote, becoming the group's leader. Returning home, her boss demanded she withdraw the application and when Hamer refused, she was fired and ordered off the plantation. After several attempts, she managed to register, but then was unable to vote because of the poll tax. During this time, Hamer and her family were continuously harassed by local authorities and shot at from speeding cars. Undaunted, Hamer became active in the civil rights movement, serving as a field secretary for SNCC, helping develop welfare programs for needy Black families, and all the while working to get more African Americans registered to vote.[87]

Fannie Lou Hamer

LIBRARY OF CONGRESS

Between 1960 and 1964, the extensive voter registration drives in the Southern states led to the most dramatic increase in the African American vote of any four-year period since Reconstruction. Still, registration rates of Black voters remained low, due to poll taxes, tests designed to suppress the Black vote, and violence or threats of violence against African Americans who wanted to vote. In early 1965, the registration rate for voting-age African Americans was less than twenty percent in Alabama and less than seven percent in Mississippi.[88]

For lower income people of all races, it was a big step forward when the Twenty-fourth Amendment, ratified in 1964, abolished poll taxes. However, it was a big disappointment that during Freedom Summer of 1964, when African Americans in

Marchers on the Edmund Pettus Bridge during the
Selma to Montgomery March in 1965. ALABAMA DEPT. OF ARCHIVES AND HISTORY

Mississippi launched a major voting rights effort that was countered by massive white violence, the federal government *still* failed to protect African Americans' voting rights.[89]

In 1964, Hamer was a co-founder of the Mississippi Freedom Democratic Party (MFDP), which promoted voter registration while also challenging the legitimacy of the all-White "Mississippi Regulars." The official Democratic Party in the state, the Regulars protested the national party's support for the civil rights movement and barred African Americans from its activities.[90]

Hamer was frustrated and "sick and tired of being sick and tired" about Mississippi's continued efforts to oppress African Americans and disenfranchise Black voters. When the state Democratic Party sent its usual all-White Democratic delegation to the party's national convention in Atlantic City, New Jersey in 1964, Hamer and sixty other representatives of the MFDP traveled to Atlantic City, insisting that the Mississippi Regulars' segregated delegate selection process had violated party rules and demanded that the party seat *them* instead of the all-White state delegation.[91]

National Democratic Party leadership, fearful of losing the Southern White vote, offered the MFDP an insulting compromise of two seats, which they rejected and walked out. Before leaving, Hamer gave a fiery speech, covered on national television, iconic in the history of the voting rights movement in the United States. She told of the brutal beatings and assassination attempts she had endured in Mississippi as a result of simply claiming her right to vote—a right she did not even know she had until she was in her forties.[92]

Brutalizing marchers on "Bloody Sunday." The late Georgia Congressman John Lewis, then a young SNCC leader (on the ground, center) is severely beaten.

LIBRARY OF CONGRESS

The Voting Rights Act of 1965

The following year, Alabama police shocked the nation by brutally attacking hundreds of non-violent demonstrators peacefully marching from Selma to Montgomery in support of the voting rights of African Americans. Martin Luther King, Jr., John Lewis, and other civil rights leaders had chosen Selma, Alabama as the center of the campaign for voting rights because only two percent of eligible African Americans in that city were registered to vote, despite the concerted efforts of local people. The police responded violently and after a protestor was shot and killed, the activists set out to march to Montgomery, the state capital, fifty-four miles away, to publicize the worsening situation for African Americans and demand the vote.[93]

On March 7, 1965, with John Lewis of the Student Nonviolent Coordinating Committee (SNCC) and Reverend Hosea Williams of the Southern Christian Leadership Conference (SCLC) in the lead, about 600 marchers began walking across the Edmund Pettus Bridge, only to be blocked by state troopers and local policemen who viciously attacked the crowd with clubs, whips, and tear gas as White onlookers cheered.

National television coverage of what became known as "Bloody Sunday" sparked national outrage; two days later, about two thousand marchers, including large numbers of clergy, poured into Alabama to join King and other civil rights leaders to complete the march across the bridge and to the state capitol. This time, federalized Alabama National Guardsmen and agents of the Federal Bureau of Investigation (FBI) protected the marchers.[94]

The public outcry over the brutality in Selma forced President Lyndon Johnson to encourage Congress to pass the Voting Rights Act of 1965, one of the most consequential laws in U.S. history. The Voting Rights Act of 1965 banned election-related practices, including literacy tests, that states used to keep African American women and men away from the polls. The Voting Rights Act directed the Department of Justice to monitor voter registration in Southern counties where less than half of African American residents were registered. It also required counties and states with a history of discrimination against African American enfranchisement to get advance approval ("pre-clearance") from the Department of Justice before applying any new voting regulations.[95]

The results were dramatic. By the end of 1965, some 250,000 new African American voters had registered to vote, a third of them registered by federal examiners. Within two years, Black voter registration rates in Mississippi increased to around sixty percent. Before the Voting Rights Act of 1965, an estimated twenty-three percent of African Americans of voting age were registered nationally, but by 1969, sixty-one percent had registered. Not surprising, while many Southern White Democrats left the party to become Republicans, African American allegiance to the Democratic Party solidified. Over time, African American women would prove to be the Democratic party's most loyal supporters, turning out in large numbers for every election.[96]

For the rest of the century, the federal government continued to take action to expand voter eligibility and to facilitate registration and voting. In 1971, the Twenty-sixth Amendment lowered the voting age to eighteen years. In the 1990s, Congress passed the Americans with Disabilities Act (ADA) requiring states to ensure that people with disabilities could vote. In 1993, Congress adopted the National Voter Registration Act ("Motor Voter") to make voter registration easier and to encourage turnout. And in 2009, through the Military and Overseas Empowerment Act, Congress mandated reforms to facilitate military troops voting while serving overseas, as well as voting by expatriates.[97]

Congress also expanded or extended the Voting Rights Act of 1965 several times under both Democratic and Republican administrations. In 1975, it added provisions requiring bilingual election materials in areas of the nation with a significant number of "language minority" voters. As a result, Native Americans, Asian Americans, Alaskan Natives, and Spanish-speaking voters gained protection against discrimination at the polls.[98]

A Surge in Women's Political Activism

Like the civil rights movement, a renewed movement for women's rights that began in the 1960s brought about a major increase in voter turnout. Often called the "Second Wave" of the women's movement, relative to the "First Wave," which fought for women's enfranchisement, it heightened women's group consciousness and interest in politics. The Second Wave led to increased political activism among both women's rights activists—who during this time generally embraced the term "feminist"—and later, conservative women who in the 1970s launched what they called the "pro-family" movement in opposition.[99]

The amorphous Second Wave began in the early 1960s and grew rapidly. It was initially spearheaded by older, politically moderate women who served on federal and state commissions that identified laws negatively impacting women and recommended reforms. Many were White, but women of color also played crucial roles as the movement got underway. Operating in a completely different political climate regarding race than the suffragists who fought for the vote in the late nineteenth and early twentieth centuries, Second Wave feminists did not avoid association with the civil rights movement and its leaders. Rather, many women's rights activists of the 1960s supported both movements and borrowed many tactics and strategies from the civil rights movement, which was then experiencing considerable success.[100]

One of the feminists' earliest and most important victories came as an addendum to a major civil rights bill. Title VII of the Civil Rights Act of 1964 extended the Act's ban on race-based discrimination in employment to prohibit sex-based discrimination as well. Ironically, Virginia Senator Howard Smith, a White Southern conservative who adamantly opposed the civil rights movement, introduced Title VII, and at first, Smith presented it in Congress as if it were a joke. Many thought he added the provision banning sex discrimination as a poison pill to kill the bill.[101]

In fact, Smith acted at the behest of Alice Paul and other aging members of the National Woman's Party (NWP) who had for years urged him to support the Equal Rights Amendment (ERA) and other measures to enhance women's equality. In the 1960s, NWP members were still working with scant success for passage of the ERA, which they had first introduced in 1923. They perceived an opportunity to promote equal rights for women by attaching the Title VII clause to the civil rights measure. With strong support from Congresswoman Martha Griffiths, a Democrat from Michigan, and Senator Margaret Chase Smith, a Republican from Maine, Congress adopted Title VII. At first, the Equal Employment Opportunity Commission (EEOC) created to enforce the Civil Rights Act of 1964, ignored complaints based on sex discrimination. But in time, Title VII proved to be one of the most important pieces of legislation in advancing gender equality and the basis for many feminist victories.[102]

In 1966, feminists disturbed by the EEOC ignoring Title VII and wanting to lobby more effectively for the reforms recommended by the state and federal women's commissions, created a new non-government organization modeled somewhat after the National Association for the Advancement of Colored People (NAACP). The National Organization for Women (NOW) was dedicated to promoting women's equality in all aspects of American society—public and private. Betty Friedan was one of NOW's founders and its first president. Friedan, a journalist, was the author of the 1963 best-seller, *The Feminine Mystique*, which articulated the frustrations of many White middle-class women and brought many of them to feminism. Friedan's fame helped attract thousands to the new feminist organization.[103]

Pauli Murray, an African American lawyer and civil rights activist, also played a leading role in the founding of NOW, and co-authored with Friedan NOW's eloquent and comprehensive "Statement of Purpose." It began with the declaration:

> We, men and women who hereby constitute ourselves as the National Organization for Women, believe that the time has come for a new movement toward true equality for all women in America, and toward a fully equal partnership of the sexes, as part of the world-wide revolution of human rights now taking place within and beyond our national borders.
>
> The purpose of NOW is to take action to bring women into full participation in the mainstream of American society now, exercising all the privileges and responsibilities thereof in truly equal partnership with men.[104]

Aileen Hernandez, an African American activist and union organizer who succeeded Friedan as NOW president in 1970, worked to make NOW more inclusive and to focus attention on issues facing women of color. The women's movement grew rapidly as thousands of women, mostly younger and more radical who had come from the civil rights movement and the anti-Vietnam War movement, joined the fight for women's rights.[105]

In 1967, NOW adopted the ERA as one of its key goals, much to the delight of Alice Paul and other NWP members who had pursued this goal for so long and with so few allies. They were thrilled to see younger women become excited over the amendment. Soon thereafter, NOW also voted to work for legalization of abortion—and in the early 1970s, for protection of the rights of lesbians.[106]

By 1970, the fiftieth anniversary of the Nineteenth Amendment, the women's rights movement was vast, vocal, and highly visible. On August 26, 1970, feminists took to the streets to celebrate the suffrage victory and to press for more change.

Across the nation, there were huge demonstrations and parades sponsored by NOW that had challenged women to take the day off in a "Women's Strike for

"Women's Strike for Equality" marchers, August 26, 1970,
the Fiftieth Anniversary of the Nineteenth Amendment. LIBRARY OF CONGRESS

Equality." The largest and most spectacular march was along New York's Fifth Avenue with an estimated fifty thousand marchers, which exceeded even the largest suffrage marches in the city a half a century earlier. Elsewhere in the city where public monuments to famous females were conspicuously absent, women erected temporary statues to honor suffragists and other famous women. On that day, women participated in many moving tributes to their feminist forebears. A caravan of women visited graves of famous suffragists, ending at Seneca Falls where the governor of New York proclaimed August 26 a state holiday.[107]

Promoting Women in Politics

The creation of the National Women's Political Caucus (NWPC) a year later underscored feminists' awareness of women's severe underrepresentation in elected office and their determination to increase women's political power. The organization was founded after Betty Friedan reached out to prominent women in politics who were eager to move more women and women's issues to the forefront of American politics.

In 1971, Friedan and Bella Abzug, a newly-elected Democratic Congresswoman from New York, along with Congresswoman Shirley Chisholm of New York, the first African American woman in Congress, and Congresswoman Patsy Takemoto Mink of Hawai'i, the first Asian American woman in Congress, brought together a diverse group of women that established the NWPC. Other prominent women in the organization included journalist Gloria Steinem, editor of the new feminist magazine *Ms.*; Dorothy Height, president of the National Council of Negro Women; Eleanor Holmes Norton, attorney; Fannie Lou Hamer, civil rights movement leader; LaDonna Harris, Comanche Leader and founder of Americans for Indian Opportunity; Lupe Anguiano, Mexican-American civil rights activist; Margaret Heckler, Republican Congresswoman from Massachusetts; and Jill Ruckelshaus, who worked within the Nixon and Ford administrations to promote women's equality. Through the NWPC, feminists from both political parties worked together to boost women's influence in political parties, promote feminist legislation, and get more women elected to office. In addition, as the NWPC statement of purpose made clear, they sought action "against sexism, racism, institutional violence, and poverty."[108]

In 1972, more women ran for Congress than ever before. There were dramatic successes, including Barbara Jordan, a feminist Democrat from Texas, who became the first African American women to be elected to Congress from a Southern state. That same year, Congresswoman Shirley Chisholm launched a campaign for president of the United States. As she announced her candidacy, Chisholm declared: I am not the candidate of Black America, although I am Black and proud. I am not the candidate of the women's movement of this country, although I am a woman, and I am equally proud of that.... I am the candidate of the people of America. And my presence before you now symbolizes a new era in American political history." Though not successful in gaining the Democratic nomination, Chisholm stayed in the race all

Shirley Chisholm, 1972

the way to the national convention, running on the same slogan that had helped her win her seat in Congress, "Unbought and Unbossed." It would be several decades more before women made sizable breakthroughs in politics, and still more before winning the highest offices in the land. But women and women's issues were now at the forefront of national politics and so they would remain. It *was* a new era.[109]

All of this activity, together with public opinion polls that showed widespread support for women's equality, caught the attention of lawmakers in both parties. This resulted in a second honeymoon for women reformers, reminiscent of the early 1920s. In the early 1970s, even politicians who were not fans of feminism were supportive. All three branches of the federal government took action that advanced the feminist agenda. This included legislation to end sex discrimination in jobs and education, aid for women and families, and a new cause for the women's movement: protection of a woman's right to control her own body—what feminists called "reproductive freedom." In 1973, the Supreme Court issued a landmark decision for women, *Roe v. Wade,* legalizing abortion.[110]

In the 1971-1972 session, Congress passed more women's rights bills than in all previous legislative sessions combined. The greatest indicator of congressional support for the women's rights movement was its approval of the Equal Rights Amendment (ERA) by overwhelming majorities. Since the 1920s, the ERA had languished in Congress despite support from Republicans. Democrats had remained opposed to the ERA because women reformers and organized labor objected. But by the early 1970s, protective legislation for workers had been extended to men as well as women and these groups dropped their objections. At last, the League of Women Voters (LWV) and the National Woman's Party (NWP) were on the same page regarding the ERA. In 1972, the opposition would come from an entirely different source.[111]

Conservative Women Organize

After Congress sent the Equal Rights Amendment (ERA) to the states for their consideration in March 1972, many states rushed to ratify it, and it appeared the amendment would soon be added to the U.S. Constitution. Within a year, thirty of the required thirty-eight states had ratified. However, conservative women organized in opposition, seeking to prevent further ratification and to persuade states that had ratified to rescind even though legal precedents suggest rescission is invalid. Though Congress extended the ratification period from seven to ten years, only five more states ratified before the 1982 deadline and five states voted to rescind.[112]

Phyllis Schlafly of Illinois, an experienced political activist from the Republican Party's right wing, together with conservative women activists from across the nation, mobilized thousands of women in a powerful anti-ERA movement. Most of their recruits were politically inexperienced women from a variety of conservative religious groups that saw the ERA as a threat to the traditional patriarchal family. Lottie Beth Hobbs of Texas, a leader among women in the Church of Christ, brought many of these women into the anti-ERA movement through an organization she founded, Women Who Want to be Women (WWWW). The anti-ERA coalition included conservative Catholics, Mormons, evangelical and fundamentalist Protestants, and Orthodox Jews—groups previously hostile to one another but now united against the ERA and feminism.[113]

The anti-ERA coalition also included old-line political conservatives such as the John Birch Society and a number of prominent Southern senators who had fought against the civil rights movement and now applied the politics of backlash and obstruction to the fight against the women's movement. In the South, many women who had actively resisted racial integration now worked to oppose the ERA and feminism. As in the case of the Nineteenth Amendment, most states that refused to ratify the ERA were in the South.[114]

Outside the White House, Phyllis Schlafly protests First Lady Rosalynn Carter's advocacy of the ERA, January 21, 1977. LIBRARY OF CONGRESS

Through the rest of the 1970s until the ERA deadline of 1982, American women became even more polarized and politicized as the two women's movements competed to influence politicians and policies. Tensions accelerated in 1977 as feminists and conservative women faced off during a series of state and federal conferences sponsored by Congress. The United Nations had declared 1975 to 1985 "The Decade of Women" and sponsored a 1975 International Women's Year conference in Mexico City where a "World Plan of Action" was adopted. Inspired by the conference, U.S. feminist leaders had suggested these conferences so American women could elect delegates and produce a "National Plan of Action" to guide future federal policy on women's issues.[115]

After fierce battles for control of the state conferences—which feminists won— the elected delegates and thousands of observers gathered in Houston, Texas for a culminating National Women's Conference. Feminists had worked hard to encourage the participation of women from diverse racial, ethnic, and economic groups, including veterans of the civil rights movement, hoping to unite them all in an even more powerful women's rights movement. The National Plan of Action the feminist majority adopted to send to Congress called for ratifying the ERA, protecting minority rights, and supporting reproductive rights, including publicly funded abortion. The delegates shocked many Americans by supporting lesbian and gay rights—then a new issue in American politics.[116]

However, the conservatives had expanded their ranks and strengthened their coalition during the year as anti-ERA and anti-abortion groups joined forces. During the National Women's Conference, they organized a massive "Pro-Life, Pro-Family Rally," also in Houston, and wholeheartedly denounced the National Plan of Action and federal support for feminism. Announcing the start of a "pro-family" movement, conservatives vowed to remain politically active, to roll back the gains of the feminists, and to take back their country from the moderate and liberal politicians who supported feminism. The 1977 IWY conferences—a major turning point in U.S. history—had further polarized American women and made them more politically active as both sides mobilized more supporters and clarified their political agendas.[117]

The battle between advocates of women's rights and their conservative opponents had a major impact on American political culture, making it clear to politicians that women had become a force to be reckoned with, though bitterly divided in their goals. In 1980, while Democrats continued to support the women's rights movement, the Republican Party chose to side with the conservative women's movement. Abandoning the ERA, which the party had supported for many decades, and embracing a strong pro-life position, the Republican Party cast itself as the party of "family values."[118]

Watershed Election in 1980

By 1980, the successful drive to gain federal protection of voting rights had led to dramatic increases in African American voters in the South. This, along with two decades of feminist activism and almost a decade of conflict between advocates of women's rights and family values, led far more women to turn out to vote. In the 1980 election in which President Jimmy Carter lost to Ronald Reagan, women voted at a higher rate than men for the first time in the history of the United States. This proved to be the start of an enduring trend.[119] By 2000, even African American and White women of the South, whose voter turnout had previously lagged behind women from other regions of the United States and behind Southern men, voted at levels that approached women in other regions and at a higher rate than Southern men.[120]

There was still no "woman's bloc." The 1980 presidential election, however, saw the emergence of a differential between women's and men's voting preferences in which women tended to be more supportive of Democrats and men more supportive of Republicans, which also proved to be an enduring trend.[121] Feminists, including National Organization for Women (NOW) leader Eleanor Smeal and former Congresswoman Bella Abzug, moved quickly to identify and name this differential the "gender gap," hoping it would enhance their political clout, especially within the Democratic Party. In any case, the gender gap attracted considerable attention from the press, pundits, and political strategists—all seeking to explain it. Many attributed the gender gap to the women's movement, which had taught women to see their own values in political terms. Women who embraced the movement generally embraced the Democratic Party as the party more amenable to political action on behalf of women's equality.[122]

On the defensive, Republicans were quick to point out that the gender gap could also be read as men's declining support for the Democrats. This is supported by political scientists who note that men are less likely than women to favor the social welfare programs as well as the civil rights positions that the Democratic Party has advocated increasingly since the 1960s. Republicans also pointed out, correctly, that White married women tended to vote for their party while women of color and single women of all races favored the Democrats. Republican strategists insisted that the gender gap was really a "racial gap" or a "marriage gap." Thus, while GOP leaders understood the enhanced importance of women's votes, they would try to win them, not by increased support for feminism but by symbolic appointments and gestures, and by fidelity to policies that appealed to their pro-family base.[123]

Two Parties, Two "Women's Blocs"

Over the next several decades, Republicans continued to court pro-family voters, becoming increasingly reliant upon them, and alienating many moderate voters in the process. Republican feminists largely vanished from the party. At the same time, the GOP continued to attract large numbers of disaffected White Democrats from the South, becoming more uniformly conservative as well as racially homogenous. In fact, in the South, anti-feminism became a crucial part of the GOP's "Southern Strategy" to grow the party—quite useful in an era when overt racism had become increasingly unacceptable. Many leaders of the anti-ERA effort in the South had earlier battled the civil rights movement, which suggested a sizable overlap between White supremacist and anti-feminist constituencies in the region. White Southern conservatives became a crucial part of the Republican base and Southern White women consistently demonstrated great party loyalty when casting their votes.[124]

Democrats continued to support women's rights along with civil rights for minorities, and became increasingly supportive of gay rights. Barack Obama, a Democrat, a feminist, and the nation's first African American president, was elected in 2008 with a seven-point gender gap; four years later, he was re-elected with an even larger gender gap of ten points. As president, Obama also became a champion of LGBT rights and eventually, same-sex marriage. During his presidency in *Obergefell v. Hodges* (2015), the Supreme Court ruled that married same-sex couples are entitled to be treated equally under the law. In celebration of this landmark decision, President Obama had the White House illuminated in rainbow colors, the symbol of LGBT pride and solidarity. A great many voters who identify as racial and ethnic minorities, including African Americans and Latinos, continue to support the Democratic Party in all elections.[125]

In the twenty-first century, the differences of opinion on women's and gender issues that divided American women in the 1970s, continue to divide the two major political parties and the nation: Democrats are still firmly aligned with women's rights advocates, while Republicans still cater to their traditional pro-family base.[126]

There continue to be dramatic differences in party identification related to race. According to one study, African American voters' overwhelming support for Democratic candidates in presidential elections is "stunning," especially among Black women who consistently cast less than ten percent of their votes for Republican candidates. The unified "woman's bloc" that many predicted as women gained the vote in 1920 never materialized. Instead, the United States has two women's blocs; a racially diverse feminist bloc closely aligned with the Democratic Party, and a largely White conservative bloc closely aligned with the GOP.[127]

Gutting the Voting Rights Act

The ever-expanding differences between the Democratic and Republican Parties in their racial composition and race-related policies had a negative effect on state and national policies regarding voting rights. After decades of expanding and enforcing voting laws, eliminating barriers that suppressed turnout especially of African Americans, and adopting new measures to encourage participation in elections, in 2013 the United States took a major step backward. In *Shelby County v. Holder*, the Supreme Court ruled unconstitutional a crucial section of the Voting Rights Act of 1965, the "pre-clearance" section. As a result, states were free to make changes to voter qualifications without having to first prove that the new voting rules did not discriminate on the basis of race.[128]

Almost immediately, the legislatures in many states adopted new laws and procedures regarding voting, including restrictive photo I.D. requirements, purges of registration lists, cuts to early voting, and relocating or closing polling places. These changes have disqualified countless numbers of women and men who are unaware of, or unable to satisfy, the new voting requirements. Most advocates of these new voting restrictions are Republicans who promote these changes as a means of preventing election fraud—despite neutral studies that show that such fraud is extremely rare. Critics, mostly Democrats, insist that the measures are intended to suppress voter registration and participation by minorities and the poor—and they have had that effect. Research has shown that some of these voter requirements are particularly hard on women.[129]

As of 2021, equal suffrage advocates are demanding that Congress restore the power of the Voting Rights Act while also fighting to stop voter suppression at the state level.[130] Clearly, in the United States equal voting rights are not only hard to acquire, but difficult to keep. It appears that the suffrage battle never ends.

Almost the First Woman President

The two trends that first became visible in 1980—women turning out to vote in greater numbers than men and, as a group, being more likely than men to support Democratic candidates—have accelerated in recent elections. In addition, women's and gender issues continue to play a crucial role in national politics.

In the 2016 election, the major party platforms indicated that the tendency of Republicans to promote conservative family values and of Democrats to support women's rights, was stronger than ever.[131] The two parties took diametrically opposing positions on the issue of abortion, and both presidential candidates appealed for support by reminding voters of the importance of future Supreme Court appointments. For many conservative women and men, that issue was paramount. Still, pundits predicted that the majority of women—including Republicans—would vote to elect Democrat Hillary Rodham Clinton who had served previously as a Secretary of State, a Senator from New York, and a First Lady. In a contest between a woman with extensive experience in government and a strong record of supporting women's rights, and a man with no political experience who proudly opposed feminism, pundits reasoned there was a strong possibility that the first woman president would be the result.[132]

On election day 2016, large numbers of women voters visited Susan B. Anthony's grave in homage, leaving their "I voted" stickers, fully expecting to witness the election of the first woman president of the United States. Clinton won the popular vote by 2.9 million more votes than the Republican candidate, Donald J. Trump, but Trump's electoral college victory made him president of the United States.[133]

Hillary Rodham Clinton accepts the Democratic Party's
nomination for president, 2016. LIBRARY OF CONGRESS

Clinton benefitted only slightly from crossover voting. For the most part, in the 2016 presidential election the persistent pattern of voters remaining loyal to their parties held. As a Pew Research Center report stated, "Voter Choice and party affiliation were nearly synonymous." Over ninety percent of women who identified as Republicans voted for Trump, the same rate as Republican men. Democrats also voted overwhelmingly for their party's nominee with ninety-four percent supporting Clinton. The roughly one-third of the electorate, thirty-four percent, who identified as "independents" divided their votes almost evenly between the two candidates or voted for a third-party candidate.[134]

Hillary Clinton did win the women's vote by a sizable margin: over-all fifty-four percent of women voted for Clinton compared to forty-one percent for Trump. Exit polls also estimated that among her voters, women outnumbered men by thirteen percent—a thirteen-point gender gap. However, as before, the Democrats' advantage with women was largely due to solid support from women of color. Nearly one hundred percent of African American women voted for Clinton, along with a large majority of Latinas and other women of color. Across the board, women of color voted Democratic to a far greater extent than the men in their communities, though the men also voted heavily for Democrats. Most White voters, both male and female, voted for Trump, although far more college-educated White voters (fifty-five percent) supported Clinton. Non-college Whites were a majority of Trump's voters (sixty-four percent).[135]

After the election, pundits and the press expressed shock that, according to exit polls, most White women (fifty-two percent) had voted for Trump. Later, more accurate analysis put the figure at forty-seven percent for Trump, and fifty-five percent for Clinton, a plurality but a statistical tie. The expression of shock revealed the persistence of the enduring but inaccurate expectation that women's gender is the main determinant of women's politics.[136]

Analysts seeking to explain White women's support for Trump emphasized that the majority of college-educated White women voted for Clinton. However, nearly all failed to point out that that there were strong regional differences in women's choices. Most White women living outside the South supported Clinton; fifty-two percent of them voted for her compared to the forty-eight percent who voted for Trump. But he won the votes of White women living in the South by a margin of sixty-four percent to thirty-six percent. That many White women residing in Southern states shared Trump's anti-feminist views made a huge difference in his election.[137]

In post-election analysis, much of the narrative explaining Trump's victory focused on economic displacement and anxiety as motivating factors among his supporters, especially non-college-educated Whites. However, research shows that Trump's advantage with these voters, usually attributed to differences in education, was more the result of sexist and racist attitudes, and that men do not have a monopoly on either. When White women are asked to respond to statements such as "women are taking privilege and power away from men," or "gender bias is not a real problem or not as much of a problem as many women make it out to be," or "women need to be protected," many of them agreed. And those beliefs had a powerful impact on their vote choices in 2016. Many women as well as men who voted for Trump strongly disliked Hillary Clinton's feminism.[138]

Younger voters were significantly more supportive of Clinton. Notably, voters under age thirty—just thirteen percent of the voters—reported voting for Clinton over Trump by a margin of fifty-eight percent to twenty-eight percent. Voters between thirty to forty-nine years old favored Clinton by a fifty-one percent to forty percent margin. However, the majority of voters over fifty years old went for Trump.[139]

Women March, Resist, Organize, Run, and Win

Clinton's defeat set off an immediate chain reaction culminating in massive public protests led by women, many of them young women, both White women and women of color. The result was the largest public protest in U.S. history. The Women's March on Washington, held on January 21, 2017, the day after Trump's inauguration, was accompanied by more than five hundred marches nationwide with an estimated turnout of between three-and-a-half million and five million marchers. The Washington March alone drew more than 450,000 participants to the nation's capital. The U.S. marchers were joined by women-led marches in more than a hundred cities around the world.[140]

Women who had supported Hillary Clinton were fired up after the defeat. Across the country, women formed new grassroots "resistance" organizations and besieged their Republican representatives. The largest of these groups founded in response to Trump's election, Indivisible, reported that three-quarters of its members were female. Many women decided to seek office themselves, leading to a record number of women filing to run for office at every level of governance—from school boards to state offices to the U.S. Senate.[141]

There had been other periods in U.S. history when women's outrage with their government led to surges in the number of women seeking power to right wrongs through political action. Most notably, in 1992, anger over White male senators' dismissive treatment of Anita Hill, an African American law professor who denounced Supreme Court nominee, Clarence Thomas, for sexual harassment, prompted a spike in women's candidacies that resulted in many victories, especially by Democrats. Five women senators were elected and the number of women in the House of Representatives doubled—but only to forty-seven. But after that, the number of women in Congress had inched up gradually and only slightly. In 2016, Congress remained still less than twenty percent female.[142]

Trump's election inspired many more women to run for public office. As one political analyst explained, "It was if a switch had been flipped.... Suddenly, women were eager to run, as if they'd realized that the men were screwing everything up and they were going to have to do the job themselves." After Trump's victory, EMILY's List (an acronym for "Early Money Is Like Yeast"), founded in 1985 to fund campaigns for pro-choice Democratic women, was contacted by an astounding forty-two thousand women interested in running for everything from school board to Congress.[143]

Women's March, Washington, D.C., January 21, 2017

In the 2018, mid-term election—which attracted the highest voter turnout in a midterm election in at least forty years—a record number of women emerged victorious. Women's high turnout played a major role in producing a "blue wave" that turned the House of Representatives back to a Democratic majority, led by House Speaker Nancy Pelosi. In the House,102 women won election, including forty-three women of color; in the Senate, fourteen women were elected or re-elected; and for state governorships, nine women won.[144]

In one of the most publicized races of 2018, Stacey Y. Abrams, a lawyer, voting rights activist, and the minority leader in the Georgia legislature, was narrowly defeated in the state election for governor. Georgia's election was marred by major controversy over apparent attempts to suppress the minority vote. Abrams was the first African American female nominated by a major party to run as a gubernatorial nominee in the United States. Her opponent was a White male Trump supporter, Bryan Kemp, who was serving as Georgia's Secretary of State during the election, and thus, in charge of safeguarding the state's elections. From the beginning, there were problems. In the months leading up to election day, Kemp oversaw highly suspicious purges of some 300,000 voters from the rolls in a contested but court-sanctioned move claimed to be "list maintenance" that disfranchised a large number of African Americans who supported Abrams. On election day, voters encountered poll closures, long lines, and malfunctioning voting equipment, especially in largely minority areas.[145]

Similar to 2016 when defeat inspired action, Abrams's loss in 2018 set off yet another major, woman-led political battle that focused on the issue of voting rights. Abrams launched a national voter protection program, Fair Fight, focusing on twenty battleground states. The ongoing goal of Fair Fight is to end systematic voter suppression, and to press for free and fair elections.[146]

Woman Suffrage at 100

In 2020, the United States celebrated the centennial of the passage of the Nineteenth Amendment. As the year began, there were festivals, symposia, and countless new books, documentaries, and films about the long and dramatic struggle American women waged to gain the right to vote. The participation of African American women and other women of color in the struggle received long overdue acknowledgment. Historians, museum curators, and the media alike more fully documented the discrimination

Stacey Y. Abrams

Black women and women of color faced within the woman suffrage movement and their post-1920 fight against disfranchisement by Southern states.[147]

In Washington, D.C., the Smithsonian, the Library of Congress, the National Archives, and the National Portrait Gallery all featured major exhibits commemorating the fight for woman suffrage and the ratification of the Nineteenth Amendment. The congressionally appointed Women's Suffrage Centennial Commission (WSCC) sponsored numerous events, including the "Forward Into Light Campaign" in which buildings and landmarks across the nation were lit up in the suffrage colors purple and gold on August 26, 2020. That week the WSCC also sponsored a massive mosaic of Ida B. Wells-Barnett on the floor of Washington, D.C.'s Union Station, a mosaic created from thousands of small photos of women who fought for the vote. The U.S. Mint issued the 2020 Women's Suffrage Centennial Coin and the U.S. Postal Service issued a commemorative stamp.[148]

In January 2020, House Speaker Nancy Pelosi, the most powerful woman in the federal government, along with many congresswomen, honored the suffragists who fought so hard for the vote by wearing white to the State of the Union Address. Also in January, Virginia made history by becoming the thirty-eighth state to ratify the Equal Rights Amendment (ERA) as women in suffrage banners cheered from the galley of the state house after witnessing this historic vote. Whether or not the ERA can become law, given that the deadline Congress had set for ratification was 1982, remained unclear.[149]

Beyond Washington, D.C., state governments as well as local historical societies throughout the nation also hosted exhibits on woman suffrage. Many states

and cities celebrated by erecting new statues, in particular Tennessee, which took special pride in its role as "The Perfect Thirty-Six" and began its commemoration of the Nineteenth Amendment early. In addition to the Women's Suffrage Memorial dedicated in 2006, Knoxville dedicated a statue in 2018 in honor of Harry T. Burn and his mother, Febb Ensminger Burn, who, together played a pivotal role at the end of the long suffrage saga. In August 2020, two more statues went up in the state; the Tennessee Triumph Women's Suffrage Monument in Clarksville and the Tennessee Woman Suffrage Monument in Nashville's Centennial Park.[150]

In Virginia, a nonprofit, volunteer organization, The Turning Point Suffragist

House Speaker Nancy P. Pelosi

Memorial Association, worked to complete a national memorial to American suffragists on the site of the Occoquan Workhouse where suffragists were once imprisoned for picketing the White House. This new museum and memorial, the Turning
Point Suffragist Memorial, will provide an overview of the suffrage movement and
include bronze statues donated by the National Suffrage Center Commission, honoring three suffrage leaders: Alice Paul, co-founder of the National Woman's Party
and author of the Equal Rights Amendment; Mary Church Terrell, co-founder of
the National Association of Colored Women (NACW) and the National Association for the Advancement of Colored People (NAACP) who was also a NWP member who had picketed the White House for woman suffrage; and Carrie Chapman
Catt, President of the National American Woman Suffrage Association (NAWSA),
founder and president of the International Woman Suffrage Association (IWSA),
and founder of the League of Women Voters (LWV).[151]

On the fiftieth anniversary of the Nineteenth Amendment, feminists had set up
temporary statues in New York City's Central Park to call attention to the absence
of statues honoring *actual* women—rather than fictional or allegorical figures. For
the centennial of the Nineteenth Amendment, Monumental Women, a volunteer
nonprofit organization, installed a *permanent* statue of suffragists. The group had
been at work on the project since 2014, determined to break the "bronze ceiling"
and create "the first-ever statue honoring real women in the 167-year history of
New York City's Central Park."[152]

On August 26, 2020, Monumental Women unveiled the Women's Rights Pioneers
Monument, a statue of Susan B. Anthony, Elizabeth Cady Stanton, and Sojourner
Truth created by noted sculptor Meredith Bergmann. Hillary Rodham Clinton

Women's Rights Pioneers Monument, Central Park
NYC PARKS/DANIEL AVILA

spoke at the dedication, saying: "There is nothing more important to honor the women portrayed in this statue than to vote" and that "a century later, the struggle to enforce the right to vote continues."[153]

The Pandemic of 2020

In March 2020, all commemorative events for the Nineteenth Amendment suddenly had to be postponed, canceled, or conducted online because of a new and deadly virus, COVID-19, which spread rapidly around the world and by the end of the year, killed more than 350,000 Americans.[154] The pandemic forced people in the United States and worldwide to isolate themselves in their homes. Ironically, the 2020 pandemic brought new attention to a little-known part of the woman suffrage story; how suffrage activities were disrupted by the deadly influenza pandemic that began in 1918 and killed between twenty million and fifty million worldwide.[155]

The 2020 pandemic affected all parts of life in the United States, including voting, leading to bitter partisan debates about how to safely conduct elections in the midst of an epidemic. Many called for national voting by mail, while others insisted that would lead to voter fraud. By the summer, election officials and voting-rights experts who had earlier predicted a high level of participation in the November 2020 election, expressed concern that the "Pandemic Threatens Monster Turnout in November."[156]

However, several events during the summer, and the fact that an extremely controversial president was seeking re-election, led voters in 2020—especially women and people of color—to be highly motivated, despite the pandemic.

Events Inspire Massive Voter Registration

A series of killings of African Americans, mostly by police officers, inspired a national outpouring of support for racial justice. In late May and early June, millions of women and men from all walks of life—all ages, races, and religions—took to the streets despite the pandemic to demonstrate in support of the Black Lives Matter movement. The protests peaked on June 6, 2020 when over half a million people turned out for demonstrations in more than five hundred sites across the United States. Analysts estimated that about fifteen million to twenty-six million people participated in Black Lives Matter marches over a period of weeks—in some cities, months—becoming the largest protests in the nation's history.[157]

The massive marches were accompanied by voter registration drives. In the midst of the protests, Congressman John Lewis, who had nearly been killed in 1965 marching for voting rights, died on July 17, 2020. After the civil rights icon's death, voting registration efforts surged, as did calls to restore the pre-clearance part of the Voting Rights Act of 1965, and to name the bill in Lewis's honor.[158]

That some of the marches were also accompanied by riots, arson, and violence—much of it by right-wing saboteurs—alienated many conservatives. This reaction was compounded by protestors' calls for "defunding the police" and removing statues of Confederate heroes. President Trump responded by demanding "law and order" and sending unmarked federal police to restrain mostly peaceful demonstrators. When White supremacist groups engaged in counter protests and acts of violence, the president insisted that they were acting in self-defense. All of this galvanized many conservatives and led to efforts to bolster conservative turnout in the coming election.[159]

Many voters, especially critics of the Trump administration, were also angered by numerous efforts to undermine public trust in the voting process and to suppress the vote. These included attacks instigated by the U.S. President on the U.S. Postal Service and its ability to handle massive voting by mail, casting doubt on the credibility of the election itself. Trump predicted massive voter fraud would result from mailed-in ballots and encouraged his supporters to volunteer as "poll watchers," which was largely interpreted as the latest version of voter intimidation and disfranchisement. Ultimately, Trump shocked the nation with his unprecedented refusal to commit to a peaceful transfer of power if defeated. Many feared that the very survival of the United States as a democracy was in danger.[160]

After Democrats nominated former Vice President Joseph R. Biden as their candidate for president, he announced his intention to select a woman as his running mate. In August, Biden announced his choice for vice president, California Senator Kamala Devi Harris, the daughter of immigrants from India and Jamaica. This nomination energized women and people of color to get behind the Democratic ticket. This was a major step forward for women. Democrats had nominated Congresswoman Geraldine Ferraro in 1982 and Republicans had nominated Governor Sarah Palin in 2008, both unsuccessful. Harris became the third woman—and the first woman of color—to be nominated for vice president by a major political party.[161]

In late September, Supreme Court Justice Ruth Bader Ginsburg, who had served on the high court for twenty-seven years and solidified the court's liberal block, died. She was a beloved champion and icon of equal rights for women, racial minorities, and the LGBTQ community. Immediately, supporters of women's reproductive rights understood the implications of Ginsburg's passing for *Roe v. Wade*, the Supreme Court decision of 1973 that had legalized abortion. Within days of her death, Trump and Senate Majority Leader Mitch McConnell, a Republican, made clear their intention to quickly replace Justice Ginsburg with a woman who was conservative and pro-life. Suddenly, the issue of abortion and the protection of women's rights loomed even larger as factors in the presidential election.[162]

Trump's choice, Judge Amy Coney Barrett, pleased many conservatives who admired her legal credentials and judicial philosophy, and expected her to be a solid defender of conservatism on the Court for many decades to come. But the choice *thrilled* White Christian conservative women, who saw in her a new kind of

Speaker Nancy Pelosi and other Congresswomen, wearing white because of the suffrage centennial and masks due to the Covid 19 pandemic, pay tribute to the late Supreme Court Justice Ruth Bader Ginsburg, October 2020.

icon, one who reached the heights of her profession while unabashedly religious and who openly prioritized her conservative Catholic faith and her family, which included seven children, among them two children adopted from Haiti and a young son with Down syndrome. Trump's choice of Barrett enthused not only Catholics but conservative evangelical Protestants, as she was part of an ecumenical Christian community whose worship practices and ideas were similar to some Protestant traditions, including the authority of the husband in the family. The Eagle Forum, founded by Phyllis Schlafly in 1975, was jubilant; The headline in its newsletter declared, "Finally, a Woman of Faith and Family on Supreme Court."[163]

With no historic understanding of woman suffrage or sense of the irony involved, Trump courted conservative women by pardoning suffrage icon Susan B. Anthony for voting illegally in 1872—a radical act of civil disobedience Anthony hoped would lead to arrest and conviction so she could take her case to the higher courts. Representatives of the Susan B. Anthony List, a conservative group whose mission is to end abortion rights by electing pro-life national leaders, surrounded Trump in the Oval Office as he ceremoniously signed Anthony's pardon on the anniversary of Tennessee's ratification of the Nineteenth Amendment. Feminists had long rejected the Susan B. Anthony List's claim that Anthony was anti-abortion and were quick to denounce this symbolic pardon that Anthony would never have sought or accepted.[164]

Trump also made overtures to women in the suburbs, a group that had supported him heavily in 2016 but, according to polls, were turning away from him in droves. At rallies, he appealed to suburban women: "Please, Please Like

Me," and rather ham-fistedly referred to them as "housewives" whose husbands' jobs he protected. And assuming falsely that suburban women were all White and racist as well as married, he also boasted of "saving the suburbs" from destruction by opposing Democratic proposals for low-income housing that Trump claimed would invite crime and ruin their neighborhoods.[165]

President Trump's handling of the Coronavirus crisis also roiled women voters. As women navigated careers and taking care of families, or in so many cases, were on the frontlines as healthcare personnel or teachers, the president downplayed the seriousness of the illness. He flouted the guidance of public health experts and urged "reopening" the country. He also persisted in holding large campaign rallies, defying many states' recommendations against large gatherings and for mask wearing in public. Eventually, Trump contracted the virus, along with several family members, numerous staff members, Secret Service agents, and politicians who followed his lead. Yet, he seemed to have learned nothing from his illness, continuing to hold large public gatherings and generally downplaying the seriousness of the pandemic as casualty rates soared to unimagined heights.[166]

Many predicted that Trump's reckless approach to the pandemic would cause many women supporters to abandon him, and pundits predicted the largest gender gap in U.S. history. However, while it alienated many women, Trump loyalists defended him, agreeing that reopening the country was important for saving jobs and keeping children in school.[167]

Women Vote, Women Win in 2020

The November 2020 election saw the largest voter turnout in a century. Again, women cast far more ballots than men, but both sexes voted in record numbers. There was an unprecedented amount of absentee voting and mail-in-voting, as well as early, in-person voting that resulted in long lines of voters—most wearing masks to avoid the deadly virus—daily for weeks before the election.

Results were not clear on election day, but within a week, Joseph R. Biden and Kamala D. Harris were declared President and Vice President Elect of the United States. But while the Democrats fared well in the presidential race, in other elections across the nation Republicans held their own. The results were a clear rejection of President Trump and his leadership. Biden defeated Trump by more than seven million votes, receiving more than eighty-one million votes, the highest number of votes ever cast for a presidential candidate in U.S. history. However, about seventy-four million cast votes for Trump, the second highest number of votes for a presidential candidate.[168]

Early reports of the results in this record-shattering election indicated that trends regarding women's voting that had been in place for decades persisted. The gender gap, which had averaged about eight points in the past ten presidential elections, was approximately the same with a nine-point difference between the percentages of women and men that favored Biden and Harris over Trump and Vice President Mike Pence.[169]

Women were crucial to the Biden/Harris win, and African American women played an even greater role in Democratic success than usual. The Democratic ticket received ninety-three percent of African American women who turned out to vote in large numbers.[170] In addition, they took the lead in mobilizing large numbers of other Democratic voters, including many who were previously unregistered. Some of the fervor African American women demonstrated in the election was inspired by Biden's choice of Harris as his running mate. Like Melanie Campbell, head of the Black Women's Roundtable and president of the National Coalition on Black Civic Participation, many African American women interpreted Harris's nomination as a sign that the Democratic Party had finally come to realize and appreciate their essential contributions as the most consistent part of its voting and organizing base.[171]

African American women's most celebrated contributions were in Georgia where the Democratic presidential candidate won for the first time in twenty-eight years. The victory astonished many Americans, including Trump, who refused to accept the results in Georgia as legally cast votes. He quickly filed numerous lawsuits challenging election results in some other key states where Democrats had prevailed. Trump relentlessly pressured Republican election officials to overturn the results and flip electoral votes into Trump's column. His attempts to overturn election results and to convince supporters that the election had been stolen eventually led to Trump's second impeachment after he incited his supporters to storm the Capitol and "Stop the Steal" by interrupting the Senate's final certification of the electoral votes on January 6, 2021.[172]

The Biden/Harris victory in Georgia was the result of years of work by Stacey Abrams and two organizations she founded, along with several other women-led groups that together beat back efforts at voter suppression and registered hundreds of thousands of new voters, including disengaged voters of color and many young people. This vast number of first-time voters put the Biden/Harris ticket over the top, and within a few months delivered the Democrats control of the U.S. Senate by helping elect two new senators, Rev. Raphael Warnock, an African American pastor at Martin Luther King, Jr.'s historic church in Atlanta, and Jon Ossof, Georgia's first Jewish senator who began his political career as an aide to voting rights champion John Lewis.[173]

The Democratic victory in Georgia owed much to the votes of suburban women—a group that is varied in terms of race, ethnicity, marital status, and occupation. But the Democrats narrowly lost to Trump among White women, largely due to Trump's support from White women in rural areas. Trump won handily among White women without college degrees, garnering support from about sixty percent of this group. Biden got thirty-nine percent of the votes of non-college White woman, but won the votes of White women with college degrees by about sixty percent.[174]

One of the most significant demographic changes from the 2016 presidential election to the 2020 election was the number of men who switched their preferences from Trump to Biden. Exit polls indicated that forty-six percent of all men supported Biden, while in 2016, forty-one percent had supported Democrat Hillary Rodham Clinton. Some analysts, including Eleanor Smeal, a former president of the National Organization for Women (NOW) and head of the organization Feminist Majority, interpreted this outcome as the result of some men's discomfort—or misogynist attitudes—in relation to Clinton.[175]

Women made major gains in Congress in the 2020 elections. Overall, a record number of women—at least 141—serve in the 117th Congress, including 105 Democrats and thirty-six Republicans, breaking the record of 127 women lawmakers in the 116th Congress. The new Congress in 2021 also has a record number of women of color, including three Native American women, the most in U.S. history.[176]

In sharp contrast to the 2018 mid-term election, the surprise was the number (eighteen) of Republican women who were elected to the House of Representatives. All are opposed to abortion, prompting Marjorie Dannenfelser, president of the pro-life political action group, the Susan B. Anthony List, to celebrate their victories and the re-election of two pro-life Republican women senators as "breathtaking progress, something that Republican insiders and even some staunch pro-lifers doubted could be done." Since the 1970s, far fewer Republican women than Democratic women have run for office and been elected. The Republican Party historically has a poor record of recruiting and supporting women candidates compared to the Democrats. However, after losing so many seats to a diverse group of Democratic women candidates in the 2018 midterm elections, Republican leaders had come to see female candidates as an asset. In 2020, they put aside their disdain for "identity politics," at least temporarily, and actively recruited a diverse group of Republican women to run.[177]

The election of these Republican women more than doubled the number of GOP congresswomen, though at twenty-eight their numbers are still fall far short of the number of Democratic congresswomen, which numbers eighty-eight in the 117th Congress. The record-breaking diversity of the new Congress was also due largely to the Democrats: of the fifty-one women of color elected, forty-six are Democrats. The Georgia runoff victories meant that Democrats would control the Senate. As the two Independent senators normally caucused with the Democrats, the two parties would had equal numbers of votes, with Vice President Harris playing a crucial role as the "tie breaker" when the Senate votes were evenly split. This also meant that when President Biden nominated the most diverse cabinet in history, including twelve women, eight of them women of color—including Biden's pick of the first Native American cabinet member, Representative Deb Haaland of New Mexico as Secretary of the Interior—their chances of confirmation were high.[178]

However, the major gain for women—all women—was the historic, glass-ceiling-shattering election of Kamala Devi Harris as Vice President of the United States. She is not only the first woman to reach the second-highest office in the nation, she is the first person of color. It had taken a century for women to reach the top tier of American elections.[179]

A Beacon of Achievement

On August 26, 1920, the day the Nineteenth Amendment was ratified, Carrie Chapman Catt, president of the National American Women Suffrage Association (NAWSA), addressed the "women of America" in a victory speech. She reminded them of the years of struggle by generations of suffragists, and the many sacrifices made so that "you and your daughters might inherit political freedom."[180]

One hundred years later, on November 7, 2020, the night the Biden/Harris victory was declared, Vice President-Elect Kamala Devi Harris reminded the nation of that heritage. Wearing White in honor of the suffragists, she gave an acceptance speech in which she thanked "all the women who worked to secure and protect the right to vote for over a century: a hundred years ago with the Nineteenth Amendment, fifty-five years ago with the Voting Rights Act and now, in 2020, with a new generation of women in our country who cast their ballots and continued the fight for their fundamental right to vote and be heard."[181]

As Harris paid homage to her late mother, Shymala Gopalan Harris, who left India for the United States at age nineteen, she offered special praise to the countless African American, Latina, and Native American women "throughout our nation's history who have paved the way for this moment tonight."[182]

Harris was also mindful of the impact of her election on children, including the starstruck girls in her vast television audience. "Every little girl watching tonight sees that this is a country of possibilities." As Harris concluded, she declared, "While I may be the first woman in this office, I will not be the last."[183]

Kamala D. Harris giving her acceptance speech as Vice President elect

In her remarks and in her choice of colors, Vice President-Elect Harris sent a message to the nation and the world. As one *New York Times* reporter observed, dressing in white—which suffragist Alice Paul said symbolized "the quality of our purpose"—had been a celebrated symbol of women's rights for decades. Over the last four years, the reporter noted, wearing white had "taken on even more potency and power." Now, finally, it was "transformed into a beacon of achievement."[184]

Kamala D. Harris taking oath for vice presidency,
January 20, 2021. "I stand on the shoulders of
those who came before."

A new Vice President, a woman, now stood before the world, embodying and celebrating the achievements of American women as a century of woman suffrage concluded and a new one began.

Notes

1 Louise Merwin Young, and Ralph A. Young, *In the Public Interest: The League of Women Voters, 1920-1970* (Greenwood Press, 1989), 33-38; Meilan Solly, "What the First Women Voters Experienced When Registering for the 1920 Election," *Smithsonian Magazine*, July 30, 2020; Lorraine Gates Schuyler, *The Weight of Their Votes: Southern Women and Political Leverage in the 1920s* (University of North Carolina Press, 2006).

2 Jo Freeman, *A Room at a Time: How Women Entered Party Politics* (Rowman & Littlefield, 2000), 81-85; Catherine E. Rymph, *Republican Women: Feminism and Conservatism from Suffrage*

Through the Rise of the New Right (University of North Carolina Press, 2006),14-29; J. Stanley Lemons, *The Woman Citizen: Social Feminism in the 1920s* (University of Illinois Press, 1973), 85-89; Cartoon from the *Philadelphia Inquirer*, in Marjorie Spruill (Wheeler), ed., *Votes for Women: The Woman Suffrage Movement in Tennessee, the South, and the Nation* (University of Tennessee Press, 1995), 319.

3 Freeman, *A Room at a Time*,124-29; Rymph, *Republican Women*,16-22; Young and Young, *In the Public Interest*, 33-38; Nancy F. Cott, "Across the Great Divide: Women in Politics

Before and After 1920," Chapter Twenty-two, in Marjorie J. Spruill, ed., *One Woman, One Vote: Rediscovering the Woman Suffrage Movement*, Second Edition (NewSage Press, 2021).

4 Liette Gidlow, "Beyond 1920: The Legacies of Woman Suffrage," National Park Service Series: The 19th Amendment and Women's Access to the Vote Across America, nps.gov/articles/beyond-1920-the-legacies-of-woman-suffrage.htm; Lemons, *The Woman Citizen*, 73-81, 103-108; Elisabeth Israels Perry, "Women in Action: Rebels and Reformers, 1920-1980," League of Women Voters Educational Fund, 1995, 6; Freeman, *A Room at a Time*, 230-32.

5 Ibid.; 203; Christina Wolbrecht and J. Kevin Corder, *A Century of Votes for Women: American Elections since Suffrage* (Cambridge University Press, 2020), 1-2; Rymph, *Republican Women*, 23.

6 Lemons, *The Woman Citizen*, 55-58, 151-76.

7 William H. Chafe, *The Paradox of Change* (Oxford University Press), 1972,1991), quotation, 27; Lemons, *The Woman Citizen*, 153-76. Lemons quotation,153.

8 Ibid., 63-68, 72-73.

9 Cott, Chapter Twenty-two; Wolbrecht and Corder, *A Century of Votes for Women*, 2; J. Kevin Corder and Christina Wolbrecht, *Counting Women's Ballots: Female Voters from Suffrage Through the New Deal* (Cambridge University Press, 2016); In the 1920 presidential election, approximately 36 percent of eligible women and sixty-eight percent of eligible men voted, compared to sixty-three percent of women and fifty-nine percent of men in the 1920 presidential election. Solly, "What the First Women Voters Experienced."

10 Ibid., 3-5; Cott, Chapter Twenty-two.

11 Ibid.

12 Alison M. Parker, *Unceasing Militant: The Life of Mary Church Terrell* (University of North Carolina Press, 2021), 160-78; Rymph, *Republican Women*, 34-35, 46, 52-60; Freeman, *A Room at a Time*, 99.

13 Ibid., 85-89; Elisabeth Israels Perry, *Belle Moskowitz: Feminine Politics and the Exercise of Power in the Age of Alfred E. Smith* (Routledge, 2018).

14 Lemons, *The Woman Citizen*, 85-112, quotation, 90; Cott, Chapter Twenty-two.

15 Ibid.; Anne Bail Howard, *The Long Campaign: A Biography of Anne Martin* (University of Nevada Press, 1985); Lemons, *The Woman Citizen*, 41-62.

16 Ibid, 123-24,172-73; Gidlow, "Beyond 1920."

17 Lemons, *The Woman Citizen*, 181-204; Christine A. Lunardini, *From Equal Suffrage to Equal Rights: Alice Paul and the National Woman's Party, 1910-1928* (New York University Press, 1986), 150-68; Kathryn Kish Sklar, "Why Were Most Politically Active Women Opposed to the ERA in the 1920s?" in Kathryn Kish Sklar and Thomas Dublin, eds., *Women and Power in American History*, Vol. 2 (Prentice Hall, 2002): 154-161.

18 Susan Ware, *Why They Marched: Untold Stories of the Women Who Fought for the Right to Vote* (Harvard University Press, 2019), 75-76; Freeman, *A Room at a Time*, 57-58.

19 Lunardini, *From Equal Suffrage to Equal Rights*,164-65.

20 Ibid.,150-68.

21 Ibid.; Freeman, *A Room at a Time*,129-30,135-38, 203-205; Lemons, *The Woman Citizen*,142-44,181-204, 238-39.

22 Ibid.

23 Ibid., 233-34; J. Kevin Corder and Christina Wolbrecht, "For Women's Equality Day, Here's the Key Question: Was Women's Suffrage a Failure?" *Washington Post*, Aug. 26, 2017.

24 Lemons, *The Woman Citizen*, 234.

25 Estelle B. Friedman, "The New Woman: Changing Views of Women in the 1920s," *Journal of American History* 61, no.2 (1974): 372-93 Quotation from William Leuchtenburg, *Perils of Prosperity: 1914-32* (University of Chicago Press,1958), 160.

26 Cott, Chapter Twenty-two; Chafe, *The Paradox of Change*; For examples of scholars asserting that women reformers kept Progressivism alive through the 1920s, see Clarke A. Chambers, *Seedtime of Reform: American Social Service and Social Action, 1918-1933* (University of Minnesota Press, 1963); Anne Firor Scott, "After Suffrage: Southern Women in the Twenties," *Journal of Southern History*, XXX (Aug. 1964): 298-318; Lemons, *The Woman Citizen*; Perry, "Women in Action."

27 Perkins was also Secretary of Labor under President Harry Truman. Serving from 1933 to1945, to date she remains the longest serving Secretary of Labor. Kirsten Downey, *The Woman*

Behind the New Deal: The Life of Frances Perkins, FDR's Secretary of Labor and His Moral Conscience (Anchor, 2009); On women "New Dealers," see Susan Ware, *Beyond Suffrage: Women in the New Deal* (Harvard University Press, 1987).

28 For examples of the recent emphasis on the positive impact of woman suffrage, see Alia Wong, "How Women's Suffrage Improved Education for a Whole Generation of Children," Aug. 28, 2018, *The Atlantic*, theatlantic.com/education/archive/2018/08/womens-suffrage-educational-improvement/568726/; Schuyler, *The Weight of Their Votes*; Gidlow, "Beyond 1920."

29 See for example Liette Gidlow, "Resistance after Ratification: The Nineteenth Amendment, African American Women, and the Problem of Female Disfranchisement after 1920," in *Women and Social Movements in the U.S., 1600-2000* (Alexandria, VA: Alexander Street, 2017), womhist.alexanderstreet.com/index.html.

30 Carrie Chapman Catt and Nettie Rogers Shuler, *Woman Suffrage and Politics: The Inner Story of the Suffrage Movement* (Charles Scribner's Sons, 1923), 5; The Supreme Court ruled against the challenge to the Nineteenth Amendment in 1922 in *Fairchild v. Hughes* and *Leser v. Garnett*, Lemons, *The Woman Citizen*,14.

31 Marjorie Spruill (Wheeler), *New Women of the New South: The Leaders of the Woman Suffrage Movement in the Southern States* (Oxford University Press, 1993),181. Florida called a special session only after a state supreme court justice reminded the governor that if the state failed to put the amendment into effect, the enforcement clause of the Nineteenth Amendment and perhaps of the Fifteen Amendment might be invoked.; Gidlow, "Resistance after Ratification."

32 Marjorie J. Spruill, "Bringing in the South: Southern Ladies, White Supremacy, and State's Rights in the Fight for Woman Suffrage," Chapter Nine, and Rosalyn Terborg-Penn, "African American Women and the Woman Suffrage Movement," Chapter Ten, in Spruill, *One Woman, One Vote*, Second Edition; Schuyler, *The Weight of Their Votes*; Gidlow, "Resistance after Ratification."

33 Examples: Australia enfranchised white women in 1902 but did not extend the vote to aboriginal people of either sex until 1962. Canada enfranchised white women in 1918 but no "First Canadians" of either sex could vote until 1960. Chinese Canadians of both sexes were enfranchised in 1947. In 1919 Kenya and Rhodesia enfranchised only white women: in 1956 Kenya extended the vote to African women and men with educational and property requirements that were abolished in 1963; Rhodesia (which became Zimbabwe in 1980) adopted universal suffrage without regard for race in 1987. Mart Martin, *The Almanac of Women and Minorities in World Politics* (Westview Press, 2000); Jad Adams, *Women and the Vote: A World History* (Oxford University Press, 2014).

34 Wanda A. Hendricks, "Ida B. Wells-Barnett and the Alpha Suffrage Club of Chicago," Chapter Seventeen, and Terborg-Penn, Chapter Ten, in Spruill, *One Woman, One Vote*, Second Edition; Parker, *Unceasing Militant*.

35 Gidlow, "Resistance after Ratification"; Schuyler, *The Weight of Their Votes*; Martha S. Jones, *Vanguard: How Black Women Broke Barriers, Won the Vote, and Insisted on Equality for All* (Basic Books, 2020); On North Carolina see Glenda Elizabeth Gilmore, *Gender and Jim Crow: Women and the Politics of White Supremacy in North Carolina, 1896-1920* (University of North Carolina Press, 1996), 220-24.

36 Ibid.; on Columbia, see Schuyler, *The Weight of Their Votes*, 48-49; quotation, Gidlow, "Resistance after Ratification."

37 Gilmore, *Gender and Jim Crow*, 218; quotations, Gidlow, "Resistance after Ratification."

38 Ibid.

39 Ibid.

40 Ida E. Jones, "Mary McLeod Bethune, True Democracy, and the Fight for Universal Suffrage," *Yellow Rose Journal*, Women's Vote Centennial Commission, nps.gov/articles/000/mary-mcleod-bethune-true-democracy-and-the-fight-for-universal-suffrage.htm; "Mary McLeod Bethune," Turning Point Suffragist Memorial, suffragistmemorial.org/mary-mcleod-bethune-1875-1955/.

41 Terborg-Penn, Chapter Ten; Terborg-Penn, *African American Women in the Struggle for the Vote* (Indiana University Press,

1998),154-55; Archibald Grimké and his two brothers were the sons of Sarah Grimké's and Angelina Grimké Weld's brother Henry and Nancy Weston, enslaved by the Grimké family. In the 1860s, the Grimké Sisters first learned of the brothers and welcomed them as family members, providing financial support for their education. Archibald graduated from Harvard Law School. He named his daughter Angelina Weld Grimké, a poet and writer, for her aunt.; Dickson D. Bruce, Jr., *Archibald Grimké: Portrait of a Black Independent* (Louisiana State University Press, 1993); Schuyler, *The Weight of the Votes*, 52-56.

42 Carolyn Jefferson-Jenkins, *The Untold Story of Women of Color in the League of Women Voters*, (Praeger, 2020), 88-115; Terborg-Penn, Chapter Ten.

43 Freda Kirchwey, "Alice Paul Pulls the Strings," *The Nation*, March 2, 1921, 332-33. In "How Did the National Woman's Party Address the Issue of the Enfranchisement of Black Women, 1919-1924?" by Kathryn Kish Sklar and Jill Dias, in *Women and Social Movements of the United States,1600-2000* (Alexandria, VA: Alexander Street), documents.alexanderstreet.com.

44 Ibid.; Terborg-Penn, Chapter Ten, and Katherine M. Marino, "The International History of the U.S. Suffrage Movement Chapter," Chapter Eleven, in Spruill, *One Woman, One Vote*, Second Edition.

45 Cathleen D. Cahill, *Recasting the Vote: How Women of Color Transformed the Suffrage Movement* (University of North Carolina Press, 2020).

46 Ibid.

47 Ibid.; The American-born children of Chinese immigrants had citizenship rights after 1898, when the U.S. Supreme Court ruled that a person born in the United States to Chinese immigrant parents was a U.S. citizen at birth, a decision based on the Fourteenth Amendment. *United States v. Wong Kim Ark*, 169 U.S. 649 (1898).

48 Laura Prieto, "Votes for Colonized Women," *Process: A Blog for American History*, Organization of American Historians, May 28, 2020, processhistory.org/prieto-votes-colonized/.

49 Ibid.; Allison L. Sneider, *Suffragists in an Imperial Age: U.S. Expansion and the Woman Question, 1870-1929* (Oxford University Press, 2008).

50 "Alaska's Suffrage Star: Alaska Women And The Vote in the 1910s and 1920s," Alaska State Libraries and Archives and Museum, lam.alaska.gov/suffrage-star.

51 Ibid.

52 Sneider, *Suffragists in an Imperial Age*, quotation, 106; Jason Daley, "Five Things To Know About Lili'uokalani, the Last Queen of Hawai'i," *Smithsonian Magazine*, Nov. 10, 2017; Rumi Yasutake, "Women in Hawai'i and the Nineteenth Amendment," *Journal of Women's History*, Vol. 32, No.1, Spring 2020, 32-40.

53 Ibid.; Shawn Gilbert, "Suffragists You Need to Meet: Wilhelmina Dowsett (1861-1929)," League of Women Voters of Diablo Valley, my.lwv.org/california/diablo-valley/article/suffragists-you-need-meet-wilhelmina-dowsett-1861-1929.

54 Yasutake, "Women in Hawai'i and the Nineteenth Amendment."

55 Ibid.

56 Gilbert, "Suffragists You Need to Meet: Wilhelmina Dowsett."

57 Yasutake, "Women in Hawai'i and the Nineteenth Amendment"; Sneider, *Suffragists in an Imperial Age*, 128.

58 Prieto, "Votes for Colonized Women"; Juan R. Torruella, "Ruling America's Colonies: The Insular Cases," *Yale Law & Policy Review*.

59 Sneider, *Suffragists in an Imperial Age*,123-24; Eva-Lotta E. Hedman and John T. Sidel, *Politics and Society in the Twentieth Century: Colonial Legacies, Post-Colonial Trajectories* (Routledge, 2000), 14-15.

60 Sneider, *Suffragists in an Imperial Age*, quotation 124.

61 Leonora C. Angeles, "Philippines Suffragist Movement," *Woman Suffrage and Beyond*, Feb. 22, 2012.

62 Ibid.

63 Prieto, "Votes for Colonized Women"; "More to the Movement," Library of Congress, loc.gov/exhibitions/women-fight-for-the-vote/about-this-exhibition/more-to-the-movement/?st=gallery.

64 Angeles, "Philippines Suffragist Movement."

65 Prieto, "Votes for Colonized Women."

66 Ibid.; Hedman and Sidel, *Politics and Society in the Twentieth Century*, 15.

67 Sneider, *Suffragists in an Imperial Age*, 114-17.

68 Prieto, "Votes for Colonized Women"; G. Jiménez Mu oz, "Deconstructing Colonialist Discourse: Links Between the Women's Suffrage Movement in the United States and Puerto Rico," *Phoebe: An Interdisciplinary Journal of Feminist Scholarship, Theory, and Aesthetics*, 5 (Spring 1993), 9–34; Frances R. Grant, "Porto Rican Women Out for Reform," *Brooklyn Eagle Magazine* (Brooklyn, NY), Oct. 2, 1932, 89.

69 Hahna Cho, "Luisa Capetillo: Feminism and Labor In Puerto Rico," *Backstory*, Sept. 7, 2018, backstoryradio.org/blog/luisa-capetillo-feminism-and-labor-in-puerto-rico/; "Luisa Capetillo: Puerto Rican Changemaker," Library of Congress, blogs.loc.gov/international-collections/2019/11/luisa-capetillo-puerto-rican-changemaker/; Prieto, "Votes for Colonized Women."

70 Ibid.; Milagros Benet de Newton, "More to the Movement," Library of Congress; Grant, "Porto Rican Women Out for Reform"; María de Barceló-Miller, "Halfhearted Solidarity: Women Workers and the Women's Suffrage Movement in Puerto Rico During the 1920s," in Felix Matos-Rodriguez, and Linda Delgado, Linda eds., *Puerto Rican Women's History: New Perspectives* (Routledge 2015):126–142.

71 Anne S. Macpherson, "The 19th Amendment Didn't Grant Puerto Rican Women Suffrage," *Washington Post*, Aug. 26, 2020.

72 Ibid.; On the NWP's aid to Puerto Rican suffragists, see Sneider, *Suffragists in an Imperial Age*, 117-34.

73 Jennifer Johnson, "After the 19th Amendment: Women in US Virgin Islands Secure the Vote," National Archives, rediscovering-black-history.blogs.archives.gov/2020/12/16/virgin-islands-secure-the-vote/.

74 Ibid.; Prieto, "Votes for Colonized Women."

75 Ibid.; Johnson, "After the 19th Amendment."

76 Prieto, "Votes for Colonized Women"; "Guam and the 19th Amendment," National Park Service, nps.gov/articles/guam-and-the-19th-amendment.htm; Becky Little, "How the United States Ended Up With Guam," history.com/news/how-the-united-states-ended-up-with-guam.

77 "American Samoa and the 19th Amendment," National Park Service, nps.gov/articles/american-samoa-and-the-19th-amendment.htm; Ann M. Simmons, "American Samoans Aren't Actually U.S. Citizens. Does That Violate the Constitution?" *Los Angeles Times*, April 6, 2018.

78 Meagan Flynn and Teddy Amenabar, "Could D.C. Become a State? Explaining the Hurdles to Statehood, *Washington Post*, Jan. 8, 2021.

79 Ibid.

80 Ibid.

81 Wolbrecht and Corder, *A Century of Votes for Women*.

82 Barbara Ransby, *Ella Baker and The Black Freedom Movement: A Radical Democratic Vision* (University of North Carolina Press, 2005).

83 Ibid.; Ramachandra Guha, "How the Suffragettes influenced Mahatma Gandhi," *Hindustan Times*, New Delhi, India, Feb. 24, 2018.

84 Ransby, *Ella Baker*.

85 Katherine Mellen Charron, *Freedom's Teacher: The Life of Septima Clark* (University of North Carolina Press, 2012).

86 Chana Kai Lee, *For Freedom's Sake: The Life of Fannie Lou Hamer* (University of Illinois Press, 2000).

87 Ibid.

88 "Introduction: The Origins and Evolution of the Voting Rights Act," in *50 Years of the Voting Rights Act*, Joint Center for Political and Economic Studies, jointcenter.org/wp-content/uploads/2019/11/VRA-report-3.5.15-1130-amupdated.pdf.

89 In 1964, five states had a poll tax: Alabama, Arkansas, Mississippi, Texas, and Virginia. The amendment applied only to federal elections. In 1966, a Supreme Court decision, *Harper v. Virginia Board of Elections*, made poll taxes unconstitutional in elections at any level, not only federal. *Harper v. Virginia Board of Elections*, 383 U.S. 663 (1966); John Dittmer, *Local People: The Struggle for Civil Rights in Mississippi* (University of Illinois Press, 1995).

90 Bettye Collier-Thomas and V. P. Franklin, *Sisters in the Struggle: African American Women in the Civil Rights-Black Power*

Movement (New York University Press, 2001); Vicky L. Crawford, Jacqueline Anne Rouse, and Barbara Woods, *Women in the Civil Rights Movement: Trailblazers and Torchbearers, 1941-1965* (Indiana University Press, 1993).

91 Keisha N. Blain, "'God Is Not Going to Put It in Your Lap.' What Made Fannie Lou Hamer's Message on Civil Rights So Radical—And So Enduring," *Time*, Oct. 4, 2019.

92 Ibid.

93 Robert A. Pratt, *Selma's Bloody Sunday: Protest, Voting Rights, and the Struggle for Racial Equality* (Johns Hopkins University Press, 2017).

94 Jon Meacham, *His Truth Is Marching On: John Lewis and the Power of Hope* (Random House, 2020).

95 John Lewis, *Walking with the Wind: A Memoir of the Movement* (Simon & Schuster, 2015); German Lopez, "How the Voting Rights Act Transformed Black Voting Rights in the South," *Vox*, vox.com/2015/3/6/8163229/voting-rights-act-1965.

96 ACLU: "Voting Rights Act: Major Dates in History," aclu.org/voting-rights-act-major-dates-history; Lopez, "How the Voting Rights Act Transformed Black Voting Rights in the South"; Library of Congress, "Voting Rights for African Americans"; Jo Freeman, "Gender Gaps in Presidential Elections," *Political Science and Politics*, Vol. 32, No. 2, June 1999, 191-92; Wolbrecht and Corder, *A Century of Votes for Women*, 236-37.

97 Carnegie Corporation, "Voting Rights: A Short History," Nov.18, 2019.

98 Rosen, "'Give Us the Ballot'"; In 1982 the Voting Rights Act was extended for another twenty-five years. In 2006 it was extended for an additional twenty-five-year period. Carnegie Corporation, "Voting Rights: A Short History."

99 Marjorie J. Spruill, *Divided We Stand: The Battle Over Women's Rights and Family Values That Polarized American Politics* (New York: Bloomsbury, 2017), 14-29; Historian Cynthia Harrison noted that most women's rights advocates in the 1940s through mid-1960s strenuously avoided the word "feminist" which some people associated with "selfish" and "strident" women, and that even National Woman's Party members "employed the word feminism cautiously, generally restricting its usage *en famille*." Furthermore, "not until the appearance in 1966 of the National Organization for Women...did women fighting on behalf of women reclaim the word." Cynthia Harrison, *On Account of Sex: The Politics of Women's Issues 1945-1968* (University of California Press, 1988), xi.

100 Spruill, *Divided We Stand*,14-29; On the origins and development of the modern women's rights movement, see Harrison, *On Account of Sex*; Ruth Rosen, *The World Split Open: How the Modern Women's Movement Changed America* (Penguin, 2003); Sara M. Evans, *Tidal Wave: How Women Changed America at Century's End* (Free Press, 2003); Susan M. Hartmann, *From Margin to Mainstream: American Women and Politics Since 1960* (Knopf, 1989); Dorothy Sue Cobble, Linda Gordon, and Astrid Henry, *Feminism Unfinished: A Short, Surprising History of American Women's Movements* (W.W. Norton & Company, 2014).

101 Spruill, *Divided We Stand*, 17-18.; Harrison, *On Account of Sex*,176-82.

102 Jo Freeman, "How 'Sex' Got into Title VII: Persistent Opportunism as a Maker of Public Policy," in Jo Freeman, *We Will Be Heard: Women's Struggles for Political Power in the United States* (Rowan and Littlefield, 2008),171-90.

103 Flora Davis, *Moving the Mountain: The Women's Movement in America since 1960* (University of Illinois Press, 1991, 1999), 14-93; Daniel Horowitz, *Betty Friedan and the Making of "The Feminine Mystique": The American Left, the Cold War, and Modern Feminism* (University of Massachusetts Press, 1998); Spruill, *Divided We Stand*, 14-41.

104 "NOW Statement of Purpose, 1966," now.org/about/history/statement-of-purpose/.

105 "Aileen Hernandez, 90, Ex-NOW President and Feminist Trailblazer Dies," *New York Times*, Feb. 28, 2017; "NOW Mourns the Loss of Aileen Hernandez," NOW press release, Feb. 27, 2017, now.org/media-center/press-release/now-mourns-the-loss-of-aileen-hernandez/; On women coming to the feminist movement from the civil rights movement and the New Left, see Sara M. Evans, *Personal Politics: The Roots of Women's Liberation in the Civil Rights Movement and the New Left* (Vintage Books, 1980); Alice Echols, *Daring to be Bad: Radical Feminism in America, 1967-1975* (University of Minnesota Press, 1997).

106 Davis, *Moving the Mountain*, 66-68; Spruill, *Divided We Stand*, 20.

107 Ibid., 21-22; Friedan, *It Changed My Life, Writings on the Women's Movement*, 184-92 (Harvard University Press, 1998); Rosen, *The World Split Open*, 92-93.

108 Ibid.,14-15, 20, 25-29; Liz Carpenter, *Getting Better All the Time* (Simon and Schuster, 1987),121-128; Barbara Winslow, *Shirley Chisholm: Catalyst for Change* (Routledge, 2018); Friedan, *It Changed My Life*, 208-32; Tanya Melich, *The Republican War Against Women: An Insider's Report from Behind the Lines* (Bantam Books, 1994); Leandra Ruth Zarnow, *Battling Bella: The Protest Politics of Bella Abzug* (Harvard University Press, 2019).

109 Spruill, *Divided We Stand*, 28-29; Max Sherman, *Barbara Jordan: Speaking the Truth with Eloquent Thunder* (University of Texas Press, 2007); Barbara Winslow, *Shirley Chisholm: Catalyst for Change, 1926-2005* (Westview Press, 2014).

110 In *Roe v. Wade* (1973), the U.S. Supreme Court declared that a woman is legally entitled to have an abortion until the end of the first trimester of pregnancy and that a state could not proscribe abortion until after the fetus became viable. Spruill, *Divided We Stand*, 29-30, 32-50.

111 Ibid., 29-32.

112 Jone Johnson Lewis, "Which States Have Ratified the Equal Rights Amendment,' *ThoughtCo*, Aug. 26, 2020, thoughtco.com/which-states-ratified-the-era-3528872.; Jane J. Mansbridge, *Why We Lost the ERA* (University of Chicago Press, 1986).

113 Ibid.; Spruill, *Divided We Stand*, 71-113; Ruth Murray Brown, *For a "Christian America": A History of the Religious Right* (Prometheus Books, 2002); Donald T. Critchlow, *Phyllis Schlafly and Grassroots Conservatism: A Woman's Crusade* (Princeton University Press, 2008).

114 Spruill, *Divided We Stand*, 32, 84-85, 95, 187-88, 306, 127, 201-202; Donald G. Mathews and Jane Sherron De Hart, *Sex, Gender, and the Politics of ERA: A State and the Nation* (Oxford University Press, 1998).

115 Spruill, *Divided We Stand*.

116 Ibid.; *The Spirit of Houston: The First National Women's Conference: An Official Report to the President, the Congress and the People of the United States* (U.S. Government Printing Office, 1978).

117 Spruill, *Divided We Stand*; For a first-person account from the conservative perspective, see Rosemary Thomson, *The Price of LIBerty* (Creation House, 1978).

118 Spruill, *Divided We Stand*, Chapters 13 and 14; Melich, *The Republican War against Women*.

119 Spruill, *Divided We Stand*, 316-17.

120 Wolbrecht and Corder, *A Century of Votes for Women*, 236-37.

121 Ibid. Though women split their votes almost equally between Reagan (46%) and Carter (45), men favored Reagan by a large margin. Exit polls showed that men gave 54% of their votes for Reagan, creating an unprecedented eight-percent-age-point difference between women's and men's choices. news.gallup.com/poll/158588/gender-gap-2012-vote-largest-gallup-history.aspx.

122 Wolbrecht and Corder, *A Century of Votes for Women*, 7-8; When referring to the "gender gap," most scholars and pundits mean the difference in the percentage of women and men who support a given candidate, usually the winning candidate, not the gap within a gender. Susan J. Carroll, "The Gender Gap as a Tool for Women's Political Empowerment: The Formative Years, 1980-84," in Angie Maxwell and Todd Shields, eds. *The Legacy of Second Wave Feminism in American Politics* (Cham Palgrave Macmillan, 2018); J. Ryan-Hume, "The National Organization for Women and the Democratic Party in Reagan's America," *The Historical Journal*, 1-23. doi:doi:10.1017/S0018246X20000175; Spruill, *Divided We Stand*, 316-318.

123 Ibid.; Wolbrecht and Corder, *A Century of Votes for Women*, 7-8.

124 Spruill, *Divided We Stand*, 316-17, 325; Melich, *The Republican War against Women*; Marjorie J. Spruill, "Feminism, Anti-feminism, and the New Southern Strategy," in Maxwell and Shields, *The Legacy of Second-Wave Feminism in American Politics*; Angie Maxwell and Todd G. Shields, *The Long Southern Strategy: How Chasing White Voters in the South Changed American Politics* (Oxford University Press, 2019).

125 CAWP 2017 Fact Sheet, "The Gender Gap: Voting Choices

in Presidential Elections," cawp.rutgers.edu/sites/default/files/resources/ggpresvote.pdf; Juliet Eilperin, "For Obama, Rainbow White House Was 'A Moment Worth Savoring,'" Washington Post, June 30, 2015.
126 Spruill, Divided We Stand, 325-44.
127 Ibid.; Wolbrecht and Corder, A Century of Votes for Women, 216.
128 Rosen, "'Give Us the Ballot'"; Carnegie Corporation, "Voting Rights: A Short History"; ACLU: "Voting Rights Act: Major Dates in History."
129 Ibid.; Lisa Rab, "Why Republicans Can't Find the Big Voter Fraud Conspiracy," Politico, April 2, 2017; Andrew Gumbel, "Election Fraud and the Myths of American Democracy," Social Research 75, no. 4 (2008): 1109-134. jstor.org/stable/40972109; Rosen, "'Give Us the Ballot'"; LWV, "How Voter ID Laws Disproportionately Impact Women – And What We're Doing About It." lwv.org/blog/how-voter-id-laws-disproportionately-impact-women-and-what-were-doing-about-it; Danyelle Solomon and Connor Maxwell, "Women of Color: A Collective Powerhouse in the U.S. Electorate," Center for American Progress, Nov.19, 2019 americanprogress.org/issues/race/reports/2019/11/19/477309/women-color-collective-powerhouse-u-s-electorate/
130 Luke Broadwater, "After Death of John Lewis, Democrats Renew Push for Voting Rights Law," New York Times, July 21, 2020.
131 Editorial, The Most Extreme Republican Platform in Memory," New York Times, July 18, 2016; Editorial, "The Democratic Platform is Far More Liberal than Four Years Ago. Here's Why That Matters," Washington Post, July 7, 2016.
132 Spruill Divided We Stand, 334-43; Wolbrecht and Corder, A Century of Votes for Women, 228-229.
133 Cleve Wootson, "Susan B. Anthony's Tombstone Covered in 'I Voted' Stickers, Washington Post, Nov. 8, 2016; Drew DeSilver, "Trump's Victory Another Example of How Electoral College Wins are Bigger Than Popular Vote Ones," Dec. 20, 2016, Pew Research Center, pewresearch.org/facttank/2016/12/20/why-electoral-college-landslides-are-easier-to-win-than-popular-vote-ones/.
134 Wolbrecht and Corder, A Century of Votes for Women, 230-31; Of independents, the vote was 43 percent Trump, 42 percent Clinton. Pew Research Center, "An Examination of the 2016 Electorate, Based on Validated Voters August 9, 2018," pewresearch.org/politics/2018/08/09/an-examination-of-the-2016-electorate-based-on-validated-voters/.
135 Ibid. In 2018, the Pew Research Center estimated the 2016 presidential election gender gap was 13 percent, based on validated voters. Exit polls conducted in 2016 by Edison Research had reported an eleven-point gender gap. CAWP 2017 Fact Sheet, "The Gender Gap: Voting Choices in Presidential Elections"; Wolbrecht and Corder, A Century of Votes for Women, 230-31.
136 Ibid., 228-33; Pew Research Center, "An Examination of the 2016 Electorate, Based on Validated Voters August 9, 2018"; Molly Ball, "Donald Trump Didn't Really Win 52% of White Women in 2016," Time, Oct. 18, 2018.
137 Angie Maxwell, "What We Get Wrong about the Southern Strategy," Washington Post, July 26, 2019; Angie Maxwell, "Why Southern White Women Vote against Feminism," Washington Post, Sept. 11, 2019; Maxwell and Shields, The Long Southern Strategy.
138 Wolbrecht and Corder, A Century of Votes for Women, 229-30, 235.
139 Trump had a fourteen-point advantage with voters from fifty to six-four and an eleven-point lead among voters sixty-five and older. Pew Research Center, "An Examination of the 2016 Electorate."
140 On the action inspired by women's outrage over the 2026 election, see Rebecca Traister, Good and Mad: The Revolutionary Power of Women (Simon and Schuster, 2019); Michael Hais and Morley Winograd, "The Future is Female," Feb.19, 2020. Brookings Institute, brookings.edu/blog/fixgov/2020/02/19/the-future-is-female-how-the-growing-political-power-of-women-will-remake-american-politics/; Anemona Hartocollis and Yamiche Alcindor, "Women's March Highlights as Huge Crowds Protest Trump: 'We're Not Going Away,'" New York Times, Jan. 21, 2017; Kaveh Waddell, "The Exhausting Work of

Tallying America's Largest Protest," The Atlantic, Jan. 23, 2017, theatlantic.com/technology/archive/2017/01/womens-march-protest-count/514166/.
141 Ball, Pelosi (Henry Holt and Company, 2020), 258-60.
142 Ibid.; Traister, Good and Mad; Spruill, Divided We Stand, 322.
143 Ibid; Ball, Pelosi, quotations, page 259; Traister, Good and Mad.
144 Politico: The WOMEN Candidate Tracker, A Collaboration with the Center for American Women and Politics at Rutgers and the Women in Public Service Project at The Wilson Center, Nov. 28, 2018, politico.com/interactives/2018/women-en-rule-candidate-tracker/; Jens Manuel Krogstad, Luis Noe-Bustamante, and Antonio Flores, Pew Research Center, "Historic Highs in 2018 Voter Turnout Extended Across Racial and Ethnic Groups," pewresearch.org/fact-tank/2019/05/01/historic-highs-in-2018-voter-turnout-extended-across-racial-and-ethnic-groups/.
145 Reis Thebault and Hannah Knowles, "Georgia Purged 309,000 Voters from Its Rolls," Washington Post, Dec. 17, 2019; Adam Edelman and Dartunorro Clark, "Democrat Stacey Abrams Ends Bid for Georgia Governor, Accuses Winner of Voter Suppression," NBC News, Nov. 16, 2018, nbcnews.com/politics/elections/democrat-stacey-abrams-ends-candidacy-georgia-governor-race-blasts-process-n937356.
146 Vanessa Williams, "Stacey Abrams Chooses Building a National Voter Protection Program Over Running for President in 2020," Washington Post, Aug.13, 2019; Stacey Abrams, Lead from the Outside: How to Build Your Future and Make Real Change (Henry Holt and Company, 2018); Stacey Abrams, Our Time is Now: Purpose, and the Fight for a Fair America (Henry Holt and Company, 2020).
147 For examples, see: Martha S. Jones, Vanguard: How Black Women Broke Barriers, Won the Vote, and Insisted on Equality for All (New Basic Books, 2020); Cathleen D. Cahill, Recasting the Vote: How Women of Color Transformed the Suffrage Movement (University of North Carolina Press, 2020); Library of Congress, "More to the Movement," loc.gov/exhibitions/women-fight-for-the-vote/about-this-exhibition/more-to-the-movement/?st=gallery; National Portrait Gallery "Votes for Women: A Portrait of Persistence," npg.si.edu/exhibition/votes-for-women?utm_source=siedu&utm_medium=referral&utm_campaign=spotlight.
148 Women's Vote Centennial, womensvote100.org/ and ourstory100.com/; DeNeen L. Brown, "Ida B. Wells Gets Her Due as a Black Suffragist Who Rejected Movement's Racism," Washington Post, Aug. 25, 2020; United States Mint Announces Design for 2020 Women's Suffrage Centennial Silver Medal, usmint.gov/news/press-releases/united-states-mint-announces-design-for-2020-womens-suffrage-centennial-silver-medal; "Forever Stamp Honors Centennial of Women's Suffrage," Aug.14, 2020, about.usps.com/newsroom/national-releases/2020/0814ma-forever-stamp-honors-centennial-of-women-suffrage.htm.
149 For a review of ERA history since 1972, including the "three states strategy" and twenty-first century efforts to complete ratification, see Lewis, "Which States Have Ratified the Equal Rights Amendment?"; "Why Democratic Congresswomen Wore White Again to Send a Message at the State of the Union," Time, time.com/5777514/women-wearing-white-state-of-the-union/; Veronica Stracqualursi, CNN, "Virginia General Assembly Passes Resolutions Ratifying ERA," Jan.15, 2020, cnn.com/2020/01/15/politics/virginia-general-assembly-equal-rights-amendment/index.html.
150 Kylie Hubbard, "Suffrage Coalition to Unveil Burn Memorial on Saturday," Knox News, June 7, 2018, knoxnews.com/story/news/2018/06/07/suffrage-coalition-unveil-harry-burn-memorial-downtown-market-square/677044002/; Tennessee Triumph Women's Suffrage Monument, artsandheritage.us/tn-triumph-womens-suffrage-statue/; Tennessee Woman Suffrage Monument in Centennial Park," / tnsuffragemonument.org/.
151 Mary Tyler March, "Virginia Gets New Museum Honoring Suffragists," wamu.org/story/20/01/24/virginia-gets-new-museum-honoring-suffragists-100-years-after-women-got-the-right-to-vote/; Turning Point Suffragist Memorial, suffragistmemorial.org/memorial-dedication-postponed/.
152 Monumental Women, monumentalwomen.org.

518 ☆ ONE WOMAN, ONE VOTE

153 Sarah Cascone, "Hillary Clinton Urged Americans to Vote
During the Unveiling of a New Monument to Suffragists in
Central Park," Aug. 26, 2020, Artnet News, news.artnet.com/
art-world/central-park-womens-rights-pioneers-monu-
ment-1904271.
154 Amy Harmon, "The Number of People with the Virus
Who Died in the U.S. Passes 300,000," New York Times, Dec. 14,
2020; according to the Center for Disease Control Covid Date
Tracker, by January 5, there had been 352,464 deaths, covid.cdc.
gov/covid-data-tracker/#cases_casesper100klast7days.
155 Ellen Carol DuBois, "A Pandemic Nearly Derailed the
Women's Suffrage Movement," National Geographic, April 20,
2020.
156 Zach Montellaro, "Pandemic Threatens Monster Turnout
in November," Politico, March 21, 2020, politico.com/
news/2020/03/31/states-struggle-voting-pandemic-155700.
157 Larry Buchanan, Quoctrung Bui and Jugal K. Patel, "Black
Lives Matter May Be the Largest Movement in U.S. History,"
New York Times, July 3, 2020.
158 Luke Broadwater, "After Death of John Lewis, Democrats
Renew Push for Voting Rights Law," New York Times, July 21,
2020; David Greenberg, "A Civil Rights Legend Who Saw
Humanity in His Oppressors," Dec. 26, 2020, Politico, politico.
com/news/magazine/2020/12/26/john-lewis-civ-
il-rights-legend-obituary-2020-445135.
159 Eugene Scott, "Democrats are Avoiding 'Defund the
Police,' While Republicans Harp On It," Washington Post, June
11, 2020; Aimee Ortiz and Johnny Diaz, "George Floyd Protests
Reignite Debate Over Confederate Statues," New York Times,
June 3, 2020; Michelle Mark and Connor Perrett, "Trump Said
He Intends to Declare Antifa as a Terrorist Organization. Here's
What We Know about the Decades-old, Leaderless Group,"
Business Insider, June 2, 2020, businessinsider.com/what-is-an-
tifa-movement-charlottesville-va-trump-news-2017-8.
160 Jane C. Timm, "GOP Recruits Army of Poll Watchers to
Fight Voter Fraud No One Can Prove Exists," NBC News, nbc-
news.com/politics/donald-trump/gop-recruits-army-poll-
watchers-fight-voter-fraud-no-can-n1217391; Allan Rap-
peport, "Postal Service Pick With Ties to Trump Raises Concerns Ahead of 2020 Election," New York Times, May 7, 2020.
161 Alexander Burns, "Joe Biden's Vice-Presidential Pick:
Kamala Harris," New York Times, Aug. 11, 2020.
162 Peter Baker and Maggie Haberman, "McConnell Vows
Vote on Ginsburg Replacement as Her Death Upends the 2020
Race," New York Times, Sept. 18, 2020.
163 Ruth Graham, "For Conservative Christian Women, Amy
Coney Barrett's Success Is Personal," New York Times, Sept. 28,
2020; Eagle Forum, Oct. 26, 2020, eagleforum.org/publica-
tions/press-releases/amy-coney-barretts-confirmation-to-the-
supreme-court.html.
164 Samantha Schmidt, "Susan B. Anthony Was Arrested for
Voting When Women Couldn't. Now Trump Will Pardon Her,"
Washington Post, Aug. 18, 2020; Ellen Carol DuBois, "Taking the
Law into Our Own Hands: Bradwell, Minor, and Suffrage Mili-
tance in the 1870s," Chapter Six in Spruill, One Woman, One
Vote, Second Edition.
165 Lisa Lerer, "'Please Like Me,' Trump Begged. For Many
Women, It's Way Too Late," New York Times, Oct. 17, 2020;
Christina Wolbrecht and Erin Cassese, "President Trump's
Appeals to Women Show That the More Things Change, the
More They Stay the Same," Center for American Women and
Politics (CAWP), Nov. 2, 2020, cawp.rutgers.edu/election-anal-
ysis/trump-appeals-suburban-women.
166 Erin Haines, "The Pandemic is Political—and Women are
Angry at the President, USA Today, Oct. 16, 2020.
167 Ibid.; Courtney Subramanian, "Trump Campaign's Pitch
to Women Voters: Let's Get Back to Pre-pandemic 'Normal,'"
USA Today, Oct. 10, 2020.
168 Domenico Montanaro, "The 2020 Election Was a Good
One for Republicans Not Named Trump," NPR, Nov. 11, 2020,
npr.org/2020/11/11/933435840/the-2020-election-was-a-
good-one-for-republicans-not-named-trump; Kate Sullivan
and Jennifer Agiesta, "Biden's Popular Vote Margin over
Trump Tops 7 Million," CNN Politics, Dec. 4, 2020, cnn.
com/2020/12/04/politics/biden-popular-vote-margin-7-mil-
lion/index.html.
169 These statistics about the election come from VoteCast.

Jocelyn Noveck, "Women Crucial to Biden's Win, Even as Gender Gap Held Steady," AP News, Nov. 16, 2020 apnews.com/
article/election-2020-joe-biden-donald-trump-voting-rights-
elections-84ef3db79532c0029894ff25a316370b.
170 Ibid.
171 Astead W. Herndon, "Georgia Was a Big Win for Democrats. Black Women Did the Groundwork," New York Times,
Dec. 5, 2020.
172 Amber Phillips and Peter W. Stevenson, "What Happens
Next in Trump's Impeachment?" Washington Post, Feb. 12, 2021.
173 Ibid.; Eric Lipton, "Trump Call to Georgia Official Might
Violate State and Federal Law," New York Times, Jan. 3, 2021;
Joan Walsh, "Democrats Did What They Had To Do: Beat Back
Voter Suppression and Keep Voter Turnout High," The Nation,
Jan. 22, 2021.
174 Jocelyn Noveck, "Women Crucial to Biden's Win."
175 Ibid.
176 Deena Zaru, Kiara Brantley-Jones , and Arielle Mitropoulos, "Record Gain for Women in Congress Highlights Lack of
Diversity among Republicans," ABC News, Dec. 5, 2020, abc-
news.go.com/Politics/record-gain-women-congress-high-
lights-lack-diversity-republicans/story?id=74023373.
177 Ibid.; Marjorie Dannenfelse," Election of Pro-Life Women
Shows Tide Is Turning," Nov. 18, 2020, RealClear Politics, real-
clearpolitics.com/articles/2020/11/18/election_of_pro-life_
women_shows_tide_is_turning_144687.html#!; Erin Delmore,
NBC, "Inside the Movement that Swept Republican Women
into Congress," Nov. 20, 2020, nbcnews.com/know-your-val-
ue/feature/inside-movement-swept-republican-women-con-
gress-ncna1248394; Rachael Bade, "GOP Women's
Record-Breaking Success Reflects Party's Major Shift on
Recruiting and Supporting Female Candidates, Washington
Post, Dec. 7, 2020; Swanee Hunt, "Republican Women in the
House Could Change Everything," CNN Opinion, Jan. 2, 2021,
cnn.com/2021/01/02/opinions/republican-wom-
en-117th-congress-hunt/index.html.
178 Zaru, Brantley-Jones, and Mitropoulos, "Record Gain for
Women in Congress Highlights Lack of Diversity among
Republicans"; Alexa Mikhail, "Women Are at the Table: Biden
Nominates a Record Number of Women for His Cabinet," The
19th, Jan. 22, 2021, 19thnews.org/2021/01/biden-women-cabi-
net-nominations/?utm_campaign=19th-social&utm_source=-
facebook&utm_medium=social&fbclid=IwAR3d-
ZQkwhmYOChNF6JN4kVgSRZkbOt8HNfN8gouCqHtp-
gNsZWFDGhMX6dTY.
179 Vanessa Friedman, "Kamala Harris in a White Suit, Dressing for History: This Wasn't about Fashion, It Was about Politics, Past and Future," New York Times, Nov.8, 2020.
180 Quotation from The Woman Citizen, Sept. 4, 1920; Barbara
Stuhler, For the Public Record: A Documentary History of the
League of Women Voters (Greenwood Publishing Group, 2000),
26.
181 Sarah Maisey, "Why Kamala Harris's Suffragette White
Suit is a Beacon of Hope for the Future," The National, Nov. 9,
2020, thenationalnews.com/about-us.
182 Ibid.
183 Ibid.
184 Friedman, "Kamala Harris in a White Suit."

October 28, 1920

Life

Vol. 76. Copyright, 1920, Life Publishing Company No. 1982

Price 15 Cents

"Congratulations"

Appendix I

THE ELECTORAL THERMOMETER

Woman Suffrage Won by State
Constitutional Amendments and
Legislative Acts Before the Proclamation
of the Nineteenth Amendment

		Electoral Vote
1890	Wyoming was admitted to statehood with woman suffrage, having had it as a territory since 1869.	3
1893	Colorado adopted a constitutional amendment after defeat in 1877.	6
1896	Idaho adopted a constitutional amendment on its first submission.	4
1896	Utah, having had woman suffrage as a territory since 1870, was deprived of it by Congress in 1887. It was reinstated by constitutional referendum when admitted to statehood.	4
1910	Washington adopted a constitutional amendment after defeats in 1889 and 1898. The territorial legislature twice enacted woman suffrage, but lost it by court decisions.	7
1911	California adopted a constitutional amendment after defeat in 1896.	13
1912	Oregon adopted a constitutional amendment after defeats in 1884, 1900, 1906, 1908, 1910.	5
1912	Kansas adopted a constitutional amendment after defeats in 1867 and 1893.	10
1912	Arizona adopted a constitutional amendment submitted as a result of referendum petitions.	3
1913	Illinois was the first state to get presidential suffrage by legislative enactment.	29
1914	Montana adopted a constitutional amendment on its first submission.	4
1914	Nevada adopted a constitutional amendment on its first submission.	3
1917	North Dakota secured presidential suffrage by legislative enactment, after defeat of a constitutional amendment in 1914.	5
1917	Nebraska secured presidential suffrage by legislative enactment after defeats of a constitutional amendment in 1882 and 1914.	8

APPENDIX I ☆ 521

| 1917 | Rhode Island secured presidential suffrage by legislative enactment after defeat of a constitutional amendment in 1887. | 5 |

1917   Rhode Island secured presidential suffrage by legislative enactment   5
after defeat of a constitutional amendment in 1887.

1917   New York adopted a constitutional amendment after defeat in 1915.   45

1917   Arkansas secured primary suffrage by legislative enactment.   9

1918   Michigan adopted a constitutional amendment after defeats in 1874,   15
1912, and 1913. Secured presidential suffrage by legislative enactment
in 1917.

1918   Texas secured primary suffrage by legislative enactment.   20

1918   South Dakota adopted a constitutional amendment after six prior   5
campaigns for suffrage had been defeated, each time by a mobilization
of the alien vote by American-born political manipulators. In that state,
as in nine others in 1918, the foreign-born could vote on their "first
papers" and citizenship was not a qualification for the vote. The last
defeat, in 1916, had been so definitely proved to have been caused by
the vote of German-Russians in nine counties that public sentiment,
in addition to the war spirit, aroused a desire to make a change in the
law that resulted in victory.

1918   Oklahoma adopted a constitutional amendment after defeat in 1910.   10

1919   Indiana secured presidential suffrage by legislative enactment in 1917.   15
Rendered doubtful by a court decision, the law was re-enacted with
but six dissenting votes.

1919   Maine secured presidential suffrage by legislative enactment after   6
defeat of a constitutional amendment in 1917.

1919   Missouri secured presidential suffrage by legislative enactment after   18
defeat of a constitutional amendment in 1914.

1919   Iowa secured presidential suffrage by legislative enactment after   13
defeat of a constitutional amendment in 1916.

1919   Minnesota secured presidential suffrage by legislative enactment.   12

1919   Ohio secured presidential suffrage by legislative enactment after   24
defeat of referendum on the law in 1917 and of a constitutional
amendment in 1912 and 1914.

1919   Wisconsin secured presidential suffrage by legislative enactment after   13
defeat of a constitutional amendment in 1912.

1919   Tennessee secured presidential suffrage by legislative enactment.   12

1920   Kentucky secured presidential suffrage by legislative enactment.   13

Total of presidential electors for whom women were entitled to vote
before the Nineteenth Amendment was adopted, 339.
(Full number 531).

In 1913 the territory of Alaska had adopted woman suffrage.
It was the first bill approved by the governor.

From: The National American Woman Suffrage Association, *VICTORY: How Women Won It*
(New York: H.W. Wilson Company, 1940), Appendix 4, 161-164.

Appendix II

CHRONOLOGY OF CONGRESSIONAL ACTION

1868   Passage of the Fourteenth Amendment, which introduced the word male into the Constitution.

1869   First woman suffrage bill introduced into the House.

1869   Hearing on woman suffrage.

1878   Introduction by Senator Sargent of the Woman Suffrage Amendment in its final form.

1887   January 25, first vote in the Senate, yeas 16, nays 34, 50 voting.

1914   March 19, second vote in the Senate, yeas 35, nays 34, 69 voting.

1915   January 12, first vote in the House, yeas 174, nays 204, 378 voting.

1917   September 24, creation of Woman Suffrage Committee in the House.

1918   January 10, second vote in the House, yeas 274, nays 136, 410 voting.

1918   October 1, third vote in the Senate, yeas, including pairs, 62,

1919   February 10, fourth vote in the Senate, yeas, including pairs, 63, nays 33.

1919   May 21, third vote in the House, yeas 304, nays 89.

1919   June 4, fifth vote in the Senate, yeas, including pairs, 66, nays 30.

1920   August 26, proclamation by the Secretary of State of the Nineteenth Amendment.

From: The National American Woman Suffrage Association. *VICTORY: How Women Won It* (New York: H.W. Wilson Company, 1940), Appendix 8, 172.

Appendix III
RECORD OF ACTION ON NATIONAL SUFFRAGE AMENDMENT IN THE STATES 1919 -1920

	STATE	DATE OF RATIFICATION	VOTE SENATE	VOTE HOUSE	PARTY OF GOVERNOR	PARTY CONTROLLING LEGISLATURE
1	Wisconsin	June 10, 1919	24-1	54-2	Rep.	Rep.
2	*Michigan	June 10, 1919	Unan.	Unan.	Rep.	Rep.
3	*Kansas	June 16, 1919	Unan.	Unan.	Rep.	Rep.
4	*Ohio	June 16, 1919	27-3	73-6	Dem.	Rep.
5	*New York	June 16, 1919	Unan.	Unan.	Dem.	Rep.
6	Illinois	June 17, 1919	Unan.	133-4	Rep.	Rep.
7	Pennsylvania	June 24, 1919	32-6	153-44	Rep.	Rep.
8	Massachusetts	June 25, 1919	34-5	184-77	Rep.	Rep.
9	*Texas	June 29, 1919	Unan.	96-21	Dem.	Dem.
10	*Iowa	July 2, 1919	Unan.	95-5	Rep.	Rep.
11	*Missouri	July 3, 1919	28-3	125-4	Dem.	Div'd
12	*Arkansas	July 20, 1919	20-2	76-17	Dem.	Dem.
13	*Montana	July 30, 1919	38-1	Unan.	Dem.	Rep.
14	*Nebraska	Aug. 2, 1919	Unan.	Unan.	Rep.	Rep.
15	*Minnesota	Sept. 8, 1919	60-5	120-6	Rep.	Rep.
16	*New Hampshire	Sept. 10, 1919	14-10	212-143	Rep.	Rep.
17	*Utah	Sept. 30, 1919	Unan.	Unan.	Dem.	Dem.
18	*California	Nov. 1, 1919	Unan.	73-2	Rep.	Rep.
19	*Maine	Nov. 5, 1919	24-5	72-68	Rep.	Rep.
20	*North Dakota	Dec. 1, 1919	38-4	103-6	Rep.	Rep.
21	*South Dakota	Dec. 4, 1919	Unan.	Unan.	Rep.	Rep.
22	*Colorado	Dec. 12, 1919	Unan.	Unan.	Rep.	Rep.
23	Rhode Island	Jan. 6, 1920	37-1	89-3	Rep.	Rep.
24	Kentucky	Jan. 6, 1920	30-8	72-25	Rep.	Div'd
25	*Oregon	Jan. 12, 1920	Unan.	Unan.	Rep.	Rep.
26	*Indiana	Jan. 16, 1920	43-3	Unan.	Rep.	Rep.
27	*Wyoming	Jan. 27, 1920	Unan.	Unan.	Rep.	Rep.
28	*Nevada	Feb. 7, 1920	Unan.	Unan.	Dem	Div'd

Appendix III *(cont)*
RECORD OF ACTION ON NATIONAL SUFFRAGE AMENDMENT IN THE STATES 1919 -1920

	STATE	DATE OF RATIFICATION	VOTE SENATE	VOTE HOUSE	PARTY OF GOVERNOR	PARTY CONTROLLING LEGISLATURE
29	New Jersey	Feb. 10, 1920	18-2	34-24	Dem.	Rep.
30	*Idaho	Feb. 11, 1920	29-6	Unan.	Rep.	Rep.
31	*Arizona	Feb. 12, 1920	Unan.	Unan.	Rep.	Dem.
32	*New Mexico	Feb. 19, 1920	17-5	36-10	Rep.	Rep.
33	*Oklahoma	Feb. 27, 1920	24-15	84-12	Dem.	Dem.
34	*West Virginia	Mar. 10, 1920	15-14	47-40	Dem.	Rep.
35	*Washington	Mar. 22, 1920	Unan.	Unan.	Rep.	Rep.
36	*Tennessee	Aug. 18, 1920	25-4	49-47	Dem.	Dem.

From: Doris Stevens, *The Story of the Militant American Suffragist Movement*, (New York: Boni and Liveright, 1920), Appendix 1.

About the Suffragists on the Book Cover

Marie Louise Bottineau Baldwin, Chippewa attorney and advocate for Native American and woman suffrage

Fannie Barrier Williams, educator and activist for African American and women's rights, and the first Black woman to become a member of the Chicago Woman's Club

Mabel Ping-Hua Lee, Chinese-born immigrant who worked for U.S. woman suffrage though unable to naturalize and vote herself

Susan B. Anthony *(center)*, leader of the woman suffrage movement from the 1850s through the early 1900s

Dora Lewis, National Woman's Party leader, one of the oldest suffragists jailed for picketing the White House

Rose Winslow, also known as Wenclawska, Polish-American factory worker and union organizer who endured hunger strikes and forced feedings for the cause of woman suffrage

Nannie Helen Burroughs, educator, religious leader and activist for African American and women's rights

All photos from the Library of Congress, except Anthony's photo, which is from Elizabeth Cady Stanton's book, *Eighty Years and More,* 1898

Contributors

BEVERLY BEETON was well known for her scholarship on the woman suffrage movement in the Western United States. Her books on the subject include the influential *Women Vote in the West: The Woman Suffrage Movement 1869-1896* (Garland Publishing, 1986). She also published numerous articles on the Western suffrage movement, including "Susan B. Anthony's Woman Suffrage Crusade in the American West," (with co-author G. Thomas Edwards) in *Journal of the West* (1982). Beeton obtained her Ph.D. from the University of Utah. She was a university administrator and history professor for twenty-five years, serving at four different universities in Utah, Illinois, and Alaska. She retired as Provost and Vice Chancellor for Academic Affairs at the University of Alaska Anchorage. After retirement she continued to write and speak on women's history, including on woman suffrage and the 1918 influenza pandemic. After moving to Seattle, Washington in 2010 she wrote a family history about the development of Northern Utah through the lives of her ancestors who were among the first homesteaders. Beeton died in 2020.

VICTORIA BISSELL BROWN is Professor Emerita of History at Grinnell College where she taught for twenty-five years. She received her Ph.D. from the University of California, San Diego. Her scholarship has focused on the Progressive Era, particularly Jane Addams and Woodrow Wilson. Brown is the author of a biographical study of Addams, *The Education of Jane Addams: Politics and Culture in Modern America* (University of Pennsylvania Press, 2003, 2004, 2007), and editor of an edition of Jane Addams's memoir, *Twenty Years at Hull-House* (Bedford /St. Martin's,1999, Second Edition 2018). She has also published articles on Woodrow Wilson's gender politics and appeared in the PBS "American Experience" documentary on Wilson. Her current research is on the history of the American grandmother in the twentieth century. Brown resides near Philadelphia, Pennsylvania.

NANCY F. COTT is the Jonathan Trumbull Research Professor of American History at Harvard University. After earning her Ph.D. from Brandeis University, she went on to write extensively on American culture, focusing on women's history. Cott is one of the founders of the field of U.S. Women's History. Her publications range widely over questions concerning women, gender, marriage, feminism, citizenship, and sexuality from the eighteenth century to the contemporary United States. She explored a new area in her most recent book, *Fighting Words: The Bold American Journalists Who Brought the World Home between the Wars* (Basic Books, 2020). Her other books include *The Bonds of Womanhood: "Woman's Sphere" in New England, 1780–1835* (Yale University Press, 1977), *The Grounding of Modern Feminism* (Yale University Press, 1987), and *Public Vows: A History of Marriage and the Nation* (Harvard University Press, 2000). Cott served as president of the Organization of American Historians in 2016-17, and she is an elected member of the American Academy of Arts and Sciences. She lives in Cambridge, Massachusetts.

ELLEN CAROL DUBOIS is the author of numerous works on the woman suffrage movement, including *Suffrage: Women's Long Battle for the Vote* (Simon and Schuster, 2020). Among her other works on suffrage are *Feminism and Suffrage: The Emergence of an Independent Woman Suffrage Movement, 1848-1869* (Cornell University Press, 1978); *Harriot Stanton Blatch and the Winning of Woman Suffrage* (Yale University Press, 1997); and *The Elizabeth Cady Stanton-Susan B. Anthony Reader: Correspondence, Writings, Speeches* (McFarland Press, 2022; first published 1987). She is the co-author, along with Brenda Stevenson of the sixth edition of the leading textbook on U.S. women's history, *Through Women's Eyes: An American History with Documents* (Bedford/St. Martin's, 2022), and was the original co-editor, with Vicki L. Ruiz, of *Unequal Sisters: An Inclusive Reader in U.S. Women's History* (Routledge; 4th edition,

2008). Her current project is a comprehensive biography of Elizabeth Cady Stanton, with Basic Books. Du Bois received her Ph.D. from Northwestern University. After teaching at the University of Buffalo, she taught for thirty years at the University of California, Los Angeles (UCLA) where she is now a Distinguished Research Professor in the History Department.

LINDA G. FORD is the author of three books on women's history, including *Iron-Jawed Angels: The Suffrage Militancy of the National Woman Party* (University Press of America,1991), which won the Gustavus Myers Award for human rights. She also authored *Lady Hoopsters: A History of Women's Basketball in America* (Half-Moon Books, 2001), and *Women Politicals in America: Jailed Dissidents from Mother Jones to Lynne Stewart* (2018). After receiving her Ph.D. from Syracuse University, she taught at Keene State College in New Hampshire and at Colgate University in New York. Ford, a feminist activist, is also the author of numerous articles on feminist history and issues of the left, particularly in the publications *Counterpunch* and *Dissident Voice*.

ROBERT BOOTH FOWLER is Professor Emeritus in the Political Science Department at the University of Wisconsin, Madison. He received his Ph.D. from Harvard University. Fowler is the author of *Carrie Catt: Feminist Politician* (Northeastern University Press, 1986) as well as numerous articles about Catt as the National American Woman Suffrage Association leader. He has published numerous books and articles in his areas of specialty, political thought and religion, and American politics. He lives in Madison, Wisconsin and Tucson, Arizona

CAROLYN DE SWARTE GIFFORD is an authority on American women's religious experience and social reform activity. She earned her Ph.D. in Religion from Northwestern University. She has published numerous books and articles on Frances Willard and the WCTU. Among her books are *Writing Out My Heart: Selections from the Journal of Frances E. Willard, 1855-1896* (University of Illinois Press, 1995); *Let Something Good Be Said: Speeches and Writings of Frances E. Willard*, co-edited with Amy R. Slagell (University of Illinois Press, 2007); *Women in American Protestant Religion, 1800 to 1930* (Garland, 1987); and *Gender and the Social Gospel*, co-edited with Wendy Deichmann (University of Illinois Press, 2007). Gifford served as an associate editor of both *Past and Promise: Lives of New Jersey Women* (The Scarecrow Press, 1990) and *Women Building Chicago 1790-1990: A Biographical Dictionary* (Indiana University Press, 2001). She resides in Reno, Nevada.

SARA HUNTER GRAHAM was an associate professor at Louisiana State University and a specialist in women's history and political history. She received her Ph.D. from the University of Texas, Austin. Her highly acclaimed book, *Woman Suffrage and the New Democracy* (Yale University Press, 1996), was published posthumously, shortly after her death in 1996. Her work on the woman suffrage movement also included "Woman Suffrage in Virginia: The Equal Suffrage League and Pressure-Group Politics, 1909-1920," published in *The Virginia Magazine of History and Biography*.

WANDA A. HENDRICKS is a Distinguished Professor Emerita at the University of South Carolina. She received her Ph.D. from Purdue University. Hendricks is the author of *Gender, Race, and Politics: Black Club Women in Illinois* (Indiana University Press, 1998); senior editor of the three-volume *Black Women in America: Second Edition* (Oxford University Press, 2005); and an editor of the *Women, Gender, and Sexuality in American History Series* at the University of Illinois Press. Her many published articles and essays include, "On the Margins: Creating a Space and Place in the Academy," which appeared in *Telling Histories: Black Women Historians in the Ivory Tower* (University of North Carolina Press, 2008). Hendricks's most recent book, *Fannie Barrier Williams: Crossing the Borders of Region and Race* (University of Illinois Press, 2014) was awarded the Letitia Woods Brown prize by the Association of Black Women Historians for the best book by a senior scholar in African American Women's

History. Hendricks's current book on the transnational activism of Madie Hall Xuma, the African American wife of South African and African National Congress president Alfred Bitini Xuma, will be published by the University of Illinois Press. Hendricks resides in Columbia, South Carolina.

SHERRY J. KATZ has taught U.S. women's and gender history and other courses for over twenty years in the Department of History at San Francisco State University. She received her Ph.D. in History from the University of California, Los Angeles (UCLA) in 1991. Katz has written extensively on early twentieth century socialist feminist activists in California and their coalition-building work for woman suffrage, protective labor and social welfare legislation, birth control legalization, and equality in partisan politics. She has published a number of essays and articles, including "'Researching Around Our Subjects': Excavating Radical Women," *Journal of Women's History* (Spring 2008). Katz co-edited a collection of essays on women's history methodologies, *Contesting Archives: Finding Women in the Sources* (University of Illinois Press, 2010), which won the Western Association of Women Historians' Barbara "Penny" Kanner Prize. Her most recent publications include biographical sketches of socialist feminists for the "Online Biographical Dictionary of the Woman Suffrage Movement in the U.S." Katz is currently writing on socialist feminist Estelle Lawton Lindsey, the first city councilwoman elected in a major U.S. city (Los Angeles, 1915).

LINDA K. KERBER is the May Brodbeck Professor in Liberal Arts & Sciences and Professor of History Emerita at the University of Iowa, as well as a Lecturer in the College of Law. She received the A.B. from Barnard College in 1960 and the Ph.D. in history from Columbia University in 1968. She has served as President of the American Studies Association, the Organization of American Historians, and the American Historical Association. In 2006-2007 she was Harmsworth Professor of American History at Oxford University. Kerber is an elected member of the American Philosophical Society and a Fellow of the American Academy of Arts and Sciences. In 2020, she offered the Charles Homer Haskins Prize Lecture "A Life of Learning" for the American Council of Learned Societies. In her writing and teaching, Kerber has emphasized the history of citizenship, gender, and authority. Her book *No Constitutional Right to Be Ladies: Women and the Obligations of Citizenship* (Hill and Wang, 1998) won best book in women's history and in legal history (both prizes awarded by the American Historical Association). Among Kerber's other books are *Toward an Intellectual History of Women* (University of North Carolina Press, 1997, 2001); *Women of the Republic: Intellect and Ideology in Revolutionary America* (University of North Carolina Press, 1980-2014); and *Federalists in Dissent: Imagery and Ideology in Jeffersonian America* (Cornell University Press, 1970, 1980, 2018). Kerber also co-edited *Women's America: Refocusing the Past* (Oxford University Press, ninth edition 2020); and *U.S. History as Women's History: New Feminist Essays* (University of North Carolina Press, 1995).

ANDREA MOORE KERR, a women's historian and independent scholar in Washington, D.C., earned her Ph.D. from the University of Maryland. She was the author of *Lucy Stone: Speaking Out for Equality* (Rutgers University Press, 1992). Kerr served on the board of directors of the Humanities Council District of Columbia, the Eastern Market Preservation Corporation, Washington, and on the steering committee of Washington Women Historians. Kerr died on December 1, 2018.

KATHERINE M. MARINO is an Associate Professor of History at the University of California, Los Angeles. She obtained her Ph.D. from Stanford University in 2013. Her research and teaching explore histories of women, gender, and sexuality in the United States and Latin America, as well as human rights and transnational feminism. Her book *Feminism for the Americas: The Making of an International Human Rights Movement* (University of North

Carolina Press, 2019) received the Latin American Studies Association Luciano Tomassini Latin American International Relations Book Award, the Western Association of Women Historians (WAWH) Barbara "Penny" Kanner Award, and co-won the Ida Blom-Karen Offen Prize in Transnational Women's and Gender History. It also received Honorable Mentions for the Organization of American Historians Mary Jurich Nickliss Prize in U.S. Women's and/or Gender History and for the WAWH Frances Richardson Keller-Sierra Prize. Her articles have been published in the *Journal of Women's History* and *Gender & History, Frontiers: A Journal of Women's Studies*, as well as in several news media outlets, including the *Washington Post*. Marino lives in Los Angeles, California.

JUDITH N. MCARTHUR received her Ph.D. from the University of Texas at Austin and taught at the University of Houston-Victoria. She is the author of *Creating the New Woman: The Rise of Southern Women's Progressive Culture in Texas, 1893-1918* (University of Illinois Press, 1998). She is co-author (with Orville Vernon Burton) of *A Gentleman and an Officer: A Military and Social History of James B. Griffin's Civil War* (Oxford University Press, 1996); and co-author (with Harold L. Smith) of *Minnie Fisher Cunningham: A Suffragist's Life in Politics*, and of *Texas Through Women's Eyes: The Twentieth-Century Experience* (Oxford University Press, 2003). McArthur is the co-editor (with Ruthe Winegarten) of *Citizens at Last: The Woman Suffrage Movement in Texas* (Texas A&M University Press, Reissue edition 2015), and (with Angela Boswell) of *Women Shaping the South: Creating and Confronting Change* (University of Missouri, 2006). Her essays include, "A. Elizabeth Taylor: Searching for Southern Suffragists," published in *Reading Southern History: Essays on Interpreters and Interpretations* (ed. Glenn Feldman); and "Maternity Wars: Gender, Race, and the Sheppard-Towner Act in Texas," published in *Texas Women: Their Histories, Their Lives* (ed. Elizabeth Hayes Turner, Stephanie Cole, and Rebecca Sharpless.) McArthur lives in Fort Collins, Colorado.

ALICE S. ROSSI, a leading scholar and activist, was the Harriet Martineau Professor of Sociology Emerita at the University of Massachusetts, Amherst. She received her Ph.D. from Columbia University. Rossi was a founder of the National Organization for Women (NOW) and a member of NOW's original governing board. She was president of the American Sociological Association and the first president of Sociologists for Women in Society. Rossi also served as Vice President of the American Association of University Professors, Chair of the Social Science Research Council, and a member of the Advisory Council for the National Institute on Aging. Appointed by President Jimmy Carter, Rossi served on the National Commission for the Observance of International Women's Year (1977) and then published a scholarly analysis of it, *Feminists in Politics: A Panel Analysis of the First National Women's Conference* (Academic Press, 1982). Her extensive publications also include *Sexuality Across the Life Course* (University of Chicago Press, 1994); *Caring and Doing for Others: Social Responsibility in the Domains of Family, Work and Community* (University of Chicago Press, 2001). Rossi was the editor of four books, including the classic anthology, *The Feminist Papers: From Adams to de Beauvoir*, first published in 1973. Alice Rossi died on November 3, 2009.

ANASTATIA SIMS is Professor Emerita of History at Georgia Southern University. She received her Ph.D. from the University of North Carolina at Chapel Hill. Sims wrote *The Power of Femininity in the New South: Women's Organizations and Politics in North Carolina, 1880-1930* (University of South Carolina Press, 1997); and co-edited *Negotiating the Boundaries of Southern Womanhood: Dealing with the Powers That Be* (University of Missouri Press, 2000). She has also authored several articles on women's organizations and woman suffrage in journals and anthologies. Sims is currently working on a biography of Juliette Gordon Low, founder of the Girl Scouts of the United States. She lives in Statesboro, Georgia.

MARJORIE J. SPRUILL is Distinguished Professor Emerita of History at the University of South Carolina. She received a B.A. from the University of North Carolina, Chapel Hill, an M.A.T. from Duke University, and an M.A. and Ph.D. from the University of Virginia. In addition to *One Woman, One Vote: Rediscovering the Woman Suffrage Movement* (NewSage Press, 1995; Second Edition, 2021), she is the author or editor of five books on woman suffrage, including *New Women of the New South: The Woman Suffrage Movement in the Southern States* (Oxford University Press, 1993), and *Votes for Women! The Woman Suffrage Movement in Tennessee, the South, and the Nation* (University of Tennessee Press, 1995). Spruill also co-edited a two-volume textbook on the history of the American South and two multi-volume anthologies about the "lives and times" of women in South Carolina and Mississippi. Her most recent book is *Divided We Stand: The Battle Over Women's Rights and Family Values That Polarized American Politics* (Bloomsbury 2017). During her career, Spruill was a professor at the University of Southern Mississippi; Vanderbilt University, where she was an Associate Provost; and at the University of South Carolina. She served as President of the Southern Association for Women Historians (SAWH), as well as on the Executive Council of the Southern Historical Association, (SHA), and on the editorial boards of the SHA *Journal of Southern History* and the British Association for American Studies (BAAS) *Journal of American Studies*. In 2018, Spruill was inducted into the Society of American Historians. She currently serves on the Scholar's Advisory Council of the National Women's History Museum and on the South Carolina Archives and History Commission. Spruill lives in Folly Beach, South Carolina.

ROSALYN TERBORG-PENN earned her Ph.D. at Howard University and was a professor of history at Morgan State University in Baltimore for more than three decades. Terborg-Penn published extensively on topics in African American women's history, and edited (with Sharon Harley) a groundbreaking book, *The Afro-American Woman: Struggles and Images* (Kennikat Press, 1978). At a time when many scholars failed to recognize the important role of African American women in the suffrage movement, Terborg-Penn persevered in highlighting and celebrating their work, as well as focusing attention on racism among White suffragists. Terborg-Penn first wrote about African American suffragists in a well-known dissertation that evolved into a highly recognized article and later, into her seminal book *African American Women in the Struggle for the Vote, 1850-1920* (Indiana University Press, 1998). Another major contribution was Terborg-Penn's anthology, *Women in Africa and the African Diaspora: A Reader*, which was co-edited with Sharon Harley and Andrea Benton Rushing, published in 1987, and revised and expanded in 1996. The volume grew out of the first national symposium held by a new organization that she co-founded, The Association of Black Women Historians. Terborg-Penn was also one of the editors of *Black Women in America: An Historical Encyclopedia* (Carlson, 1993). In 2000, Terborg-Penn became a founding member of the Association for the Study of the Worldwide African Diaspora. Her most recent work focused on writings on race and race relations in Suriname. Terborg-Penn died on December 25, 2018.

MANUELA THURNER is an editor, translator, and writer. She received her Ph.D. in American Studies from Yale University with a doctoral thesis on *Girlkultur* and *Kulturfeminismus*: Gender and Americanism in Weimar Germany, 1918-1933. Her other publications include an essay, "Subject to Change: Theories and Paradigms of U.S. Feminist History," published in the *Journal of Women's History* in 1997 and anthologized in *Major Problems in American Women's History*, edited by Mary Beth Norton and Ruth M. Alexander (Houghton Mifflin Co., 2003). Thurner lives in Munich, Germany.

Acknowledgments

I would like to thank several people who were essential to the development and production of this second edition of *One Woman, One Vote: Rediscovering the Woman Suffrage Movement*. The first edition, published in 1995, was originally designed as the companion book to the PBS "American Experience" documentary *One Woman, One Vote*, produced by the Educational Film Center (EFC). In particular, I am grateful to Steve Rabin, who was EFC President at the time, and to Ruth Pollak, the writer and producer of the documentary, for inviting me to design and edit the companion book. I will always be grateful for the support EFC provided for the first edition.

None of this would have been possible, however, without the dedication and skill of the publisher of NewSage Press, Maureen R. Michelson, who moved mountains to produce the first edition of the book in record time for the 75th anniversary of the Nineteenth Amendment in 1995. Twenty-five years later, we have worked together again in close partnership to bring out this new and expanded edition for the 100th anniversary.

As the 2020 suffrage centennial approached, Maureen and I were inspired to produce a new and expanded edition of *One Woman, One Vote*. Our goal was to add new chapters that incorporate the latest scholarship, offer new material on the role of race and region, and further diversify the cast of characters in this account of how women won the right to vote. We also wanted to place the story of the U.S. suffrage movement in an international context, and to bring the story of women and the vote up to the present.

The original plan was to release the book in 2020. However, there were extraordinary events in that year in which women played essential roles as voters and as organizers and candidates. In addition, voting rights were once again under attack, proving to be so relevant and important to the story that we decided to remain at work throughout the year. We were eager to provide a fuller account of the long suffrage struggle, which has proven to be never ending

Maureen has gone far beyond the usual role of a publisher, encouraging me to take as long as necessary to make the story complete and timely, skillfully editing all new material. In addition, we worked together to add more than a hundred new photographs that greatly enrich the book. For both of us, it has been a labor of love.

Maureen's dedication to publishing work by and about women, specifically the second edition of *One Woman, One Vote*, was recognized by the writing organization Soapstone as the recipient of its 2021 "Soapstone Bread and Roses Award." The award traditionally honors a woman whose work has sustained the writing community and includes a generous donation, which was used toward the production of this book. I congratulate Maureen and thank Soapstone for honoring her and supporting *One Woman, One Vote*.

Special thanks to the book designer, Sherry Wachter, for her great work in designing this book—expertly and patiently working with us through several drafts. Sherry, too, is a woman of tremendous talent and dedication to quality.

She has gone above and beyond the duties of a designer, putting in countless hours to help bring the suffrage story to readers in a visually inspiring format. On several occasions, Sherry went the extra mile, telling us she wanted the book to be the best it can be. Thank you, Sherry!

I also thank Angie Maxwell, Anastatia Sims, and Christina Wolbrecht for their assistance with fact checking, and Carole Bucy, Connie Lester, and Corinne Porter for aid in locating and identifying photos. I am grateful to Adele Logan Alexander for allowing me to include the photo of her grandmother, Adella Hunt Logan, and to Pam Elam, President of Monumental Women, for the photo of the Women's Rights Pioneers Monument.

I extend a heartfelt thanks to the eighteen authors of the essays, distinguished scholars who tailored their essays to make them accessible and inviting to a general audience. I offer a special tribute to Rosalyn Terborg-Penn, the first historian to capture the story of African American women in the suffrage movement, who inspired others to follow in her footsteps. Her unexpected passing on the eve of the suffrage centennial was greatly mourned by the entire community of suffrage scholars.

During the production of this second volume, pioneering scholar of the Western suffrage movement, Beverly Beeton, died. Still earlier, authors Sara Hunter Graham, Alice Rossi, and Andrea Kerr, passed away. I have been proud to work with these scholars, and with all the authors of essays in *One Woman, One Vote*. I am deeply grateful for their contributions. This book is dedicated to them, and to generations of scholars, past, present, and future, of the woman suffrage movement and the struggle for equal voting rights in the United States.

Finally, I would like to thank my historian husband Don H. Doyle for his help with editorial and technical support, and for his constant encouragement.

—*Marjorie J. Spruill*

About the Editor

Marjorie J. Spruill, Distinguished Professor Emerita, University of South Carolina, is the author or editor of numerous books on the woman suffrage movement. Recently retired from a career of teaching and writing women's history, she is a frequent speaker on woman suffrage nationally and abroad, as well as a media consultant and an advisor for documentaries, films, and museum exhibits on suffrage and the larger subject of women's history and politics.

Marjorie J. Spruill

Spruill was an advisor to the National Archives for its centennial exhibit, "Rightfully Hers," and was commissioned to participate in several projects sponsored by the Women's Suffrage Centennial Commission. As an authority on the American South, she worked with Nashville Public Television on the recent documentary *By One Vote: Woman Suffrage in the South,* and with South Carolina Educational Television on *Sisterhood: SC Suffragists.* Earlier, she was the historical advisor for the 2004 HBO film, *Iron Jawed Angels.* Spruill currently serves on the Scholar's Advisory Council of the National Women's History Museum and on the South Carolina Archives and History Commission.

As editor of the Second Edition of *One Woman, One Vote,* Spruill has continued the story of women and the vote up through the 2020 election, bringing to the task her expertise on modern feminism and anti-feminism. Her publications in those areas include *Divided We Stand: The Battle Over Women's Rights* and *Family Values That Polarized American Politics* (Bloomsbury 2017) in which she described the rise of the modern women's rights movement, the mobilization of conservative women in opposition, their competition for influence on federal policy, and the role this played in the development of modern American political culture. Spruill's work has been supported by the Radcliffe Institute for Advanced Study, Harvard University; the Woodrow Wilson International Center for Scholars; the National Endowment for the Humanities; the National Humanities Center; the Gerald R. Ford Presidential Foundation; and the American Association of University Women.

Spruill lives in Folly Beach, South Carolina, where she continues to research, write, and consult about women's history.

Other Books by Marjorie J. Spruill

Divided We Stand: Women's Rights, Family Values, and the Polarization of American Politics. Bloomsbury.

New Women of the New South: The Leaders of the Woman Suffrage Movement in the Southern States. Oxford University Press.

VOTES FOR WOMEN! The Woman Suffrage Movement in Tennessee, the South, and the Nation, editor. University of Tennessee Press.

Jailed for Freedom, memoir by suffragist Doris Stevens, first published in 1920. Editor. Lakeside Classics, R.R. Donnelley & Sons.

Hagar, pro-suffrage novel by Mary Johnston, first published in1913. Editor. University Press of Virginia.

South Carolina Women: Their Lives and Times. Co-edited with Valinda W. Littlefield and Joan Marie Johnson. University of Georgia Press, Volumes 1-3.

Mississippi Women: Their Histories, Their Lives. Co-edited with Martha Swain and Elizabeth Payne. University of Georgia Press, Volumes 1-2.

The South in the History of the Nation: A Reader. Co-edited with William A. Link, Bedford/St. Martin's, Volumes 1-2.

Index
Page references for illustrations are in italics.